MUSINGS
OF A
ROGUE COMET

MUSINGS

OF A

ROGUE COMET

Chiron,
Planet of Healing

Martin Lass

Galactic Publications
Nyack, New York

12745-LASS

Galactic Publications, Nyack, New York.

Library of Congress Number:		2001118878
ISBN #:	Hardcover	1-4010-3204-4
	Softcover	1-4010-3203-6

This book was printed in the United States of America.

To order additional copies of this book, contact:
Xlibris Corporation
1-888-7-XLIBRIS
www.Xlibris.com
Orders@Xlibris.com

CONTENTS

12745-LASS

12745-LASS

12745-LASS

7 ~ CHIRON IN ASPECT 358

8 ~ CHIRON IN TRANSIT 446

12745-LASS

By The Same Author

Star Traveler
A Planetary Guide to Your Spiritual Growth and Evolution

Love Makes the Worlds Go Around
The Living Planets Speak

Mirror, Mirror, Body & Mind
(Musings of a Rogue Comet – Book Two)

The Story of Life – *The Journey of Wounding & Healing*
(Musings of a Rogue Comet – Book Three)

Practical Healing – *A Chiron Workbook*
(Musings of a Rogue Comet – Book Four)

12745-LASS

Through the Darkness lies the Light . . .

12745-LASS

Healing is the gradual awakening
to the perfection of your life . . .

12745-LASS

If the Universe is a cosmic symphony
then we are the music
and Healing is our ascending melody . . .

12745-LASS

Love is the Beginning and the End
of our journey of Wounding and Healing.

12745-LASS

"Suddenly everything changed before me.
Reality was opened out in a moment.
I saw the boundless view.
All became dissolved in Light –
united within one joyous Love.

Yet the Light cast a shadow,
Grim and terrible,
Which, passing downwards,
Became like restless water;
Chaotically tossing forth spume like smoke.
And I heard an unspeakable lament –
an inarticulate cry of separation.
The Light then uttered a Word,
Which calmed the chaotic waters."

— from The Hermetica.[1]

---

[1] A collection of 2nd and 3rd century Alexandrine texts in Latin, Greek and Coptic, referred to as *Corpus Hermeticum,* which had its ideological origins in the ancient Egyptian Mystery traditions. Translation from: Freke, Timothy & Gandy, Peter. *The Hermetica – The Lost Wisdom of the Pharaohs.* Judy Piatkus Publishers, London, 1997, pp. 37-38.

Dedicated to Giordano Bruno,
Burned at the stake on February 17, 1600 . . .
in ceaseless pursuit of Truth.

12745-LASS

ACKNOWLEDGMENTS

Love and Gratitude to all my teachers
in Spirit and in person
who have helped me on my journey
of Healing and evolution of consciousness . . .

Yehudi Menuhin, Kathy D'Amico, Ray Bradbury, John Gould, Lobsang Rampa, J. R. Krishnamurti, Paul C. Bragg, Maurice Ravel, Claude Debussy, Martin Schulman, Barbara Hand Clow, Melanie Reinhart, G. I. Gurdjieff, P. D. Ouspensky, Rudolf Steiner, George M. Adie, Rickie Hilder, Stephen Bishop, Gail Pisani, Dr. John F. Demartini, Chiron and the planets

Love and Gratitude to all my teachers
and loved ones in Life
who have shaped me
like a blacksmith's hammer,
gradually awakening me
to the Divine Design of my life . . .

Mom, Dad, Kurt, Tim, Leigh S., Mrs. Tootelian, Roger B., Phillip S., Diana B., Paul H., Ron G., Betsy Brown, Robert Pikler, John Painter, Fran Jelly, Lim Kek Tjiang, Gabby, Uncle Igor, Bert Newton, Lynne James, Marty M., Peter K., Brenda K., Christiana, Graeme B., Yvette B., Cameron L., Fred McKay, Steve E., Alan H., all at the Newport Work, Jill Sykes, Dobbs, Margaret Birken, Del, Rob, Gene, Jo B., Ken T., Leo Drioli, Golden Age Magazine, all my clients, Chris W., Chris N., Tim M., all in the Demartini school, and particularly my Soul-mate partner and wife, Inge, and my beautiful and challenging children Alex, Saskia & Eliza.

12745-LASS

Apart from the previous acknowledgments, there are four special thanks I wish to give. Without these four influences, three of them people and the third, extra-terrestrial, so to speak, this series of book would not exist. The logical framework of ideas and the esoteric knowledge upon which these books are founded comes directly from these influences.

To my beloved teacher, George Adie, now passed away, who was himself a pupil of G. I. Gurdjieff and his protégé, P. D. Ouspensky: you brought the "dry-biscuit" ideas of Ouspensky alive for me and led me into a direct experience of the living work that lay behind the external teachings of Gurdjieff. You taught me the power of Silence. You awakened my sleeping consciousness to the Being that lies within my Heart. You showed me what it was to experience Gratitude for my given life.

To my teacher and soul-friend, Rickie Hilder, a gift from the angels: you nurtured my awakening to the livingness of the Universe, not as a dead knowledge, but as a living experience. You introduced me to Chiron, planet of Healing. You showed me that I was a Healer.

To my teacher and fellow traveler in the Mysteries, Dr. John Demartini: you gave me a framework into which I could put the *knowing* in my Heart – the ideas, the knowledge and the words. You gave me a process whereby I could repeatedly come into the experience of Love. You helped me touch the Universe again with my Heart. You kindled, once more, the awe, the wonder and the reverence for the magic, the magnificence and the mystery of the cosmos, at once ponderable and imponderable. You showed me that, in Truth, I Shine like a star, as we all do, and that I can Sing my Song of Love without fear or guilt.

And to my special teachers, the planets: you have challenged me to understand your messages, your wisdom, your secrets. You have guided me all the way, challenging me to expand my consciousness and my understanding all the way to the limits of the solar system. Each of you has given me a different perspective on the universal message of Love, a different path to the same end: the realization of the integral Oneness of everything in the Universe. You helped me see that the stars I loved to look at so much in my childhood were truly *within* me, in my Heart. You knew that this was always the Truth, and you did not rest until I knew it, too, with utter certainty, Gratitude and Love.

PREFACE

from the Author

One of the greatest spiritual teachers of the first half of last century, George I. Gurdjieff, always exhorted his students to read his written material in a certain way that, in his opinion, made sure that the material was understood and fully assimilated into their very essence. I have found his exhortation extremely valuable and set it out now for the consideration of you, the reader, as you embark upon these hefty tomes!

"Read each of my written expositions thrice:

Firstly – at least as you have already become mechanized to read all your contemporary books and newspapers.

Secondly – as if you were reading aloud to another person.

And only thirdly – try and fathom the gist of my writings."[2]

---

[2] Gurdjieff, G. I. *Beelzebub's Tales To His Grandson – All and Everything*, First Series, First Book. Arkana, London 1985, preface.

12745-LASS

INTRODUCTION

"A subtle chain of countless rings
The next unto the farthest brings;
The eye reads omens where it goes,
And speaks all languages the rose;
And, striving to be man, the worm
Mounts through all the spires of form."[3]

-Ralph Waldo Emerson

The Brink of a New Paradigm

It has been said that nothing is as powerful as an idea whose time has come. The greatest advances in the consciousness of the human race have come from just such ideas that were presented at the time Humanity was ready for them. With the discovery in 1977 of the 'planet' Chiron, we now stand at this kind of threshold in human history.

Historically, Humanity's discovery of each of the planets, in turn, has heralded the awakening of new ideas and understandings. Every new discovery made by Humanity, astronomical and otherwise, expands its scope of awareness, adds to its overall understanding and challenges it to continue to push past the boundaries of the unknown. Astronomically, scientifically and astrologically, we can correlate the discovery of each planet with new scientific breakthroughs, new technologies, new ideas and a wider view of our existence on planet Earth.

The discovery of the 'planet' Chiron has been no different. Its discovery has heralded a quantum leap in the consciousness of the human race of the same magnitude and importance as the birth of quantum

[3] Emerson, Ralph Waldo. *"Nature" (1836)*, edition: *"Selected Essays"*, ed. Larzer Ziff. Penguin Classics, New York, 1985, p.35.

12745-LASS

physics[4] and the breaking of the microscopic boundary of the atom in quantum physics[5], both interrelated with the discovery of Pluto[6]. Although, from the pragmatic surface of it, the discovery of Pluto and quantum physics' journey into the secrets of the atom seem unrelated, astrological data and correlation makes this connection self-evident now. It will be the same for Chiron in the near future. Humanity's journey into the macrocosm is paralleled by its journey into the microcosm throughout history; its outer journey and its inner journey are mirror reflections. Nowhere is this more evident than during the last 150 years with the parallel explorations of the astronomical and the sub-atomic worlds.

Just through the portal of the new century, marked by Chiron and Pluto's first conjunction since Chiron's discovery, we are truly at a revolutionary crossroads with respect to Chiron's themes and issues. The previous conjunction of Chiron and Pluto was in the midst of World War II in the sign of Leo. This latest time they met in Sagittarius. Chiron can already be astrologically correlated to the revolution of consciousness that has been taking place since its discovery. It is only a matter of time before scientific proofs of such correlations are at hand. In the meantime, such astrological correlations form the basis of Part Three of this first book.

Previous work on Chiron broached many themes, some old and some new. The tapestry of these themes was, for a long time, a paradoxical and patchy one, generating more questions than answers. To quote from the Introduction to Melanie Reinhart's book on Chiron of 1989:

> "This book ["Chiron and the Healing Journey"] is in the nature of a mosaic; the long process of researching and writing it has been rather like the experience of trying to piece together a jigsaw for which initially there was no picture, and eventually several different pictures! The reader will find many irreconcilables

---

[4] Max Planck, December 14, 1901, while Pluto in Gemini exactly opposed Uranus in Sagittarius and quincunxed Jupiter, Saturn and Mars.

[5] Otto Hahn, 1938.

[6] Clyde Tombaugh, February 18, 1930.

> sitting here side by side, sometimes with no attempt to resolve them. The archetypal nature of Chiron himself is also thus: the opposites of horse and human being are yoked uncomfortably into one form, awaiting the more inclusive synthesis that only a journey into the depths of his own inner nature can bring. Latching on to ready-made philosophies does not necessarily work where Chiron is involved, for this archetypal pattern suggests the need, and brings the opportunity, for each of us to make our own personal and unique quest for the meaning of our lives. During this process, we inevitably come up against many imponderables, paradoxes and unanswerable questions."[7]

How true! In this present work, building on the basis of deep personal experience and extensive research, we seek to offer the "more inclusive synthesis" that Reinhart speaks of, building upon the invaluable work that Reinhart and others have done. We seek to offer a view from 'on high' that resolves many of the paradoxes, dilemmas, seeming inconsistencies and irreconcilables brought into conscious light by the discovery of Chiron.

So what are Chiron's themes?

The primary emerging theme of Chiron is *Healing* – Healing in relation to evolution of the consciousness of Humanity and of each of us personally.

At the outset of this series of books, it is necessary to clarify some literary conventions that I will employ. I will draw a distinction in this series of books between "healing" and "Healing". When I use "healing" with a lower case "h", it will refer to healing in the ordinary sense, particularly physical healing. When I use "Healing" with an upper case "H", I will be referring to Healing in the broadest sense, physical, emotional, mental and spiritual, covering the full gamut of life, physical and metaphysical, terrestrial and celestial. The fuller definition of "Healing" will become gradually revealed and illuminated as we proceed, as such definition is intimately tied to Chiron's themes and musings.

Similarly, the use of the word, "Pain", as opposed to "pain", and

[7] Reinhart, Melanie. *Chiron and the Healing Journey.* UK: Arkana, 1989, p.5.

12745-LASS

"Wound" as opposed to "wound" will also be indicative of these concepts in their broadest sense, physical, emotional, mental and spiritual, again covering the full gamut of life. Finally, any other word used in the book that seems to be unnecessarily capitalized, will indicate that the word's underlying meaning is also to be taken in the broadest sense.

The issues of health, healing, illness and disease – physical, emotional, mental and spiritual – have long been on Humanity's agenda. Particularly in the 20th century, though, we attacked the problems of health and disease with a renewed fervor. Modern medicine has catapulted ahead in leaps and bounds in the last 50 years. In the same way that science is meeting spirituality in the microcosmic world of quantum physics and in the macroscopic world of astronomy, modern medicine is destined to meet Spirit through its ever-deepening study of physiology, molecular biology, neuroscience and psychology of all different kinds.

Scientific evidence to support the connection between our emotional states and the state of health and disease of our physical organism now exists. This is the beginning. Medical science now knows that emotions affect the endocrine and neuropeptide transmitter systems of the body, that this then affects the electrochemical balance of the physiology and that, ultimately, this affects the cellular functions, manifesting in health or disease.

Conversely, drugs in their many forms, which alter the body's chemistry, can have marked effects on our emotions and moods. This is particularly evident in the use of psychiatric and psychedelic drugs, stimulants and depressants.

Increasingly, these facts illuminate the question of which of mind or body is the cause and which is the effect. What if it were both and neither? What if both mind and body were mirror reflections of each other and both were reflections of a consciousness that lies beyond both? This is what the Chiron paradigm suggests.

Advances in physiology, molecular biology, neuroscience and medicine, etcetera, leapfrog advances in psychology, psychotherapy, psychiatry and behavioral sciences and vice versa. Despite the attempts of conservative factions to keep the two areas separate, increasingly there are pioneer individuals pursuing the dream of a Grand Unified Theory of the Body/Mind. To this end, the new Chiron paradigm represents a quantum leap of understanding not only in healing *per se*, but in physiology, psychology, psychotherapy, psychiatry, behavioral science, remedial therapies, criminal rehabilitation, family dysfunction, substance abuse, morals, ethics, philosophy, education, spirituality, metaphysics and sociology in general. The new paradigm of "Healing" encompasses all this and more. Such a claim, I hope, will entice readers to explore this series of books deeply and to build upon the ramifications herein.

Ultimately, however, proof is a personal journey and is dependent upon seeing and experiencing the reality of Chiron's musings in relation to our own lives. From here, we can grab the bull by the horns and ride it to larger social and global understandings. The intuition of the genius leaps ahead of proven scientific findings and then works backwards towards developing workable theories and experimental proofs, followed by practical and financially viable applications. In the same way, the Healer works from his own intuitive experience, subsequently developing workable theories, experimental proofs and subsequent practical therapies. What I offer in this book is a quantum leap of intuition from our rogue friend, Chiron. From here, it is up to each one of us to challenge, develop, refine, prove, disprove, accept, reject and expand the material offered.

Astrology Today

> "Astrology is a science in itself and contains an illuminating body of knowledge. It taught me many things, and I am greatly indebted to it. Geophysical evidence reveals the power of the stars and the planets in relation to the terrestrial. This is why astrology is like a life-giving elixir to mankind."[8]
>
> -attributed to Albert Einstein.

When the world hears the word "astrology", what does it think of? On the surface of it, the first reaction of many people is to think of the

[8] Quoted in: Calaprice, Alice ed. *The Expanded Quotable Einstein.* Princeton University Press, Princeton, 2000, p. 321.

12745-LASS

daily newspapers, magazines and the horoscope column. Astrology, for many, is about predicting the future. It is about fun and entertainment. If we go a little deeper, we begin to see that there are people who take astrology more seriously. Amongst these are punters, stock market players, progressive companies, politicians, the 'alternative' community and, of course, astrologers themselves, to name a few. Then there are people who recognize it as a way of coming to understand themselves and their lives better – a way of shining a light on the meaning behind their existence. Deeper still, we find people who look at astrology as one of the great tools for understanding the nature of the cosmos and the very questions of existence, as a link between the externally observed and the internally experienced, as a link between the physical and the metaphysical, between the terrestrial and the celestial. Amongst these last people were such great historical figures as Ptolemy, Pythagoras, Tycho Brahe, Galileo[9] and Keplar.

Astrology in the modern day is the attempt to correlate the movement of astronomical bodies with every facet of human behavior, endeavor, belief and striving. It is then the aim, in reverse, to draw meaning from the movements of astronomical bodies, which can potentially impact our understanding of our lives and ourselves, personally and globally. Astrology is a mirror for understanding ourselves, physically, mentally, emotionally and spiritually.

A concept that supports this premise, and one that is emerging in scientific circles as well as in alternate or 'new-age' endeavors for cosmological understanding, is the *holographic* view of the Universe. The holographic view of the Universe can be summed up in the poetic words of William Blake:

"To see a World in a Grain of Sand.
And heaven in a Wild Flower,
Hold Infinity in the palm of your hand
And Eternity in an hour."[10]

---

[9] Refer to "Gli 'Astrologia Nonulla' di Galileo" by Serena Foglia and Grazia Murti, *Linguaggio Astrale*, Autumn 1992, pp. 5-45.

[10] Quoted in "William Blake" by Kathleen Raine, Thames and Hudson Ltd., London, 1970, 1988, p. 50.

According to the holographic view, every smallest part of Creation reflects the whole Creation in miniature. The Hermetic axiom, "As Above, so Below" asserts the holographic view of the Universe. If we know how to read it, the study of atoms can reveal the secrets of the stars and vice versa. Physicists know this and currently work with this idea as a foundation concept. As British astrophysicist, Sir Arthur Eddington, once said:

> " . . . the road to a knowledge of the stars leads through the atom; and important knowledge of the atom has been reached through the stars."[11]

Science strives for a Grand Unified Theory (GUT) of the Universe, a Theory of Everything, a theory that supports a belief in universal laws that stand true for all of Creation from the micro to the macro. By this, science tacitly and perhaps unwittingly acknowledges an inherent and deep belief in the holographic view. The quest of science, from mathematics to astronomy to physics and beyond, has been to discover a simple set of laws that can describe all of Creation.

Another idea that is becoming increasingly accepted, which has been given a mathematical proof and has been experimentally verified, is the idea of the interconnectedness of everything in existence.[12] The seeming separateness of anything is due solely to the limitations of our perception and understanding at any given time in history.

Three facts stand out when considering the idea of universal interconnectedness. The first is the fact that everything in existence is comprised of fields of energy that, theoretically, extend to infinity, each field overlapping and interacting with all others in existence. That is to say, we are electromagnetically connected to everything else in existence.

The second fact is that, as scientist and writer, Paul Davies, points out, we are made of stardust. Not just poetically speaking, but *actually.* The atoms in our bodies have their origins in the stars. Furthermore,

---

[11] Eddington, Sir Arthur. Stars and Atoms, 1928, Lecture 1.

[12] Refer to Bell's inequality, 1964, the Einstein-Podolski-Rosen paradox (EPR) and the Hundredth Monkey Principle.

each one of us has atoms in our bodies that once belonged to Julius Caesar, Buddha, Genghis Khan and Moses. Not theoretically, but *actually.* Given that atoms are particles of consciousness, as we shall explore in the ensuing series of books, this means that our consciousness and the consciousness of others are linked, beyond the limitations of time and space.

The third and final fact is that, according to the theory of the Big Bang, every particle of matter in the Universe is connected by virtue of having the same origin. The Big Bang was the splitting of singularity into diversity. It has been shown that when singular particles split into secondary particles, these secondary particles remain 'entangled' or connected, beyond our normal concepts of time and space. Each appears to 'know' where the other is and what it is doing.

Due to these aforementioned facts, theorists in physics, such as Bernard d'Espagnat and David Bohm, argue that we must accept that all things in the Universe are interconnected, that we must take the wholistic view and that consciousness probably arises from this interconnectedness.

Considering the above, the interconnectedness of the planets and our lives is not such a far-fetched idea. Our exploration of the perceived world is, ultimately, the exploration of ourselves, of our perception and of our consciousness. Quantum physics is showing us that they are one and the same. The boundaries between the Seer, the Seeing and the Seen are blurring with every new discovery and each new theory in quantum physics. *If all this is so, then to study astrology is to study ourselves.*

The progress to date of scientific exploration of these two ideas – the holographic view of the Universe and the idea of universal interconnectedness – is beautifully summed up in Michael Talbot's book, "The Holographic Universe"[13] and in Fritjof Capra's book, "The Tao of Physics"[14].

We find ourselves in an ambiguous situation concerning the existence of astrology in the modern world. On the one hand, we have those who call themselves astrologers and proceed as such, researching and practising astrology, *per se*. The other camp is the scientific world, which is in itself split on the question. One side of science emphatically refutes

[13] See bibliography.
[14] See bibliography.

astrology as superstition, wishful thinking and ignorance. The other scientific camp researches and studies astrology, except under different names, as pointed out by writers such as Valerie Vaughan[15], Percy Seymour[16] and John West[17]. I believe that science and spirituality will meet in the future. Similarly, science (astronomy) and *astrology* will eventually meet. The differences of opinion or the labels used are merely perceptual. I believe that we are all talking about the same thing, but in different languages. Both perspectives are necessary, however, at this time in history. In the future, they will be synthesized. Part of the intent of this series of books is to present the beginnings of such a synthesis.

Whatever language we speak, the paradigm emerging in the collective consciousness of Humanity is that there is a connection between astrology and our 'ordinary' reality that goes beyond wishful thinking, beyond superstition and beyond fortune-telling. This series of books seeks to bring to light understandings and ideas that come from astrological experience and connect them with astronomy, Healing, evolution, psychology, physiology, sociology, mythology, theology, physics, metaphysics, mathematics and music. How these ideas and understandings are meaningful or relevant, personally or globally, historically or in the future, will be seen in their further application, research and testing. Let's close this section with the words of Thomas Moore:

> "Astrology is a form of imagination emerging from nature and having direct relevance for everyday life. It is applied poetics, a vision of life on earth stimulated by movement in the heavens, which can take us into areas of self-reflection as no other system of symbols and images can." [18]

---

[15] "The Acceptance of Astrology in the 'Real World': Revival or Revisionism", The Mountain Astrologer (journal), December/January 1996-97, Cedar Ridge CA, USA.
[16] "The Scientific Basis of Astrology" and "Astrology: The Evidence of Science".
[17] "The Case for Astrology".
[18] Moore, Thomas. *The Re-Enchantment of Everyday Life.* Hodde & Stoughton, 1996, p. 317.

12745-LASS

Overview of This Series of Books

Each of the four separate books of this series, under the common banner of "Musings of a Rogue Comet – Chiron, Planet of Healing", explores different aspects of our journey of Healing and the evolution of consciousness. These books are:

BOOK ONE: Musings of a Rogue Comet – Chiron, Planet of Healing

This book firstly relates the story of my personal introduction to Chiron, the planet of Healing. It then goes on to relate my subsequent journey of Healing and evolution of consciousness with Chiron as a guide. As such, it is an inspirational tale – a testament – of the real possibility of Healing our lives.

It then explores Chiron and its themes of health and disease – Wounding and Healing – *astrologically,* providing insights into the workings of Chiron in our lives, personally and collectively, as seen through the astrological horoscope.

BOOK TWO: Mirror, Mirror, Body and Mind

The second book explores the *psychological* and *physiological* aspects of Chiron's musings in relation to health, disease, dysfunction and disorder. As such, this book outlines the 'mechanics' of Wounding – i.e. the causes of health, disease, dysfunction and disorder – and then explores Chironic methods of Healing. It also touches on questions of morals, ethics and accepted social paradigms.

BOOK THREE: The Story of Life

The third book brings together all the previously discussed elements of Chiron into a bigger picture. As such, it expands the primary themes of Wounding and Healing into a broader understanding, an understanding encapsulated in the Great Story of why we are here, where we come from, where we are going and who we are, i.e. the *Story of Life.*

The Story of Life is to be found throughout history, culture and science in many diverse forms. To this end, the third book explores the connections between Spirit and Matter, between physics and metaphysics, between light and consciousness, between astrology and astronomy, between astronomy and spirituality, connecting all this to the mythological, the theological and the spiritual questions of our lives.

Here we see that Healing is not just about health and disease, but covers the entire gamut of human experience and expression. We see that awakening to the Story of Life *is* the Healing journey.

BOOK FOUR: Practical Healing – A Chiron Workbook

The fourth and final book in this series puts the musings of Chiron into a step-by-step workbook of Healing, enabling us to systematically take advantage of the powerful processes that Chiron has offered us. It incorporates physical, emotional, mental and spiritual exercises, meditations, cutting-edge processes, personalized projects and step-by-step guidance for attaining our dreams, visions, inspirations and our Purpose in life. Its aim is to help us to begin to answer the four fundamental questions of existence, i.e. where do come from, who are we, why are we here and where are we going? Ultimately, the aim of this book is to assist us in attaining the real experience of Gratitude and Love for ourselves and our lives by gradually awakening us to the perfection of our lives and of the world around us. This awakening is the *essence* of Healing.

12745-LASS

PART ONE
A Personal Journey

12745-LASS

1 ~ MEETING CHIRON

A Personal Encounter

The quest for knowledge and understanding is invariably preceded and inspired by the direct experiences of life itself on a day-to-day basis. Experiences lead to questions that, in turn, lead to journeys and quests. This was certainly the case for me concerning Chiron. One might argue that personal experiences, being subjective in nature, are not the best basis upon which to build an objective appraisal of a given subject. However, as we shall see later in our explorations (and because *all is consciousness),* the line between the *subjective* and the *objective* is an illusion. The Seer, the Seeing and the Seen are One. Even in orthodox psychology, for example, it is acknowledged that psychologists' theories are heavily influenced by their own early life and subsequent life experiences. Less acknowledged, but equally true, is that the early lives of scientists influence their way of thinking, the specific areas of their interest and the theories they develop thereof. This is why we are interested in the personal lives of the great names in science, like Einstein, Edison and Feynman.

So let's begin at the beginning, as my personal introduction to Chiron through the various experiences of my life will necessarily throw light on our first introduction to Chiron's messages and meaning.

In the first half of 1992, I felt that I had reached an impassable barrier in my search for meaning in my life. I had spent the preceding 5 years, with the help of a spiritual school, pondering the questions of who I was, where I came from, where I was going and why I was here in this life. My beloved spiritual teacher had died several years before the time in question. After his death, the school he set up continued in the best way it could.

During this time, I felt as though I was in a vacuum. I felt alienated, alone and plagued by inexplicable sadness. I would often sit in cafés in Sydney, watching people go by, trying to understand the meaning of the feelings that plagued me. I felt like a stranger in this world – an alien. I felt that people in general, although on the surface of it busy, happy and enterprising, were really quite lost. I felt that the ways in which people escaped from and avoided their own inner emptiness and Pain were becoming increasingly sophisticated in the technological age. The reality of it, I felt, was that people were asleep, unaware of the existence of their true selves and their inherent potentials. In retrospect, I know now that the way I saw others at this time was a reflection of my own sense of inner meaninglessness, lack of direction and disconnection from my real Self. I felt that I was powerless to change any of it – myself or anything outside myself.

At the same time, though, I struggled to remain free from what I considered the curse of my own negativity, striving to become impartial to what I observed within me and outside me. The emptiness remained – a kind of acute Pain in the middle of me that fuelled my Wish for Contact with life and for a sense of meaning.

In the midst of this acknowledgment of my situation and my powerlessness to do anything about it, I called out to the Universe for answers. I asked for help from whatever guidance there might be around me. I realize, in retrospect, that this was *praying* in the truest sense of the word. Not in the way we are taught in church, but praying from a very real acknowledgment of my smallness in the face of what I perceived about myself and about the world at large. I needed help. I was on my knees. In asking, I was handing power back to the Universe, so to speak.

During this time, I was already a practising astrologer. The emphasis of my astrological viewpoint was soul-centered. I sought to help others along their spiritual paths, aided by the tool of spiritual astrology. I had searched long and hard for the keys that would bring orthodox modern astrology alive again – an astrology that I considered to be cluttered with dead information and cold out-moded Saturnian structures. There was something missing that I could not put my finger on. Martin Schulman's books on karmic astrology were my bibles at this time. I felt that they offered an uncommon depth to the astrological view of why we are here.

Just before this time, during the first half of 1992, I was browsing through the astrology section of the Adyar Bookshop in Sydney, as was my wont, when a book literally fell off the shelf and landed at my feet. I laughed to myself, thinking, "What a cliché!" I picked up the book. It was called, "Chiron and the Healing Journey" by Melanie Reinhart. I had heard about the asteroids in astrology. (At the time, Chiron was considered by to be an asteroid.) However, at this time, I didn't feel inclined to pursue the study of asteroids. I had enough planets on my plate, so to speak! So I put the book back on the shelf and forgot about it. The relevance of relating this event will become clear shortly.

Shortly after my aforementioned prayer to the Universe, I received a telephone call from a person with whom I was acquainted through the music industry. Her name was Rickie. *(See **Chart 30 – RICKIE HILDER,** p.566.)* We hadn't had much to do with each other up until this time, although I knew she was into 'psychic stuff' (as I put it to myself at the time). When she called, she said to me that she had been receiving messages for me. She wanted us to meet so that she could tell me what these messages were. She didn't say who they were from. We made a time to meet, which, due to our busy schedules, was not for several weeks. As I put the phone down, I had the sense that perhaps my calls for help had been heard. I eagerly awaited the planned meeting.

Two days before meeting with Rickie, I had a powerful dream. *(See **Chart 31 – CHIRONIC DREAM,** p.567.)* In this dream, I was holding a woman in my arms – perhaps it was a girl, my wife, my daughter, a lover, my mother. In any case, the form was definitely feminine. What was also clear was that she was dying in my arms. I remember, in the dream, feeling such anguish and Pain in the knowledge that she was dying. Then she died. The feelings of loss, Pain, anguish and despair were overwhelming. Still in the dream-state, however, I went within myself, following the Pain, deeper and deeper, towards its source, as though diving into deep, dark and cold waters. The closer I approached the source, the more unbearable the Pain. When I had gone so deep that I felt I could truly not bear any more Pain, the woman in my arms came alive again.

The Pain – the feelings of loss, anguish and despair – were transformed into joy, love, release and a sense of connection. I awoke with tears streaming down my face, fully conscious of the process that had taken place, my whole Being alive with new energy and life. I wrote the dream down, although to this day I can recall every detail. More about this in minute . . .

Two days later, I met with Rickie. She spoke to me about many things. She relayed messages that she had received from her 'channeled' guidance. Two things that she conveyed to me from her spiritual guides changed my life forever. Not that the things that she said were particularly earth-shattering on their own, but it was the timing and context. What she told me acted as a catalyst for my current understandings to be transformed to another level of understanding. A quantum leap of consciousness and understanding took place from that time onwards.

Our meeting, I realize in retrospect, was a kind of initiation. If I had not been prepared, by my own 'work' on myself over a period of many years, it would not have been like this. It would have perhaps been no more that an interesting conversation. I understand now that our potential access to revelations or 'connections' to higher levels of consciousness and understanding is paralleled exactly by the amount of earthly experience we have had. Not only this, but it is also dependent on our efforts to assimilate and synthesize our experiences into a more unified understanding. Otherwise, new revelations can find no context within us.

Anyway, the first thing that Rickie told me was that I needed to know that *the planets were alive* – that they were living, with consciousness, purpose, karmic paths, etcetera, just like us. Well, not exactly like us, but like us on a different level and scale of livingness and consciousness. She indicated that we could have a conscious relationship with the planets – that we could communicate with them for our mutual evolution.

When she told me this, I felt something move within me. I don't really know how to describe it – it was a kind of recognition. I realized that something in me had known all along that this was so, i.e. that the planets were alive. My conditioning, education and upbringing, however, prevented such ideas from ever being believed or tested. Such ideas had not even been given space in my conscious thoughts.

The practical result of these revelations was that I almost immediately began searching for, exploring and sensing the reality of conscious contact with the planets. An expansion of awareness took place, which I found I could maintain for short periods. More about this shortly . . .

The second thing that Rickie told me at this meeting was that I needed to know about Chiron. Chiron, she told me, was the planet of the Wounded Healer. It was the planet, only recently discovered, that had to do with the Healing of our Wounds (physical, emotional, mental and spiritual). She told me that Chiron's message was that, by working consciously towards the Healing of our own Wounds, we could become Healers in the Service of others.

Up until this point, I had not calculated the position of Chiron in an astrological natal (birth) chart. When I calculated the current position of Chiron in relation to my natal horoscope, I found that Chiron was entering a transiting conjunction to my natal Uranus and my natal Sun. That is to say, it was currently coming back to the same place that Uranus and the Sun were in when I was born. I was confounded. Astrologically speaking, such a coincidence points to deeply relevant issues and connections being brought to the fore.

I began to piece together the puzzle . . . the book on Chiron falling out of the shelf, the call for help, the answer from Rickie, the dream, the meeting, the sensing of Contact with the living planets and the discovery of Chiron during a major Chiron transit to my natal horoscope. There was no way that all of this could have been just a coincidence. At the time, I hadn't yet been introduced to the idea of *synchronicity.*

Revelations

As the next weeks and months went by, a pattern began to unfold, as did the beginning of the next stage of my own personal Healing. The discovery of Chiron was also the next key in my search for meaning in astrology. It brought astrology into the realm of experiential knowledge. No longer did astrology have to be dead information taken from dry studies of personality types or from boring treatises on the codified at-

12745-LASS

tributes of planetary influences. Here was the key to living astrology – the key to the receipt of knowledge and understanding directly from the horse's mouth, so to speak. The key was the *direct and conscious experience* of planetary energies and their effects on our lives.

Shortly after the meeting with Rickie, I went and bought the book on Chiron by Melanie Reinhart. I sifted through its reams of dissertations on the mythological and archetypal relevance of Chiron, trying to understand and connect to the living energy of Chiron. I realized, during this time, that one of the greatest values of studying other peoples' interpretations of the attributes of individual planets was to help us to 'tune in' to the specific 'frequency' of a planet – like tuning into a distant radio station. Once the frequency is recognized and imprinted sufficiently upon our consciousnesses, we can 'call up' the station anytime we wish and receive the latest direct messages from the planets.

I realized this was one of the ways ancient astrology had been practised. Ancient astrology was 'shamanic' in the sense that the Contact with the planets was a sacred, living initiation, in which the astrologer became 'one' with the particular planet, thus being able to 'speak' or 'channel' the messages of the planet. Some ancient societies had much more Contact with the livingness of the Universe around them than we do in modern times. They were not yet affected by the Age of Reason and the march of the scientific method. To this end, they developed systems of 'gods' and higher 'powers' that acted as icons and waystations for the facilitation of conscious connection to real living consciousnesses in the living Universe. The dissolution of these societies into the rigidity and dogmatism of superstition, organized religion and ritual practices – the true Mysteries becoming mythology, mythology becoming history and history becoming dogma – happened *subsequent* to the real experiences of conscious Contact with these higher realms. The primarily Saturnian process of dissolution of living experiences into dead forms and structures is the subject of another study, beyond the scope of this book.

Suffice to say, with the so-called Age of Enlightenment and the Age of Reason, proceeding in Western society, there came the loss of the belief in the livingness of the Universe, i.e. the loss of the *animistic* view. The Age of Reason brought the *mechanistic* view into dominance. The mechanistic view makes a clear distinction between what is obviously alive and what is ostensibly inanimate.

This was a necessary step in the evolution of our consciousness. All sides of our multifold nature – physical, emotional, intellectual and spiritual – must be developed equally and eventually synthesized into one true Being. To this end, in the last so many hundreds of years, the world and Universe increasingly were considered mechanical and inanimate structures ruled by observable laws of cause and effect. Modern Humanity's one-eyed interpretation of the Newtonian paradigm prevailed. Even our view of biological life suffered from this kind of reductionism. A gradual mistrust of our spiritual and intuitive perceptions came into being. Science became very pragmatic and suspicious. If something could not be observed and measured under controlled conditions then, for all practical purposes, it did not exist. Thousands of years of rich experience that was beyond the limitations of body and intellect – beyond the known senses – was temporarily discarded in favor of the certainty of the measurably known.

Only now, in the age of quantum physics, is the scientific world beginning to see the incompleteness of the Newtonian paradigm, i.e. that this paradigm is only part of a greater picture. With this, there has been a resurgence of the recognition, amongst 'new-age' circles, of the value and validity of ancient knowledge and understandings. Again, I believe science and spirituality will eventually meet. As Albert Einstein once said:

"Science without religion is lame,
religion without science is blind." [19]

Science and Spirit will eventually come to the same understandings, each seeing the same picture from a different side of the coin. We need both understandings in the same way that we need two eyes to have any sense of distance or perspective.

With respect to my initial despairing call for Contact and guidance, I realized, in retrospect, that the Universe is actually waiting for us to

---

[19] Quoted in: Calaprice, Alice ed. *The Expanded Quotable Einstein.* Princeton University Press, Princeton, 2000, p. 213.

make Contact with it. Furthermore, I realized that *we* are the ones who have cut ourselves off from conscious Contact with the living Universe. We have created the blockages and fragmentation, albeit not consciously. To begin to understand how this became so and how to turn the situation around, we need, initially, to reach a point where most of our normal beliefs and conditioning have failed to give us the answers we need. We almost need to be in despair, acknowledging our inability to find the answers by ourselves. In a sense, we must be brought to our knees by our need and Wish for Contact and Healing. At this point, we are able to pray. At this point, we are able to ask for help. At this point, we have sufficient humility to bare our souls to the Universe at large. At this point, we are finally ready for answers. Furthermore, it is only at this point that our prayers *can* be answered.[20]

I also realized, in retrospect, that, somewhere along the track of our evolution, we 'chose' to experience the Pain of separation, cutting ourselves off from rest of the living Universe. In doing so, we cut ourselves off from our guidance. Our spiritual guidance could do nothing except take a step back for a time and wait until it was called upon again. We 'chose' to experience separateness from the Universe. We needed to experience the other side of the coin of Creation. We needed to enter the world of duality . . . to enter the world of reflections, so that we might ultimately awaken to our true nature.

When we finally reach a point of true humility and ask for help and Contact, it will be given. When asked, the consciousnesses of the Universe, in their multitudinous variety, will come forth and give us guidance. The ways in which this Contact will manifest are also manifold, some more obvious and straightforward than others are. For me, the initial answer came through the channel of my friend Rickie. From that point onwards, I was increasingly able to hear the messages directly.

It is perhaps important to mention here that, during this entire process, there was a part of me that did not believe what was going on.

---

[20] This point of despair is most often reached during Saturn Returns and Uranus half-Returns, otherwise known as *mid-life crises.* During these times, all that we thought about ourselves and our lives is put into question, our self-righteousness and illusions given a veritable beating.

Despite the coincidences, synchronicities and confirmations that took place, there was a part of me that doubted everything. At times, I felt I was just imagining these things. I felt that I might have been making it all up in my head for, as yet, unseen psychological reasons. I felt, at times, that I might be crazy. However, as confirmation after confirmation took place, I increasingly learned to trust the guidance and experiences that I was given. The results themselves were undeniable. I felt more Healed and more Whole than I had ever felt in my life. At times, I felt reconnected to my Heart. I began to be able to find my path, my meaning and my mission in this life. The creative output from these experiences remains a testament to their power of transformation – poems, angelic/devic messages, books, articles, music, photography and art.

Perhaps the most powerful testament to the validity and veracity of this entire process was, and still is, the Healing of people around me. These were people with whom I had the privilege of interacting, of sharing, of doing astrological readings and of working with in a Healing way. Chiron's motif, "Healer, Heal Thyself" is experientially verified when one sees that one's own Healing results directly and indirectly in the Healing of others (and vice versa). Ultimately, many people all working in this way amplifies the Healing, growth and evolution of Humanity at large and promotes the Healing of Mother Earth. Let's return to the main story, though . . .

In retrospect, I realized that my dream of the dying woman was a Gift from Chiron. The dream was the beginning of the symbolic and actual Healing of my feminine side – my intuition, my gentleness, my creativity, my caring, nurturing and sensitive side. It was also the beginning of the Healing of my sense of living Contact with life. These parts of me had become cut off from me for reasons that became clear to me much later. More than this, though, the dream from Chiron illustrated, in a practical example, a process of Healing our Wounds. This process will be discussed in more detail in Book Two. Chiron's message is that total Healing of our Wounds and blockages is possible if we consciously undertake to do so. The path of Healing lies in integrating, embracing and Loving the Wound, *not* by trying to get around it, *not* by running away from it and *not* by trying to destroy it.

Concerning the meeting with Rickie, she became and remains one of my dearest soul-friends. She was an angel of mercy. Later, in my astrological studies, I discovered that Rickie has Chiron conjunct her natal Sun (both in the same place at birth) and Chiron parallel Mercury (at the same declination of longitude). Who better to initiate me into the secrets of Chiron than this? Another coincidence? I think not. Just by the way, as it turns out, another two spiritual teachers whom I met later also have Chiron-conjunct-Sun in their natal charts. This was further confirmation for me. We will explore these planetary aspects in Part Three of this first book.

Living Contact

Another result of this meeting/initiation was the spontaneous conscious Connection to the living consciousnesses of various species of plants, flowers, trees and the natural elements. In short, I began receiving guidance from the 'angels' or 'devas' of the world of Nature. These devas are the conscious co-Creators of the patterns of every diverse living species in the Universe. They hold the patterns of creation handed down to them from 'on high', holding these patterns until they become manifest in the world as we know it. They are servants of the Creation, filled with Light and Love. They can be Contacted and can give us higher guidance. The guidance, for me, came in the form of poems and consciously-'channeled' messages that I diligently typed into my hand-held computer over a period of a year.

Incidentally, during the early stages of this period of devic Contact, I was synchronistically introduced to the work of biologist, Rupert Sheldrake. Sheldrake expounds a theory of *morphic resonance.* Morphic resonance represents a theoretical scientific basis for what I have referred to as devas or angels. In Sheldrake's view, *morphogenetic fields* are the *non-physical* organizing forces behind every living species, evolving in parallel with the evolution of the species themselves, spanning time and space in a *non-local* way. We will discuss fields, time, space and *non-locality* in relation to Chiron in Book Three.

It became clear to me, close to the outset of this intense period of devic Contact, that one particular higher consciousness or Being was helping me in my Healing, reconnection and, more specifically, in putting together my journal of poems and angelic messages. This archetypal consciousness, I felt, had taken me on as a kind of foster son for that period of time. The ancient Greeks personified it as the god, Apollo. Apollo, in the Greek tradition, was the god of the Sun, of music, poetry, prophecy, light and Healing, although I didn't know all of this at the time. The following poem was the fifth poem of this journal:

"When I was a child,
when the world was full of Gods and Magic,
Poetry and Music came easily..
. . . I knew not that I conversed
with the Gods.
The world and my Ego sealed away the Truth
and my Soul went into hibernation.

I've walked a Dark Passage,
to Wake my Soul
from its heavy Slumber . . .
. . . I've asked for help
and the Gods have responded.

This morning,
Apollo laughed at me, with me,
for my Blindness;
Laughter that was filled with
so much Joy and Love.
"Come on then . . . let's Play!"
And I felt again as a Child,
and the World was again
a Miracle of Creation . . ."

It was only at the time of writing this current series of books, many years later, that I discovered that Chiron, in the Greek myth, was the foster son of Apollo. (I must have missed this point in Reinhart's book, not being particularly interested in mythology at the time!) Apollo took

Chiron under his wing after Chiron was abandoned by his mother, the sea nymph, Philyra. Recently, I have traced the beginning of my own Healing journey back to a perception of abandonment by my mother as a baby and small child. We will explore the illusion of abandonment in greater detail later in this series. Who better to introduce me to Chiron and initiate me into Chironic experience than Apollo?

The confirmations and coincidences that took place during this period with respect to the poems and angelic messages are too numerous to mention here, so I will mention just two.

Firstly, during the typing of these poems and transmissions, which took place 'on the fly', often a word or two would come up on the screen in capital letters as I typed and then the typing would continue in lower case again. There was no way that I had accidentally pressed the Caps Lock key because this process would start and stop by itself and happened numerous times. The words that ended up in capitals in this way were always words of deep import and meaning, bringing alive the whole context of the message being conveyed. This did not occur before this time and has not occurred since. I believe that this was the devas' way of saying to me, "Here we are! You are not merely imagining all of this!"[21]

The second confirmation was one of many that took place in a similar way. I was receiving a poem/transmission from the deva of the *mountain paper-flower* at the time. My office was at the end of a long house with a window overlooking an embankment. These yellow paper-flowers were growing wild along this embankment. As I looked at them and sensed their wonderful Healing yellow color, I began to receive their message, which I then proceeded to type into my hand-held computer. While I was typing this, my eight-year-old daughter and her friend were playing outside around this embankment. I had paused from my typing for a moment when I heard my daughter entering the room from behind me. She had walked *all the way around the long house to enter the front door and all the way through the house to get to my office.* She was carrying one of these yellow paper-flowers. She came straight up to me,

---

[21] This journal of poems and angelic messages is called, "Angels, Apollo and I AM – A Journal of Inner Healing and Angelic Contact". I will be releasing this work for publication in the near future, with accompanying black-and-white art photos.

giving me the flower, saying, "This is for you, daddy." She ran off and went back to playing with her friend. I was overwhelmed by the sense of confirmation and love behind the incident. The devas were saying to me once more that this was real, not imaginary. There were many other experiences like this one.

Past Lives and Inner Archetypes

The other thing that occurred after this extraordinary meeting with Rickie was that I began to reconnect with the unconscious archetypes and symbols of my psyche. At the time, I felt that these were related to memories of previous lives. I have a slightly different understanding of this now, which we will explore later in this book and again in Books Two and Three.

The idea of reincarnation was not new to me at this time, but I hadn't had any direct experience of its validity. In the several weeks following the said meeting, not only did I experience a sense of release, Healing and expansion of my awareness, but also I began simultaneously to become aware of unHealed Pain within me (emotional and physical, centered in my solar plexus). During these weeks, the Pain became increasingly acute. Related to this, I had a curious and inexplicable conviction that, in a previous life, I had lost someone very dear to me through death, and that I had never recovered from it in that life. I couldn't say why I felt this. I felt that the Wound had been carried into this life. Many of the key experiences of my life up to this time had served to amplify this Wound of separation and loss.

The growing Pain reached a peak in Townsville (north-eastern Australia) at the end of July of that year (1992). (A Chiron transiting conjunction of my natal Uranus was exact and Venus was exactly conjuncting my natal Sun. *See* ***Chart 32 – PAST LIVES REVEALED, p.569***). At the time, I was browsing through a bookshop again and happened to pick up a book on American Indian wisdom. As I read this book, page after page, I realized that, somehow, somewhere, I knew this wisdom. I knew this way of life. I felt like I had come home. I *knew* I had been there and that I had lived amongst these people. Line after line I read, confirmation growing within me. However, the joy and sense of reconnection

2745-LASS

was quickly overshadowed by anguish and an acute attack of my inner Pain. I felt that it was in this Indian life that I had lost someone dear to me. Although I have a different interpretation of this now, it was entirely real to me at the time.

I was so overwhelmed that I had to leave the bookshop. I also felt I knew who the person had been and who they were in *this* life now. (I now know that the person in this present lifetime was *symbolic* of the Wound that I was experiencing and that the specific Wound very much related to *this* lifetime. More on the subject of past lives a little later.) As I walked along the street mall, I met up with my wife and her best friend, who had been shopping elsewhere. As we walked, the friend asked me what was wrong. He said I looked "black". The floodgates opened and I was seized by a powerful release of inner Pain – a cathartic reaction that physically immobilized me for a short time.

Gradually, as understanding and Healing took place, I was able to become quiet again. Over the next few days, I began to see how all the pieces of the puzzle were put together with respect to this previous life symbol and its manifestation in my current life. I felt changed inside. I felt I would not suffer this particular Pain again. I now realize, in retrospect, that Healing of this Wound had taken place during this process. As part of the Healing process, I realized the role that this 'past-life' experience had played in the gradual process of cutting me off from life. The initial Wound couldn't be dealt with at the time that it happened – whether it was an actual past life or symbolism for some event earlier in this lifetime. As a protection from its Pain, and from the possibility of the same thing recurring, I had unconsciously begun to close down the doors of my Soul – to protect myself against further Pain. I felt that, in lives subsequent to the past life in question (and in the psychological spaces of this present lifetime), I had become a recluse – a kind of hermit – burying myself in either self-pity and emotional isolation or in the ascetic spaces of monastic-type environments. Here was part of the answer to my sense of aloneness and separation from the world in this current lifetime.

This was not the end of it, however. The more primal origins of this Wound were still to be revealed. However, this would take place much later. In the meantime, when one layer is peeled off, we begin to see new

Wounds, related to the first, and are taken on a journey of dealing with these. Due to the first cathartic experience, on the exact date of my Chiron half-Return (Chiron transiting opposition to natal Chiron), I went to have a professionally conducted past-life hypnotic regression. Bear in mind that past-life therapy itself does not require a belief in actual past lives – it works whatever the belief system (providing there is a willingness to Heal). It works because the 'memories', whether real or not, are the symbolism and archetypes of our minds on an unconscious (or *supra-conscious)* level, speaking to us about the state of our psyche.

During my regression session, I discovered several 'lives' where I had failed to act upon my inner knowings and upon my sense of shamanic contact with the Universe at large. Not understanding why this had happened, we went deeper into the regression. I was quickly thrust back into a life where I was in a dungeon, chained at wrists and ankles. I was dying. I had been locked up for speaking my truth – for speaking about things that I understood and had perceived to be true. People did not like what I had to say and some were frightened by me. I believe that I had also spoken about things that people were not ready to hear – that confronted and challenged them beyond their capacity to accept or assimilate. Consequently, I was locked up, starved and allowed to die there.

This, as I understand now, was symbolic of a survival pattern in me, which was carried throughout this life. The essence of the pattern was, "speak your inner truth and you will be abandoned and left to die again". In my current lifetime this was translated into "keep your mouth shut, don't talk back or Mommy won't love you". More pieces of the puzzle were falling into place.

Later, I also experienced what I regarded at the time as past-life recall in various dreams and in lucid moments while awake, further unlocking the bigger picture of my total existence. It is, however, not necessary to go into the detail of these here. What is important to emphasize here is the real connection between my experiences of Chiron and the unresolved traumas and issues that I attributed to past lives. These unresolved issues and traumas are unconscious influences in our lives until we delve into them and resolve them. Chiron can point the way and can facilitate the Healing of these issues. We will cover this material in much more detail as we proceed.

Issues

In the meantime, it is perhaps relevant at this early stage of our exploration to offer a definition of a word that we will be using a lot. The word is thrown around a lot in 'new-age' circles, and, as such, covers a multitude of sins, omissions, commissions and confusions created by unfocused thought. Nonetheless, with proper definition, the word becomes invaluable in quickly referencing important aspects of our theme without going into detail each time, i.e. aspects of Chiron's musings in relation to our potential Healing and evolution of consciousness. The word is "issues".

"Issues", from a 'new-age' perspective, is used to denote the things in our life that we are currently 'dealing with', 'working through' or from which we are learning 'lessons'. Implicit in its connotation are potentially all aspects of our psyche – physical, mental, emotional and spiritual – and all areas of our lives – health, finance, relationship, family, social, career, spirituality, etcetera. What are we talking about?

"Issues" are our *perceptions* of events, circumstances and situations, often involving other people, that have thrown us off-center from a place of inner (and hence, outer) balance.

For example, disagreements and arguments that we have with others, transient or ongoing, are our "issues". Childhood events of a 'traumatic' nature are our "issues". Poverty can be an "issue". Resentment, anger and their causes can be "issues". Diseases can be "issues". A death near to us can be an "issue". Guilt, fear and their causes can be "issues". Unanswered questions that perplex us can be "issues". Success and failure can both be "issues". The meaning or lack of meaning of our lives can be "issues". Our whole life is comprised of "issues", great and small. Some are short-term and others are long-term. The degree to which we are thrown off balance defines the magnitude of the "issue".

Another word for "issues" could be "problems". However, the connotation of "problem" is primarily negative. "Issues" is more neutral and carries a tacit implication that something positive will come of it in the end. Every issue carries with it definite benefits, blessings, lessons and Gifts. This is true despite negative appearances and despite the Pain we may experience while going through an issue.

"Issues", by definition, and by virtue of being singled out as such, take the focus of our current attention. Other areas of our life pale in significance, taking a back burner, so to speak, in the wake of our current "issues". Furthermore, the implication behind "issues" is that they are something that we need to 'deal with' and 'work through' before we can go on with our 'normal' lives in the way that we think they *should* be going. There is the implication that something is 'wrong' in our lives that needs 'fixing', changing, attending to or getting rid of. (In this way, partners, spouses and relatives, too, can be "issues"!)

We will see, as we proceed, that "issues" are, in fact, our *Woundedness* surfacing at certain moments of our lives, begging attention, begging resolution, dissolution and Healing. Their origin is *internal,* not external, despite the illusion we all suffer from that anything that happens outside of us is not of our own making.

Let's continue our story, though . . .

The Mirror of Astrology

Since 1992, when Chiron thrust its way into my life, I have spent a great deal of time, thought, feeling and effort getting to know Chiron – the messages, the influences, the correlations, the correspondences and the deeper meaning behind each of these. I have done hundreds of readings for people, personal and postal, and conducted numerous seminars, all with Chiron as a major focal point. I have participated in the Healing journeys of many of these people. I have personally drawn up and studied thousands of charts. I have also made statistical studies of Chiron in the lives of more than 20,000 people using third party databases. I stand in awe of the relevance and accuracy of Chiron's revelations. I am touched to the depths of my Being by the Love and understanding that comes from Chiron when we work consciously with its energy. I feel deeply privileged to have been given the opportunity to look into the depths of the lives of others. I am eternally Grateful for this Gift.

I am also constantly astounded at the truth of astrology when it is approached from the soul-centered perspective, with the Moon's Nodes and Chiron as the major keys and focal points. The messages of the living planets can be heard using the chart as a focusing tool. The natal horoscope is a key to tune into the frequency of another's life pattern. The planets themselves reveal that living pattern. I say living pattern, because that's exactly what it is. The natal horoscope is not a dead, fixed representation of a person. It is the doorway to the perception of a person's Plan for this lifetime.

As a person grows in their life, the influence of the natal horoscope changes. The planets, their aspects and their placements take on higher octave meanings. Orthodox modern astrology does not even scratch the surface of these deeper levels of potential. We are moving into an Age where we will be studying astrology concurrently with studying ourselves and the physical Universe around us. They are all the same thing. We are moving into the Age of holographic astrology – the understanding that our lives, internally and externally, and the lives of the planets are interconnected at every point and reflect each other perfectly. As we have previously asserted, astrology represents a supreme mirror by which we can see ourselves more clearly and awaken to our true nature.

The Next Step

This was not the end of the story either! When we reach what we regard as the pinnacle of understanding in any given area of our lives, *we begin to stagnate.* The march of evolution will not let us sit still for too long. I reached that point around the middle of 1996. I felt like I was in a kind of limbo. Many old doors were closing and I was out looking for new ones. My astrology understandings and practice had reached a point of nil growth. My restlessness took me on the search yet again. My mother had died in mid 1995 – a state of affairs that was, despite the obvious feelings of grief and loss, nevertheless full of hidden blessings, Healing and resolutions of Love. Furthermore, I felt that the spiritual school I had attended for so long had lost its way, despite any of our efforts to keep it on track – so I left. My marriage was coasting along in a 'no man's land' for reasons that I could not fathom. The career opportunities I had expected to manifest for many years had not yet manifested.

In the midst of all this, a former astrology client of mine was continually contacting me, trying to get me to come along to see his new mentor. In fact, he was beginning to become quite a nuisance. I wasn't impressed at first, thinking he had been duped by a cult of some sort! However, despite my growing irritation, on each new occasion I listened to what he had to say. I heard many ideas that rang a bell in me. I recognized the intimation of higher universal laws in what he related to me. His mentor/teacher was Dr. John F. Demartini, a teacher, philosopher and Healer.

After many attempts to entice me along to a meeting or seminar, I relented. I attended a Demartini lecture entitled, "Sacred Healing". Despite my initial reluctance in going, during this six-hour lecture, I knew without a doubt that here was my next step. At the conclusion of the lecture I immediately enrolled for a two-day seminar called "The Breakthrough TM Experience". Since then, I have worked closely with Dr. Demartini in many seminars, in his mystery school, "The Concourse of Wisdom School of Philosophy and Healing" and have become a certified practitioner of his special method of Healing and psychological integration. Now, every time I think about this whole incident, I am filled with Love and Gratitude for my former astrology client, now my dear friend, for having had the dogged and insensitive(!) persistence to continue to badger me until I relented. He was a true salesman of Spirit!

Remarkably, but predictably, Dr. Demartini has Chiron in opposition to Uranus in his natal horoscope, an aspect that is a feature shared by many Healers and teachers in the latter part of the 20th century. This feature is discussed at length later in this first book. He also has strong twelfth house influence, which also has many Chironic implications, as will shall also see later. I believe Dr. Demartini is one of the great Teachers and Healers of our time. He is certainly bringing Chironic messages to Humanity. He is also responsible for the development of "The Quantum CollapseTM Process[22] of Healing", a process designed to bring about

---

[22] *The Quantum Collapse ProcessTM Dr. John F. Demartini © 1988 Property of the Concourse of Wisdom School of Philosophy and Healing, www.drdemartini.com.

integration of our psyches, wholeness and the real experience of Gratitude and Love. I believe this process is destined to have an immortal effect on the planet. The process is described in detail in Book Two and again in Book Three.

Due to the Healing and new perspectives obtained from my application of the Demartini work, I experienced some striking awakenings regarding the nature of my life and the paths taken. I will present a short review of just one aspect of that awakening, as it illustrates an important Chironic theme. As for the rest, the remainder of this treatise on Chiron will elaborate in detail.

Learning to Love All of Me

As background to my illustration, it is necessary to mention that my first and primary career was as a classical musician. Through circumstances of my life, I had been thrust into the popular entertainment arena in my early twenties. In my mid-twenties, I had reached quite a high point in my career as a popular entertainer. I was playing many prestigious shows for many important occasions, I had several very successful albums on the market, I was becoming a household name and I was commanding very high fees. In short, I was, to the outside view, on top of the world.

However, in my perception, my inner life was languishing away. I felt I needed to 'find' myself, to know a more 'true' part of me that had been neglected or forgotten. This took me on a spiritual quest. During this time, I became part of an esoteric school of wisdom and spirituality – a school based on the teachings of G. I. Gurdjieff, its teacher a pupil of Gurdjieff himself and of Gurdjieff's chief protégé, P. D. Ouspensky. After a short time in this school, I had a huge awakening. I realized that 1) most of my life had been spent trying to please other people and that 2) because of this, my life was not my own. I felt that my career and success had been created, managed and maintained by others around me . . . parents, spouse, managers, agents, audiences, etcetera.

Certainly, there was truth in this. It was an important revelation, no doubt. However, in the elation of my newfound understanding, I made the decision to gradually start 'phasing out' "Martin Lass—Popular

Entertainer" in favor of a more serious and 'spiritual' Martin Lass. In short, *I pulled the plug on that part of my life, because I felt that it did not fit the 'new me' that I envisioned.*

So what happened? Naturally, my career started dying and my income began falling, my public appeal diminished and my market started drying up. When we do not Love something, it dies or disappears from our lives. When we do not Love a part of ourselves, it, too, begins to die. It is paramount to a kind of partial suicide. We will discuss these concepts in Book Two.

In the meantime, I was busy building my astrology career. There are benefits and blessings to every situation in our lives, no matter how difficult and no matter whether the situation is self-inflicted or not. The astrology and Healing areas of my life seemed to be taking the place of the previous entertainment and music career. Something dies and something is born. The astrology journey for me was also a Healing journey. Along the way, I met Chiron, the planet of Healing. Although it took me a long time to hear it clearly, one of Chiron's messages was:

> "Love all parts of yourself . . . there is no part of you that is not worthy of Love, from the Darkest to the Lightest. All parts of you and all parts of your life are Serving you and others towards your highest possible spiritual purpose. No aspect of your life is superfluous, it is all Serving you. Healing is the journey of connecting all the parts and loving them equally. All the parts of you are One. All the parts of you are Love . . ."

As we mentioned above, anything that we do not Love, dies or disappears from our lives. "Martin Lass—Popular Entertainer" was dying and disappearing. Assured, though, "Martin Lass—Astrologer and Healer" was growing.

Now for the crunch . . . I was reaching the point in my life many years later, mentioned at the beginning of the chapter, when I seemed to be up against a brick wall. The astrology business was stagnant and I was losing my inspiration for it. I was already in financial straits to a degree I had not previously experienced. I lost everything. In this space, I tried to re-invent "Martin Lass—Popular Entertainer", but this time in the new-age music world. I wrote music designed for Healing, meditation and relaxation – 'deep' music, as I portrayed it to others and to myself. This was received well in very small circles, but again, I came up against the same brick wall . . . stagnation, loss of inspiration and material adversity. During this entire time, too, my relationships were going into crisis. My marriage was in danger and my social circles were becoming increasingly limited and, paradoxically, more co-dependent.

What was going on? I couldn't figure out why my life was falling apart around me. After all, I had acted according to a revelation – an inspiration of a 'higher' level of consciousness. Again, I put this and many other questions out there into the Universe. The answer came from my former astrology client, aforementioned, who refused to accept "no" for an answer! It was at this time that I met Dr. Demartini.

To cut the story short, in this next stage of my journey, with the help of my new teacher and with the help of Chiron and the other planets, I came to realize that, in an effort to become 'more spiritual' and to 'find myself', *I had effectively cut off a part of myself and was trying to run away from it.* That part of me was "Martin Lass—Popular Entertainer". It was the part of me that gave me the very tools by which I could express my greatest Gift. It was the interface between my Spirit and the outside world. Because I had cut this part of me off, I had cut off my main lifeline to the world. It is a two-way street. If we cannot Give, we cannot Receive. If we stop the flow of Spirit *through* us, we stop the flow of Spirit *into* us. This explained perfectly the current state of my life, internally and externally.

Through this next stage of my life, I learned to Love the *performer* part of me once again. I learned how to Heal it and reintegrate it within me. My life began to become more fulfilled again. My bankbook began to look better, my relationships were Healed, my marriage saved and my career began to flower again. As we Heal, reconnecting the parts of ourselves that we have not been Loving, our external lives begin to manifest the abundance we deserve. Our lives begin to shape themselves, on the outside, into vehicles that can better manifest the glory, the magnificence and the beauty of the Gift of Spirit that lies within each one of us.

More Pieces of Me

One would have thought that this would have been the end of the story . . . but no. I guess I am as thick as anyone else and it takes just as long for the penny to drop. A little later on, I found myself in a similar plight. Due to revelations and new understandings that I had, I decided to abandon various aspects of my life in favor of an inspired Vision I received of my highest Purpose in this lifetime, i.e. in favor of dedicating all my energy to writing and performing my own original music. To this end, I decided to stop doing all astrology, all Healing work for others, all orchestral and musical 'session' work, all writing of articles, poetry and books.

Can you guess what happened? Again, after a short time, I found myself in financial straits, work drying up and inspiration flagging. Again, I was shaking my fists at the Universe saying, "Why, if I have agreed to dedicate my life to my primary inspiration and Love in life – writing and playing my original music – why are you not supporting me by giving me the means and resources by which I can carry out that purpose?"

Using the benefit of hindsight and the Gift of friends and teachers on similar paths, I looked back at the previous 12 months of my life. I asked myself, "What parts of me have I left behind *this* time? What parts of me have I stopped loving, appreciating, acknowledging and embracing?" The answer? *All the parts of me that were giving me the means and resources to be able to carry out my primary purpose of writing and performing my original music.* That is, astrology, Healing, orchestral and musical 'session' work, the writing of articles, poetry and books, etcetera! These were all the parts of me that were giving me 1) Inspiration 2) Healing 3) Lessons & Understanding 4) Relationship satisfaction and networking 5) Financial resources 6) Broader view of existence 7) Mental stimulation and challenges 8) Personal worth of helping others 9) Outlet for Spirit in ways that music alone cannot fully provide. The list goes on . . .

The Universe had given me all the means and resources necessary for me to carry out my primary Purpose in life, but I threw them away in favor of the elation of pursuing a single-minded vision, *not realizing that all the parts that I was throwing away were the very things out of which my primary Purpose was and is evolving.* I was removing the foundation stones that supported the whole edifice of my higher Purpose. I had thrown the baby out with the water. Again, I had cut myself into parts . . . on the one side, the parts that I embraced and Loved and, on the other side, the parts that I rejected and did not Love.

What was it that Chiron had said?

> *"Love all parts of yourself . . . there is no part of you that is not worthy of Love, from the Darkest to the Lightest. All parts of you and all parts of your life are Serving you and others towards your highest possible spiritual purpose. No aspect of your life is superfluous, it is all Serving you. Healing is the journey of connecting all the parts and loving them equally. All the parts of you are One. All the parts of you are Love . . ."*

I realized that I had been trying to jump ahead of myself by becoming elated and infatuated with the Vision I had been given. My self-righteousness had said to me that I didn't need these other aspects of my life, that I could go straight to the pinnacle without climbing the mountain. As if the pinnacle could exist without the foundations of the rest of the mountain!

Life is a great teacher. I was brought to my knees once more. The Truth of this Vision of my life's Purpose had again become distorted and I needed to go back and pick up the pieces and learn to Love the whole picture rather than just the separate fragments.

So, with the tools I had been given, enabling me come to a state of Unconditional Love concerning any issue in my life, I went back and embraced and Loved these aspects of my life once more. I dissolved, once more, my illusions and charges against each of these aspects of my life and myself, one at a time. Consequently, my outer life soon reflected my new consciousness and continues to do so as long as I continue to work towards Loving all aspects of myself and my given life.

The Guiding Hand and Life's Purpose

I realize now, as planet Chiron has been trying to teach me for years, that every part of my life Serves me. I realize that the perfection of my life needs no 'fixing' or changing. I realize that there is truly a Guiding Hand showing me the way to Unconditional Love. The secret is to include all that I am in my understanding . . . to Love all that I am, as I am, without exceptions. The big picture is already there. I just need to discover it, unveil it, understand it and embrace it. The more I discover and unveil it, the more I realize in my Heart that there truly is a Guiding Hand in my life. The more I embrace the abundance of all that I am, the more my life on the outside is a reflection of that abundance.

When we get 'successful', we have a tendency to forget the basics that got us where we are. By forgetting the basics, we undermine the foundations of what we are trying to build. Life then forces us, by our subsequent failures, to take stock and get back to basics. This applies to every area of life from business to relationships to spiritual pursuits.

When we think that we have received a divine revelation or understanding, we tend to abandon where we are and go off in search of a 'better' life. *In truth, there is no better life than our current life.* We have everything that we need right here and now – all the resources, all the support, all the opportunities. Whether we see this or not, whether we embrace this or not, determines the degree of Gratitude and fulfillment we are able to experience in our lives. Furthermore, it determines the state of our external affairs, i.e. the state of 'success' or 'failure' of our given calling. It is a measure of our Healing or lack thereof.

Whatever we do not Love in ourselves and in our lives *runs our lives.* The more we Love ourselves *just as we are* and the more we Love our *lives* just as they are, the more freedom we experience to express and manifest the Gift of Spirit that lies within us and the more we can openly embrace and freely live the Divinely-Designed calling we each have been given.

There is an old Zen saying that seems apt with respect to the lessons of my life in the last few years:

"Before enlightenment,
chopping wood, carrying water.
After enlightenment,
chopping wood, carrying water."

In any case, I am now realizing that Healing *is* evolution . . . the evolution of consciousness. As we grow, Heal and evolve, we increasingly connect consciously to who we are, where we have come from, where we are going and why we are here. In short, as we grow, Heal and evolve, our Life's Purpose becomes gradually more clear as does the Guiding Hand that is leading us toward our awakening.

Gradually, I have begun to see yet another octave of understanding about Healing. I am hearing Chiron's next phase of teaching. With it comes exact scientific methods of Healing and evolution of consciousness. This phase will revolutionize the world. It is in these higher messages, understandings and methods that the world will come to understand Healing from a new perspective that will literally change history. The time has come, as the very discovery of Chiron prophesizes.

This is the subject of this series of books. It presents a new and revolutionary view of Healing, consciousness and human evolution for those who are ready. For those that are not ready, the older, more tried and tested Healing and growth paradigms will always offer the stepping stones to greater understanding in the future. To deny the stepping-stones of our previous understandings is to spit upon the path that has taken us to where we are today. Nature herself never discards old patterns. She simply builds new ones on top. That is what we will be seeking to do in this book.

Let's now delve into the details of this new paradigm of Healing and evolution of consciousness, led by our rogue comet friend, Chiron. Prepare to be challenged, entertained, confronted, awakened and Healed by the material that follows!

Key Points

- The Seer, the Seeing and Seen are One.
- All is consciousness.
- The line between subjective and objective is an illusion.
- The planets are alive! Ancient astrology was 'shamanic'.
- The *animistic* view of the Universe was lost to the West in the Age of Reason.
- Today, the connections between science and spirituality are being rekindled.
- The Universe is waiting for us to make Contact.

- One's own Healing facilitates the Healing of others.
- The path to Healing lies in integrating and loving the Wound.
- Devas (angels) are the conscious co-Creators of all the diverse forms of life.
- Chiron, in the Greek myth, was the foster son of Apollo.
- Past-life experiences and dream-states can hold the key to our Healing.
- "Issues" are the things that take us away from inner balance.
- Every issue carries with it benefits, blessings, lessons and Gifts.
- "Issues" are our Woundedness, surfacing at certain moments of our lives.
- The messages of the living planets can be heard through the astrology chart.
- Astrology represents a supreme holographic mirror.
- Dr. John Demartini is arguably one of the great teachers and Healers of our time.
- Dr. Demartini developed "The Quantum Collapse ™ Process" of Healing and integration.
- When we do not Love something, it dies or disappears from our lives.
- Chiron says there is no part of us that is unworthy of Love.
- Every part of our life Serves us. Nothing needs fixing or changing.
- There truly is a Guiding Hand in our lives.
- Whatever we do not Love in ourselves and in our lives runs our lives.
- Healing is evolution . . . the evolution of consciousness.
- Nature never discards old patterns – she simply builds new ones on top.

2 ~ WHO IS CHIRON?

"Dost thou love picking meat?
Or wouldst thou see a man in the clouds,
and hear him speak to thee?" [23]

-John Bunyan

The Essence of the Argument

A native American prophecy states that when the planet of Healing is discovered in the sky, the ancient sacred warrior teachings will return to the Earth. Enter Chiron. Chiron is reawakening teachings that have their origins in antiquity. These origins pre-date recorded Western history and subsequently show up in the mythologies, philosophies, religions, arts and customs of virtually every culture, worldwide.

One of the forms these teachings took was *the Hermetic teachings*, derived from the ancient Egyptian Mystery traditions. It is important to point out that the Hermetic traditions we find *after* the 1st century AD had their origins in the Egyptian culture. However, even the Egyptian teachings were passed down from far earlier sources. We will refer to the ancient teachings as *the Mysteries.* We will be exploring their origins, sources and some of the mythologies that evolved from them in this series of books, particularly in Book Three. In the meantime, what is the essence of our rogue comet's message?

The essence of the new paradigm that is emerging since the discovery of Chiron is this:

---

[23] Bunyan, John. *The Pilgrim's Progress.* London, 1678, section entitled "Author's Apology for his Book", html version courtesy of Judith Bronte, http://acacia.pair.com/Acacia.John.Bunyan/.

Healing is synonymous with the evolution of consciousness, globally and personally. Healing is the journey of our consciousness towards greater wholeness, greater integrity, greater balance, greater harmony and, ultimately, greater Love. When our consciousness around any given issue remains stuck for too long, resisting our innate need for evolution, disease manifests. Disease, dysfunction, disorder and disharmony – our *Wounds* – are our teachers, teachers mirroring the lessons we are resisting learning.

In terms of the awakening of consciousness, we are a balance of Light and Dark. The Healing process (that we are equating with the evolution of consciousness) is the gradual, on-going and eternal process of bringing our Darkness into the Light. Along the journey, we gain greater understanding, greater knowledge, greater Truth and greater Being. In this way, Healing is not a pursuit limited to one profession or one area of human endeavor. It encompasses areas of all human endeavor and human expression. It entails a striving towards unity and concordance of all human knowledge and understanding on all levels – physical, mental, emotional and spiritual.

Orthodox medical, psychological and psychiatric therapies attack *symptoms* first. Deeper therapies look for *root causes.* The current trend in medical, psychological and psychiatric research is to search for the root 'cause' of a disease/disorder. Current thinking (that pervades orthodox medicine and therapy) is that disease or imbalance – physiological, emotional, mental or spiritual – indicate that something needs to be *fixed.* If we can find the root cause, then we can 'fix' it. We go to the doctor asking them to 'fix' us – to make us 'better'.

Both orthodox and alternative Healing professions are leading us into ever-finer realms of human energy systems – of the body *and* the mind – in search of root causes to 'fix'. In the process, we are learning, in ever greater detail, all there is to be known about ourselves. This will ultimately Serve us in ways that we do not yet see. In the beginning, we employed physical remedies, e.g. surgery, and then moved to chemical and herbal remedies, i.e. drugs, then to electrical, radiative and magnetic remedies. Then there is vibrational medicine and spiritual Healing. Where will it end? The Chiron paradigm says it ends with Spirit itself. It ends with the acknowledgment that the natural evolution of consciousness includes health and disease as *homing beacons,* pointing us toward ever greater wholeness, consciousness, Truth and, ultimately, Love. In the end, Love will be acknowledged as the greatest Healer. Let's look at this a little deeper . . .

The Chiron paradigm calls the root cause of disease, dysfunction, disorder or imbalance: *the Wound.* By "Wound", we mean a sense of inner hurt, missingness, fragmentedness, injustice, unfairness, incompleteness, aloneness, etcetera. We mean the unresolved, undissolved, unreconciled, and unHealed issues that lie buried within our psyches, awaiting the Healing process. These issues drive us, run us and point us in particular directions in our lives. The *Wounding,* i.e. the descending journey of fragmentation, separation, disorder, imbalance and disease, is the flip-side of the *Healing.* One cannot exist without the other. They are two sides of the same coin, as we shall see.

Chiron says there is a Gift in every Wound . . . further, that Healing is the process of discovering the Gift. Seeing the perfection of the whole process, we are inspired to say "thank you". Gratitude takes us to Love. So we Heal. Disease, dysfunction, disorder and imbalance – our Wounds – arise from *ingratitude.* Ingratitude for what? Ingratitude for the 'root causes' of our Wounds, for our lives, for the people in our lives, for the lessons of life, for life itself.

Ingratitude, as such, arises from misperceptions and misinterpretations of the happenings of our lives, i.e. it arises from events, situations and circumstances *that we have distorted in our mind's eye.* This is the Wounding. We will be exploring the *physiological* basis of our distortions and misperceptions (and the psychological and spiritual ramifications therein) in Books Two and Three.

Traditional thinking says the root cause or Wound is 'bad' and that it needs to be 'fixed', changed or otherwise expunged. Chiron says the Wound contains a Gift. By discovering, acknowledging and embracing the Gift, *so we Heal.* If we could remove the Wound, we would be throwing the baby out with the water, so to speak. In truth, the root cause or Wound *cannot be removed,* because doing so would be amputating a part of our psyche. If we *appear* to have removed the root cause, *then we have merely succeeded in changing its form.* It will invariably show up in some other form until the lesson is learned. How then do we deal with the root cause? Here is the essence:

Chiron says nothing needs fixing. Disease, dysfunction, disorder and imbalance – our Wounds – are created by our *perception* of the events, circumstances, situations and people of our lives. In Truth, the world and our lives are already in perfect order and balance. *The Wound is our inability to see perfect order and balance.* The Healing process consists of awakening to the perfect order and balance that already exists. Such is the process of the evolution of consciousness. The Wound, whether manifested physically, mentally, emotionally or spiritually, is a result of our lopsided perceptions, *perceptions that exaggerate and express one side of a situation while discounting, minimizing and repressing the other side.*

Most importantly, our lopsided perceptions of disorder, disharmony, imbalance, injustice, etcetera – i.e. our Wounds – *take us on a journey.* They take us on a journey in search of greater consciousness, greater wholeness, greater Truth and greater Love. The specific way in which this happens *is the Gift.* Complete Healing only occurs when we look back at a Wound and acknowledge the miracle of how it has Served us in our lives . . . how it has helped us to discover greater meaning, fulfillment, Truth and Love . . . how it has given us our special and unique place in the world.

In the final analysis, it is Gratitude that Heals . . . Gratitude for the Wound, Gratitude for our lives, Gratitude for being exactly who we are, Gratitude for every event, situation, circumstance and person in our lives. It is seeing, acknowledging and embracing the way in which each event, situation, circumstance and person has Served us on our journey of Healing and evolution of consciousness.

Said another way, when we have learned the lesson of the Wound and are fully Grateful for the experience, the Wound Heals. *At this point, we move on to the next issue in our lives.* Each issue is a Gift. Each issue represents another opportunity for Healing, another opportunity for awakening, another opportunity for learning to Love ourselves and our lives.

In Truth, our whole life is about Healing. Healing is the journey toward greater wholeness, integrity, Truth, consciousness and Love. Ev-

12745-LASS

ery minute of our lives, our innate longing for Oneness and Love pushes us to learn our lessons. Some lessons take a lifetime; others are learned more quickly. If we could understand what the processes of life, learning, evolution and Healing were all about, we could encapsulate all this into a scientific, verifiable, repeatable process of Healing that would change history and Humanity. Instead of taking a lifetime to Heal a Wound, resolve an issue or see the events, situations and circumstances of our lives with greater consciousness, we could move through it all in a fraction of the time. *This is exactly what Chiron offers us.* The process is known. The knowledge and understanding exist now. The methods and application exist now. The process is already being used. Quantum leap breakthroughs of individual Healing and evolution of consciousness are happening now. Such Chironic processes of Healing will be described in detail in Book Two.

Key Points

- The Hermetic teachings were one of the ancient forms of Chiron's messages.
- The Hermetic teachings were derived from the Egyptian Mystery traditions.
- Healing is synonymous with the evolution of consciousness, globally and personally.
- Healing is the journey of consciousness towards unity, Truth and Love.
- When we resist evolution, disease manifests.
- Disease, dysfunction, disorder and disharmony are our teachers.
- Healing is the process of bringing our Darkness into the Light.
- Healing encompasses all human endeavor and expression.
- Healing is the search for unity and concordance of knowledge and understanding.
- Health and disease are homing-beacons toward unity, Truth and Love.
- The root cause of disease, dysfunction, disorder and imbalance is called the *Wound.*
- Chiron says there is a Gift in every Wound.
- Disease, dysfunction, disorder and imbalance are the result of ingratitude.
- Ingratitude arises from misperception and misinterpretation.
- Chiron says nothing needs fixing.
- In Truth, perfect order and balance already exist.

- Seeing the existing order and balance *is* the Healing process.
- Our lopsided perceptions of the world create our diseases.
- Our Wounds take us on a journey – the journey is the Gift.
- Gratitude Heals.
- Our whole life is a Healing journey.
- Chiron offers us proven, scientific, repeatable processes of Healing.

The Astronomical View

So *what* is Chiron? Initially it was considered a planetoid – a small or *minor* planet. Other sources refer to it, even now, as an asteroid – astrological sources in general, for example. In most scientific circles, Chiron is now considered a cometary body, i.e. a comet.[24] It is the largest periodic comet in the solar system, some 10,000 times the mass of Halley's comet. It was discovered on November 1, 1977.[25] *(See **Chart 1—BIRTH OF CHIRON**, p. 536.)* The previous description – "planetoid" – was in deference to Chiron's size, i.e. somewhere between a planet and a large asteroid. It measures roughly 300–400 km in diameter.

It has also been conjectured that Chiron may have been 'captured' by our Sun whilst passing through the neighborhood of our solar system and, furthermore, that it may not remain within our solar system for an indefinite time. Another theory is that Chiron is a stray from the Kuiper Belt of objects that orbit beyond Neptune. To quote from NASA's Internet website:

> "Two separate arguments indicate that Chiron has not been in its present orbit for more than a few million years. The first is that Chiron's orbit is unstable on time scales of about a million years to perturbations from the large outer planets. The second argument involves the super-volatiles sublimating from Chiron's

---

[24] See New Scientist, 13 May 1989: Astronomers at the University of Hawaii, having observed a coma or halo of light around Chiron, now believe it is a giant comet.

[25] Chiron was discovered by Charles T. Kowal of the Hale Observatories at Pasadena, California at about 10am on November 1, 1977.

> surface. It is estimated that at Chiron's current orbit these substances would completely vaporize in a few million years, so the fact that Chiron is still active means it has not been in this orbit that long. The fact that Chiron must have come to its present state from another location in the solar system has led investigators to look towards the Kuiper belt . . .
>
> " . . . the argument that Chiron is an escaped member of the Kuiper belt is based on a number of lines of reasoning. Gravitational perturbations from the giant planets should occasionally force Kuiper belt objects into Neptune-crossing orbits from which they can evolve into orbits like the Centaur's. The similarity in size between Chiron and the discovered Kuiper belt objects makes this a likely source. Asteroids are also in this size range, but the observations of a coma on Chiron appear to rule out an asteroidal origin. The evidence that Chiron still retains super-volatiles which would only persist for long times at lower temperatures than it presently experiences indicates a colder source region, beyond Chiron's present orbit."[26]

Out around the orbit of Neptune lies a belt of cosmic objects and debris (many are comets) known as the Kuiper Belt. It seems that Chiron properly belongs to this belt, rather than being a planet with its own individual orbital path in the solar system. This has some interesting ramifications that will be explored in later chapters. At this stage, it is sufficient to say that each planet or asteroid belt theoretically has its energetic origins in a specific place *outside the solar system.* The Kuiper Belt's energetic origin, and hence Chiron's, appear to be tied to the same energetic origins as that of Neptune and/or Pluto. We will explore these energetic origins in Book Three.

Chiron is the largest of a group of cometary bodies, strayed from the Kuiper Belt, collectively referred to as *the Centaurs,* all of which have their orbits in the outer solar system. For more information on the Centaurs, refer to the work of Zane Stein at http://www.geocities.com/SoHo/7969/chiron.htm.

---

[26] http://nssdc.gsfc.nasa.gov/planetary/chiron.html

In any case, it appears that Chiron is a celestial visitor – perhaps temporary, but definitely timely.

In addition, it has been suggested that, if Chiron had been given the description of cometary body or comet when it was first discovered in 1977, it may not have been noticed astrologically. For this reason, perhaps it is just as well that it was first called a "planetoid" or "asteroid". In the context of this series of books, however, we will call Chiron a planet, as it is a commonly accepted term for Chiron amongst astrological circles. In this context "planet" simply means a celestial body.

Chiron's orbit is quite eccentric when considered from a planetary perspective. Not so from a cometary viewpoint. Its orbit, which has a period of between 49 and 51 years, is tipped steeply in relation to the plane of the ecliptic . . . 6.9° to be exact. Its orbit is also very elliptical. If zero is a circle and 1.0 is a line then Chiron's orbit has an ellipticity of .3786. The next nearest to this is Pluto at .2482 and Mercury at .2056.

From an astrological point of view, Chiron's ellipticity means that it does not spend an equal amount of time in each sign of the zodiac. Chiron's shortest transit of a sign occurs in Libra – about 1 ¾ years. It was, coincidentally, in this sign at the time of commencement of writing this book. The longest transit of a sign occurs in Aries – about 8 ¼ years. The ramifications of this unequal transit of the zodiac signs are explored in later chapters of this first book, as are the ramifications of eccentricity and ellipticity of planetary orbits in general.

To confuse matters even more, Chiron's orbit, primarily between Saturn and Uranus, sometimes wanders inside the orbit of Saturn. Furthermore, as we have mentioned, Chiron may be related to Neptune and the Kuiper belt. All this has interesting ramifications when one considers, metaphorically, the soul's journey of awakening as a passage from the innermost planets to the outermost, as we will see.

Overall, Chiron appears to be somewhat of a rogue in the general scheme of the solar system. For this reason, some early astrologers gave Chiron the keyword, *maverick*. This accolade will be seen to be increasingly fitting as we delve into Chiron's musings in this series of books.

12745-LASS

Key Points

- Chiron is considered a cometary body.
- Chiron may be a temporary visitor.
- In this book, we will refer to Chiron as a "planet".
- Chiron may belong to the Kuiper belt of astronomical objects.
- Chiron may be more akin to Neptune and Pluto than Saturn or Uranus.
- Chiron's spends the most time in Aries and the least time in Libra.
- Chiron appears in all ways to be a rogue in the general scheme of things.

Astrologers' Early Studies

Amongst the early pioneers of Chironic astrology were Erminie Lantero, Richard Nolle, Zane B. Stein, Barbara Hand Clow and Melanie Reinhart. Without their work, books such as mine would not exist. I freely acknowledge that my work is built upon their foundations and thank them for this. The initial task of figuring out what a new astronomical body means in astrological terms is a long and painstaking process. Once enough data and understanding are collected, it allows us all to 'tune' in to the 'frequency' of a planet – the 'station' has been found, so to speak. It is then the task to refine that connection further and to begin to hear the messages of the planet more directly, endeavoring to assimilate those messages into our current understanding. Sometimes the assimilation process can mean turning our current views upside-down. However, we never fully discard our previous understandings. We simply keep building and refining. This series of books does just that – it builds upon the previous foundations, turns current views upside-down, refines and adds to the understanding of the messages of Chiron.

The early studies of Chiron very quickly revealed the themes of Healing, transformation, bridging the gap between Matter and Spirit, re-awakening our intuitive and higher faculties, breaking through to new levels of awareness and the process of attaining psychological integrity. On the down side, there were the themes of Wounding, escapism, drugs, crime, mental imbalance, inner fragmentation, alienation, aloneness and disease. Taken each on their own, all of these themes are valid, but incomplete. The total picture includes and integrates all these themes and many more into a unified understanding. Such is the intent of this series of books. The very process of integrating these themes is, itself, a Chironic process, i.e. the process of Healing, taken in its broadest sense. Chiron says that, ultimately, everything in the Universe is connected and that the gradual awakening to this connectedness *is* the Healing Journey.

Key Points

- This book is built upon the foundations laid down by others.
- We can 'tune' into the planets and 'hear' their messages directly.
- Healing and Wounding are Chiron's primary themes.
- Chiron says everything in the Universe is connected.
- Becoming aware of universal connectedness *is* the Healing process.

2745-LASS

3 ~ MYTHOLOGY & SYMBOLISM OF CHIRON

Much has been written about the mythological origins of Chiron. We will cover a little of this here and much more in Book Three of this series. For those interested in further details of the mythological aspects of Chiron and their interpretations, I also recommend the books of Barbara Hand Clow and Melanie Reinhart on Chiron as a background to what we will be presenting here.[27]

Many correlations, connections, theories and conclusions about Chiron's astrological influence can be made just by studying the mythology. However, any analogy or metaphor on its own – and a myth is a symbolic metaphor – eventually falls short of the whole truth, because it is not the thing itself . . . it is a description. The whole truth of any matter can only be truly and gradually revealed by 1) experiential interaction with the matter itself, 2) by mental synthesis of the fragments of knowledge gleaned from the experience into a complete understanding and 3) by the confirmation of the completion of the first and second steps, i.e. by a Heart-felt recognition.

Having said this, however, it is necessary to acknowledge the power of myths and archetypal symbols as potential *keys* to the portals of higher consciousness. This is because these symbols emerge, in part, from our subconscious or *supra-conscious*. Symbols act as catalysts for intuitive and inspired connection to remote people, things, realms and consciousness. By dwelling on and meditating upon symbols, we empower them,

---

[27] "Chiron - Rainbow Bridge Between the Inner and Outer Planets" by Barbara Hand Clow. And "Chiron and the Healing Journey – An Astrological and Psychological Perspective" by Melanie Reinhart. See bibliography.

which in turn invokes a response from the symbol's object. The symbol, analogy or metaphor is a kind of waystation for the receipt and transmission of 'messages' between different realms of consciousness. However, when the initiate begins to regard a symbol itself as being the main point of focus, then they are in danger of losing perspective. This often happens when what was initially an experiential process becomes too ritualized. History gives us innumerable examples of this, beginning with many of the codified practices of the major religions.

From another point of view, symbols, archetypes and myths represent energetic templates. Each symbol attracts or repels us depending upon our current questions and issues. Particularly when we are at crossroads, certain symbols and/or archetypes come forth into our lives, illuminating our quest. All symbols and archetypes have their true origins in antiquity and are quite literally part of the substance of our creation and subsequent evolution. The energetic patterns they represent are built into the fabric of space/time and come from conscious origins, from our Creator and co-Creators.

In this way, all mythologies, symbols and archetypes – and indeed the origin of every major world religion – can be traced back to the one Story of Life that predates recorded history. The circumstances, events, locales and personages may differ from one version to the next, but the essence is the same. Such assertions will be supported and explored at length in Book Three.

From these aforementioned considerations, it can be seen that symbols, archetypes and mythologies offer mirrors in which we can see ourselves more clearly, by which we can understand our lives a little better. So let's briefly explore some of the main mythic, symbolic and archetypal themes that revolve around Chiron, bearing in mind that we will cover this area in greater detail in Book Three.

Key Points

- Analogies, metaphors and symbols are not the thing itself.
- Analogies, metaphors and symbols are way-stations for understanding.
- Analogies, metaphors and symbols emerge from the supra-conscious.
- Symbols, archetypes and mythology are our mirrors.

- All mythologies, symbols and archetypes can be traced back to the one Story of Life that predates recorded history.

The Myth of Chiron

Chiron, in mythology, took the physical form of a centaur – upper half man, lower half horse. He was born of an illicit union between Kronos (Saturn) and Philyra, a sea nymph, although his parents have also been said to be Kronos (time) and Rheia (space). His grandparents were Uranus (the Sky father) and Gaia (the Earth mother). In the Greek myth, Chiron was abandoned by his mother due to her disgust at his appearance. He is said to have never known his father. He was raised and tutored by Apollo, the god of the Sun, light, music, poetry, Healing, truth and prophecy. Chiron, having become a master Healer himself, taught Aesclepius, the father of medicine.

Furthermore, Chiron was said to have been wounded in the leg through various causes (depending on the version of the myth). We might imagine that this further inspired him to study the Healing arts. However, although he became a master Healer of others, his own wound remained unhealed. For this reason, Chiron is associated with the archetype of the *Wounded Healer.*

Chiron, in an extraordinary arrangement with Zeus (Jupiter, in the Roman pantheon), the god of the gods, exchanged his mortal life for the release of Prometheus, the god of fire. He was then immortalized in the constellation of Sagittarius.

In more recent times, Chiron has been further associated with the idea of a shamanic journey into the underworld. The reasons for this will be explored in a minute.

In addition, Chiron has been recently linked to the symbolic idea of the *Rainbow Bridge.* Again, we will explore this in a minute.

The Centaur

The symbol of the centaur expresses the predicament of our dualistic existence: we are spiritual beings (the human torso and head of the centaur) having an earthly experience (the lower horse part). The more we emphasize one part of the partnership of Spirit and Matter to the partial or complete exclusion of the other, the more separate, isolated, cut-off and alienated we feel. A life of the senses, without Spirit, can never satisfy or fulfill us. A spiritual life, without the appreciation of the Gift of the material world, leads us into an impotent unreality where we are unable to manifest purpose, meaning and direction on Earth.

The centaur symbolizes the potential for a balanced acknowledgment, appreciation and purposeful utilization of both sides of our dual nature – the lower material nature and the higher spiritual nature – for the natural evolution of our consciousness.

This symbol says that, without our earthy origins (Virgo), our connection to heaven (Pisces) is not possible. Healing is the reconnection of our earth-self and our heaven-self. In short, we must have our feet on the ground and our head in the sky. The path of Healing necessarily includes a process of *recapitulation.* By this, we mean breaking down stagnant patterns (old Saturn), getting back to basics (earth signs of Virgo, Capricorn and Taurus) and rebuilding new, more appropriate and relevant patterns (new Saturn) that correspond to our new consciousness. This then allows us to better connect with our divine nature. The process of recapitulation was seen unmistakably in the hippie movement of the 1960s and in the new-age ecology, self-sufficiency and bio-sustainability movements.

The path of recapitulation can be seen clearly in the planets, too. Chiron's path of Healing takes it *inside* the orbit of Saturn at times, connecting it with the inner planets and the unresolved issues therein. We will discuss this theme a little later in the book.

Finally, Chiron's wounded leg is symbolic of the inherent Woundedness of our lower material nature. Our lower nature is dualistic, fragmented, isolated and separates us from our divine potential, which is, in essence, unified and whole. The themes of duality vs. unity arise from this, themes we will cover shortly.

We will explore many more aspects of the centaur in Book Three.

2745-LASS

Key Points

- We are spiritual beings having an earthly experience.
- The centaur symbolizes the gulf between our 'lower' and 'higher' natures.
- The process of *recapitulation* takes us back to our earthy nature, back to basics.
- We are dualistic beings, both material and spiritual.
- Our lower material nature is dualistic, i.e. fragmented or Wounded.
- Our higher nature is potentially unified, i.e. whole or Healed.

Abandonment – The Wounding

In the myth, Chiron was abandoned by his mother and, we are told, never knew his father. If we read the myths carefully and apply the principles of the Mysteries to them (for this is where the Greek myths originated), we will see that Chiron was abandoned *through* rather than *by* his mother. The Mother is a symbol of the Creation, i.e. the generative principle. The Creation is a process of 'descending' from Oneness (the Father) into Manyness (the Mother), as we shall explore in depth in Book Three. The process of fragmentation – descending into the earthly experience, where our dualistic illusions rule – is the essence of what we define as the *Wounding* process.

From this perspective, Chiron lost the Father (the Oneness of Spirit) *through* the Mother (the material Creation). The Return journey is the *Healing* journey, ascending back to Oneness, back to Spirit, back to Love, back to the Father. (Immediately, it is necessary to dispense with any misinterpretation of the ideas of Mother and Father. We are deriving these symbols neither from a patriarchal or matriarchal slanted viewpoint. We are simply employing them as symbols of a cosmic picture of Creation and evolution. In this way, we can avoid accusations of gender-specific political and/or social incorrectness.)

From this perspective, the Fall into the material condition is the *abandonment* from divinity or *the Wounding.* Conversely, the Return to Spirit is the Healing.

When Apollo, the Sun god, took Chiron as a foster son, he took on the role of father to him. Astrologically speaking, our Healing journey takes us to Saturn (Kronos), where we must take conscious personal responsibility for ourselves and our lives. We must become, as it were, our own father. We Return to the Father (the Oneness of Spirit, i.e. Love) by awakening to the Spirit within us. The Father can take many forms in our lives. When we miss, reject or have lost our biological father, we seek the Father in other ways, e.g. through career or through spiritual pursuit.

Astrologically speaking, when Father is acknowledged, embraced and activated within us, i.e. by *owning* our Saturnian issues, we are ready for the next stage of the journey, represented by Chiron. This stage brings us yet closer to the Father, i.e. to Spirit, Love and Oneness. The acceptance of personal responsibility and accountability for our lives leads us naturally to Chiron, epitomized in the expression: "Healer, heal thyself".

Furthermore, Chiron's experience of rejection and abandonment symbolize the feelings of rejection and abandonment experienced by Humanity at large. Our lower nature sees the incarnation process as a wrenching away from the world of Spirit, away from the loving bosom of the Creator. Such is the core Wound of Humanity, collectively and well as personally. This idea will be expanded in Book Three.

Key Points

- Chiron was born to Kronos (Saturn) and Philyra, who abandoned him.
- Mother represents the generative principle, the bosom of Creation.
- Mother represents the dualistic, fragmented illusions of reality.
- Father represents the divine Oneness, Love, Spirit.
- Chiron's Fall into the material condition was the abandonment or the Wounding.
- The search for the Father is the Healing journey, the Returning to Spirit.
- Chiron was fostered by Apollo, the Sun god.
- Personal responsibility (Saturn) is the first step towards Chiron, towards Healing.
- Chiron's abandonment mirrors the core Wound of Humanity;
- This core Wound is the feeling of being wrenching from the bosom of Spirit.

The Wounded Healer

The Wounded Healer is a modern archetypal symbol. The Chiron myth, however, illustrates the essence of this archetype. There are various versions of the story of Chiron's Wounding. We will explore the subtleties of these different versions in Book Three.

Firstly, the placement of the Wound (in the leg – the lower animal nature) represents the separation and alienation of the two halves of our physical/spiritual nature, as previously discussed.

Further, we can regard the Wound as the blind unawakened consciousness that cannot yet see the inherent perfection and 'rightness' of life and of the Universe at large. It is a consciousness blinded by the dualistic illusion of separateness, a consciousness that sees only imbalance, imperfection, unfairness, wrong-doing, neglect, abuse and dysfunction, a consciousness that is in *judgment* of the world, of people and even of the Creator.

As our eyes are gradually opened to the perfection that lies all around us at every instant of our lives, the Wound is Healed. The experience of Gratitude and Love is the result. Healing means *our dualistic illusions give way to a greater unity of consciousness, to greater Oneness and greater Love.* The Healing process is a matter of connecting all the pieces of our lives and seeing that there truly is a divine Guiding Hand behind it all, no matter what the circumstances, situations or events.

The archetypal symbol of the Wounded Healer is also the symbol of the Healer who can Heal others, but who has an incurable Wound. On the one hand, having searched heaven and earth for a cure for our own Woundedness, we gain Healing skills and understanding that can help others. On the other hand, our own Wound remains mysteriously uncured.

Alternately, the Wounded Healer can symbolize the person who tries by whatever means to avoid feeling the Pain of the Wound. This takes us constantly outside ourselves, our attention turned toward helping others, all the while feeling like the helpless victim of our own inner Wounding. In this scenario, the weight of the suffering of the world is upon our shoulders, always triggering and exposing our own unconscious Pain. The image of the saintly martyr is appropriate here. The Wound is accepted as incurable and, curiously, as a mark of saintliness.

There is another way of understanding the incurable Wound. From a higher perspective, the Wound is a Gift, taking us on a journey of Healing and reconnection, awakening us to our True and Divine nature.

Along the path, new understanding and new levels of consciousness are attained. Along the path, we become that which we have been Divinely Designed to become.

However, if, as Healers (and we are *all* Healers in some form), we fail consistently to address our Wounds, there comes a point when our Woundedness becomes increasingly counter-productive. At this point, the Universe impels us to move onward. It can be outside events and circumstances that motivate us or it can be the very Pain of the Wound itself. If we remain in the same place for too long, we stagnate. If we stagnate long enough, we become self-destructive and begin breaking down our lives. Our self-destructiveness represents an unconscious effort to return to a point where growth can begin anew . . . we backtrack, recapitulate, retrace our steps. This is a natural and valid part of the evolutionary process and can be seen throughout Nature.

The avoidance of the Wound and the Pain of the Wound can exacerbate and perpetuate the situation. The need to avoid and escape from this kind of inner hell manifests in abusive and self-abusive ways, mirrored in a version of the myth where Chiron Wounds himself. In short, we become our own worst enemy.

Once a Wound is cured, it does not mean we are suddenly without Woundedness. It simply means we move on to the next issue, the next Wound, the next lesson. The journey never ends. It is eternal. This, perhaps, is the deeper meaning behind the idea of the incurable Wound. Although we may constantly be moving toward greater wholeness, Truth and Healing, we are never finished. There is always a greater sphere of consciousness to be attained. *From this point of view, disease represents one of evolution's tools, impelling us onwards towards greater consciousness.* More on this in Book Two . . .

Ultimately, our greatest Wound proffers our greatest Gift. The Gift is the very essence of our life's purpose, calling, direction, drive, etcetera. The greatest Wound and its associated Gift are the homing beacons of Healing and of the evolution of consciousness. For this reason, our greatest Wound can never be completely Healed. We are constantly approaching total Healing, but we never 'get there'. There will always be greater levels of Healing, 'wholing', unity, Truth and Love, relative to where we are. From this point of view, we are all Wounded Healers eternally.

Key Points

- The origin of Chiron's Wound depends on the version of the myth.
- The Wound symbolizes the separation of our lower/material and higher/spiritual nature.
- The Wound can be considered the unawakened consciousness.
- The Wounded Healer, driven by his own incurable Wound, learns to Heals others.
- The Wound is a Gift that takes us on a journey of Healing.
- If the Wound remains uncured, we stagnant, self-destruct, and must recapitulate.
- The Healing of one Wound is not the end of Healing. We are never finished.
- Disease is one of evolution's tools, impelling us towards greater consciousness.
- Our greatest Wound gives us our greatest Gift.
- The Gift in the Wound is the Wound's motivating role, impelling us toward our life's purpose, calling, direction, drive, etcetera.

The Shamanic Journey

Another of Chiron's themes is the idea of the *shamanic journey.* The initiate relinquishes the ordinary world for a time, journeying into the unseen world of the unconscious, to the place of the primal source of Nature, to the world beyond death or to realms inaccessible to our ordinary states of consciousness.

On the one hand, it is a journey of reconnection to our earthy roots. Here, we gain wisdom and understanding from the spirits of ancestors, animals, the natural elements and Mother Earth. It is a reconnection to our genetic roots. It is interesting to note that in Nature, all life forms recapitulate the entire evolution of life to the present day *within their one lifetime.* We have within our genetics (and their associated vital fields), access to the entire history of organic life on Earth. Healing can mean recapitulating evolutionary steps that have either been missed or are as yet incomplete within us.

On the other hand, the shamanic journey can be a journey into the underworld, facing death and the Dark side of our nature. Having gained the awakening, wisdom and Gifts sought, we return to the world of Light, a transformed being. The true meaning behind the mythic theme of the underworld will be explored in depth in Book Three.

Still further, it can be a journey into the 'higher' realms – the angelic, the devic, the world of the after-life, etcetera. Near death experiences (NDEs) fall into this category. Gaining a transcendent glimpse of the larger picture of life, the initiate returns to the ordinary world, forever changed in consciousness, bringing his message to Earth.

In all cases, the need for the shamanic journey tacitly acknowledges that we are disconnected from higher understanding. We have lost touch with something that previously *united* our fragmented and disconnected psyche. It is also an acknowledgment that a journey of some sort is necessary – to undergo suffering, trials and tribulations – in order to transform us and lift us into a higher state of consciousness. It is a journey that seeks to Heal the rift between our inner Heaven and inner Earth. Along the journey we are training to become co-Creators who will eventually bring Heaven and Earth together – within us and outside of us. Later, we will pave the path for others to follow.

The shamanic journey – being but another guise of the Healing journey – must be undertaken consciously and willingly. The rituals of many indigenous races have written this journey into their social and religious customs, formalizing the process in the form of initiations. Ultimately, though, in whatever circumstance we find ourselves, *we* must make the decision to embark upon the journey of Healing and reconnection. No one else can decide for us. No one else can do it for us. We must make the decision, fully aware of at least some of the pitfalls and suffering that we may encounter along the way. Then, having walked the path, we can guide others, encouraging them to follow their own path of Healing, their own reconnection to divinity.

Chiron, we might imagine, walked this path and has now returned from the shamanic journey, incarnate within the planetoid/comet we have named after him. He will help us walk the path of reconnection to Spirit, the path of Healing and evolution of consciousness.

Key Points

- The shaman journeys into realms 'above' and 'below' the visible world, seeking wisdom, understanding and connection;
- This journey seeks to bridge the rift between Heaven and Earth within us;
- This journey paves a path upon which others may follow.
- Chiron's journey was a shamanic journey.

Divination

Another of Chiron's themes is divination, i.e. the art of prophecy and of connecting to higher realms of understanding through oracular means. According to the myth, Chiron was tutored in the art of prophecy by Apollo. He was also the *chiromancer:* the reader of the Tarot. Interestingly, the linguistic origins of the word *chiromancy* are, of course, the same as Chiron. The Greek derivation of the word "Chiron" (whose archaic spelling is "Cheiron", according to Robert Graves) is *cheir*, meaning "hand", combined with *Centron*, meaning "goat".

In physics, *chiral* refers to the right-handedness and left-handedness of the particles *(fermions)* produced by the *polarization* of Light. Polarization is the splitting or fragmenting of Light into secondary particles. Thus Oneness becomes Manyness. We will explore this topic in detail in Book Three.

Chiropractic is the technique of bringing the two 'polarized' sides of the body into greater alignment and unity via the manipulation of the spine. We will be exploring more linguistic connections later in this series. Suffice to say, the derivation of the word "Chiron" intimates that *something that was initially unified later became fragmented.* In terms of our journey of consciousness, this is the Wounding. The ultimate aim of all Healing is to return to the unified state – spiritually speaking, *to a state of Grace.*

The theme of divination echoes again the idea of the need to connect to levels of understanding from which we have been disconnected – levels that exist beyond our normal sensory perceptions. The process of connecting to higher realms of understanding is an *alchemical* one. It requires transcending our earth-bound logic. It requires a state of inner Stillness and balance. In the inner Stillness, we can hear the messages of the higher realms.

The form of the divination itself is a kind of ritual, whether it be Tarot, astrology, palmistry, pendulum swinging, casting of the stones, reading of tea leaves or whatever. At the core of all these practices lies the holographic paradigm, i.e. the belief in the connectedness of everything in existence. If we know how to connect in the right way, casting a handful of sand can tell us the secrets of the Universe.

From the point of view of our own personal Healing and reconnection to divinity, divination offers a key to transcend the limitations imposed by our Wounds and blockages. Our limitations, astronomically and astrologically speaking, keep our consciousness within the confines of the orbits of the inner planets. The transcendence of these limits is seen in the quantum leap represented by the movement from Virgo to Pisces, from the sixth to the twelfth house and from Chiron through to Neptune. The action of Uranus also facilitates this leap, particularly when linked with Chiron in the horoscope. These astrological aspects will be discussed at length in Part Three of this book.

A key is needed to help us jump beyond the confines of our narrow understanding, beyond the limits of the inner solar system, beyond the Asteroid barrier. Our narrow understanding keeps us captive to our dualistic lower nature. Chiron offers just such a key. Divination is but one of Chiron's tools. Divination allows us to pull ourselves up by the spiritual bootstraps, so to speak. It allows us to elevate our consciousness to a higher pinnacle than we were previously able to reach through normal efforts. In this way, new things become possible in terms of Healing and reconnection.

It should also be mentioned that Chiron was an astrologer in some versions of the myth. We might imagine that his astrology was the astrology of Healing, of alchemy and personal transformation, i.e. spiritual astrology. Chiron's own journey in search of Healing brought him knowledge and tools in many diverse areas.

Key Points

- Chiron was the chiromancer: the reader of the Tarot.
- Divination allows us to reconnect with higher states of consciousness.
- Divination is a form of inner alchemy.

- At the core of divination lies the belief in the holographic nature of the Universe.
- Divination 'bootstraps' consciousness into a potentially higher state.

The Rainbow Bridge

The symbol and theme of the Rainbow Bridge was first applied to Chiron by astrologer Barbara Hand Clow.[28] She refers to Chiron as the Rainbow Bridge between the inner and outer planets. We will be exploring the astrology of this idea a little later. In the meantime, what is the Rainbow Bridge?

Briefly, Creation is, symbolically, the descent of white light (unpolarized) into the many colors (polarized light) of the rainbow, i.e. a descent from the Oneness and the purity of the Creator to the colorful diversity of Creation. Such a view of Creation is in line with many ancient religious and spiritual teachings. Throughout history, consciousness and Spirit have been compared to light. We even say "the *light* of Spirit" and "the *light* of consciousness". Significantly, the Big Bang theory and current theories in particle physics support the idea of the Creation consisting of the descent of light from an unpolarized or unified state into a polarized or fragmented state. We will explore this at length in Book Three.

White light, as we know, *contains* all colors. When diffracted by a prism, it breaks down into seven primary colors and innumerable shades and tints thereof. Interestingly, the number "7" appears to be built into the very fabric of Creation. It comes up repeatedly the more we delve into the mysteries of the cosmos. We will explore this subject, too, a little later in this series.

Symbolically, if the descent of Spirit into Matter is considered to be white light diffracting into its many colors, then, conversely, *the Return to Spirit from Matter, i.e. the evolutionary journey, must be the reintegration of the many colors back into white light.* Healing consists of returning the many 'colors' of our lives into the white light of our divinity. This is what is meant by the Rainbow Bridge. The Rainbow Bridge is the path of Healing and evolution of consciousness.

---

[28] Ibid.

Chiron can be considered just such a Rainbow Bridge, as we shall see. It is a bridge from lower consciousness (represented by the affairs of the inner planets) to higher consciousness (represented by the affairs of the outer planets). Chiron's path is the Healing path of *reintegration.* By this, we mean that Healing consists of rescuing the lost or rejected fragments of our psyche and merging them – rejoining them – with our one true Self (Being).

Key Points

- Chiron is the Rainbow Bridge between the inner and outer planets.
- The Rainbow Bridge is the journey of consciousness, as Light, from duality to unity;
- It is the Return to our divinity;
- It is the Healing journey of our fragmented selves;
- It is the Return to Oneness.

Joining Heaven and Earth

The attainment of higher states of consciousness is symbolized by the joining of Heaven and Earth (or the bringing of Heaven *to* Earth, depending on how it is perceived). Such states are facilitated by the Healing of our Wounds, by the dissolution of our blockages and by the transformation of the dualistic and fragmented aspects of our lower nature. The joining of Heaven and Earth symbolizes our awakening and reconnection to divinity.

Our reconnection to divinity is further symbolized by the reconnection of the inner and outer planets via the Rainbow Bridge, aforementioned. Thus, we awaken to the all-encompassing consciousness of the solar system as a whole. The consciousness of the solar system as a whole transcends the consciousness of any individual planet or life form on a planet.

Our reconnection – our Healing – affords us the possibility of becoming a *link* between Heaven and Earth. It allows us to 'channel' Light, Love and higher consciousness into the Earth plane. From another perspective, our reconnection raises Earth consciousness to a higher level.

Either way, we stand as way-stations, as receiving and broadcasting systems, connecting Heaven and Earth. The 'clearer' we are in our consciousness and the more awakened we are to the inherent unity of the Universe – i.e. the more Healed we are – the more actively we act as way-stations.

Chiron, as a planetary messenger, points the way. The first step is to consciously recognize and acknowledge our Wounds and blockages. The second is discerning the path towards Healing these Wounds and blockages, as indicated by Chiron. The last step is walking the path. In this way, we transcend the limitations of our consciousness, as defined by the inner planets and move into a higher awareness, as defined by the outer planets.

In astrological terms, 'Earth' is seen through the sign of Virgo and the sixth house and 'Heaven' is seen through Pisces and the twelfth house. The journey of bringing Heaven and Earth together within us – our Healing journey – can also be traced astrologically by the planets themselves. The journey begins at the inner planets, tracing a path through Saturn, Chiron, Uranus, Neptune, Pluto and beyond. These ideas will be explored and further elucidated a little later.

Lastly, the theme Heaven and Earth is also reminiscent of the Centaur symbol inasmuch as they both symbolize the disconnection and reconnection of our lower and higher natures.

Key Points

- Heaven and Earth are joined together by the Healing process.
- The bridging of the inner (Earth) and outer (Heaven) planets symbolizes our reconnection to divinity.
- We act as way-stations – receiving and broadcasting systems – between Heaven and Earth.
- Chiron helps us consciously recognize our Wounds and blockages;
- Chiron then illuminates a path of Healing.
- Whether we walk the path of Healing or not is up to us.
- Earth and Heaven are seen through Virgo and Pisces, through the 6th and 12th houses.

- The Healing path begins at the inner planets, tracing a path through each planet, as far as Pluto and beyond.

Balancing Polarities

There is a common thread emerging from much of what we have discussed so far. The joining of Heaven and Earth requires the reconciliation of seeming opposites, the balancing of what is seen to be polar extremes. The same can be said for the zodiac pairs, Virgo and Pisces, and for the 6th and the 12th houses. Although these may initially seem like one-way 'journeys' – Earth to Heaven, Virgo to Pisces, 6th to 12th house, Manyness to Oneness, Woundedness to Healing – we will gradually see that we cannot 'travel' from one polarity to another without embracing each side equally. Furthermore, as shall also see, by embracing both sides equally, we transcend both and enter into a new state of consciousness. But we get ahead of ourselves . . .

Of the other previously-discussed symbols and themes, the centaur, too, requires the balancing of polarities, this time those of our animal and human natures, our terrestrial and celestial existence. The idea of balancing polarities or reconciling seeming opposites is encapsulated in the Yin-Yang symbol and in the Zen *koan* (a seemingly-irrational and unanswerable question posed to initiates.) In fact, as we shall gradually see, our entire existence, from the structure of the brain and nervous system to the dilemma of morals and ethics, arises from the pitting of one polarity against another. Nature does not produce monopoles. Chiron epitomizes this idea.

Astrologically, the *opposition* aspect is very much related to the Chironic theme of balancing polarities. In the astrological *opposition*, issues needing to be seen, acknowledged, reconciled, Healed and resolved are brought into acute focus. Under such circumstances, avoidance is difficult, often making confrontation with these issues inevitable. Resolution and Healing can only take place when both sides of a polarity (an issue) are seen, acknowledged, embraced and finally Loved. Both ends of the proverbial stick are indispensable to the whole. When we see, acknowledge, embrace and Love both sides, the illusion of duality – i.e. the illusions of fragmentedness, separateness, disconnectedness, aloneness, etcetera – is shattered. From this, a third point emerges, completing the Holy Trinity. Consciousness is expanded . . . Love is experienced. Paradox becomes *metadox*, i.e. a transcendent consciousness of the initial dilemma. The new understanding contains both sides, is neither and is more. Unity is achieved, the unity of Truth and Love . . .

By seeing both sides of an issue, we gradually awaken to the order and balance that already exists in the world and in our lives. We see the *implicate order*, hidden within the *explicate disorder*. We come to sense aspects of the divine perfection. Such states of expanded consciousness are natural products of the Healing journey.

Key Points

- The joining of Heaven and Earth consists of reconciling and balancing seeming opposites.
- The resolution of opposites lies in embracing both sides of a polarity (issue).
- When the illusion of duality is shattered, a third point emerges, completing the Holy Trinity.
- The Holy Trinity ultimately becomes unity.
- Healing is the act of resolving paradox, of balancing polarities.
- Healing is the process of attaining consciousness that transcends a dilemma.
- Expanded consciousness is a natural by-product of the Healing journey.

Duality and Trinity

The resolution, balancing and Healing of polarities is a very Chironic subject. Every issue (Wound) we have represents a polarity seeking resolution. Polarities or seeming opposites are the natural by-product of the descent of the Creation. The Creation is *built* upon such duality. Disconnection, fragmentation, isolation, aloneness and separation are inherent in this process. This is what we define as the *Wounding*. For the resolution, balancing and/or Healing of a polarity (or of a disconnection), a third or reconciling 'force' is needed. This third 'force' must be a higher conscious 'force' that can *transmute* the denser material of conflict, disconnection, separation, dilemma, etcetera. Ancient esoteric science and spirituality acknowledged the existence of the third 'force' as a primal cosmic law – a law upon which Creation and evolution rely. The third 'force' facilitates the descending and ascending octaves of Creation and evolution. The third 'force' has had many names from antiquity to the present day. The three 'forces' taken together as the cosmic Law of Three – the active/positive, the passive/negative and the reconciling/neutral – are perhaps best known in the western world as the Holy Trinity. The third 'force' is known in western religious circles as the *Holy Spirit.*

We invoke the third 'force' – the Holy Spirit – when we remain, in our consciousness, *present* and poised between seeming opposites. We invoke it when we remain poised between our inner contradictions, poised between what we see that we are and what we Wish to Become. We invoke it when we remain poised between our inner Pain and our Wish for Healing. By acknowledging, embracing and Loving both sides of an issue, simultaneously, equally and Unconditionally, we are, in a sense, invoking the third 'force'. If we remain consciously centered in this place, with Gratitude, we can receive a glimpse of Light from Above – we can be touched by Grace. When we remain consciously poised in this place, we are allowing the influx of energy and consciousness from higher realms. This is Healing. We are allowing a reconnection to our higher Self and to our divinity. Such is the essence of divine illumination.

Chiron facilitates this kind of process in the solar system. Working with Chiron, we can invoke the third 'force' or Holy Spirit in our lives. However, for this to take place, we must make room in our consciousness. Further, it must be a conscious inner action, one that requires effort, intention and willingness.

Once touched by Grace, the issues at hand, having Served their purpose, dissolve into the Oneness of true understanding and Love. Thus, *duality becomes unity via trinity.* This is what Christianity truly means when it says that the Son Returns to the Father via the Holy Spirit. The Son represents our dualistic condition, symbolized by Jesus, the man. The Father represents Oneness. The Holy Spirit was personified as Jesus, the Christ – the way back to the Father. Chiron offers the same path and process. Healing and religious/spiritual illumination are synonymous. The Healing process, in its many guises, will be discussed at length in Book Two. The religious symbolism – not only the Christian symbolism, but the symbolism of other religions, as well – will be discussed in Book Three.

Key Points

- Polarities and opposites are created in the process of Creation.
- By remaining *present* and poised in the face of seeming opposites, we invoke the third force – the Holy Spirit.
- By embracing both sides of a dilemma/issue, equally and with Gratitude, we Heal.
- When we are centered and *present*, all apparent paradoxes dissolve into Oneness and Love.
- We Return to the Father via the Son by invoking the Holy Spirit.
- Healing and religious/spiritual *illumination* are synonymous.

Chiron and the Law of Octaves

The Law of Octaves is also referred to as the Law of Seven. Its basic premise is that the Universe is built upon rising/evolving and falling/involving energies that manifest patterns of sevens, both in the macrocosm and microcosm. One octave is like a scale of seven musical 'notes', rising or falling from beginning to end. At the end of each octave, another may begin, again comprised of seven 'notes'.

Between the last 'note' of one octave and the first 'note' of the next is a point of transformation, of death and rebirth, of endings and beginnings. Astrologically, this point is aligned with Pluto and the hypothetical planet, Vulcan. In science – from chemistry to systems analysis – the point of transformation is called a *phase transition*. In terms of consciousness, this point is where we can experience a quantum leap of understanding. From Chiron's perspective, this is where the *completion* of Healing takes place. The *process* of Healing, however, occurs along the *steps* of the octave. The most important place *within* the octave lies between the first four steps – representing the four *material* planes or realms – and the last three – representing the three *spiritual* planes or realms. This place in the octave corresponds to what religion calls the *firmament.* If the solar system as a whole is taken as an octave, then the Sun sits at this junction. More on this subject in Book Three.

The next most important place in the octave lies between the first three steps – representing the planets taken as a whole – and the fourth – representing the consciousness of the Sun. If the metaphysical journey from the planets to the Sun is taken as a *whole* octave, overlaid on the first three (and a half) steps of the larger octave of the solar system, then the Sun represents a point of transformation into a new octave, aforementioned. Metaphysically, Chiron sits at this point, i.e. at the junction between the planets and the Sun. In considering what we have just covered, we must remember that the cosmos is a *hologram,* each part reflecting the whole.

If we are to pass from one octave into the next, we must entirely synthesize, integrate, make whole, rejoin, Heal all the seven 'notes' of the preceding octave, one step at a time. Here is where Chiron comes in. Chiron sits at each point of transformation, similar to Pluto, but acting as a Healing and 'wholing' force. If we are ready to see, acknowledge, embrace and finally Love Unconditionally all issues pertaining to the previous step of the octave, then we can Heal. That is, we integrate, we become more whole, we become more conscious, we become more awake, perceiving higher Truth and experiencing greater Love and Oneness. If we are not ready, we are cast back down the octave so we can continue to learn our lessons, pass our tests and Love our issues a little more. In other words, whatever we haven't Loved, we keep bumping into, keep creating or keep repeating until we do. Reincarnation is an example of being cast back down the octave.

The Law of Octaves exists everywhere and in all things. For example, the planets and their orbits express sevens. Saturn has a 28-year cycle (4 x 7) that rules our growth and maturity. Our important ages, corresponding to the Saturn cycle, are 7 (self-identity), 14 (puberty), 21 (coming of age) and 28 (becoming a responsible adult), etcetera. Uranus's orbit is 84 years, i.e. 12 x 7 years. Chiron's orbit, although currently about 51 years, is actually 49 years if we take an average over many centuries, i.e. 7 x 7 years.

Chiron's orbit of 49 years represents a great potential for Healing and evolution of consciousness due to its 7 x 7 nature, i.e. seven octaves tracing a larger macro-octave.

We will further explore the Law of Octaves and sevens in Books Two and Three.

Key Points

- The Law of Octaves describes the seven-fold nature of the cosmos.
- The transition from one octave to another constitutes transformation, death and rebirth, Healing and the evolution of consciousness.
- The transition from one step to another within the octave is the *process* of Healing.
- Failure to move to a new step or into a new octave requires recapitulation.
- Reincarnation is a form of recapitulation.
- Planetary orbits demonstrate the Law of Octaves, some more obviously than others.
- Chiron's 49-year orbit (7 x 7 years) represents great potential for Healing and evolution of consciousness.

The Koan

In the Zen tradition, there is an exercise given by the master to his students. It takes the form of a seemingly-unanswerable question or untenable statement, i.e. a paradox or contradiction. An example of a koan might be, "What is the sound of one hand clapping?" Another might be, "The flowers of conflict." Or, "What movement in Stillness?" Or, "Love is neither side, but both." The koan challenges us to rise above our earth-bound logic that sees things as being disconnected, fragmented, dualistic, two-sided and either/or. We are challenged to unify opposites, resolve paradoxes and dissolve conflicts. Such a state of consciousness includes both sides, is neither, and is more. (Another koan!) Such a state transcends our dualistic illusions and reveals to us greater Truth.

Chiron's challenge is the same. It is to look beyond what *seems* to be true. It is to look beyond seeming imbalance, seeming chaos, seeming opposites, seeming dysfunction and glimpse the Divine Plan encompassing it all. It is to see connections and connectedness, to which our dualistic lower mind is blind. It is seeing both sides – the visible and the hidden – of a given issue, i.e. seeing the higher Truth that encompasses all aspects of the issue. Seeing higher Truth, we turn and say "thank you". Healing takes place. The process of transcending our lower-natured/emotional illusions is at once both an evolution of consciousness and a Healing journey.

The above ideas encapsulate the essence of Chiron's message. The Healing processes arising from this message will be explored in ever-greater detail in this series of books.

Key Points

- Beyond all opposites, beyond all dualistic illusions, lies greater Truth.
- Truth encompasses both sides of every issue, the visible and the hidden.
- Chiron's challenge is to look beyond what *seems* to be true.
- Our journey of Healing and evolution of consciousness is about awakening to greater Truth.

Master Alchemist

When we remain *present* and poised in the face of our inner contradictions and polarities, acknowledging and embracing them as described above, we are allowing the influx of higher influences. We are invoking the influences of the third 'force' or Holy Spirit. We are rising above the perceived duality or illusion. Duality becomes unity via trinity. What takes place in this space is *alchemy*. This is the deeper meaning that lies behind the symbolism of alchemical practices and ideas.

Chiron's Healing quest led him to become a kind of master alchemist, for which he was immortalized in the constellation of Sagittarius. He bargained with Zeus (god of the gods) for the release of Prometheus from his bondage. Prometheus's fire is the fire of alchemy, releasing the Spirit from the bondage of the dualistic illusions of the lower nature. Alchemy is an inner spiritual process. The transmutation of lead into gold is an analogy, a symbol, a metaphor. The entrance of higher influences (the fire of Spirit) into our organism facilitates the transmutation of the substances of our lower nature (lead) into finer Matter (gold). Such is the alchemical transformation of our blockages, our inner Pain, our contradictions, our illusions. Such is Healing. Our vibrational level rises. Our very atoms change. We become more akin to light or fire, as symbolized by Prometheus. We will explore the physics of this very real process in Book Three.

Chiron teaches us that the fire of alchemy is nothing less than our efforts to consciously attend to our issues. As we attend to our Wounds, blockages and contradictions, with the intention of understanding, Healing, balancing, resolving and dissolving them, so we are reconnecting with our divine nature.

Another word for the fire of alchemy is *conscience.* When we stand in the face of our inner contradictions, without denial, without judgment, we are *standing in our conscience.* Conscience is the action of the 'third force' or Holy Spirit, aforementioned. Contrary to popular belief, conscience has nothing to do with guilt, fear, shame, remorse or feelings of unworthiness, although these emotions do call us to action. Rather, conscience is the call of Unconditional Love, beckoning us to awaken to a more expansive and inclusive view. Atonement (at-*one*-ment), which follows conscience, is a kind of Healing . . . it is the resolution of an inner battle. The battlefield is *within* us, not, as we often think, outside of us. The battle is not a battle between 'good' and 'bad' in us, as we might think. Rather, it is a battle between our polarized *perceptions* – perceptions of ourselves, our lives and the world – and Actuality. The 'good' and the 'bad' we perceive within us and around us are our *perceptions,* our *judgments, not* Truth or Actuality. Conscience – inner alchemy – means balancing our polarized perceptions, dissolving our judgments, resolving our paradoxes and inner contradictions and bringing our Darkness into the Light. Conscience is the act of Unconditionally Loving.

Thus, Chiron pertains, amongst other things, to the awakening of real conscience.

Key Points

- Alchemy is an inner spiritual process.
- When higher influences enter our organism, transmutation of the substances of our lower nature takes place.

- Healing is the alchemical transformation of our Wounds.
- Conscience has nothing to do with guilt, remorse, shame or feelings of unworthiness.
- 'Good' and 'bad' are our perceptions, our judgments.
- Real conscience is the act of Unconditionally Loving.

The Fall from Paradise

The Fall from Paradise – the Casting Out from the Garden of Eden – is also an appropriate metaphor for our Wounding. Our spiritual predicament is that we are cut off from divinity, bound to cycles of earthly incarnations. In the version of the story inherited by the 21st century, Man was cast out of the Garden of Eden for eating from the Tree of Knowledge of Good and Evil. This constituted the Original Sin. For this, as the story goes, Man was condemned to live out a life of suffering "'til thou return unto the ground."[29]

The inherited story leaves much to be desired in relation to its original meaning. This, however, we will elaborate in greater detail in Book Three. Suffice to say, Chiron says the Original Sin was the original Wound, i.e. the illusion of separation from Oneness, from Love, from divinity, from God. Rather than being a failure by Humanity to obey God, the separation was actually part of a larger Plan. In the larger Plan, we are being given the opportunity of becoming conscious of our true nature as divine aspects of God, as beings of Light. The descent or Fall from Grace gives us the opportunity to see ourselves in the mirror of duality, thus awakening to our true nature. This opportunity is part of what Chiron calls the *Gift in the Wound.*

In our interpretation, the story of the Tree of Knowledge of Good and Evil was not the story of sin, condemnation and punishment, but the story of a Gift – the Gift of free will. The Gift opened our eyes and allowed us to freely explore the many sides of Creation. We needed to experience the Dark side of Creation – the other side of the coin, so to speak. Why? Partly, as training to become special helpers of the Creator. As we descended into the Creation, we began to know fear, to become

---

[29] Genesis 3:19.

aware of our 'nakedness', to know separation, alienation and to know 'evil'. Only in Darkness could we choose Light. Only *from* Darkness could we walk back towards God as conscious and willing helpers of Creation. If we cannot Love the Darkness, seeing how it Serves us on our path of awakening, how can we recreate it?

The Return to Grace is the Healing journey. It is the same, symbolically, as the Rainbow Bridge, as joining Heaven and Earth, as invoking the Holy Spirit, as solving the koan, as Healing the incurable Wound, as balancing all polarities, as resolving all paradoxes and contradictions, as alchemically transmuting our lower nature and as ascending the octave. The Return to Grace is *dependent* on Loving our Darkness. Chiron says there is no part of us that is unworthy of our Love.

Unfortunately, certain churches and various self-serving factions throughout history have twisted the meaning of Original Sin in order to sway the masses. The modern interpretation of Original Sin asserts that we are somehow flawed from the start, that we are unworthy, that we are lowly creatures, almost without hope of redemption. Others use our real Wounds of guilt, fear, blame, unworthiness and abandonment as tools with which to subjugate us. The idea that we are flawed is itself a symptom of our Woundedness, Woundedness being a symptom of our descent into the material world (the Creation).

If, as Chiron suggests, Original Sin is actually the original Wounds that arise from our descent into Creation (our trek into the world of free will), then the Original Sin can be Healed. Just as we chose to walk into Darkness, so we can now choose to walk toward the Light, conscience at the helm, Healing our Wounds as we go. Jesus Christ, whether real or symbolic, tried to teach us this. We are divine, we are Loved and we can learn to Love ourselves. We will Heal ourselves by forgiving, accepting, embracing and finally Loving ourselves Unconditionally. Chiron teaches us, as Jesus did, that Healing means facing our Wounds, standing in our consciences and bringing our Darkness into the Light. We can Heal Original Sin (the original Wound). We can re-enter the Garden of Eden. A condemning God is replaced by a Loving Creator, one who masterminded a Plan of enlightenment on our behalf. Such is the Plan of Man's journey into Darkness and Return to Light. Such is the Wounding and the Healing. Free will was a Gift, not a Sin stolen from God because of a "serpent of evil". The real serpent of 'evil' lies in our lopsided perceptions, i.e. in our dualistic illusions about ourselves and the world around us. With this change of perspective, we graduate from spiritual kindergarten. With this change, we begin to awaken to the Divine Design of our Creation and evolution.

Key Points

- Original Sin is the original Wound, i.e. the initial separation from divinity.
- The story of the Tree of Knowledge of Good and Evil was the story of a Gift – the Gift of Free Will.
- The Fall from Grace allows us to see ourselves in the mirror of duality and awaken to our divine nature.
- The Fall from Grace provides a training ground for us as potential helpers of the Creator.
- As we chose Darkness, so we can choose Light.
- We Heal ourselves by forgiving, accepting, embracing and finally Loving ourselves Unconditionally.
- There is no part of us that is unworthy of our Love.
- The Return to Grace is the Healing journey.
- The "serpent of evil" represents the dualistic illusions of our lower nature.

Lemuria

The story of Lemuria closely parallels the story of the Fall from Paradise. The story has re-surfaced in the 'new-age' movement and, as such, remains relatively free of the distortions of organized religions. The story of Lemuria is the story of our initial descent into Matter. The promise of Lemuria is that we will ultimately Return to Spirit. Chiron's message and appearance on Earth at this time are part of this story. The story of Lemuria will have its culmination in the theme of the Second Coming, which we will cover in the next section.

Deep in antiquity, there was a place called Lemuria. Exactly where it was is not exactly known. It is likely, though, that it sat somewhere between the physical world, as we know it, and the next higher dimensional reality. The Lemurian race was an *astral* or *semi-discarnate* race, existing before biological life was sufficiently evolved to host (incarnate) souls such as ourselves. In long-past previous lives, we were all astrally incarnate as Lemurians.

As Lemurians, we lived, in a sense, closer to the Grace of the Creator. We had more of an innate sense of the Oneness of everything around us. We were connected to each other, to Nature, to Mother Earth, to the planets in a living way. We were connected to the higher angelic realms. We Served the cosmic purpose of bringing Light into the Earth realm, which we did with Joy and Love. However, our consciousness was not as fully awakened as it is now. We were, in a sense, still asleep to our *individual* potential, still innocent of our divinity and of the higher Designs for which we were created. We basked in a more collective consciousness. Neither did we yet know the same experiences of Darkness that we have experienced since (in our physical incarnations). We were what we might call *Innocent Angels.*

At a certain point, according to the designs of the Creation, sufficiently-evolved physical vehicles appeared on Earth and the Gift of incarnation was bestowed upon us. The next stage of the great Plan was set in motion. In the subsequent and innumerable incarnations, racially *en masse* and individually as souls, we, the former Lemurians, freely walked into worlds previously denied to us. We walked the material world, the world of physical incarnation, the world of duality and illusion, the world of Darkness. We have explored separateness, aloneness and individuality, along with all other dualized emotions of the human psyche. We have explored the lower realms of illusion, unconsciousness and sleep. We have delved deep into materiality.

At the point of the Earth's greatest density or greatest materiality (when we had long since been incarnate in *physical* form) we were known as the *Atlanteans.* This was about 85,000 years ago, some conjecture. In this incarnational guise, we explored all aspects of the Dark side of Creation. In doing so, we accumulated great density and fragmentation of consciousness. However, we also gained much experience and learned many lessons.

When we had sufficiently explored this side of Creation, we were then given the choice between the Darkness of dualistic materiality and the Light from which we had come. At this time, Avatars of Light descended from Above with the specific purpose of guiding us back to Light. They sewed the threads of the Great Story of Creation and Evolution into the fabric of all cultures on Earth. Such is the Story of Life that we will explore at great length in Book Three.

For many, the choice has been made to journey back to the Light – back toward the Creator – carrying with us the knowledge and experience we have accumulated and, most importantly, the awakened consciousness we have attained.

On the Return journey, it is necessary to transform our density . . . to rejoin our fragmented consciousness . . . *consciously and intentionally.* Such is the journey of Healing and the evolution of consciousness. This is played out through many trials and tribulations over countless incarnations. In this way, we gradually reach for the Light.

The Return journey consists of dissolving, Healing and resolving our issues – i.e. our Wounds, blockages, misperceptions and illusions. Such is the path back to Light, the Path back to Lemuria. However, we Return with awakened consciousness and self-determination, borne out of the acknowledgment of the Oneness of human will and divine Will.

This is where we stand presently. We are engaged in the on-going process of Healing our fragmented consciousness. We are reconnecting with our Lemurian origins and bringing back the treasures of our long journey: knowledge, wisdom, humility, understanding, conscience, consciousness and awakened individuality. We are walking back towards Lemuria, back toward Light, Oneness and Love, but *we do so awakened. We do so with our individuality and our free will intact.* This may seem like a contradiction, i.e. becoming One, but remaining Many. There is no contradiction; we are individual and yet we are One with All. We are the hologram. This is the great paradox, a paradox dissolved by the Healing journey.

We now stand on the threshold of the culmination of the Creator's Plan for us. We are poised to become conscious, willing servants of Light and of the Creation – to become conscious co-Creators, engaged in the process of Creation.

For this to occur, the illusions perpetuated in the Darkness must be purged. That is to say, all our Wounds must be Healed, all our polarities reconciled and all our fragmented parts rejoined, Healed and 'wholed' in Love and Light. This is where Chiron comes in. Chiron offers us a concise and focused process of 'whole-ing', integration, growth and evolution, allowing us to Heal in optimal time.

Key Points

- The story of Lemuria is the story of our initial descent into Matter.
- The promise of Lemuria is that we will ultimately Return to Spirit.
- The Lemurian race was an astral or semi-discarnate race.
- As Lemurians, we were closer to the Grace of the Creator, but with less awakened consciousness.
- As Lemurians, we were Innocent Angels basking in a collective consciousness.
- When evolved physical vehicles became available, we were given the Gift of incarnation.
- In the time of Atlantis, we reached the point of greatest density or materiality.
- Avatars of Light descended to the Earth realm to help us Return to the Light.
- The Avatars sowed the seeds of the Great Story of Life into many diverse cultures.
- The Return journey requires conscious and intentional effort, taking innumerable incarnations.
- The Return to Lemuria is the Return to Light, but with awakened consciousness.
- The Return to Lemuria is the merging of human will and Divine Will.
- The last stage of the Lemurian Plan is to become co-Creators in the process of Creation.
- We are One and we are Many; we are the hologram.
- Chiron offers us concise, focused and swift processes of Healing.

The Second Coming

The Second Coming of the Christ is a symbol of our rejoining with divinity. The Second Coming is occurring within each one of us as we Heal and 'whole' ourselves. It is the individual and collective attainment of Christ Consciousness.

Jesus, the man, whether actual or symbolic, was a messenger, a symbol and a facilitator of Christ consciousness some 2000 years ago. Since its discovery in 1977, Chiron, too, facilitates the attainment of Christ

Consciousness by offering a path whereby we can Heal our separation from divinity.

What do we mean by "Christ consciousness"? Simply, a state of higher consciousness, closer to Truth, Oneness and Love. Chiron encourages us to open our inner eyes to all those things within us that prevent us from attaining these ideals, that prevent us from reconnecting to life and to Spirit. Chiron encourages us to look into our Darkness and to Love what we find there. The Light of awakened consciousness allows us to see what we need to see. The Second Coming is a shifting of consciousness within each one of us into the next dimensional reality – closer to the Creator, closer to Love, closer to Oneness. As we shift, so the world shifts.

The Parting of Ways is symbolic of the way in which each of us reacts to the increase of Light as the planet increases its consciousness. Those who are ready for the quantum leap will move with the changes. Others will not yet be ready and will shy away from the brightness of the Light. This is in alignment with cosmic justice. Those who are not ready will continue their lessons, plying their spiritual paths in different directions – directions that are 'lateral' within the current dimensional reality.

As a symbol, the Parting of the Ways was distorted into the story of sinners going to Hell and the 'righteous' going to Heaven after physical death. This distortion was perpetrated by those wishing to control others for their own self-serving aims. In Truth, Heaven and Hell are an inner state arising from our self-judgment and appraisal of our current level in the hierarchy of consciousness. Such judgment is determined by how much we have learned to Love and what we have yet to Love.

Lastly, the story of the Second Coming as the physical reappearance of Jesus, the man, is, I believe, a device invented by the early Christian church to help the general (and, for the most part, uneducated) populace retain their Faith. All things Serve. However, the true meaning of the Second Coming lies in the attainment of Christ Consciousness, i.e. in the rejoining of our earthly selves with our divine origins. Such is the final aim of all Healing.

Key Points

- The Second Coming is the personal and collective attainment of Christ Consciousness.
- In the 20th century, Chiron facilitates the attainment of Christ Consciousness.
- Christ Consciousness is a state of consciousness closer to Truth, Oneness and Love.
- Chiron encourages us to look into our Darkness and Love what we find there.
- The Parting of the Ways means some choose to move more quickly towards the Light, whereas some choose to move not so quickly.
- The personal experience of Heaven or Hell is related to what we have Loved and what we have yet to Love.
- The Second Coming – the rejoining of our earthly selves with our divine origins – is the final aim of all Healing.

Wounding and Healing

The descent of Spirit into Matter and the re-ascent of Matter into Spirit are the Creation and evolution, respectively. We have compared these to white light splitting into seven colors and merging back into white light via the Rainbow Bridge.

On the descending journey, Oneness becomes Manyness, unity becomes diversity (duality) and Actuality becomes the illusory reality we perceive. In the Chiron paradigm, the descending journey is *the Wounding.*

On the Return journey—the ascent – Manyness returns to Oneness, diversity (duality) returns to unity and our illusions of reality dissolve into the Truth of Actuality. In the Chiron paradigm, this is *the Healing.*

All life is either descending or ascending, either Wounding or Healing. Healing is synonymous with our evolutionary journey of consciousness. This is one of Chiron's great messages, the essence of our explorations in this series of books.

Key Points

- The Wounding is the Creation.
- Wounding takes us from Oneness into Manyness, from unity into duality, from Truth into illusion, from Actuality into illusory reality.
- The Healing is evolution.
- Healing takes us from Manyness to Oneness, from duality to unity, from dualistic illusion to Truth, from illusory reality to Actuality.

The Gift in the Wound

"The disgusting and rejected frog or dragon of the fairy tale brings up the sun ball in its mouth [from the bottom of the pond]; for the frog, the serpent, the rejected one, is the representative of that unconscious deep ("so deep that the bottom [of the pond] cannot be seen") wherein are hoarded all of the rejected, unadmitted, unrecognized, unknown, or undeveloped factors, laws, and elements of existence. Those are the pearls of the fabled submarine palaces of the nixies, tritons, and water guardians; the jewels that give light to the demon cities of the underworld; the fire seeds in the ocean of immortality which supports the earth and surrounds it like a snake; the stars in the bosom of immortal night. Those are the nuggets in the gold hoard of the dragon; the guarded apples of the Hesperides; the filaments of the Golden Fleece. The herald or announcer of the adventure, therefore, is often dark, loathly, or terrifying, judged evil by the world; yet if one could follow, the way would be opened through the walls of day into the dark where the jewels glow."[30]

-Joseph Campbell

Chiron's primary emerging theme is the symbol of the *Gift in the Wound.* Chiron says that every Wound bears a hidden Gift, a hidden Service, a hidden blessing. Other ways of expressing this are:

There is a blessing in every crisis.

---

[30] Campbell, Joseph. *The Hero with a Thousand Faces.* Fontana Press, 1993, pp.52-53.

Every cloud has a silver lining.
There are benefits to every negative situation.
Every Void has a Value.
Every thing and every happening is a Service of Love.
Through the Darkness lies the Light.
Beyond the Pain lies Love.

Chiron's message is that there is not a thing – no circumstance, event, situation, person or thing – that does not Serve us in every way on our journey of Healing and evolution of consciousness. All things Serve. All circumstances, events, situations, people and things are acts of Love from a Guiding Hand. There is a Guiding Hand looking after us in every way as we ply the path of Healing, as we strive for a Return to Love.

Further to this, there is nothing we can *do or say,* nothing that we can *neglect to do or say,* that is not also a Service to others on their paths of Healing and evolution of consciousness.

Divine order and balance already exist in the world and in our lives. From this perspective, there can be nothing that does not Serve order and balance. Every aspect is part of the larger Plan.

At first, this may seem a little difficult to accept and overly idealistic. We look into the world and we see much evil, wrongdoing, injustice, imbalance and Darkness. We see these in us, in our lives, in others, in others' lives and in the world at large. *Chiron says the Healing and evolutionary journey consists of the transcendence of these very perceptions.* Chiron says that our journey is to discover the hidden order, hidden balance, hidden meaning and Love that lie behind all things, even those things we initially judge and condemn. The Healing journey is to see the perfection and to become aware of the Guiding Hand. To this end, Chiron offers us the idea of the Gift in the Wound.

Our judgments, blame and condemnations are inherent parts of the Wounds that lie buried within us, awaiting the Healing effect of higher perspectives and broader understanding. Part of the Healing process is to begin to look for blessings, benefits, service, opportunities, possibilities and lessons within what we initially judge negatively and within what we initially condemn. When the picture is sufficiently clear to us, we are ready for Chiron's next step (that we will cover as we proceed).

When the blessings, benefits, lessons and Service of the Wound have been seen, acknowledged, embraced and Loved, we are left with a glimpse of a bigger picture of our lives. The bigger picture reveals answers to the four basic questions of our spiritual journey: *Who are we? Where do we come from? Where are we going? Why are we here?* The *Divine Design* of our lives is embedded in the answers to these questions. Our Divine Design is the deeper meaning and higher purpose of our lives, revealed as a *vision* and a *calling* in the spaces of our open Heart. Our Divine Design is the special Service we offer the world, as an act of Love and Gratitude for the acknowledged blessing of our lives. The ultimate Gift in the Wound is the discovery of our Divine Design.

We will explore these themes in greater detail later.

Key Points

- Every Wound has a hidden Gift, a hidden Service, a hidden blessing.
- All things Serve our Healing and evolution of consciousness.
- All happenings, people and things are acts of Love from a Guiding Hand.
- There is a Guiding Hand helping us as we ply the path of Healing.
- Our journey is to discover the hidden perfection and Love that lie behind all things, even those we initially judge and condemn.
- When we see the benefits, blessings, lessons and Gifts of what we initially judged and condemned, our Hearts open.
- The Divine Design of our lives is revealed as a vision and calling in our open Hearts.
- Our Divine Design is our special Service, offered as an act of Love and Gratitude.

Chiron's Promise

The place of Return, symbolized by the mythical fire of Prometheus, is, astrologically speaking, the Sun. The astrological and metaphysical journey from Earth (the material world) to Sun (the spiritual world) will be elaborated shortly.

Chiron was immortalized as a star in the constellation of Sagittarius, as we mentioned previously. Becoming a star represents a Return to Spirit, Oneness and Love, a Return to greater Light. Whether we Return to the Sun or to a star, it is the same thing. (The Sun is a star.) However, the symbol of the constellation of Sagittarius goes one step further. Sagittarius lies in the direction of the galactic center of the Milky Way. The implication here is that Chiron, having finished his purpose on Earth and having become enlightened *beyond the confines of the solar system* now resonated with the greater spiritual Light of the galactic center. The further significance of these metaphors will become apparent when we explore their astrological, astronomical and metaphysical meanings in Book Three.

Chiron's Promise is that we shall all eventually Return to the Light. The path to the Light *lies through the Darkness.* By walking into our Darkness, shining the light of Love, we will find the greater Light that lies within us; we will awaken to the ocean of Light and Love that surrounds us. The Light of Love is all around us. *We* are the Light of Love. Awakening to this Truth *is* the Healing journey.

Key Points

- The Return to Light is symbolized, astrologically, by the journey to the Sun;
- It is further symbolized by Chiron's Return to the greater Light of the galactic center in Sagittarius.
- Chiron's Promise is that we shall all Return to Light.
- The Light lies through the Darkness, accessed by our Love.
- The Light of Love is all around us. *We* are the Light of Love.

4 ~ JOURNEY'S THROUGH THE PLANETS

"Know that you are another world in miniature and have in you Sol and Luna and even the stars." [31]

-Origen, a 3rd century Church father.

Dual Journeys

If we are to put Chiron into its proper context in the bigger cosmic picture, we will need to understand the weave of the entire fabric, so to speak. Therefore, we will need to understand the whole planetary picture and its relationship to our lives, personally and collectively. Furthermore, working with Chiron, as I have done for so many years now, has given me a view of the whole planetary picture that is quite different in some respects to the traditional view accepted by most astrologers. The difference lies in the metaphysical framework that gives each planet its special place in the larger Plan of Creation. We will explore this framework briefly in this chapter, offering much greater detail in Book Three.

With a view to putting Chiron into its proper context in the bigger cosmic picture, let's take a look at the map of our solar system. This map is, metaphysically speaking, a map of our potential Healing and evolution of consciousness. Let's take the solar system *and the relative positions of the planets in relation to the Earth* as a metaphor and symbol for our journey.

---

[31] Translated and quoted in: Moore, *op cit.*, p.320.

The process of our Healing and evolution of consciousness is a process of awakening in two 'directions'. It is a dual process of 1) *focusing* our inner will and attention and 2) *expanding* our awareness.

As we grow from childhood to adulthood, self-awareness grows, as does will, focus, attention and self-determination – an inner journey that parallels the outer expansion of our consciousness. This journey is a gradual process of focusing our consciousness into a laser-like point. To a certain extent, this growth happens naturally over time, as it is the innate striving within every living creature to evolve.

It is true, however, that sometimes we get stuck along the way, lose the vision or become too comfortable in our particular sphere. At these times, we tend to attract some difficult circumstance – some kind of wake-up call – and, in an instant, our comfortable illusions are destroyed again. The inexorable march of evolution is written into every fiber of our bodies and souls, into every atom in the Universe. To continue, however . . .

Simultaneous with this inward-tending focusing process, our outward sphere of awareness, initially limited to the immediate world around us, gradually expands. As we grow, experiencing repeated awakenings and realizations, we gradually become aware that the world is bigger than we thought. Our scope widens, our vision extends farther and we include more of the outer world in our inner picture. The way we view the Universe and ourselves at any particular time in our lives is destined to be superseded by an ever-greater picture of reality. In this way, we are always learning, always expanding.

The first aspect of our journey – that of *focusing* consciousness, will, attention and self-determination – is paralleled by the astrological and astronomical journey from the relatively dark consciousness of the Earth to the enlightened consciousness of the Sun.

If we consider the Creation to be analogous to the descent of white light into the seven colors of the rainbow – specifically, what we call the *Seven Rays* of Creation – then the merging of these colors, returning to white light, *initially occurs at the Sun.* The planets each represent various manifestations of the Seven Rays as those Rays pass through the solar system on their way to the Sun. We, as aspects of the light of the Rays on planet Earth, are on a journey to the Sun, the focal point for the consciousness of the solar system. We will explore the Seven Rays and these related questions, astronomically, astrologically and metaphysically, in Book Three.

The second aspect of our journey is that of *expanding* consciousness, i.e. becoming aware of an ever-larger, ever-more-expansive picture. This is paralleled, in our metaphor, by the astrological and astronomical journey from the narrow sphere of Earth to the widest sphere of Pluto and beyond . . . all the way to the *magnetopause*[32] of the solar system. Again, we will explore the astronomical, astrological and metaphysical details and ramifications of this in Book Three.

There are, of course, many ways to look at the planets and their relation to our evolutionary journey of consciousness. Each way of looking at the larger plan serves a valuable purpose in terms of our Healing and expansion of consciousness. However, the *actual* journey that we take through the solar system – as Light passing through the magnetopause, 'descending' to Earth, 'rising' to the Sun and then 'rising' back to the magnetopause – is a little more complex than the metaphors that we will present below. In Actuality, the exact planets touched on our journey may be different and in a different order from the simplified metaphors that follow. However, what we will present below will form the basis for further understanding. One step at a time. Detailed aspects of the actual journey will be explored in Book Three.

Let's take a closer look at each of these dual journeys, one at a time . . .

Key Points

- The first aspect of our two-part journey is the *focusing* of consciousness – the journey from Earth to Sun;
- The second aspect is the *expanding* of consciousness – the journey from Earth to Pluto to the magnetopause and beyond.
- The Sun is the focal point for the consciousness of the solar system.

[32] The magnetopause is the astronomical boundary of our solar system where all electromagnetism, i.e. Light in its infinite frequencies, becomes unified. It lies over 4000 *astronomical units* (AU) from the Sun, where an astronomical unit equals the average distance from the Sun to the Earth.

The Journey from Earth to Sun

Consider the journey of awakening and development of self-awareness, self-determination, will and focus. This journey consists of *synthesizing* all we have gleaned from our expanding consciousness of the world around us. It is a process of bringing our unified awareness and understanding into the intensity of laser light or nuclear fusion. This is represented by the journey from the relative darkness of the Earth to the enlightened consciousness of the Sun. In terms of consciousness, the Sun is 'where it's at', so to speak; it's 'the place to be'.

The journey from Earth to Sun, via Moon, Venus and Mercury, is a journey of bringing duality, fragmentation and illusion back into Oneness and Truth. It is about transcending our judgments, biases, misperceptions and illusions. It is about merging the fragments of ourselves – our *personas* – into the unity of our true Being. It is about Healing our Wounds. It is about awakening to the perfection and divinity all around us at every moment in our lives. Our lives are perfect and divine in ways that we do not initially see. It is about acknowledging the Guiding Hand that is with us at every moment of our lives, hidden from our unseeing eyes.

We begin the focusing journey of consciousness on planet Earth, of course. Without going into too much detail at this stage, our consciousness, when 'dense', 'heavy' and relatively unawakened, is trapped by the gravity of the Earth and by the density of its electromagnetic field. Thus, we begin our cycles of incarnation. As we awaken, becoming 'lighter' and more 'transparent', our consciousness rises from the Earth (even while still attached to the physical body during incarnation) toward spheres of greater consciousness. Specifically, our consciousness rises towards the Sun (our body being a kind of diving suit on Earth). At a certain point between the Earth and the Sun, the Sun's gravity and electromagnetic influence overrule the Earth's gravity and we are 'attracted' towards and 'captured' by its greater Light. This all has to do with electromagnetic fields, their density and frequency and their interaction with each other. *Our consciousness is an electromagnetic field,* as we shall discover, inhabiting a physical body but temporarily. We will explore the physics and metaphysics of this in Book Three.

The first stepping-stone to the Sun is the Moon. As our consciousness rises from the Earth in gradually higher concentric spheres, it is primarily under the influence of the gravity and electromagnetic field of the Moon.[33]

The Moon, in part, represents protective patterns – particularly emotional ones – that keep us from having to deal with difficult life issues before we are ready. These patterns can be reactive or passive – reactive helps us fight for our safety, while passive helps us 'sleep' through it all. These patterns remain with us for the whole of our lives. These patterns are part and parcel of our animal nature or *lower mind.* Our lower mind is also referred to (in some circles) as the *lower self,* as opposed to the *higher Self.* Our lower mind is the part of us that seeks pleasure and flees from pain. It protects our physical existence. It is summated in the autonomic nervous system. It is a survival-oriented being. Most importantly, *the lower mind perceives the Universe through the duality of the senses.*

In order to evolve our consciousness toward greater Oneness and Truth, we must transcend the illusions of the lower mind. Our lower mind 'sees' through the physical senses, perceiving the world only in terms of duality, illusion, judgment, half-truths and lies. We will be exploring the physiology and psychology of this at length in Book Two. In short, our journey entails transcending the emotional patterns represented by the Moon. This means addressing these patterns and their associated issues and seeing them for what they are. Such is the journey of self-knowledge. Although these patterns Serve us up to a certain point in our lives, eventually they become counter-productive to our quest for Healing and evolution of consciousness.

Inherent in the lessons of transcending the Moon is the struggle against the inertia, laziness and complacency of our lower nature, the

---

[33] Science does not yet acknowledge the Moon as having a planetary electromagnetic field (magnetosphere), considering it a dead planet. However, recent discoveries show that its core is capable of inducing a magnetic field when it passes through the Earth's magnetosphere. New Scientist Magazine, June 1999, p. 15.

struggle against the 'heaviness' and pull of the body and the struggle against the material illusions of the senses. It is a process of listening, not to the messages of the lower mind, but to the messages of the Soul that already sees the big picture. (We will define "Soul" as we proceed.) It is learning the lesson of *effort.* Without effort, gravity takes hold of us and pulls us back into the Darkness.

It is also a process of dissolving our illusions of pain and pleasure, realizing that pleasures have their pain and pain has its benefits and blessings. To this end, Chiron will help us to see the Gifts in our Wounds. In addition, each of the planets, from Jupiter outwards, will assist us in overcoming the illusions of the Moon-ruled lower mind. We will explore this a little later. Back to the Moon, however . . .

Considering the above, the influence of the Moon relates primarily to our *identification* with *the material world and with our physical bodies.* We are both attracted to and repulsed by this world. We both infatuate its pleasures and resent its pains. We are *emotionally attached to it.* In this way, *the material world rules us as long as we listen to the messages of the Moon-ruled lower mind.*

Transcendence of the influence of the material world and the dualistic illusions of the senses entails a realization, acknowledgment and growing emphasis on our *spiritual* or non-material nature. We need to break free from the hypnosis of the sensory experience, i.e. from our identification with our material nature.

Paradoxically, for this to be realized and transcendence to be attained, a balanced appreciation and wise utilization of the body and of the material world is required. If we seek to escape from the physical world whilst infatuating the spiritual, we are destined to remain here until we Love the material world Unconditionally. Our task is to *master* the material world, not escape from it. Mastery of the material world *is a spiritual attainment.* The two – the material and the spiritual – are, in Truth, inseparable. Equal mastery of both brings the freedom we seek.

The journey through the waters of space, under the influence of the Moon, represents a major portion of our journey from the Earth to the Sun. From here, we pass to Venus. Venus, in this case, represents a *higher octave* of emotional illusions, biases, judgments and lies. Our emotions pull us this way and that, constantly swinging from one extreme to another. *Each emotion, as a fragment of our whole being, represents but a fragment of the greater Truth of Unconditional Love.* Yet, each emotion, when we experience it in the moment, demands our total attention, making us feel as though this is the only reality. One minute we feel a certain way and cannot imagine feeling any differently. Yet, in next moment, due to influences external and/or internal, we do (feel differently). The seesawing of our emotions accounts for our often-illogical, one-sided and judgmental viewpoints, opinions and attitudes. In our daily lives, the emotional extremes of *elation* and *depression* follow each other as inevitably as sunshine follows rain.

Venus's lesson is about *balance.* It is about learning to see both sides of a given issue – the *yin* and the *yang* – and come to a balanced emotional state about it. It is about learning to *manage* our emotions. It is about realizing where and how we are emotionally 'colored' on issues. It is about seeking the middle ground between the eternal 'tic-tocking' of our emotions. It is about becoming free from the attraction and repulsion of these emotions.

The mid-point between the tic-tocking of all emotions is Unconditional Love. *Unconditional Love is not an emotion. It is the synthesis of all emotions into Oneness.* Yet, paradoxically, each emotion offers a Service. Fear, guilt, jealousy, anger, etcetera, as well as happiness, excitement, affection, determination, etcetera, *all Serve our journey of Healing and evolution of consciousness.* Each emotion points us back towards the center, back towards the middle point, back to the point of maximum growth. The transcendence of Venus entails the acknowledgment of the Service each individual emotion plays in the greater picture of our personal evolution. Our Healing and evolution depend on us embracing each emotion *and its polar opposite.* We transcend Venus by transcending our emotional nature. We transcend our emotional nature by Loving each aspect of ourselves – every emotion, every 'anti-emotion', every personality trait, every crease and fold of the psyche. Such is the path to Unconditional Love. In this way, Venus is aligned to Neptune. This, however, is a future topic.

Next, we come to Mercury. Mercury, after Venus and the Moon, represents the next octave of duality we wish to transcend in favor of greater unity of consciousness. Mercury relates to the intellect . . . the thinking and communicating mind. Initially, our minds are a myriad of thoughts and opinions, ideas and attitudes *that all vie for attention, more often than not conflicting, disagreeing and canceling each other out.* We are not aware of the majority of our mental contradictions. The 'thinker' in us is constantly changing hats! This is why we say that Mercury rules the astrological sign of Gemini, the sign of the chameleon! *When we are expressing one opinion, we are repressing another part of us that thinks the opposite in a different moment.* However, in our relatively unawakened state, we think that our thoughts, ideas, opinions and attitudes are coherent, logical, consistent and more-or-less permanent. We are blind to many of the inconsistencies of our thought . . . until others point them out! Even then, we do not always listen or believe it!

The path through Mercury demands that we bring our mental inconsistencies, contradictions, biases, illusions and lies into a consistent and synthesized whole. It demands that we see things as they truly are and not how we *think* they are. It demands that we awaken to the fact that our contradictory *personas* express and espouse contradictory ideals at different times. It demands that we look out into the world and begin to see how things really are, not how our one-sided thinking perceives things to be. It implores us to realize that *there are two sides to every coin, two ends to every stick, two sides to everything in existence. There is an 'up' side and a 'down' side to everything.* If we judge something or someone as being 'bad', where is the equal 'good'? If judge something or someone as being 'good', where is the equal 'bad'? If we look hard enough and long enough, we will discover that the 'goods' and the 'bads' in anything *are equally balanced. Further, that 'goods' and 'bads', 'rights' and 'wrongs', positives and negatives are all a matter of perception, not Actuality.* We will explore this radical statement and the mechanics of perception in Books Two and Three.

Ultimately, the lesson of Mercury, as we approach the Sun, is to begin to see, decipher, appreciate and finally embrace the perfection of the magnificent Plan of life around us. Mercury's lesson is to see that there is nothing out of place in the Universe, that each piece is connected, has its place and fits perfectly into the jigsaw of life. It is to see that there are no mistakes, no accidents, no injustices and nothing to fix. Every part of Creation Serves us and points us back towards Love and Oneness. In this way, Mercury is aligned with Uranus . . . but again we digress.

The intellectual mind is a tool, through which we can ultimately see and appreciate the blueprints of Creation. It is a tool that allows us to stand back and see the whole picture before us. This is the quest of both science and spirituality. Science seeks the Grand Unified Theory of the Universe. Spirituality seeks the meaning of existence; it seeks to touch the face of the Creator, so to speak. When science and spirituality meet, some time in the future, realizing that their quest *was* the same and that their final answers *are* the same, Humanity will have reached the Sun in consciousness.

The three planets we 'travel through' on our way to Sun consciousness – Moon, Venus and Mercury – roughly represent body, emotions and intellect, respectively. I say, "roughly", because the physical body is definitely Earth-ruled, although influenced greatly by *all* the inner planets. Mercury represents a higher octave of consciousness than Venus, which, in turn, represents a higher octave of consciousness than does the Moon. As we bring each aspect of ourselves into greater balance and unity, the hidden factor behind them all gradually becomes apparent . . . i.e. the invisible Spirit within us. *The consciousness of the Sun is the blending of all three aspects of ourselves into a unified whole.* This blending is our *spiritual* nature.

Each of us has the potential to attain Sun consciousness. This journey – this quest – has been the underlying theme behind every 'hero' story since the dawn of man. It lies behind all solar worship and behind our eternal fascination with the Sun. The symbols and events in each case may differ vastly, but the essence remains the same, i.e. the triumph of Light over Darkness.[34]

Such is Chiron's journey, too, as we elaborated in the mythology section. Chiron, either by the symbolic release of Prometheus, the god of fire, or by his mythical transformation into a star, returned as a hero to greater Light and Oneness. We all have this potential. These stories and myths were designed – designed consciously by awakened beings (Avatars) in antiquity – to awaken the part of us that longs for Light,

---

[34] Refer to Joseph Campbell's "The Hero with a Thousand Faces". See bibliography.

that longs for Truth, that longs for Unconditional Love and that longs for the ultimate Return Home.

Key Points

- The journey from Earth to Sun is the journey of self-awareness, self-determination, will and focus;
- This journey is a journey of *synthesis* towards the Sun.
- The consciousness of the Sun is like laser light or nuclear fusion.
- This journey returns duality, fragmentation and illusion into Oneness and Truth.
- This journey brings together the fragments of ourselves into unified Being.
- Our task is to transcend our judgments, biases, misperceptions and illusions.
- Our lives are perfect and divine in ways that we cannot initially see.
- Our consciousness, when 'dense' and 'heavy', is trapped by the gravity and electromagnetism of the Earth.
- As we awaken, becoming 'lighter' and more 'transparent', our consciousness rises from the Earth towards the Sun.
- The Moon represents our lower nature (lower mind).
- Our lower mind perceives the Universe through the duality of the senses.
- Our task is to master the material and spiritual worlds simultaneously.
- The material and the spiritual are, in Truth, inseparable.
- Freedom comes from mastering both the material and the spiritual equally.
- Venus represents our emotional illusions, biases, judgments and lies.
- Our emotions pull us this way and that, constantly swinging from one extreme to another.
- Each emotion is but a fragment of the greater Truth of Unconditional Love.
- Venus teaches us to see the balance of any given issue – both sides: the *yin* and the *yang*.
- Venus's lesson is about learning to manage our emotions.
- The mid-point between the tic-tocking of our emotions is Unconditional Love.
- Unconditional Love is not an emotion, but the synthesis of all emotions into Oneness.
- Our minds are a myriad of conflicting thoughts, opinions, ideas and attitudes.
- When we express an opinion, we are repressing another part of us that thinks the opposite in a different moment.

- Mercury's lesson is to bring our mental inconsistencies, contradictions, biases, illusions and lies into a consistent and synthesized whole.
- There are two sides to every coin, two ends to every stick.
- There is nothing out of place in the Universe, each piece having its perfect place.
- There are no mistakes, no accidents, no injustices and nothing to fix.
- Every part of Creation Serves us, pointing us back towards Love and Oneness.
- Moon, Venus and Mercury relate to body, emotions and intellect, respectively.
- The consciousness of the Sun is the blending of our physical, emotional and mental aspects;
- This blending constitutes our spiritual nature.
- The Return to Light is the theme of all the great hero stories throughout history.

The Journey from Earth to Pluto and Beyond

Paralleling the *focusing* journey of consciousness, represented by the journey from Earth to Sun, is the journey of *expanding* our consciousness. This journey traces the ever-expanding orbits of the planets, from Earth to Pluto and beyond.

How can we be *focusing* and *expanding* simultaneously? The answer lies in the nature of time and space and its connection to light and consciousness. We will discuss these questions in detail in Book Three. Suffice to say, as we Heal and evolve, our consciousness approaches the speed of light and our perception of time and space collapses towards timelessness and spacelessness. To a being with galactic consciousness, the entire solar system appears as a *non-local* point, timeless and spaceless. All is Here and Now.

Back to our journey of expansion from Earth to Pluto and beyond . . .

Before Copernicus, western Mankind considered the Earth the center of the Universe and that the planets, Sun and stars revolved around it. This was a *geocentric* view of the cosmos, i.e. the Earth at the center. In the evolution of our understanding, we eventually realized that this view was flawed. We discovered that the Sun was the center of our solar system and that the Earth was subordinate to it. This is the *heliocentric* view of the cosmos, i.e. the Sun at the center. This understanding was further superseded by modern astronomy and astrophysics with the realization that our solar system was subordinate to the larger order of the galaxy. Furthermore, our galaxy is subordinate to the larger order of the local cluster of galaxies, and so on.

To understand the celestial map of our potential Healing and evolution of consciousness, we need to return to the geocentric view for a moment – i.e. the Earth at the center. In this astrological plan, the Earth is our starting point. From here, the astronomical distance of the orbit of each next nearest planet to Earth – Moon, Venus, Mars, Mercury and Sun – traces our astrological path of growth from birth to adulthood. Our consciousness expands, gradually encompassing the solar system, one planet at a time. When our conscious awareness approaches the Sun, we are said to have grown up – we have reached the age of self-determination. Astrologically, the Sun relates to ego, will, attention, focus, self-determination and consciousness in general.

At this point, our awareness *potentially* becomes heliocentric – the Sun at the center. When this happens, we begin to have the possibility of manifesting our true Will (as opposed to our little *wills)* in relation to our lives. At this point, we are said to have come of age; that is, we begin to operate within spheres of activity in life that correspond to the interplay of the affairs of the inner planets. The inner planets are Earth, Moon, Venus, Mars, Mercury and Sun. (The Sun, although a star, and the Moon, although a satellite, are astrologically referred to as planets.)

Now our potential growth is poised on the edge of the inner solar system – at the Asteroid belt. Much of our conscious life does not extend beyond this point – we remain transfixed by the compelling illusion and sleepy comfort of our ordinary lives. The Asteroid belt, from one point of view, is an important factor in the natural inhibition of Humanity's growth and evolution. It is a safety belt, holding us back until we are ready to continue our evolution, until we are ready for greater Truth.

The Asteroid belt divides the inner planets from the outer planets. Modern astronomers have tried to understand what the Asteroids are, how they came to be there and what is their part in the cosmic plan. If the bigger picture of the solar system is a macro-reflection of our inner constitution, as we are proposing, then we, too, need to understand their significance.

Science has yet to decide what are the origins of the Asteroids. One theory is that the Asteroids were part of an ancient cosmic calamity. Consider the following ideas. Firstly, the astronomical law called *Bode's Law* leads some astronomers to believe that there should have been a planet where the Asteroids are now. One theory is that a stray planet, meteor or comet came into the solar system in antiquity and collided with this hypothetical planet. The Asteroids are the resultant debris of this cosmic collision. However, some scientists shy away from this theory because there is not enough mass in all the Asteroids to make up a planet even the size of our Moon. However, the total mass of the destroyed planet may not have ended up in the Asteroid belt. Some of it may have ended up as other planets, moons of other planets, comets, meteors, cosmic debris or been ejected entirely from the solar system by the force of the collision.

For the purposes of this book and our journey, though, let's assume that there was a planet there and that the Asteroids are part of the debris of an ancient cosmic collision. The scientific fact that there is not enough mass in all the resultant Asteroids to make up for the hypothetical missing planet suggests that the solar system, if taken as an integrated system, has an inherent imbalance. In truth, the imbalance is only in our perception. When we discover where the missing mass went and where it is now, we will see how balance has been maintained. Furthermore, *when we see how the perception of imbalance has helped us to evolve, grow and Heal, we will have solved the mystery.*

This brings us to our point, which is, in part, a theory of why human psychological and spiritual evolution have seemingly proceeded so slowly, at times almost at a standstill. If we accept that our natural growth and evolution as a species is reflected in the ever-widening orbits of the planets and, further, by our consciousness of each of them at their discovery, then we are confronted by a missing rung on the evolutionary ladder – or, at best, a seemingly-damaged one. The Asteroids represent this missing or damaged rung. Our consciousness reaches the orbit of Mars, encompassing, as we have said, all the affairs of our ordinary existence. At this point, the next stepping-stone is missing or damaged, appearing to condemn us to lives confined to the inner planets. Without this rung in place, how are we to find our way to the affairs of the outer planets, to our potential as consciously-awakened spiritual beings?

There are two potential answers to this dilemma. The first has been already explored by some astrologers. This consists of deciphering the messages of the various Asteroids from an astrological point of view. There are messages to be heard from some of the larger Asteroids – Vesta, Juno, Pallas Athene, Ceres, Toro, Psyche, Hidalgo, Eros, Icarus, Sappho, Urania, Pandora, Amor and Lillith, to name a few. The Asteroids, astrologically and psychologically speaking, represent special missionaries or guides to help us bridge the gap between Mars and Jupiter. In our natal (birth) horoscopes, they represent special talents, gifts and guidance.

We won't go into too much detail here about the Asteroids. It is relevant to mention, however, that the Asteroids' represent a primarily *feminine* influence. When taken within the context of the journey from the inner to the outer planets, this makes sense as a counter-balance to Mars's masculine influence that precedes the Asteroid belt. What is important, though, is that the Asteroids, on their own, seem to have been unsuccessful in providing a total bridge to the outer planets.

It is necessary, on our evolutionary journey, to come back to the Asteroids (and even back to the inner planets) after touching Jupiter, Saturn and Chiron before we can move out to Uranus, Neptune and Pluto. The specific issues of Saturn and Chiron (which we will touch upon briefly in a minute) outline this path of recapitulation. (Chiron traces a path of recapitulation by its wayward orbit that sometimes comes inside the orbit of Saturn.)

Chiron's discovery may be the discovery of a counter-balance to the missing Asteroid mass. Whether this is true or not, Chiron certainly offers a potential answer to our missing-rung dilemma, as a kind of foster-brother to the planets. The discovery of Chiron and the recapitulation of our lives as per Chiron's indications are part of the Healing journey that allows us to move into higher spheres of consciousness (represented by the affairs of the outer planets). Humanity's growing awareness of the existence of Chiron – the 'planet' of Healing – means that a key has been found. This key represents a quantum leap in Humanity's potential understanding of itself and its place in the Universe. However, we have jumped ahead of ourselves . . . we will come back to Chiron in a minute.

From across the Asteroid belt, Jupiter calls us to a higher potential, calls us to break out of the limitations of our ordinary view of life, call us to acknowledge the extraordinary potential that is truly ours. In terms of the expansion of consciousness, it is from Jupiter that the real journey of the higher Self begins. The continued journey of our potential Healing and evolution of consciousness is traced by the ever-expanding orbits of the outer planets – Jupiter, Saturn, Chiron, Uranus, Neptune, Pluto and beyond.

It is interesting to consider that each of us is destined in each lifetime to recapitulate the entire journey of evolution up to the present time. We recapitulate the biological evolution of life up to human status, the global evolution of Humanity up to the present and our own personal evolution up to where we left off in our last lifetime. At this point, we take up where we left off and continue the journey, taking new steps and meeting our next lessons.

Let's take a closer look at the affairs of each of the planets in turn. In addition, let's look at the chronology of our lives in relation to our ever-expanding awareness, awareness that is mirrored in the ever-expanding orbits of the planets. Let's look at the bigger picture of our lifetimes, finally putting Chiron in its proper place.

Before we are born, as an embryo and a fetus, we remain within the energetic egg of our mother's body and energy field. We mustn't forget the energetic influence of the father, though, coming via the sperm. In is interesting and relevant that the sperm – our 'Father' half – leaves the energetic egg of the father at conception. In a sense, we are further removed from the Father than the Mother. Psychologically and metaphysically, we long more for a Return to the Father – for a Return to Spirit. In any case, as a fetus, our mother's 'atmosphere' or *aura* shields us from outside influences. Our life, at this point, is subordinate to the greater intensity and consciousness of her electromagnetic field. Some would argue that this remains so to a greater or lesser degree well into adulthood! We spend a good deal of our life trying to break out of this egg fully. In the meantime, we become subject, increasingly, to other influences. This occurs unconsciously at first and later more consciously, as we strive to develop our focus, will and self-determination.

When we are born, we emerge from our mother's protective 'atmosphere'. At the moment of birth, with our first breath, the influences of the Earth and the planets are imprinted upon us. This becomes our 'signature' – our special, individual energy pattern. Inherent within this imprint are all our potential personality traits and characteristics and all our lessons, challenges and difficulties. This is when we become truly human. Before our first breath, we are more animal than human. Before the first breath, we are only *lower mind.* At the first breath, the *Higher Mind* (higher Self) incarnates. Our subsequent life is about trying to *awaken* the Higher Mind, trying to transcend the dualistic illusions and messages of the lower mind.

The first planetary influences that hit us after emerging from the birth canal are the influences of Mother Earth (Gaia). We are birthed to the Earth as much as we are to our human mother. We represent an integral part of the collective consciousness of Gaia. We also represent a potential for Gaia, so it is in her interests to look after us. She will watch patiently as our life unfolds and as our consciousness grows, waiting for the day when we will consciously acknowledge her.

The next planetary influences that enter us are the influences of the Moon. While still a baby, the Moon's energy protects and nurtures us, giving us a safe, soothing and sleepy place in which to grow. Part of the Moon's service to us is the creation of protective patterns – particularly emotional ones – that keep us from having to deal with difficult life events before we are ready. These patterns can be reactive or passive. Reactive patterns help us fight for our safety whilst passive ones help us 'sleep' through it all. These patterns remain with us for the whole of our life. When we are ready to deal with our issues, then we need to become conscious of these patterns, reassessing our attitude towards them, Loving them for their part in our journey, but at the same time transcending them. These patterns become the fuel for the fire of our further Healing and evolution of consciousness.

The next planetary influences come from Venus. Venus provides an environment of emotional security. She relates to our need for emotional harmony, peace, love and nurturing. Venus corresponds to our innate wish for harmonious contact with others and with life in general, expressed in our closest personal relationships. We search for contact by seeking relationship with others, by seeking beauty, harmony and peace in our life.

The next closest planet is Mars. Mars corresponds to our physical existence. After incarnation into our physical body, we spend our first few years learning how it works and exploring the physical world. Such are the toddler years up to about age seven. As a baby, we begin by exploring sensations – comfort, discomfort, pain, pleasure, physical love, etcetera. During the first few years, everything goes into the mouth for oral examination!

Then we learn to walk, run, jump, push, pull, talk, feed ourselves, control our bodily functions and, in general, gain the first stages of mastery of movement and bodily functions. We also begin to assert ourselves as individuals, particularly in physical ways. Mars helps us to understand very early in life, through our bodies, that we have the capacity for self-motivated action and self-determination. Later this evolves into the capacity to make decisions, to take on responsibilities and to have conscious intentions.

Then we come to Mercury. Here, our intellect and communication skills begin to be developed. This kicks in with full force from about 7 years old. Granted, some children begin this earlier and some later. We are generalizing for the sake of the illustration.

From this age onward, the development of the mind accelerates. We develop logic, mathematics, ideas and concepts, verbal interaction, communication and writing, etcetera. From this age, our brain is filled at an accelerated rate with facts, information and ideas. We spend the rest of our life trying to make sense of it all – to connect the pieces to form a logical picture of ourselves and of life in general.

During this time, our first more-or-less conscious contact with the Sun gives birth to the first elements of individual self-expression. Our ego and self-image are being formed. We are learning how to express ourselves in different ways – to express ourselves through the vehicles of Mercury, Venus and Mars: mind, feeling and body. In addition, during these years, we gradually begin separating our own world from the world of others. The acknowledgment of our individuality is implicit in the realization of the 'otherness' of the outside world and the people around us. From the relatively undifferentiated state of embryonic consciousness, we move into greater differentiation, fragmentation, specialization and individuality.

We are also experimenting with our will and focus. Our need for self-determination grows, generally flowering in the late teens. Our innate striving to become the master of our life is initially expressed through self-will and willfulness – the little 'wills' of the lower mind. Later, as we work consciously towards our Healing and evolution of consciousness, our true Will begins to emerge, more in alignment with our divine nature.

In the meantime, Jupiter has been there, whispering to us about the magical Universe. We 'hear' Jupiter's voice clearly as small children. As we grow, Jupiter keeps an eye on our education, always trying to excite us with the prospect of new learning and new adventures.

Due to circumstances both cosmic (such as the Asteroid dilemma) and earthly, Jupiter's call becomes decreasingly audible as we grow up. Our conditioning comes down upon us like a fog. We call this fog: adulthood.

Due to this fog of adulthood, we find it increasingly difficult, as we get older, to learn new things. The other factor in this decelerating learning curve is that, as we get older, our three basic centers – mind, body and feeling – become increasingly disharmonized, fragmented and 'sleepy'. These centers become set in their ways and do not wish to be disturbed by having to learn new tricks! Our protective Moon patterns become increasingly fixed.

As far as the decelerating learning curve goes, this is reversible. Contrary to popular belief, we can regain close to the learning capacity we had as children. It is all a matter of consciousness. Consciousness is a matter of synthesis and connection – synthesis and connection of our fragments, our knowledge, our personas, etcetera. This is the Healing journey. The descent of consciousness into Darkness in the first place is part of the overall plan. We become increasingly 'material', 'dense' and fragmented until approximately age 36. From here, the body begins to break down, gradually returning to the 'dust' of the Earth. However, from this point on, the Soul (Spirit) can be heard more readily, providing we work actively on ourselves, seeking resolution and Healing of our issues.

As an adult, Jupiter calls us to our higher potential. It calls us to recognize and acknowledge that our existence is far greater, more magnificent, more amazing and more wonderful than we had ever previously thought. It calls us to awaken to the fact that we have infinitely more potential than we ever imagined. It calls us to expand our consciousness beyond its current limitations. Jupiter's influence remains throughout our life, of course. Whether we continue to hear or acknowledge its messages is another thing.

Naturally, Saturn, too, has an influence on our growing process. However, Saturn does not really come into our life in a conscious way until around 28–30 years old. Until then, as we are growing up, Saturn's influences come via the adults around us. They come in the form of discipline, authority, control, restriction, lessons, etcetera, coming in both negative and positive ways, manifesting in 7-year cycles (aforementioned).

By the time we reach the age of 28–30, we have experienced much of what life has to offer. It has been a kind of apprenticeship. Up until this age, we have been gathering material, so to speak – material that will be the basis of our further Healing and evolution of consciousness. Up until this age, we think we know what life is all about. We think we are in control. We think we are the masters, already. At this age, all that changes.

Around this age, something happens within us that corresponds to what is called, in astrology, the Saturn 'Return'. This is when Saturn is completing its first orbit around the Sun within our lifetime, i.e. it is coming back to the same place in the sky where it was when we were born.

At this time, Saturn encourages us to get serious about our life – to get serious *consciously*. Many of us will know what we went through during these years. Our whole image of ourselves comes into focus, as does the question of who is really in control. Perhaps, during this time, we realize that our life, up until that point, was not really in our own hands. We thought we knew what it was all about. Now we begin to question this. If you have been through this time of life, think back and remember what you went through during these years. Some of the decisions we make during this time change the course of our life. Often, drastic external events form the catalyst for Saturn's awakening process.

During this time, we are encouraged to ask ourselves questions about our life. "What has my life been about up until now?" "How did I get here?" "Where have I failed?" "Where have I succeeded and why?" "Where am I now?" "What would I change if I could?" "Where am I going?" "How am I going to get there?" "Who am I really?"

Saturn says the pathway towards the answers to these questions lies in the acceptance of *personal responsibility* and *accountability*. Whether we accept these or not determines our future potential for Healing and evolution of consciousness.

If we begin to accept responsibility and work towards these goals, we then meet Chiron. When we accept personal responsibility for ourselves and our life, our Wounds, blockages, contradictions, omissions, commissions, judgments, misperceptions, illusions, etcetera, will tend to surface. Chiron offers us the key to the Healing of these things. We are given a period of roughly 10 years around a particular fulcrum point for the *beginning* of the conscious resolution and Healing of our Wounds and unresolved issues. This period of time lies somewhere between the ages of about 13 and 37, different for each of us; it is different for each of us, due to Chiron's highly elliptical orbit. The fulcrum point for this period is when Chiron has come halfway around the Sun from the time when we were born. This is known as the *Chiron half-Return* or *Chiron opposition.* Due to its elliptical orbit, Chiron reaches the halfway point in its orbit at different times in each of our lives, depending on the year we were born. For some, it happens in their teens, for some in their twenties and for others in their thirties. *(See GRAPH 1—CHIRON CYCLE, p. 576.)*

In any case, this astrological milestone is the fulcrum point for the possibility of Healing and evolution of consciousness and revolves around our specific Wounds and unresolved issues. The years shortly before this and many years afterwards are earmarked for Healing and 'wholing' processes.

Chiron's occasional transgression inside the orbit of Saturn has some interesting ramifications. In a sense, this allies Chiron with Jupiter and the inner planets for short times. This alliance acts as a beacon to Humanity, giving us a taste, if we are receptive, of what we can look forward to on the path of Healing. In addition, by giving us a 'pre-Saturnian' look at our Wounds and illuminating the possible path through them, it encourages us to move on to Saturn, where the real work begins. Otherwise, with no gold at the end of the rainbow to inspire us onward, we might choose to ignore these paths and possibilities. Furthermore, Jupiter corresponds to the Inner Child within us. The fact that Chiron crosses the orbit of Saturn and approaches Jupiter indicates that Chiron can facilitate the Healing of Inner Child Wounds. This is a necessary process if we are to truly grow up and awaken to our divine potential. Our path to the stars, via the outer planets, is paved with the resolution and Healing of our inner-planet issues. It is thus that we lay down the earthly foundations required for heavenly connection, as previously mentioned.

By the time we reach 38–44, however, we need to have seriously started work on ourselves. We need to have had some kind of realization and taste of the extraordinary potential that awaits us. This is due to the fact that, at this age, Uranus reaches *its* halfway point in its orbit. Uranus represents the next step of our journey. The Uranus *half-Return* or *opposition* occurs for each of us, when Uranus has traveled halfway around the Sun from the point at which it was when we were born. This represents a potential major milestone in our life. This time can be our coming-of-age, our entry card into the conscious Universe. During this time, Uranus steps in and attempts to align all our faculties. It tries to make Contact with us. It tries to wire us into the conscious Universe.

Imagine it this way: Dr. Frankenstein has just finished creating his monster. All it needs now, to bring it to life, is a very large bolt of electricity! (I apologize for this analogy!) Uranus provides the bolt of electricity we require at this age.

If Uranus meets blockages, Wounds, illusions, biases, judgments and misperceptions within us, which we have not yet dealt with, we cannot be aligned correctly. The energies do not get through. If we cannot deal with the remaining blockages as they surface during this Uranian time – and they will surface, sometimes with great force – then the alignment is partially or totally aborted. The result is a so-called 'mid-life crisis'.

Conversely, if Uranus's energies *can* get through, due to 1) having done sufficient work on ourselves up to this point, 2) being able to deal with the remaining issues as they emerge and 3) becoming consciously responsible and accountable for ourselves and our life, then this major transit has the effect of connecting us to the main power grid of the cosmos. It has the effect of opening the doors of our consciousness to the Universe. We are awakened to the consciousness of all life around us. We begin to become a conscious citizen of the solar system. At this point, we begin to directly experience the reality of our true potential – i.e. our inner eyes are opened (to a greater or lesser degree).

The next life cycle occurs around 50–51 with the so-called "Chiron Return". Chiron has then completed a full revolution of the Sun, returning to the place where it was when we were born. (We mentioned previously that Chiron's true orbital cycle averages out to 49 years if taken over many centuries, but at present, it is roughly 51 years. We will use this figure throughout this book.)

This time of our life can be a culmination point – a milestone – of Healing and evolution of consciousness. It can be a time of reaffirmation of our highest purpose. Whether it is or not, again depends upon the degree to which we have consciously worked for the resolution and Healing of our Wounds and unresolved issues.

If we have done so, then Chiron becomes a conscious force in our life. The way is cleared for a more conscious connection to, and communication with, the higher planets – i.e. Uranus, Neptune and Pluto. Chiron helps us cast away the veils of illusion and enter the world of Light.

The Uranian activation, aforementioned, sets the stage for a more conscious contact with Neptune. If we are ready, the messages of Love, Harmony, Inner Peace and Oneness can be experienced directly, becoming a way of life – not external to ourselves. We have become sages compared to our beginnings. We have become clearer channels for the infinite diversity of experiences and influences that the planets represent. We have awakened to our first experiences of Unconditional Love. We have started to reconnect with Oneness, whilst retaining our sense of individuality. No longer does the idea of being simultaneously One and Many present a conflict, a paradox or a contradiction. We have come closer to our Creator. We are Returning Home.

From here, we meet Pluto, face to face. Up until now, the forces of change – death, transformation and rebirth – have acted upon our life in an unconscious way. Unconsciously, we have reacted, resisted, agonized over and despaired of the processes to which Pluto corresponds. Now we look back and realize that our greatest moments of Healing and evolution of consciousness were at just those times in our life that we previously considered the worst times. The big picture of our life reveals itself. We become aware of the overall perfection of every smallest detail of our life. We see each detail in relation to the whole. We realize that nothing was superfluous. Everything had its right place. Everything led us to becoming who we are today. Our life was, is and will always be *a perfect balance;* it was our limited perception that caused us to think otherwise.

When death approaches, Pluto is there, waiting for us. The final Journey of Transformation is about to take place again. We have lived an entire octave of existence . . . an incarnation . . . our life. Now, in death, we transcend the earthly experience and are born into another octave of existence. After a time, if we still have more work to do, then the great cycle begins again, i.e. we are cast back down the octave, into another incarnation.

Alternately, if we have expanded our sphere of consciousness to the limits of the solar system, we are rejoined with the Oneness and Love that encompasses the solar system. Our cycles of incarnation are finished. We are ready for the next step in our eternally-evolving journey.

The above illustration of life cycles is not to say that some of the mentioned activations, Healings, reconnections and greater understandings cannot and do not take place at other times in our lives. They certainly do. However, this possibility will always be dependent upon the degree of our readiness and preparation. The above illustration of life cycles is a rough framework of major milestones where certain things become more possible than at other times due to specific planetary transits. When we touch on the subjects of the illusions of space and time, we will see how we need not be limited by our life cycles and their corresponding planetary cycles. We will see that Healing and evolution of consciousness, through any of the issues of any of the planets, are holographically possible at any conscious moment in our lives.

It is pertinent to mention that, if we do not take advantage of the influences and opportunities in our lives in a conscious way, then our lives are lived out in a way that is *subservient* to planetary influences. In this case, we come under the influence of the greater fate of Humanity and are subservient to the mass movements of the collective unconscious, i.e. the consciousness of Gaia (planet Earth). Humanity, as a whole, when relatively unconscious and psychologically 'asleep', also falls under the automatic laws of planetary influence. All cultural, racial, political, philosophical and social patterns, etcetera, are the reflections of unconscious interactions with planetary influences and their cycles.

If, however, Humanity begins to 'awaken' to its higher possibilities, already it begins to have the possibility of 'digesting' planetary influences in a different way. For Humanity to awaken to these possibilities, the conscious efforts of individuals all over the planet must reach a critical mass. If we wish to help Humanity to wake up to its higher potential, we need only begin with ourselves. Every effort we make towards our own Healing and evolution of consciousness will assist Humanity's awakening and evolution. It begins with us and our own lives.

We have sought, in the above section, to gain an understanding of the way in which our awareness grows and expands in our lives, reflected in the expanding orbits of the planets of the solar system. We are all connected to this. Our lives and the lives of the planets are intimately connected at every point. How we work with this knowledge will depend on our individual willingness to pursue a more conscious and focused life. In addition, it will depend on how willing we are to bear the responsibility of being a conscious being.

Key Points

- The journey from Earth to Moon, Venus, Mars, Mercury and Sun traces the path of our growth from birth to adulthood.
- The Moon protects us until we are ready for greater awakening and Truth.
- Venus provides an environment of peace, harmony, nurturing, balance and beauty.
- Venus represents our need for intimacy and personal contact.
- Mars relates to our physical development and sense of self.
- Mars encourages our potential self-assertion and self-determination.
- Mercury relates to the development of our intellect and our communication skills.
- The Sun represents individual self-expression, Will, focus and creativity.
- As we grow up, our conscious awareness approaches the Sun.
- At the Sun, we have attained relative individuality, self-determination, attention, focus and conscious control of our lives.
- The Asteroids limit our lives to the affairs of the inner planets.
- They represent a natural protective barrier against greater Truth.
- To move beyond the Asteroids, recapitulation of our lives is necessary.
- Chiron offers a bridge of Healing and evolution of consciousness across the Asteroid barrier.
- Jupiter calls us towards our higher potential and higher possibilities.
- The voice of Jupiter is 'heard' by us as children.
- Jupiter whispers to us of the magical, mysterious and adventurous Universe around us.
- We naturally lose Contact with the child's view of the Universe as the fog of adulthood descends.
- Saturn is the gatekeeper to higher consciousness.
- Saturn requires seriousness, responsibility and accountability.
- Saturn encourages us to take stock of our lives, notably around the age of 28–30.
- After Saturn, Chiron offers us a path of Healing of our Wounds and issues.
- As we Heal our Wounds and issues, with the help of Chiron, we approach Uranus.
- Uranus has the capacity to plug us in to the cosmic power grid.

- Neptune is the portal to the experience of Unconditional Love.
- Neptune points us back to Oneness . . . we are Returning Home.
- Paradoxically, on the Return journey, we retain our individuality amidst Oneness.
- Pluto awakens us to the secrets of creation and destruction.
- Pluto relates to the forces of death, transformation and rebirth.
- Pluto shows us that even the worst events of our lives led us perfectly to who we are today.
- When our consciousness encompasses the entire solar system in Unconditional Love, we are rejoined with the Oneness from which we came.
- Activations, Healings, reconnections and new understandings can take place at any time in our lives.
- If we fail to live consciously and intentionally, the planets rule us;
- We then come under the influence of the collective unconscious of Gaia.
- By attending to own Healing and evolution of consciousness, we assist Humanity as a whole.

5 ~ THE GIFT IN THE WOUND

"It is by going down into the abyss
that we recover the treasures of life.

Where you stumble,
there lies your treasure.

The very cave you are afraid to enter
turns out to be the source of
what you are looking for.
The damned thing in the cave
that was so dreaded
has become the center." [35]

-Joseph Campbell

"Disease is the ultimate whack on the head. It requires that we acknowledge misalignment and work to learn the real truth about life. For any person who learns to overcome this kind of thing, what you get for the experience is priceless. It is so rare and valuable that you become the envy of many. I know that sounds weird, but even though the average person on the street hasn't suffered the fear and restriction that you have felt, he will probably never be motivated to go after life's true meaning and experience the peace you will come to know through your extraordinary journey."[36]

-Stephen C. Parkhill

---

[35] Campbell, Joseph. Edited by Diane K. Osbon. *A Joseph Campbell Companion.* HarperPerennial, 1998, p. 24.

[36] Parkhill, Stephen C. *Answer Cancer – Miraculous Healings Explained.* Health Communications Inc., Florida, 1995, pp. 188-119.

2745-LASS

> "... curiously, one of [Einstein's] explanations [refuting the label of "genius"] relies not so much on any special ability *but on a reaction to a disability.* Einstein claimed that he was very late learning to speak and even after he did, he found whole sentences tricky, rehearsing them in an undertone before speaking them out loud. That delayed development, Einstein said, meant that he went on asking childlike questions about the nature of space, time and light long after others had simply accepted the adult version of the story." (Italics and bracketed additions mine)
>
> -from "New Scientist Magazine" [37]

Chiron says there is a Gift in every Wound. Out of all the themes, symbols and messages of Chiron, this one is perhaps the most relevant and pertinent to our study. If we can understand this one idea, then we have the primary key to understanding Chiron. This idea underpins the majority of what we will explore in the remainder of this book and in Books Two, Three and Four. For this reason, it is worth exploring further.

Perception

In order to discover what the Gift in the Wound might be, we need to understand Wounds from a higher perspective. *Wounds are a matter of perception, i.e. our perception of events, situations, circumstances and people in our lives.* Let's explore this idea ...

Firstly, *all events are neutral.* Events are neither good nor bad, neither right nor wrong, neither positive nor negative, *until we make them so by our perception.* By our judgment of perceived events, *we make a heaven or a hell out of them.*

How is this so? Our perceptions and their resultant judgments are based upon sensory input, i.e. the senses. The senses, for physiological reasons that we will explore in Book Two, perceive the world in terms of

---

[37] *New Scientist (magazine),* Reed Business Information, London, Vol. 162, No. 2192, 26 June, 1999, p 3.

black and white, yes and no, positive and negative, pain and pleasure, right and wrong, good and bad. The senses are *dualistic.* The senses *lopside the Truth of what is.* Therefore, *every perception we have is actually a misperception of the Truth, i.e. it constitutes a half-truth or illusion.* Furthermore, we all have *selective* senses. Neuroscience acknowledges that we register only a small fraction of what comes in through the senses. The rest of the picture is filled in by the brain, *by our existing conceptions, ideas, beliefs, emotions and mental images, by memory and imagination.*

The psychology and metaphysics of what we are speaking about will be explored at length in Books Two and Three. In the meantime, we can say that, due to the nature of our perception, we tend to *exaggerate* one side of an event or issue and *minimize* the other side. Further, we tend to *express* one side of an event or issue and *repress* the other. One side is *visible* to our waking consciousness and the other side becomes *hidden.* In short, *we dualize the event or issue and end up with a lopsided view of what actually occurred.* This lopsided view is what we *express* when we say, "It was such and such . . ." and "It made me *feel* such and such . . ." and "It *caused* such and such . . ." and "Such and such was to *blame . . ."* and so on and so forth.

As a quick example, imagine we have experienced a calamity of some sort – a hurricane, an earthquake or a car accident. At the time of the happening, we saw more negatives than positives, more pain than pleasure, more wrong than right, more senselessness than sense, more chaos than order, etcetera. However, as the years pass, we tend to look back and see things that we could not see at the time. Hindsight is a great teacher. We see things like how the event changed our lives in certain directions, resulting in positive outcomes. We see how the event resulted in positive actions from people around the event. We see how the event awakened appreciation, Gratitude and even Love for things and people we previously took for granted. Perhaps we gained a new awareness of and appreciation for the Gift and fragility of our lives. None of this would have occurred if we had not experienced the event. We don't see this at the time, though. The nature of our perception is to initially lopside – distort – the Truth of what is. *This takes us on a journey, as we shall see.*

One can imagine that, if every perception we have through the senses

2745-LASS

is inherently lopsided, then every subsequent perception must be built upon the foundations of other lopsided perceptions. An entire edifice of misperceptions is erected, layer by layer. *This is the basis for our personal Voids and Values.* We will discuss Voids and Values in a moment.

Now we come to the crux of our argument: *misperceptions are Wounds. Wounds are our misperceptions.* Every time we lopside the Truth of what is, we create a Wound. The original misperception is the original Wound, i.e. the illusion of separation from Oneness, from divinity. Subsequent misperceptions are subsequent Wounds, built upon the foundations of the original Wound.

So, having understood this, what could be the path towards the Healing of our Wounds? Healing is discovering the Truth that lies hidden from our lopsided consciousness, i.e. the Truth of the events, situations, circumstances and people upon which we have passed judgment. The process consists of discovering the flip-sides of the happenings and issues we judge. We express one side whilst repressing the other. One side is visible to us, the other hidden. Healing means revealing and learning to Love the repressed and hidden sides of any given issue.

Healing our Wounds (misperceptions) consists of discovering the benefits, blessings, lessons and Service that lie behind the events and issues that we initially judged negatively.

Can it be that simple? Yes it is. This is Chiron's most important message. The process itself may not be easy, however, because our expressed *personas*[38] will fight for their existence, fight to retain their lopsided stance on these events and issues. Nonetheless, this is the path. We will discuss actual Healing methods and processes of this kind in Book Two. Further, we will directly experience some of them in Book Four.

In the meantime, we can suggest that where we see 'bad', we might look for the *equal* 'good'. Where we see 'wrong', we might look for the *equal* 'right'. Where we see 'pain', we might look for the *equal* 'pleasure'.

---

[38] Every emotion, thought, feeling, judgment, bias, stance, illusion or half-truth we have constitutes a *persona*. When we *express* a certain view, a particular *persona* temporarily holds the reigns of our waking consciousness. Contrary to our mistaken certainty concerning continuous and coherent waking consciousness, we change personas as frequently as Imelda Marcos changed shoes. We will explore personas at length in Book Two.

Where we see negative, we might look for the *equal* positive. The flip-sides we seek were repressed in us at the time of perception, based on our previous misperceptions. We may have to dig deep in order to find the flip-sides. However, as we do so, we are gradually dissolving our charges, dissolving our judgments, coming into a more balanced state of consciousness and gradually perceiving greater Truth. *In this way, we are Healing our Wounds and approaching the experience of Unconditional Love.*

We can also look at the whole matter from the psychological point of view of *personas.* Every perception we have *births two personas,* one that sees one side of the event or issue and one that sees the other side. At the moment of perception, due to the nature of the dualistic senses and our brain-function, one persona is *expressed.* This becomes our view, our opinion, our belief, our stance, our lopsided reality. When this persona is expressed, we call it "me". The other persona (actually an anti-persona) becomes repressed and hidden. It is still there, but we do not see it consciously. We are in denial of it.

By seeking out the flip-sides of events and issues, *we are searching for the repressed and hidden anti-persona, i.e. the part of us that knows the other side of the picture.* When persona meets anti-persona, the two balance each other, dissolving into an equilibrium of consciousness. We are left with the greater Truth of the matter. We are left in a relative state of Love.

As we continue working in this way, discovering more flip-sides of an event or issue, a bigger picture of reality begins to emerge. We begin to see things that we did not see before. We begin to see things that we saw previously, but now in a new light. We begin to connect the pieces, building a larger picture and expanding our understanding. We begin to see the balance, harmony and perfection of the whole matter. *In short, we begin to glimpse the Gift in the Wound.*

So, how do we get to the 'root cause' – the original Wound – of an issue? Simply by working backwards through the layers of misperceptions, until we reach the original misperception. The cumulative effect of working in this way gradually reveals to us a higher perspective on the issue. Understanding dawns.

When we reach the 'root cause', we work with this in the same way as all other Wounds. We look for the benefits, blessings, lessons, Gifts

2745-LASS

and Service that lie within the Wound. As we approach equilibrium of consciousness by working in this way, we reach a kind of critical mass. We cross a certain threshold and, all of a sudden, all paradoxes dissolve, all questions disappear, all remaining charges collapse and we are left with the bigger picture of the event or issue. We experience the Truth of the matter, beyond our previous illusions. We see how the pieces fit together, how every aspect of the matter Served and Serves a higher purpose.

The test for determining whether we have attained this critical mass and have fully balanced our perception of the 'root cause' is if we can feel Gratitude for the whole affair. If we can, then, as we turn and say "thank you" for the whole affair, we experience an orgasm of consciousness as the Heart opens and we are illuminated with Light and Love. This is Healing. This is the evolution of consciousness.

Do we exaggerate? Not a chance! If anything, we fail to express fully the power of this moment of Healing. I have been witness to the results of this process innumerable times, in myself and in others. The actual methods and process will be discussed in detail in Book Two. The intensity of the experience will be directly proportional to the magnitude of the original Wound (misperception). The magnitude of a Wound can be measured by the degree to which it is running our life.

Once we have Healed an issue, we simply move on to the next issue. We are never finished. There will always be greater levels of consciousness, greater degrees of Truth, greater magnitudes of Love. After all, Love, in its purest state, is infinite and eternal.

The Gift in the Wound is the perfection of the journey we have had, from the original happening into Wounding and from Wounding back to Healing. *In the process of Happening, Wounding and Healing, we have become who we are meant to become in this lifetime.* We see, at the moment of Healing, a piece of the puzzle of who we truly are, of who we have been Divinely Designed to be, of what we have come here to do, of what Service we offer the world and of what we would truly Love to do.

Love is the Beginning and the End of our journey of Wounding and Healing.

Key Points

- Wounds are a matter of perception.
- All events are neutral.
- By judging events, we make a heaven or a hell out of them.
- Perception is based upon the dualistic senses.
- The senses lopside the Truth of what is.
- The senses are selective, the brain (memory and imagination) filling in the details.
- Every perception is a misperception, a half-truth, an illusion.
- We tend to *exaggerate* one side of an event or issue and *minimize* the other.
- We *express* one side of an event or issue and *repress* the other.
- One side of an event or issue is visible, the other hidden.
- Perception *dualizes* events and issues, giving us lopsided views.
- Our personal Voids and Values are built upon the edifice of misperceptions and their subsequent misperceptions.
- Misperceptions are Wounds. Wounds are our misperceptions.
- Every time we lopside the Truth, we create a Wound.
- Healing is discovering the Truth behind our misperceptions.
- Healing consists of discovering the benefits, blessings, lessons and Gifts behind our Wounds.
- Every perception births two personas;
- One persona we call "me"; the other is repressed, hidden, denied.
- When persona meets anti-persona, they balance each other, dissolving into Truth.
- By working backward through layers of misperceptions, we approach the original Wound.
- Healing occurs at the threshold of equilibrium of consciousness.
- Gratitude is the test for whether Healing of a particular Wound is complete.
- Gratitude takes us to Love.
- The moment of Healing is an orgasm of consciousness, an influx of Light and Love.
- The intensity of Healing is proportional to the depth of the Wound.
- The magnitude of a Wound is determined by the degree that it runs our life.

- The Gift in the Wound is the perfection of our journey of life.
- Moments of Healing reveal pieces of our Divine Design.
- Love is the Beginning and the End of our journey of Wounding and Healing.

Divine Design

> "We might ask, what is the cause or purpose of the original wound? The original wound is created by the fading of the connection between the newborn and its deeper spiritual wisdom within its core. Why, from the evolutionary perspective of humankind, would this take place? The answer lies in the difference between the core connection in early life and the connection gained through life experience. *The early connection to the core is unconscious. The connections to the core that are made during the process of living are conscious.* Adults' connection to their core, which is brought about through life experience, creates conscious awareness of their inner divinity. Adults become aware that they are a spark of divine Light in the Universe. They are localized divinity. This evolutionary process creates more conscious awareness in our species. We are finding out that we are co-creators of the Universe. *The purpose of incarnation is the creation of awareness of self as divine co-creator of the Universe.*" (Italics mine)
>
> -Barbara Ann Brennan [39]

The Gift in the Wound represents a piece of the puzzle of the deeper meaning of our lives. Each original Wound we Heal uncovers yet another piece of the puzzle of who we are, where we come from, where we are going and why we are here. The answers to these four primary spiritual questions are contained in what we have been calling our *Divine Design.* Each of us has a Divine Design. The number of misperceptions we have about ourselves and our lives (and their degree of polarity or 'charge') determines whether we are aware or ignorant of our Divine

[39] Brennan, Barbara Ann. *Light Emerging - The Journey of Personal Healing.* New York: Bantam, 1993, pp. 11-12.

Design. It determines whether we embrace or deny our Divine Design. It determines whether we accept or resist our Divine Design. As we dissolve our charges, resolve our issues, balance our misperceptions, Heal our Wounds, so our Divine Design begins to become apparent to us.

Divine Design encapsulates what we call *Purpose, mission* and *calling.* It encompasses the very thing that we would most Love to do in our lives, once it is awakened, acknowledged and embraced. Paradoxically, before Healing, this can represent the thing we are most in fear about doing or acknowledging and so it remains buried within the muffled recesses of our Wounded Hearts.

In the Healing process, our Divine Design becomes clear to us, because, as we clear ourselves of the 'static' of our 'charges' – the fog of our misperceptions – we can begin to hear the messages of the Soul more clearly. The Soul holds all the answers to our questions. It holds the pattern of our Divine Design within what we might call the *Akashic Record.* We will explore the astronomy and metaphysics of this in Book Three. Suffice to say, our Soul represents consciousness that encompasses the solar system, consciousness that knows Truth, Oneness and Love, consciousness that knows our Divine Design.

Carl G. Jung was aware of a paradox involved in the emergence of our Divine Design. He described the integration, balancing and 'wholing' process of our being – conscious with the unconscious – as the process of *individuation.* We have defined this as the Healing process. One of the results of this process, Jung realized, is a simultaneous and paradoxical realization that we are both the *same* as all others and part of the *whole*, but we are *unique* from others and *individual.* This is the paradox of being both One and Many, simultaneously. This paradox and its relation to the ultimate Wound that will never be Healed will be explored more in Books Two and Three.

Suffice to say, when we have dissolved the illusions that separate us from others and from the Universe at large, becoming One with all, Loving all Unconditionally, so we simultaneously become aware of our *unique* and *individual* Divine Design. It speaks to us, as it were, from our Hearts. Thus, we know our place in the greater cosmic Plan.

Key Points

- Our Divine Design contains the answers to our primary spiritual questions.
- Consciousness of our Divine Design depends on the number and polarity of our misperceptions (Wounds).
- Divine Design encapsulates our Purpose, mission and calling.
- Our Soul holds the pattern of our Divine Design.
- Our Soul knows Truth, Oneness and Love.
- We are both One with others and yet unique and individual.
- As we approach Oneness and Love, our unique Divine Design becomes apparent.

Voids and Values

A way to look at the question of Divine Design from a more practical perspective is to understand the nature of Voids and Values. Our Wounds represent our deepest Voids. Our Voids are those things that we feel are missing in our lives (remembering that these feelings are ultimately misperceptions). Our Voids determine our Values; i.e. we seek what we think is missing in our lives, whether it be love, wealth, contact with others, justice, truth, retribution or something else. Smaller Voids determine lesser Values that are transient and easily swapped for others. Larger Voids determine greater Values that are more long lasting and not so easily changed. Our greatest Voids determine our greatest Values, i.e. those things that form the core Values of our life. Our core Values take us on a journey towards becoming what we become in life. Without the greatest Voids, we would have no core Values and hence no journey of 'becoming' in life. Our Voids and Values are beacons, pointing us towards Healing and the evolution of consciousness, *pointing us towards our Divine Design.*

Our greatest single Value is the Purpose for which we are here in this lifetime. The Void that pointed us towards our greatest Value – our life's Purpose – was the deepest Wound. This is the Gift in the Wound. The whole process and its result is our Divine Design.

Without the perception of Wounds, we could not have Values. Without Values, we would have no motivation or Purpose in life. Our Divine Design is given to us via our Wounds. As we Heal and begin to see this miraculous picture, and we turn to the Universe and say "thank you", we enter increasingly into a state of Unconditional Love.

We can now begin to understand what the placement and role of Chiron is in the astrology chart. Chiron in the natal horoscope, put simply, represents the place of our deepest Wounds, i.e. our greatest Voids. It represents a key to understanding the forces in our lives that drive us towards our Divine Design, towards our higher Purpose. It represents a potential path of Healing and holds the key to the discovery of our Gifts and potential Service.

As we uncover piece after piece of the puzzle of our Divine Design, we are increasingly motivated by Gratitude and Love for the miracle of our lives. We awaken to the perfect order and balance around us and in our lives. We are able to embrace the perfection of our Divine Design and carry it out with Gratitude and Love. At this point, we realize that human will and Divine Will are One.

Although we are growing, Healing and evolving constantly, *our greatest Void is never filled.* This is the Wound that is never completely Healed. This is what is meant by the Chironic symbol of the Wounded Healer. The Wound that will never Heal constantly drives us towards our highest calling, towards our Divine Design. Such is the longing for Oneness, for Truth, for Love, for God.

Our deepest Wound (greatest Void) is the rudder, the driving force, the very impulse of evolution. Our greatest Value (the Gift in the Wound) is the beacon, enticing us towards the manifestation of our Divine Design.

Here, we can define the experience of Love as the awakening to the divine order in the world and in our lives. The more we realize and awaken to the Love that lies behind Creation, the more we experience Love and realize that *we are Love.*

Our degree of conscious evolution is determined by how much we have Loved. It is determined by how much of our life we have Loved, by how many of the people in our lives we have Loved (Unconditionally) and by how many happenings and issues in our lives we have Loved.

Ingratitude is defined by the denial of, rejection of and lack of awareness of Unconditional Love. That which we have not Loved Unconditionally is that for which we are still ungrateful. Ingratitude takes us *away* from Unconditional Love. When we see and acknowledge divine order and balance in the world and in our lives, we can experience Gratitude. Gratitude, inspired by dissolving our charges, dissolving our judgments, resolving our issues, balancing our perceptions and seeing the divine perfection, takes us to Love.

The things we have yet to Love are the things about which we still have 'charges' or judgments. These are the things that run our lives, that take us on journeys, that 'attract' happenings and issues into our lives and that drive us in particular directions, creating corresponding behavior patterns. *Our Divine Design in a given lifetime is borne out of what we have Loved and what we have not yet Loved.* From birth, this translates into the neural patterns of the brain as we grow up, shaped by our perceptions and misperceptions of the influences and environment around us as we are growing up. *Nature* – what we bring with us into life – and the influences and environment around us – *nurture* – combine to manifest our Divine Design. More on this subject in Book Two.

Key Points

- Our Wounds represent our deepest Voids.
- Our Voids determine our Values.
- Our greatest Voids determine our core Values.
- Our greatest Value is our divine Purpose, driven by our greatest Void.
- Chiron, in the horoscope, represents the place of our deepest Wounds;
- It represents the potential path of Healing;
- It holds the key to the discovery of our Gifts and Service in life.
- Human will and Divine Will become One when we are Healed.
- Our deepest Void (Wound) is the rudder, the driving force, the very impulse of evolution.
- Our greatest Value (the Gift in the Wound) is the beacon, enticing us towards our Divine Design.
- Love is the awakening to the divine order.

- The more we see Love, the more we experience Love and the more we realize that we are Love.
- Our conscious evolution is determined by how much we have Loved.
- Ingratitude is the denial of, rejection of and lack of awareness of Unconditional Love.
- Divine Design is borne out of what we have and have not yet Loved.

Going into the Wound

"Come to the edge," he said.
They said: "We are afraid."
"Come to the edge," he said.
They came.
He pushed them . . . and they flew. [40]

-Guillaume Apollinaire

We have said much on the subject of the Gift in the Wound. It is all very well to talk about it, but the reality of it is that, in order to grow, Heal and evolve, we must put in the required effort. Further, we must walk *towards* the Pain rather than away from it. Ultimately, it is by going *into* the Wound that we see what we need to see, awaken to the larger Plan and are then able to Heal. What is going to entice us to do this, against the inclinations of our lower nature?

After remaining stuck in our Wounds and unresolved issues for longer than our Heart and Soul will allow, the Pain of regret begins to outweigh the Pain of moving forward, in spite of the obstacles. An anonymous poet said this more poignantly:

And the day came,
when the risk to remain tight in a bud
became more painful
than the risk it took to blossom.

---

[40] As quoted in: Toms, Michael & Toms, Justine Willis. *"True Work"*. Bell Tower, New York, 1998, p. 60.

Healing requires that we stand in the face of our Wounds and unresolved issues. It requires that we stand in the face of our Pain and hurt. It requires that we go into the Wound, with an intention and a deep Wish for Healing and resolution. Can we face our Darkness, Loving what we find there, bringing our disparate, disowned, denied and negatively-judged aspects back into the Light?

Our Heart will not let us rest until we awaken to and acknowledge the Love within us and around us. It will use any device in order to get us to move down the path of Healing, for it already knows what is store for us. It knows that the journey is worth it, the Pain worth it, the effort worth it. It knows that nothing else matters except the awakening of Love. The Heart holds the key.

What is the Heart? It is the waystation between Spirit and Matter. It is the receptacle for Divine Love. It is the portal, through which our higher Self (Higher Mind) and Soul can be heard and felt. It is our spiritual Sun. It brings us our spiritual food, without which, we would soon die. When the Heart is closed, we are Wounded. When the Heart opens, we Heal. Love is the greatest Healer.

How then are we to open our Hearts? The first step is to stop running, stop trying to escape, stop trying to avoid our Wounds and unresolved issues. The next step is to become aware of our Pain, physically, emotionally, mentally and/or spiritually. We need to remain in the place of our Pain whilst trying to listen to the Heart.

What is the nature of our Wound? What are the issues that plague us? Can we identify them, even if only partially? Then, *what are the hidden positives, blessings, benefits, flip-sides, lessons and Gifts behind the mask of seeming Darkness?* We need to dig deeply into our Wound, despite the resistance, despite the protestations of our lower mind, despite the Pain and Darkness. If we continue to seek the answers to where these hidden positives, blessings, benefits, flip-sides, lessons and Gifts might be, gradually Light begins to enter the Wound. We begin to see and understand the Wound and its attendant issues a little more. We begin to be able to breathe again. In short, we begin to Heal.

As we proceed in this way, the Light dawning within us, we are gradually able to integrate our Dark aspects, learning to Love them increasingly. As we do so, a larger picture begins to emerge. We see more of ourselves. We begin to see how our lives have led us in specific directions. We begin to see that these directions were not accidental or malicious, but were the orchestrations of higher consciousness, the ministrations of Love. Gradually, the picture becomes clearer . . . we are beginning to see our Divine Design. There are no accidents, no mistakes, no injustices . . . just the machinery of Love.

Does this sound as though it is worth the effort, worth the Pain, worth the trials and tribulations? Chiron says that Healing lies *through* the Wound, not around it or by running away from it. Through the Darkness lies the Light. There is a Gift in the Wound, if we have the courage to enter this place.

Ultimately, the Gift in the Wound is the revelation of our Divine Design. Our Wounds (Voids) determine our Values. Our Wounds and Values take us on a journey of Healing and evolution of consciousness. On this journey, we become what we have been Divinely Designed to become. We awaken to our Divine Design and to the Guiding Hand of Love that led us there. The Healing journey is awakening to, acknowledging, embracing and saying "thank for" for the perfection of our lives and for our Divine Design. The celebration and prayer of thanks for our Divine Design is to align with the Divine Will and carry out our Purpose, according to our Divine Design, with Gratitude and Love. Here is a poem . . .

"What if I should Wake in the day,
without past or future,
and find myself
amidst a spiraling of galaxies,
amongst flowers and music,
in a Dance of Life
that is eternally Now?

And what if I should Wake in the day,
not resenting who I was,
not imagining who I might have been,
and find myself where I am,

amidst the spinning stars,
amongst gods and men,
close to kings, princes and paupers,
in a Dance of Oneness
that is an eternal Song?

And what if I should Die in the day,
so to speak,
without painful memories,
without unfulfilled dreams,
and find myself
within the Stillness of the Creator,
within the spiraling galaxies,
full of flowers and music
and spinning stars?
How then,
could I keep from Singing my Song?"[41]

All Things Serve

"We can recall the late Joseph Campbell speaking to this point when he referred to an essay written by Schopenhauer called "An Apparent Intention of the Fate of the Individual." Campbell said, "He points out that when you are at a certain age – the age I am now (seventy-five) – and look back over your life, it seems to be almost as orderly as a composed novel. And just as in Dickens's novels, little accidental meetings and so forth turn out to be main features in the plot, so in your life. And what seem to have been mistakes at the time, turn out to be directive crises." And then he asked, "Who wrote this novel?" He went on to say that life seems as though it is planned and that there is something inside of us that causes these occurrences. It's a mystery. All of us can look back at our lives and see events that appeared to be disasters at the time but shifted us to

[41] Martin Lass, 1996.

a new course and led us into important aspects of our journey. It's as though nothing can happen for which we're not ready."

-Michael & Justine Toms
(quoting Joseph Campbell paraphrasing Schopenhauer)[42]

If there truly is a Gift in every Wound, as Chiron asserts, then, from all that we have discussed so far, it should be becoming clear that Chiron's perspective is that *all things Serve the march of the evolution of consciousness.* All things Serve our Healing and evolution of consciousness, no matter what the form, no matter what the prevailing social attitudes, no matter what judgments and condemnations we or others may have. All paths lead to the Way. There are no mistakes or accidents. All things are part of a larger Plan. Mostly, though, we do not see this Plan and consequently think that things were not, are not and cannot be as they *should* be or *could* be.

When we do glimpse this larger Plan, in a moment of higher consciousness, in a moment of Healing, in a moment of awakening, we become aware that there is truly a Guiding Hand at work in the Universe. We become aware that our lives have been orchestrated down to the finest detail in such a way as to 1) give us the optimum opportunity to awaken to our divine nature as Love and Light and 2) fulfill the Destiny that is inherent within our Divine Design. *These two factors encompass the entire meaning of life.*

When we begin to glimpse this reality, so we begin to experience the magnitude of Love that lies behind our creation. We begin to see that there is nothing in the Universe that is not borne out of Love, that is not a manifestation of Love, that is not Love itself. We begin to see that *we* are Love and that every aspect of our lives has been an expression of that Love. Healing and the evolution of consciousness are the journey back to the Truth of Love. All things Serve this journey.

"There is nothing we have done or not done that is not worthy of Love."

-Dr. John Demartini

---

[42] Ibid., p.25.

2745-LASS

Key Points

- All things Serve the march of the evolution of consciousness.
- All things Serve our Healing.
- Moments of Healing awaken awareness of the Guiding Hand.
- Our lives are orchestrated in the finest detail.
- All things are borne out of Love.
- We are Love.
- Healing is the awakening to the Truth of Love.

Keys

So what are the keys to awakening to these great Truths? What keys can facilitate our accelerated Healing and evolution of consciousness? What are the keys to the doors of our perception, which would enable us to stand witness to the Divine Masterpiece of Creation? What are the keys that can open our Hearts, enabling us to Love ourselves and our lives Unconditionally?

We have touched upon some of these keys already. Further and more detailed keys are given in a variety of processes that I have summed up in what I call the "Chiron Process". We will explore these various keys, including their ultimate culmination in The Quantum Collapse™ Process[43] of Dr. John Demartini, in Book Two.

All these various methods seek to shine a Light into our Darkness, illuminate what we find there and bring what we find back into the whole of our Being. These methods serve to balance our misperceptions – Heal our Wounds – by seeking to discover the blessings, benefits, lessons and Gifts within the happenings and issues that we initially judged negatively. The final key is saying "thank you" to the Universe for the whole experience. The final *experience* of Healing is the Silence of Love.

One Healing key worth mentioning briefly comes in the form of *hindsight.* Hindsight is a great tool for awakening to the flip-sides of a

---

[43] *The Quantum Collapse Process™ Dr. John F. Demartini © 1988 Property of the Concourse of Wisdom School of Philosophy and Healing, www.drdemartini.com.

happening or issue. In moments of great crises or calamities, we inherently see more negative aspects than positive and judge these happenings accordingly. Over time, however, it becomes increasingly apparent that certain things in our lives would not be the way they are if the crises or calamities had not taken place. Amongst these things are hidden blessings, benefits, lessons and Gifts. We have explored this previously. In short, the bigger picture becomes apparent with hindsight. If we could develop a process by which we could expand our consciousness, as though we were looking back at a happening or issue from 50 years in the future, we could Heal our Wounds – our misperceptions – in a fraction of the time. Such a process exists and will be elaborated in Book Two and further explored in Book Three. Practical application of *all* the Healing processes and musings of Chiron will be set out in Book Four.

Key Points

- The keys to Healing are given in Chironic processes;
- These processes seek to shine Light into our Darkness;
- They seek to balance our misperceptions;
- They seek out the benefits, blessings, lessons and Gifts of our Wounds.
- The final key is Gratitude.
- The final *experience* of Healing is Love.
- Hindsight is a great tool for Healing.

6 ~ CHIRON KEYWORDS

Here, we offer a list of keywords that relate to the messages and musings of our rogue friend, Chiron. This will be useful in summarizing what we have explored in this book so far. It will also be useful in fine tuning the radio frequency of our consciousness to Chiron's frequency, thus connecting us in consciousness to Chiron and his musings in a more direct and intuitive way.

Bear in mind that many of these keywords, their deeper implications and the rationale in assigning them will be explored in Part Three of this book and in Books Two and Three.

The Nature of Chiron

Healer, alchemist, divinatory, shaman, maverick, outsider, loner, visitor, special missionary, emissary, intercessory, Christ-figure, intermediary, isthmus, way-station, connector, negotiator, counselor, metaphysician, ferryman, guide through the Darkness.

The Wounding

Wound, Wounding, Woundedness, incurable Wound, Pain, separation, disconnection, aloneness, alienation, distanced, far from Home, stranger in a strange land, irreconcilable, fragmentation, duality, Darkness, abandonment, deprivation, isolation, meaninglessness, lost, cast out, rejected, forsaken, cut-off, ostracized, denied, repressed, hidden, disowned, unacknowledged, misperception, illusion, lopsidedness, imbalance, half-truth, lie, judgment, stance, persona, emotion, Matter, 'charge', kinetic, particulate, fermionic, hylotropic, density, gravity, spacetime, local, heavy, material, polarization, maya, samsara, 'identification', hypnosis, 'sleep', fundamentalism, entropy, descent, involution, the Fall.

The Journey

Healer, shamanic, underworld, alchemical, ferment, enzyme, catalyst, transmutation, search, quest, longing, driven, evolutionary, illuminating, revealing, surfacing, unveiling, uncovering, mirror, reflection, paradox, dilemma, complementary opposites, koan, Yin/Yang, divination, Tarot, channel, intercessory, waystation, transmitter/receiver, Holy Spirit, bridge, intuition, *kundalini*, quantum leap, dark night of the soul, inner journey, turning point, finding Self, seeking the flip-sides, expressing the repressed, unveiling the hidden, into the Darkness, into the Wound, into the Pain, medical, cosmogonic cycle.

The Healing

Heal, Healing, Healed, Healer, The Gift in the Wound, the blessing in the crisis, connectedness, rejoining, reconciliation, transcendence, communication (metaphysical), 'wholing', unity, unified field, the *collapse,* Light, wavicle (wave/particle unity), photonic, bosonic, holotropic, the Light in the Darkness, back into the fold, coming Home, the Return, Loving Self, greater Truth, balance, harmony, seeing perfection, Unconditional Love, true Being, Stillness, Silence, motionless, omnipresence, the Now, eternal, non-local, Actuality, Oneness, awakening, finding, prodigal son, closeness, merging, integration, individuation, synthesis, Light-ness, levity, spiritual, metadox (union of opposites, beyond paradox), universal, syntropy, the Ascension, ascent, evolution.

Shortly, we will explore how all these ideas, themes and processes can be seen and worked with, through Chiron, in the astrology chart. This will form the bulk of our remaining material in Book One. Before this, though, let's take a sidetrack and present some material designed to give us a taste of the *feeling* of Chiron. Without the feeling of Chiron, our understanding of Chiron could remain somewhat dry and intellectual. Our final aim is, after all, to awaken the Heart to the Truth and experience of Love . . .

2745-LASS

PART TWO

An Interlude

What is the *feeling* of Chiron, beyond the intellect, non-verbally, felt in the gut, felt in the Heart? It is a feeling I have come to know well over the last so many years, but how to share this with others has been the challenge as a Healer, astrologer and writer. I have shared this feeling for years through music, but it is more challenging (and frustrating at times) to try to share it through words.

What follows in the next section consists of a short fiction story, an inspirational excerpt and a selection of poetry. I have chosen them because they represent a sideways glance at the themes of Chiron. They appeal primarily to our *feeling* and *intuitive* nature. The short story and the poetry are mine and the inspirational excerpt comes from Australian Aura-Soma therapist, Healer and singer, Rickie Hilder.

1 ~ THE TRAIN (A SHORT STORY)

by Martin Lass

(The following short story was written in 1981, during my first Chiron-square-natal Chiron transit, although I only realized this in retrospect. It is full of the symbolism of the Wounds of abandonment and separation from which we all suffer, to a greater or lesser degree, as a result of the incarnation process. As we grow up, we become increasingly alienated from our pre-birth roots. As children, we are far more connected to where we have come from, although innocent in consciousness. As the world and life's circumstances crowd in, however, not only do we lose contact with our origins, but also we often lose Faith in the reality or future possibility of such a connection even existing.

The first Chiron square in our lifetime, depending on what age we are when it occurs, calls up our specific Wounds and calls up the past events of our lives, which have been a reflection of those Wounds. Chiron says that we must fully incarnate – i.e. fully descend into the material world – before the Return journey is possible. In a sense, the separation from our pre-birth roots must be total. Then, from the depths of despair and aloneness, can come a Wish – a Wish for reconnection to our divine origins. It is here that the conscious Healing journey often begins.

The story itself, a mixture of fact, fiction and symbolism, was for me an unconscious affirmation of the possibility of Healing through reconnection to, and emotional understanding of, our past. At the time, the process of writing this story remained an affirmation of the future potential for Healing, i.e. a Return to Faith in the 'rightness' and perfection of all that we experience. The greater part of the Healing took place much later.

The main factual background of the story revolves around the external circumstance of my family's emigration from America to Aus-

tralia when I was eleven. The symbolism in the story, however, goes far deeper, showing that outside circumstances are often a pale reflection of what goes on inside us, even when the external events are, in themselves, major upheavals.)

*

Not so long ago, I met a person who, as it turned out later, had been a close friend in my childhood. Not so much a close friend, I guess, as a childhood sweetheart. She had certainly meant a lot to me back then. You don't think about those sorts of things when you are young – you just live in the wonder of each day, not expecting anything to change. At the height of our friendship, though, my family, for reasons I didn't understand at the time, packed up our bags and moved to the other side of the country. I hadn't seen or heard from my childhood friend since – she was all but forgotten.

I remember that when I saw her again after so many years, I didn't recognize her. I do recall experiencing a vague feeling in my chest – a kind of longing that I didn't understand. The chance meeting took place in the local orchestra. I was a violinist trying to eke out a living through music. Music was my passion as well as my savior in difficult times.

On this particular day, the orchestra rehearsal had been in progress for about ten minutes when a woman, arriving late, came in quietly and sat in the empty chair to my left. The orchestra had been trying to fill a vacancy for quite some time. It had been announced recently that the position had been given to a young lady from the other side of the country – a woman by the name of Cathy Wenton. It was not uncommon for people to relocate great distances for the sake of work in the music field – work was scarce.

The name, Cathy Wenton, meant nothing to me at first. The fact that a woman changes her last name when she gets married didn't occur to me then. When she sat down next to me, I stopped playing for a moment to adjust the music stand for her and to say hello. Her hair was a mass of flaming red and her eyes were deep green. I was shocked, not really understanding why at first. She acknowledged my greeting with a look, holding my gaze for what seemed to be an uncommon time. I remember being a little disappointed by her eyes at second glance. They should have sparkled more or something. It was a strange thought, considering I had just met her – so I thought.

The rehearsal continued with no time for chat, but my mind was elsewhere. I kept seeing Cathy Wenton's face superimposed upon my own vague memories. I could see her laughing. I could see her crying. I could see her gazing at the clouds and running like a deer across a childhood landscape. I searched through my memory, trying to give this face a place, but it eluded me. The rehearsal went on in the background of my consciousness.

Before I knew it, the conductor had called a coffee break and people were moving swiftly from their chairs in search of coffee. Cathy Wenton stayed seated. She turned to me, regarding me for a moment, as if to reconfirm her thoughts, and then said,

"Hello Allan." She looked at me as though I should have recognized her. Surprised that she had known my name, I sat there looking back blankly.

"Cathy Wenton . . ." I said searchingly, as though saying it would conjure up some kind of recollection. Slightly embarrassed, I shook my head. Seeing this, she offered,

"You would probably remember me as Cathy Avery. I've been married since you last saw me." In a breath, it all came back to me – Cathy Avery, my childhood sweetheart. I asked her how she had been for the last so many years, what she was up to now and where she had been in between. We exchanged polite questions and answers about each other – more out of embarrassment than anything – the way people do when they don't know what to say.

Going home after the rehearsal, my thoughts were of Cathy. I was remembering our childhood together – the wonderful times, the adventures and the special moments. It didn't occur to me, as I indulged in my reverie, that people change after such a long time, particularly between childhood and adulthood.

*

It is late at night. Allan lies on his bed, thinking of Cathy and of the meeting that had taken place that day. He is very drowsy. One thought mingles with another, the boundaries blurring. He reminisces of times when he and Cathy were children. As he drifts closer to sleep, a dream is in the making . . .

A solitary cone of lamplight settles softly on the desktop next to the bed, giving the room a warm and secret atmosphere. It is three o'clock in the deep morning. The silence is alive. A train calls from across a distant and dark valley. A dream is in the making . . . softly, the world drifts away. The cone of lamplight is shifting its rays . . . shifting and turning like the rays of the autumn sun, flaming through maple trees. The light alters, the scene changes . . . changed by an autumn afternoon . . .

. . . all across the neighborhood, people are sweeping dead leaves into piles and setting them alight. It's autumn and there are many fallen leaves to burn – leaves of elm, oak, maple and poplar. Smoke rises from the burning piles, quickly at first, then slowing as it rises. Dispersing, the autumn smoke casts a hazy net over the world, capturing the afternoon in drowsy fingers. The sun flames quietly in the maple trees, filtering through to the lawns below, a mottling of molten gold.

Along the wide maple avenue, a boy is running. There are many old and beautiful houses along the street, but the boy doesn't see them. He runs wildly through the autumn afternoon, searching for his child-friend, Cathy. He must find her. He must find her and warn her, before it's too late. He must tell her of the impending doom. The train whistle sounds again, this time closer. Heart pounding, legs aching, the boy runs faster. She can still be saved, he thinks. Got to reach her, before it's too late . . .

As he runs, his memories carry him back to an even earlier world . . .

. . . he is sitting high above the Earth. All around him are apple blossoms and leafy windows opening out into the deep blue sky. Next to him sits Cathy . . . tomboy, ponygirl, christened "Eagle" by the children of the neighborhood. This place, high in an apple tree, is their secret place. None of the other children of the neighborhood are able to climb this particular tree. It's their special place.

The summer envelops them as they sit and talk, playing make-believe games about their imagined future. There are endless hours, it seems, disappearing into forever, like dandelions in a meadow disappearing into the distance. The shouts and laughter of the other children in the neighborhood seem to be so far away . . . as far away as Autumn and the faces that Autumn augurs.

The boy's little brother comes running up to the foot of the apple tree, laughing with excitement, calling up into the tree.

"See train! See train!" he says, pointing. The train disappears around the bend, smoke puffing from its stack. What people has the train brought to town this time? Who will it take away? The train brings strange things and strange people from far away places. The train is augury itself, hinting of changes in the coming years.

What does it matter, though, when there are kites to fly in the wild blue sky, when there is basketball to play, fences to jump, ravines to explore and a whole host of other adventures to go on? What does it matter when the sun comes out after a summer thunderstorm and boys and girls stream out of houses after dinner, beating the wet pavement with sneakers and bare feet in the lingering light? There are thousands of trees to climb, tree houses to build, games to play and replay a hundred times. Who would give a thought to the coming of Autumn? Growing up seems so far away. Every childhood morning, waking with the birds, the cool summer air entices children from their dreams of adventure out onto the stage of life where their dreams are enacted.

The years pass like centuries . . . slowly, inexorably, inevitably. And in the passage of years, the old makes way for the new. So now, the train brings a visitor. As she steps off the train, she takes a deep breath of late summer air and she knows from this that her time has come. The trees are just ready to drop their leaves, their youth exhausted. Watermelons and pumpkins lie in their respective patches, on the threshold of full ripening. There is a lull in the summer wind as it drowsily awaits the word. And when the word is spoken, its sound invokes the winds of change, blowing away the ghosts of summer . . . Autumn has arrived.

Every year now, Autumn comes to visit . . . each time she comes, she stays a little longer. She is a mummified woman. She sits in her rocking chair, knitting into the late afternoon, as dry and wrinkled as a

2745-LASS

dead leaf. Her fingers are like spiders, working away at her knitting, the knitting needles clicking together like dry sticks.

The boy sits at her feet, listening to tales of graveyards, spooks and specters, of jack-o-lanterns that came to life and carnivals inhabited by strange and misshapen people. Together they press autumn leaves between wax paper, they collect acorns, seeds and pinecones and they make bats' wings and witches' cloaks for trick-or-treating. The boy collects chestnuts from below the solemn chestnut tree that stands on a quiet corner of the neighborhood. Some of these he polishes and gives to the old woman. In return, she gives him father's old tobacco tins in which to store his autumn riches.

Sometimes they sit on the front porch in the late afternoon, watching the figures of smoke rise from the piles of burning leaves. They watch the curling fingers drawing in the air, speculating on the designs drawn. They dream and talk of far away places and of great things to come.

Then it comes time for Autumn to leave. She will be gone for three seasons, the train whisking her away and returning her again in the late summer. Each time she comes, though, her visit becomes longer, her place in the world more permanent. Soon the train will no longer take her away in between, her silent coup going unnoticed . . .

*

Little brother has received a train set for his birthday. It's shiny and new and has seven carriages. The little engine pulls the carriages around the circular track, puffing out pretend smoke. As the child watches the train going around, suddenly his joy turns to anguish as a premonition overwhelms him. He is crying now, not understanding his vision, tears falling on the train like the first drops of an Autumn storm . . .

*

Now the tables have turned . . . every year it's Summer who comes to visit. As she steps off the train, the children spill out of school, running to greet her. She runs across the fields in the amber wind, beckoning them to follow. Her flaming hair is like a lion's mane, her green eyes filled with the coolness of a deep forest. She and the boy play together . . . the world is theirs. They make plans to go away together to the mountains, to get married and to do all the things that summer people do. They can see the years stretching out in front of them without end. But then the train whistle sounds and it's time for Summer to go once more. The boy asks his mother,

"Why can't Summer stay a little longer? I remember a time when it was always Summer."

"Do you now?" his mother says, stopping her knitting for a moment. "You do talk nonsense sometimes! Anyway, she will always comes for visits." She sits back in her rocking chair, smiling knowingly to herself. She's a dry and wrinkled old thing, her knitting needles clicking together like old bones . . .

*

. . . jolted from his reverie, the boy, running down the long maple avenue, remembers that he's searching for Cathy. He knows that there is something very wrong going on. He needs to tell her. He must warn her of the danger before it's too late. As he runs, he hears little brother's voice again, calling out.

"See train! See train!" little brother cries distraughtly, tears streaming down his face. The boy runs faster, pushing his young body to the limit. He rounds the corner and there is Cathy's house. She's playing on the front lawn and looks up as he approaches. The train whistle blows again, this time closer, louder, more insistent. He runs up to her, puffing and panting, talking franticly. He is telling her how their apple tree is changing colors, its leaves wilting around their secret place, falling to the ground below. He is telling her how Autumn has stolen away the Summer and painted all the summer leaves with gold and crimson, burning them in giant pyres. Summer is dying, he says, dying five billion deaths, its spirit rising from the piles of burning leaves, into the afternoon sun, a hazy net of smoke. As he is saying this, he is looking into her eyes and then he knows . . . he knows that it's already too late. Her eyes have changed.

Behind her, sitting on the front porch in a rocking chair, is Cathy's mother. Her mother smiles at the boy with a look of satisfaction as the train comes around the bend, smoke pouring from its stack. She calls out politely to the boy to run along home now or he will miss the train. She resumes her knitting, her dry and wrinkled fingers working swiftly now.

Suddenly the boy looks up, as if from a deep sleep, and sees that he is traveling at a great speed away from Cathy, away from his home, away from his childhood landscape. The autumn smoke in the trees has become the smoke pouring from the train's stack. His family is with him, his little brother still crying, softly now. Together, they are speeding towards a new home on the other side of the country.

And now, in his mind's eye, he sees his childhood falling away from him like an old coat. He senses the inevitability of this and waves a silent farewell to Cathy, knowing that she, too, must grow up. Somehow, he knows, in a silent place in his heart, that his journey will eventually bring him back home . . .

A vision comes to him in the last stages of dreaming – a vision of flaming autumn dissolving into the deep blue coldness of winter. In the vision, a solitary moonbeam traverses the deep morning darkness. Its radiance cuts a path across a silent snowfield. Along the path, there is the shadow of a spider making its web.

The moon glows.
The silence is alive.
In the winter coldness
there is the promise of an unborn Spring.

*

2 ~ CHIRON BY RICKIE HILDER

A channeling

(Rickie Hilder in an Australian Healer, Aura-Soma color therapist, counselor, channeler, writer, teacher and performer. She works extensively and consciously with Chiron's energy.) [44]

*

"My love for you is such that I am always there to offer you the opportunity for 'wholing', for Healing.

"This opportunity was a commitment each of you undertook as a reflection of my service to humanity – 'hue-manity' (the rainbow that is humanity!) It is there in every moment.

"The Healing of the individual reflects the possibility of the Healing of the whole. The service I bring is dormant within each of you and I am the key to unlock this potential for wholeness within each of you.

"It is simple. I am there for you. Indubitably. Always. We are never separate. We are each part of the Whole.

"Each elected their path to Unity, as individuals, to promote the Healing of the Whole. The Healing of each promotes the Healing, ultimately, of the Planet. And the Healing Mother Earth undertook promotes the Healing of 'hue-manity'. That is Her service to you.

"What you do to yourselves affects each other down to minute detail. Your compassion, your acceptance, your generosity of spirit can only shine forth when it shines within – when it shines the Light on the Wounds that lie unHealed, unresolved in the darkness of your psyche.

"There is a joy and spontaneity that is lacking in your lives, of paths

---

[44] See Rickie's natal chart p. 566.

untrodden, of passions unfulfilled because of the lack of Unity, because of the openness of the Wound.

"How can the aspect in the dark be in joy?

"By bringing it back into the fold. By accepting the unacceptable. By rejoicing in the fact that separation is a lie. That the need for separation is a lie.

"There are various of you who have undertaken much in the Healing of this beautiful Planet – those who undertook to reflect their personal Healing to communities at large – those who undertook a larger mission. That was a choice of service. An illumination for 'hue-manity' is under way, is in full flow – the flowering, so to speak.

"Rejoice that you are here at this time. You can express the joy of the Beloved and the Unity of all through the expression of your personal Healing.

"Afford others the opportunity of learning through your experience. Of seeing the possibility of easing the dis-ease. Of loving and accepting their other parts, hitherto denied. The position and the placement of the Wound affords the particular avenue of service, once Healed.

"The Healing is the potential. The placement defines the potential.

"And the potential is a process. Not just one day, one moment. But every day, every moment. The Wound is the gift of every day, whilst in 'hue-man' form.

"The gift of connection – that is the gift. Of Unity. Of Wholeness. Of Oneness.

"Take my hand and I will teach you how to love the unlovable. For indeed I do.

"I bring joy. The joy of wholeness. I bring peace. The peace of wholeness. I bring love. The love in wholeness.

"Know that I am there. Know that you are never alone. Know that you only have to call my name. Know I can hear you, can recognize you, and see the true beauty of your being.

"Connect with me and I will connect you to yourselves. You will see you through my eyes. As an aspect of the Divine, there is no part of you that I do not see, that I do not love.

"You are whole and perfect as the Beloved made you perfect. I see all that is hidden about you, hidden from you, and I see it with tenderness.

I love the unlovable. I love all, as it is part of the All. Through me, you can learn to love all. Let me teach you.

"Turn towards me – turn towards the Light I shine, and I will mirror back your true beauty and courage."

*

3 ~ POEMS BY MARTIN LASS

Juvenilia

The moon,
full of ancient youth,
is a clock face,
milk-crystal white
against a twilight blue sky,
counting away unaccountable time . . .

People, like children, wander softly
in a twilight world,
the faceless of a fleeting civilization;
a civilization haunted by ghosts of ghosts,
a resigned anonymity,
inevitably, ineluctably captured.

The moon,
milk-white clock crystal,
watches her children
as they watch her,
with empty faces and exiled hearts,
lost in a blue twilight . . .

At dusk,
across the turquoise horizon
and the pink-flame wisps of clouds,
the birds fly,
towards some distant twilight,
silhouetted . . .

The sky deepens
and the stars blink.
In the silence of departure,
the air is very loud.

Grandma

Tattered quilt and ancient linens
in the afternoon sunlight,
a watercolor wash,
faded and shifting . . .

Sarcophagus soon . . .

A flame is flickering,
soon to smolder,
soon to die . . .

A pale yellow ghost
moves silently
within faded drapery
and timid light,
then sleeping, now dreams . . .

Flickering shadows
of afternoon
go unnoticed.
Pale ghost,
then sleeping, now dreams . . .

Smoldering embers
of the twilight hour,
pale ghost moving,
then sleeping, now dreams . . .

Dying hues
into blackest night,
pale ghost silent
on tattered quilt and ancient linens,
then dreaming, now sleeps . . .

Having passed
through so many seasons,
so many summer storms,
where will I go next?
I am like dandelion fluff
born gently, inevitably, by the wind
to every end of the world,
through lands far removed
from where I began.
I am at the mercy
of subtle shifts of breeze,
tasting all winds
but staying with none.
Time forbids this.
Time and the inevitable fate
of an endless journey.
A melancholy pervades my thoughts
knowing that my journey
cannot be broken,
but that I must travel all the way,
until I eventually come upon my beginnings,
and truly know them for the first time.[45]

Perhaps, then, I may rest . . .

[45] Acknowledgments to T. S. Eliot, "Four Quartets", i.e. "We shall not cease from exploration/And the end of all our exploring/Will be to arrive where we started/And know the place for the first time." Eliot, T. S. *Four Quartets.* Faber and Faber, London, 1944, 1959, 1979.

There's a little road
in the country,
a few houses
along its leafy way . . .

There are quiet trees
in a sunny wilderness,
a few fields of corn
and meadows of tall grasses
broken by rabbit-runs,
spotted with wild-flowers,
soft with summer abandon . . .

On rabbit-run, children run,
laughing and calling,
now stopping: listening: waiting:
(a gentle open silence) . . .
at the end,
in the distance,
a wooded area . . .

Then run again,
playing down the road
(hide and seek),
suddenly alone,
the houses behind,
back beyond a tree-hidden bend.
The road comes to another
which disappears silently,
alone in the woods,
the blue sky empty above,
and the barren birds' cries
intimating of the wild, wide
wilderness beyond . . .

A shiver in the body,
a wrench in the heart,
now running back
to the familiar land . . .

There's a little road
in the country . . .

Early morning light
invades the sleeper's silence . . .
silence outlined by curve of breath
and rise of bosom
in the darkened room,
silence that falls softly,
like a mist, from the gray clouds,
enveloping the world.

What lies beyond
the chiaroscuro of sleeping forms,
beyond the parted curtain
(which frames a flower,
silhouetted against the grayness),
beyond the twilight tranquility
that descends on the garden's waiting,
beyond the autumn numbness,
settling on a quiet day?

This compressed eternity
(the trains are silent,
red against the soft green rain),
this suspended Being,
world in a glass ball,
what beyond?

Soft, the rain,
soft, the silence:
early morning light invades . . .

Later Poems

My Love . . . Tonight,
I saw what lies within your Bud . . .
I see how you Struggle
in your Opening . . .

When your Flower is fully Open,
and you Breathe in Trust and Love,
you will have such Strength!

Strength not born of hardness,
but of gentle firmness;
Strength not of rigidity,
but of the supple reaching up
of a tree's branches;
Strength not born out of fear,
but out of knowledge and understanding;
Strength not born out of Battle,
but that which resides
in the heart of Peace and Stillness.

And when your Flower is Open,
Accepting of your Life's Pattern,
of the Pattern of your Being,
You will know Power
that is in Harmony with ONE . . .
. . . and then,
you will hold your own Patterns,
bringing them into Creation,
Breathing Life into their four corners.
Such is the Work of Angels.

(. . .)

And then, my Love,
all will look to you
for your gentle Strength,
for your single-minded determination,
for your impartial insight,
and for your Real Will.

And I will look at you,
as I look at you tonight,
in your womanly beauty,
and remember the Child within you
that lost her Trust,
but had the Courage,
despite the Pain,
to walk the Path back Home.

(*to my wife, Inge*)

Finally I am Still..

So many machinations and manipulations,
So many tracks and side-tracks . . .
. . . even these very words
pull me away from my Being.
How complicated my world becomes sometimes . . .

I Wish for Being.

Without Being,
I am dead,
I am empty,
I am NOT.

In the Stillness,
In the Great Quiet,
In the Living Silence,
I AM.

My plate is empty
and Now I am Full.
When there is no room for my Meal,
then I cannot sup with the Angels.
Only into emptiness
can the World pour.
Having no Need,
I am Given my Fill.
I make room for the Divine,
and Become One with All.
There is no Holding on to,
no wishing for more or different,
no questions unanswered,
no fear, no Pain . . .

. . . just the Symphony of All,
Singing through me,
in me,
around me,
IS me.

I stand on the edge of an Abyss,
a fierce Wind holding me there.

First I turn my back to it,
calling out for help,
but none can hear me in the gale.
Then I try to claw my way
away from the Cliff,
but to no avail.
I have no option
but to turn and face the Void . . .
. . . the Wind urges me.

What will I do now?
I have no options.
So I listen and wait.
Will I die if I Leap?
Will I fall?
Or will I Fly?
I must Release my Chains
and Step into the Unknown . . .
. . . an Act of Inner Trust.

All that was before
must die in the Leap,
so that I may meet my Destiny
as pure as a newborn baby.

Friend of many years,
I have only just Seen you.
In my retreat,
In my conceit,
In my arrogance,
In my judgment,
I have cheated myself
of the Possibility
of real Connection.

Then I heard your Call
across the Void,
across the barriers of loneliness
and isolation . . .
. . . and we Connect,
and I See you.

You have remarkable Courage
to choose to experience
Darkness and Isolation,
and then to Speak from this Place.
In the vast gray Ocean of your Life,
your 12th house prison,
you drift without rudder, without oars,
without sight of land,
without Hope of Escape . . .
. . . and yet, from here
you turn inwards,
towards the Darkness
and towards the Light beyond,
and from here you Reach out
and Touch GOD . . .
. . . in you
and outside you.

(. . .)

And then,
through your Love of Words,
you Sing of your Life,
that it may Connect with others,
as it Connected with me.

You ride the waves
between Light and Dark,
between Joy and Suffering,
between Love and Pain . . .
. . . and, denying neither,
you Invoke the Angels,
the Holy Spirit,
that others might Resonate, too,
and Touch GOD with you.

Have Courage to continue
your sacred Charter.

(*for Amanda*)

When all crying is done,
When all tears are spent,
When the Heart becomes Still,
Listen . . .
in the Emptiness . . .
in the Silence . . .
and know with every breath
that you are Loved.

Where did I lose
my Pocketful of Dreams,
and enter into
Sadness and Separation?

Long ago,
I slammed the cupboard door
and had almost forgotten that it was there.
And now I approach the door,
a little scared,
a little excited,
a little still not believing.
I open the door
and I start to sort the jumble.
Where did I put that
Pocketful of Dreams?

Look . . .
Here is my Pain,
which I can now Accept
and Reconcile and HEAL.
Here is my Joy,
as fresh as when I left it.
Here is the Child Within,
crying out for Contact.
Here are the clothes
that I played dress up with.
Here is my Quiver,
and my Arrows.
Here is my Brush,
and my Ink.
Here is my Harp,
and my Manuscript.
Here is my Medicine Chest,
full of Gems, Oils, and Stars.

(...)

And there!
There is my
Pocketful of Dreams. . .
… my Connection, my Joy,
my Love, my Gratitude,
MY LIFE.

I am Earth,
I am Heaven,
I AM MAN.
"I am This,
I am That,
I AM."

(for George Mountford Adie) (1901–1989)

PART THREE
The Astrological Perspective

It is important to mention, at the beginning of this Part Three of Book One of Chiron's musings in relation to Healing and the evolution of consciousness, that many of the astrological points of view that follow are based upon the elaborations, explorations, premises and conjectures that have been laid out not only in Parts One and Two of this first book, *but in the subsequent Books Two and Three of this series.* From this perspective, because it is redundant to re-state or preempt the details of these past and future musings, I will simply refer to these relevant ideas in general, referencing where further discussions about them can be found. By doing this, I leave it to you, the reader, to explore these ideas in detail by referring to Parts One and Two of this Book One and by exploring Books Two, Three and Four of this series at some time in the future. It is my fervent hope and wish that all will read the entire series from beginning to end, as this will give the best chance of a full understanding of all the material covered.

Part Three of this book represents the essence of Chiron's musings, seen from the astrological point of view. As such, it is written for professional astrologers, laypersons and well-informed non-professionals alike. Whatever your interest in the material I have presented, I hope to entice you to a new appreciation of Chiron's place in the astrological tapestry. In addition, I hope to give you enough material with which to start or continue working with Chiron in a practical way.

2745-LASS

1 ~ THE DISCOVERY OF CHIRON

"Not only have the external relationships in the human world changed since the 1960s towards an increasing awareness of being connected with the environment in space and time, but so have the internal relationships of man with himself. The keen occupation with the phenomenon of human consciousness *per se,* the rising interest in a "humanistic" (that is, a non-reductionist) psychology, the techniques of a "holistic" medicine partly imported from other cultures – for example, acupuncture – the interest in non-dualistic Far-Eastern philosophies and exercises such as meditation and yoga, all this is but another important aspect of the metafluctuation which touched a large part of mankind at the beginning of the last third of this [the 20th] century."

-Erich Jantsch, Center for Research in Management of the University of California, Berkeley.[46]

Planetary Characteristics

Before we launch into the body of *astrological* considerations about Chiron, let's recap some of the *astronomical* planetary characteristics of Chiron and their astrological ramifications.

We have previously elaborated on the astronomical details of Chiron. Amongst these details, we pointed out several important characteristics that can help us draw a picture of Chiron's astrological influence. These points were 1) Chiron's highly elliptical orbit, 2) its degree of inclination from the ecliptic, 3) its possible association with the Kuiper belt

[46] Jantsch, Erich. *The Self-organizing Universe.* Pergamon Press, Oxford, 1980, p. 3.

and 4) its erratic orbit between Jupiter, Saturn, Uranus and Neptune. Let's look at each of these in turn . . .

1) Chiron's highly elliptical orbit means that it spends more time at one end of the zodiac than the other. It spends the least time Libra and the most in Aries. The cycle of its apparent acceleration and slowing will be discussed later in terms of the generational cycles of Healing and spiritual quests that correspond to this movement. In the meantime, the fact that Chiron spends the most time in Aries means that Arian aspects are, comparatively speaking, exaggerated and expressed, whereas Libran aspects are minimized and repressed.

We will take the view of Arian and Libran characteristics according to the Mysteries in this case, as we will set out in Book Three. This view asserts that Aries represents the height of material consciousness, individuality, fragmentedness, disconnection and aloneness. It is associated with the Moon and our dualistic *lower* nature. Libra, according to this same view, represents the ultimate balance of consciousness, where we are awakened to our unity and divinity. It is associated with the Sun and our unified *higher* nature.

In defence of this position, acknowledging that a fuller exposition of this subject will be given in Book Three, it is important to point out that the fact that the zodiac has changed over the last many thousand years is *not* relevant *and* relevant in different ways. Firstly, it is not relevant inasmuch as the zodiac according to the Mysteries is symbolic and its messages are universal no matter to which time or culture they are applied. Secondly, taking the holographic view, the fact that Chiron's orbit is shortest in Libra and longest in Aries *at this time in history* is an indication that its messages are relevant to us *now*, synchronistically speaking. In another thousand years or more, the definition of each zodiac sign will have changed according to the paradigms, issues and evolutionary needs present in the culture at that time. Astrology is a fluid art as much as it is a science. As we evolve, so does our astrology.[47]

Therefore, from the point of view of the Mysteries, what the planet,

[47] Many astrologers become unnecessarily stressed by science's dismissal of astrology on the basis of the precession of the equinoxes and the movement of the zodiac against the astronomical background. Astrologers try to defend their position using purely scientific argument,

Chiron, exaggerates and expresses – the Arian side – is separation, isolation, aloneness, fragmentation, duality, lopsidedness, individualization, abandonment, deprivation, rejection and diffusion of consciousness expressed through a material Moon-centered orientation. What the planet minimizes and represses – the Libran side – is connectedness, togetherness, wholeness, balance, unity, Oneness with everything, belonging, nurturing, being wanted, being Loved and the focusing of consciousness expressed through a spiritual Sun-centered orientation.

In short, Chiron, from the apparent view, exaggerates and expresses *Woundedness* and minimizes and represses *Healing.* Having said this, it is important to be reminded that *Woundedness* and *Healing* are *perceptions.* A truer formulation would then be that Chiron accentuates the *perception* of *Woundedness* and understates the *perception* of *Healing* in our lives.

Herein lies the essence of our entire journey. We come into life, to a greater or lesser degree, with an innate sense of being separate, cut off, isolated, alone, fragmented, without meaning, without direction, in chaos, forsaken, abandoned and without Love. This expresses itself in our life in many ways, depending on who we are, where we come from, why we are here and where we are destined to go. The specific nature of our individual Woundedness can be seen in the placement of Chiron in the natal chart and Chiron's relationships with the other planets.

From this perception of Woundedness comes the innate drive towards connectedness, togetherness, wholeness, unity, Oneness with everything, belonging, nurturing, being wanted, being Loved, finding meaning, finding direction, finding harmony, finding balance, finding

---

[47 cont].entering an arena where they will surely be defeated. This is because what science says is true: the zodiac has changed over thousands of years and we are still using it as though it was as it was then. We should simply agree with science. Then we should point out that the astrology we have today is *not* the astrology of thousands of years ago. Nor will it be the same in a thousand years or more. The definition of Arian or Libran characteristics, for example, will be different in a thousand years, holographically mirrored in the precession of the equinoxes. Astrology is a fluid art that is a reflection of the cultural, social, philosophical and spiritual paradigms of the time. It cannot be 'proven' any more than the theories of quantum physicists (regardless of what they try to tell us!) Proving it is irrelevant to the point of the matter. The astrology that we have today is relevant to *today,* but, at the same time, holographically connected to a picture of Actuality that is ultimately beyond all separate cultures and civilizations, beyond time and space as we know it.

Inner Peace and finding Love. The specific ways in which we strive for these things – broadly called *Healing*, according to our paradigm – can also be seen in the placement of Chiron in the natal chart and in the relationships of the others planets to Chiron.

The placements of Chiron and Chiron's relationship with the other planets in the natal chart will be the primary substance of the remainder of this Book One.

It is important perhaps, though obvious, to point out that Chiron's placement and relationships in the natal chart are but parts, albeit integral parts, of the total picture of the natal chart. As such, in the natal chart, all planets interact in a dynamic interplay that forms the totality of a holographic representation of our lives and us. Furthermore, the transiting planets at any given time of our lives must equally be considered a part of that holographic picture.

Taking this into account, any study that seeks to isolate one planet and define it and its influence upon us and our lives, such as our current study, is bound to sacrifice the bigger picture, if only temporarily. Once a basic understanding and the feeling of the planet are grasped, then it is equally important to put it back into the context of the bigger picture. This process is simply the nature of our innate dualistic perception. In order to see the whole, of which we are a part, we must separate the world into the Seer, the Seen and the Seeing. Once enlightened or awakened, we can merge into a greater Oneness where no such distinctions exist. Following this rationale, we will first pick Chiron to pieces, so to speak. At the conclusion of our in-depth study, we will put Chiron back into the big picture with a full chart delineation in Chapter Eleven.

It is also important to acknowledge that different people react differently and to different degrees to the same planetary influences. The mechanisms that make this so – the differing conditions of *opacity, translucence* and *transparency* to planetary influences – will be discussed later in this section. Back to our present discussion . . .

2) Chiron's degree of inclination from the ecliptic makes it somewhat of a rogue in the general scheme of things. It also gives it an unusual perspective. Both these aspects align it with Uranus and Pluto in many ways.

Astrological studies of both ellipticity and angular inclination of planetary orbits show that a planet's astrological influence is exaggerated by these features. This, combined with the size of the orbit, gives a starting point for an appraisal of comparative planetary influence. Let's consider the solar system a unified Being of higher consciousness and the planets its major *personas*. From this perspective, ellipticity, angular inclination and orbital size determine the degree of *polarization* of the consciousness of these personas. Greater ellipticity, angular inclination and orbital size will give greater extremes of expression, greater nonconformity of viewpoints and greater influence overall, compared to the other planets. *From this perspective, comets represent some of the solar system's most extreme emotional expressions.*

The rotational characteristics of a planet also tell us a lot about its astrological influence. For example, Uranus's axis of rotation points 98 degrees away from its orbital axis, its magnetic field is 59 degrees from the rotational axis and it rotates in the opposite direction to most of the other planets. These features correlate with Uranus's known astrological characteristics as being non-conformist, unpredictable, erratic and presenting revolutionary ways of looking at things.

Chiron's degree of angular inclination suggests that it is somewhat of a loner. At the same time, it receives a different perspective from its conformist planetary siblings who keep to the more socially acceptable tracts of the solar ecliptic. In addition, Chiron alternates between being close to other planets, Saturn and Uranus in particular, and being far removed from them. There is much time for deep and solitary introspection. The astrological correlations of the resultant influences certainly concur with these features as part of its astrological make-up.

3) Chiron's possible association with the Kuiper Belt is also an interesting point. The Kuiper Belt, a collection of comets, asteroids and interplanetary debris, lies, for the most part, outside the orbit of Neptune, extending some 1000 AU[48] from the Sun. Pluto, it is now believed, may be a part of this belt, rather than occupying the domain of one of the primary Seven Rays from the galactic center, as is the case for most of the other planets.

---

[48] Astronomical Units. One AU is a measurement of distance corresponding to the mean distance between the Sun and the Earth.

Before continuing to elaborate on the ramifications of Chiron's possible association with the Kuiper Belt, it is necessary to elaborate briefly on the Seven Rays and the origins of the planets. Then we can put the Kuiper Belt, Pluto and Chiron into a larger perspective. We will give a basic outline here. Later, in Book Three, we will explore these astronomical ideas and their metaphysical ramifications in detail.

We postulate that the origin of the solar system and of the planets is a 'cone' of Light originating from the galactic center that diffracts, as it goes, into the Seven Rays of Creation. Each of seven sacred planets and seven non-sacred planets is associated with one of these Rays. The diffraction, deflection or reflection of each Ray on its incoming journey accounts for the orbital characteristics of each planet, as we will set out in Book Three. The more diffraction, deflection and/or reflection of the incoming Light of a Ray, the more extreme and non-conformist the orbits of its associated planets.

Apart from the Seven Rays and their associated planets, our solar system also hosts planets and other celestial bodies, such as some comets, *that have their origin not directly from the galactic center.* Some of these planets and bodies are *secondary reflections* of the original cone of Light of our own solar system. Still others do not hail from the same cone of Light that formed the majority of our solar system. They come from Rays that have been deflected, reflected or diffracted *from other Rays of other solar systems apart from ours.*

Examples of these indirect manifestations are many of the comets that orbit the Sun in wildly elliptical orbits that are tipped to the ecliptic at extreme angles. Such comets are the extreme emotional expression of the solar system, *but they may have their origins in other solar systems.* In this way, *they possibly represent the interactions of consciousness between star systems.* If star systems were atoms, these type of planets and other bodies might be *shared electrons* between atoms, i.e. *ionic bonds.*

Further examples of this are possibly the Kuiper Belt collection of interplanetary objects, lying outside the orbit of Neptune, and the so-called Oort Cloud of comets, lying up to 40 to 50 thousand AU from the Sun. The angle of inclination to the ecliptic is the clue that suggests to us that the origin of a planet or other cosmic body is not directly from the galactic center, but comes via secondary processes or from other star systems.

This would seem to be the case with the Kuiper Belt. Although it is not a singular planetary object, its many objects taken as a whole indicate a degree of unified consciousness such as the Asteroid Belt between Mars and Jupiter. The nature of such celestial consciousness is to see the solar system from an outside perspective, from a different point of view than its native inhabitants. This is directly analogous to getting input from an impartial observer, in this case, *possibly from the consciousness of other star systems.* The benefits of considering the views of such interstellar-originating immigrants, such as Chiron and Pluto may be, are then obvious. To step back from issues that we are too close to can give us perspective and impartially.

Pluto is tentatively taken to be part of this Belt by some astronomers. Chiron, being cometary in nature, having an orbit that approaches Neptune at times, being tipped to the ecliptic and having an elliptical orbit, may well be a stray from the Kuiper Belt as well. Although astronomers are not totally sure, the astronomical data to date backs up this assumption.

4) Chiron's erratic orbit, moving primarily between Uranus and Saturn and approaching Jupiter and Neptune at times, is indicative of the wide scope of ideology and experience that is available to Chiron. As we consider the affairs of these other planets, we begin to see that Chiron represents a kind of bridge between them, a necessary bridge that allows us to move from one level of consciousness to another. The bridge from Saturn to Uranus has been well explored by other astrologers, such as Barbara Hand Clow and Melanie Reinhart, and well as in this present study. We explored it here in Chapter 4, "Journeys Through the Planets".

The ramifications of interaction with Jupiter are:

Moving beyond exaggerated and infantile action and reaction into a more sober sense of responsibility and hard work in relation to Healing and the evolution of consciousness.

Uncovering the Inner Child aspects of ourselves that have been covered, repressed, forgotten, ignored or otherwise negatively condemned by our Woundedness.

Awakening to, acknowledging and embracing our innate knowledge and wisdom.

Balancing our perceptions of positives and negatives, i.e. our dualistic illusions, thus revealing the perfection of our lives.

The ramifications of interaction with Neptune are:

Moving beyond the necessity for obtuse and contrary reactions to challenges and confrontation in favor of seeing the unity of seemingly-opposite viewpoints (this is *compassion,* in its truest sense).

The Healing of seeming opposites of intellectual formulations into the unity of Heart-felt understanding.

Moving beyond the tendency and need for definition and dualistic ideation, merging into the unified and Silent space of Truth and Love.

In a sense, Chiron's message would be sufficient if it only served to illuminate and bring together the issues of Saturn, Uranus, Jupiter and Neptune into a unified understanding. As it happens, it does this and more. The unification of all these issues brings a new level of consciousness, new understanding and associated ideas and messages. The whole is greater than the sum of the parts.

We are now ready to embark upon a more detailed astrological appraisal of Chiron. Let's begin by setting the scene that led to the discovery of Chiron in 1977. For this, we will go back to 1952 . . .

A Tapestry of Planets

Our tale begins in 1952. Why 1952 and not some other year? It was in 1952 that Chiron first made an opposition to Uranus in the 20th century; and this was one of the longest relationships of Chiron and Uranus in the last 1000 years. The first instance in this century took place in February 1952, the last in May 1989. There were altogether 41 occurrences as the two planets danced around this opposition over a period of 37 years, 32 times being before Chiron's discovery in 1977.

During this same time, Saturn, Neptune and Pluto also made numerous aspects to Chiron and to each other and Uranus, peaking in the 1960s. The combined effect was a social and cultural conflagration that brought to light many issues that prepared us and set the scene for the discovery of Chiron. Let's look at some of these planetary aspects.

Uranus's Role

Let's begin with the Chiron/Uranus oppositions. Having worked extensively with clients born with this opposition in their natal charts, we can say that the effect of this opposition is to make it extremely difficult for us to ignore, bury or escape from our individual Woundedness. In this opposition aspect, Uranus shines a light on our Wounds, blockages and unresolved issues. It is the Light of greater Truth shone into our Darkness. Appropriately, many persons with this aspect in their natal chart are either Healers or they are involved in Healing in some way, directly or indirectly. We will explore the individual expressions of this aspect in detail a little later.

From a global perspective, Uranus illuminated Chiron via 41 oppositions between 1952 and 1989, gradually awakening us to its existence and to the nature of Chiron's influence and messages. As its influences became increasingly difficult to ignore and its manifestations increasingly acute, it became inevitable and ultimately necessary for Chiron to be discovered, if only to 'explain' what was going on in the world and in the lives of all those personally affected by the oppositions.

In this way, Uranus was the major force in awakening us to the existence of a new planet and providing a new astrological factor for us to work with.

Saturn's Role

As we have just said, the first opposition of Uranus and Chiron in the 20th century took place in February 1952. This was closely followed by Saturn squaring Chiron only a month later. Prior to this, Saturn and Chiron had been squaring each other on and off *since 1935*. There were 21 exact squares during this period, with the two planets being within loose orb most of the time. In a sense, this square represented *the establishment* inasmuch as it caused us to seek to erect edifices of material protection against our Woundedness and our unresolved issues. It represented a *repression* of these issues until Uranus came along and shone a light upon our inner Darkness. In terms of breaking down the repression, we must also take into account the Chiron/Pluto conjunction of 1941. However, no Healing path was offered by Pluto, just an exacerbation of long-standing issues, expressed through WW2.

Saturn's role, as ever, is to force us to stop and take stock of ourselves, in particular to take stock of long-standing issues that are begging for resolution. It brings these things to our attention, but does not necessarily facilitate their immediate resolution, particularly in a square aspect. From this perspective, the year Uranus came into the picture (1952) was the year we were first encouraged to take stock of long-standing and unresolved issues that related to repressed, unacknowledged, denied, disowned, ignored, unseen or otherwise negatively-judged Wounds and issues. Uranus offered its help in breaking down the residue of this aging standoff between Chiron and Saturn.

We might suggest that the Wounds that remained as a result of World War II were high on this agenda. This is the short-term picture. The years of the so-called 'baby boomers' were a reaction to these Wounds. In an effort to avoid, ignore or escape from these Wounds, all energy and attention was put into the bearing and raising of children and into assuring material security and prosperity. The Healing of the Wounds of the parents of this generation was to be begun in earnest by their children, in particular, those born between 1952 and 1989.

From a more long-term perspective, Humanity was at a point, after several hundred years of the scientific revolution and the so-called Age of Reason, where the swing of the pendulum was to come back towards Spirit and spiritual matters. The first step was to impel us towards introspection, to take our attention away from the practical, pragmatic affairs of the material world and force us to look within. What better way to do this than to bring our unresolved and unHealed Wounds and issues to the forefront of our consciousness? Uranus shone the light and Saturn made us sit down and take stock.

Saturn's influence in these matters peaked in 1966 when it conjuncted Chiron. The mid-1960s, as we shall see in a moment, were the height of the ferment and turmoil – a "metafluctuation", as Erich Jantsch put it in the quote that opened this chapter – that brought

Chiron's influence to the fore, paving the way for its discovery in 1977. By the time it was discovered, its messages were already well established within our consciousnesses. We simply needed a frame of reference, ideas and concepts with which to explain what we had been going through. Chiron's discovery gave us exactly this.

The message of the conjunction of Saturn and Chiron in Pisces in 1966 was that *we* are the ones that need to take responsibility and accountability for our Woundedness. Ultimately, no one else can do it for us. Our journey requires effort . . . effort that some of us are not yet willing to make. It requires seriousness, resolve, humility and a sense of responsibility. It also requires that we forsake our illusion of being victims to anything at all. It requires giving up our attachment to our unnecessary suffering. It requires the Healing of our sense of aloneness, disconnectedness and fragmentedness. The psychological aspects of this journey will be elaborated in Book Two. The further ramifications of Chiron's relationship to Saturn during these years will be discussed a little later in the book.

Pluto's Role

The next aspect, relevant during this time, was the opposition of Pluto and Chiron, occurring 11 times between 1961 and 1965. This aspect reflected, more than any other aspect, the turmoil of the 1960s. It also had strong associations with the space race. One of the two most important fulcrum points in the discovery of Chiron was when Humanity put the first man into space in 1961. *(See **Chart 8 – FIRST MAN IN SPACE**, p.543.)* We will explore many of the events and people involved in these revolutionary times shortly.

As a prelude to the Chiron/Pluto oppositions, it is perhaps relevant to mention two facts. Firstly, Chiron played an important role in Pluto's birth chart (February 18, 1930, Flagstaff, AZ). In this chart, Chiron conjuncts the North Node in Taurus: Pluto's life's path is to bring the intangible into tangible manifestation, to bring what is in the dark into the light, to show that where there is loss and destruction there is also gain and birth, but in new forms. Chiron squares Mars in Aquarius, T-square with the Moon in Scorpio: active and intentional efforts are required to bring the understanding of loss, death, destruction, etcetera, to a new level, showing that nothing is ever truly lost or gained – things just change form. Furthermore, Chiron trines Saturn in Capricorn while Saturn sextiles the Moon in Scorpio: the Healing of the Wounds of loss of safety, security, Trust, etcetera, will be facilitated by serious study into the tangible nature of the intangible, i.e. by finding the spiritual (energy) in the material world and the inseparability of these two sides – the very knowledge given to us by quantum physics. Moreover, as we can gather from the preceding, Chiron loosely opposes the Moon in Scorpio: indicating the need for Healing of the Wounds of loss, death, destruction, which have created mistrust, suspicion, secretiveness, manipulativeness, etcetera. From the association of Chiron and Pluto in 1930, we can see that the respective natal issues of these Kuiper brothers are in empathy with each other's.

Secondly, Chiron and Pluto conjuncted in July 1941, in the midst of WWII. The revolutionary and destructive power of Pluto was channeled into deep Wounds during this time, Wounds that were unable to be accessed without knowledge of Chiron's existence. The plight of the Jewish people was perhaps the most expressed aspect of these Wounds. The hidden Gift and blessings of WWII and of the experiences of the Jews during this time still have yet to emerge fully into the global consciousness. The discovery of Chiron has given us the tool by which Healing of these Wounds is possible. However, the process will certainly be an extended one. The Healing will take place, I believe, not through the first generation – those who experienced the events personally – but through those many generations that will follow.

In any case, the global cycle of the Wounds created during this conjunction of Chiron and Pluto reached its halfway point in the mid-1960s with the Chiron/Pluto oppositions. We will explore Chiron's cycles of Wounding and Healing, globally and personally, shortly. The nature of the Chiron/Pluto oppositions of the 1960s was to bring the unresolved and unHealed issues of the first part of the cycle (1941–1961) to the fore. The form that these issues took in the 1960s was different, but the essence was the same. The Vietnam War was one example of the emergence of the old Wounds of WWII.

It is interesting to note that Chiron and Pluto conjuncted once more on December 30, 1999, representing the end of the cycle that began in 1941. These issues – issues that are part of Humanity's entire history – emerged once more, for us to address and work through a little more. What still remains after such a cycle is then carried over into the next cycle.

Those persons born with the Chiron/Pluto opposition in their natal charts – in the first half of the 1960s – have taken considerably longer to come to terms with their issues and Woundedness than those with the Chiron/Uranus opposition. The apparent depth of the Woundedness (Pluto being a more extreme and powerful influence than Uranus) has meant that many of these people have tried every imaginable way of burying, avoiding, ignoring and denying their Woundedness. The lateness of the 1st Chiron square in their personal Chiron cycles has a lot to do with this, too. We will discuss this Chiron cycle a little later.

In a sense, Pluto's role in the discovery of Chiron was to shake Chiron out its millennia-old sleepy state and encourage its Kuiper brother to get out there and start making waves, fulfilling the mission for which it came. If Uranus shone the Light, then Pluto was the catalyst that activated Chiron. Together, Pluto and Chiron activated the eons-old Wounds of Humanity, inspiring yet another quantum leap search for meaning, connectedness, divinity and Healing. The so-called new-age movement, birthed in the 1960s, is perhaps the most striking example of the result of this activation.

Neptune's Role

Neptune's main influence in the Chiron saga took place between May 1963 and January 1968 when it trined Chiron 11 times. Perhaps the most obvious expressions of this aspect were the hippie culture, the flower children and the catch-cry "Make love, not war". Love was touted as the answer to everything. "All the world needs now is love, sweet love", they said. There was a great Truth encapsulated in their messages. Love is indeed the answer to all questions, as we will explore in Book Two.

The drive towards a more spiritual, peaceful, loving and harmonious world where Man could live as a brotherhood was the simultaneous attempt to escape from the Wounds of the material condition and to Heal those same Wounds. The material world, the scientific method and the establishment, economically, socially and politically was condemned. The swing of the pendulum went to the other extreme. The role of the individual was repressed and the role of the brotherhood – the collective – was expressed. In a sense, Humanity banded together in the wake of Wounds that they could not individually deal with. This was all part of the Healing journey that followed.

Neptune's influence while trining Chiron contributed to the wish to break through to a new level of consciousness, unbounded by mundane rational thought. This was certainly manifested in the escalation of psychedelic drug use. It also manifested in the explosion of creativity that we saw in the 1960s, in particular in music. So many musicians seemed almost divinely connected to the Muses during this time.

Chiron's Gift, too, particularly when aspecting Neptune in this way, is to help us to make quantum leaps of consciousness, intuitively, psychically, mystically. Neptune activates the divinatory powers of Chiron. From such revelations, we must then work backwards in order to try to put the new understandings into a context that makes them practical and conversant with current paradigms. Otherwise they remain impotent and soon dissipate until we are more ready to assimilate them into our consciousness. This process can take decades.

In July 1989 until May 1990, several months after the last Chiron/Uranus opposition, Neptune went into opposition with Chiron (three exact hits). *(See Chart 6 – CHIRON/NEPTUNE OPPOSITION 1989, p.541.)* From here, Chiron was on it own, so to speak. It was well and truly established in astrological circles, it influence and messages being brought into conscious awareness by the many astrologers working with it.

The sense of this final opposition of Chiron and Neptune was to reflect Chiron's essential message. That message is that the way to Healing, the way to reconnect with the Oneness of the Universe, the way to evolution, is *through* the Wound, not around it. Healing is effected by Loving the Wounds and their associated issues, by dissolving our judgments around them. Having established Chiron's position in our consciousness, Neptune could then step back, taking away the training wheels, so to speak. We were left to connect with the divine and mystical realms by our own devices, using tried and tested tools of Chiron's design. Chiron became the intercessory, the intermediary, the divine way-station, the ferryman, so to speak.

So, if Uranus's role was to shine a Light into our Woundedness, Saturn's role to impel us to take stock of ourselves and take responsibility for our Woundedness, Pluto's role to be a catalyst to begin a new wave of Healing and introspection, then Neptune's role was to attract us to the possibility of Returning to Oneness, Returning to Unconditional Love, Returning to Spirit.

The Sun's Role

We could not leave out the major influence of the Sun during this time. Although the Sun makes virtually every possible transit to every other planet every year, there is another factor that contributes to cyclical waxing and waning of its influences. That factor is the *sunspot cycle.* This is a cycle of some 11 years, during which the electromagnetic output of the Sun waxes and wanes periodically. During a period of 11 years, the Sun reverses its polarity, returning to its original polarity after about 22 years.

The peak of the cycle – also called the *solar maximum* – has been variously linked to weather patterns, power outages, computer failures, communications difficulties, psychiatric episode increases, climatic changes and increases in the evolutionary pace of humans, both physically and culturally.

In addition to this, there are larger cycles of approximately 80–90 years and of about 500 years, during which the 11-year cycle becomes alternately less and more active. The last trough of the 500-year cycle occurred between 1645 and 1715 (called the *Maunder minimum)*, after which sunspot activity began to increase again.

The significant point is that the solar maximums of 1946 and 1957 were the largest in recorded history and corresponded to the peak of the 500-year cycle. Add to this the fact that, during 1955–1970, sunspots dominated the northern hemisphere of the Sun (and hence its influence on the northern hemisphere of the Earth) and we can begin to see that the activity of the Sun during this period was a major influence on the Earth. Lastly, the solar maximum following the 1946 and 1957 peaks was in the crucial year of 1968. As we proceed, we shall see that the latter half of the decade of the sixties was the fulcrum point in a major evolutionary movement of consciousness.

In astrological and metaphysical terms, this increased solar activity represented a call to action, a confront and challenge to our comfortable illusions, a wake-up call to our sleeping Spirit. Its illumination contributed to the discovery of Chiron, the planet that is the external mirror of our innermost Wounds and their hidden Gifts. When combined with all the other planetary aspects, we can begin to see why this period in history was such an important spiritual and Healing awakening, albeit a dramatic and difficult one.

A Menagerie of Planets

The interaction of Saturn, Uranus, Neptune and Pluto with each other during this time was also an important factor in the whole awakening to Chiron. These four planets and Chiron danced up a storm that left us gasping at the end of the 1960s. The actual discovery of Chiron in 1977 was almost a letdown in comparison. The main work had already been done. Let's look briefly at some of the interactions of the outer planets during these important years. These interactions trace a chronology of awakening to, activation of and culmination in the discovery of Chiron . . .

Saturn and Uranus

In April 1952, only two months after the first Chiron/Uranus opposition, Saturn squared Uranus. The square aspect often requires 'outside' help in order to break down the *impasse*. The square of Saturn and Uranus inferred the necessity of a bridge between these planets. The Saturnian 'old guard' of ingrained and out-moded paradigms was being challenged by the revolutionary Uranus. Squaring each other, they were in a standoff, so to speak. Uranus tried to shine a light on Chiron (via the opposition of the two) while Saturn tried to block it. The mediating force between Saturn and Uranus would be Chiron, assisted by Pluto. This mediation would eventually culminate in 1977 with the discovery of Chiron, only months after the very next time Saturn and Uranus squared each other. The final stage was yet to come, though.

In the meantime, apart from several trines and other minor aspects, Saturn and Uranus also *opposed* each other 5 times between April 1965 and January 1967, further adding to the power of the fulcrum point of 1966. This was part of the ongoing confrontation between the hardened and inflexible paradigms of the establishment and the groundbreaking, unexpected, fresh, eccentric revelations of the dawning new age. Pluto certainly stirred the pot during this time, too. All three planets – Saturn, Uranus and Pluto – danced with Chiron in these vital and lively mid-1960s.

The final stage, in 1988, a year before the final Chiron/Uranus opposition and Chiron/Neptune opposition, was when Saturn and Uranus *conjuncted.* This was the culmination . . . the bridge between Saturn and Uranus, and between the inner and the outer planets, was complete, thanks to Chiron. After 1989, Uranus light on Chiron ceased with their final opposition and Neptune left Chiron to its own devices. Chiron was, so to speak, a fully-fledged planet and in full view of the collective consciousness of Humanity. It was now necessary for us, personally and collectively to make sense of Chiron's messages and build upon them, ever growing, Healing and evolving.

Saturn and Neptune

From November 1952 to July 1953 Saturn and Neptune conjuncted. The next time this occurred was between March and November 1989. There are those dates again! In the midst of this, only months after Saturn trined Neptune in 1977, Chiron was discovered.

The first conjunction of these two planets, in 1952, was in the midst of the first Uranus/Chiron oppositions and Uranus/Saturn squares. On the one hand, Saturn would tend to restrict and inhibit the flow of Neptunian energies in this conjunction, leading to a need for outside intervention in order to access them. This, in a sense, was again a call to Chiron to bridge this gap.

From another perspective, access to Neptune, via Chiron and Uranus, could only be achieved by Saturnian seriousness, personal responsibility and hard work. This, in turn, brings us to Chiron naturally and inevitably. Once Chiron has been invoked and inner work undertaken, the path to Uranus and Neptune also opens.

From a final perspective, the conjunction of Saturn and Neptune gave us a taste of what was 'missing' in our lives during the post-war years. We 'missed' an intuitive connection to divine and ethereal realms, rather than the spiritual bondage of out-moded and empty religious traditions and rituals. Once the goal was sensed within our collective consciousness, the race was on.

In early 1977, Saturn and Neptune trined, auguring the discovery of Chiron. The inner work undertaken and under way, the channels were open for a bridge to be discovered between the inner and outer planets, represented by Saturn and Neptune, respectively.

When we get to 1989, the year of the next Saturn/Neptune conjunction, Chiron had been discovered and Uranus and Neptune were about to take leave of Chiron. The birth process and early childhood of Chiron was complete as was the bridge between the inner and the outer planets. The longing for a reconnection to divinity and Oneness, inspired by the Saturn/Neptune conjunction, could be answered by walking the Healing path as set out by Chiron.

Saturn and Pluto

Between November 1952 and August 1953, Saturn and Pluto sextiled each other. The sextile aspect, being an open channel for planetary influence to pass freely, allowed Saturn and Pluto to converse freely, so to speak, during this important time. In a sense, with the lines of communication open, the intervening planets, including Chiron, were illuminated. Again, there is the hint of the idea of a bridge between the inner and outer planets. Due to the issues of all five planets in question – blockages, obstacles and confrontation – this sextile sent out an appeal, so to speak, to Chiron to help complete the bridge.

Between April 1965 and February 1966, Saturn and Pluto opposed each other. This was one of the fulcrum and focal points of the discovery of Chiron, culminating in the inception of the "Star Trek" television series. We will explore this rather interesting and unusual perspective shortly!

In any case, the effect of the opposition of Saturn and Pluto was to bring to light the Wound of our separateness from the outer planets and beyond. It illuminated the Wound of our separateness from the greater consciousness of the solar system and galaxy, our separateness from divinity and our separateness from our higher spiritual functions. As we will have already explored, our Wounds Serve to drive us towards our Healing and the evolution of consciousness. The innate need for connection to our divine source, not having been addressed by the industrial revolution, drove us towards the stars, on one hand, and towards the microscopic origins of matter on the other. The space race throughout the 1960s was the outward expression of this, as we shall see.

From the surface of it, one might ask what is the possible connection between the search for Spirit and the space race. If we take the analogy of our expanding consciousness mirroring the ever-expanding orbits of the planets in our solar system, then the space race is merely an outward expression of our inward urge for this expansion. We will explore this in detail in Book Three. We will explore Star Trek and the space race in detail shortly.

Again, between January and May 1977, while Saturn and Neptune trined, Saturn and Pluto sextiled. The channels between the inner planets, Saturn as the spokesperson, and the outermost planet, Pluto, were open once more. The illuminating light of the sextile came with full force this time, auguring the discovery of Chiron only months later.

In May 1989, Saturn sextiled Pluto once more, while Saturn conjuncted Neptune. The channel between inner and outer planet was open again, but merely to celebrate, as it were, the completion of the Chiron bridge, the Rainbow Bridge.

Uranus and Neptune

From September 1966 to May 1968, Uranus and Neptune sextiled each other. Uranus represents the *Soul's Message* and Neptune, the *Soul's Vision.* Taken together, they reveal the Divine Design of the Soul (at the magnetopause of the solar system) transmitted to the higher Self on its journey through the planets. Saturn's opposition to Uranus during the first part of this time indicated earthly resistance to hearing the messages of the Soul (the resistance of the establishment or *status quo)*. Nonetheless, the message and vision were held by sextiling Uranus and Neptune, the channel of their communication held open by the aspect, overcoming Saturn's opposition and paving the way for their receipt by Humanity via Chiron.

Uranus and Pluto

Uranus and Pluto conjuncted between October 1965 and June 1966. During this time, Chiron opposed each of them at different times. As we previously mentioned, 1966 was one of the fulcrum points in the panorama of the discovery of Chiron. The power of Uranus and Pluto together is unparalleled in terms of their awakening and revolutionizing effect. Uranus shines a bright light, illuminating the big picture, and Pluto turns the world upside-down, wiping away static and dead forms. Pluto is about the transformation of consciousness; Uranus is about elevating consciousness to new heights; both are about the *evolution* of consciousness.

In a sense, Pluto stirred up the deepest Wounds while opposing Chiron during this conjunction of Uranus and Pluto and Uranus shone a light on those exposed Wounds. Humanity called out for assistance. Chiron, stirring from its eon-long slumber, answered.

Furthermore, the Virgo placement of Uranus and Pluto at this time was fair indication of the issue of Healing that was being illuminated. This was the beginning of a revolution that birthed the alternative health, healing and medicine movement.

The Chiron placement in Pisces at this time illuminated the Wounds of separation from divinity, from Oneness and from Love that is a feature of the incarnation process itself. This inspired the wish for a Return to Oneness and a rejoining with the greater cosmos from which we were sundered. Again, this was expressed in the acceleration of the development of space travel. Our Home, astronomically and metaphysically, *is* the greater cosmos, beyond the confines of our Earth-bound consciousness.

The three main themes were set: Healing, consciousness and evolution. The evolutionary journey *is* the Healing journey; the Healing journey is a journey of consciousness, reflected in the material hologram.

Neptune and Pluto

Neptune and Pluto sextiled each other from 1950 through to 1956, then again from 1976 through to 1979, again from 1980 through to 1986 and will again between 2026 and 2032. *The sextile is the only aspect of Neptune and Pluto between 1892 and 2061.*

As with the Uranus/Neptune and Saturn/Pluto sextiles, this opened the communication channel between these two outer planets during times crucial to the eventual discovery and activation of Chiron. The linked chain of sextiles – Pluto to Neptune, Neptune to Uranus and Pluto to Saturn – was only broken between Uranus and Saturn. This created an intensified need for a mediating bridge, ultimately filled by Chiron. The conjunctions of Saturn and Uranus in 1988 sealed the deal, so to speak.

It was as though the awakening and activation of Chiron was coming from both directions. Firstly, it was coming from *beyond* the solar system, channeled through Pluto, Neptune and Uranus. Secondly, it was coming from *within* the solar system in the form of challenges to the Saturnian *status quo*, i.e. the need for Healing and Connection felt by Humanity, individually and collectively. It is interesting that, during 1977, when Chiron was discovered, Neptune was in Sagittarius and Pluto was in Libra. Sagittarius points us to the greater Truth of galactic consciousness, as we will discuss further in Book Three, whereas Libra, according to the Mysteries, represents the ultimate balance of consciousness that opens our Hearts to Love.

The Dynamic Picture (1952–1989)

From all that we have discussed, we can now see that the focal dates for the entire symphony of Chiron's discovery were 1952, 1957 1961, 1966, 1968 (and the 1960s in general), 1977 and 1989. The year 1952 was the exposition, introducing the main themes. The 1960s were when the major work was done, the themes developed in a complex counterpoint, climaxing in 1961 and 1966. The year 1977 was the actual discovery, the main themes now clear and in the tonic key, so to speak. Finally, 1989 was the coda and the final cadence.

The coda of this planetary symphony, in 1989, went as follows:

On 4 March, Saturn and Neptune conjuncted, affirming the Rainbow Bridge.

On 5 May, Mars conjuncted Chiron, giving extra impulse to get on with its task now.

On 19 May, Chiron and Uranus opposed each other for the final time, a kind of farewell salute. *(See Chart 4 – LAST CHIRON/URANUS OPPOSITION, p.539.)* Chiron was on its own now.

In June, Saturn and Neptune again made an exact conjunction, again affirming the Rainbow Bridge.

On July 12, Chiron and Saturn opposed one another, Saturn impelling Chiron to take the reins, so to speak. *(See Chart 5 – CHIRON/SATURN OPPOSITION 1989, p.540.)*

On July 18, Chiron and Neptune opposed each other, Neptune now taking a loving but firm leave of Chiron. *(See Chart 6 – CHIRON/NEPTUNE OPPOSITION 1989, p.541.)*

On August 6 through to mid 1990, Chiron and Pluto trined, resonating in a newfound kinship, Chiron supported by its Kuiper brother. The channel for extra-solar influences remained open, feeding Chiron and encouraging us all to seek the Light of greater consciousness by walking towards Pluto through the doorway of Chiron (the Wound).

During this time, on November 27, 1989, Pluto conjuncted Mars while they both trined Chiron. *(See Chart 7 – NOVEMBER 1989, p.542.)* This was like a final burst of cosmic energy, after which, Chiron was a truly initiated and fully-fledged member of the consciously-acknowledged planetary club.

Let's now look at some of the actual events that took place during the years 1952–1989. We will explore these events with astrological references and charts. Note that we will not necessarily present these events in chronological order. In addition, if some of the events' astrological charts we look at do not look like they are astrologically significant, we must remember that we are looking at a dynamic picture. To see the big picture, according to the Chiron paradigm, we need to step back and include more. We need to include all that transpired in the dynamic picture between 1952 and 1989 and even beyond. The astrological process is a dynamic one. By this fact, an astrological snapshot at a particular moment in time can only hope to illustrate individual points within that larger context in an incomplete way. The greatest service of such snapshot charts is when they are used to reflect the nature of *beginnings* of events and processes, such as a birth chart of an individual. Transits serve to map out milestones along that journey. Dynamic aspects, combined with transits to snapshot charts, give us a more satisfying and encompassing view of the picture we seek to illuminate.

Events and Issues

Any appraisal of events and issues of a period of time is bound to be incomplete unless encyclopedic in length and breadth, so we will pick out a few of the more obvious ones that have particularly Chironic implications. In other words, don't be upset if we miss out on your favorite subject!

The events and issues that we will explore here were all part of the *lead-up* to the discovery of Chiron. In a sense, Chiron's presence was highly evident even before it was discovered. The need to explain the issues and events of the 1950s and, in particular, the 1960s, required us to discover Chiron and then look back, applying Chiron's indications to what were the most tumultuous years of the 20th century.

Science Fiction & Star Trek

> "Picard, you are about to move into areas of the galaxy containing wonders more incredible than you can possibly imagine . . . and terrors to freeze your soul."
>
> -Star Trek – The Next Generation, episode "Q Who?", Q speaking to Captain Picard.[49]

> "For that one fraction of a second, you were open to options you had never considered. That is the exploration that awaits you . . . not mapping stars and studying nebula . . . but charting the unknown possibilities of existence."
>
> -Star Trek – The Next Generation, episode "All Good Things . . .", Q speaking to Captain Picard.[50]

When confronted by the possibility of expanding our current sphere of consciousness, we generally react in a two-fold way. On the one hand, we are excited by the prospect and on the other hand, we react with fear, suspicion and trepidation. At worst, we react with violence, trying to 'kill off' the imagined enemy of the unknown.

No better was this witnessed than in the spate of science fiction movies that appeared from 1951 and throughout the 1950s into the early 1960s. Although science fiction existed well before this, as far back as last century with H. G. Wells and Jules Verne, it was somewhat of an aficionado pastime. In the 1930s and 1940s, it came in the pulp magazine format: *Amazing Stories* and *Astounding Science Fiction,* for example. However, in the 1950s, science fiction became mainstream in the cinema with releases such as "The Day the Earth Stood Still" in 1951, "Red Planet Mars" in 1952, "War of the Worlds" in 1953, "The Day the World Ended" in 1955, "Forbidden Planet", "Invasion of the Body

---

[49] Quoted in: Sherwin, Jill ed. *Quotable Star Trek.* Pocket Books, New York, 1999, p. 54.
[50] Ibid., p. 55.

Snatchers" and "World Without End" in 1956, "The Fly" in 1958 and "The Day the Earth Caught Fire" in 1961.

In many ways, the type of science fiction produced during these years has parallels in Cold War fears that we will discuss shortly.

During these years, we felt the chains of the Saturnian *status quo.* The existing paradigms were impotent to answer the deep questions, longing and Wounds we experienced as Chiron's influence began to be illuminated after World War II. When faced with such an *impasse,* we reach outwards, beyond the safety of tried and tested ways, beyond the accepted paradigms, beyond the out-moded and stagnant ways of dealing with life. This journey generally begins in the imagination, in the symbols and archetypes of the sub-conscious and supra-conscious mind.

As we test the waters of formerly unacceptable propositions, we are immediately confronted with all that is within us that resists change and fears the unknown. On the one hand, the science-fiction films of the 1950s expressed optimism, adventure and excitement. On the other hand, they simultaneously expressed the fear of the unknown, personified in the guise of hostile alien beings, catastrophic astronomical events, deadly terrestrial and extraterrestrial mutant organisms and the horrors of atomic war.

It is interesting to note the resurgence of such themes in the 1990s as we approached the momentous Pluto/Chiron conjunction of at the end of 1999. *(See **Chart 10 – CHIRON/PLUTO CONJUNCTION 1999,** p.545.)* These themes came out in such TV series as "The X-Files", "Millennium", "American Gothic" and "Profiler". Chiron's passage through Scorpio in the 1990s had a lot to do with this, too.

Ultimately, our fear is the fear of greater Truth than we may not be able to handle. Our contradictory and charged personas will do anything to preserve their right to exist unchallenged. In the Light of greater Truth, some of these personas must die to make way for higher consciousness. In the 1950s, on the one hand, we were driven outwards into the cosmos in search of answers, welcoming space and extraterrestrial 'friends'. On the other hand, our fear of the unknown manifested in the images of hostile aliens, the personification of the Other, the Darknesses 'out there' that, in Truth, mirrored the Darknesses within ourselves that we feared to see.

In a sense, the threshold that Humanity stood upon during the 1950s and 1960s was the threshold of awakening to the outside. The consciousness of Humanity had come to a threshold of potential new awakening. The infantile illusion of being alone, unique and special must eventually give way to the more mature recognition of the Other in our lives. The acknowledgment that we may not be alone in the Universe was a momentous one. It mirrored our innate need to reconnect to the spiritual parts of ourselves that had been all but forgotten in the Age of Reason and in the Industrial Revolution.

This awakening is represented astrologically by the journey from the lower to upper hemispheres of the natal chart. It also has associations with the transition from the anaretic degree to the next and with the leap from one octave into a new octave of consciousness, as previously discussed. These represent the orgasm of consciousness that takes place when critical mass is reached in any given issue in our lives. It is further represented by the transition from Virgo (the final integration of the Healing journey) to Libra (balanced consciousness, acknowledging Self and Other as mirrors of each other.) Also within this awakening is the transition from Virgo (the fragmented Many, particulate and disconnected) to Pisces (the unified One, whole and connected.) The Virgo placements of Uranus and Pluto and the Chiron placement in Pisces during the 1960s certainly illuminate this last point.

We will discuss some of these astrological themes with reference to Chiron a little later. In the meantime, let's return to space, so to speak!

Although the trend of science fiction diminished in the first half of the 1960s, attention and focus turning towards other matters, such as the Cold War, we were far from finished with the archetypes and symbols of the psyche expressed through science fiction. The most momentous occurrence, in this respect, and one which formed one of the two most important fulcrum points in the tapestry of Chiron's discovery, was the approval for a new series of TV shows called "Star Trek". *(See Chart 3 – STAR TREK APPROVED, p.538.)*

When we find ourselves at an *impasse* of consciousness, in an untenable situation, in irreconcilable Pain, with no answers forthcoming, we have the impulse to 'get off the planet', so to speak. We will discuss this idea at length in Book Two. The are two-fold reasons behind this impulse. Firstly, it is an obvious attempt to escape from our situation. Secondly, it is not so obvious attempt to seek a higher perspective, to make a non-rational leap into a new dimension of consciousness, to see a bigger picture whereby understanding, resolution and Healing of our predicament become possible.

The impulse itself can manifest in numerous ways. One of those ways, as we are now beginning to see, is in the impulse to travel in space, to explore the planets and the stars. In the 1960s, we did this actually, via the so-called *space race*, and in virtual reality through science fiction, no better exemplified than by Star Trek. Both ways were ultimately going to provide us with a mirror in which we would find ourselves staring back at ourselves. They would provide new ways of looking at issues that we had lost sense of back here on Earth. As astronauts returning from space relate, once you see the Earth from space, your perspective about *everything* changes and you can never see things in the old way.

As we have explored, the evolutionary expansion of consciousness and the search for spiritual meaning in our lives is directly paralleled by the astronomical picture. We seek the stars because we seek to find out who we are, where we come for, where we are going and why we are here. The aliens that we meet in science fiction are but disguised aspects of ourselves that we are learning to Love. The places that we visit are but disguised aspects of home. The more we see ourselves in the mirror of the cosmos, the more we feel at Home, the more we feel a sense of belonging, of Connectedness, of Oneness with all around us. Until then, no journey that we take can fill the sense of aloneness and emptiness within us. Even in the exploration of space, we are cut off by the walls of our consciousness, feeling like strangers in strange lands. This is reflected in the Pisces placement of Chiron in the 11th house in the Star Trek natal chart. ***(Chart 3 – STAR TREK APPROVED, p.538.)***

Conversely, Uranus in opposition to Chiron impels us to strike out into uncharted territory *(start opening credits music . . . roll cameras. . . !)* " . . . to explore strange new worlds, to seek out new life and new civilizations, to boldly go where no man has gone before."[51] Incidentally, the technology aspect of Uranus is worth noting in relation to space travel.

[51] Ibid., p. 301.

Mars, occulting Saturn (loosely conjuncting, but parallel within less than a degree), both opposing Uranus and Pluto, seeks to break down the limitations, restrictions, repressions and stagnant thinking of the establishment, paving the way for innovative advances in technology.

The walls of our consciousness are like the walls of a spaceship, protecting us and nurturing us, but, at the same time, imprisoning us and cutting us off from Contact and from a sense of Home. No better was this Chironic feeling summed up than in an episode of Star Trek called, "The Naked Time". In this episode, the crew of the Enterprise has been stricken by an alien organism that causes what is psychologically hidden, repressed, unacknowledged, etcetera, to surface and dominate the personality. (The Chiron relevance is immediately apparent.) Towards the end of the episode, Captain Kirk, under the power of the alien organism, in a poignant and Piscean melodramatic soliloquy, waxes lyrical about his love for his ship. However, he simultaneously realizes with deep Pain that these same walls cut him off from Home. ('Home' he associates with love for a woman, as opposed to his love for his ship, and with the freedom to lay aside his responsibilities and burdens for a time, away from the constraining and jealous walls of his ship) . . ."No beach to walk on . . .", he says. Constrained by these walls, he cannot reach out and allay his aloneness. We seek Connection and Contact (Pisces Chiron), but we are stuck in forms (Saturn-conjunct-Chiron).

In another episode – "Is There in Truth No Beauty?" – Spock's body becomes the vehicle of expression for the alien, Kollos. Kollos soliloquizes about the human condition . . ."How compact your bodies are. And what a variety of senses you have. This thing you call . . . language, though . . . most remarkable. You depend on it for so very much. But is any one of you really its master? But most of all . . . the aloneness. You are so alone. You live out your lives in this shell of flesh. Self-contained. How terribly lonely."

Apart from these more obvious considerations, other themes in Star Trek are also eminently relevant to our musings in relation to Chiron and its discovery. Let's look at these now . . .

One of the main themes in the series was the juxtaposition of the intellectual and analytical (Spock) with the emotional and intuitive

(Captain Kirk). This is clearly seen in the chart in the opposition of Virgo Pluto and Uranus (Spock) and Pisces Chiron, Saturn, Mars and Mercury (Kirk). On the one hand, our journey of consciousness and Healing is ever to seek a higher logic, a higher perspective, a glimpse at the bigger picture. Uranus and Pluto certainly intimate these aspects. On the other hand, we seek a connection – or, rather, a reconnection – to our intuitive, spiritual side, to a noble view of the essential Oneness of all creatures and all things, intimated by the 11th house Piscean planets. Ultimately, we need a balance of both sides of this equation.

The expressed issue of the latter part of the 20th century, poignantly expressed in the 1960s, was the over-emphasis of Reason and logic and the neglect of all things spiritual and intuitive. This stance was certainly made clear in Star Trek, with Spock coming out looking ridiculous more often than not and Kirk forever saving the Universe from inevitable destruction by relying upon his emotional and seemingly-irrational instincts.

From this perspective, Spock was somewhat stuck in the analytical and anal sides of Virgo, cut off from a sense of belonging and connection to life. In rare moments, we see Spock's sense of aloneness and inner vulnerability. Kirk, on the other hand, often allowed the Piscean planets to hold sway over logic, quick to defend human emotion as evolutionarily superior to pure logic.

Paradoxically, Spock was the one that expressed the humanitarian and collective ideals, summed up in the Vulcan saying, "The needs of the many outweigh the needs of the few or the one."[52] This essentially expresses the Aquarian Sun and the quartet of Piscean planets in the 11th house. Moreover, Kirk, although expressing high ideals and a wish for Contact with the Universe (he was always off kissing alien women!) was, in practice, a self-aggrandizing individualist to a fault. This is more indicative of Pluto and Uranus in the 5th house. Kirk turned the aforementioned Vulcan ideal back to front in one of the later Star Trek films ("The Search For Spock") when, after rescuing Spock from a presumed death, he indicates to Spock that he saved him "because the needs of the one outweighed the needs of the many."[53] In Truth, we tick-tock be-

[52] Ibid., p. 307.
[53] Ibid., p. 133.

tween the polarities of the One and the Many, as we shall explore at length in Books Two and Three. The reconciliation and synthesis of the two sides is what the Chiron paradigm of Healing seeks.

So, we can see that there were many conflicting issues raised in Star Trek, mirroring the opposition of Uranus-conjunct-Pluto and Chiron-conjunct-Saturn. The main dichotomies were the individual vs. the collective, the intellect vs. the emotions, science vs. spiritual and philosophical idealism and separateness vs. Oneness. The exploration of the human psyche and of consciousness, mirrored in the voyages of the Starship Enterprise, although seemingly trite in the Hollywood dialogue of TV in the 1960s, was well served by this TV series.

Another interesting point is that, although bound by the so-called "Prime Directive" to not interfere in the lives of alien races, the crew of the Enterprise was forever saving alien races from otherwise inevitable destruction or subjugation at the hands of 'evil'. There always seemed to be something to 'fix', something to 'set right', something to redress. Chiron's perspective tells us that what we try to 'fix', change, Heal or save *are actually aspects of ourselves, mirrored in the outside world.* The Piscean relevance of this lies in the perception of victimhood and injustice, whereas the Virgoan relevance lies in the need and desire to 'fix', 'set right' and Heal. Chiron, as the Wounded Healer, totally personifies both sides of this axis. In the series, Dr. McCoy, the ship's doctor, was continually challenged to push beyond the boundaries of known medical science and practise, expanding his craft on different species of alien life. In a classic moment (episode: "The Devil in the Dark"), McCoy, challenged with healing a being that was made more of rock than flesh, spouts out, "I'm a doctor, not a bricklayer!"[54]

Various episodes of Star Trek also explored the dual nature of the human psyche, i.e. the dark, hidden side and the lighter, visible side. The nature of Chiron in opposition to Uranus, particularly given that Uranus was conjuncting Pluto at the time, is to bring our dark aspects into the light, to place our paradoxes side by side, to challenge us to Love all aspects of ourselves equally. With respect to this theme, we have already mentioned "The Naked Time". There was also "The Enemy

---

[54] Ibid., p.263.

Within", where Kirk suffers a transporter malfunction and is split into two people – his 'good' side and his 'bad side. This story illustrates that a person needs both sides to function in life. In the words of the character, Dr. McCoy: "Jim, you're no different than anyone else. We all have our darker side. We need it. It's half of what we are. It's not really ugly, it's human."[55] In the episode, "Mirror, Mirror", universe and anti-universe cross paths resulting in an exploration of the two sides of the psyche and, again, in the realization that one side of us cannot function without the other.

Then there was the so-called "Vulcan mind-meld". The idea of merging two minds into one is the epitome of the Piscean ideal. However, the Pain of seeing one's own inner Truth, not to mention exposing it to someone else, was made patently obvious in dramatic scenes with Spock and a variety of unsuspecting victims. This theme certainly expressed Chiron's placement in Pisces and its opposition to Uranus and Pluto.

The exploration of time and its relation to consciousness was also a recurring theme in Star Trek. The relevance of this will become clearer when we consider the relation between time and consciousness in Book Three. Similarly, the interchangeability of energy and matter is a theme well explored, the most obvious example being the so-called Transporter that converts matter to energy, transports it and reassembles it back into matter. This theme we will also cover in Book Three.

Still on the Star Trek chart, the trine of Chiron with Neptune in Scorpio in the 7th house further amplifies the call of Spirit *through* our Wounded feelings of aloneness, separateness, isolation and disconnectedness. By walking through the Wound, dealing with its issues, we begin to resonate with higher frequencies. As we resonate to higher frequencies, we come into greater alignment with the consciousness of our higher nature. The trine of Chiron and Neptune ensures that, having walked through the Wound, so to speak, Spirit will be waiting to welcome us.

The trine of North Node in Gemini and Venus in Capricorn on the Midheaven reflects the destiny of the series. Its task was to bring our

---

[55] Ibid., p. 76.

deep innate knowledge and wisdom (Sagittarius South Node) into a tangible and communicable form (Gemini North Node). Its task was to put this knowledge and wisdom into a form easily understandable, accessible and graspable to the world at large. That form took the metaphor of the physical journey (Node in 1st house) into space, a journey that mirrored our inner psychological journey of discovering who we are, where we have come from, etcetera.

The Capricorn Midheaven gave the series the practical foundations it required to be a material and financial success and achieve widespread recognition, albeit that success was not immediately forthcoming. Capricorn Venus retrograde made it a labor of love, destined to bring fruit at a later stage. The trine of North Node and Venus-conjunct-Midheaven brought the labor of love into alignment with a higher destiny.

After Star Trek was approved in February 1966, by the end of March, the conjunction of Saturn and Chiron had become exact, as had the Uranus Pluto conjunction. Saturn and Chiron were out of orb by the beginning of May, Uranus and Pluto by the end of August.

The first episode of Star Trek went to air on September 8, 1966. *(See Chart 11 – STAR TREK 1ST EPISODE, p.546.)* The stellium of planets in Virgo, primarily in the 5th house overwhelms the chart, the Healing theme in the broadest sense more than apparent. The trines and sextiles of these planets to North and South Nodes, respectively, give the stamp of destiny to the series. The conjunction of Uranus, Pluto and the Sun (Sun and Uranus in occultation), all sextiling Neptune-conjunct-South Node and trining the North Node is the most powerful call to higher consciousness that one could ask for. The show was destined (North Node) to have a powerful (Pluto) and revolutionary (Uranus) effect for years to come (Neptune), inspiring us to Shine (Sun) through the vehicle of space travel (Uranus). The underlying theme, however, that lies behind these external manifestations is the journey of Spirit into higher realms of consciousness and awakening.

Chiron, now in very loose separating opposition to some of the Virgo planets, remains nonetheless in the background. Its 12th house Pisces placement gave the series an indefinable mystique and it called out to us to acknowledge our hidden longing for Spirit. Chiron in the 12th house requires divinatory and/or mystical means in order to access its power. It was as though the Star Trek series could offer us a magical path of Healing – or an escape from our Pain, as the case may be. Neptune conjuncting the South Node affirms that, somewhere in the recesses of our Soul, we already know where we have come from and, hence, where Home is, even if we cannot put it into words.

Chiron-conjunct-Saturn, trining Jupiter, represents an affirmation and intimation of the miraculous and mysterious Universe that awaits us, delighting the wise but childlike Inner Child within each of us. Jupiter's promise, in this aspect, is that by attending to our Wounds, blockages and unresolved issues that have their primal origins in childhood, we will Return to a view of the world that delights as well as confounds. This view constantly intimates that there is a Guiding Hand at work. In the end, we will realize that the limitations we perceive around us in the world and in our lives are self-imposed; further, that they are limitations of perception only, overcome by the expansion of our consciousness. The outward journey to the stars is symbolic of the expansion of our consciousness beyond its present confines.

The power of Star Trek becomes apparent when we consider its longevity and its huge cult following that stretches right into the new millennium. Spin-off series abound, not to mention numerous full-length feature films. The themes explored are universal themes that all come back to the four basic questions that we began with: who are we, where do we come from, where are we going and why are we here?

The Pain of our inner fragmentedness, isolation, aloneness and separateness, combined with our generally low self-worth in the 20th century, drives us ever outward and inward, simultaneously. The outward journey – trekking into space – mirrors the desired expansion of consciousness. This expansion of consciousness is a Healing journey of rejoining our fragmented nature, forging connectedness with the Universe, feeling not alone or separate and feeling validated as worthy citizens of a starry cosmos. Such is Chiron's own Healing path as it orbits the solitary tracts of the outer solar system. The themes of Pain, separateness, isolation from the Divine and the longing for a Return to the Divine are most aptly and openly explored in the 5th of the Star Trek spin-off feature films, "The Final Frontier". In this story, the revolutionary/renegade Vulcan, Sybok, represents the Healer/Seeker on a Quest for the origin of our existence. Although the culmination of a Return to God is not achieved in this particular story, the nature of our hidden Pain and our longing for a Return to God/Oneness/Love/All are openly illustrated and explored.

All in all, our journey is a journey of consciousness . . . one that is ultimately undertaken in the recesses of the psyche, mirrored symbolically, holographically and supra-consciously in the external world, whether that world is real or virtual. It is a journey that we have all undertaken, sometimes from the comfort of an armchair, sitting in front of the TV, carried away to distant times and places by programs such as Star Trek.

Other TV science fiction series of note in the 1950s and 1960s were Rod Serling's "Twilight Zone", "Lost in Space" and "The Outer Limits". As with Star Trek, these programs were an expression of the major aspects of Pluto, Uranus, Chiron and Saturn.

A final mention is the movie, "2001 – A Space Odyssey", the Stanley Kubrick classic of 1968, based on a novelette by Arthur C. Clarke called "The Sentinel". Its world premiere occurred in Washington D.C. on April 2, 1968.

In this chart, Chiron is at zero degrees Aries, representing new beginnings combined with primal Wounds. This is interesting when we remember the opening of the film with prehistoric ape-like ancestors of Man. This placement of Chiron also illustrates the eternal question of who we are and what are our origins, themes that this film certainly raised in rather obtuse ways. Chiron in the 5th house (given a natal time of between 8pm and 10pm) speaks of a feeling of inadequacy in the face of the larger Universe. It speaks of a fear of stepping out and being seen, a fear of exposing our Inner Light. However, we are drawn forward in this film, beyond our primal fears and doubts. The singleton nature of Chiron is indicative of our feeling of aloneness, isolation and disconnectedness from the greater Universe.

Lastly, Pluto and Uranus, in a loose conjunction, oppose a tight conjunction of Venus and Mercury. Here, destiny and technology call us from the limits of the solar system, challenging us to move beyond the confine of the inner planets and the consciousness associated with it. This was certainly exemplified in the main plot of the film, mankind being drawn ever outwards into the cosmos by a mysterious black monolith.

The Space Race

The other of the two most important fulcrum points in the tapestry of Chiron's discovery was the momentous occasion of the first man in space. *(See Chart 8 – FIRST MAN IN SPACE, p.543.)* This event was sandwiched into what became known as the "space race". We have already explored the reasoning behind our assertions of the importance of the space race, so let's go straight to the chart of The First Man in Space . . .

This is perhaps the most extraordinary chart at which we will look. Pluto conjuncts the North Node in the 4th house, calling us toward our destiny that ultimately lies beyond our home on Earth, beyond the solar system, physically and metaphysically. Its message is one of hope and possibility of attaining that destiny; when dreams become reality, the world changes. Pluto in Virgo opposes Chiron, shaking our Wounds in their foundations, for it is through the Healing of these that we will attain our destiny. Chiron conjuncting the South Node in Pisces brings the entire collection of Humanity's unHealed Wounds throughout history into the focus and Light of the moment, particularly our sense of disconnectedness, isolation and aloneness. The call to Return Home to Spirit comes through strongly. This conjunction illuminates Man's smallness and the paradoxical insignificance of his achievements in the face of the vastness of the Universe (10th house placement). Conversely, the brilliance of intellect, technology, creativity and innovation (Uranus in Leo in the 3rd house) supports the bold and public achievement of putting the first man in space (Uranus trining Sun and Venus in Aries in the 10th house).[56] The public profile of the event and the technological

---

[56] For astrologers, the heliocentric version of this chart is worth looking at, too. Earth and Venus are conjunct, as are Jupiter and Saturn, as well as Mars and Uranus. These three conjunct pairs form a square, sextile, quincunx triangular arrangement. Chiron forms an exact conjunction with the MC in Pisces. Chiron and Pluto still oppose one another but with a 5 degree applying orb.

vistas opened as a result of this event are seen in the parallel of declination of Sun and Uranus.

Another occasion of great importance and relevance to our theme is the occasion of the first man on the moon. *(See Chart 9 – MAN LANDS ON THE MOON, p.544.)* Again, Pluto is highly prominent, this time conjuncting the South Node in the 10th house. Childhood has finished . . . Humanity has taken the first step away from home and stands upon the threshold of cosmic adulthood.

The North Node in the 4th house and in Pisces calls us toward our destiny, toward our true spiritual Home, toward the Oneness and all-encompassing Love of the cosmos.

Sun and Mercury, conjunct in Cancer in the 8th house, express the fragility and danger of the mission. These planets form one of the points of a loose grand water trine. Chiron in Aries in the 4th house is on the second point and Neptune in Scorpio conjunct Mars in Sagittarius in the 12th house is on the third point. Our achievement is tempered within the more tentative spaces of our psyches by the sobering and humbling realization of our smallness in the face of what we are encountering (Chiron retrograde in Aries). Only the thinnest tangible lifeline holds us in our precarious position as we step boldly onto another planet. Then there is still all that we have to deal with and answer for back on planet Earth (Chiron in the 4th house). Chiron asks us to ask ourselves, are we yet truly worthy of such an achievement? Mars in Sagittarius on the Ascendant, boldly poking its fiery finger in the grand water trine, supplies the raw power, boldness, energy, sense of adventure for the mission.

Uranus and Jupiter, conjunct and parallel (occultation) in Libra in the 10th house beckon us from across the great divide . . . from across the Asteroid belt and from across the psychological divide of the Descendant. They beckon us step away from home, toward our ultimate admission into the outer planetary and, eventually, galactic community.

For those interested in further investigation of this event, Man's first step on the Moon occurred at exactly 10:56:20pm EDT, announced and transmitted from Houston.

For even more accurate charts of these two events, one would need to calculate the charts from a *lunar-centric* perspective.

Another interesting chart is that of Man's 1st satellite in space by the Russians, occurring on the October 4, 1957, as reported from Moscow. Here, a Chiron/Uranus opposition is given expression by a trine/sextile to Sun conjunct and parallel (occultation) Jupiter in Libra. In short, our exposed Woundedness (Chiron/Uranus opposition) and feeling of isolation from the Universe (Chiron in Aquarius) drives us off the planet in search of Contact and connection to spheres of consciousness as yet unknown (called by Jupiter and Sun in Libra).

A last chart worth looking at, related to the space race, but occurring much later, on January 28, 1986 (11:39:17am EST), was the Challenger space shuttle disaster. Here, Chiron in Gemini (Wound of feeling out of touch and/or ignorant) in the first house (the physical environment) opposes Saturn in Sagittarius (clipped wings) on the cusp of the 7th and 8th houses (ending of relationships). Chiron (parallel the Sun) and Saturn (Wounds of restriction, repression, limitations, responsibility) make a trine and sextile, respectively, to the Sun, Venus and Mercury conjunct parallel Sun and Venus in Aquarius in the 10th house (in the public eye, achievement, answerability), all squaring Pluto in Scorpio (death, endings, loss) on the cusp of the 6th and 7th houses (anaretic degree – growing up, turning point, expansion of consciousness), loosely conjunct the South Node (old issues and repressed past, resurfacing, demanding resolution).

Star Wars and Other Films

It is worth taking a quick look at some other films that reflect the issues raised during this time, issues of Chironic importance.

The release of the film "Star Wars" on May 25, 1977, and its extended season throughout the northern summer was a fitting preamble to the actual discovery of Chiron. Again, the adventure into space mirrored the adventure of our Spirit into the metaphysical cosmos. The themes of "The Force" and "The Dark Side" were very Chironic. Darth Vadar, hidden behind his mask, initially a representative of the Dark Side, ultimately turns out to be a part of all of us all. He ultimately triumphs in a Return to Light and an unveiling of Self from behind the mask. The Force itself is a kind of generic representation of Spirit or God or Oneness that connects us all, if we are able to 'tune in' to it. It is the Guiding Hand that we spoke of previously.

Many other themes were broached by this series of movies. One of these was the idea that the power of belief is the power to move the world. Consciousness and certainty rule the world.

We do not pretend that movies of this kind hold all the deepest secrets of philosophy and the psyche . . . neither do they purport to do so. They are designed for the entertainment of the masses. Nonetheless, when such things have such an unparalleled effect on people, they do so because some of their basic ideas resonate with us at a deep level at the time. This is fair indication of the relevance of these ideas and their importance to the onward march of the evolution of consciousness. Whether these ideas are put there consciously and deliberately or not, the synchronicity of their appearance at a particular moment in time is undeniable.

Another film worth looking at is "Close Encounters of the Third Kind", released in November 1977, only weeks after the actual discovery of Chiron. *(See **Chart 13 – CLOSE ENCOUNTERS,** p.549.)* In the chart, the conjunction of Pluto and the North Node in Libra is carried through from the actual discovery of Chiron, indicating a far-reaching destiny of Humanity to reach the outer boundaries of the solar system and beyond. Being in the 4th house, though, the house of home, Nature and planet Earth, it poses the question, "where *is* home?" The cosmos comes right into our backyard in this film. We are united, with a sense of kinship, to other life in the cosmos. Chiron retrograde in Taurus in the 11th house, parallel the Moon, sextile Jupiter in Cancer and trining Saturn in Virgo, asks us tentatively, "Is our home as safe, secure and permanent as we thought? Or do we need to expand our definition of "home" to include a larger picture?"

Then there was "ET", released on the 13th June 1982. *(See **Chart 14 – ET,** p.550.)* The *yod* of Chiron, Pluto and Neptune again illuminates the question, "Where is home?" A new perspective was required, indicated by Chiron at the focal point of the yod formation. We saw ourselves in the mirror of the displaced ET, cut off from home, a stranger in a strange land, but finding Contact, connection and empathy with the Child within. We were witnesses to the power of the Heart and Love to breathe life into the cosmos and to connect us all beyond all illusions of distance or superficial differences. Further, the parallel of declination of Chiron and Mercury bring our Wounds, blockages and unresolved issues into our immediate consciousness and we are, for a moment, able to communicate, express and share our aloneness with others.

Another film to consider briefly is "Ghostbusters", released on the June 8, 1984. *(See **Chart 15 – GHOSTBUSTERS, p.551.**)* This seemingly-innocuous and ridiculous film reflected a serious movement of consciousness that was going at the time. We speak of the trend of trying to contact life after death and consciousness beyond the realms of the physical world. This was most prominently seen in the advent of "channeling". This phenomenon was directly related to the conjunction of Chiron and the North Node in Gemini in 1984. We will be discussing the recurring conjunction of Chiron and the North Node in different signs in some depth a little later. Suffice to say, in my experience, the phenomenon of channeling – Contact with discarnate consciousness – is more often than not associated with the sign of Gemini and with the planets Uranus, Mercury and Chiron. The involvement of the North Node merely gives the phenomenon an extended destiny and relevance to the point in history in which it occurred. All of these elements are certainly present in the "Ghostbusters" chart in addition to an extraordinary five-planet enhancement comprised of parallels and contra-parallels (Sun, Venus, Uranus and Neptune), indicating the power of the underlying themes broached in the film. The flippant treatment of the subject matter in this film is indicative of the Gemini sense of humor, but does not diminish its relevance. Charged subjects such as these, that raise as many fears as interested eyebrows, are often better treated lightly at first. These fears were certainly put into a humorous form in this film.

A final film to look at, which does not fall into the category of science fiction, is "Dead Poets Society", released on the 2nd of June 1989. *(See **Chart 16 – DEAD POETS SOCIETY, p.552.**)* Having already discussed the relevance of 1989 in the emergence of the newly discovered Chiron, the relevance of the timing of this film should be apparent. As Chiron was doing its last passing oppositions to Uranus, Saturn and

Neptune, it was passing into the 8th house of death at the time of the film's release, challenging the illusion of death with its newfound strength. Mercury retrograde, T-squaring the Nodes, unable to speak of what was truly in the Heart – that which the Heart knows to be its destiny – is faced with a choice: acknowledge the Inner Truth or die. Interestingly, this chart has an unprecedented 15 major parallels and contra-parallels, including an occultation of Saturn and Neptune, all indicative of the film's power, influence and relevance of its messages.

This was all personified by the main character in the film, a student studying English literature. His dilemma was whether to honor the passion in his Heart, which was, for him, a career in acting, or whether to succumb to the cold virtual-death of his parents wishes for him (Saturn). In the end, not able to face either, stuck at an *impasse* of consciousness, he chose to die. As we will discuss in Book Two, when confronted by an irreconcilable, untenable and insurmountably Painful situation, it is sometimes necessary for us to take steps backwards before we can resume forward evolution. Sometimes death of the stagnant and entrenched forms is necessary.

In the end, though, Cancerian Chiron speculates: did he truly die? Where was the simultaneous birth? Where did consciousness grow, Heal and evolve from the ashes of seeming death? In the film, the triumph of the Spirit was exemplified in the final scene where the remaining students stand upon their desktops, in rejection of the Saturnian *status quo*, chanting "Captain, my Captain . . ." to their teacher and spiritual mentor. Spirit was awakened within these remaining students, who were now willing to "seize the day" and to Shine in the face of the stagnant *status quo* of the establishment.

The Cold War

Towards the late 1950s and up to 1962, the world gradually turned its attention from the imaginary enemies of science fiction movies to the perceived enemies of the Cold War. This illustrated and illuminated our innate fear of the hidden, the unknown, the Dark side of our psyches. This fear was personified in the form of the opposing 'enemies' of capitalism and communism, leading to unprecedented build up of arms around the world. It became a world of subterfuge, of spies and secrets, of diplomatic parrying and rhetoric. Pluto was certainly in its element during these years.

The focal points of the Cold War included the erection of the Berlin Wall in 1961, subsequent riots in Berlin in 1962 and the Cuban Missile Crisis in the latter year.

In *Chart 17 – THE BERLIN WALL, p.553,* we see Chiron in Pisces and the South Node in Aquarius in opposition, more or less, to Pluto and Moon in Virgo, North Node and Uranus in Leo and, to a lesser degree, Sun and Mercury in Leo. Note that the exact timing of this chart is dubious – it was some time in the early hours of the morning – so we will not consider the house positions. The Wound of separateness, aloneness, isolation and disconnectedness (Chiron in Pisces) was exacerbated by the separatist aspects of Virgo Pluto and Moon. These Virgo planets are generally quick to draw lines of delineation, to define, compartmentalize, to separate, to see differences rather than similarities. The Healing journey, of course, entails the unification of differences, the raising of boundaries and the merging of disparities into a common ground. The Leo planets in this chart, however, say, "What is mine is mine . . . what is your is yours . . . we *take* what is ours." Their concern is maintaining authority, maintaining rule and position and affirming their rights in an outwardly flamboyant way. Retrograde Saturn and Jupiter in Capricorn, loosely conjunct, quincunxing Uranus and the North Node, is indicative of the restriction of freedom, the affirmation of authority and the revolutionary exercising of power.

In the riots that followed in 1962 *(See Chart 18 – BERLIN RIOTS, p.554),* we see the extraordinary alignment of Chiron and Jupiter, conjunct in Pisces, opposing Pluto and Mercury, conjunct in Virgo. (Again, we will ignore the house placements due to doubt about exact timing.) These two pairs of conjunctions further trine and sextile Neptune in Scorpio, respectively. The Wound of separateness aloneness, isolation and disconnectedness (Chiron retrograde in Pisces) is joined by the Wound of the Inner Child that has lost its freedom and joy of life (Jupiter retrograde in this conjunction in Pisces). This finds extreme expression through the opposition challenge, through the voice of Mercury-conjunct-Pluto in Virgo. The wish for a higher unity and resolution to the *impasse* (represented by the Berlin Wall) comes through Neptune in Scorpio in aspect to all the aforementioned planets. Furthermore, the restrictions, limitations and stifling authority of the past (Saturn retrograde-conjunct-South Node in Aquarius) had us wishing for a more idealistic, humanitarian and free way of living. Trining Venus in Libra gave us the wish for a more balanced relationship with each other, dissolving the self-imposed boundaries laid down by our fear and suspiciousness.

Another chart worth looking at is the day the Berlin Wall fell. This was on the November 9, 1989, CET. Jupiter in Cancer exactly opposes Saturn and Neptune conjunct and parallel (occultation) in Capricorn . . . the old guard (Saturn and Neptune in Capricorn) falls to new found freedom (Jupiter) and the birth (Jupiter in Cancer) of a new Germany. Chiron in Cancer, very close to Jupiter, trines Sun, Mercury and Pluto conjunct in Scorpio . . . the awakening, expression (Sun), communication (Mercury) and transformation (Pluto and all three Scorpio planets) of the Wounds of the mother country (Chiron in Cancer).

Finally, perhaps the most acute expression of the Cold War years came in the form of the Cuban Missile Crisis. *(See **Chart 19 – CUBAN MISSILE CRISIS**, p.555.)* Again ignoring house placements, this series of events is exemplified by the North Node and Mars, conjunct in Leo, opposing Saturn and South Node, conjunct and parallel (occultation) in Aquarius, The underlying issues and tensions are a feature of Chiron in Pisces opposing Uranus in Virgo. They are also a feature of Chiron opposing Pluto, but, this time, to a lesser degree. Jupiter is also loosely conjunct Chiron in this arrangement of planets. These underlying issues – the same mentioned in relation to the previous two charts we examined – are brought to a head by the Nodes/Mars/Saturn opposition. Sun in Libra, trining Chiron and Jupiter, seeks a resolution to the underlying issues, Leo Mars-conjunct-North Node pushing the point towards its ultimate destiny. The Mars/North Node conjunction quincunxing Chiron and Jupiter, and the Saturn/South Node conjunction quincunxing Uranus, indicates that a new consciousness about the prevailing issues and conditions is required.

Woodstock

On August 15, 1969, at exactly 5.07pm EDT, the first strains of music started up at what would become the cultural and sociological event of the decade, perhaps even of the century. *(See **Chart 21 – WOODSTOCK**, p.557.)* Perhaps the most striking astrological transient of the event was the transit of the Moon from Virgo through to Libra, conjuncting South Node, Pluto, Uranus and Neptune on the way and opposing Chiron. The Bohemian aspects of Virgo were certainly expressed through this Moon and its transits. Also, the transition from the self-absorbed lower hemisphere (the last sign of the natural horoscope being Virgo) into the more outwardly reflective consciousness of the upper hemisphere (the first sign of the natural horoscope being Libra) was intimated here. The messages of the festival certainly reflected the Healing qualities of the Virgo Moon and the artistic, harmonious and peaceful qualities of the Libran Moon. The Moon's transit of the Virgo South Node indicates the resurfacing of issues still to be dealt with on the Healing journey towards Oneness (Pisces North Node).

Chiron in Aries, opposing Jupiter in Libra, reflects the Wounds of low self-worth (Chiron) expressed through the desire to return to a simpler, more innocent way of life (Jupiter – Inner Child). When things become overwhelming, too complicated and the evolutionary path is lost or blocked, we seek a way out that ultimately takes us back to basics. In short, when we cannot move forward, we must take backward steps to a point where evolutionary movement again becomes possible. The seeking of a simpler, more innocent way of life is an expression of this. We will discuss this evolutionary principle in more detail in Books Two and Three.

Pluto in Virgo in the whole equation, combined with the Sun moving strongly into a square aspect with Neptune (Neptune sextiling Pluto) over the course of the festival, give influences that suggest alternate ways of attaining altered consciousness and Healing, i.e. sex, drugs and rock-n-roll.

The Beatles

The Beatles first single, "Love Me Do", was recorded in September 1962. *(See **Chart 20 – BEATLES 1ST SINGLE**, p.556.)* Although the recording probably took a good part of the day, and remembering that the dynamic picture is more encompassing than a snapshot in time, we have arbitrarily taken midday for our chart analysis. This recording was the significant point at which the Beatles' rise to fame began, although some of the individual members had worked together before this. The cultural and psychological effect of the phenomenon of The Beatles broke down old paradigms in music, in culture at large and in sociology. The Beatles became an icon for the youth of the day, giving them a focal point for the expression of that which was unspoken within them, i.e. feelings and issues that Chiron and Pluto were bringing to light.

Chiron and Jupiter retrograde, conjunct in Pisces in the 4th house, indicates Wounds of the repressed and forgotten Inner Child being experienced through the family dynamic and the larger community family. This became a public expression through the Sun, Pluto and Uranus in Virgo in the 10th house and, for the youth of the day, represented a way of expressing and Healing these Wounds. The seemingly-misplaced cathartic-type reactions of teenagers at Beatles concerts now make much more sense when considered in this context.

The Moon and Neptune conjunct in Scorpio in the 1st house accounts for the charisma and mysterious, almost religious, attraction of the Beatles. When we put Mars in Cancer in the 9th house into the picture, we see a grand water trine embedded in a kite formation, the tip of the kite being Sun and Pluto. Not to mention the yod of North Node, Mercury and Chiron/Jupiter. The focal point of this yod was Chiron and Jupiter, indicating that the destiny (North Node) and message (Mercury) of the phenomenon was to give a new level of understanding about the aforementioned Wounds (Chiron and Jupiter). The outward expression of these inherent Wounds and their Healing journey was then directed through the opposition to the 10th house planets, i.e. through the focal point of the kite formation. The Beatles were destiny. All the ingredients were there.

The Hippie Generation

Various factors contributed to the explosion of the hippie and psychedelic cultures and the so-called flower children. The influence of Neptune and its aspects to Chiron, both natally and at the time, perhaps contributed the most to these phenomena.

Firstly, however, those born between 1947 and 1952 experienced either their first Chiron-square-natal Chiron or Chiron-trine-natal Chiron somewhere between 1961 and 1971 between the ages of 14 and 19. *(See GRAPH 1—CHIRON CYCLE, p.576.)* These transits contributed to the surfacing of Wounds in the consciousness of the youth during the 1960s. This generation was also the last generation bearing the Saturn/Chiron square that occurred 21 times between 1935 and 1952.

The way in which the youth of the day dealt with these Wounds was more in the domain of Neptune, i.e. in the experimentation with drugs, sexual freedom and communal living. The unprecedented artistic out-pouring of these years, particularly in music, was also a way in which we expressed our Wounds during these years. Then there was the bringing of Eastern religion, spirituality and mysticism into the West.

The most important Neptune aspect during this time was between May 1963 and January 1968 when Neptune trined Chiron 11 times. We have already discussed this aspect. Suffice to say, the influence of this aspect certainly contributed to the hippie and psychedelic cultures. In addition, these aspects would most certainly have set off the natal placements and aspects of Chiron during the 1960s in those born between 1947 and 1952 in particular.

Furthermore, the conjunction of Neptune to natal Chiron for those born 1948–49 accentuated the Neptunian influences of the mid-1960s. *(See GRAPH 3 – NEPTUNE CONJUNCT NATAL (1947–48) CHIRON, p.578.)*

Finally, Chiron's placement in Pisces during most of the 1960s and its opposition to Pluto and Uranus in Virgo brought to the fore the issue of *earthing.* This theme was emphasized even more by the conjunction of Saturn and Chiron in Pisces in the mid-1960s, in particular in 1966. The hippie culture emphasized the need to 'get back to basics', to return to a more earthy existence, i.e. to reconnect with our earthy origins. This is what we have called the process of *recapitulation.* Old

Saturn forms (the establishment) no longer served the requirements of the evolution of Spirit, hence the backlash by the youth of the day towards the establishment (arising out of the years of Saturn-square-Chiron between 1935 and 1952). The old Values were seen to be dead-ends and so we experimented with new ideas, new ways of interrelating, new social paradigms, etcetera. We temporarily discarded the pre-emptive fruits of advanced civilization in favor of a simpler life and a return to community and brotherhood. This was, of course, the seed of the new-age movement, which, in turn, birthed the ecology movement.

During the ensuing years, having walked a path of Healing and having reconnected, to a greater or lesser degree, to our sense of connection to Spirit, we were then able to re-embrace the technological society anew. *The seesawing between spiritual and material concerns in our lives, personally and collectively, is a universal and inevitable law.* Chiron traces this ebb and flow, as we shall see in a later chapter in this book.

It is interesting to note that the new-age movement, birthed during the 1960s as a backlash against the establishment, material values, capitalism, big business, etcetera, is now becoming the new 'establishment' and is itself big business! Conversely, big business is turning increasingly to new-age inspired techniques, seminars and work-practices in order to ensure the smooth running of the their communities of employees.

Drugs & Holotropism

The planetary influences of the 1960s impelled the search for new, different and higher consciousness. They impelled us to break through the out-moded and stagnant Saturnian *status quo* and to find answers, resolution and Healing of the Wounds that Chiron, Pluto and Uranus were exposing. Again, Neptune was at the helm of this reaction to our exposed Wounds. Experimentation with drugs was 1) an attempt to escape from, alleviate or dull the Pain of the exposed Wounds and 2) an innate if unconscious striving for higher consciousness. The underlying issues of drugs will be elaborated at length in Book Two of this series.

With respect to the latter aspect – the innate striving for higher consciousness – drugs provided a means, albeit haphazard and emotionally driven at times, for accessing *holotropic* states of consciousness. In holotropic states, connections between otherwise seemingly-disconnected aspects of the world are revealed. The underlying Oneness of the Universe becomes more apparent. Our innate Soul-wish to reconnect with Oneness is fuelled by the experience of our exposed Wounds. Intensive studies of holotropic states in connection with mental health and illness and in connection with drugs have been carried out, in particular, by psychiatrist and consciousness researcher, Stanislav Grof. He has since developed drug-free techniques of achieving the same holotropic-type experiences. It is true to say that without the explosion of drug use and abuse in the 1960s, such research may have remained on the back burner, so to speak.

The question of the use and abuse of drugs certainly comes under the umbrella of Chiron. As we shall see in Book Two, drugs are simultaneously escape routes from our inner Pain and stepping stones to higher consciousness. The use of drugs – whether alcohol, narcotics, nicotine, caffeine, refined sugars or psychological virtual drugs, whether legal or illegal, whether medical, recreational or religious – arises from our deep, innate and often unrecognized need for unitive experience and transcendence, i.e. our need for Healing and evolution of consciousness. Drugs, like divinatory practices, identity crises, major life catastrophes, divine revelations and near-death experiences, have the potential to 'bootstrap' us into higher states of consciousness, where we can see meaning and connections that were previously hidden to us.

In any case, during the sixties, our innate wish for Healing and the evolution of consciousness was *catalyzed* by Pluto, Uranus and Chiron and was *expressed* primarily through Neptune. The culmination of this was, of course, the discovery of Chiron. The most interesting chart in relation to drugs, however, is the chart of the Second International Conference on Hallucinogenic Mushrooms held on the Olympic Peninsula, Washington, on 28 October, 1977, just days before Chiron's discovery. At this conference, three scholars presented material that linked the use of hallucinogenic mushrooms to many religious traditions of the past, including the Eleusinian Mysteries.[57] It was suggested that the use of

[57] Refer to: Wasson, Gordon & Hoffman, Albert & Ruck, Carl A. P. *The Road to Eleusis.* Hermes Press (William Dailey Rare Books Ltd.), Los Angeles, 1998.

such mushrooms was one of the chemical catalysts for the arising of unitive and transcendent experiences that formed the basis of religions and spiritual practices from antiquity to the present day.

The chart in question has Chiron in Taurus (our Wounds stuck in the material and dualistic illusion) in opposition to the Sun in Scorpio (the seeking of the hidden essence behind material illusions, i.e. the Gift in the Wound). Mercury (lower intellect) occults Uranus (higher intellect, potential connection to higher understanding and transcendent integration of seeming paradoxes) in Scorpio, bringing higher understanding to our Earth-bound consciousness. Pluto (death and rebirth) conjuncts Venus (the Earthly heart) in Libra (potential for balanced consciousness), shaking our emotional nature out of its usual duality of lopsided emotions and judgments, paving the way for the more unitive experience of Unconditional Love. The North Node conjuncts Pluto and Venus, auguring the destiny that awaits us all when we transcend our illusions and Wounds. Neptune in Sagittarius (intimating the Oneness of galactic consciousness) sextiles this trio of planets, opening the path to Love and Oneness.

We are not, of course, condoning the use of drugs as a regular means of attaining Healing and the evolution of consciousness. The drawbacks and dangers of drugs are well documented. We are simply pointing out that drugs have been used in consciousness-raising capacities throughout history and have ramifications beyond modern society's primarily negative judgments.

Protests, Rioting, Wars and Racism

The escalation of rioting during the latter part of the 1960s and the early 1970s was indicative of the reaction to the challenge of Chiron and Pluto during these years. We react to difficult situations, unacceptable truths and to the constraints of the *status quo* in many different ways. Violence, in the form of protests and riots, was the way some chose to react during these years. Many of the riots were concerned with black civil rights, with clashes between blacks and whites commonplace during these years. Chiron and its planetary associates during this time shone a light on the Wounds of the black people, bringing what was formerly repressed into the open. Such a challenge necessarily brings conflict. Other racial struggles were evident during these years, too. These racial issues began emerging in the early 1950s and continued to escalate into the late 1960s.

Rioting was seen in on the streets of London, Paris, Washington DC, Johannesburg, Limassol, Berlin, Northern Ireland, Milan, Buenos Aires, amongst many others.

Amongst the racial tensions that escalated during these years was the whole plight of the Jewish people after WWII. The role of Pluto conjuncting Chiron during WWII cannot be overemphasized. We will explore this in greater detail in a later chapter in this book. During the late 1950s and the early 1960s, the demand for retribution, recompense and justice for the atrocities inflicted upon the Jews reached a new intensity. The focal point was the trial and sentencing of Adolf Eichmann in Israel. He was tried and sentenced to death between 1960 and 1962 for his part in the war crimes against the Jews. *(See CHART 22 – EICHMANN SENTENCED, p. 558* and *CHART 23 – EICHMANN HANGED, p. 559.)*

Ignoring house and Moon positions due to uncertain time, the sentencing chart clearly shows the Sagittarian striving for justice with Sun, Mercury and Mars, all conjunct and parallel (triple occultation), trining and sextiling North and South Nodes, respectively. Venus joins the other three in Sagittarius. Uranus opposes Chiron, as is so common throughout these years, throwing light on old Wounds.

The hanging chart, again ignoring the Moon and house placements, exemplifies Chiron's negative theme of victimhood with a grand water trine between Chiron and Jupiter on one point, and Venus and Neptune on the other two. The occultation of Saturn and the South Node says it all in terms of the past coming back to haunt. The quincunxing of Chiron and Jupiter with the North Node impels us to seek a new and higher understanding of events and issues concerning which we are stuck in a lower-natured consciousness.

Wars and conflict are another way in which we react to Plutonian and Chironic challenges. The 1950s saw the Korean War. The 1960s saw the Vietnam War, The Six Day War between Israel and the Arab states, the Cuban missile crisis and the Bay of Pigs debacle, the taking over of Peking by the Red Army, the Soviet invasion of Czechoslovakia, Soviet and Chinese border clashes, flare-ups in Northern Ireland leading to deployment of British troops, Colonel Gadaffi's coup of Libya, Biafran capitulation to Nigerian troops, post Six Day War clashes between Syria and Israel, US troops invading Cambodia, Israel and Lebanon in border clashes, the Yom Kippur War between Egypt, Syria and Israel, the Turkish invasion of Cyprus, the Biafran War, the struggle for independence of Algeria, Kenya and Aden, the Sharpeville massacre in Africa and so on and so forth . . .

Pluto, classically associated with war and birth through destruction, played the major role in this respect during the 1960s, spurred on by Chiron's awakening of our Wounds and our unexpressed, unresolved issues. The next major aspect of Pluto and Chiron occurred in December 1999, when they conjuncted in Sagittarius. This aspect augurs the 21st century awakening of repressed and unexpressed issues and Wounds around spirituality, religion, philosophy, morals, ethics, etcetera. The reaction to these may be somewhat violent. An escalation of religiously-based wars and conflict seems inevitable. Shortly into the new millennium, we already we see an escalation of tensions between Israel and Palestine, catalyzing hatred between the Moslem, Jewish and Christian worlds. We also see tensions and conflict between the Chinese government and the Falun Gong sect and between religious factions in Northern Ireland.

JFK

Very few events had as devastating and poignant an effect on people during the 1960s as the rise and fall of John F. Kennedy. Just into the new century, over 30 years later, we are still somewhat obsessed with the whole saga. It has been kept alive by the ongoing misfortunes and deaths of the Kennedy family members who survived the death of JFK. Was the allure and the magnitude of the whole series of events a case of JFK's own personal energy, charisma and influence or was it that he was merely the outward manifestation of the underlying planetary influences of the time? Personally, I think it was a combination of both.

Looking at JFK's natal chart *(See* ***CHART 24 – JOHN F KENNEDY,*** *p. 560),* we see very strong earth influence with the triple conjunction Taurean planets Mars (7th house), Mercury and Jupiter (8th house) trining Virgo Moon (11th house). The 8th house, sharing not only Mercury and Jupiter, but also Sun and Venus (in Gemini), seems to augur an emphasis on collective ownership of material and spiritual resources. However, the square of Uranus retrograde in Aquarius with the 7th and 8th house Taurean planets appears to make unexpected obstacles to the expression of this potential. His life's path North Node in Capricorn suggests a lifetime of learning how to look after others whilst taking responsibility for his own life. The 3rd house placement of this Node indicates his path as a communicator above all else. The presence of Pluto in the 9th house with the South Node, however, particularly as it squares Chiron, indicates old Wounds and issues coming back to haunt in dramatic and violent ways.

The most important planets, however, in relation to his charisma and public appeal, and ones that played a key role in the drama of the surrounding events and issues of the whole JFK saga, are Saturn, Neptune and Chiron. Saturn and Neptune are conjunct in the 10th house, straddling the cusp of Leo and Cancer. They trine Chiron in Pisces in the 6th house. Neptune offers a charismatic and indefinable air of mystery to his public persona, whereas Saturn speaks of responsibility, practicality and ability to lead. Chiron in Pisces – the Wound of loss of faith in a Divine Plan – sits in the 6th house of potential Healing. This Wound motivates one to either succumb to the forces that be, as a victim, or to try to organize one's life in such a way as to maintain control of external circumstances. The more we try this, however, the more the Universe shows us the ways in which events and circumstances of our lives are out of our control, rather responding to a higher power, albeit hidden to our unseeing eyes. Despite our efforts to hide from it and hide it from the eyes of others, the Wound is worn clearly upon our countenance, *felt* rather than logically understood. Herein lies the attraction that people felt to JFK.

The trine of Chiron and Saturn/Neptune accentuates the air of mystery by displaying a vulnerability that others find attractive as it mirrors their own hidden and unexpressed vulnerability and sensitivity. This aspect says, "Together we can Heal, together we can do it, together we have strength to conquer all Wounds, to move through all issues, to resolve all differences". This is, of course, the Truth. However, the outward expression of this Truth and its worldly manifestation may not be what we expect when viewed from our lopsided standpoints and paradigms.

The square of Chiron with Pluto, however, intimates that the Healing of the Wounds can only be accomplished by radical and violent change. It even goes so far as to say that the ultimate Healing will only take place much later, when the form of JFK is dissolved into the general events and issues of the populace at large. This has certainly been the case since JFK's death.

Looking at the election chart *(See **CHART 25 – JFK ELECTED,** p. 561.)*, ignoring the house placements, we see the familiar Chiron/Uranus opposition. Scorpio planets, Sun, Mercury and Neptune, give intensity, focus and allure to the event. The trine and sextile arrangement of the Nodes with Mercury in this Scorpio group brings destiny and an important message together. The conjunction of the North Node and Pluto in Virgo trining Saturn in Capricorn also speaks of the power of this event, but represents a double-edged sword due to its unparalleled power. The issues of Wounding and Healing come through in the Virgo placement of the North Node and Pluto.

The transits of the election chart to the natal chart have the Moon in Leo transiting JFK's Saturn and Neptune in the 10th house, setting off the natal trine with Chiron. Here we have emotional attachment to the power, allure, magic and mystery of public office. Personally, JFK was experiencing the major transit of Uranus opposition natal Uranus (half-Return), a time of major activation and awakening to a higher purpose in life. There was a sense of destiny and purpose. The way this destiny and purpose were carried out is not so obvious if we erroneously think that his death was the death of that purpose.

Looking at the assassination chart *(See **CHART 26 – JFK ASSASSINATED,** p. 562)*, we again see Chiron opposing Uranus. However, this time it is embedded in a yod formation of Uranus, Jupiter and the Moon, with Uranus at the focal point. This is further complicated by another yod of Uranus, North Node and the Moon, this time with the Moon as a focal point. Saturn conjuncts the Ascendant, with Chiron in the 1st house. The Sun sits on the Midheaven in the final anaretic degree of Scorpio.

Many complicated influences prevailed at this moment in time, some more obvious than others were. For example, the focal point of Saturn on the Ascendant, combined with Chiron in the 1st house and the Moon in the 12th, indicates the Wounds of the physical/emotional body, cut off from its earthy origins (Aquarius Ascendant, Moon and Saturn) and the Wounds of the higher Self, cut off from its divine origins (Chiron in Pisces). The Sun in Scorpio (death) on the Midheaven (public spectacle) shines a spotlight on the moment. The North Node in Cancer suggests that sometimes we need to relinquish our need for control (South Node in Capricorn) and acquiesce to the Guiding Hand of the Universe. If we continue to live without faith in the Universe (Chiron had returned to JFK's natal sign of Pisces), the Universe must ultimately bring us to our knees. The lesson is humility. The aim is opening our Hearts to the messages of the Soul once more.

The astrological feature that brings the whole assassination chart alive, summing up the essence of the message given to us personally and collectively via the whole JFK saga, is the placement of the Nodes in relation to JFK's natal chart. *The transiting Nodes, in Capricorn and Cancer, are in exact opposition to the natal Nodes.* Destiny asked us, "Who will look after you now?" Placing so much faith, trust and responsibility for our lives into the hands of another is ultimately unbalanced and unhealthy. We also need to look *within* for the support, caring, nurturing and protection we desire. Simultaneously and paradoxically, we need to place our lives into the hands of an even *higher* power, freeing ourselves from the illusory icon of a man who promised us our security, safety and future on a silver platter. To be inspired by another is one thing. To give away our own self-determination and inner inspiration is quite another. The death of JFK required us to reassess our own role in our lives. It required us to take back responsibility, not only for the practical aspects of our collective lives, but for the spiritual aspects of our personal lives, i.e. for our Vision, Inspiration and Purpose.

Furthermore, Chiron in Pisces trining and sextiling the Nodes, both at the time *and* in transit to Kennedy's natal Nodes, brings the Wounds into sharp relief. The personal issues of JFK reflected the collective issues of the times: in a world gone seemingly mad, who or what could we put our Trust and Faith in? The Wound of loss of faith in the Divine (Chiron in Pisces) was illuminated by the Chironic aspects of the time, particularly those involving Uranus and Pluto. The Healing journey necessarily entails the ultimate reconnection to our own inner divinity as a beacon and guiding force in our lives, personally and collectively. If we have our spiritual currency invested in another person, we have little left for inner work. From this point of view, due to the nature of the awakening influences of Chiron during these years, it was almost inevitable that the icon of JFK be kicked out from under our feet. Although the world – and particularly America – lost much by his death, we also gained . . . his death caused us to introspect even more deeply than we would have otherwise been inclined.

Nuclear Protests

The protests against nuclear research and its use in both war and peace illustrate the backlash against the establishment, its dead forms and its technological fruits. It illustrates, again, the innate calling to 'get back to basics', to 'earth' ourselves and re-establish a connection to our earthy origins. In effect, we said that we were not yet ready to handle nuclear power responsibly. The push for nuclear power necessarily requires an equal push towards more spiritual power and responsibility. The seesawing between technology and spirituality is, again, a universal and inevitable law. As we seesaw between the two, over time, the two gradually become merged and we realize that each represents but a different facet of a greater picture. The aspects of Saturn, Pluto, Uranus and Chiron during the 1960s more than mirror these themes and trends as expressed through nuclear protests of the time. For example, 1961, as Pluto opposed Chiron, was a year of demonstrations in London against the nuclear arms race, supported by 89-year-old philosopher, Bertrand Russell.

Paradoxically, the rise of nuclear power reflects the inexorable and inevitable march of the evolution of consciousness. The challenge of nuclear energy is holographically synonymous with the challenge of evolution to Return our material nature to Spirit. It is inevitable that

Humanity invest its time and effort into nuclear power. Whether this is popular or not, or indeed safe or not, is not the issue. Economics will dictate. The survival of Humanity will dictate. The future of Humanity will dictate. The rise and use of nuclear power on a global scale will mirror further advances in the evolution of consciousness of the planet. We will discuss these ideas in Book Three. Suffice to say, when we are challenged to evolve our consciousness faster than we are ready, we resist and move to recapitulate to a simpler past. In this case, in the 1960s, we fought to *retain* the *status quo* by opposing technology, i.e. by opposing nuclear power, research and weapons.

Such apparent paradoxes are necessarily the domain of Chiron and challenge us to see the unifying principle hidden within the paradox. In this case, the unifying principle is revealed by Healing of the illusion that Matter and Spirit are somehow separate. But we digress . . .

Martin Luther King Jnr

The issues of racism, aforementioned, were brought into significant focus in the 1960s by civil rights activist, Martin Luther King Jnr. *(See CHART 27 – MARTIN LUTHER KING JNR., p. 563.)* His natal chart shows a life's path of bringing the intangible (Scorpio South Node) into tangible manifestation (Taurus North Node). These Nodes also indicate the issues of Trust and openness as being lifetime lessons. The trine of North Node and Capricorn Sun emphasizes King's practical nature, the ability to organize and manifest tangible results in the physical world and the potential to be recognized and respected for his life's achievements. The conjunction of Sun and IC indicates a deep connection with and a subsequent expression of his roots, background and history, personally and collectively.

Chiron and Jupiter are conjunct in Taurus in the 7th house, accentuating the Nodal issues of Trust and openness. Chiron in Taurus indicates a Wound of loss of Trust, faith and belief in all-encompassing Love. This Wound is expressed through his personal relationships (7th house) and, of course, through the championing of social causes and moral values. Chiron's trine with Neptune in Virgo in the 11th house further indicates the connection with the Healing of old Wounds of a collective nature, in King's case, the Wounds of the Afro-American people. This aspect, combined with the square of Neptune and the Nodes, indicates that the Healing of these Wounds and the fulfillment of King's life's path are dependent upon an opening to higher influences. They are dependent on the acknowledgment of all-encompassing Love as the driving force behind life.

In the assassination chart *(See CHART 28 – MARTIN LUTHER KING JNR. KILLED, p. 564)*, we see the Sun and Saturn exactly conjunct in Aries with the North Node just over 3 degrees away, also in Aries. The check-mating of the individual, in this case King, poses the question as to whether we can rely on others to put all our trust, faith and belief in. As a balance, we must also develop a strong sense of our own individuality, self-reliance and self-motivation. Both sides of the question are necessary, i.e. dependence and independence. History teaches us that when we put too much of our lives into the hands of another, we are eventually bound to have the rug pulled out from under us. Conversely, when we try to be entirely independent, relying on no one and no thing, eventually we must be brought into a position where outside help is required. Balance is maintained by the Universe.

Certainly, this was the case with the assassination of Martin Luther King Jnr. The unexpected and sudden death of King (Uranus and Pluto in Virgo, Pluto in the 12th house of the secret enemies) gave an unexpected and difficult twist to his message (Uranus and Pluto in Virgo opposing Venus and Mercury in Pisces), his message being freedom from oppression and victimization. Chiron, in the 1st degree of Aries in the 6th house, contra-paralleling the occultation of Mercury and Venus, emphasizes the Wounds of the self in need of Healing, expressed through the struggle with the mirror-reflection of outside oppressors. Chiron squaring the Moon in Cancer again raises and further accentuates the issue of dependence versus independence via the perceived loss of support, nurturing, caring and motherly championing of our causes.

The poignant trining of Mercury and Venus in Pisces to Neptune in Scorpio retrograde in the 2nd house and their quincunx/square aspects to Jupiter in Leo retrograde in the 11th leaves the door open for a return to reliance on Spirit, as expressed from within us via the Inner

Child doorway. The message of the whole incident, as always, was "look within".

Natural Disasters

The 1960s were also a time of many natural disasters, as the Pluto/Uranus conjunction, the Pluto/Chiron, Uranus/Chiron, Pluto/Saturn and Uranus/Saturn oppositions and the Saturn/Chiron conjunction all suggest. Millions died of famine in the Peoples Republic of China. Soviet Russia suffered enormous crop failures. Typhoons devastated Japan's crops. Monsoon rains failed in Pakistan and India suffered a crippling drought. Deadly drought also struck the Sahel – the 2600-mile strip south of the Sahara Desert. Red Sea countries, including Saudi Arabia, suffered the worst locust plagues since 1944. A devastating earthquake struck Yugoslavia.

Chiron's Birth

Having looked at the years before and following the actual discovery of Chiron and seen the larger context in which this occurred, let's now look at its birth, seen through its natal chart. *(See **Chart 1—BIRTH OF CHIRON**, p.536.)*

Perhaps the most striking and immediately apparent feature of Chiron's 'natal' chart (based on the time when Chiron was 'birthed' into our waking consciousness) is the conjunction of Pluto, the North Node and the Midheaven in Libra, with Venus close by. Even if the birth time is inaccurate (this is possible) and this puts the Midheaven away from the others, the Libra placement of Pluto and the Node, Venus close by, says it all. Libra, when considered from the perspective of house rulerships, represents the 'coming out' or 'coming of age' point in the chart. It is the cusp between the lower and upper hemispheres of the natural horoscope, the point where our focus begins to turn outwards from our previous hypnotic focus on ourselves as being the center of existence. It is the acknowledgment of the 'Other' in our lives.

Given the new perspective of ourselves *within* the context of a larger picture that includes the 'Other', this cusp also represents the point at which we begin to ask questions like, 'Where have we come from?', 'Where are we going?', 'Who are we?' and 'Why are we here?'

If the birth time *is* accurate, the public significance of Chiron's discovery (Node/Pluto/Midheaven conjunction) is vindicated.

Taken more metaphysically, pre-empting the material we will present in Book Three, the Pluto/Node conjunction in Libra represents the possibility of a Return to Balance via the death of old illusions. Specifically, these are the illusions that have kept us captive to our bodies, to our lower nature and to our self-absorbed state. It represents the evolution of Spirit. Within the context of Chiron's natal chart, it clearly says that Healing and the evolution of consciousness/Spirit are the same issue. The Return to Balance (of consciousness) *is* the Healing path. The death of our naïve and nascent illusions via the Healing path will ultimately take us back to Spirit, back to Love, back to Oneness, back Home.

According to the Mysteries, this Return path is clearly seen in the zodiac symbolism of the journey from Aries/Earth consciousness to Libra/Sun consciousness.

The Sun and Uranus, conjunct and parallel (occultation) in Scorpio in the 11th house, with Mercury close by, illustrates the revolutionary and revelationary nature of this discovery for Humanity at large, a doorway offered into the next world. The trine made by these two planets with the Moon in Cancer in the 7th house tells us that the way is opened to us by the transformation of the emotions of the lower nature. Our lower nature consists of all our polarized personas, emotions, thoughts, half-truths, lies, illusions, biases, lopsided perceptions. We will discuss our lower nature in great detail in Book Two.

Jupiter's presence near the Moon, also in Cancer in the 7th house, but retrograde, intimates that the doorway to higher consciousness lies through the Inner Child doorway in the Heart. This is a Return to Innocence, but now awakened and active rather than being sleepy and passive. Neptune's presence in Sagittarius in the 12th house, sextiling/trining the Nodes and quincunxing the Moon, says that the way to higher consciousness and our destiny is via the intuition. It is via seemingly-irrational leaps of mystical insight and divinatory means. The lower/higher octave partnership of Moon (lower emotional nature) and Neptune (higher emotional nature, i.e. Love) is apparent here. The Moon also sits in its disseminating phase, expressing Chiron's wish, aim and major motivation to share its knowledge, wisdom and Healing ability with the world.

Chiron's own square with Mars in Leo and its parallel aspect with Saturn indicate the blocking of the old paradigms – masculine, outwardly active, inwardly passive, competitive, physically-based, individualistic, action-based, Saturnian paradigms, etcetera. In this way, it tacitly emphasizes a new paradigm that is more intuitively based, feminine, inwardly active, outwardly passive, supportive, network-based, Neptunian and outwardly spiritual. Astrologically, the path to the outer planets is clearly bridged by the feminine aspects of the Asteroids. At the same time, the Chiron/Saturn parallel aspect indicates that now is the time for the real work to begin on our collective journey of Healing and the evolution of consciousness.

It is important to acknowledge that both sides of the equation, as illustrated above, are equally necessary. The discovery of Chiron, in this respect, was but the reverse swing of the pendulum of the consciousness of Humanity, personally and collectively, from what it had been expressing for some hundreds of years prior.

Next, it is important and relevant to point out that, although it is not indicated on the chart printed in this book, five major asteroids – Vesta, Pallas, Astraea, Ceres and Juno – are clustered together with the North Node, Pluto, Venus, the Sun, Uranus, Mercury and Neptune. These planets are all splayed out opposite Chiron in the chart. Chiron is illuminated greatly by this pattern, standing center stage, acting as a kind of focal point. Recalling our previous discussion about the asteroids and their place in the cosmic scheme, Chiron represents a kind of 'spokesplanet' for the other asteroids at the moment of its discovery. Astraea and Pallas make proper oppositions to Chiron, whereas Vesta conjuncts Pluto and the North Node, Ceres conjuncts Mercury, and Juno sits just out of conjuncting orb to Neptune.

Finally, we come to Chiron's own placement, retrograde in Taurus in the 4th house. Chiron's own path, and, hence its promise for Humanity, is the Return to Love and Trust in the Universe (Taurus). It is seeing that what we previously feared, suspected, quarantined from our lives and judged negatively (Scorpio) was all part of a larger Plan of Love. It is the breaking down of the barriers of our protective mechanisms (expressed through the Moon) by truly seeing what is, rather than what was lopsidedly perceived from the perspective of our lower-natured consciousness. It entails the realization that we are, *in all ways and without exception,* looked after by the Universe (the widest view of the 4th house). There are no accidents, no mistakes, no oversights. All things truly Serve us in our lives. Love is everywhere when we have the eyes to see it and the open Heart to feel it.

Furthermore, it is our *perception* of accident, mistake, oversight, imbalance, injustice, abuse, neglect, wrong-doing, inequity, etcetera, that takes us on the journey of our lives, resulting in a Divinely Designed life's path, Purpose and Service. In this way, Love even lies at the root of our misperceptions. Our misperceptions take us on a path that ultimately awakens us to Love. The feeling or judgment of a lack of Love drives us toward this awakening, impelling us to seek Love and to discover it in places that we would have never previously thought possible.

The Wound of Chiron in Taurus in the 4th house says Love is missing and the Universe is not looking after us. The Healing Journey is the Return to Love and the awakening to the ways in which we are truly looked after. The Gift in the Wound is our Divine Design, orchestrated by our misperceptions, and the experience of Love via this Divine Design.

Furthermore, the Taurean placement of Chiron in this chart clearly intimates the issue of *missingness,* not only in emotional terms, but also in physical and sensory terms. The lesson here is that, ultimately, nothing of the senses will ever satisfy us . . . when all illusions of physical and sensory *missingness* are dissolved, we become aware of the abundance of Love within us and all around us. This *missingness* has its seat in the very nature of our dualistic senses, discussed briefly previously and discussed at length in Book Two. When the illusions of Pain and pleasure – mirrored in the duality of the senses – are dissolved into higher consciousness, we come closer to Truth, closer to Oneness, closer to Unconditional Love. The feeling of *missingness,* as the Wound, drives us towards wholeness, completeness and unity. That is its Gift.

2 ~ FRIENDS, ASSOCIATIONS & RULERS

Let's distill the essence of what we have discussed so far and add yet other issues and themes to our tapestry by exploring some of Chiron's zodiac friends, associations and some candidate signs for its rulership.

Saturn as Master Trainer

Saturn prepares the way for an introduction to Chiron. Without Saturn's strict training, the path to Chiron is either closed or precarious and uncertain. The placement of Saturn in the natal chart, its aspects thereof and its transiting relationships in a person's life determine the possibilities and opportunities for approaching Chiron at any given time in a lifetime. Whether we take up the opportunities and explore the possibilities is up to us.

The relationship of Saturn to Chiron – placement, aspect and transit – in the natal chart, in transit to the natal chart and in real time aspect at any given time, will also determine these same opportunities and possibilities.

The question arises, then . . . is it possible that a person may not have favorable opportunities and possibilities of approaching Chiron due to the nature of his/her natal chart and the subsequent lifetime aspects of Saturn and Chiron? To answer this, we must remember that the picture of planetary influences in relation to our lives is a holographic picture, i.e. the planets mirror our consciousness and our consciousness is mirrored in the planets. We could say that our consciousness before incarnation *attracts* us to a particular point in time and space that corresponds to our issues and thus we are born. The physics and astronomy of this picture will be explored in Book Three. Furthermore, what we might normally classify as "unfavorable" aspects and transits, when looked at from a higher perspective, offer the same opportunities and possibilities as any others. The challenge is to see the ways – i.e. the *form* – in which this is so. Seeing these ways is an integral part of our journey of transformation of consciousness; it is all about the *awakening* of higher consciousness. The differences from one chart to the next lie merely in the *form* that the inherent possibilities take. This is what astrology seeks to reveal.

In any case, Saturn represents the real, practical stepping stone to Chiron. It is, however, a step that must be taken consciously and intentionally in order to derive the maximum benefit and opportunity to deal with the Chironic issues that we will ultimately meet. Saturn is the gatekeeper to the outer planets, Chiron being the portal.

Saturn's key issues in this respect are responsibility, seriousness, discipline, intention, resolve, attention, focus, persistence, steadfastness and effort.

Saturn requires that we take *responsibility* for our lives. This requires the end of *blame.* It requires that we acknowledge the part we have played in making our life and its circumstances the way they are today. Forgiveness is a stepping stone on this path. Beyond forgiveness is the acknowledgment that the outside world is a true reflection of our inner state of consciousness, our issues and our Wounds. Said another way, we get back what we put out, no more, no less.

Saturn requires *seriousness* in our attitude towards our potential Healing and the evolution of our consciousness. It requires that we stop trying to run away from, avoid, make light of or ignore the calling of evolution from within our Hearts. It asks us to take stock, looking at where we have come from, where we have been, where we are now and where we wish to be in the future. It requires us to become students in the study of ourselves and our lives.

Saturn requires *discipline.* Anything worth pursuing is worth pursuing in a disciplined way. Sporadic efforts bring sporadic results. Consistent effort over time brings long-term and permanent results. This is common sense. However, for some reason, we are not naturally inclined to apply the same discipline to our spiritual growth, Healing and evolution of consciousness as we are to more seemingly-tangible pursuits, such as building a business, pursuing a hobby, learning a trade or making ourselves comfortable and secure in life. Yet, it eventually catches up with us when we realize, through ill health or adversity, that the Quality of our lives is not what we expected it to be. Something is still missing in the equation. At this point, Saturn again impels us to take the spiritual aspects of our lives more seriously and begin to be more disciplined in our approach to our Healing journey. As they say, an ounce of prevention . . .

Saturn requires that we have an *intention,* consciously, to pursue avenues of Healing and evolution of consciousness. Nothing in the world ever happened without there first being an intention. When we have no intention ourselves, we are subject to the intentions of others.

Intention is very closely related to *resolve.* When we are confronted by the circumstances of our lives and challenged to awaken to a higher understanding, we are impelled towards making a resolve to attend to our lives, our issues and our Wounds. A long-term lack of intention can ultimately throw us into adverse circumstances and ill health in our lives, impelling this kind of a resolve.

Saturn says that *attention* is one of the major keys in the conscious pursuit of Healing and the evolution of consciousness. Without consciously directed attention, we are slaves to our lives, slaves to others and slaves to every emotion that arises within us. In short, we are slaves to our lower nature. Attention is the muscle we must develop in order to master our lives. The failure to develop conscious attention causes attention to atrophy, chaos being the ultimate result in our consciousness.

Without attention, we are at the mercy of every emotional and sensory impulse, meaning that we will run from perceived Pain and seek perceived pleasure. In this way, we have not the tool by which we can approach the Wound, through which the Gift of our lives is revealed. To remain in the *presence* of the Wound within us, using the tool of attention, is the key to transcending its illusion and awakening to a higher consciousness of the world around us, our lives and our true nature.

Focus comes from the conscious use of the tool of *attention,* applied with *intention,* towards a specifically understood and acknowledged goal or purpose. An understanding of the goal or purpose towards which we strive comes with the responsibility, seriousness, discipline and resolve of self-study. It comes when we take stock of our lives. Focus represents the relatively unified light of consciousness as it consciously acknowledges and pursues a goal or purpose of Healing and evolution of consciousness.

Saturn requires *persistence,* persistence in the *intention, resolve, attention* and *focus* towards our goal or purpose of Healing and evolution of consciousness. Only through persistence can a true and permanent change of Being (awakening) occur. Challenges and setbacks are but the milestone along the way, milestones that are perceived as failures and blockages by the uninitiated who turn back at the slightest hiccup. Persistence comes when challenges and setbacks are seen in their true light, i.e. as calls to awaken to a higher reality, beyond the illusions of our dualistic, lower-natured consciousness. Persistence allows us to move beyond these transient illusions. The fuel for persistence comes from acknowledging the wordless *knowing* that lies within our Hearts, a knowing that impels us towards conscious understanding and awakening.

Steadfastness is closely aligned with *persistence.* Steadfastness is the act of holding the *knowing* in our Hearts in the forefront of our consciousness, in the face of all outside circumstances, despite the protestations of our lower nature. The knowing in our Hearts is *Love.* Steadfastness is the steady and continued acknowledgment of Love.

Effort is the Saturn's currency. Without effort, i.e. plain hard work, nothing of value can be achieved. Involution – the Wounding – is an *effortless* action, taking us further and further into duality, into illusion, into fragmentation of consciousness. Evolution – the Healing – is an *effortful* action, bring us closer to unity, Truth and integrity of consciousness. *Effort* challenges our lower-natured illusions, it shines Light into the Darkness, it brings the Wound into view, helping us to grow, Heal and evolve.

Without the master training of Saturn, we would forever remain in bondage to the illusions of our lower nature. Without the aid, help and lessons of Saturn, we would remain trapped within the inner planets. We would remain barred from the greater consciousness of the solar system, barred from the possibility of galactic consciousness. Without passing the gatekeeper – Saturn – we cannot approach Chiron. Without embracing and working with Saturn's lessons, we cannot consciously work with Chiron's energy or revelations.

At yet, having said this, the Wound itself – the domain of Chiron – ever drives us towards our destiny, towards our higher purpose, towards our Divine Design. At a certain point, we are inevitably driven up against Saturn. We reach an *impasse* of consciousness, more often than not reflected in an *impasse* in our external lives. (Astrologers, look for the Saturn transits.) At this point, we are impelled to reassess our relationship to Saturnian issues and themes in our lives. Chiron, itself, drives us to take up Saturn's requirements. It drives us to get serious about our lives and our potential Healing and evolution of consciousness.

In these ways, the issues and themes of Saturn and Chiron go hand in hand.

The Moon and Chiron

The Moon and Chiron are intimately connected.

The Moon is the expression of our dualistic emotional nature, which is formed in childhood as a response to our lopsided perceptions and reactions to the world around us. (We will discuss the psychology of this in Book Two.) *As such, it is inherently the expression-vehicle for our Woundedness. It is Chiron's face seen through our lower nature, so to speak.*

We cannot understand the Moon and its influence and expression in our lives without understanding Chiron and its place. This is because our lower emotional expressions (Moon) have their ultimate origins in our Woundedness (Chiron). Conversely, we cannot fully see and appreciate the way Chiron manifests in real life without understanding the Moon and its mechanisms. This is because our Woundedness is *expressed* in the mirror of our Moon-ruled lower emotional nature. As we can see, the two planets are integrally linked.

The Moon represents, to a large degree, the routes of 'escape' and avoidance we take when things get too difficult to deal with in our lives, i.e. when the Wounds become too Painful.

This brings us to an important point. That is, that what seems like an 'escape' route or avoidance tactic *has inherent within it the factors and environment whereby Healing can take place.* This applies equally to all Moon placements. The Moon represents, on the one hand, a kind of governor, regulating the degree of reality and Truth we are capable of dealing with or not, i.e. the Moon protects us and wraps us up in cotton wool. On the other hand, it takes us, by virtue of our 'charges' and lower emotional issues that attract or repel us from things, into the situations and environments where our Wounds, blockages and unresolved issues may be illuminated, Healed and resolved.

Said another way, *the Healing path is already contained within the Wound.* If Chiron *drives* us by virtue of our Wounds, i.e. our Voids and Values, then the Moon, through our lower emotional charges and issues, *steers* us along that path.

As the Healing journey proceeds, as our Wounds are Healed and as our issues are resolved, the expression of the Moon changes, reflecting the Healing in our lower emotional nature. We align to a higher octave of the Moon's expression. Moreover, in a sense, as we Heal, we gradually transcend the Moon. Said another way, we become the masters of the Moon, i.e. the masters of our emotional nature. As masters of our emotional nature, we are then free to make use of the palette of emotional colors in the pursuit of our life's path and purpose.

Said yet another way, as we master our emotional nature, initially the realm of the Moon, our emotional nature increasingly enters the realm of the Sun, i.e. it becomes more unified, coherent, conscious, intentional and self-determined. From being unconsciously *reactive* and Moon-ruled, our emotional nature becomes Sun-ruled and consciously *active.* In this way, our Healing journey takes us to our Divinely Designed life's purpose and its outward expression and manifestation. This brings us to another point . . .

The other aspect of the Moon that is intimately connected to Chiron is the Moon's Nodes. On the one hand, the Moon's Nodes represent the direction of our lives, our purpose, goal, aim, major lesson, etcetera, as well as our Gifts, talents and Service to the planet (North Node). On the other hand, the Nodes tell us where we have come from and what Gifts, talents, lessons, issues, etcetera, we bring with us into this lifetime (South Node). Because our Wounds, indicated by Chiron, drive us *toward* our life's path and purpose and *toward* the expression and manifestation of our Divine Design (by virtue of our Voids and Values), thus Chiron is connected to the Moon's Nodes, which are the indicators of our life's path and purpose.

Again, Chiron drives and the Moon steers. Chiron is the *experience* of our Woundedness and the Moon is the *expression* of our Woundedness. The two work hand in hand. Therefore, we must relate them in an astrological reading.

Virgo/Pisces Polarity

The polarity of the zodiac signs of Virgo and Pisces holds many keys to understanding Chiron and its issues and themes.

Perhaps the most important theme of Virgo and Pisces in relation to Chiron is the law of the One and the Many. Virgo, on the one hand, traditionally speaking, represents the height of fragmentation, separateness and discreteness – the mass of innumerable disconnected data in need of synthesis. On the other hand, the positive aspect of Virgo entails this very synthesis, without leaving out any seemingly-small and insignificant detail. This attention to detail stresses the importance of the practical and the pragmatic, as well as the somewhat cynical side of Virgo.

Pisces, however, traditionally speaking, represents the *loss* of fragmentation, separateness and discreteness, i.e. the merging into a singular and undifferentiated mass unconsciousness. On the other hand, the positive side of Pisces is the *conscious* merging back into Oneness, wholeness, Truth and Unconditional Love. This is the result of the Healing journey.

What we speak about here is the *cosmogonic cycle,* as we shall explore in depth in Book Three. This is the law that pervades the Universe. It says that, on all scales from the microcosm to macrocosm, the Universe is comprised of cycles of Oneness becoming Manyness and Returning to Oneness. Our journey from Spirit into Matter and the Return to Spirit is just one such cycle.

Chiron and its themes exemplify this journey. Initially, we see that the journey from Oneness (Pisces) to Manyness (Virgo) is the Wounding. The journey from Manyness (Virgo) back to Oneness (Pisces) is the Healing.

Virgo separates and defines – the act of dualistic perception, without which the world as we know it would not exist. The world – the Creation – is built upon duality. For any act of Creation, the greater the detail envisioned, the more firm and long-lasting its manifestation. Differentiation is one of Virgo's keywords. It is this separating and differentiating process that, at the same time, fragments our consciousness. This is the essence of the Wounding. However, it is the fragmentation of *sleeping* or *innocent* consciousness. The descent into duality offers us the opportunity to *awaken* our consciousness to the eternal Oneness from which we are born. This is the purpose of the Creation and of our cycle of lives.

On the other hand, Pisces *merges* and dispenses with definition. It recognizes that Truth has no words, no definitions, no names. However, the two sides of the Piscean paradox are represented by the *unconscious* and *conscious* aspects of merging. The *unconscious* side is *pre-awakening* – our consciousness as *innocent* angels, so to speak. The *conscious* side is *awakened* merging – our consciousness as *experienced* angels, so to speak. This latter case is the essence of the Healing.

The Wounding, seen through Virgo, is mirror-reflected in Pisces. Through Virgo, the Wounding is experienced as fragmentation, differentiation and consciousness-isolating specialization. Through Pisces, the Wounding is experienced as a penchant for feeling like a victim to outside circumstances. The wish for a Return to Oneness in the face of the fragmentation of our consciousness often leads us into self-pity, into 'poor-me' reactions and into feelings of powerlessness. The theme of surrendering to a higher power is also associated with this Pisces reflection.

On the other hand, this theme of surrendering to a higher power – the Healing journey – is mirror-reflected in the Virgo theme of responsibility and attention to small matters. If we forget the small things and the details, we leave behind the very things that comprise the totality of the unified consciousness we seek. If one small detail is left behind, we are still fragmented. Therefore, one of Virgo's higher octave themes is *inclusion,* i.e. including increasingly more into our conscious awareness.

All things are connected . . . *how* they are connected is the Virgo question. This is the question that unconsciously drives the Healer to explore all possible connections between body systems and between Body, Mind and Soul. This is the path of *synthesis,* of connecting the dots, so to speak. This is the Healing journey.

Virgo consciousness seeks to 'get it right', to master a thing or process to the 'nth' degree. All things must be in balance. This requires focus, attention, concentration and intention. It requires that we are awake to each and every detail. Virgo is the training ground for self-mastery and for us as potential co-Creators. When we 'get it right', we can merge (Pisces) back into Oneness *without losing ourselves.* The eternal paradox of the One and the Many remains within us, but as *awakened* or *experienced* beings of Light.

Lastly, the polarity of Virgo and Pisces represents the Earth-focused cynic and the Heaven-focused faithful adherent, respectively. The Earth-focused cynic denies that anything exists outside what can be touched, seen, smelled, heard or tasted. In doing so, we cut ourselves off from an awareness of our inherent divinity. We remain in a state of fragmentation that is filled with dualistic illusions. The Heaven-focused faithful adherent, on the other hand, denies the efficacy and reality of all things of the visible world. In doing so, we cut ourselves off from the possibility and potential of true awakening to our divine nature. We remain in an undifferentiated sleep state that is filled with fantasy and dream-images. In this state, we are unable to fulfill our ultimate role as co-Creators in training. These complementary opposites of Virgo and Pisces epitomize the nature of our Woundedness.

On the other hand, paradoxically, we *require* both personas within us for balanced consciousness to be born. The cynic keeps us practical and earthed, and guards against blind faith and susceptibility. The faithful adherent continually challenges the cynic within us, challenging the illusions of the dualistic material world. Ultimately, we will awaken to the Truth that we are Spirit *and* Matter, One *and* Many. One side cannot exist without the other. Our focus (perception) on one side of the equation, to the exclusion of the other side, epitomizes our Woundedness. *An awakening to the Actuality of the simultaneous existence of the One and the Many within us is the true Healing journey.* It is here that the illusory paradox of the Virgo/Pisces polarity dissolves and a higher understanding is revealed. *Nothing has changed . . . the One has not become the Many. Neither has the Many become the One. We have merely awakened to our true nature, which is inherently both One and Many simultaneously.*

Chiron illuminates and mirror-reflects all of the above issues and themes and leads us to musings and explorations of the ramifications of those issues and themes.

6th/12th house Polarity

The polarity of the 6th and 12th houses also expresses Chironic themes and issues. Perhaps the most important theme is that of the paradox of the *inner* and the *outer.* The 6th house essentially remains inwardly focused. It is the final stop of the inwardly focused lower hemisphere of the natural zodiac. The 12th house essentially remains outwardly focused. It is the final stop of the outwardly focused upper hemisphere of the natural zodiac. At the 6th house, we sit at the threshold of the acknowledgment of the Other, the outside world, when we pass beyond the anaretic degree into the 7th house. At the 12th house, we sit on the threshold of acknowledgment of our individuality when we pass beyond the anaretic degree into the 1st house.

Yet, paradoxically, in the 6th house, we are concerned with the manifest world around us and, in the 12th house, we are concerned with the world within us, beyond the senses. In the 6th house, we see the outside world and ultimately recognize it as a reflection of ourselves. In the 12th house, we see our inner world and ultimately recognize it as a reflection of the outside world. Neither inner nor outer make sense without the other. Which is real, inner or outer? Neither, on their own. Taken together, we finally begin to taste Actuality.

The 6th house is the house of the *tangible* and the 12th, the house of the *intangible.* The parallels to the Virgo/Pisces polarity are obvious, as these are the natural signs of their respective natural houses.

How does all this relate to Chironic themes? Chiron, as we have seen, represents the border line, the potential bridge between consciousness turned upon itself, in denial of a greater reality (the Other), and consciousness turned outward, seeking Contact and Connection to a greater reality, as represented by the outer planets and beyond. At this borderline threshold, we are as children, suddenly realizing that the world is not just for us. We realize that there are other consciousnesses around us, interacting with us. This act of perception is, paradoxically, an integral part of the Wounding *and* the Healing. As the Wounding, the act of perception is a process of separation, differentiation, definition and consciousness-isolating specialization. As part of the Healing journey, the act of perception is an acknowledgment of higher consciousness, ever including more within our concentric sphere of awareness.

The paradox of the One and the Many is similarly encapsulated in the 6th/12th-house polarity. From 12th to 1st house the One becomes the Many again (individuality as a manifestation of the Many). From the 6th to 7th house, the Many (fragmented individuality) becomes the One again (realization of the connectedness to others in an inseparable symbiotic relationship). The two hemispheres of the natural zodiac – lower and upper, summated in the 6th and 12th houses respectively – are but two halves of Actuality. Like the Yin and the Yang, each complements the other *and contains elements of the other.* The seeds of fragmentation are contained in the upper hemisphere with a separation of consciousness into Self and Other. The seeds of unity are contained in the lower hemisphere with the realization that the Universe is contained *within us.*

On a more practical note, the 6th house, traditionally being the house of work, methodology, Healing and Service, provides the solid basis for subsequent *inclusion* and *synthesis* required for ultimate awakening to our inherent Oneness and divinity. The 12th house, traditionally being the house of the psyche, the unconsciousness, the isolated, the repressed, the domination of the unseen collective, etcetera, provides the material and environment whereby the impulse to Soul-search is engendered. Such Soul-searching will inevitably awaken us to our *individual* value, purpose and place in the larger Plan. Both journeys are part of the Healing journey as outlined by Chiron.

The Anaretic Degree

So, what about the anaretic degree itself? Moreover, what is its relation to Chiron? Traditionally, the anaretic degree, being the final degree in a given zodiac sign or house, represents the point where transcendence and evolution *must* take place, otherwise recapitulation – cyclic repetition – will occur. In this way, the anaretic degree is related to the point where one octave becomes a new octave. Issues and themes are brought to a head in this degree, demanding attention and resolution. A quantum leap of consciousness is required to thrust us through into the next concentric sphere of consciousness. The anaretic degree shines a light on all unresolved, undissolved and unHealed aspects of the issues at hand. It brings the repressed into sharp relief. Thus, the Chiron connection becomes clear.

In terms of the Law of Octaves, the anaretic degree, represents the final or 7th step of the ascending octave. If this step is 'successful', a new octave of consciousness is entered and new issues and themes become apparent, i.e. our next lessons. At this final step, something must die for something new to be born. More often than not, it is our illusions that must die, making way for the revelation of greater Truth. The association of the anaretic degree with Pluto thus becomes apparent.

From this point of view, the anaretic degree represents the vessel in which the orgasm of consciousness can take place. *In Chiron terms, it represents the alchemical retort in which all elements are made visible, allowing Healing to take place.* Healing, as we have explored, is the awakening and expanding of consciousness beyond its current confines. It is aligning to a greater concentric sphere of understanding. The process itself is akin to the birth process. It contains both pleasure and Pain, chaos and order, loss and gain, confusion and understanding. The anaretic degree is the journey down the birth canal. It is also the *transition* phase of the birth process, well known to women in childbirth. It is a leap into the void, leaving behind the illusions of what we thought we knew. It is Chiron's journey through the underworld, through the perceived Darkness, into the Void, into the Wound.

We emerge from the other side with a quantum leap of understanding, a larger scope of consciousness and a vista that dwarfs our previous views of the world and of ourselves. Our consciousness is more integrated, more whole, more awakened and more Healed.

The discovery of Chiron was preceded in the 1950s and the 1960s by a virtual anaretic degree: the melting-pot turmoil of these years. We are now experiencing the orgasm of consciousness, i.e. the emergence of the new paradigms that we have explored in this book so far. It is a chain reaction that may take many years, perhaps many generations, to fully complete and fully integrate into the collective consciousness of Humanity.

Virgo to Libra Transition

We have spoken about the transition from Virgo to Libra and from the 6th to the 7th house in terms that are more traditional. Let's now look at it from the perspective of the zodiac of the Mysteries. When we consider this transition, we must take into account the issues we have previously discussed. We must take into account the symbolism of the lower and upper hemispheres, the Self and the Other, the anaretic degree, the Virgo penchant for attention to detail and *inclusion* as a principle. When we do, we can begin to see the connection to the meanings of Virgo and Libra according to the Mysteries that preceded our current understanding.

Virgo, according to the zodiac of the Mysteries, represents the final step before potential enlightenment. It is the step where we finally 'get it right'. It is where we finally *include* everything, without leaving any detail behind. It is where we finally see the connections between all seemingly-disconnected things. It is where we have attained mastery over the physical reflections of our spiritual being and where we have attained mastery over the dualistic illusions of our lower nature. In short, we have finally achieved a relatively *balanced* consciousness.

Libra, therefore, represents the point of balanced consciousness, freed from dualistic illusions. It represents the fire of awakened and focused consciousness – the consciousness of the Sun.

The transition from Virgo to Libra represents the final step in the Healing journey via the anaretic degree, i.e. via the final step of the current octave. If this final step is not achieved, we play out the cycle repeatedly until we 'get it right' and evolve to the next octave, i.e. until we move on to the next issue or lesson.

The synthesis process – the Healing journey – is a journey from *earth* to *water* to *air* to *fire*. The journey from Virgo to Libra encapsulates them all, Virgo being traditionally an earth sign, an air sign according to the Mysteries and Libra being traditionally an air sign and a fire sign according to the Mysteries. According to the Mysteries, the transition from air (Virgo) to fire (Libra) is most important. The fire of Libra – representing the Sun – is the portal to the spiritual realms, i.e. the realms of ether, space and time. It is the portal to higher consciousness, a gateway to worlds beyond paradox and duality.

Chiron mirrors this portal in the *expansion* of consciousness. Chiron is the Rainbow Bridge between the inner and the outer planets, between the small consciousness of our current state and the larger consciousness of our true potential.

The practical and material achievement of balance is a pre-requisite for awakened higher consciousness. Put simply, we require our feet to be on the ground if we wish to put our head in the heavens. Such is the requirement of the zodiac sign of Virgo if we are to attain Libran balance.

One interesting aspect of the Virgo requirements is what the world and the current paradigm call "obsessive-compulsive disorder" or OCD. We will discuss OCDs at length in Book Two. However, let's elaborate briefly here . . .

When our focus keeps coming back to the same issue, repeating actions, thoughts and feelings, driven by guilt or fear, we are being given a golden opportunity. We are being given a wake-up call, so to speak, by which we can finally get to the bottom of a given issue in which we may be 'stuck'. As we shall see in Book Two, OCDs are a perfect mirror of our state of consciousness. Furthermore, each one of us has elements of OCD, whether diagnosed or not.

Beyond this simple fact, lies an even more important implication. In order to transcend our current sphere of consciousness, we must *remember* everything, we must *include* everything, we must *connect* everything and we must put ourselves into the picture of what we are observing. Such effort, seen from the perspective of the current paradigm, could be defined as an OCD. More generically and colloquially speaking, we often accuse others of being "obsessive" or "compulsive" when their focus in life does not make sense to us or does not afford us the attention we expect from this person. Yet, this focus is required by the force of evolution within us.

Our final and most all-encompassing OCD is the primary focus on our Divine Design, i.e. on our Purpose in life, as 'heard' within the spaces of our awakening Heart. It is an OCD driven not so much by guilt and fear (our blessed companions and driving forces in the march of evolution of consciousness, as we shall see later), but by Love and Gratitude.

OCDs reflect our need for Healing. Simultaneously, they drive us *towards* that Healing. Lastly, they reflect our acceptance of Healing in the form of our consciously-embraced Divine Design. OCDs do not change, neither are they ever cured or fixed . . . they just change form. For an elaboration of these radical views, see Book Two.

From both the traditional point of view and from the point of view of the Mysteries, the Virgo affiliation with OCDs is now apparent. Healing (Virgo) = Balance (Libra). Balance can only be achieved by *inclusion, synthesis* and *connection* of all seemingly-disparate and fragmented pieces of the puzzle of our lives. In the same way as a master musician practises music repetitively until mastery is achieved, so we must repeat our lessons of life until we master them. When mastered, as an act of Love and Gratitude, we celebrate our life by 'obsessively' pursuing our Divine Design.

Lower to Upper Hemispheres

We have said that the lower and upper hemispheres of the natural zodiac represent the polarity of Self and Other. The separation of the world into Self and Other is a necessary requirement in the awakening and enlightening process. The Wounding is necessary for the Healing. In the final analysis, nothing changes except our conscious awareness. Wounding and Healing are eternal.

The lower hemisphere is the "Self" part of the Yin-Yang pair, the upper being the "Other" part. "Self" – the lower hemisphere – is cut off from the outside, neither acknowledging it nor being aware of it. It represents the world we know, the world we have come to understand, the world we may have even come to Love. In a sense, this is the place of *unconscious* Oneness where the dualistic idea of an 'outside' does not yet exist. The "Other" is awakened to the idea of an 'outside', drawing a boundary between the known and the unknown, the Loved and the yet-to-be-Loved. The distinctions and differentiations Serve to illuminate our true nature to ourselves via the mirror of dualistic reality. Fragmentation of consciousness precedes *conscious* Oneness.

From Chiron's perspective, the Wound is required for a conscious awakening to Oneness. The Wound is a Gift. Both the Wounding and the Healing are encapsulated in the symbolism of the lower and upper hemispheres.

Chiron/Neptune

The descending journey into duality, into materiality, via Chiron, is the Wounding. Here, Unconditional Love (Neptune) becomes conditional love (Venus). The Return journey – the Healing journey via Chiron – entails the synthesis of illusory half-truths of our perception into greater Truth and, thus, greater Love. The path from Venus (lower-octave conditional love) to Neptune (higher-octave Unconditional Love) is paved by Chiron and the Healing journey. Chiron says that there is not one small aspect of ourselves that is unworthy of Love.

In a sense, Chiron, probably associated with the Kuiper Belt of objects *outside* the orbit of Neptune, orbiting *within* the orbit of Neptune, give us a pre-emptive taste of the consciousness of Neptune and beyond. It offers us the possibility of a quantum leap of consciousness, propelling us outwards in an expansion of our definition of Love.

For these reasons, Chiron and Neptune are closely aligned in the horoscope. Chironic processes impel us to see both sides of given issues, exhausting all definitions, answering all questions, dissolving all illusions and taking us into a wordless state where the Truth of Oneness and Love can be felt relatively directly. This is the domain of Neptune. In the horoscope, the interpretation of Neptune and its influences and meaning is often problematic, i.e. a mystery. When taken together with Chiron and the path Chiron offers, Neptune's place and role become clearer.

The Sagittarius Connection

There are many associations between Chiron and the sign of Sagittarius, some superficial, others deeper.

Ironically, the most superficial connection lies in the symbol of the centaur. We have explored the Chironic implications of this symbol previously. Although the centaur is one of the deepest and most important symbols of Chiron, the connection thereof to the sign of Sagittarius is at best a namesake and pictorial comparison. This connection quickly prompted early astrologers in the study of Chiron to ascribe Chiron as the ruler of Sagittarius. We need to look beyond appearances to find the deeper connection between Sagittarius and Chiron.

Sagittarius, as a constellation, lies in the direction of the galactic center when viewed from our distant planet. From all that we have discussed and explored and all that we will explore in Book Three, we know that the galactic center represents greater Truth, consciousness and Love, beyond the confines of the solar system. We also know that Chiron, in the myth, was immortalized as a star in this constellation, representing the possibility for attaining this higher state of consciousness. The Healing journey – our journey of evolution in consciousness – offers us the possibility of Returning to galactic consciousness, symbolized by the constellation of Sagittarius.

Therefore, the symbolism of Truth, Oneness and Love exemplifies Sagittarius, *not* the symbolism of the Wound between the lower and higher selves, as expressed by the symbol of the centaur. Chiron represents a *pathway* to Sagittarian ideals.

Sagittarius/Gemini Polarity

If anything, it is in the Sagittarius/Gemini polarity that Chironic issues and themes become apparent.

Gemini and Sagittarius represent the *particular* and the *general,* respectively. This is a form of the Many and the One.

The Gemini side is concerned with Knowledge, whereas the Sagittarius side is concerned with Wisdom/Being. Knowledge without Wisdom/Being is empty. Wisdom/Being without Knowledge is impotent.

The Sagittarian side is concerned with *experience,* whereas the Gemini side is concerned with intellectual *understanding.* Experience without understanding is impotent. Understanding without experience is empty.

The Sagittarius side is concerned with *knowing,* whereas the Gemini side is concerned with *communicating* and *expressing.* Knowing without communicating/expressing is impotent. Communicating/expressing without knowing is empty.

Sagittarius ultimately represents the Wisdom/Being of undifferentiated Oneness, but *innocent* or *unawakened.* Gemini represents the Knowledge of the Many, of the dualistic and material world. Via Chiron, this Knowledge of the Many, *gained through the experience (Sagittarius) of the dualistic world,* can be synthesized into a greater understanding, i.e. the Wisdom of Oneness, *but this time experienced and awakened.*

Chiron, as the Wounding, represents the journey from Sagittarius to Gemini. Chiron, as the Healing, represents the journey from Gemini back to Sagittarius. Beyond all journeys, Gemini and Sagittarius are two sides of the Yin-Yang of Knowledge and Being.

Complementary Opposites in the Zodiac

This brings us to an important realization. We have explored the Virgo/Pisces polarity and the Gemini/Sagittarius polarity in some detail and found that Chiron sits in the middle of each polarity, offering us a way of transcending the seeming paradoxes presented by these zodiac pairs. Even the issue of transforming paradox into *metadox* (the union of opposites), revealing a greater understanding that both encompasses and transcends both sides, is a Chironic theme, as we have explored. What if we examine each of the complementarily opposite zodiac pairs? Will we find Chiron sitting in the middle of each, offering a path of transcendence to greater Truth, Oneness and Love? I believe so. Let's explore this a little . . .

A little while ago, I wrote an article for a magazine that explored each of the zodiac pairs and offered a synthesis of the seeming opposites.

Let me quote from this article, filling in the details of the four other zodiac pairs that we have not yet covered:

Aries/Libra

This polarity is the expression of self/others, me/we, egoism/altruism, inner strength/outer weakness, solitude/relationship, etcetera. If the pendulum swings too far towards Aries, then we believe that we need no one else. We are a law unto ourselves. The inner loneliness and isolation that this kind of stance brings naturally encourages us to swing back the other way if we are ready. The expression, 'No man is an island' is the balance for this Arian stance. One of the chief features of the Aries signature person is the hidden need for approval from others. In this way, the door to potential acknowledgment of the value of others is kept ajar.

If the pendulum swings too far towards the Libran stance, then we find ourselves invariably giving our power away to others. Inner truth is sacrificed for the sake of social harmony and a peaceful life. The thorn in this peaceful life is the inevitable feeling of self-deprecation and of resentment towards others. Consequently, the Libran signature person will always find themselves in situations of great imbalance and conflict. This is the other side of the coin saying to them, 'When are you going to stop being a doormat?'

The perfect marriage of the Aries/Libra polarity is the balance between self and others. There is an invisible line around us, over which no other shall step. There is a line, beyond which we do not step into the space of others. Paradoxically, there is no line between others and us because what we do for ourselves, we do for others. What we do for others, we do for ourselves.

The highest understanding and resolution of the Aries/Libra paradox is the realization that others are a perfect reflection of us. What we see, judge or love in another is what we see, judge or love in ourselves. If we infatuate another, we are seeking to love that part of us that we ascribe to them. If we are resentful of another or judge them, we are in judgment or resentful of the parts of ourselves that they reflect – we are seeking to love those parts in us.

Taurus/Scorpio

This is the polarity of organization/chaos, construction/destruction, material security/material chaos, total trust/suspiciousness, peace/war, etcetera. If we swing too far towards Taurus, we become too fixed, complacent, materially oriented, trusting to a fault, indolent and attached to our comfort. When we find ourselves in these states for too long, we either get bored and are impelled to make changes or life deals us some swift and dramatic crises to wake us from our slumber. Within this pole is the need to control everything material.

If we swing too far towards the Scorpio pole, we become excessively destructive, chaotic, materially scornful, jealous and envious, suspicious and over-protective. This pole is the 'shoot-first-and-ask-questions-later' stance. Within this pole is the need to control Spirit.

Everything in the life of these two polarities points us towards the real security that can only be found in Love. The Taurean security leads to boredom and stagnation – the Scorpio security leads to hatred and resentment of the things that it strives to control. The two poles together are a good illustration of the 4th Ray of Creation – the Ray of Harmony through Conflict. Only when we relinquish our need to control, handing over our will to the higher power of our higher Self, do we begin to understand that only in Love do we need no security. Love is the answer to all questions.

In addition, the Taurus/Scorpio polarity requires a balance between Spirit and matter. In the real world, this blended dichotomy acknowledges equally the processes of construction and destruction – of war and peace. War without peace brings chaos. Peace without war brings stagnation. Real harmony is a balance of both.

Cancer/Capricorn

This dichotomy is the expression of the polarities: being cared for/ caring for, dependence/independence, support/non-support, public recognition/private recognition, fluid/solid, organic/structured, warmth/

lack of warmth, embryonic/fully formed, growth/decay, idea/form, Spirit/matter, etcetera.

The Cancer extreme seeks warmth, caring, nurturing, looking after, etcetera. This hearkens back to a time before self-determination and before responsibility was required. There never seems to be enough love for us when we are at this extremity – it is a bottomless pit. We are dependent upon others for our emotional needs. The world around us, however, seems cold and uncaring. This is literally a fetal response, where we do not want to accept personal responsibility for our lives. The cold and uncaring world around us (Capricorn) is trying to get us to grow up – to take responsibility – to nurture ourselves, to look after ourselves. At this Cancerian extreme, we are in birth without growth and maturity.

The Capricorn extreme is only interested in practical matters. Responsibility, achievement, respect and recognition are more important than care. In this space, we don't have time to worry about those who cannot worry about themselves. We bury ourselves in work, creating structures against the emptiness we feel inside. We see the world as a commodity that we can shape – beat into form. The trouble is, once we have built the structures, who is going to inhabit them? In our extreme coldness and pragmatism, we repel others who could teach us the warmth that could fill these empty structures. At this extreme, we are in death without having lived.

The lesson here is that we are each seeking a balance between care and responsibility, between being nurtured and nurturing self, between being supported and supporting self, between being looked after and looking after self. Warmth, caring, nurturing (Cancer) without form and structure (Capricorn) remains embryonic and unmanifest – thus it turns inwards into the bottomless pit of despair. Form and structure without warmth, caring and nurturing remains empty – it remains inanimate and lifeless. This also leads to isolation and despair.

Where then is the blending of these polarities? It is a question of a balance of dependence and independence. The perfect marriage of the Cancer/Capricorn dichotomy includes both dependence and independence in every person. In caring for others, we seek to learn how to care for ourselves. In caring for ourselves, we are preparing to care for others. In taking responsibility for our lives, we are preparing for taking responsibility for others. In taking responsibility for others, we are learning to take responsibility for ourselves. The blending of these two sides is Love.

Leo/Aquarius

This is the polarity of ego consciousness/collective consciousness, individuality/blending with the masses, autocracy/sociocracy, inner focus/outer focus, self-approval/collective approval, individual creativity/ the creative masses, the sun/the stars, the local picture/the galactic picture, my will/thy will, geocentric/heliocentric, I am/we are, etcetera.

When the pendulum swings too far towards the Leo pole, we begin to think that we are the center of the world. We begin to think that everything revolves around us. We are the stage, the actors, the play, the playwright and the light. All others are stagehands and audience. We are the chosen – the ones born to lead and to hand down to others from 'on high'. The trouble is, that deep inside, the truth is known, if not consciously. The seeking of approval, adulation and attention is no more than an unconscious desire to rebalance the lack of self-esteem that we feel inside. Our self-worth is deprecated privately and exaggerated publicly. Without others, where would we be? While outwardly espousing our superiority, we are really run by our need for adulation, approval and attention from others. We are slaves to others' opinions.

When the swing towards Aquarius is exaggerated, we espouse high ideals of brotherhood and collective benefit, technology and spirituality while doggedly asserting our own independence, being deliberately contrary and going against the flow! While outwardly being a 'people person' we are inwardly cut off, aloof and alienated. Without other people to interact with, we feel empty and alone – we are dependent upon other people being around. Yet, we outwardly assert our independence! This Aquarian stance is one of the more perplexing puzzles to those around it.

A healthy sense of self-worth (positive ego – Leo) is a necessary requirement for a collective society (Aquarius) to function properly. We only need to look at the failures of Communism around the world to see illustrations that support this statement. A society with no individual leaders becomes a society run by committee. According to the joke, the definition of a committee is a life form with more than six legs, but no brain! Anywhere we look in nature we see hierarchical structures, i.e. class systems and pecking orders. To think that Man can rewrite nature's plan and introduce a classless system is not so much an Aquarian stance, as one would think, but is redolent of Leonine arrogance. Conversely, true self-worth and a healthy ego are not possible until we witness our actions having a true benefit to all around us; and this does not necessarily mean that we seek to please everybody around us all the time!

The synthesis of this Leo/Aquarius polarity consists of true self-appreciation – not inflated or depreciated. Each person in such a society recognizes his or her true place. We learn from those who have walked further down paths that we wish to travel. We teach others who wish to walk down the paths that we have traveled. We are all teachers and students, leaders and followers amongst geniuses. The Leo/Aquarian leader will acknowledge and draw upon the individual talents of each person in their group, acknowledging that the whole is greater than the sum of its parts. True self-worth of each member is the result. True self-worth has another name: Love.

The synthesis of the Leo/Aquarius polarity engenders the Heart-felt Wish that lies within each of us to Shine and to Celebrate our existence as a "thank you" to the Universe for the Gift of Life.

It is clear from our explorations of the zodiac pairs that the resolution of their seeming paradoxes is to be found in a synthesis of both sides into a greater unity, that unity being Love. The journey of resolution and synthesis is a journey of consciousness. It is the Healing journey.

The resolution and Healing of these opposites is a process of revealing the flip-sides of each opposite stance. It is a process of revealing the Yin in the Yang and the Yang in the Yin. In psychological terms, as we will explore in depth in Book Two, it is a process of bringing the *repressed* and the *hidden* into the Light of higher consciousness and thus seeing a larger picture. In this way, we balance our consciousness, aligning it with higher Truth, bringing us closer to the experience of Unconditional Love.

Such is the work and promise of Chiron.

From this, we can then propose that Chiron does indeed sit in the middle of each of the zodiac pairs. This itself points to an even greater Truth that is hidden within the zodiac: we are required by evolution – indeed, it is our destiny – ultimately to balance, synthesize, resolve, integrate, blend, transcend, Heal, etcetera, *every polarity/opposite/paradox within our personal horoscope.* This includes the *apparent* opposites, such as each zodiac pair and such as planetary oppositions (that we will discuss in the next section), as well as the *hidden* opposites, such as the signs and houses *opposite* each of our natal planets and the *virtual* planets opposite each *actual* planet. This topic, however, goes beyond the scope of this present work.

Chiron and the Opposition Aspect

Building on our conclusions in the previous section, we can now suggest that Chiron has a definite relationship to opposition aspects in the horoscope.

Oppositions represent the lowest and most polarized state of consciousness, whereas conjunctions – particularly occultations – represent the most unified. Said another way, oppositions represent Woundedness – the result of the descent of Spirit/Light into the material Creation. The subsequent ascent or Healing journey is a metaphoric and metaphysical journey through the planetary aspects from the opposition, through the quincunx, the trine, the square, the sextile and the semi-sextile to the conjunction/occultation. Each of these angular aspects represents one of the Rays we are working through on our way to Sun consciousness. Chiron's role in the resolution and Healing of planetary oppositions thus becomes apparent.

In the natal chart, we tend to exaggerate one side of a planetary opposition and minimize the other. Furthermore, this does not remain the same over time. We tend to swing back and forth between the poles, first exaggerating one side and minimizing the other, now exaggerating the other side and minimizing the first. The opposition represents seemingly-opposite, contradictory, conflicting and disconnected issues that are seeking resolution, Healing and synthesis. Only a quantum leap of understanding can transcend the seeming paradox. Here is where Chiron comes in, offering us a path of Healing and synthesis.

It is important to point out that Chiron can give us a potential path of resolution and synthesis of an opposition *even if it does not aspect the opposition in question.* Chiron is the key that unlocks the specific Woundedness that fuels such natal features as the opposition. Once unlocked, by attention, intention and directed effort, we can use this fuel for transformation, i.e. to resolve, dissolve and transcend the seeming paradoxes of the opposition. The resolution of opposition aspects *is* part of the Healing journey. This resolution opens us to a new perspective, a larger reality, a greater Truth beyond the apparent duality.

This transcendence of the paradox of the opposition aspect via Chiron immediately associates Chiron and the opposition aspect with Uranus. Chiron, as we have said, is the Rainbow Bridge between the inner and outer planets, represented by Saturn and Uranus, respectively. Uranus represents a higher logic, a glimpse at a larger plan, an understanding that resolves paradoxes and confounds the ordinary logic of our lower nature. Ultimately, the resolution of all planetary oppositions is their *conjunction/occultation,* as manifested simultaneously in the unified Light of the Sun and at the solar magnetopause.

Oppositions, like the zodiac pairs, ultimately represent the lessons of Love. Chiron says that all things Serve us on our Healing journey back to Love. All things are borne of Love and Serve Love. Seeing how this is so is part of the journey of awakening.

The Journey from Aries to Pisces

Taking the natural zodiac now, let's look at the cycle from Aries to Pisces, around the zodiac wheel. Aries represents the individual, separate, disconnected, fragmented from the whole. It represents the most material, most dualized point in our journey. It is the place of the greatest Woundedness. Chiron takes the most time through Aries and thus exaggerates Arian issues the most.

From one perspective, it is also a starting point in the cycle. From here, Healing becomes possible after the long journey into the duality of the material world. Aries represents the very beginning of the Return journey. Pisces will be our final destination in this Healing cycle, i.e. Oneness, wholeness and Unconditional Love. Chiron will be our companion all the way. Chiron exemplifies the Woundedness at the same time as offering a path of Healing. Evolution is the Gift in the Wound.

From Aries, we move to Taurus. If Aries is about *being,* i.e. the differentiated individual, the "I am", then Taurus is about *having.* By the reflection of abundance or lack of abundance in the material world, abundance or lack of abundance in our emotional world, we awaken to the abundance that lies within us, in our Hearts. This gives us the key to mastery of the material world. This key will be put to good use much later in the cycle.

From Taurus, we move to Gemini where, by outer reflection of knowledge, intellect and communication, we awaken to the knowing in our Hearts.

Then, in Cancer, through reflection of issues of caring and not caring, nurturing and not nurturing, being looked after and not being looked after, etcetera, we are awakened to our inner capacity for providing care, nurture and support to ourselves. This reflects the truth that the Universe is always looking after us. However, sometimes do not immediately recognize the form that this takes.

Then, in Leo, we are given the first glimpse of our true nature as Light by the outward reflection of our creativity, self-expression, etcetera. We look in the mirror for the first time and we are spellbound by the reflection.

In Virgo, we are challenged to bring together all that we have discovered in the first five signs into an integrated and synthesized whole. In doing so, we suddenly catch a glimpse of ourselves reflected in the outside world.

In Libra, we are confronted with the Other, the outside world, seen as distinct and separate from ourselves. The mirror is now extremely detailed, although we do not yet realize that it is a mirror. The mirror gives us the opportunity to awaken to many aspects of ourselves.

In Scorpio, we are confronted with the illusions of life and death, existence and non-existence, loss and gain, etcetera. We are challenged to realize our own innate physical mortality that masks our spiritual immortality, beyond the illusions of form.

In Sagittarius, we seek greater Truth; we turn our attention further and further outwards in search of deeper meaning and more inclusive answers to our questions.

In Capricorn, we achieve mastery over all that we see in the mirror reflection, still without fully realizing that *we* are the mirror.

In Aquarius, it begins to dawn upon us that perhaps we are One with all that we see, that we are part of the collective, not separate from it.

In Pisces, we finally realize that the mirror is us and we are the mirror. We merge into the Oneness from which we are borne, but with an awakened consciousness.

Chiron's place in this journey is, as always, integrating, joining, wholing, Healing, synthesizing, etcetera.

The Rulership Question

Initially, Chiron's rulership sign was considered Sagittarius. The reasons for this, aforementioned, were the symbol itself – the centaur – and the myth of Chiron, where he was immortalized as a star in the constellation of Sagittarius. Although these aspects are worthy of consideration, all my experience working with Chiron has shown me little connection between Chiron and Sagittarius in a practical sense. As an ideal – i.e. Truth, Wisdom, the Big Picture, galactic consciousness, etcetera – Sagittarius certainly represents the epitome of the Healing journey as we have laid it out. However, this is the long-term goal and result of the Healing journey. It does not speak of the details and stepping-stones along the way, which Chiron so perfectly epitomizes.

The details of the Healing journey and the practical application of Healing methods thereof rightly belong to the sign of Virgo. The real association of Chiron with Virgo is easily demonstrated in the innumerable case histories I have done. Our previous discussions about Chiron and its relationship to Virgo represent the distillation of these case histories.

Yet, the Healing journey aspect of Chiron is not the whole picture of Chiron. There is also the Wounding and the Journey into the Wound.

745-LASS

The *Wounding* aspect of Chiron has more association with and connection to the sign of Pisces and the 12th house. It is here where we express our sense of hurt, our feeling of being Wounded and our feeling of being abandoned by the Universe. The Virgo/Pisces polarity is eminently important in relation to Chiron and both the issues of Wounding and Healing.

The *journey* into the Wound has more association with and connection to the sign of Scorpio and with Chiron's Kuiper brother, Pluto. This is the Journey into the underworld, into the Darkness, before the Light is revealed.

Then there is the Libra connection. The Healing journey aspect of Chiron leads us inevitably and inexorably toward Libran balance of consciousness, particularly from the perspective of the Mysteries, aforementioned. However, like Sagittarius, Libra represents the *result* and *goal* of the Healing journey. Similarly, the sign of Aries represents the *culminating point* of the Wounding, not the Wounding *per se.* In addition, I have not found sufficient practical evidence in my case histories to suggest a working connection between Chiron and Libra when considered on their own.

Overall, it would seem that Chiron rules *not* a given sign or signs specifically, but rather rules the *processes* that occur between signs. Chiron is a bridge, a catalyst, an intermediary, an intercessory, a way-station, a go-between, a ferryman, a linking factor and an alchemical force. For example, Chiron sits on the path between Virgo and Pisces, between Virgo and Libra, between Pisces and Aries, between Aries through the signs to Pisces, between each of the opposite zodiac pairs, etcetera, as previously discussed. If Chiron were involved in digestion, it would be an *enzyme, not* the food itself or the conduit of the food tube.

From the point of view of Chiron being a comet rather than a planet *per se,* it represents an emotional expression of the solar system. It represents a reflection of a need within the consciousness of the solar system for a new perspective, an expanded horizon, a quantum leap of consciousness. From the point of view that Chiron may well be a temporary visitor, it again represents a connecting agent, a catalyst, an alchemical ingredient.

From the psychological point of view, emotional outbursts (which we have proposed that comets represent on a cosmic scale due to their highly elliptical orbits and their angles of inclination to the ecliptic) draw attention to issues and themes that are begging for attention, resolution, dissolution and Healing. Chiron, being discovered at this time in history, reflects issues and themes that are just under the surface of our evolving consciousness. These themes and issues are merely waiting for the catalyst to impel their emergence, when they can then be dealt with.

If I had to ascribe Chiron's rulership to one sign, I would have to say Virgo. Although Mercury is traditionally the ruler of Virgo, it leaves a lot to be desired in terms of representing the complete scope of Virgo. Mercury more rightly rules Gemini. Moreover, Chiron's issues and themes cross the borders of Virgo substantially into other signs, as we have seen. I believe that a more complete planetary ruler of the sign of Virgo has yet to be found. On the other hand, perhaps we need to move beyond the paradigm that attaches a planet, as ruler, to one or two particular signs. In the meantime, Virgo will certainly suffice, particularly at this time in history when old paradigms of Healing are giving way to new ones. In this case, Mercury certainly deserves to be at least the secondary ruler of Virgo.

3 ~ LIFE CYCLES

" . . . life exists at the edge of chaos, moving from chaos into order and back again in a perpetual exploration of emergent order."

-Brian Goodwin, biologist.[58]

Cycles of Spirituality and Healing

Due to Chiron's elliptical orbit, its influence waxes and wanes over time, creating cycles of more or less intensity and involvement in spiritual and psychological matters pertaining to issues of Wounding and Healing. If we combine this with the ever-changing tapestry of aspects with other planets, we get rich and complex patterns of rising and falling impetus to pursue and deal with these issues.

The most basic pattern is created from Chiron's own aspects to its position in peoples' natal charts. *(See **GRAPH 1—CHIRON CYCLE, p. 576**)* The important life transits are:

* Chiron sextile natal Chiron
* Chiron square natal Chiron
* Chiron trine natal Chiron
* Chiron quincunx natal Chiron
* Chiron opposition natal Chiron (half-Return)
* Chiron quincunx (2nd) natal Chiron
* Chiron trine (2nd) natal Chiron
* Chiron square (2nd) natal Chiron

---

[58] Goodwin, Brian. *How the Leopard Changed its Spots – the Evolution of Complexity.* Charles Scribner's Sons, New York, 1994, p. 182.

* Chiron sextile (2nd) natal Chiron
* Chiron Return

Some of these transits are more important and more influential than others are. We will be discussing these transits as a cycle in each of our lives, shortly. However, let's look at ***GRAPH 2 – CHIRON CYCLE MAJOR ASPECTS (HISTORICAL)***, *p.577.* Here we see the way in which the number of these Chiron/natal Chiron transits, taken collectively, waxes and wanes over time, making some years more intense in terms of the outward manifestation of issues pertaining to Wounding and Healing. For the purposes of the graph, we have taken only the squares, trines, opposition and Returns as these are the most influential.

The points of greatest intensity occur when Chiron is in Libra (1945, 1996, 2047) and the least intensity when it is in Aries (1970–71, 2021–22). This may seem counter-intuitive to our previous assertions inasmuch as we said that Aries represents the most disconnected, fragmented, isolated and dissipated time of our journey of consciousness. However, if we think about it, we will see that the times of our greatest Darkness *birth* the impulse to move towards the Light, i.e. to move towards Healing. During Arian times, Chironically speaking, we are the most impelled to seek meaning and connection in our lives because we perceive these to be missing. Hence, the escalation over the ensuing 25 years of interest and pursuit in spiritual and Healing matters.

The peak of intensity, occurring during Libran times, Chironically speaking, represents the most awakened time, full of planetary connections and, hence, consciousness of these matters. It is not an easy time. However, in retrospect, it is a most rewarding time in terms of Healing and the evolution of consciousness.

At these peaks, closer to Sun consciousness, we are assaulted by the brilliance of the Light. *Reacting* to our *unpreparedness* or *acting* out of our *preparedness*, we either back away from the Light, seeking the solace and solitude of the Arian realms once more, or we embrace the Light and move more towards Sun consciousness. The analogy of this cycle to our cycles of incarnations is striking. We will explore this in Book Three. Suffice to say, *when we are in Darkness, we seek the Light and when we are in the Light, if too bright, we seek the Darkness.* This represents the self-regulating mechanism of our evolution of consciousness. It is the driving force behind the cosmogonic cycles of the cosmos.

Historically, the collective peaks of Chiron-natal-aspect-intensity in this century were in 1945, and in 1996. In a sense, the Light became too bright in the late 1930s and early 1940s. Compounding this was the effect of Saturn squaring Chiron during the years between 1935 and 1952. This made dealing with our Wounds and unresolved issues a Painful and tedious task. We were not necessarily ready for this task. WWII was a manifestation of our reaction to the extreme illumination of our Woundedness. Further compounding this situation was the aforementioned *solar maximum* of 1946. The manifestation of our effort to retreat from the Light and from our exposed Wounds and unresolved issues came in the form of the post-war years. These were times when we focused more on our material comfort and its associated structures; i.e. it was a time of economic growth and family values – the 'baby-boomer' times.

The year 1996 represented perhaps the saturation point of the new-age movement, i.e. when people had had enough of a 'good thing' and were getting sick of hearing the same ideas dished up in the same way. The new-age movement will become increasingly integrated into the establishment, more materialistic and more economically oriented. This must occur if it is to survive. *It will become part of the new establishment. It will become the new expression of Saturn.*

After a time, as we approach the next trough in 2021–22, it will become necessary to slough off the dead forms of what was originally the new-age movement, to break down the now stagnant patterns of this particular Saturn expression. From here a new cycle of Healing and evolution of consciousness will begin. It will be the same themes as the 1960s and the 20th century new-age beginnings, but in different forms more appropriate to the times. The next peak of activity from these new beginnings will occur around 2047.

The last trough of influence was in 1970–71, at the end of the 1960s. In a sense, the 1960s represented the force that turned the cycle back towards the Light. We had, over the ensuing time from WWII, become increasingly attached to our material world and less connected to spiritual concerns. As this sense of disconnection from Spirit grew, we began to express it outwardly. The result was the 1960s. The obvious growth of the new-age and ecology movements from the early 1970s onwards mirrors the intensifying of the Chiron aspects until 1996. The next trough occurs in 2021–22. In the meantime, we are moving into a time of technological acceleration. We are moving into a time of accelerated mastery of the material world through science, technology and most importantly, communications. The Internet is just one of these manifestations, having taken off in a big way in the last few years.

Having said all this, it is necessary to realize that Chiron's aspects to other planets, in particular the outer planets, adds to or subtracts from this basic Chiron Cycle. The intensity of the 1945 peak was accentuated by the Saturn/Chiron squares during this time, by the 1941 Chiron/Pluto conjunction and by the 1946 solar maximum. The intensity of the 1960s, during a trough time, was accentuated by the intense aspects of Chiron to Pluto, Uranus and Saturn, not to mention the ongoing oppositions of Uranus to Chiron over a period of an unprecedented thirty-seven years. We have discussed these aspects already and seen how they contributed to the intensity of Chironic themes and issues during this time, culminating in the discovery of Chiron.

Similarly, the Libra to Aries retreat of Chiron in this present cycle, from 1996, was accentuated by the Chiron/Pluto conjunction of late 1999.

These other planetary aspects to Chiron are part of the rich tapestry we mentioned at the start of this section. These aspects form the colors, hues and tints of the basic Chiron Cycle, as well as determining the intensity at any given part of that cycle.

Perihelion, Perigee and Aphelion

Another aspect that we need to be aware of from our earthly perspective in the solar system is the times when Chiron is closer or farther away from the Earth and the Sun. This is particularly relevant in Chiron's case due to its highly elliptical cometary orbit. This necessarily affects the intensity of its influence upon us. The *perihelion* of Chiron is the point at which it is the closest to the Sun in its orbit.[59] The *perihelion opposition* or *perigee* of Chiron to the Earth is its closest point to the Earth in its orbit. The *aphelion* of Chiron is its point of greatest distance to the Sun in its orbit.[60]

Obviously, the closer to the Earth a planetary body is, the greater its influence upon us. More than this, however, the closer a *cometary* body like Chiron is to the Sun, the more *active* it becomes as frozen material on its surface volatilizes into the gases that surround the comet like a halo.

Chiron's last perihelion was at the peak of the Chiron/natal Chiron aspect cycle aforementioned, i.e. on the February 14, 1996 at 14 Libra 04. Its last perigee (or perihelion opposition), the point where Chiron is at its closest point to the Earth, was on April 1, 1996 at 11 Libra 07. Interestingly, it was in August of the same year that it was announced that a meteorite, having its origins on Mars, may have contained evidence of extraterrestrial life. This is interesting when we consider it in the light of what we have explored previously in relation to the Space Race.

The fact that the perihelion and perigee correspond to the fastest moving part of Chiron's cycle and that they occur in Libra emphasizes the importance of the signs of Libra (perihelion sign) and Aries (aphelion sign).

Zane Stein[61] points out that the Sabian Symbol[62] for this last perihelion at 14 Libra 04 was: "A stack of machinery parts; all are new and all circular. Perfect and effortless participation in the universal order."[63] This certainly corresponds to our view of Chiron at its peak in Libra and to the symbolism of Libra according to the Mysteries. The essence of Sun-ruled Libra in the zodiac of the Mysteries is the realization of perfect order, perfect balance, supreme consciousness, where all seemingly-

---

[59] Approximately 8.46 AU from the Sun.

[60] Approximately 18.94AU from the Sun.

[61] Astrologer who was one of the early pioneers of Chiron astrology.

[62] From Dane Rudhyar's "The Astrology of Personality". The Sabian Symbols were developed by Marc Edmund Jones and a clairvoyant friend, Elsie Wheeler, in the late 1920s.

[63] Paraphrased from Zane Stein's website at http://www.geocities.com/SoHo/7969/page3.htm.

disparate and disjointed factors are seen to be a part of a larger divinely-designed Plan of Creation. When perfection is seen and Loved, we no longer resist or oppose the Plan and we participate in it from a place of Love and Gratitude rather than from fear and/or guilt.

The symbol of the circle in this Sabian Symbol also implies the divine perfection, unaffected by the see-sawing of our illusions and their associated lopsided emotions and perceptions. The shapes of the orbits of the planets reflect greater or lesser alignment with the balanced consciousness of the Sun. As we have said, the more elliptical the orbit, the more emotionally charged are the issues of a given planetary body. More on this in Books Two and Three.

The perigee, at 11 Libra 07, "marking Chiron's most intense seeding of lessons to Humanity here on Earth", says Zane Stein, is given the Sabian Symbol: "Miners are emerging from a deep well into the sunlight. Depth of participation in the world's work. Whole-souled giving of self to service; or inability to bring self to effort."[64] Again, this certainly corresponds to Chiron's musings in relation to our Healing and evolution of consciousness. By balancing our consciousness, unifying it and bringing dualistic emotions into unified Love, we unveil the Gift of our Divine Design. We unveil our special Service to the world. This Service encapsulates the one thing we would most Love to do with our lives. At this point, we have said, human and Divine Will become One.

If, however, we are not ready for the intensity of the Light, we retreat and begin a new cycle of descent into Darkness and Return to Light, i.e. another *cosmogonic cycle.* (More on this in Book Three). The intensity of the Light, in terms of Chiron's issues of Wounding and Wounds, becomes unbearable if we are not yet ready to face the Darknesses (Wounds) within us. The Pain of having our Wounds revealed, brought to the surface and having then to deal with them becomes too much. Even in our Healing and evolution of consciousness, we waver. We tic-tock between times when we wish to consciously pursue our Healing and times when we wish to know nothing about it whatsoever. This cyclic tic-tocking applies equally to individuals, groups and Humanity taken as a whole.

Taking all of the above into consideration, it follows that where

[64] Ibid.

Chiron was in its cycle when we were born is vitally important and must be considered in the chart reading process. If Chiron was at or near perigee, perihelion or apogee, this has certain ramifications. In addition, the *direction* of its travel towards or away from the Sun and/or Earth will be important to consider, too. From mid-Aries through to mid-Libra, Chiron is approaching us, whereas from mid-Libra to mid-Aries it is receding from us. The Aries to Libra journey of approach represents our growth from being self-centeredly isolated to acknowledging and embracing the 'other', i.e. the mirror reflection of ourselves in others and in the outside world. The receding journey from Libra to Aries represents our widening of consciousness to include more of the Universe, but, paradoxically, feeling increasingly isolated, impersonal, disconnected and alone.

Another ramification of Chiron's movement towards and away from us arises from its corresponding movement towards and away from Saturn and Uranus on either side of the main part of Chiron's orbit. As Chiron approaches us in its cycle, it is also approaching Saturn. As our Wounds become increasingly illuminated and therefore difficult to deal with, we tend to move into more conservative Saturnian values. In other words, we seek solace and safety in the known, in the material, in the tangible and in 'safe' structures.

Conversely, as Chiron moves away from us in its cycle, it is also approaching Uranus. As our Wounds become more distant, our sense of disconnection and aloneness increases, particularly as Chiron moves through Aquarius. As it approaches Uranus, our sense of connection to the Earth recedes and we tend to move more towards revolutionary values and anarchistic ideals. In short, we react to our sense of isolation by shaking the place up, trying anything and everything to break out our exiled consciousness.

This pattern can be seen in the conservatism of the 1940s and in the radical nature of the 1960s. The cyclic swinging from one extreme to the other is a feature of our consciousness, collectively and individually. Interestingly, those born up to seven years or so *before* perigee/perihelion or apogee, i.e. before their first Saturn/natal Saturn square, are blessed to experience Chiron in both directions in their early life.

This gives them a chance to find a balance between the polarized elements in their lives, represented by Saturn and Uranus.

Now let's widen our exploration of Chiron's eccentric orbit and discuss the Chiron Cycle . . .

The Chiron Cycle

The Chiron Cycle itself is the cycle and its sub-cycles derived from Chiron's elliptical orbit and ensuing uneven transit through the signs of the zodiac. These two factors contribute to the fact that each of us, depending on when we were born, will experience Chiron's transits to our natal Chiron at different times in our lives. We have outlined these major lifetime transits in the section above entitled, "Cycles of Spirituality and Healing". Before we examine each of these transits in detail, let's look at the cycle as a whole. *(See **GRAPH 1—CHIRON CYCLE**, p. 576.)*

This graph outlines the Chiron Cycle for those born between the years of 1930 and the end of 1999. It traces the age at which each of these major transits occurs in a given lifetime, depending on the birth year. As we can see, the only transit that occurs at roughly the same age, regardless of birth year, is the Chiron Return at around the age of 50–51. Our previously examined graph (Graph 2, showing that 1996, for example, was, collectively, a year of maximum Chiron/natal Chiron transits for people born across a wide range of years) was derived from this first graph.

We might also notice that those *born* around 1945 and again around 1996 have the greatest spread in the intervening times between these major transits. The first major transit occurs as early as 5 years old for some born between 1941–44 and 1991–94.

On the other hand, those born around 1970–71 have the least time between transits with the 1st square not beginning for most people born between 1953–69 until after the age of 20.

These two extremes must necessarily have significance not only for the individuals born in these years, but also for the *generations* born in these years, taken as a whole. From one point of view, the later we experience the first major transit, i.e. the 1st square, the more we tend to feel a sense of disconnectedness, isolation, fragmentedness, Woundedness and aloneness. This is particularly so, considering we have come all the way through puberty into adulthood without having had Chiron's aid. Without this aid, there is little help in awakening a path of Healing and in addressing our Wounds as expressed through the natal placement of Chiron in our charts. Furthermore, as it turns out, those of us born with a late 1st square are part of the latter stage of the outward sweep of Chiron towards its Arian aphelion. This intensifies the feeling of being abandoned by the Universe and being left in the Darkness of our own Wounds.

From this is birthed the need for a return to a sense of connection to the Universe, a need for Healing, a need for a way of bringing our fragmented consciousness into a greater unity and wholeness. The people born during these years were the people that birthed the new-age movement and all its associated offshoots. Such offshoots included alternative medicine, ecology, a return to the ways and beliefs of indigenous races and the resurgence of interest in spiritual matters. They were the people who aided the discovery of Chiron and contributed to the manifestation of Chiron's messages and musings, even if they themselves were personally unaware of Chiron.

Conversely, those born between 1970 and 1996, will have an ever-*decreasing* interest in the so-called new-age movement and its offshoots and in Chironic matters as Chiron approached its perihelion and perigee in 1996. The generation of my children, for example, all born in the 1980s, is not the least bit interested in in-depth pursuit of spiritual or Healing matters, despite the fact that I can see the workings of Chiron in their lives. They simply are not consciously aware of these workings nor are they interested in finding out about them. This is not to say that these years did not produce some spiritual people. They certainly did. They just operate and express their spirituality in more practical and materially-oriented ways. It is just that the specific issues of Wounding and Healing are not high on their agendas. They are, in a sense, unable to understand why my generation is so concerned with the things that we are concerned with and spend so much time in our lives trying to understand these matters and issues.

In addition, they have the 'answers' ready-made for them by my generation and so do not feel the need to question these areas of life. The other side of this is the fact that they will have only ready-made 'answers' for their own children and not self-experienced truths. Their children will feel unfulfilled by this and will seek their own answers to their spiritual questions, as so the cycle goes on . . .

In short, *those born between 1971 and 1996 represent the balance to the views, ideals and concerns of those born between 1945 and 1970.* They are the two halves of the cycle. We have said that Humanity seesaws between interest in spiritual matters and interest in material matters. This is another example of this universal cycle. Having said this, however, *within society, all stages of the cycle are represented at every point in time.* It is just that, at certain times, our *conscious* focus, collectively speaking, is more towards one pole than the other. At other times, it is the reverse. At certain times, we *express* one side and at other times, we express the other. The psychology behind this interesting observation and its Chironic connection is explored in depth in Book Two.

The Chiron Cycle can show us which side of the Spirit/Matter duality will be expressed and which will be repressed at any given point in time. At the beginning of this new century, we are currently moving *away* from the peak of an *expression* of the spiritual side of our lives (1996) and *towards* an expression of the material side (2021–22). This is the case, despite what the new-agers would like to believe.

However, there *are* larger cycles, of which the Chiron Cycle is but a sub-cycle. Uranus, Neptune and Pluto all represent larger cycles, but pertaining to focal points of key issues somewhat different from Chiron's.

The most striking larger cycle that pertains to our Chironic study was mentioned previously. This cycle is the larger cycle of expression and repression of the spiritual/material paradox. If we put the beginning of this larger cycle at around the Age of Enlightenment or Age of Reason, around the time of Newton, then we are not much more than halfway through this cycle. The Age of Reason was a return to the scientific, mechanistic, material view of the world. In the 1900s, we saw the beginning of a return to the mystical, animistic, spiritual view of the world. In addition, this return was amplified by the approaching peak of the 500-year solar cycle aforementioned. Therefore, we can conjecture that the *expression* of the latter view will continue for some hundreds of years into the future before being subdued by the former view again.

However, within this major cycle, the shorter Chiron Cycle will cause an ebbing and flowing of emphasis on, and outward expression of, the mystical, animistic, spiritual view of the world *within* the larger cycle for the next several hundred years.

Interestingly, the current outward-journeying phase of the Chiron Cycle will see a backlash against the trend in theoretical physics, itself the 'spiritual' end of the material science, and its pseudo-religious assertions of connections and correlations to metaphysics and spirituality. This phase of the cycle will demand concrete proof and will look more towards the practical applications of the strange and unpredictable theories of quantum physics rather than conjectures about finding "God particles" and the like. The trend back towards the concrete and the materially verifiable was given quite a boost by the Taurean current, manifesting in early May 2000. At this time, six planets lined up in Taurus, many of them quincunxing a loose conjunction of Chiron and Pluto. To quote astrologer, Roderick Kidston:

> "For several centuries theoretical physics has been the king pin, but during this Taurus mini-epoch, biology and genetics will probably overthrow, at least for a time, the old monarch. After all, what use has nitty-gritty biochemistry for the pseudo-religious ravings of the new physics, which sound more like mystic mumblings than real, hard science?!"[65]

We can certainly see the evidence of a swing away from the new-age ideals of the last 30 years. Having said this, however, we will explore, in depth, the connections between the concrete physics of light and the metaphysical intimations of Spirit in Book Three! I guess I am beginning to show my age!

Another indicator of the trend of the out-going phase of the Chiron Cycle was, strangely enough, the billion-dollar merger of Internet gi-

---

[65] *WellBeing Magazine Astrology Guide 2000.* Wellspring Publishers, North Sydney, Australia, 2000, article entitled, "Year 2000", p.10.

ant, AOL and media giant, Time Warner. This merger was first proposed shortly into the new century in a lead-up to the Taurean current of the following months. This was one of the biggest mergers in history and had intense effects on markets around the globe. Up until this time, Internet and IT (information technology) companies had been floating shares on the stock market and producing market capitalization absurdly more than the companies' real dollar values. Some of these companies had never turned a profit and yet were worth millions of dollars on paper. This side of business was, up until this merger, *intangible* and driven by hype, optimism, the promise of the future and an infatuation with technology. Once a large Internet or IT company like AOL had teamed up with a *tangible* company like Time Warner, based on real customers, real products, real services, real sales and real profits, it brought the otherwise intangible world of IT to earth. This set the trend for the next phase of Information Age. We can speculate that, in what we formerly called the "new-age" arena, there will be a similar process, bringing otherwise intangible and ephemeral ideas and practices to earth in practical and materially-viable ways.

Furthermore, the demand for tangibility and hard-cash accountability manifested very clearly leading up to and during the Taurean alignment of May 2000 and in the 'bear' markets of the year 2000. Led by Wall Street, this trend particularly affected the technology sector worldwide, in which some technology stocks lost as much as 95% of their value and many simply hit the wall. Technology stocks, which had ridden an extended and inflated wave of speculation and hype, were pruned mercilessly, leaving only those that were able to prove themselves in terms of down-to-earth financial strategies and tangible earnings and assets. Nonetheless, these technology survivors will form the solid foundations for the next phase of the Information Age.

All in all, these movements in the finance sector are directly analogous to evolution's requirement that spirituality be based upon tangibility. It is all part of the ultimate meeting of science and Spirit, the secular and the sacred, the terrestrial and the celestial, the tangible and the intangible, the material and the spiritual.

Lastly, as we have intimated previously, major aspects of the outer planets to Chiron will also contribute to the intensity of the ebbs and flows of the Chiron Cycle or lack thereof. The intensity of such aspects between 1952 and 1989 represents a good case in point. We will look more closely at this topic in Chapter 10 when we explore Chiron and the new millennium.

Phases of the Chiron Cycle

Let's now look at each of the major Chiron/natal Chiron transits. Taken together, these transits trace the ebbing and flowing of our impulse to either delve into our Wounds and unresolved issues or not. It traces times when our Wounds and issues are thrust to the fore, demanding that we look at them and deal with them to the best of our ability at the time. Our degree of preparedness and willingness to do this necessarily varies from person to person and at different times in our lives. Furthermore, due to our general level of evolution, *opacity* to planetary influences may prevent us from becoming aware of the influences of Chiron at these times. We will discuss this point a little later. With this last point in mind, here are the influences and potentials for each of the Chiron transits of our lives . . .

Natal Position

Although not strictly speaking a transit, the natal position of Chiron determines the sensitive point in the natal chart with respect to later transits; it also outlines the specific Wounding, Voids and subsequent Healing paths and Values for a person. It represents what we feel is the most missing in our lives. This, in turn, determines what we seek in life, who we relate to or not, the paths we walk, things that we will attract or repel and the destiny we will meet.

The natal position of Chiron is the backdrop against which the drama of subsequent Chiron/natal Chiron transits will take place.

The 1st Sextile

This transit manifests in a relatively unconscious way. The period in which it can occur ranges from 3 to about 16 years old. In short, in represents the appearance in our lives of opportunities and connections to Healing possibilities. Although we are primarily unconscious to the nature of our Woundedness and the possibilities that this transit brings, it is like a window opened upon our Woundedness that offers a potential path of Healing. It may be a person who comes into our lives. It may be the discovery of an interest, representing a future career path. It may be a place of solace discovered. It is often accompanied by an awakening of creativity, which reflects, unconsciously, our inner secrets. If it occurs later, say in the early teens, it can be an awakening to the world, its mysteries, its joys and its sorrows. This was certainly the case for me at the age of 15–16.

Because of the early nature of this transit for some, it can be difficult to pinpoint the exact events and circumstances to which it corresponds. What we can say, though, with relative certainty, is that the later it occurs, the more a sense of Woundedness mounts within us, impelling us to seek a Healing and/or spiritual path. This, again, is the nature of the Chiron cycle, aforementioned.

In many ways, the 1st sextile transit of Chiron/natal Chiron sets the path of Healing and evolution of consciousness that we will subsequently follow, albeit unconsciously until the Chiron/natal Chiron opposition. Our Values that arise from our Voids (Wounds) will be expressed, manifested and cemented during this transit. This is a time of the outward manifestation of our Divine Design, although still embryonic and often difficult to see at the time.

The 1st Square

The 1st Chiron-square-natal Chiron represents the time in our lives when we are first made *conscious* of our specific Woundedness. This transit can occur as early as age 5 and as late as 23. Although we are made conscious of our Woundedness during this time, we are, for the most part, unable to deal with it, grasp its deeper meaning or soothe its effect upon us. It is, in a sense, a reaffirmation and deeper etching of our original Wounds. These Wounds subsequently drive us on the evolutionary path towards our ultimate Healing and towards the expression

45-LASS

and manifestation of our Divine Design. The deeper the Wounds (Voids), the greater the Gifts (Values). Core Wounds create core Values.

During this time, our Woundedness, the nature of which is set out by Chiron's sign and house placement at our birth and its aspects to other planets, surfaces. That which we feel to be missing in our lives is brought into Painful awareness. We may be missing a sense of Connectedness or a feeling of Love. We may have a deep need for security. We may have lost our Faith or Trust. We may have a deep need for companionship, and so on and so forth.

Whatever it may be, the first Chiron/natal Chiron square represents an *impasse* of Healing, but an illumination of our inner Woundedness, a glimpse at our inner fragmentation and, at times, a glimpse at our Dark side. Akin to Saturn, this square impels us to make an inner resolve, although we cannot carry out our resolve until the ensuing period, after the transit has finished. The resolve is invariably in the nature of a Healing wish, whatever the form may take, even if the native does not equate this inner resolve with Healing at all.

The 1st Trine

The 1st Chiron/natal Chiron trine represents a time when we are highly likely to meet opportunities for Healing and evolution of consciousness to a degree not previously encountered. We may meet teachers, spiritual or otherwise. We may encounter Healers, whatever the modality. We may simply be inspired at the time to pursue Healing and/or spiritual matters. It is a time when answers seem to be forthcoming and pathways open that allow us to resolve some of our issues and Heal some of our Woundedness. It can be either externally engineered, so to speak, or internally pursued. This transit can occur as early as age 7. Obviously, the earlier the transit occurs, the more likely it is to be externally engineered rather than the latter case.

The exact nature of these opportunities will be mirrored in the transiting planets to Chiron during this time, as well as in its sign and house placement at the time.

For example, from my own experience, I was inspired during the 1st trine to seek the source of a teaching that I had studied in books for the previous 5 years. This search led me to meet my first consciously-acknowledged spiritual teacher. Interestingly, it was during the 2nd Chiron/natal Chiron trine that I met my next most influential spiritual teacher and mentor, Dr. Demartini, in 1996.

It is the same for many of the persons whom I have worked with astrologically. The 1st trine is a time when we resonate to those people, things, situations and places that we sense will offer us Healing possibilities, even if we do not call it "Healing" as such.

It can also be a time when we begin to sense with greater clarity what we may be here to do. That is, we may begin to sense our Divine Design, even if we cannot rightly put it into words at the time. This comes much later, closer to the 2nd Chiron/natal Chiron trine.

The 1st Quincunx

This transit can occur as early as age 10. It represents a time of questions, reassessments, new perspectives and assimilation of the events, circumstances and outcomes of the previous trine transit. It can be a perplexing time, but a time that impels us to gain greater clarity, to come to a new level of consciousness about the Wounds and unresolved issues that plague us. It can be a time of shedding old skins and, in this way, it is akin to Pluto in its effect, albeit far more diluted.

During this time, it is as though we are working our way through an obstacle course, complete with puzzles we must solve and decisions we must make about our next steps.

In addition, during this time, we may recognize allies in those people, things, events and situations that we previously viewed as our enemies. In other words, we may begin to see the blessings in the crises, i.e. the Gifts in the Wounds, a new level of consciousness thus emerging.

The Opposition

Except for the Chiron Return, the Chiron/natal Chiron opposition (or half-Return) is by far the most important and influential of the transits of the Chiron Cycle. It can occur as early as age 13 and as late as 37.

This transiting opposition represents the fulcrum point of our potential journey of Healing and evolution of consciousness. There are about ten years on either side of the transit when we must consciously awaken to our Woundedness, whatever the form it takes, and take positive steps towards Healing and the evolution of our consciousness. If we do, we are awakened, to a greater or lesser degree, to the answers to the four basic questions of existence, i.e. "Where do we come from, where are we going, who are we and why are we here?" In short, our Divine Design becomes clearer.

The opposition transit itself is a time of intense illumination of our Wounds, blockages and unresolved issues. Unlike the square transits, however, we are certainly able to take positive steps during this time towards the Healing of those Wounds and the resolution of those issues. It is perhaps the most acute and most active time of our conscious journey of Healing and evolution of consciousness. We could liken it to the birth pangs of Spirit.

Anything that stands in the way of our integration, our awakening and the activation of our Divine Design can surface, sometimes in dramatic and cathartic ways. The opposition is akin to Uranus inasmuch as it shines a bright light into the Darkness of our unawakened consciousness. It impels us to seek a higher understanding and synthesis of the otherwise dualistic illusions and lopsided perceptions of our lower nature. Beyond our contradictions, paradoxes and conflicts there is a hidden unity, concordance and metadox (union of opposites). The Healing journey is awakening to a larger picture, seeing the connections and sensing the perfection and 'rightness' of those things, people and events that previously we judged negatively. In short, it is a process of seeing the blessings in the crises and of discovering the Gifts in the Wounds.

If we do not attend to our Woundedness or seek resolution of our issues during the ten or so years either side of the fulcrum point of this transit, we enter a 'mid-life crisis'. During this crisis, the meaning of our lives becomes more distant and seemingly unattainable.

This mid-life crisis is linked with the Uranus/natal Uranus opposition (half-Return), occurring roughly between the ages of 38 and 44.

This represents a time when the work we have done or not done towards our potential Healing and evolution of consciousness is 'paid' or not 'paid'. If we have done the work, Uranus can connect us to a higher state of consciousness, linking us with the affairs and consciousness of the outer planets. The balancing and integration of our consciousness, corresponding to the alignment of our chakras, makes it possible for this Uranian activation to take place. Chiron's role in the chakra energy system of our Body/Mind is explored in Book Two.

If, on the other hand, we have not done the work of Healing and evolution of consciousness before this Uranian transit, we experience a withdrawal from this potential Contact and, hence, a 'mid-life crisis'. More on this in a moment . . .

The 2nd Quincunx

The 2nd Chiron/natal Chiron quincunx, similar to the 1st, represents a time of assimilation, reassessment and redefinition of the issues brought up by the previous transit – in this case, the opposition transit. It is a time when we are impelled to try to make sense of our journey of Healing and evolution of consciousness up to the present and to come to a more integrated understanding of it all.

Conclusions we may have come to during the preceding Chiron/natal Chiron opposition may now seem incomplete or not totally satisfactory. Something seems to be still out of place but we cannot tell what it is. We are simply being encouraged by this quincunx transit to come to a higher understanding of all that we have been through. We are being encouraged to see more of the big picture, to connect more of the dots, so to speak.

During this time, the odd pieces that do not appear to fit the big picture will plague us, irritate us and generally intrude upon our peace of mind. We may feel, at times, like a secretary trying to file a backlog of paperwork in a disorganized filing cabinet. Nonetheless, it is a time that can be very fruitful if we pursue each disparate piece of the puzzle with a view to understanding its unique place as well as its part in the larger scheme. Ultimately, everything in our lives is connected to this larger scheme. The Healing journey is discovering how each thing fits and interrelates with all others.

The 2nd Trine

The 2nd Chiron/natal Chiron trine, similar to the 1st, is a time when our vibratory frequency is aligned to people, places, things and circumstances that offer great possibilities for our potential Healing and evolution of consciousness. However, during this second trine, we are more likely to recognize these opportunities and possibilities more quickly and to consciously pursue them. We are clearer about ourselves and our path, presuming we have done sufficient work on ourselves up until this time.

In a sense, this transit represents an affirmation of our path, our purpose, our vision and inspiration. It is a time when many things will come together in our understanding, naturally and consciously. It can be a time of deep Healing, resolution and Connection. This transit, like the trine aspect in general, resonates to Neptune and, as such, awakens us to the possibility and actual experience of Unconditional Love that is the final result of all Healing.

Interestingly, this transit can occur *after* or *during* the Uranus/natal Uranus opposition, aforementioned, as well as before it. There is a definite similarity between the two transits inasmuch as they both bring together the results of all previous work we have done on our Healing and evolution of consciousness. The Uranus transit, however, tends to be more upsetting – more dramatic and *revolutionary.* The 2nd Chiron trine is more harmonious and less confronting, although still *revelationary* in its effect.

If this Chiron transit *precedes* the Uranus/natal Uranus opposition, its acts as a prelude, i.e. a taste of things to come. If the two transits take place *simultaneously*, one adds to the other, the overall effect amplified. If the Chiron transit occurs *after* the Uranus transit, then it acts as kind of a postlude, affirming and finalizing the effects of the Uranus transit.

The 2nd Square

The 2nd Chiron/natal Chiron square, like the preceding trine, can occur before, during or after the Uranus/natal Uranus opposition. This timing will determine the specific nature of its effect.

In general, however, this transiting square tends to bring to the fore any of our unHealed and/or unresolved Wounds and issues. Our ability to deal with these at the time is generally limited again, but will depend again on the nature of accompanying transits and aspects, such as the aforementioned Uranus half-Return. In this way, this transiting square, like the first Chiron/natal Chiron square, is aligned with the energy of Saturn.

If we have done little in the way of attending to our Healing and evolution of consciousness, this square will bring up all kinds of regrets, resentments, painful memories and core Wounds. It is often accompanied by an inexplicable sense of loss and a feeling of the meaninglessness of our lives. We may feel that if we could but turn back time, things might be different. Again, this represents a kind of mid-life crisis. Chiron's answer to this is to learn to Love things just as they are and see the benefits, blessings, lessons and Gifts in them, despite the pain and suffering they seemed to have caused at the time.

If, on the other hand, we have attended to our Healing and evolution of consciousness, this transit will still bring up regrets and painful memories. However, our ability and willingness to deal with these effects as they come up is evident during this time. It is as though we are being given a chance to go deeper into the Healing process, to finalize any loose ends, to resolve any regrets, painful memories and continuing issues.

If this transiting square occurs *after* the Uranus opposition, we are generally better equipped to deal with whatever comes up, providing we have done sufficient work in the past. If this square occurs *before* the Uranus opposition, it is generally more difficult and represents a time when we are being given a chance to 'clean up our act' in preparation for the activating effect of the Uranus transit. If this Chiron square occurs *simultaneously* with the Uranus opposition, then the depth, intensity and acuteness of the Healing journey are increased manifold, but so, too, is the potential Healing result.

The 2nd Sextile

The 2nd Chiron/natal Chiron sextile, like the 1st sextile, represents opportunities and connections to possibilities for Healing and the evolution of consciousness. Unlike the 1st sextile, however, we are more conscious and can recognize these potential pathways better.

It is a time, too, when there can be an increase in creativity, which is simultaneously one of the *keys* to Healing and one of the *results* of Healing. There can be fruitful meetings, events and journeys during this time, i.e. an exchange of Healing energies between us and people, places and things. This transit, like the sextile aspect in general, is akin to Mercury in its influence.

The Return

The Chiron Return, when Chiron has completed a full cycle of the zodiac and Returned to its natal position in our charts, is the culmination of the journey of Healing and the evolution of consciousness up to the age of 50–51.

Its effect will lie somewhere between two extremes, depending on our level of attention and conscious work on the themes of Healing and evolution of consciousness in our lives to date. In all cases, our original Wounds and their attendant issues will surface again. Whether we respond with Love or with fear, guilt, remorse, anger and resentment will depend on our previous work.

If we have not attended to our Wounds and issues during our lives and have not worked towards Healing and higher consciousness, ultimately aspiring to Unconditional Love, we will be thrust back into the thicket of our Woundedness. In this case, our core Wounds and issues will surface again, demanding attention, Healing and resolution. In a sense, we are required to repeat a grade of school. However, the likelihood of truly beginning in-depth work on our subsequent Healing and evolution of consciousness definitely diminishes with time. This is due to our age, to the general level of crystallization of our personality and to associated emotional habits, masks, protective mechanisms and ingrained escape routes. This is not to say that it is impossible. It simply becomes more difficult over time and we become less inclined to bother with it.

In this case, the Chiron Return can be, paradoxically, a time that we hardly notice due to the success of our long-standing patterns of avoidance and evasion. Conversely, it can be a time of monumental regret. The Chiron Return can open the Pandora's Box of our core Wounds and long-standing unresolved issues. Unable to deal with or answer the tortured callings that arise from our fragmented consciousness, we go into crisis or, alternatively, even deeper into retreat. Only in the final moments of death, maybe many years later, will we have an opportunity to feel Healing and sense the Truth of the Love around us and in us. It is only then that the stranglehold of our personality mechanisms finally relaxes with the weakening of our physical vehicle. I venture to suggest that, if you are reading this book and have gotten this far in it, you will not have to fear the aforementioned scenario!

If, however, we have attended, to a greater or lesser degree, to our Wounds and issues during our lives, the best we can look forward to is a deep sense of completion and peace during this transit. Although our core Wounds and issues will arise again during this time, our previous work will help us to appreciate and finally Love these Voids that have given us our core Values and, ultimately, our Divine Design.

It will be a time when we can move into another octave of Healing and evolution of consciousness. The cycle repeats, but on another finer energetic level, i.e. another octave. We are given an opportunity to move to deeper levels of Healing and higher levels of consciousness, forever expanding to the limits of the solar system and, simultaneously, approaching the focused consciousness of the Sun. Increasingly, Love is our guide rather than fear and guilt.

In Truth, the effect of the Chiron Return lies somewhere between these two extremes. Some issues – those that we have fully worked through – we will transcend, moving into a new energetic level of Healing and a new cycle. Others we will have to recapitulate in the next Chiron Cycle, striving for more understanding, higher consciousness pertaining to the issues themselves and deeper Healing of old Wounds. Still others will be deeper Wounds only just uncovered by the previous cycle and representing our next lessons.

The Uranus/natal Uranus opposition (half-Return) and the Chiron Return work hand in hand to align us with and connect us to the outer planets of Uranus, Neptune and Pluto. It can be a spiritual coming-of-age if we are ready. If we are not, then the destructive forces of Pluto will accelerate our decay, seeking to spade us in, so to speak, in preparation for our physical death and rebirth in a new cycle, i.e. a new incarnation.

4 ~ CHIRON IN THE CHART

Opacity, Translucence & Transparency to Planetary Influences

Before embarking upon the subject of Chiron in the chart, in the signs, in the houses and in aspect, it is necessary to preface this with a discussion on the varying nature of the effects of planetary influences upon us.

As we mentioned previously, the degree to which we are aware of and are personally influenced by the planets varies from person to person and from lifetime to lifetime. This is one of the reasons that astrology has been so elusive in terms of proving its veracity in controlled studies. The other reason is that studies of this kind do not take into consideration the changing cultural consciousness of Humanity over time and its reflection in the changing *interpretation* of the zodiac signs and houses themselves. Astrology is not just a science, not just an art, but a cultural expression.

Those wishing to prove astrology would do well to look at the influences of the planets themselves and their aspects to each other at any given time, *aside from their sign and house placements.* These angles, whether current, transiting or progressed, and when taking parallels and contra-parallels of declinations and occultations into account, offer the most promise for the proof that astrology really does work. The work of the Magi Society is at the forefront of this particular tack.[66]

In any case, one of the reasons that the personal awareness and effect of planetary influences upon us varies is due to each of our current level of evolution and degree of awakening in a given lifetime.

---

[66] See www.magiastrology.com on the Internet. Magi Society: 847A Second Ave, Suite 245, New York, NY 10017.

When we are extremely unawakened and are early on in our evolutionary journey through the solar system, planetary influences do not tend to affect us in a personal way. However, we do fall, almost entirely, under the mass influence of the planets. We are subjugated to the overall movement of consciousness of the whole of Humanity, i.e. the collective consciousness of Gaia. In this case, free will is almost non-existent, despite our illusions that tell us otherwise. We are buffeted this way and that without our intervention or ability to resist. As Gurdjieff said of the 'ordinary' man, we are but automatons, reacting to external and internal influences, unaware that we are but machines with no free will.

In this case, there is little sense in trying to read the personal horoscope of a person in this stage of their evolution. They will not understand what you are saying nor will you, as a reader, be able to correlate the areas and events of their lives with the planetary positions. One of the signs of such an unreadable horoscope lies in a distinct lack of major aspects, i.e. conjuncts, oppositions, squares, trines, sextiles, quincunxes, parallels, contra-parallels and occultations. This mirrors a lack of focused consciousness, the sign of the earlier stages of a person's evolution.

This first case scenario is what we are calling being *opaque* to planetary influences.

The second case scenario we are calling *translucence* to planetary influences. This is perhaps the most common case, although the degree of *translucence* varies from person to person in a spread throughout Humanity that covers all degrees. By *translucence,* we mean that planetary influences have an effect on our lives *personally* as well as collectively. We are, to a greater or lesser degree, *aware* of these changes of energy and the effects they have on the different areas of our lives. We may not be aware of astrology, as such, but we are certainly aware of the changing energetic landscape of our lives.

It is at this stage of evolution that an astrological reading becomes both possible and meaningful. At this stage we can speak about the real influences of Chiron and about the nature of our Woundedness and unresolved issues. Before this, our words fall on deaf ears. Even the level of *interest* in these themes is dependent upon our stage of Healing and evolution of consciousness.

This book is written primarily for those who fall, for the most part, into the category of being *translucent* to planetary influences.

The third and final stage in our journey of Healing and evolution of consciousness corresponds to being *transparent* to planetary influences. In this case, having worked entirely through our issues, learned our lessons and Healed our Wounds, the influences of the planets no longer affect us either personally or collectively. They simply pass through us, unaffected and not affecting us. In this case, we correspond to the consciousness of the Sun. We are entirely expanded in consciousness beyond the planets to the limits of solar system whilst simultaneously being entirely focused at the Sun. (Again, we will explain this seeming paradox in detail in Book Three when we discuss the physics of time and space in relation to astronomy, psychology and metaphysics.)

At this third and final stage, an astrological reading, such as we prepare these days, again becomes meaningless and inapplicable. A reading for this stage of our evolution would require a new astrology that is based upon the Sun and the surrounding stars, i.e. a *stellar* astrology.

In Truth, we each have areas of our psyche that are *opaque,* some that are *translucent* and some that are *transparent.* If we average these areas, we get a combined *frequency* of resonance that is our unique signature and determines our overall stage of Healing and evolution of consciousness.

If we were entirely *opaque*, we would also not be alive. Conversely, if we were entirely *transparent*, we would not be here on Earth. We would be in another realm of existence, beyond this one. The astrology reading process, and indeed astrology itself in its current form, is the most useful when we are *primarily translucent* to planetary influences. During this stage, we are, to a greater or lesser degree, at least aware that we are here for some reason other than to eat, defecate, breathe, sleep and reproduce, even if we do not know the reason yet. We are on a relatively conscious search for meaning, for connection, for Contact. We have in our consciousness the four age-old spiritual questions, i.e. "Where have we come from, where are we going, who are we and why are we here?"

The search for the answers to these questions *is* the Healing journey.

Fate vs. Destiny

Leading on from the previous section, we can now offer a definition of the difference between *fate* and *destiny* in our lives.

Fate is the action, on a collective scale, of planetary influences upon those parts of our consciousness that are *opaque*, i.e. relatively unawakened. Concerning these unawakened and unresolved issues and Wounds, we fall under mass influence. We are led along by the mass movements of the consciousness of the whole planet, i.e. the consciousness of Gaia. In short, our judgments, charges, lopsided perceptions, illusions, etcetera, send us this way and that way and all the while we are thinking that we have free will. In Truth, it is merely *fate* at work. We are guided unconsciously to where we have the greatest possibility of seeing the nature of our issues.

Destiny, on the other hand, is the action, on a personal scale, of *stellar* influences upon those parts of us that are relatively *translucent* or *transparent,* i.e. relatively awakened in consciousness. This corresponds to the inner state of being able to hear and consciously act upon the vision, inspiration and purpose that lie in our Hearts, to hear the callings of the Soul. This corresponds to Sun-consciousness. We are aware, to a greater or lesser degree, of our Divine Design in relation to these parts of us and can consciously act towards its fulfillment; further, we consciously choose to do so. We are guided, not by the planetary influences we have called *fate,* but by the higher consciousness of the Sun and the stars themselves. We have *certainty* and *resolve* and, as such, are the *masters* of the world around us, rather than being a slave to it. The world cannot stop a person who is in contact with his *destiny.* Destiny shapes the world.

Chiron's Place and Emphasis in the Chart

Chiron, in the natal chart, represents the place of our greatest Void, our deepest Wound. It mirrors that which we feel is the most missing in our lives. It represents the area of our consciousness where we are the most fragmented, scattered, disconnected, isolated, alone, hurt, etcetera.

Conversely, it also sets out the potential path of Healing, of resolution of our issues and of our greatest final Service. It defines the *nature* of that Service that we have called Divine Design, although its *manifestation* will be mirrored more in the North Node, the Sun, the Midheaven and the Ascendant and their attendant aspects.

A sparsely aspected Chiron indicates a relatively low awareness of the nature and manifestation of the native's specific Woundedness and its Healing path. This does not mean to say that the person is unevolved. It simply means that their focus in life is not specifically in the area of Healing, as such. Such people will learn the same lessons, walk the same Healing journey, but unconsciously, without the benefit of conscious knowledge of their Healing and spiritual path.

Conversely, a well-aspected Chiron generally, but not exclusively, indicates a high awareness of the nature and manifestation of the native's specific Woundedness and the Healing path thereof. The questions of existence are more likely to be in the forefront of their consciousness.

Either way, sparsely aspected or well-aspected, Chiron represents the driving force of evolution, causing us to seek Values that are the antithesis of our Voids or Woundedness. So much psychology could be explained if Chiron and our deepest Voids were understood by psychologists. We will explore Chiron and psychology in depth in Book Two.

The power of Chiron must not be underestimated. It is akin to Pluto in its intensity and power to drive us. Chiron's influence and effect may appear hidden at first, but when the key is found, Chiron opens up the rest of the natal chart in a way that was previously impossible. So many of the other features of a person's chart will fall into a bigger picture when we understand Chiron's place and its specific manifestation in that person's life.

Working with Chiron in the Chart

Having said all this, it is necessary to point out again that the natal chart is an integrated and dynamic picture. To take one feature out of the context of the whole and proceed to draw conclusions from it without reference to the whole will bring unsatisfactory results. The job of the astrologer is to integrate all the features and reveal the Plan behind all the pieces, which unifies it into a grand tapestry. The evolved astrologer seeks to reveal the Divine Plan that is already there, rather than trying to make the pieces fit into their own pre-conceived illusions about life and about the person they are reading for.

To work successfully with Chiron in the chart, we must treat both aspects of its message equally, i.e. the Wounds *and* the Gifts, the Wounding process *and* the Healing path. We must also put these into the context of the other major features of the chart. In particular, we must consider the Nodes of the Moon, representing the life's path and direction. We must consider the Sun, representing the *higher* Self and its potential expression and manifestation. In addition, we must consider the Moon itself, representing the *lower* self, its wiles and its emotional mechanisms. We must consider the Moon's role as the *expression vehicle* of our Woundedness.

The astrologer must have a conception of the dualistic nature of the psyche as expressed through the planets. We must consider the planets' light and dark sides, their higher and lower natures, their positive and negative manifestations and, ultimately, the higher synthesis of both sides of a given feature. Otherwise, the reading process becomes lopsided and is colored by the reader's own charges, judgments, Voids, Wounds, lopsided perceptions, illusions and biases, etcetera. A tall order, no doubt, but we can approach this ideal by steps. As we aim to help others, so we are helped. As astrologers, we must not forget that the clients' issues are *our* issues. If we can work through them during the reading, so we can help the client work through them. We get as much out of the reading as the person we read for, if we are open and humble.

Working with Chiron in the chart, it is first necessary to *touch* the Wound, even if it is very softly. From here we can then begin to work with the Wound, beginning to illuminate the paths and possibilities for Healing and beginning to balance some of the issues that relate to the Wounds.

Before this, though, we must try to understand the overall nature of the life's path of the native. For this, we look to the Moon's Nodes. Martin Schulman's book on the Nodes is an excellent reference if we remain cautiously aware that his bias is primarily towards the negative side of the total picture. The Nodes can tell us what we have come into life with – our lessons, our Gifts, our issues, etcetera. It can then tell us in which direction our life is pointed – our potential, the general nature of the life's purpose and the area of life in which it will be played out.

Having thus determined the life's path we then look to the Sun to see in what ways and in which areas we will *express* that life's path. This puts our higher nature into the picture we are building.

We might then look at the aspects the Nodes and Sun make to other planets to see the context in which they operate.

We can then look at Chiron and see how we will be driven along the life's path and its related expression. Looking at the Moon and relating it to Chiron, we will be able to see how our Wounds will express through our lower nature. We will see the evolution of protective patterns and escape mechanisms that help us to deal with our Wounds and issues at an acceptable and bearable rate.

Then we might look at the aspects that Chiron makes to the Nodes, the Sun, the Moon, the Midheaven and the Ascendant and try to interrelate these features of the chart.

From here we may then deal with the others planets, each in turn, looking at their issues separately, in relation to planets other than Chiron and then in relation to Chiron.

Gradually, working with the native, a bigger picture begins to emerge, the pieces falling into place. Gradually we will see how our Wounds drive us perfectly towards the fulfillment of our life's purpose. From a higher perspective, the Wounds, the Healing journey and the Gift of the Divine Design are One. In a well-read chart, there will be no superfluous pieces, no loose ends. Such a complete synthesis is the aim of the dedicated reader. The chart will all make sense, each feature a part of the overall tapestry. When we see our life spread out before us and we see and feel the perfection of this Plan, we connect with the Guiding Hand that lies around and within us at every moment, waiting for us to awaken.

Such a revelation of our lives, made possible by this type of astrological reading, is, in itself, a Healing Gift. Astrology and Healing are natural partners.

We will give a detailed example chart delineation in a later chapter.

5 ~ CHIRON IN THE SIGNS

As we launch into specific definitions of Chiron in the signs, houses and in aspect, we must remember at all times, that the power of any planet, such as Chiron, is, to a great degree, manifested or not in our lives due to the aspects it makes with the other planets. Chiron as a singleton will not be nearly so powerful as, say, Chiron-conjunct-Sun or Chiron-trine-Saturn. In general, a planet without aspects is a planet without context, without definition and, for all practical purposes, without meaning. A singleton will rely on transiting and progressed aspects to give it context and meaning and to activate it in our lives.

Furthermore, the aspects that Chiron makes will modify Chiron's basic influence according to the other planets' influences, their placements and their aspects with yet other planets. The astrological chart is an integrated and dynamic picture.

Still further, each of us has within us, holographically, *all* manifestations of *every* planet in *every* sign, in *every* house and in *every* aspect. This is perhaps the hardest statement to comprehend, but is the ultimate basis of the great Truth of astrology at its most esoteric. The aspects of a planet that we manifest and that show up in the astrological chart of a given lifetime are merely the ones that we tend to *express* in this lifetime, tempered or intensified by its aspects to other planets.

It is for the aforementioned reasons that I was initially reluctant to offer isolated definitions of Chiron in the signs, houses and in aspect. However, if we bear in mind the preceding thoughts, we can gain our first insights and understandings of Chiron's workings and messages.

It is important to clarify one thing, however. Through my personal research and study, I have found that the sign and house placements of Chiron – and indeed of any given planet – *are not nearly so important and significant as the angular aspects that the planets make to each other.*

The angular aspects and each planet's own intrinsic energy signature, *aside from its sign and house placement,* represent the *essence* of what we seek to study, i.e. ourselves. The sign and house placements represent the clothing or context in which that essence lives and, as such, are only rightly considered *after* the essence. It is for this reason that I will spend a good deal of time and energy in the later chapter on Chiron in aspect. However, bowing to popular feeling and belief, I offer detailed definitions of Chiron through the signs in this chapter and through the houses in the next chapter.

Finally, concerning the Wounds that are reflected through Chiron in the chart, we must reiterate that the Healing path alone does *not* indicate our life's path and purpose. Neither can it wholly tell us how that life's path and purpose will manifest in reality. The Wound *is,* however, the primary driving force. The Healing journey is the journey of *discovering* our life's path and purpose, i.e. our Divine Design. That is Chiron's Gift, i.e. the *discovery*. The life's path and purpose itself can seen more clearly in the Nodes of the Moon, whereas our *expression* of that path and purpose can be seen in the Sun, the Ascendant and the Midheaven. The exterior face of our Woundedness, as we have said, can be seen in the Moon. The *synthesis* of all these features will give a glimpse at the total picture.

Having said all this, I leap . . .

Chiron in Aries

The Wound:

A profound sense of loss of self-worth, a core feeling of worthlessness, unworthiness and even undeservingness of life itself. Self-denial. A feeling of not being wanted, needed or useful. A feeling of being uncentered, unfocussed, lacking solidity.

The Search:

The search for Self, for identity.

The Wound's Expression:

A tendency to put others first. To seek to please others. To sacrifice self, even sabotage self. To give away power to others. To fail to stand up for self. To be afraid to take a stand. A tendency to meander through life, influenced by the slightest change of atmosphere or energy.

I am reminded of a client of mine with Chiron in Aries. He has sacrificed himself and his true life's passion for the sake of a partner who keeps him well under thumb, threatening to leave him or take their baby away if he does not give her one hundred percent attention. He fails to take a stand and thus meanders through his life in a seemingly purposeless fashion, his self-worth at an all-time low.

Alternately, as a reaction, the Wound can express a tendency towards futile grandstanding, bravado, aggressive reactions to what we perceive to be others' putting us down, misplaced stoicism, championing the causes of others in order to feel valuable and worthy and/or stubborn resistance to ask others for help despite our desperate plight.

Escaping the Wound:

A tendency to live vicariously through others, to wish to help others (altruism overruling all egoism, positive and negative). Tendency to try to rescue others who also lack self-worth. Tendency to retreat from conflict, confrontation and challenge. Tendency to avoid circumstances and situations where taking a stand or expressing an opinion is required.

The Healing Path:

The people we try to please, that we sacrifice ourselves to, help, rescue or live vicariously through will mirror our true worth back to us, ever encouraging us to discover, acknowledge, embrace and ultimately Love ourselves and our unique Gifts. Simultaneously, the part of us that will never be put down – the Spirit – will ultimately fight back against the belittling of ourselves by our lower nature and against its reflection in the outside world, i.e. against others putting us down. When enough is enough, we will stand up and affirm our true worth. We are not designed to be doormats.

Where are we unique, special and gifted? No person on the planet is superfluous or identical to another. Each of us Serves a special and unique purpose and Service or we would not be here.

The Gift:

The discovery, acknowledgment, embracing and Loving of our special and unique Divine Design. The realization of the indestructibility of Spirit, despite the transience of forms. The acknowledgment of the Divine within us. The growth of *presence* and spiritual solidity. To share this with others by our mere *presence,* true self-Love and positive ego. To remain firmly but gently in our own space despite the opinions and actions of others.

Notable People with Chiron in Aries:

Pope John Paul II, Richard Burton, George Bush, Winston Churchill, Nat "King" Cole, Mohandas K. Gandhi, Judy Garland, Queen Elizabeth II, Carl G. Jung, Henry Mancini, Paul Newman, Albert Schweitzer, Johnny Carson, Doris Day, Leonardo DiCaprio, Betty Ford, Steffi Graf, Hugh Hefner, Benny Hill, Lee Iacocca, Robert Kennedy, Henry Kissinger, Liberace, Spike Milligan, River Phoenix, Gene Roddenberry (creator of Star Trek), Claudia Schiffer, Peter Sellers, Aaron Spelling, Margaret Thatcher, Uma Thurman.

Chiron in Taurus

The Wound:

A deep sense of insecurity. A core fear of losing safety, security, abundance and, ultimately, Love. The Wound says these were taken away, were lost or are missing. A loss of Trust. A deficit of Values.

The Search:

The search for security, Trust and Love, often through material values. The search for universal Values.

The Wound's Expression:

The tendency to try to grasp, hold on to, cling to, covet and/or hoard security, safety, abundance and love (our interpretation of love), whether it be with respect to people, things or core ideals. Tendency to be materially and/or emotionally demanding, clinging and self-centered. Tendency to align self with transient values. Alternately, to devalue self and life. Ultimately, however, it is all a quest for Love.

Escaping the Wound:

There can be the tendency to cling to material things and to emotionally safe and secure environments. Avoidance of risks. Immersion in comfort and 'good living', yet cautious with money.

The Healing Path:

Ultimately, we will realize that the safety, security, Values and Love we seek are not to be found in the tangible world (the world of material forms). It can only be found in the Heart, in the wellspring of Spirit and in the Love that invisibly pervades all things.

In the meantime, our efforts to find and keep safety, security, values and love in its material forms will gradually become less and less able to answer our needs. Nothing of the senses can ever satisfy. Abundance in the material world is but a reflection of the true abundance . . . that of the Heart, of Spirit and of Love. Love is the ultimate Value.

The Gift:

Understanding the connection between the material and spiritual worlds. The Gift of learning how to manage and increase the abundance of the material world. The Gift of financial prudence, investing skill, management ability with material resources, steady persistence with these Gifts and a long-term view.

Ultimately discovering, acknowledging, embracing and Loving the true wellspring of safety, security, abundance and values, i.e. the Heart, Spirit and Love. The material world is the playground of Spirit, the schoolroom of the higher Self, the mirror of the Soul, enticing us to awaken.

A Return to Trust that Love will always be there, always is there and was never missing. The realization that when we lose, we simultaneously gain . . . this is the universal law of conservation and compensation. Also, that we can cannot lose Spirit or Love because it is eternal, omnipresent and indestructible. It is us and we are it.

I am reminded of a client of mine who has been a financial advisor and planner for the whole of her life. She has recently intensified her spiritual search, finally discovering that the security and abundance she has sought throughout her life and has tried to assist others in finding was always in her Heart, in Spirit, in the wellspring of Love. She has now turned her vision and inspiration towards helping children to find their security and abundance, both materially and spiritually, drawing upon the wealth of experience and knowledge she has accumulated over the many years of her life. In short, she has become aware of her Divine Design and is honoring it in Gratitude and Love.

Notable People with Chiron in Taurus:

Buzz Aldrin, Neil Armstrong, Marty Brill (comedian and comedy writer for such television shows as "M.A.S.H."), Miles Davis, Bob Hawke (former Australian prime minister), James Joyce, Martin Luther King Jnr, Elizabeth Kubler-Ross, Jayne Mansfield, Marylyn Monroe, Arnold Palmer, Pablo Picasso, Franklin D. Roosevelt, Elizabeth Taylor, Tom Wolfe (writer), Burt Bacharach, Shirley Temple (Black), Sean Connery, Albert Einstein, Mata Hari, Audrey Hepburn, Grace Kelly, Jim Jones (Jonestown cult leader), Edward Kennedy, Rupert Murdoch, Willie Nelson, Jacqueline Kennedy Onassis, Ross Perot, Stephen Sondheim, Leopold Stokowski.

Chiron in Gemini

The Wound:

A deep-seated feeling of not being able to communicate with others, of being verbally inept, of not being able to fit in socially, of not being intelligent, of not being able to see the connections between one thing and the next. Hidden feeling of being uneducated or stupid compared to others. A feeling of not being up with the times.

The Search:

The search for understanding, awareness, integration and for rapport with others.

The Wound's Expression:

Putting others with intelligence, with social, communication and writing skills, with higher education, with scientific minds, etcetera, on a pedestal or, conversely, putting them down. Tendency to depreciate, denigrate and hide our own skills, intelligence and talents, particularly in early life. Can find it difficult to believe in self and own ideas. This can either manifest as an extreme drive to develop these same attributes or, conversely, to avoid them altogether. Can manifest as a need to gather allies against our perception of the world as being unsupportive of us and denigrating us for our perceived lack of intelligence or understanding, i.e. the formation of secret and/or subversive social groups. Tendency toward gossip. Obsessive need to gather knowledge and understanding to allay an inner fear of disintegration.

Escaping the Wound:

As aforementioned in the previous paragraph. In addition, hiding own talents, intelligence, skills in these areas so as not to be put on the spot or compared with others. The development of a fortress of protection, i.e. an area of life expression and skill where no one can criticize. Avoidance of social situations. Reclusive behavior. Inner communication with other entities, imagined or real, sometimes manifesting as an outward announcement of personal contact with 'higher' powers.

The Healing Path:

Remembering that what we think is missing in our lives is what we unconsciously strive to obtain, here the Healing path is awakening to, recognizing, embracing and finally Loving the specific *form* of our intelligence and communicative expression. Time spent in the recesses of the mind (due to avoidance of social contact, avoidance of confronting intellectual exchange and the feeling of being inferior to others in this respect) later bears useful fruit. It bears the fruit of unique, coherent, intuitively intelligent self-expression and communicative methods and it gives a unique perspective to be shared in the world. Healing questions include, "Where is the unique expression? Where is there innate intelligence and intuition? Where is there a deep understanding growing? Where is there an advanced form of communication growing within?" Those that we laud and put upon a pedestal or, conversely, put down and ridicule, mirror those aspects of ourselves that we have yet to recognize, acknowledge, embrace and Love. The Healing path is recognizing the unique forms that our Gifts take.

An example comes to mind from my studies. A teenage girl with Chiron in Gemini puts herself down for her lack of educational prowess compared to her peers. She excels outside school at dancing. As a young child she had constant dialogue with imaginary friends and was her own best company. As a teenager, it was eventually discovered that she had been writing song-lyrics for years, but hiding them from others. The lyrics were those of someone far in advance of her years, showing an intelligence, power of observation and innate sense of the logic of lyrical form that was inspiring, poignant, dramatic and with a potentially huge future in song-writing.

The Gift:

Unique, deeply thought out, coherent, intuitively intelligent understanding. Ability to share this with others in unique ways. A valuable and unique perspective on the affairs of the world around us, personally and/or globally. A drive to explore subjects of interest with unparalleled intensity and in the utmost detail. Rapport and communication with other realms of life, on this world or in the next.

Notable People with Chiron in Gemini:

Woody Allen, Julie Andrews, Brigitte Bardot, Phil Donahue, Jane Fonda, Dustin Hoffman, Buddy Holly, Glenda Jackson, Larry King, Shirley MacLaine, Charles Manson, Jack Nicholson, Roy Orbison, Luciano Pavarotti, Elvis Presley, Eleanor Roosevelt, Jimmy Swaggart, Gene Wilder, Colleen McCullough (fiction writer), John Laws (radio personality), Carl Sagan, Jim Henson, Saddam Hussein, D. H. Lawrence.

Chiron in Cancer

The Wound:

The core belief and feeling that love will never be found, that it was lost, that it was never there, that the world is not supportive, nurturing, caring, mothering or loving. Alternatively, that although love exists, it is either forever unrequited or we are not deserving of it. The core belief that we are unlovable and/or abandoned.

The Search:

The search for our roots. Seeking to reunite with the 'mother'. The search for the cosmic bosom, the wellspring of Creation, the source of Love. Ultimately, the search for the Love within.

The Wound's Expression:

A constant background feeling, more often unconscious, of emptiness, loneliness and emotional Pain. A tendency to sabotage relationships, to withdraw love, to wish for relationship with unattainable partners. Conversely, a tendency to smother others in love, caring, nurturing, support, etcetera. The wish to wrap others in cotton wool, soothe their Pain, look after them, all the while feeling a gnawing emptiness inside. The tendency to try to rescue others that are perceived to be unloved, uncared for or abandoned. This can manifest as matchmaking and collusion in others' relationships. Love of animals, small children, Nature in general, ecology. Pursuit of softness, gentleness, peace, although our inner world can be hard, harsh and at war with itself. Alternately, going to any length to obtain the love of others . . . lying, cheating, deluding self and others, sacrificing self and innermost desires, boasting and putting on pretences, giving all of self to others, looking after others, etcetera.

Escaping the Wound:

Investing emotional energy – love, caring, nurturing, support – in others. Rallying and campaigning against perceived abandonment, neglect, deprivation, lack of care, love and support. Supporting social welfare schemes. Avoiding close personal relationships for fear of abandonment. Drowning sorrows and feeling of emptiness in various external pursuits, addictions or self-imposed seclusion.

The Healing Path:

Those that we seek to love, care for, nurture, support and wrap in cotton wool each mirror aspects of ourselves to which we wish to do the same, except we do not allow ourselves this. What did we do or not do in our lives that makes us feel as though we are unworthy of Love, undeserving of caring, nurturing and support? Why do we deny ourselves this? What is the source of our guilt? The Love that we miss lies within us, cut off from us by our own self-judgments. The Healing path will take us on a journey that will ultimately awaken us to the reality of Love within us and around us. Ultimately, by trying to aid others in their search for these things, we will see that they already exist in these peoples' lives, but are unrecognized in form and unacknowledged in existence. Ultimately, we are our own Healers, by learning to Love ourselves Unconditionally. When we Love ourselves, we are simultaneously aware of the Love that lies around us at every instant.

An example from my experience: a person who has been a Healer most of her life. She has long sought to help others, to soothe and caress their Pain away, to wrap them up in cotton wool, to Heal their Wounds. Her Service is as a facilitator and catalyst for others' Healing. She is a 'connector' of people to where they need to be and to who they need to meet at any given time in their lives.

She herself has been on a lifelong quest to Heal the Wounds of abandonment by her mother, to Heal the little girl within her that was crying out for Love. She now recognizes that there is a difference between her higher self that is wise and Loving and her lower self that is dualistic, fragmented and subject to illusions and lies. She realizes that her own Healing journey has been learning to Love her mother *and* herself Unconditionally, discovering the Divine Design behind all the happenings in her life that she has previously called the Wounding. She now works specifically with children, apart from performing as a singer and compere, allowing the little girl in her to Sing.

The Gift:

The discovery and recognition that Love lies within us and around us, that there is nothing *but* Love, that *we* are Loved, that there is no part of us that is unlovable. The ability to *receive* Love as well as give it. The ability to recognize the *form* Love takes in our lives and in the lives of others. The discovery that support, caring and nurturing exist everywhere and in all our lives in forms that we did not previously recognize, i.e. that a Guiding Hand exists and is active in our lives.

Notable People with Chiron in Cancer:

Charlie Chaplin, Bob Dylan, Adolf Hitler, Jack Nicklaus, Ryan O'Neal, Nancy Sinatra, Bret Whiteley (artist, suicide), Natalie Wood, Jeffrey Archer, Joan Baez (folk singer), Jim Bakker, John Cleese, Wes Craven, Neil Diamond, Placido Domingo, David Frost, Germaine Greer, Evel Knievel, Lee Harvey Oswald, Al Pacino, Ringo Starr.

Chiron in Leo

The Wound:

The feeling that we cannot express ourselves, our self-expression and creativity squashed, our sense of self-worth damaged or missing. A feeling that we are not part of the celebration of life. A feeling of being uncreative, unimaginative, uninspired. A feeling of being unappreciated, not recognized for our specialness or particular station in life, not given our proper due or respect, not liked or adored.

The Search:

The search for our value beyond ego and personality. The search for spontaneity, for our Inner Light, our God-spark. The search for the freedom to Sing our Song without fear or guilt.

The Wound's Expression:

Seeking to express and create, but tending initially to hide the results. Trying to join in the flow of life, but feeling inadequate, afraid, leading to attempts to create 'reasons' – achievements, accolades, artistic creations, public image, etcetera – why we are deserving of joining in. Fear of being in public, being seen, being on stage, on show or put on the spot. Feeling unworthy of being the center of attention.

Conversely, trying to stand up and be seen, recognized, appreciated, lauded, respected, loved, etcetera. All attempts made to gain appreciation, recognition, accolade, respect, the public eye – to steal the center stage, all the while feeling unworthy inside.

Alternatively, putting others' talents and creative expressions on show, supporting and looking after them, living vicariously through their achievements, recognition and accolades, particularly children's. The Love of children and of their freedom of expression and creativity.

Escaping the Wound:

Avoidance of being in public, on show, the center of attention. Reluctance to accept accolade, compliments, recognition, etcetera. General self-depreciation of our own creative talents and modes of self-expression. Hiding the results of artistic and creative output. Putting others' talents and creative expressions on show, supporting and looking after them, living vicariously through their achievements, recognition and accolades, particularly children's.

Alternately, obsession with being seen 'on stage', in the public eye, anything for attention, accolade, adulation.

The Healing Path:

Ultimately, the Pain of seeing others succeed in areas where we innately know we should succeed will drive us to the outward acknowledgment and expression of our inner worth, our creativity and our self-expression. Our innate creative urge and Wish to Shine will win out in the end, whether in this lifetime or another.

Alternatively, the others that we assist to do these same things will constantly mirror our own innate urge to Shine, to burst forth and celebrate our own existence, impelling us to do likewise.

Conversely, by building up our own public image, attempting to gain appreciation, recognition, accolade, respect, the public eye, stealing the center stage, we gradually learn where our true Light Shines. The mirror of approval and disapproval, support and reprimand, will teach us where our unique creativity and self-expression are. In this way, we come to celebrate who we are, *exactly as we are,* in Gratitude and Love for the Universe that created us. This Gratitude and Love are the true seeds of our Wish to Create, of our Wish to give something back to the Universe.

The Gift:

To allow ourselves to Shine, to Sing our Song, so to speak. To acknowledge the divine creative principle that lies at the heart of our own creation and then give this back to the Universe through our own creations, self-expression and celebration of life. To stand before others, unashamedly being who we are, inspiring others to do likewise, acknowledging the Gift of their lives and their unique Divine Designs.

I am reminded of a friend with Chiron in Leo. He has been somewhat reclusive and shy most of his life and has played down his own creative and inventive side, choosing instead to help his children bring out their talents, gifts and creativity. In the last so many years, a spiritual and Healing quest has allowed him to come out of his shell and Love his life, his inner passion and inspiration and to begin to share this with the world. It turns out that an invention of his, that he hid and played down for so many years, is quite revolutionary in his particular industry and he is now taking steps to bring his creation to the largest possible market.

Notable People with Chiron in Leo:

Muhammad Ali, Dwight D. Eisenhower, Lynn Redgrave, Dionne Warwick, Bob Woodward, Arthur Ashe, Tammy Bakker, Cilla Black, Agatha Christie, Billy Connolly, Tom Conti, Michael Crichton, Harrison Ford, Aretha Franklin, three out of four of the Beatles: George Harrison, John Lennon and Paul McCartney. Also, Jimi Hendrix, Erica Jong, Janis Joplin, Carole King, Bruce Lee, Joe Pesci, Paul Simon, Barbra Streisand, Tammy Wynette.

Chiron in Virgo

The Wound:

A deep feeling of being incomplete, fragmented, scattered, disconnected, impure. The feeling that something is 'wrong' with us, physically, emotional, mentally and/or spiritually and needs 'fixing', changing, getting rid of or Healing. An inexplicable sense of dissatisfaction with the way things are.

The Search:

The search for wholeness, connection and Soul-satisfaction. The search for integrity, subtlety, purity and exactitude.

The Wound's Expression:

Dissatisfaction with ourselves and others in our lives. Always seeking to 'fix', 'correct', change, control and get rid of aspects that we perceive to be not 'good' enough. Critical nature, particularly in regard to our line of work and our more serious pursuits. Scattered, disorganized manner of living or, conversely, a highly perfectionist nature that makes it uncomfortable for others to be around. Both poles of this can manifest a tendency towards illness as a mirror of our polarized state of consciousness. We seek, simultaneously and paradoxically, to have ourselves validated by others and yet to have them affirm to us that there is something 'wrong' with us. Can be hypochondriac. Can be zealously and/or fanatically health-conscious.

Escaping the Wound:

Criticizing others, blaming others, trying to 'fix', 'correct', change or get rid of others. Highly judgmental. Perfectionist focus on details, trying to escape the inability to integrate our understanding and our picture of the world. Ceasing to try to understand and just blindly, by rote, going through the prescribed steps of living. Can be obsessive-compulsive. Alternately, just letting everything go, living in total disorganized chaos, blaming the world at large for being imperfect. Possible bohemian, hedonistic living.

The Healing Path:

Consists of gradually putting together the pieces of our lives and the pieces of an integrated picture of life. The more pieces we collect and try to integrate, the more this picture is revealed to us. By seeking to help, Heal, 'fix', 'correct' and/or change ourselves and others, we learn the art of integration and Healing, whether we call it this or not. This is Chiron's natural sign. By seeking integration and, ultimately, wholeness, we gradually reveal the inherent unity and integrity that already exists. The Healing process itself is a raising of consciousness to be able to see the bigger picture, the Plan, the perfection, the balance and harmony that already exist. It is the journey from Virgo to the sign of balance, Libra, according to the Mysteries. It is seeing how even our illusory perceptions of imbalance and incompleteness Serve us on our journey of Healing and evolution of consciousness and lead us towards our Divine Design.

I am reminded of a compatriot with Chiron in Virgo. Her life has been a process of dissolving her judgments against others and against the world, in particular against her father whom she has viewed as the most diabolical man in existence. She has been highly critical, hugely demanding and very difficult to live with. Her own sense of isolation, due to these aspects of her nature, has taken her on a Healing path, i.e. an effort to put the pieces of her life and her psyche into a coherent picture. Her inner dissatisfaction, fragmentedness and conflict have led her to seek balance, harmony, wholeness and alignment with higher realms of consciousness. Consequently, she has become a monumental Healer, having explored innumerable modalities of Healing and having a highly developed psychic awareness.

The Gift:

The unveiling of the Divine Plan, the perfection, balance and harmony of life. The development of methods of integration, 'wholing' and Healing. Learning to Love things and people just as they are. Learning to Love ourselves just as we are. The Gift of Gratitude for life and for our Divine Design. A deep sense of Inner Peace in the acknowledgment that 'all's right with the world'. Healing. Oneness. The Return to Love.

Also, the ability to integrate masses of data into a coherent creation.

The development of the skills and arts required for our ultimate Service, i.e. to become co-Creators. Creation requires the utmost attention to detail, the utmost focus, the utmost ability to juggle all the required pieces and, lastly, the sense of the overall Plan and its Loving source of Spirit.

Notable People with Chiron in Virgo:

Billie Jean King, Danny DeVito, Michael Douglas, Joe Frazier, Hermann Goering, Julio Iglesias, George Lucas, Jim Morrison, Jimmy Page, Diana Ross, Bobby Womack.

Chiron in Libra

The Wound:

The core Wound of feeling alone, incomplete, separate. The feeling that there is something missing in our lives. This placement, more than any other, reflects our longing for our Soul-mate.

The Search:

The search for the pieces of ourselves in the mirror of others, for companionship, for Contact and for our Soul-mate.

The Wound's Expression:

Fear of being alone. Sacrificing self and inner direction for the sake of being with, staying with and keeping others around us in our lives. Constantly seeking balance, harmony, beauty and peace whilst, to a complementarily opposite degree, experiencing inner turmoil, disharmony, conflict and struggle. Deeply disturbed by interpersonal conflicts. Can express as creativity and artistic flair in an effort to create the harmony, balance, beauty and wholeness that we seek.

Escaping the Wound:

Burying ourselves in relationships, sacrificing our inner direction and our calling for the sake of finding, keeping, being with and staying with others. Seeking Contact with other realms of life, i.e. Nature, art,

45-LASS

psychic guides and life after death. Putting on masks and making up stories about self in order to attract others. Living a double life.

The Healing Path:

Every person that we have a relationship with, whether up close and personal or more at a distance, is a reflection of ourselves. More importantly, each person reflects aspects of our true Soul-mate, the other 'half' that we feel we are missing. Most importantly, however, each of the aspects of our true Soul-mate, seen through others we are in relationship with, *is an aspect of ourselves we have yet to discover, recognize, acknowledge, embrace and finally Love Unconditionally. What we sense we are missing – our incompleteness – is within us, awaiting our discovery.* The divine mirror we have been given is the reflection others offer us. The paradox is that, when we have become consciously whole and Healed, we have no more need of a Soul-mate and yet this is when we are ready to be with them.

We feel alone because we are cut off from ourselves and, being cut off in this way, we are cut from our divine origins, i.e. cut off from God/Universe/Contact.

Each piece of ourselves that we discover, through its reflection in another, gives us more of a sense of wholeness, completeness and, hence, Contact with life and Love. We feel more balanced, more harmonious, more at Peace. "I am you and you are me." Forms differ, essence is the same.

The Gift:

The realization that all that we need is within us already. We are complete and perfect the way we are; we just did not see it at first. The Gift of realizing the magnificence and the magnitude of Love inherent in the design of material life inasmuch as it offers us an unparalleled mirror through which we can awaken to our divine nature, our Light, our Divine Design. The mirror of others – the tool of duality – allows us to awaken to aspects of ourselves that we were previously oblivious to, previously denying, judging, not acknowledging and not Loving. Such is the Healing journey of integration and 'wholing'.

The Gift of discovering the harmony, balance, proportion, beauty and true perfection of all of life.

Also, the Gift of Contact with all of life on all levels and in all realms. The more whole and Healed we become, the more we see that separation and aloneness were illusions and the more we feel the real presence of others in our Hearts, beyond time, space and even death. Love goes beyond all dimensions and dissolves all boundaries.

An example of a person with Chiron in Libra is a high-profile psychic reader, a client and friend, who claims to be in Contact with spiritual guidance and to be able to read the future. She has, in her life, not been satisfied with her current partners, but has always felt that a better partner awaited her. She has, however, reluctantly stayed with these partners despite these feelings. She seeks constant contact and rapport with others and is easily hurt if others do not reciprocate to a level she feels happy with. She tries to attract others into her life by using and displaying her psychic talents.

She is creative, has written several books and has constantly sought peace and harmony in her tumultuous life. Her Gift has been to be able to witness the perfection of peoples' lives through her psychic Gift. Her further task is to learn to Love herself by Loving and recognizing aspects of her Soul-mate through her current partner(s).

Notable People with Chiron in Libra:

Annie Besant (British-Indian social reformer and feminist and former head of the Theosophical Society in India), Cher, Bill Clinton, Mia Farrow, Sally Field, Goldie Hawn, Diane Keaton, Bette Midler, Liza Minelli, Dane Rudhyar, Alexander Graham Bell, Candice Bergen, F. Scott Fitzgerald, Barry Gibb (the Bee Gees), J. Edgar Hoover, Steve Martin, Dolly Parton, Karen Silkwood, Sylvester Stallone, Donald Trump, Rudolph Valentino, Henry Winkler, Margaret Birken (New Zealand psychic).

Chiron in Scorpio

The Wound:

The core feeling of being disconnected or abandoned by Spirit, manifesting in a deep-seated fear of loss and death. The feeling that the world is against us, others seeking to bring us down, to plot against us, to manipulate us and/or undermine us.

A deep doubt concerning our own immortality, i.e. questioning whether this visible life all there is. The fear of total annihilation.

The Search:

The search for transformation and evolution of consciousness. The search for Spirit, for the Immortal and the Unchangeable within us.

The Wound's Expression:

The building of immense walls of protection, internal and/or external. The tendency to cling to others and to the sense of security they may offer and to work secretly to keep it so by whatever means required. The fear of loss, death and/or annihilation makes us highly and jealously protective of the people and things in our lives. Alternately, it may make us vindictive, destructive, maligning and backstabbing.

The striving to make some kind of immortal contribution to life and the world in order to counteract the fear of our own impermanence. The striving to understand the essence of life itself, to touch life, ultimately to touch Spirit. Conversely, a preoccupation with death and dying.

Lastly, self-destructiveness and possible suicidal tendencies as an unconscious striving to be free from our attachment to the material plane or as a self-fulfilling prophecy of annihilation.

Escaping the Wound:

Making light or entertainment of death, dying, destruction. Tendency to obsess over death and dying. Living a bohemian or hedonistic life. Clinging to partners and possessions with jealous ferocity. Exploring psychic phenomena and any indications of life after death. Being a workaholic. Potential for destructiveness towards others and their possessions. Being at war with others. Viewing the world and others as the enemy.

I am reminded of a highly jealous and manipulative client with Chiron in Scorpio who had extreme difficulty in letting go of a failing marriage. She felt as though her husband and those that supported him were her most dire enemies and that they were all manipulating and scheming against her. In the end, she lost her house, her marriage and her former life, but gained deep spiritual understanding, Inner Peace and an insatiable appetite for delving into the mysteries of life. By learning to set them free by Loving them Unconditionally, she gained her own freedom.

The Healing Path:

The deep fear of death will ultimately drive us to seek the origins of life, to seek the intangible spark that lies within all tangible life, to seek the immortal and the indestructible. In seeking this in the external world, we are looking into a mirror that reflects back our own immortal nature.

The Wounds of loss and death will ultimately cause us to introspect deeply. We will eventually see that those aspects of things and people that we have lost or who have died still exist around us and in us. They still exist, but in new forms, unrecognized at first. Their essence always remains and is accessible to us within the Loving and Grateful spaces of our Hearts. We will eventually see that those aspects of *ourselves* that we feel we have lost or have died within us still exist, just in different forms.

The Healing journey of this placement of Chiron is seeing that the world of forms is a transient illusion, behind which lies the Truth of the immortal Actuality, i.e. the Truth of Spirit, Oneness and Love. Further, it is the journey of awakening to the Service that this transient illusion offers us, i.e. a mirror in which we can eventually see ourselves, our divine nature, our Divine Design, our immortal essence.

The Healing journey will teach us that by trying to hold on to the forms of things and people we are in fear of losing, we actually *contribute* to their loss and death. When we smother the forms, we prevent them from breathing. However, when we see, embrace and Love the essence within and are no longer attached to the forms, the forms can change, but we are never in a state of feeling loss or missingness. Love brings all essences together in the Heart.

I am reminded of a poem by William Blake, he himself having Chiron in Scorpio:

He who binds to himself a joy
Doth the winged life destroy,
But he who kisses the joy as it flies
Lives in Eternity's sun rise[67]

The Gift:

The discovery, recognition, acknowledgment, embracing and Loving of Spirit. The transcendence of the dualistic illusions of material forms. The releasing of people and things to live freely in that playful illusion, knowing in our Hearts that we can never lose or miss their essence, their presence or their Love. The realization that all transient aspects of people or things that we lose or who die are still around us and/or within us, the forms different, but the essence the same.

The awakening of the immortal part of ourselves. The realization of the indestructibility of Spirit and that in every destruction of form, there is a simultaneous and entirely balancing birth. The Gift of giving something immortal to others and to the world at large. The reaffirmation of the Divine, of God/Universe.

The Gift of intensity and depth of inquiry. A passion for life, knowledge and understanding.

Notable People with Chiron in Scorpio:

Marie Antoinette, William Blake, Prince Charles, Hilary Clinton, Amelia Earhart, Johannes Keplar, Michelangelo, Mozart, O. J. Simpson, Steven Spielberg, Jose Carreras, Uri Geller, Paul Joseph Goebbels, Elton John, Stephen King, Kevin Kline, Olivia Newton-John, Camilla Parker-Bowles, Arnold Schwarzenegger, Mary Shelley, Cat Stevens, Steve Winwood.

---

[67] Erdman, David V. ed. *The Complete Poetry and Prose of William Blake.* Anchor Books (Doubleday), New York 1988.

Chiron in Sagittarius

The Wound:

A deep-seated feeling of meaninglessness, pointlessness, loss or absence of inspiration. The core Wound that says that there is no bigger picture, no Guiding Hand, no higher realms of existence. Existentialist. Can be a fear of open spaces and/or of having no boundaries. A feeling of being dwarfed by the immensity of life and the world. The feeling that we are not wise, but that wisdom is in the hands of others. Fear that we cannot know or will never find the answers to life's most important questions. The feeling that others take the air out of the balloon of our idealism, vision and optimism.

The Search:

The search for meaning, for the larger Plan, for the Master Designer. The search for the higher Self.

The Wound's Expression:

Fear of inquiry into 'deeper' matters. Reliance on others for answers to important questions of existence, putting them on a pedestal. Nonetheless, despite the fear, an insatiable appetite for gathering others' knowledge and understanding. However, there may be an innate fear of questioning what is given to us. Inclination to become involved in religious and spiritual groups that dictate a prescribed belief structure. The seeking of a safe and known environment and avoidance of challenging situations and opportunities. Alternately, at the other extreme, an obsessive need to experience all paradigms and environments first hand, even if it means discarding previous beliefs and rational constraints. Connected with this, possible foolhardy disregard for personal safety.

I am reminded of a client with Chiron in Sagittarius. He was entirely reliant upon the indications of others – psychics, scholars, Healers, mentors and friends – for the answers to the questions of his life. His own self-depreciation of his inner understanding and wisdom led him to be fearful and embarrassed around others, particularly those whom he relied upon for knowledge and understanding. He was reclusive, somewhat of an outcast and subject to fits of anger. His fear of knowledge and deeper understanding was chronic, bordering on a neurosis. At yet, despite this, he put himself into positions where he was constantly challenged in this way. The power of Spirit was driving him. His breakthrough came when, through a practical and guided Healing experience, he acknowledged and embraced his own inner Knowing.

Escaping the Wound:

Can bury ourselves in the rituals and structure of organized religions or other such groups. Can be reclusive. Tend to fear and/or avoid change. Can become dogmatic, over-zealous and/or uncompromising in beliefs and attitudes. Can be reticent and unsure of self in matters that lie beyond everyday life. Can put others on a pedestal, demeaning one's own capacity for knowledge and wisdom.

The Healing Path:

By gathering the knowledge, understanding and wisdom of others, we ultimately discover a common thread and answers begin to emerge. More importantly, by doing this, we begin to see and acknowledge our own innate wisdom and understanding through the outer reflection.

By gradually becoming too comfortable with and too entrenched in the known, with pat answers and predigested viewpoints, we ultimately long for the unknown. This is evolution's innate drive. In this way, we become more willing to approach the boundaries of our current consciousness and knowledge.

The ultimately unsatisfactory nature of stock answers and the unfulfilling nature of following beliefs prescribed by others will inevitably bring questions. We have an innate drive to expand, despite our efforts to remain in the safety of known parameters. We also have an innate feeling that there *is* meaning to life, that there *is* a bigger picture of which we are a part.

In the end, knowledge is simply a commodity . . . true understanding and wisdom come from the marriage of knowledge with Being, with our essence. Knowledge is simply a mirror we use to awaken to what we already know in our Hearts, to awaken to our divinity, our Light, our perfection.

The Gift:

The discovery, recognition, acknowledgment, embracing and Loving of our own innate wisdom and understanding. Inner Knowing. Inner certainty. Gnostic awakening. The realization that meaning lies within us, that the Divine lies within us.

The quest for adventure, to push against the boundaries of the known, to have our answers lead us to more questions. The Joy of discovery. The awakening to the miracle of existence, the magnificence of the Universe, the adventure of life and the Truth of Spirit.

Notable People with Chiron in Sagittarius:

Princess Anne, Sissy Spacek, Mark Spitz, Bruce Springsteen, Meryl Streep, Karen Carpenter, Phil Collins, Robbie Coltrane, Noel Coward, Alexander Dumas, Peter Gabriel, Bob Geldof, Ernest Hemingway, Heinrich Himmler, Victor Hugo, Chrissie Hynde, Mark Knopfler, Jay Leno, Tom Waits, Robin Williams.

Chiron in Capricorn

The Wound:

The Wound of feeling unrecognized, unappreciated, unnoticed, unacknowledged, unheard and 'passed over'. The feeling that there is no structure in life, that it is disorganized, chaotic and too ephemeral. A deep-seated fear of loss or absence of concrete and tangible realities. A fear of losing control or being out of control. A sense of inability to find or know our place in the larger Plan, i.e. our vocation and function.

The Search:

The search for order, for control, for vocation, for mastery. Richard Nolle says, "The desire to conquer time".

The Wound's Expression:

Seeking recognition, appreciation, accolade, respect and status. Seeking to be heard (can manifest as speaking loudly, ignoring others and/or interrupting others). Alternately, hiding our worthiness to be recognized, appreciated, respected, etcetera; keeping silent whilst others are being heard. The seeking to create structure and organization in our lives and the lives of those around us. The avoidance of anything that we cannot touch, smell, see, hear or taste. The compulsive need to be in control of every aspect of our lives and, sometimes, of others' lives.

I am reminded of a client of mine with Chiron in Capricorn. She tries always to be the center of attention, to speak louder than others, not always listening to what others have to say before interrupting and putting in her two cents. She makes a habit of big noting herself and associating herself with people of fame. She also needs to feel as though she is in control to an extreme degree, zealously organizing her own life as well as though close to her in her life. These aspects of her character have Served her well and have contributed to her becoming well known, highly-regarded, highly-trained, in demand and meticulously organized in her chosen profession. She is a hypnotist and always has the last word!

Lastly, with this placement, we may trip from vocation to vocation, trying to find our place, to feel useful, to feel appreciated and recognized for our station. We are like a jigsaw piece trying to find its place in the puzzle.

Escaping the Wound:

Trying to attain recognition, acceptance, accolade, etcetera, by associating ourselves with others who we feel have these attributes. Becoming 'anally' attentive to order, structure, organization. Controlling others. Alternately, placing ourselves under the control of others or organizations to bring order and structure to our lives. Tendency to talk constantly. Alternately, hiding in the shadow of others.

The Healing Path:

The need for recognition, appreciation, acceptance, respect, status and accolade gives us an insatiable drive to excel in eyes of others. This gives us a motivating force to fulfill our goals. Ultimately, the things for which we receive the most recognition, appreciation, acceptance, respect, status and accolade will be in alignment with our Divine Design.

What we truly seek is to Love ourselves – to recognize, appreciate, accept, respect ourselves – for being exactly who we are, exactly as we have been Divinely Designed.

Furthermore, the feeling of not being heard comes from our neglect of listening to ourselves, our inner voice, our inner inspiration. If others are not listening to us, it is because *we* are not listening to us. The more we learn to listen to our inner voice – the voice of our Soul or Spirit – the more others will listen, hearing the Truth and Wisdom we have to offer.

The chaos that we feel and that we fear is *within* us and is a measure of our fragmented consciousness. We innately seek to bring order to our consciousness and we begin by trying, unconsciously or consciously, to bring order, control and organization to the outside world. In the process, we are learning to create and maintain our creations.

The need for control, order and organization ultimately stems from the innate knowledge that we are destined to become co-Creators. To create and sustain something requires utmost control. It requires a clarity of mind that comes from ordered thinking and the disciplined application and organization of all available resources.

The Gift:

The recognition, acknowledgment and appreciation of who we are, exactly as we are, exactly as we have been Divinely Designed.

The recognition, acknowledgment and appreciation of the wisdom of our inner voice. The Gift of sharing our wisdom and understanding with others.

The development of the ability to organize, create order and manage ourselves, manage things and other people. The discovery of our vocation, in line with our Divine Design, our higher purpose and calling. Training as a potential (and inevitable) co-Creator. An appreciation of the nature and Gift of the material world as a training ground for us to awaken to our divine nature as co-Creators in embryo.

The Inner Peace of orderly consciousness.

Notable People with Chiron in Capricorn:

Ron Howard, Patty Hearst, Zane Stein (Chiron astrologer), Tony Blair, Jimmy Connors, Kevin Costner, Joan Crawford, Marlene Dietrich, Walt Disney, Jeanne Dixon, Chris Evert, Cary Grant, James Ingram, Chaka Khan, Annie Lennox, Christopher Reeve, Roseanne, David O. Selznick, John Travolta, Denzel Washington, Johnny Weismuller, Oscar Wilde, Oprah Winfrey.

Chiron in Aquarius

The Wound:

The core Wound of feeling alien, an outsider, of feeling isolated, cut-off, abandoned, separate, alone, distant and removed from the rest of Humanity. Feeling as though Home is very far away. Feeling different from others, as though there is something wrong with us. Feeling like a stranger in a strange land. Inability to see our place in the world. Feeling separate from the collective consciousness. Feeling exiled from society.

The Search:

The search for Connectedness, Contact, belongingness and grounding.

The Wound's Expression:

The feeling of utter aloneness and yet, paradoxically, seeking solitude. Feeling like an outsider in social circumstances. Feeling alone in a crowd. Tendency to stand apart from others, yet seeking to be amongst others. Paradoxically, relief when finally truly alone. Seeking contact with higher consciousness, i.e. a more objective view. Trying to put the pieces together into a bigger picture.

Being deliberately obtuse, contrary, reactionary, eccentric, etcetera, in order to put distance between us and others. Secretly or overtly lauding our 'differentness' from others as a kind of mark of superiority, all the while feeling inferior inside.

Escaping the Wound:

As above (last paragraph). Alternately, trying to be amongst others constantly. Conversely, becoming reclusive. Avoiding close personal relationships. Remaining friendly, but cool and distant from others. Attending to universal and humanitarian causes as a way of trying to feel connected to a bigger picture and to feel a sense of belonging.

The Healing Path:

By being in a position of feeling like an outsider, looking in at the world and people around us, we are impelled to figure out why we feel so different and so cut-off. Our position gives us the possibility of gaining more objective knowledge and seeing a bigger picture of life. The Healing journey for this placement is the process of putting each thing we observe in the world and in ourselves into a larger context, seeing how it fits and is an integral part of the whole. This, in turn, is an outer reflection of our inner predicament and the potential Healing process. Each piece we link with the whole is a piece of ourselves put back into the larger context. Gradually we feel more a part of the whole, more integrated and connected to the whole. We begin to see our place in the world. We begin to feel like we belong. Our sense of Contact with others and the Universe at large grows.

Ultimately we will grow to Love our aloneness as well as our connectedness, realizing that it gives us the space and impulse in which to make further connections and to see an ever-larger picture of life. Where are our differences in form (from others) similarities in essence?

The Gift:

The Gift of objectivity, of seeing the bigger picture, of being able to stand back and glimpse the view from 'on high'. The Gift of connection, of reconnecting with the Universe and Humanity. The Gift of aloneness in which we are, paradoxically, in silent communion with the Universe.

The Wound (Void) indicated by Chiron in Aquarius ultimately drives us towards seeing, acknowledging and embracing the higher divine logic upon which all Creation is based. From this point of view, no part is separate, disconnected or alien to the bigger picture. From this point of view, all the pieces fit into the jigsaw puzzle and no pieces are left in the bottom of the puzzle box when the puzzle is finished. When this is witnessed in all its magnificence, Love and Gratitude are the only response possible. Seeing the magnificence of this divine picture is, in itself, the ultimate Healing.

With respect to this placement of Chiron, I use myself as an example. This example was the story told in Chapter One, illustrating the Wound and its subsequent Healing journey.

Notable People with Chiron in Aquarius:

Prince Andrew, Madonna, Jean Paul Sartre, George Bernard Shaw, Bjorn Borg, Belinda Carlisle, Willem Dafoe, Christian Dior, Carrie Fisher, Greta Garbo, Bill Gates, Andy Gibb, Whoopi Goldberg, Arsenio Hall, Tom Hanks, Katharine Hepburn, Dimitri Shostakovich (20th century Russian composer), John F. Kennedy Jnr, David Koresh, Matthew Manning, Martina Navratilova, Michelle Pfeiffer, The Artist formerly called Prince, Giacomo Puccini (opera composer), Tim Robbins, Greta Scacchi, Jean-Claude Van Damme.

Chiron in Pisces

The Wound:

The Wound of a loss of Faith and Trust in the Divine and/or in the Universe. A deep-seated sense of betrayal and/or victimization by life and/or God/Universe. A loss of Faith in the power and omnipresence of Love. Fear of being hurt. A core belief in the injustice, inequity, unfairness and victimizing nature of the Universe. A feeling of being forsaken by God, mirrored in the story of Jesus Christ.

The Search:

The search for Oneness, for the Divine, for Love, for timelessness and spacelessness and for God.

The Wound's Expression:

Shutting our inner doors to the Universe, to the Divine, to God. Suffering silently within ourselves, i.e. private hurt. Yet, paradoxically, seeking to merge, to Return to Oneness, to become whole again. Developing a hard shell and a pragmatic and sometimes cynical exterior manner. This is the most common expression. Conversely, can be overly sensitive, gushing and teary. Can be susceptible or gullible to outer influences that appear to offer Love or union with something divine or mystical.

Fear of opening up to others, yet needing close personal contact. This can lead to clouded judgment when choosing partners. Yet, paradoxically, each partner will offer another reflection of what we need to see about ourselves. Often suspiciousness, fear of opening to others, fear of being hurt and lack of trust will sabotage relationships.

Nonetheless, highly sensitive inside – even overly so. Can feel like a victim of the injustices, inequities and suffering of the world.

Can manifest as agnosticism or even atheism.

Expresses very often through artistic and creative output.

Escaping the Wound:

Retreating into our shell. Not showing our sensitive nature. Making light of serious subjects in a humorous, cynical and sometimes sarcastic way. Avoiding spiritual, psychological or philosophical questions in favor of getting on with practical, pragmatic and tangible activities. Avoiding intimacy in close personal relationships.

Alternately, allowing oneself to be influenced, captivated, brainwashed, controlled, overtaken and assimilated by people, groups or organizations professing (or masquerading) divine connection or higher ideals. Giving our spiritual power to others.

Blaming the world for injustice, unfairness, inequity, victimization and hurt to self and others. Trying to rescue others. Championing lost causes, underdogs and perceived victims.

The Healing Path:

The Universe will never stop knocking at our door. Our sense of betrayal, injustice, inequity, unfairness, victimization will constantly draw us into situations that will challenge us to see a more balanced picture. These feelings will challenge us to see the justice behind the seeming injustices, to see the fairness behind the seeming unfairnesses and to return to a sense of Trust that the Universe is actually looking after us all.

The feeling as though we did not deserve to be treated a certain way or subjected to certain events and circumstances will cause us to seek retribution, redress, justice and even revenge. In this process, we will gradually see a larger picture and begin to understand the higher logic behind these things.

The path to Oneness is only attained when we can see that all things Serve us in our lives, that all things Serve our path of Healing and evolution of consciousness. All things are a divine act of Love. The more we see the hidden purpose behind seemingly-'wrong' happenings, the more we are inclined to open the doors that we shut so tightly in the beginning. The more we can do this, the more we regain Trust in a Guiding Hand, Trust in a Universal Plan, Trust in a God, Trust in the omnipresence of Love.

Paradoxically, we regain Trust by Trusting, regain Faith by having Faith. However, real Trust and Faith are based upon observed facts. They are based upon a balanced perception that sees both sides of any given situation. Balanced perception sees the justice in the injustice, the fairness in the unfairness, the equity in the inequity, the blessings in the crisis, the clouds' silver lining and the lessons, Gifts and Service inherent in every manifestation of Creation.

The Gift:

The Return to Trust and Faith in Spirit. The revealing of the Love of the Creator. A Return to Oneness, wholeness, completeness. The opening of the Heart to be able to give and receive Love freely. To be able to look anywhere in our lives and in the lives of others and see nothing except the action and presence of Love.

I am reminded of a former teacher of mine with Chiron in Pisces. In his early life he was the typical cynic and atheist, a disbeliever in anything he could not see or touch, etcetera. He had shut the door on all spiritual matters. However, his own inner turmoil, hidden from the outside world and even from his own waking consciousness, started to manifest in unpleasant psychic experiences. He was forced to delve into his issues in order to make sense of these experiences. Through the journey of Healing, reconciling the inner issues that brought about these experiences, he experienced a Return to Faith in Spirit. Not only this, he became a teacher, teaching others to develop their psychic abilities and to connect with their Higher selves. His ultimate teaching is the power of Divine Love to Heal.

Notable People with Chiron in Pisces:

Eva Braun, Princess Diana, Vivien Leigh, Richard Nixon, Tatum O'Neal, Gregory Peck, Paula Abdul, Tracy Austin, Lucille Ball, Nicolas Cage, Kurt Cobain (Nirvana), Billy Ray Cyrus, Matt Dillon, Kirk Douglas, Jodie Foster, Indira Gandhi, Billy Graham, Jimmy Hoffa, L. Ron Hubbard (Scientology), Whitney Houston, Gary Kasparov (chess grandmaster), John F. Kennedy, k.d. lang, Pamela Anderson, Carl Lewis, Karl Marx, Henri Matisse, Yehudi Menhuin, George Michael, Edith Piaf, Roy Rogers, Erik Satie (20th century French composer), Brooke Shields, Frank Sinatra, Henri Toulouse-Latrec (painter), Orson Welles, Tennessee Williams.

6 ~ CHIRON IN THE HOUSES

As we proceed to defining Chiron through the houses, we must clarify that the house position of Chiron does *not* reflect the nature of the Wound itself. This is more properly seen in Chiron's sign and its aspects to other planets in the natal horoscope. Rather, the house placement points to the area of our lives where our specific Woundedness is most likely to play out its drama, i.e. the stage upon which the actors play their parts.

Having said this, it is important to remember that, as with Chiron in the signs, each one of us has, holographically, *all* house placements of Chiron within us, i.e. we manifest our Woundedness in *all* areas of our lives. The house placement in our natal chart merely shows us where the most *visible* manifestation of Chiron's drama is likely to proceed in this lifetime. Again, this is further dependent upon the aspects Chiron makes to other houses via planetary aspects.

Unlike Chiron's sign placement, however, Chiron as a *singleton* in any given house is more likely to manifest *primarily* in that house, although its overall influence is diminished due to its absence of planetary relationships. Conversely, if Chiron is well aspected, its dramatic stage is expanded to include the other houses covered by those planetary aspects.

Interpretation is always a multi-facetted and dynamic synthesis of all the features of the horoscope.

Lastly, I will not give examples of each Chiron *sign* placement in each *house* due to lack of space, but will give two examples in each section, leaving it to you, the reader, to extrapolate the other signs placements in each of the houses from the indications given. This should be sufficient if we remember that the *nature* of the Wound is seen in the sign and aspects of Chiron and the *stage* upon which the drama of the Wound is played out is seen in the houses.

Chiron in the 1st House

Our Woundedness is most likely to be played out through our sense of self, our sense of identity and sense of self-worth. The manifestations of the Wounding will very often be physical in nature and expressed through the body and through our physical self-image. See also, Chiron in Aries.

For example, Chiron in Leo in the 1st house, say, could be a Wound where we felt that our creativity, ego, will and joy of life was repressed and/or damaged by physical abuse or restriction, or by psychological damage to our sense of self.

Or Chiron in Aquarius in the 1st house, say, could be a Wound where we felt isolated, cut-off, abandoned, an outsider to the world by the fact that we were physically ignored as a child, ostracized for being different or strange, or separated bodily from our parents, e.g. adopted, orphaned, homeless, etcetera.

Chiron in the 2nd House

Our Woundedness is played out through the issues of emotional and material security, safety, comfort, values and well being. See also, Chiron in Taurus.

For example, Chiron in Sagittarius in the 2nd house, say, could be Wound of a sense of meaninglessness and lack of wisdom due to being brought up in an environment where all physical needs and comforts were provided (born into a rich family, for example), but devoid of inner or spiritual guidance given. Conversely, being brought up in dire material adversity, the seeming injustice of it all and the frightening immensity of the world seen from the streets would give expression to the Wound of feeling as though there is no guiding force in life, no overall balancing and just Plan, and, ultimately, no God.

Or Chiron in Pisces in the 2nd house, say, could be a Wound of feeling betrayed or victimized by the world, expressed through feeling denied or cheated of emotional and/or material security (such as an inheritance), safety and comfort.

Chiron in the 3rd House

Our Woundedness is most likely to be played out in the arena of knowledge, the mind, communications, media, siblings, etcetera. See also, Chiron in Gemini.

For example, Chiron is Cancer in the 3rd house may manifest as a Wound of feeling unloved, uncared-for, not nurtured or looked after by virtue of feeling ignored, not communicated with as a fellow human, shunned by siblings and/or not being given credit for intellectual ability.

Alternatively, Chiron in Taurus in the 3rd house, say, could be the Wound of feeling deeply insecure, deprived or handicapped (lack of abundance) in the area of the intellect. Perhaps a deep mistrust of intellect. Perhaps a feeling of a lack of communication of Love and Trust.

Chiron in the 4th House

Our Woundedness is likely to be played out in the arena of the home environment, through parents and children and through Nature and the environment. Wounds and unresolved issues pertaining to our roots are illuminated here. See also, Chiron in Cancer.

For example, Chiron in Libra in the 4th house could be the Wound of feeling alone, incomplete, separate in the home environment. Something seems missing in the relationships between parents and children. It fails to fill our void, our need for contact, and even exacerbates it.

Alternatively, Chiron in Aries in the 4th house might be the Wound of feeling a deep inadequacy and low self-worth in the wake of seemingly-brighter siblings or parents with huge public profiles. Alternatively, it could be a feeling of being powerless to help the plight of the world, of Nature in crisis, feeling like a scourge upon the Earth's surface, expressed through a hatred of Humanity (which is the mirror reflection of hatred of self.)

Chiron in the 5th House

Our Woundedness is most likely to be played out in the arena of creativity, Inner Child, sexuality, self-expression, self-determination and ability to Shine or not. See also, Chiron in Leo.

For example, Chiron in Gemini in the 5th house may express as a Wound of feeling stupid or ignorant when it comes to creative matters. Alternatively, it might be a feeling of inability to communicate what is inside of us, an inability to bring what is inside of us to a wider audience.

Alternatively, Chiron in Virgo in the 5th house might be the Wound of feeling a deep dissatisfaction and/or self-criticism with any of our creative efforts or our efforts to be outwardly open and expressive. This, in turn, may be directed towards our children in the form of hypercriticism and nit-picking, causing them to fear expressing themselves or showing their own creativity.

Chiron in the 6th House

Our Woundedness is played out primarily in the area of the workplace, work methodology and in the area of our Service to the community. It can also be played out through issues of health and disease. See also, Chiron in Virgo.

For example, Chiron in Scorpio in the 6th house may manifest as the Wound of feeling as though people in our workplace are against us, constantly plotting, constantly seeking to undermine our work and work methods. Alternatively, feeling as though our work place is a kind of hell that we have been banished to by a cruel God, unable to leave due to fear of loss of income, lifestyle or contact with others. Alternately, we find ourselves working in a medical situation, close to the ill and the dying, our fear of loss and death challenged daily.

Alternatively, Chiron in Capricorn in the 6th house might manifest as a Wound of feeling unrecognized, unappreciated and not respected in the workplace. Moreover, nobody listens to us. Alternately, it might be that our feeling of not being heard, recognized, appreciated, etcetera, manifests in physical or emotional illness.

Chiron in the 7th House

Our Woundedness is most likely to be played out in the arena of relationships and social interactions. See also, Chiron in Libra.

For example, Chiron in Leo in the 7th house may manifest as the Wound of feeling unable to express ourselves, not free to explore and develop our creativity and individual gifts due to a stifling relationship that demands most of our attention and time.

Alternatively, Chiron in Pisces in the 7th house might be the Wound of feeling used and abused, victimized and betrayed by those we have had relationships with. Alternately, the Wound of feeling a deep need for contact and merging into Oneness may cause us to give ourselves away totally in relationships until we have little left for ourselves.

Chiron in the 8th House

Our Woundedness is primarily played out in the area of spiritual matters, death, dying, loss, power, sexuality, money or joint finance and immortality. See also, Chiron in Scorpio.

For example, Chiron in Virgo in the 8th house, say, may manifest as the Wound of feeling an incompleteness and dissatisfaction with life due to the death of those close to us. Alternatively, it might be that the feeling of being fragmented and incomplete may express through a deep inquiry into the nature of life and death and spiritual matters.

Alternatively, Chiron in Capricorn in the 8th house might manifest as the Wound of feeling a lack of order and control in our lives, due to the impermanence of life around us. Alternatively, it might be that our feeling of not being appreciated, recognized and respected is played out through relationships with others in the business world.

Chiron in the 9th House

Our Woundedness is most likely to be played out in the arena of the philosophical, the religious, the ethical and moral and the educational. Our Woundedness may be played out on an international stage. This placement illuminates the crisis of disconnection from our higher Self. See also, Chiron in Sagittarius.

For example, Chiron in Libra in the 8th house may express as the Wound of feeling alone, separate, cut-off from relationship and contact, expressing itself through a pursuit of spiritual matters in order to fill the void, i.e. developing a relationship with other realms. Alternately, we may seek relationship through travel or the Internet.

Alternatively, Chiron in Aries in the 9th house might manifest as the Wound of feeling inadequate, low in self-worth and unsure of our identity, causing us to pursue and become involved with religious or spiritual groups; alternatively, to study philosophy and/or psychology; alternatively, to generally gain higher education to give us a greater sense of worth.

Chiron in the 10th House

Our Woundedness is played out in the area of career, the public arena, business in general, mastery of our earthly purpose and through our need for recognition, appreciation, respect and acknowledgment of our achievements. See also, Chiron in Capricorn.

For example, Chiron in Sagittarius in the 10th house might manifest as the pursuit of business, management and public affairs as an answer to our Wound of feeling that life is meaningless otherwise and holds no secrets other than what we can tangibly make of it. A sense of achievement and accolades give respite from our inner feeling of emptiness.

Or Chiron in Gemini in the 10th house might express as the Wound of feeling intellectually stupid, ignorant or unrecognized, expressed in a career choice that is either physically and/or emotionally based, but not requiring too much thinking. Alternatively, it might be that our feeling of not being a good communicator or of being inept in social circumstances might be most prominent in our chosen career, such as acting or politics.

Chiron in the 11th House

Our Woundedness will most likely manifest in the arena of groups, community and collective expression. We will tend to be an individual expression of the collective Wounds of Humanity, seeking to play a unique role in the evolution of cultural consciousness. See also, Chiron in Aquarius.

For example, Chiron in Scorpio in the 11th house might manifest as the Wound of feeling that others are talking about us behind our backs, plotting or scheming against us and/or secretly conspiring against us. Alternatively, it might be that we fear the loss of unique cultural groups in the globalization process, these groups reflecting aspects of ourselves that we are in fear of losing through the growing process. Alternatively, it may be that we lament the loss of spirituality in the modern world and set out to make a difference by starting groups for the pursuit of spiritual matters.

Or Chiron in Cancer in the 11th house might manifest as a Wound of feeling unloved or unworthy of love by Humanity, the feeling that the world has become all so impersonal and uncaring. Alternatively, it might be that we wish to rescue groups of others who we perceive to be unloved and uncared-for, to become a Good Samaritan of sorts, a social worker, foreign aid worker or a champion of underdogs and minorities.

Chiron in the 12th House

Our Woundedness is most likely played out against the backdrop of our inner life, the unconsciousness, the psyche, spiritual longings, mysticism, etcetera, and perhaps within the walls of institutions concerned with the welfare (or incarceration) of the mind, body and spirit. In any case, the placement indicates that we tend to hide away the Wound, clinging to our Woundedness as a kind of paradoxical solace. Finding an outer divinatory expression for our mystical intuitions is necessary here. See also, Chiron in Pisces.

For example, Chiron in Taurus in the 12th house, say, may manifest as the Wound of feeling insecure, unsafe and neglected in love causing us to sequester ourselves in the relative safety of the inner recesses of the mind and fantasy world or in the cloistered walls of an institution that will give us what we need. Alternately, it could be that our feeling of having had emotional and material comfort and love taken from us or denied us is expressed in living a life of material self-denial and/or dedicating ourselves to the pursuit of Spirit.

Or Chiron in Aquarius in the 12th house, say, may express as a tendency towards becoming reclusive and non-participatory in life, licking our Wounds of feeling alienated, abandoned, cut-off, separate, different, a stranger in a strange land. Alternatively, it may manifest as a seeking for Contact and connection through the realms of the mind, Spirit, astral realms, the dream state and/or religious or spiritual groups.

7 ~ CHIRON IN ASPECT

The most important area of consideration of Chiron's influence and meaning, *even more so than the considerations of Chiron in the signs and houses,* is the area of Chiron's *angular aspects* to other planets in the natal chart. The aspects to other planets give Chiron and our specific Woundedness its character, its activation, its direction and specific manifestation. As we mentioned before, the number of strong aspects Chiron makes to other planets will determine its intensity and its specific outward manifestation. Chiron as a singleton is weak in its practical effect on our lives. *This can be said of every other planet, too. Angular aspects in the natal chart give our life focus, direction, meaning and intensity.*

This is perhaps contrary to the popular view, amongst the public and astrologers alike, that the signs and houses are the most important considerations. I have found that the signs and houses are *secondary* to the aspects in the chart. For this reason, I have devoted considerable space to the aspects in this book, more so than others books of this kind.

One of the great Gifts of Chiron and its aspects in our natal horoscope is to 'force' us, impel us or otherwise coax us to attend to our Healing and evolution of consciousness. It is the lever arm of evolution. The Gift is in the Wound.

Amongst the standard aspects, the aspect list contains *parallels* and *contra-parallels* of declination as well as *occultations* (parallel conjunctions). They have been included in the *conjunction* interpretations, as they are akin to conjunctions, but more powerful in effect. The importance of parallels lies in the fact that the aspected planets form identical angles to the plane of the ecliptic and hence to the galactic core, aligning them to a common frequency in relation to that core. The underlying astronomical, astrological and metaphysical factors behind this will be discussed in Book Three. In the meantime, I invite you to consider and ponder the *three-dimensional* angles created by parallel and contra-parallel planets, the plane of the ecliptic and the galactic core (the galactic core energy stream to our solar system lies perpendicular to the plane of the ecliptic[68]).

It is worth mentioning that the effect of the parallel aspect and that of the contra-parallel aspect are, for all practical purposes, *identical,* not opposite has been popularly thought. Practical demonstration of this is offered by the Magi Society, aforementioned.

Occultations (parallel *and* conjunct) are perhaps the most powerful of all aspects, combining and blending the energy and issues of the two participating planets in relatively perfect synthesis.

For the sake of simplicity, borrowing the terminology invented by the Magi Society, we will refer to parallels, contra-parallels and occultations collectively as *enhancements of declination.*

Before proceeding, let's speak briefly about orbs, i.e. the allowable range of radial distance between two aspecting or two transiting planets. Although many astrologers take quite wide orbs for the Sun and the Moon, gradually decreasing them for the slower-moving planets, I have found it more prudent and more accurate all around to take generally smaller orbs. It also tends to 'clean up' the chart and bring the key features into sharper relief. Otherwise, there can be a tendency in readings to waffle on about a multitude of relatively insignificant features, thereby clouding the essential issues or diverting attention from them.

When doing Soul-centered readings, for the Sun and the Moon, I tend to take a 5-degree applying orb and a 3-degree separating orb. For all other planets, I take a 3-degree applying orb and a 1 ½ degree separating orb. For quincunx aspects, however, I take only a 3 degree applying orb and a 1 and a half degree separating orb for the Sun and the Moon and a 1 and a half degree applying orb and a 1 degree separating orb for the rest. For parallels and contra-parallels, I take about a 2-degree applying orb and about a 1 degree separating orb for all planets.

However, having said this, for the sake of convenience and illustration, the examples I give of noted persons who exhibit particular aspects

---

[68] Note that we have said the "galactic core energy stream", *not* the galactic core that, from a visual perspective, is not perpendicular.

will often have wider orbs than the above. In addition, the example charts in this book also have more standardized (wider) orbs.

It is also important to remember that aspects taken in isolation cannot give a complete or entirely accurate appraisal of the dynamic and total picture of our natal horoscope. Such a total and dynamic picture can only be appreciated by looking at the overall patterns that *all* aspects of *all* planets make in the chart and integrating them into a synthesized and coherent picture. This is only possible in a dynamic reading situation. (A detailed chart delineation example is given in Chapter Eleven.)

Nonetheless, in order to begin to understand Chiron in angular aspect to the other planets, we must start with basic definitions of each aspect in isolation. We must bear in mind that these definitions must be modified as we begin to integrate the other aspects of the chart into a total picture.

Due to limitations of space, the definitions of the aspects that follow also lack the extra defining features of house and sign placements of each planet in question. Our definitions here will be more general and described in energetic terms rather than with environment-specific detail. We must leave the integration of these with their appropriate signs and houses to you, the reader. (For a brief overview of the themes and issues of each of the signs and houses, refer to Appendix C, "Affairs of the Signs" and Appendix D, "Affairs of the Houses".)

Chiron in aspect to North Node

It is important to mention that I am in the habit of taking the *true* Node positions, rather than the *mean* Nodes. It seems illogical to take a calculated average position that does not reflect the actual position of the point at the calculated time of the chart. My studies have confirmed the accuracy of making this choice, particularly with respect to the exact dates of transits to and by the Nodes.

In general, Chiron aspecting the North Node will indicate that our life's path and purpose are in some way more aligned than otherwise would be the case to the specific themes of Healing and the evolution of consciousness.

Conjunction, Parallel, Contra-Parallel, Occultation

Chiron conjunct the North Node of the Moon (the same as an opposition to the South Node) aligns the life's path and purpose with the Healing journey, *per se*. This aspect confers, more than any other, a life's path and purpose of conscious pursuit of Healing, in *our* lives and the lives of others. It is one of the marks of a person 'called' to be a Healer. Here, Chiron represents one of our life's primary planetary guides. We have been 'chosen', so to speak, to manifest and communicate Chiron's issues and messages of Wounding and Healing. This aspect can also be a tacit indication of considerable work already done on Healing and the evolution of consciousness in past lives.

The example natal chart delineation we will present in Chapter Eleven has this aspect.

Noted persons who share this aspect include Albert Schweitzer, Oprah Winfrey and Jimi Hendrix.

Enhancements of declination, i.e. parallels, contra-parallels and occultations, like the conjunction, bring the life's path and purpose into alignment with the themes of Healing and the evolution of consciousness in a conscious and outwardly manifest way. An occultation of Chiron and the North Node would be the mark of an extraordinary Healer.

Opposition

Chiron-opposition-North Node of the Moon (the same as a conjunction with the South Node) generally indicates the bringing of Healing Gifts and talents into this lifetime. It can also indicate that current issues of Wounding and Healing in this lifetime have strong connections to past lives. In any case, the awareness of issues of Wounding and Healing in the pursuit of our life's path and purpose will be very high.

Alternatively, it may be that we are now taking the lessons and Gifts of Healing attained in previous lives and directing them in practical ways in this lifetime. The specific ways are indicated by the sign and house of the North Node in this lifetime. In such a case, we may not necessarily have a life's path and purpose as a Healer, *per se*.

Trine

Chiron-trine-North Node (simultaneously sextiling the South Node) indicates a high degree of resonance between the life's path and purpose and the themes of Wounding and Healing in our lives. This indicates that Healing, whatever form it takes, will be an integral part of our life's journey and will be incorporated into the Service that we offer others.

For example, if our chosen life's path is, say, to be a musician, our music will almost certainly have a Healing element or will express our Woundedness directly.

This aspect can be a tacit indication of considerable work already done on Healing and the evolution of consciousness in past lives.

Examples of this placement include Nat "King" Cole, Bret Whiteley (artist, suicide) and Bill Clinton.

Square

Chiron-square-North Node (simultaneously squaring the South Node) indicates that our life's path and purpose cannot proceed without simultaneously attending to our Wounds, blockages and unresolved issues. In fact, because this is so, our life's path will necessarily have Healing elements in it, for us and for others, whether we call it Healing or not.

For example, let suppose our life's path and its expression is to learn to communicate our inner wisdom (North Node in Sagittarius, South Node in Gemini). We will be unable to do this until we attend to the Wounds that prevent us from *accessing* our inner wisdom. (This would be Chiron in Pisces, where we shut the door on the Universe and Spirit or Virgo, where we are so critical of ourselves that we cannot allow the outward expression of our seeming incompleteness). By attending to these Wounds, the inner wisdom that we will ultimately communicate, according to our Divine Design, cannot help but have elements of Healing knowledge and a Healing effect on others.

Examples of the aspect include Amelia Earhart, Al Pacino and Victor Hugo.

Sextile

Chiron-sextile-North Node (simultaneously trining the South Node) indicates that the energy and help of Chiron is available to us in the pursuit of our life's path. However, as with all sextile aspects, we must initiate the contact consciously and intentionally. When we do so, we can access the Gifts of our past-life Healing journeys (Chiron-trine-South Node). Whether we bring these elements to bear upon our chosen path and its expression through career, etcetera, is up to us. It is a Gift to be had, though, and we would be wise to make use of it. It means, however, attending to the Wounds of this present lifetime.

I am reminded of a friend of mine, a real estate agent who vacillates between attending to and ignoring his Healing and spiritual welfare. When he attends to these, he is extraordinary in his depth of understanding and power to help others, a vision to become a great speaker and Teacher. When he ignores these aspects of his life, he is like a little boy playing with his toys, selling real estate on the side.

It is quite common for people with this aspect to choose, unconsciously, a life's path that allows the Healing of our Wounds, blockages and unresolved issues to take place within the context of that path. In this way, this aspect of Chiron contributes to the Divine Design of our lives. A prime example of this is comedian and comedy writer, Marty Brill (writer for such television series as "M.A.S.H.", "The Mary Tyler Moore Show", "Mork and Mindy", actor on "All in the Family", appeared on "The Tonight Show with Johnny Carson" 37 times), whose childhood angst and fear still lives within him at age 69 (was six years old when his family left Romania under threat of Nazi occupation) and is translated into and drives his cutting and gritty humor.

Quincunx

Chiron-quincunx-North Node of the Moon indicates that we are being challenged to develop a new level of consciousness and awareness around our life's path and purpose. We are being coaxed to awaken to our life's higher meaning. Our Wounds, blockages and unresolved issues will be the catalyst that impels us to seek this understanding of why we are here and what we are meant to be doing from a higher perspective. The quincunx aspect is kind of like a mini-Pluto influence, encouraging transformation by coaxing us to let go of old ways of looking at things, in this case, old ways of thinking or not thinking about our life's path.

This quincunx represents a kind of niggling, irritating, frustrating nagging in our semi-conscious awareness, always insistently coaxing us to attend to our Wounds and issues.

Examples of noted persons with this aspect include Woody Allen and O. J. Simpson.

Chiron in aspect to South Node

In general, Chiron aspecting the South Node indicates that the themes of Healing and the evolution of consciousness are ones that we bring in strongly from the past, be it from past lives or from early in this lifetime. It can indicate that our life's path and purpose cannot be fulfilled without first attending to our unresolved issues and residual Wounds. It can also be the mark of person coming into this life with a specific Healing mission for themselves and as a Service to others.

Conjunction, Parallel, Contra-Parallel, Occultation

(See Chiron opposition North Node)

Opposition

(See Chiron conjunct North Node)

Trine

(See Chiron sextile North Node)

Square

(See Chiron square North Node)

Sextile

(See Chiron trine North Node)

Quincunx

Chiron-quincunx-South Node indicates that we are being impelled to develop a new level of consciousness and understanding about the Wounds, blockages and unresolved issues of our past, in particular, issues that have their ultimate origins in past lives.

When we say "origins in past lives", we must be careful not to give the impression that the specific issues of this lifetime, *in their present form,* were the same in past lives. This is erroneous. However, the *essence* of the issues is the same, their manifestation and form in *this* lifetime quite different. We will approach this interesting and misunderstood question in a later chapter.

In any case, in a sense, Chiron quincunxing the South Node indicates that we are chained to the past as long as we fail to see it in a new light. We are chained as long as we cling to the misperceptions and illusions that form the essence of our Woundedness. The fulfillment of our life's path and purpose, as indicated by the North Node, will hinge upon the Healing and resolution of the issues of the past.

Examples of noted people with this aspect include Muhammad Ali, Rupert Murdoch and Uma Thurman.

Chiron in aspect to Sun

In general, Chiron aspects to the Sun indicate that we are destined in some way to *express* the messages, issues and themes of Chiron in our lives. We are, in a sense, Chiron's emissary. The theme of coming out of the Darkness, into the Light, and allowing ourselves to Shine or not are crucial themes with these aspects.

Conjunction, Parallel, Contra-Parallel, Occultation

Next to Chiron conjuncting or making declination enhancements to the North Node, Chiron-conjunct-Sun is the most powerful manifestation of the themes of Wounding and Healing in our personal lives, particularly if it forms an occultation.

This aspect is another mark of a Healer and/or spiritual Teacher. Whether a person fulfils this task in a given lifetime or not is dependent upon many other issues and questions. In short, with this aspect, we *express* the Wound, the Healing and the themes of Chiron in our lives. We are, in a sense, Chiron's emissary. It is difficult for us to separate ourselves from our Wounds and it is certainly impossible to separate ourselves from the Healing path once initiated.

However, the area of life (seen through the houses) and the specific path and purpose of our life (seen through the Nodes), through which Chiron's messages will be expressed, will vary according. This is why we said that Healing encompasses many different areas of life. Some of these areas we would not initially consider as having a Healing effect. However, it is simplistic to associate Healing only with physical healing and the medical professions, traditional or alternate.

For example, a person with, say, the North Node in Capricorn and the Sun in Pisces conjunct Chiron in the 5th house may have a path and purpose to take responsibility for their life and for the lives of others, returning the nurturing they have been given along the way (North Node in Capricorn). They may express this through their emotional and psychic sensitivity towards others and their impulse to rescue others (Sun in Pisces). They then may play this out in the area of the arts (5th house), creating an environment and structure in which others can express themselves, like a performing arts complex (Node in Capricorn), thereby Healing their Wounds of fear of self-expression (Chiron's Gift and message as expressed through its conjunction with natal Sun).

We can see from this one example how crucial it is to consider all features of a chart in synergy with each other.

As one would expect, this aspect of Chiron and the Sun has its own difficulties and challenges because we cannot help but express our Woundedness. Whether we begin to transform our Wounds, blockages and unresolved issues or not will determine if we then express the Healing path as well.

In my own personal experience, three of my spiritual teachers, all highly psychic and all Healers, have had Chiron-conjunct-Sun, one making an occultation. Some examples of noted people who have this conjunction aspect are Jeanne Dixon (famous psychic), Tom Waits (singer), Jim Jones (Jonestown massacre), Hugh Hefner, Kevin Costner, Richard Carpenter (The Carpenters) and Shirley Temple Black.

Lastly, this aspect can be a tacit indication of considerable work already done on Healing and the evolution of consciousness in past lives.

Examples of noted persons with an occultation of Chiron and Sun include Queen Elizabeth II, Shirley Temple Black and noted Australian composer, Peter Sculthorpe.

Declination enhancements of Chiron and the Sun will act in a similar way to the conjunction aspect, although maybe not so obviously unless an occultation is formed.

Opposition

Chiron-opposition-Sun indicates that our Woundedness constantly challenges our need to self-express, our creative urge and our ability to Shine outwardly. The initial reaction is to retreat from self-expression, to close down, to become reclusive, in fear of being seen. However, the opposition aspect does not let us run away. In this way, it is Uranus's bed partner. The impulse to self-express and create are simultaneously *fueled* by the Woundedness and *held back* by the Woundedness, thus encouraging us to attend to our Wounds, blockages and unresolved issues.

In this aspect, the nature of the Wounds themselves will express as a Wounded sense of self and ego. There will be a fear of expressing ourselves, of standing out in a crowd, of being seen. There will be a fear that we are not good enough, that we are inferior to others who seem to be able to get on and be who they are without fear or reservation.

This aspect can also be the mark of a Healer and a call to express the messages and themes of Chiron to the world at large, in whatever form. In any case, it certainly calls one to introspect more deeply than one might otherwise do.

Noted persons with this aspect include Dane Rudhyar (Sabian Symbols), David Koresh (Waco), George Bernard Shaw, Johnny Carson and Madonna.

Trine

Chiron-trine-Sun indicates a high degree of resonance between our Woundedness and its path of Healing and the way in which we *express* our lives. Again, this can be an important aspect for a Healer. We cannot help but express the Wounds, in whatever form is appropriate to our life's path and purpose and its expression thereof, as indicated by our Sun's placement and other aspects. When we attend to our Wounds and unresolved issues, we cannot help but express the Healing, again whatever area of life that might be in. Again, we are Chiron's emissary in some way.

This aspect can be a tacit indication of considerable work already done on Healing and the evolution of consciousness in past lives.

Noted people with this aspect include Doris Greaves (astrologer), Erica Jong, Indira Gandhi, Luciano Pavarotti, Michelangelo and The Artist formerly called Prince.

Square

Chiron-square-Sun indicates that the outward *expression* of our life's path and purpose will be initially blocked, restricted or held back. The square aspect is Saturn's bed partner. What this means is that for us to be able to express our life, we must attend to our Wounds, blockages and unresolved issues.

As we have said, and it is worth repeating, the Gift of all major aspects of Chiron in our charts is to 'force' us, impel us or otherwise coax us in some way to attend to our Healing and our evolution of consciousness.

Having attended to our Wounds, blockages and unresolved issues, impelled by our innate need to express ourselves and our lives, we are then free to do so. We have transcended the square. Whether the Healing journey itself becomes an integral part of our life's path and purpose after this is not certain. It is not a 'given' with the square aspect. It will depend, in part, on the other aspects Chiron might make to other planets.

In my personal experience, the people I know with this aspect – some dozen or so – all have somewhat tumultuous inner lives. On the one hand, they try everything to wriggle away from their Woundedness and mostly quite successfully. On the other hand, they all *express* the wish for Healing and evolution of consciousness. This paradox creates its own ferment, making them quite deep thinkers for the most part. They vacillate between their wish for Healing and their outright avoidance of their issues. Their powers of rationalization and justification are supreme.

Noted people with this aspect include Barry Humphries (Dame Edna), Billy Connolly, D. H. Lawrence, Frank Sinatra, Merv Hughes (cricketer) and Sylvester Stallone.

Sextile

Chiron-sextile-Sun indicates that there is an open channel between our Woundedness, its Healing potential and the *expression* of our life's path and purpose. It represents opportunities and possibilities for consciously and intentionally accessing Chiron and its messages. To make use of this, however, *we* must initiate the connection to Chiron. It awaits us, but we need to activate it. To do this, we need to consciously attend to our Wounds, blockages and unresolved issues.

I have worked with at least half a dozen people with this aspect who have considerable Healing ability in some or other field, but do not pursue it for whatever reason. Still others make definite conscious use of it.

This sextile of Chiron and the Sun represents a potential color to add to our palette of life, another thread with which to express our Inner Light. It allows us to add the specific messages of Healing to whatever way we have chosen to express our life's path and purpose. If the rest of the chart indicates a specific life's path and purpose of Healing, then this will Serve us well on this path. If not, then this aspect will nonetheless Serve to help us clear the way for a free and open expression of our chosen path and purpose, whatever it may be.

Quincunx

Chiron-quincunx-Sun indicates that a new level of consciousness – a new understanding – about ourselves is being sought, one that will arise from the Healing of our Wounds and resolution of our issues.

Our view of ourselves is limited by our lopsided perceptions of ourselves and our illusory self-image. This affects the ease with which we express ourselves and allow our creativity to flow. These illusions and misperceptions have Served to keep us 'safe' from the challenge of greater

Truth, but now is the time for us to move into a higher awareness and a greater clarity about ourselves.

Chiron will bring this need home to us during our lifetime via this quincunx. Our frustration at the seeming difficulties of life that arise from our perception of ourselves and the resultant way we express ourselves will ever prick our innate wish for Healing and evolution of consciousness.

I am reminded of three persons I have worked with who all have enormous potential to do something special with their lives, but are stopped by some Wound of self, ego or illusory self-image. If, on their Healing journey, their image of themselves were to move to a different level, they would undoubtedly begin to shine their unique Gifts.

Chiron in aspect to the Moon

As we have said, the Moon represents the exterior face of Chiron inasmuch as it displays our lower emotional nature, i.e. our charges, issues, biases, judgments, etcetera. These lower emotional expressions arise from our Woundedness, as indicated by Chiron. Furthermore, we need to remember that the Wound and our life's path are intimately connected via the Moon's Nodes. The Wound drives the life's path, whereas the Moon's Nodes point us in a particular direction.

Also, as we have said, the Moon is simultaneously a safety valve and a safe haven. It protects us from too much Truth all at once *and* it is the mechanism that leads us to our lessons and unresolved issues by virtue of our lower emotional charges. As we work through our charges and issues, we begin to operate on a higher octave of the Moon's expression. We also become increasingly aligned to the Sun in consciousness, the Sun being the 'planet' of our higher nature.

Conjunction, Parallel, Contra-Parallel, Occultation

From the perspective of our lower nature, Chiron-conjunct-Moon indicates that the place we 'go' when things get too difficult or Painful is to retreat within ourselves and take a kind of paradoxical solace in our Wounds. It can be a feel-sorry-for-self, 'poor me', and/or 'look at me, I'm in Pain' kind of response.

The sign and house placement of this conjunction will give more clues as to the exact nature of the 'escape' route and the specific nature of the Wounds.

For example, if Chiron were conjunct the Moon in Taurus in the 7th house, say, it might be that the Wound of feeling denied or cheated of material and/or emotional comfort, safety and security (Chiron in Taurus) would express itself in relationships (7th house). When things get too difficult to deal with or too Painful (Moon response to Chiron's Wounds), we might seek material and emotional comfort (Moon in Taurus) in the relationship itself (7th house). However, never feeling as though we can get enough to soothe our Woundedness, we would play out the drama of the Wound *in* the relationship, 'milking it' for what we can get out of it.

This, as we have indicated previously, illustrates that the place we seek solace, 'escape' and/or avoidance can equally be the arena where we play out the Healing journey.

The higher octave manifestation of Chiron-conjunct-Moon would be an emotional nature that, when difficulties or Painful situations arise, seeks to 'escape' or 'avoid' the Pain of the Wound by immediately Healing it and resolving the issues around it! A most fortuitous aspect in terms of our potential Healing and evolution of consciousness!

Of course, the downside of that is never being able to truly 'escape' or avoid our Wounds.

Noted persons with the aspect include Barbra Streisand, Brigitte Bardot, JFK Jnr, Ron Howard, Marty Brill (comedian and comedy writer for such television shows as "M.A.S.H."), Angie Dickinson, Manuel Noriega (Panamanian dictator general) and Steven Spielberg.

Declination enhancements, as always, will have the same features as the conjunction, with the occultation of Chiron and the Moon being the most powerful. This would more than likely indicate a person of advanced evolution, being able to transform and Heal their Wounds 'on the fly', so to speak.

Opposition

Chiron-opposition-Moon indicates the tendency to run in the opposite direction when our Wounds, blockages and unresolved issues become too Painful to deal with.

Ironically, by running away from the Wound (Chiron), in its particular sign and house, we place ourselves in the opposite environment (in this case the sign and house of the Moon). By definition, the environment of lower-octave Moon can never hope to fill the Void we seek to Heal.

For example, the Wound indicated by Chiron in Scorpio, say, ultimately seeks a restoration of acknowledgment of Spirit and a transcendence of the illusions of loss and death. By running away to Taurus Moon, we will find only materiality, impermanence and illusory safety. So we try to run again, i.e. more materiality, physical comfort and the changing face of the world of forms, and still find it wanting. As William James once said, nothing of the senses can ever satisfy.

As another example, Chiron in Leo, say, ever seeking to overcome the fear of individual self-expression and to finally Shine, will ever be dissatisfied with environments where individual self-expression is lost in a sea of collective expression (Aquarius).

The nature of this opposition, as with all oppositions, is to continue to throw our issues back into our faces until we deal with them. The opposition says we cannot run away because the issues are *in* us, not outside us. Oppositions such as this are extremely difficult to deal with, but the upside is that they are extremely fruitful when grasped with both hands, so to speak.

If we continue to try to run away from our Wounds with this aspect, we will more than likely experience extreme fluctuations of mood and be hyper-reactive to outside influences.

The Gift of this aspect of Chiron and Moon is ever to impel us finally to attend to our issues and Wounds. As with all the planetary challenges we call angular aspects, whether we do attend to our Wounds and unresolved issues or not is up to us.

Noted persons with the aspect include David Helfgott (tragic pianist), Jodie Foster, John Lennon and k. d. lang.

Trine

Chiron-trine-Moon indicates that our lower emotional nature, being dualistic and reactive, will tend to illuminate our Wounds rather than offering us protection and an 'escape' route from them. We will very quickly, and in every way, witness the surfacing and action of our Wounds through our Moon-ruled emotional nature.

This gives us great potential for Healing if we do not keep futilely trying to run from our Wounds and issues. If we do continue to try, our emotional nature may tend to be hypersensitive.

If we do attend to the Wounds and issues that are reflected through our Moon-ruled emotional nature, this aspect can certainly be a mark of a person with Healing ability and focus in their lives.

Noted persons with this aspect include Karen Carpenter (who, in the end, presumably could not deal with her Wounds), Carole King, Charlie Chaplin, Diana Ross, Margaret Thatcher and Mark Knopfler.

I have also examined the charts of a multitude of patients in mental institutions and find that this aspect is very common, statistically more than the average one would expect.

Square

Chiron-square-Moon indicates that our lower emotional nature tends to stand in the way of us accessing our Wounds, blockages and unresolved issues. This is, of course, true for all of us, no matter what our Moon sign or aspects. However, in this case, the blocking effect is accentuated. The Moon, in this aspect with Chiron, represents a highly effective 'escape' route and avoidance mechanism.

However, we must remember what we have said about the dual nature of the Moon's manifestation. On the one hand, it protects us from the Pain and discomfort of bearing more Truth than we can deal with at any given time. On the other hand, it leads us, by virtue of our 'charges' – i.e. our lopsided perceptions, biases and judgments – to environments that are perfectly 'arranged' so as to offer us great possibility and potential for Healing and resolution of our Wounds and issues.

Said simply, what we judge negatively and have 'charges' against *we attract, create or become.* Conversely, what we judge positively and have infatuations about *we unconsciously drive away.*

So is the Moon square Chiron primarily 'good' or 'bad'? It is neither. On the one hand, it blocks our Wounds and makes it easier to avoid their Pain. On the other hand, paradoxically, by running away from our Wounds, blockages and unresolved issues, we will ultimately find ourselves in environments where we are constantly reminded of these.

In either case, the choice to attend to our Wounds and issues or not is up to us. It is fair to say that this square of Chiron and the Moon tends to disincline us to do so. If we do, however, chose to attend to these Wounds and issues, the Gifts are great.

This aspect, if unattended to, can manifest violence. For example, Martin Luther King Jnr was killed when The Moon squared Chiron. I have seen this aspect in high evidence in the charts of murders and murderers.

However, this same high energy can also be channeled equally successfully into productive pursuits, as in the case of tennis players John Newcombe and Arantxa Sanchez-Vicario; or into preaching as in the case of Billy Graham and Jim Bakker; or into humor as in the case of John Cleese, Vicki Lawrence and Spike Milligan; or into show business as in the case of Liza Minelli, Cher and Brooke Shields.

Sextile

Chiron-sextile-Moon indicates an open channel, able to be consciously activated and utilized, for seeing the connections between our deepest Wounds, blockages and unresolved issues clearly in the exterior face of our lower emotional nature. As we said at the beginning of this section on the Moon aspects, the Moon represents Chiron's outer face in the manifest world. If we can take our lower emotional responses, reactions and manifestations and trace them back to their origins, we will meet the Wounds in their primal state. This is true whether we have this sextile or not. However, this aspect enhances this process if we use it.

If we choose to use this Gift, we will have a great tool for our Healing and evolution of consciousness. If we do not, then this aspect is relatively benign.

Quincunx

Chiron-quincunx-Moon indicates that we will never be quite happy in the blissful ignorance and muffled womb of Mother Moon's protective shield. Something will always bother us, prick our attention and frustrate us. Something will constantly impel us to attend to our Wounds, blockages and unresolved issues, to come to a new and higher understanding about them, moving beyond the dualistic illusions of the lower mind.

From the point of view of our Wish for Healing, this simple aspect is a blessing in our lives, neither too confronting nor too sleepy.

Examples of noted persons with this aspect include Bill Clinton, George Lucas, Gillian Helfgott (astrologer and wife of tragic pianist, David Helfgott), Jeanne Dixon, Julie Andrews, Oscar Wilde, Phil Donahue and Prince Charles.

Chiron in aspect to Mercury

In general, Chiron aspects to Mercury confer a potential ability to communicate and express the messages of Chiron. However, the manifestation of this expression may tend to be more non-verbal than verbal due to Wounds to our ability to communicate verbally and intellectually with others.

Initially, before the journey of Healing and resolution of our Wounds and issues is pursued, consciously and intentionally, Chiron/Mercury aspects manifest as a Wound to our ability to express ourselves and communicate outwardly and openly. This produces the environment for deep introspection, Chiron's Gift in this case.

Once we begin to attend to our Wounds and issues, we will be invariably be guided to a form of expression and communication that is in alignment with our Divine Design, i.e. with our life's path and purpose.

With this aspect, when we attend to our Healing journey, we cannot help expressing Chiron's messages. We become, in a sense, Chiron's spokesperson.

Conjunction, Parallel, Contra-Parallel, Occultation

Chiron-conjunct-Mercury will initially express as a Wound that is unable to be expressed or communicated outwardly. It can also manifest as a fear of speaking or interacting with others, i.e. shyness or uncommunicativeness.

I am reminded of a comedian magician friend with Chiron-conjunct-Mercury in Aquarius who was so shy in early life that his parents thought there was something wrong with him. In the end, to avoid having to speak, but innately wanting somehow to express himself (Sun, Mercury and Chiron in the 5th house) and the Wound of his shyness, he started doing magic shows where he did not have to speak. Later, he incorporated his shy, bumbling and childlike character into the act as a comedy aspect. This was his Gift in the Wound.

In any case, people with Chiron-conjunct-Mercury are ultimately destined to *speak* Chiron's messages in whatever way corresponds to their Divine Design. For this to be fulfilled, we must attend to the Wounds indicated by the sign and house placement of the conjunct pair.

In practical terms, the outward reticence of this aspect leads to inward depth and deep thought, to be expressed and communicated as the messages of Chiron, in whatever form, usually later in life. The expression and communication is more often than not in a non-verbal form. For example, Martin Luther King Jnr was killed when Mercury and Chiron were conjuncting (and Saturn and Sun conjuncting). His message, at his physical death was silenced, verbally speaking, but broadcast loud and clear in another way.

As always, declination enhancements will produce similar features to the conjunction aspect with occultations being the most powerful of all.

Noted persons with this aspect include Cary Grant, Susan Sarandon, UFO contactee and channeler, George Van Tassel, Leo Buscaglia ("Dr. Hug", famous American psychologist and speaker), Cor Heiljgers (Dutch parapsychologist), and film director, George Mankiewicz.

Opposition

Chiron-opposition-Mercury indicates a battle within us between expressing ourselves and repressing our expression. There is initially a fear of revealing our Wounded nature and we hide it, putting on a brave or cool exterior. However, the Wounds seek expression, because it is only by being brought into the open that they can be dealt with, resolved and Healed.

If the Wounds do not emerge into the Light, illness can take place or the world may step in and give us a shake in some way. This opposition aspect represents an opportunity and catalyst to bring our unresolved issues and unHealed Wounds into the open.

Interestingly, the riots at the Berlin Wall of 1962 took place when Chiron opposed Mercury.

Noted people with this aspect include Muhammad Ali, Nancy Kerrigan (ice skater in the Tonya Harding knife-attack affair), Christine Keeler (British spy, prostitute) and Grace Kelly.

Trine

Chiron-trine-Mercury indicates a high resonance channel for the communication and expression of our Wounds in our lives. When we attend to our Wounds, this aspect confers the same channel for the communication and expression of the Healing path and the Healing messages Chiron.

Initially, however, it may cause us to find it difficult to express ourselves, preferring to remain reticent and guarded. Self-expression itself can be Painful due to the uncomfortable awareness of our Woundedness, like a lump in the throat.

This aspect, therefore, confers the Gift of deep introspection. When sufficient Healing and resolution has been done, we are then perhaps ready to express and communicate our thoughts and share our journey with others. In this case, depending on the other aspects to Chiron, this trine can add to our Healing ability and give us a sense of mission.

Most of the people I know and have worked with who have this aspect are guarded and reticent about speaking their innermost thoughts, although there is an obvious depth to them. The ones who have attended to their Healing journey have a message to share, but weigh their words carefully, only speaking in appropriate circumstances.

Noted people with this aspect include Billy Graham, Elton John, George Lucas, Hermann Goering, Martina Navratilova and Tatum O'Neal.

Square

Chiron-square-Mercury represents perhaps the most difficult of the Chiron/Mercury aspects in terms of expressing ourselves and communicating our innermost thoughts and feelings to others. This makes the degree and depth of our introspection all the more intense and makes the subsequent outward expression, when we attend to our Wounds and issues, all the more powerful and meaningful.

If we neglect our Healing journey with this aspect, mental instability is possible. I have studied the charts of people in institutions and involved in crime with this aspect featuring strongly in their lives. Such famous examples of this aspect include Henri Toulouse-Latrec, who suffered a mental breakdown during his life and was institutionalized for a time; also famous socialite, Brenda Frazier, who attempted suicide over thirty times in her life, suffered from bulimia and anorexia and battled alcohol and drug addictions; also Beach Boys drummer, Dennis Wilson, drowned after a drinking binge despite having entered a detoxification clinic a week before.

It is interesting how many singers have this aspect, not the least of which are Barbra Streisand, Bernadette Peters, Frank Sinatra, George Michael, Paul Simon, Paula Abdul and Patsy Cline. It is equally interesting how many people with this aspect have had throat surgery. (Mercury rules the voice and the throat.)

Also of interest is that JFK was assassinated when Chiron and Mercury squared.

Equal to the degree of intensity of this aspect, in terms of its accentuation of our Wounds of self-expression and communication, is its potential for Healing of these same issues. In addition, it increases the potential for the messages of Healing and the evolution of consciousness to come through in powerful ways.

Sextile

Chiron-sextile-Mercury confers the possibility of deep understanding of Chiron and its issues and themes and the subsequent possibility of expressing and communicating these. This, however, is not a given. As with any sextile aspect, the lines of communication between the two planets involved in the aspect must be consciously and intentionally opened and utilized.

If our Wounds and issues are not attended to, this aspect remains benign for the most part. If we do, however, then this aspect would be a welcome addition to the aspect set of someone wishing to pursue a path of Healing and evolution of consciousness for themselves and/or for others as a Service of their life's path.

Quincunx

Chiron-quincunx-Mercury indicates that a new level of consciousness about expressing and communicating our Woundedness and the subsequent Healing path and its themes is required. No better is this summed up than by the fact that this aspect is shared by Alexander Graham Bell (inventor of the telephone), Dane Rudhyar (Sabian Symbols), Jacqui Katona (Aboriginal land rights activist and spokesperson), Mohandas K. Gandhi, Vanessa Redgrave (actress and freedom fighter who turned the Academy Awards into a political platform in 1978) and Placido Domingo. Each found new ways and levels of communicating their own Wounding and Healing issues to a wider audience.

This aspect creates a constant impulse to try to express and communicate our issues and Wounds and continually to find newer and more evolved ways of doing this. It will not let us rest until we do. Neither will it give other people rest *when* we do, because we then are impelled to challenge the *status quo* and bring our new consciousness to a wider audience.

If we continually neglect the expression and communication of our Wounds and issues, an undercurrent of unrest, frustration, irritation is the result.

Interestingly, the Wall Street Crash and the recording of the first Beatles single share this aspect of Chiron and Mercury.

Chiron in aspect to Venus

Chiron aspecting Venus confers a natural empathy and concern for Chiron's issues. Our relationships will invariably have Chironic themes interwoven within them, i.e. themes of Wounding and Healing, spiritual growth and the evolution of consciousness, etcetera.

In general, Chiron aspecting Venus will tell us a lot about the ways in which we share our Woundedness and its subsequent Healing path with others. It will tell us in what ways we use the platform of relationship as a tool for our further Healing and evolution of consciousness.

Chiron in aspect to Venus can be a powerful addition to the chart of persons wishing to pursue Healing as a life's path, whether for themselves alone or in relation to others as well. Initially, however, Chiron/Venus aspects tend to create a deep longing, a deep wish for contact and for connection with others. This is mixed with a feeling that it is all futile and that the Wounds of feeling separate and alone will never be Healed.

Bearing in mind that Venus represents the lower octave of Neptune – Venus being the planet of earthly love, Neptune the planet of Unconditional Love – the issues of Venus are the foundations upon which our Return to Unconditional Love are based. When in aspect with Chiron, this provides a fertile soil – an exemplary vehicle – for the Healing of our Wounds and issues and our ultimate Return to Love.

Conjunction, Parallel, Contra-Parallel, Occultation

Chiron-conjunct-Venus initially indicates a deep longing, a deep sense of being cut off from close personal relationship, a feeling that there is not enough love to fill the void within us. This aspect confers enormous empathy and sympathy for others in emotional need. The impulse to try to rescue others, to wrap them in cotton wool, so to speak, is highly evident here.

As we attend to our Wounds, blockages and unresolved issues, this aspect will increasingly give us an awareness of the Love that is within us and around us in our lives, but that we mostly do not see or acknowledge. In this way, we are increasingly able to share our Love with others in a way that 1) does not seek to rescue them, protect them and/or 'fix' their lives, 2) does not necessitate emotional dependence on others and 3) does not involve trying to plug our umbilical cords into others. Ultimately, we will merely seek to Love Unconditionally, knowing that Love is the greatest Healer.

This aspect can indicate a high degree of Healing ability and focus and is a welcome addition to the charts of those interesting in pursuing Healing as part of their life's path and purpose.

In any case, whether we call it Healing or not, those with this aspect will have a Healing effect upon those they are around and upon those that they share their innermost feelings with. It may be in a verbal form. It may be in a musical form. It may be in some other form altogether. Whatever the case may be, these people will have a certain inexplicable attractiveness that compels us to wish to be around them and/or their creations and expressions. In short, they reflect our own Woundedness and the possibility for our own Healing. Having said this, however, being around certain types with this aspect can become high maintenance after a time.

Again, declination enhancements of Chiron and Venus will have similar features to the conjunction, with occultations being the most powerful of all in the intensity and focus of these features.

Noted persons that share this conjunction include Jacques Louis Demy (French film director, renowned for his romantic films), Marilyn Monroe, Kurt Cobain (Nirvana), Judith Durham (the Seekers), Henry Winkler, John Williamson (gentle Australian country songwriter and singer), Burt Bacharach, and Kevin Kline. The last three have occultations of Chiron and Venus.

Opposition

With Chiron-opposition-Venus, our Woundedness invariably shows itself through our relationship life, constantly challenging and confronting us to attend to our issues within this arena. We will tend to play out the drama of our issues and Wounds within our relationships. The relationships that we attract will invariably challenge and confront these same things in us. Our journey of Healing and evolution of consciousness will be facilitated by such persons that will come into our lives.

If we fail to attend to these issues and Wounds, our relationship life will tend to be tumultuous and intense to say the least. If we do, however, the rewards of Healing and evolution will be equal in power.

This aspect is a blessing in disguise if we have inclinations towards specifically pursuing a Healing path in our lives and for the sake of others. It impels us to attend to the areas of our life that will fine-tune our Healing abilities. This can be one of the aspects of a person 'called' to Heal.

The Healing and resolution of our Wounds and issues through this aspect can also take many other forms. However, the basis of all forms is the outward expression of our deepest feelings, through whatever medium is in alignment with our life's path and purpose.

Noted people with this aspect include Carole King, Antonio Banderas, Diana Ross, George Bernard Shaw, Heather Locklear and Tammy Bakker.

Trine

Chiron-trine-Venus indicates a high resonance between our earthly feeling and its expression on the one hand, and our Woundedness and its subsequent Healing path on the other, particularly in and through our close personal relationships. Relationships cannot help but bring up issues and Wounds, both in us and in those that we are in relationship with. However, with this aspect, the attendant Healing path is natural and well facilitated. This does not mean it will be easy or Pain-free. Healing always entails effort, intention and a Wish for Healing.

This aspect can be a difficult one for those that we get involved with in close relationship if they are unprepared for the level of intimacy and openness required. If they *are* prepared, however, the relationship can bear tremendous fruit of Healing and evolution of consciousness.

If there are trines of Venus and Chiron in the synastry or composite midpoint charts of two people, they will tend to be highly attracted to each other, emotionally, and more than likely develop a long-lasting bond. We will discuss this topic in greater detail in a later chapter.

Examples of noted people with Chiron-trine-Venus include Candice Bergen, Dwight D, Eisenhower, Jim Henson (the Muppets), George Lucas, O. J. Simpson and Johnny Weismuller (the original Tarzan).

Square

Chiron-square-Venus indicates that our Wounds and issues will generally stand in the way of our becoming intimate in close personal relationships. Alternately, depending on the type of relationship we have, relationships may provide a way of numbing us, sequestering us and/or protecting us from having to experience our Wounds, blockages and unresolved issues.

In the first case, we avoid intimacy at all costs because this means we must bare our Souls and reveal our Wounded nature. For this reason, this aspect can manifest as coldness, distance, hardness and/or toughness in our outer demeanor. We may even choose to avoid relationships altogether.

In the second case, we almost become like a dependent child within the relationship, burying our face in the other person's protective care, thus avoiding the subject of our inner feelings. Outside of the intimacy of this relationship, we may remain guarded, distant and cold towards others.

This aspect may also make us feel unloved, not nurtured, uncared-for and/or as though we are unlovable. Further, it can cause us to unconsciously sabotage our relationships and leave us wondering what is 'wrong' with us.

The Gift in this aspect is accessed by delving into ourselves, consciously and intentionally, attending to our Wounds, blockages and unresolved issues. This can be done the most effectively through the most difficult place, in this case through relationships. Relationships provide a perfect mirror of our Wounds, blockages and unresolved issues. Whether we have the courage to look squarely in that mirror or not is up to us.

As a part of a collection of Chiron aspects in the chart of a potential Healer, this aspect can be a welcome, if difficult, addition, particularly if it forms part of a T-square.

Noted people with this aspect include Martin Bryant (Port Arthur massacre, Tasmania), Cheiro (famous palmist and numerologist), Joe Frazier (boxer), Judy Garland, Paul Hogan, Bruce Lee, Jay Leno, Liberace and Gene Roddenberry (Star Trek creator).

Sextile

Chiron-sextile-Venus gives us the potential and possibility to access our Wounds and issues through the tool of our relationships. As with all sextiles, however, we must be the ones to consciously and intentionally activate this aspect with the Wish for Healing and resolution of our issues.

If we chose not to, then this aspect remains relatively benign. As an addition to other Chiron aspects in the chart of a potential Healer, this sextile is welcome.

Quincunx

Chiron-quincunx-Venus indicates that we seek a new level of consciousness around our earthly emotional life, our issues destined to be played out in our relationships. The key issues are whether we are Loved or not and whether we are Lovable or not. This aspect will not let these questions rest, constantly frustrating us, irritating us and prodding us to attend to the Healing and resolution of Wounds and issues that keep our consciousness at a lower level. In any case, it will tend to lead us to introspect deeply about our deepest feelings.

This aspect can be equally frustrating, irritating and confronting for those we are in relationship with as we will be constantly trying, unconsciously or otherwise, to bring *their* consciousness of these same issues to a higher level, too. Put simply, this aspect may cause us to try to 'fix' others. In this way, this aspect, like the quincunx aspect in general, is related to the sign of Virgo.

Further, this quincunx aspect is related to Pluto in terms of seeking transformation by letting go of old ideas and illusions. It is also related to Neptune inasmuch as it impels us move into the higher octave of our emotional nature and experience Unconditional Love.

This quincunx of Chiron and Venus, if combined with other aspects of Chiron, can indicate Healing ability and focus as a potential life's path. Having said this, we must bear in mind that the *form* our Healing ability will take will vary according to our life's path and purpose.

Noted examples of this aspect include Sean Connery, Leonardo DiCaprio, Phil Donahue, Whitney Houston, Walter Mondale and Charlie Sheen.

Interestingly, Chiron quincunxed Venus at the death of Jimi Hendrix; also during the 1962 Berlin Wall riots; also during the world's first heart transplant.

Chiron in aspect to Mars

Mars represents the lower octave manifestation of Pluto – the former being the planet of earthly and physical change and the latter being the planet of metaphysical and spiritual change. In general, Chiron aspecting Mars will represent the physical manifestation of our Woundedness and its subsequent Healing path, i.e. the things we *do* or *not do,* the actions we take or not take and the decisions we make or not make.

Mars works on two octaves, the octave of the lower nature, which *reacts,* and the octave of the higher Self, which *acts.*

If Mars represents a call to action, a call for us to make an intention, a decision or a resolve, then Chiron aspecting Mars will be a call for us to react or act upon our Wounds, blockages and unresolved issues. Reactions will occur if we do not intentionally attend to these things. If we *act,* however, from an intention, a resolve and/or a Wish for Healing, then our Healing and evolution of consciousness is expedited.

Conjunction, Parallel, Contra-Parallel, Occultation

Chiron-conjunct-Mars initially tends to create acute, even violent reactions when our Wounds, blockages and unresolved issues are triggered. Even when we are calm, there tends to be an unsettled emotional undercurrent within us. We tend to be hyper-reactive unless other astrological considerations counteract this aspect. Alternately, our energy can be entirely dissipated, leading to depression.

Our Wounds and issues can manifest as acute physical illness, sudden accidents or, conversely, as excess physical energy, particularly if we do not attend to these Wounds and issues. This energy can be very powerful when channeled into areas of our chosen life's path and purpose. Our Wounds, blockages and unresolved issues can form a powerful motivating force for us, whether used for Healing as such or for the pursuit of something else. There is a kind of unconscious urgency that goes with this aspect, whether an urgency to escape and avoid our Wounds, blockages and unresolved issues or an urgency to deal with them.

In the chart of a potential Healer, this aspect can confer great physical Healing ability.

Noted persons that share this aspect include Billie Holiday, Ross Perot, Gillian Rolton (Olympic equestrian), Bob Crane (Hogan on Hogan's Heroes. He was brutally murdered during his Chiron Return while Mars trined his natal Mars/Chiron.), Gian-Franco Zefferelli (film industry genius), Monica Lewinsky and Oliver Stone.

Opposition

Chiron-opposition-Mars tends to accentuate and exacerbate all the features of Chiron-conjunct-Sun, aforementioned. There will be a constant tug-of-war between our Woundedness and our reactions to them. We will initially seek to run very fast from our Wounds, blockages and unresolved issues, only to find that we crash into them again.

This aspect is perhaps the most emotionally and physically hyper-reactive of all the Chiron aspects. It augurs wars, violence and conflict when our Wounds, blockages and unresolved issues are stirred up. It can also manifest as a kind of soap-box preaching and campaigning against perceived injustice, inequality, abuse and *for* human rights, etcetera. Furthermore, this aspect features in the charts of many violent criminals I have studied.

Nonetheless, if this excess energy is channeled into our life's path and purpose, it has unparalleled physical and emotional power.

Interestingly, Chiron opposed Mars during the Wall Street Crash and during Austria's declaration of war on Serbia in WWI.

Noted people that share this aspect include Winston Churchill, Luciano Pavarotti, Manuel de Falla (composer), Stonewall Jackson, David Helfgott (tragic Australian pianist, Chiron opposes Mars, Venus *and* Moon), Tokyo Rose and Jackie Weaver (Australian actress and human rights activist).

Trine

Chiron-trine-Mars, like Chiron-conjunct-Mars and Chiron-opposition-Mars, adds enormous energy to our lives, but is potentially much smoother and harmonized than the other two. It is still hyper-reactive, but generally lacks the jagged edges of Chiron in conjunction or opposition to Mars. It is less violent, less primal and we are not so inclined to try to run away as fast as we can or to blame the world for its injustices, etcetera, towards us and others. However, this aspect can still lead to campaigning against social injustices, abuse and *for* human rights, etcetera. It can also lead to violence, apparent from numerous criminal charts studied, particular homicides.

Whether we attend to our Wounds, blockages and unresolved issues or not, this aspect can be a motivating force in our lives. On the one hand, we are driven by the impulse to escape or avoid our Wounds, leading us to our Divine Design *unconsciously.* On the other hand, we are driven by the impulse to Heal and resolve our Wounds and issues, leading us to our Divine Design *consciously.*

Interestingly, Chiron trined Mars during the time John Lennon was murdered; also, during the recording of the Beatles' first single.

Noted persons with this aspect include Azaria Chamberlain (dingo murder trial baby), Phil Donahue, Judith Durham (the Seekers), Jane Fonda, Judy Garland, Bob Geldof, Steffi Graf, Natassja Kinski, Michelangelo, Dudley Moore, Jacqueline Kennedy Onassis and Venus Williams.

Square

Chiron-square-Mars indicates that, initially, our motivation and energy can tend to be blocked due to our Wounds, blockages and unresolved issues. Initially, this aspect may manifest as a *deficit* of energy, unlike the preceding Chiron/Mars aspects we have explored.

The frustration at this lack of energy or motivation, compounded by a feeling of being thwarted at every corner in our lives, can manifest as hyper-reactions, depression or even chronic fatigue. The difficulty of revealing our life's path and purpose saps our energy reserves. Conversely, the frustration with our Wounds and issues can cause us to explode. Violence is evident with this aspect as well.

The Healing path is impelled by our need to answer these questions, i.e. why are we lacking in energy and motivation, what is the meaning and purpose of our lives and why are we seemingly thwarted in our lives? The Healing path, as ever, consists of attending to our Wounds, blockages and unresolved issues by asking balancing questions. It consists of seeing the flip-sides of happenings in our lives, seeking the lessons, blessings and Gifts behind those people, places, events and circumstances that we have otherwise been judging negatively.

This aspect is a Gift inasmuch as it tends to lead us to introspection, even against our efforts and tendency to avoid our Wounds, blockages and unresolved issues. As we begin to work through some of these things, our energy levels, inspiration and motivation return.

As a part of a potential Healer's chart, particularly if involved in a T-square, this aspect confers Healing power and depth of insight into what motivates us as human beings.

Interestingly, Chiron squared Mars at Chiron's discovery in 1977.

Noted persons that share this aspect include Michael Jackson, William Blake, Marlon Brando, Hillary Clinton, Christian Dior, Billy Graham, Jim Jones (Jonestown massacre), Jay Leno, Doug Mulray (Australian radio personality) and Jean Paul Sartre.

Sextile

Chiron-sextile-Mars represents an open channel to be able to use our Wounds, blockages and unresolved issues, consciously and intentionally, as a motivating force. Conversely, it allows us to pursue our Healing, consciously and intentionally, with vigor and purpose.

However, as with all sextile aspects, we must consciously activate this channel by our intention to Heal or be motivated by our Wound and issues. Otherwise, this aspect remains relatively benign.

The sextile of Chiron and Mars represents a welcome addition to the aspects of a potential Healer who has other major aspects to Chiron.

Quincunx

Chiron-quincunx-Mars indicates a frustrating, irritating and incessant need to know what to do next, what action to take, why things happen the way they do, what the causes are of one thing and the next. It tends to create incessant inquisitiveness and questioning. Sometimes this can be irritating to others who may perceive it as badgering. This aspect is very related to the sign of Virgo inasmuch as the need to figure out all the details of what we are questioning becomes almost obsessive.

In the final analysis, our Wounds, blockages and unresolved issues drive these needs and questions, seeking Healing and resolution. This aspect is a welcome addition to the aspect set of those wishing to pursue a Healing path and/or Healing as a specific life's path and purpose.

Interestingly, Chiron quincunxed Mars during the Cuban missile crisis; also, at the time the USSR pulled out of Cuba; also, at the death of Jimi Hendrix; also, during the 1967 Apollo disaster; also, during the LA race riots in 1965; also, during the alleged Roswell UFO incident in 1947.

Well known persons with this aspect include Billy Ray Cyrus, Alfred Gottschalk (biochemist and writer), Dustin Hoffman, Larry King, Colleen McCullough (Australian popular fiction writer), Edwin C. Moses (Olympic hurdler), Martha Raye (American entertainer), Dennis Rodman (basketball player) and Ritchie Valens.

Chiron in aspect to Jupiter

In general, Jupiter represents our Inner Child; it also represents our capacity to receive abundance in its many forms and return our inner abundance to the world in the form of our Divine Design. On the positive side, it represents good fortune and wisdom, on the negative, excessiveness, waste, childishness and folly.

Chiron in aspect to Jupiter indicates that our Wounds, blockages and unresolved issues are very much attached to our Inner Child issues and to the Inner Child's ability to express itself or not. The Healing path takes us to a reawakening of the innocence and child-like wisdom of the Inner Child. It takes us back to a *joie de vivre* that we tend to lose as we grow up. It reminds us that life is an adventure, full of magic, mystery and magnificence.

Our Wounds, blockages and unresolved issues generally have their primal origins in childhood, before the Inner Child begins to retreat with the approach of puberty. For this reason, Chiron/Jupiter aspects are extremely powerful in their potential capacity to awaken us to our Wounds and to allow us to see their inner wisdom. Jupiter presents us with our first glimpse of the Guiding Hand in our lives.

Chiron/Jupiter aspects also bring issues of freedom to the fore, physical freedom as well as spiritual, ideological, philosophical and political freedom.

Conjunction, Parallel, Contra-Parallel, Occultation

Chiron-conjunct-Jupiter represents the combination of Healing and wisdom, acquired by delving into our Wounds, blockages and unresolved issues and seeing the hidden Plan that lies behind them. This aspect can be the mark of a great Healer and/or Teacher.

With this aspect, the adventure of our lives *is* the journey of Healing and the evolution of consciousness, whatever form that adventure may take. That journey will tend to be larger than life and rich in content, our Gifts on display to the world as an inspiration and testament to the possibility of Healing in our lives.

Sensing the underlying Plan and feeling innately that we are all destined to be free to Shine, this aspect can confer a call to champion the cause of freedom in the world, freedom from oppression and freedom from ignorance.

Other people living around those with this aspect may find it difficult to take as the native's openness and inner certainty about touchy issues will be both challenging and confronting.

One the other side, this aspect can confer issues and Wounds around justice, fairness, equality, morals and ethics.

This aspect can be a tacit indication of considerable work already done on Healing and the evolution of consciousness in past lives.

One of my first spiritual teachers had this aspect. He taught us Gratitude for our given lives. He awakened us to the magic and mystery of consciousness. He helped us see the miraculous Plan of our lives.

Interestingly, this aspect occurred during the recording of the Beatles' first single *(see Chart 20 – BEATLES 1ST SINGLE, p. 556)*. In addition, it forms part of multiple aspects of Chiron at the time of the hanging of Nazi war criminal Ernest Eichmann in May 1962. It also occurred during the Berlin Wall riots of August 1962.

Noted persons who share this aspect include writer James Joyce, Jodie Foster, Pablo Picasso, Cher, Divine (drag performer), Goldie Hawn, Bette Midler, Edith Piaf, Franklin D. Roosevelt, Frank Sinatra, Sylvester

Stallone, Donald Trump, Henry Winkler and John Williamson (gentle Australian country singer songwriter).

Opposition

Chiron-opposition-Jupiter indicates that our adult idealism is initially at odds with our Wounds, blockages and unresolved issues, particularly those Wounds of early childhood or that involve our Inner Child. The initial reaction to this aspect is to assert that there is something "wrong" with the world that has dealt us our Wounds. We feel things should have been different and could be different now, if only . . . The "if only" then leads on to ideas, philosophies, morals and ethics that we feel support, encourage and engender a better world for all. This psychology may be played out solely in the spaces of our own psyche, Serving to make only our own lives more bearable. Alternately, it may be that we project this psychology onto the outside world and promote our philosophies to a wider audience. Overall, we are driven by the paradox of the child's view of the world versus the adult's view.

This first scenario illustrates the path of apparent escape and avoidance. As we attend to the Healing journey, however, in the second possible scenario, the external manifestation may not seem all that different to the outside view. However, from an internal point of view, the Healing of our Wounds and the resolution of our issues teaches us that even our Wounds Serve us; they are part of the Plan; they *support* the greater picture; they hold the Gift of our lives within their shells. The more we awaken to this, acknowledge this, embrace this and finally Love this, the more we are able to share the inherent wisdom we encounter and that grows within us. The child's view and the adult's view become merged and resolved into a greater picture of Truth. The outward manifestation of this may take the form of ideas, philosophies, morals, ethics, religious and spiritual teaching, etcetera. This wisdom may be for us alone or we may choose to share it with others, depending on our chosen life's path.

In short, Chiron-opposition-Jupiter provides us with an opportunity to begin to witness a larger plan behind our Wounds, blockages and unresolved issues, beyond our initial judgments. As such, this aspect can be an integral part of the chart of a person who wishes to pursue Healing as a specific life's path and purpose.

Noted persons who share this aspect include Charlie Chaplin, Agatha Christie, Doris Day, Dwight D. Eisenhower, Chris Evert Lloyd, Adolf Hitler, Carl C. Jung, Annie Lennox and Denzel Washington.

The startling difference between these noted people who all share this aspect is worth commenting about. We have mentioned that Chiron in the chart does *not* indicate what a person's life's path or purpose will be (this is the domain of the Nodes of the Moon). Neither does it indicate how they will *express* that life's path (this is the domain of the Sun). However, it does indicate what it is that *drives* us towards our life's path and towards initial discovery and ultimate manifestation. The Wound can drive us in one of two ways. Firstly, it can drive us by virtue of our attempts to escape from and to avoid the Wounds. Secondly, it can drive us by virtue of our attempts to Heal the Wound and resolve the attendant issues.

Either way, *we are invariably and inevitably lead to our Divine Design.* Our Divine Design may not be to the liking of other people; it may even seem wrong and evil when weighed against society's current, values, morals and ethics. Nonetheless, *every Divine Design – i.e. every person's life's path and purpose – Serves the greater picture, Serves the Plan of Creation in some way.* This is Jupiter's higher message. Awakening to the Truth of this message is part of our journey of Healing and the evolution of consciousness. We will touch on some of these points again in Book Two when we explore morals and ethics.

Trine

Chiron-trine-Jupiter indicates an uncommon potential to access the Wounds, blockages and unresolved issues of our early childhood and/or our Inner Child. The degree to which we actually Heal and resolve these things will depend on our willingness and intention to do so and upon the other aspects in our charts, particularly those to Chiron. The specific expression of our Wounds and issues and/or their Healing results will vary accordingly. The range of this aspect's outward expression can be illustrated by looking at the differences between people such as Martin Bryant (the mass murderer), Kurt Cobain (Nirvana's lead singer, now deceased) and Pope John Paul II, who all share this aspect, but express it in vastly different ways.

The Wounds, blockages and unresolved issues of our Childhood and/or Inner Child are very close to the surface with this aspect, but in a more harmonious and less confronting way than with, say, Chiron in opposition to Jupiter. However, this does not necessarily make it easier for us. The Healing journey always requires effort, intention and a wish to Heal. And there is always the possibility of emotional backlash and violence arising from childhood Wounds and issues.

This aspect is a welcome addition to the chart of a potential Healer, particularly if it is part of a grand trine. It provides access to early childhood Wounds and Inner Child issues. This is one of the first steps in the journey of Healing and the evolution of consciousness.

Lastly, this aspect can be a tacit indication of considerable work already done on Healing and the evolution of consciousness in past lives.

Interestingly, Star Trek's very first episode aired during a Chiron-trine-Jupiter aspect, although there were many other equally important aspects for this event. *(See **Chart 11 – STAR TREK 1ST EPISODE**, p. 546.)*

Noted people that share this aspect include Pope John Paul II, Lucille Ball, Martin Bryant (Port Arthur massacre, Tasmania), Kurt Cobain (Nirvana), Germaine Greer, Johannes Keplar, Chaka Khan, Henry Mancini, Michelle Pfeiffer, The Artist formerly called Prince and Giacomo Puccini.

Square

Chiron-square-Jupiter indicates that our early childhood/Inner Child Wounds, blockages and unresolved issues are initially blocked, bottled up and even hidden. This tends to cut us off from the joy, lightness, freedom and sense of adventure that we could experience through the Inner Child. Our resulting outward demeanor may be quite serious, heavy, 'adult', harsh, disciplinary, violent, reticent, shy, reserved, guarded and/or cold, amongst other possibilities.

The way in which this aspect will manifest will be determinant upon our willingness to delve into our Wounds and issues. If we are not willing, then we are more likely to take it out on the world around us, blaming it for our Woundedness, consciously or unconsciously. This is the more likely result of this aspect, particularly if Chiron has no other major aspects. Again, emotional backlash and violence can manifest as a reaction to childhood Wounds and issues.

Conversely, if we are willing to embark upon the Healing journey, this aspect will take us on a journey of rediscovering the wise but child-like part of us. Our Hearts seek lightness, freedom, joy and adventure and will ever impel us upon the Healing journey back to these experiences.

Although this is perhaps the most difficult aspect of Chiron and Jupiter, it is worth the journey as the Return to Love is the end-result. The journey will ultimately take us back to our childhood and show us the lessons, benefits, blessings and Gifts of those happenings that we have previously judged negatively since childhood. It is a process of awakening to the perfection of our lives and to the Loving Guiding Hand, which has been there from the beginning.

This aspect is a difficult but profitable addition to the chart of a person wishing to pursue Healing as a specific life's path, particularly if it is part of a T-square or another such larger planetary pattern.

Noted persons who share this aspect include D. H. Lawrence, David Koresh (Waco), Doug Mulray (Australian radio personality), Henri Toulouse-Latrec, Jamie Lee Curtis, Nat "King" Cole, Patrick White (Australian writer) and Robert Kennedy.

Sextile

Chiron-sextile-Jupiter indicates an open channel available to us between, on the one side, our Inner Child and its wise but childlike wisdom and, on the other side, our Woundedness. The potential for Healing of our childhood Wounds, blockages and unresolved issues is high with this aspect, but we must actively initiate this aspect by our conscious intention and our Wish for Healing. If we do not do this, this aspect remains relatively benign.

This aspect is a welcome addition to those interested in Healing, for themselves or for others as a more specific life's path and purpose.

Quincunx

Chiron-quincunx-Jupiter indicates that we will be continually impelled to reach a new level of consciousness and understanding about our childhood issues. We will be continually impelled to access our Inner Child wisdom and to see the Service that every happening in our childhood has given us.

There is a difference between our early-life childish reactions, arising from our lopsided perceptions, and the childlike wisdom of the Inner Child. The Inner Child innately senses the 'rightness' of all that transpires in the world and in our lives and ever impels us, as conscious adults, to awaken to the perfection of it all.

With this aspect, there will be a constant nagging feeling in the back of our awareness that there is another way of looking at the things that we currently judge negatively. That is, there is a flip-side. There is another picture. There is another attitude that we could find that would form the basis of our Healing with respect to these issues.

Noted people who share this aspect include Aaron Spelling, Bill Gates, Carl Sagan, Charles Manson, Jane Fonda, Mary Shelley (Frankenstein author), Pauline Hanson (Australia's One Nation political Party), Richard Burton and Whoopi Goldberg.

Chiron in aspect to Saturn

In general, Saturn represents restriction, limitation, repression and blockage. On the other side, it represents responsibility, seriousness, discipline, perseverance, real work and steady progress. Contrary to popular belief, the general public and astrologers alike, I believe Saturn has a lightness and a twinkle in the eye behind its stern exterior. Saturn sternly sits us down and firmly makes us take stock of our lives, knowing that by doing so, we will ultimately find freedom.

When Chiron aspects Saturn, we see an accentuation of the theme of taking responsibility for our Wounds and unresolved issues. We are impelled to take stock of our lives, to ponder where we have been, where we are and where we are going. We are encouraged, *by our restrictions, limitations, repressions and blockages,* to begin serious work towards our ultimate Healing and evolution of consciousness. Saturn and Chiron work naturally together towards our ultimate freedom, the freedom of awakened consciousness.

Conjunction, Parallel, Contra-Parallel, Occultation

Chiron-conjunct-Saturn initially indicates a high degree of suppression and/or repression of our Woundedness. Saturn's task is to keep us grounded, to balance our evolutionary inclination to approach the Light. The mythical Icarus made himself wings and flew towards the Sun, but getting too close, his wings melted and he fell back to the ground. Like Icarus, we need to stay between acceptable limits of awakening and sleeping, in accordance with our present level of conscious evolution. When we get too elated or move too quickly, Saturn steps in and brings us back to Earth, so to speak.

Saturn says to us that we need to solidify the foundations of our journey of Healing and evolution of consciousness, to take control, to become accountable, before we can take our rightful place in the Higher Realms.

Saturn-conjunct-Chiron is saying exactly this to us. Although we may feel held back, suppressed, repressed, limited and restricted, there is important work to be done in this space. The Wounds Serve us *as they are* until we are truly ready to transcend them.

From one point of view, this is a most difficult aspect and tends to make us extremely judgmental of ourselves and our perceived weaknesses; this is reflected in our attitudes towards others. We simultaneously seek to maintain ultimate control of ourselves and our lives and yet are subservient to our reactions that have their origins in our Wounds, blockages and unresolved issues. These Wounds and issues will rule us until we learn their lessons and learn to Love them with Gratitude.

From another point of view, this aspect is a Gift inasmuch as it forces us to stay in the one place, unable to run away from our Wounds, blockages and unresolved issues, until we deal with them, methodically and thoroughly. This can be one of the Chiron aspects involved in the chart of a person 'called' the Heal, providing there are other Chiron aspects that trace a freer path of Healing than Saturn on its own.

Lastly, this aspect can be a tacit indication of considerable work already done on Healing and the evolution of consciousness in past lives.

Noted persons that share this aspect include Wilhelm Keitel (Hitler's closest military advisor), Bela Lugosi (horror film actor), Sybil Thorndike (British actress), Armand Hippoly Fizeau (physicist who first successfully measured the speed of light – this is extraordinary when we remember that Saturn is the planet that brings the Light of Creation into physical and measurable form! Matter is polarized Light according to modern physics, i.e. Wounded Light, in Chiron's terminology. We will explore this topic in depth in Book Three.), William Worrall Mayo (Mayo Clinic), Getulio Dornele Vargas (Brazilian dictator), Queen Victoria (very Saturnian!) and poet/writer, Walt Whitman.

It is also interesting to note, again, that Star Trek was approved for production during a Chiron/Saturn conjunction.

Opposition

Chiron-opposition-Saturn is perhaps the most difficult of Chiron/Saturn aspects barring the conjunction aforementioned. Saturn's power to hold us in one place until we learn our lessons is somewhat broken down here. This is due to the opposition aspect giving us a place to 'run', giving us an opposite choice and giving us the power of disagreement and challenge to what is thrown our way.

In a sense, when things get difficult or Painful, we tend to run in the opposite direction, in this case towards Saturn. However, when we find ourselves limited, restricted, held back, held down and suppressed in our life's expression, we will run the other way again, in this case, back into our Wounds, blockages and unresolved issues. This tic-tocking creates the ferment and soil in which our journey of Healing and evolution of consciousness can take place.

This aspect will tend to bring father issues to the fore and will initially make us feel as though we are unable to deal with our lives due to these issues. Once we transcend blame, though, we will begin to see the Plan that lies behind the whole affair. We will gradually see the divine orchestration that has gone on in our lives, inexorably leading us to our destiny and Divine Design.

This aspect can cause us to hold ourselves back, to restrict and repress ourselves. The alternative is having to deal with our Wounds, which we are not necessarily ready to do. This can confer conservatism, pragmatism and hard-nosed attitudes towards ourselves and others. Tendency towards being a hard task-master . . . in this case, we tend become our father.

On the other hand, if we are willing to work with our Wounds and issues, Saturn will offer unparalleled support. We have mentioned previously that Saturn is the gatekeeper, guarding the entrance to the outer planets, guarding the doorway to Chiron until we are ready to take responsibility for our lives. Thus, the key to the resolution of this aspect lies in giving up blame and taking personal responsibility for our lives, our issues, our Wounds.

Noted persons that share this aspect include Aaron Spelling, George Bush, Giacomo Puccini, Joan of Arc, Anton Chekhov, Marcel Marceau, Queen Mary Stuart and Hank Williams.

Trine

Chiron-trine-Saturn indicates the potential for a high degree of serious and responsible intention and work towards our path of Healing and evolution of consciousness. This aspect innately expresses an attitude that we need to be disciplined, serious, responsible, practical and hard working towards this area of our lives, as in any other more tangible area of our lives.

This is perhaps the most fortuitous of the Chiron/Saturn aspects in this respect. It does not make it easy, it just makes it seem more profitable to embark upon our Healing and evolutionary journey to begin with.

The downside of this aspect could be that, due to our constant attention to matters concerning our Wounds, blockages and unresolved issues (and our attempts to work through these), we limit, restrict, repress and otherwise hold back other areas of our lives. Alternately, that we would continually resist and repress our Wounds, blockages and unresolved issues (negative Saturn) as a way of life, as it is the line of least resistance.

How we react to any aspect is dependent on the other aspects in our chart and on our own willingness to meet the challenges face to face.

This aspect can be a tacit indication of considerable work already done on Healing and evolution of consciousness in past lives.

Noted persons that share this aspect include JFK, Stephen Sondheim, Dean Martin, Gillian Helfgott (astrologer wife of tragic pianist, David Helfgott), James Earl Jones, Lena Horne and American writer, Tom Wolfe.

Interestingly, this aspect was in force during the release of the film, Close Encounters of the Third Kind.

Square

Chiron-square-Saturn represents a kind of double-dose of blockage and repression of our Wounds, blockages and unresolved issues. A path of Healing will be evident if this square forms part of a T-square aspect or another such larger planetary pattern. Otherwise, it will be very difficult to gain access to this area of our lives.

This aspect formed a major feature of the years between 1935 and 1952 and for those born at the time. It also contributed to what the youth of the 1960s called *the establishment.* The economic and technological growth of the 20th century world arose, in part, out of this aspect. This square, during these years, was finally broken down by Uranus's opposition to Chiron in 1952.

This aspect is prone to emotional backlashes, violence, frustration, desire to control others and deep self-depreciation. Attaining mastery of the material world – physically, emotionally, mentally, financially, politically, in terms of resources, in terms of people and populations, etcetera – seems the only defence against this.

What could be the benefits, lessons, blessings and/or Gifts of such an aspect (presuming we did not get what we were saying in the last sentence)? We must think laterally to discover this. Firstly, the Universe is trying everything it can to 1) awaken us to our divine nature and 2) help us to see, acknowledge, embrace, Love and finally fulfill our Divine Design. Secondly, our Wounds act as the driving force in our lives, inexorably leading us towards these two ends. Bearing all this in mind, we are driven towards our Divine Design and awakening *whether we Heal our Wounds and resolve our issues our not.*

This may seem contradictory to everything else we have presented so far. Let's look at it this way: we each have a calling, a mission to fulfill, a purpose for ourselves and a Purpose that goes beyond ourselves . . . *our Purpose may be best fulfilled by having our Wounds, blockages and unresolved issues remain exactly as they are. This would drive us, by reaction, to where we were needed most in the world.* One might conjecture that if every angular aspect of Chiron equally facilitated the Healing of our Wounds and issues, we would all be out there being spiritual *and nothing would get done in the material world.* We have these kind of aspects (and the people they belong to!) to thank for the fact that we are materially organized, self-sufficient, prosperous, under control and have time to think about things other than hunting our next meal. Furthermore, as we master the material world, driven by the need to escape our Wounds and issues, *we are holographically learning to master ourselves in the material reflection, i.e. the Healing journey is happening anyway, just in a different form!*

For example, say there was a need in the overall plan of Humanity for someone to champion the cause of homeless and abandoned children. If we were to be the chosen one in this case, we may come into life with a Wound specific to this aim, e.g. Chiron in Libra squaring Saturn in Capricorn, say. In this scenario, we might have been the only survivor of a pair of twins. In our primal consciousness, we may unconsciously feel responsible for the other's death. Unable to access this Wound, our greatest Value becomes *making up for this tragedy in some way, e.g. saving the children of the world.* Saving the children of the world is actually an unconscious attempt to save the parts of ourselves that are in need of Loving, caring and nurturing. All the world's a mirror, as we shall explore in depth in Book Two.

The Gift of this aspect of Chiron and Saturn is in the Divine Design it confers. Of course, we can say this regarding the Gift in *every* Wound. It is just that, in this case, this seems to be enacted more on an unconscious level rather than on a conscious level as in a consciously-undertaken journey of Healing and evolution of consciousness.

To repeat . . . Every Wound, whether Healed or not, Serves to direct us towards our ultimate Divine Design and its fulfillment.

This is not to say that a square of Saturn and Chiron, when unaspected to any other planets, is impossible to transcend and Heal directly and consciously. On the contrary, it is simply that the challenge is magnified immensely, as are the results of meeting that challenge.

In the case of this square forming part of a T-square or another such larger planetary pattern, the Healing path will be facilitated by the interaction with the other planet(s) involved, still driving us towards our Divine Design.

Noted persons that share this aspect include Phil Collins, David Helfgott (tragic pianist depicted in the movie, "Shine"), Robin Williams, Jimmy Swaggart, John Belushi, Karen Silkwood, Leonardo DiCaprio, Uri Geller, Tina Turner, Liza Minnelli, Meryl Streep, Richard Branson (Virgin Records) and Robert Redford.

Sextile

Chiron-sextile-Saturn indicates the potential for seriousness, responsibility, discipline and hard work in relation to our journey of Healing and evolution of consciousness. However, it is a channel of possibility that we must activate intentionally. Having done so, we will have the capacity to work through our Wounds, blockages and unresolved issues in an organized and systematic fashion, dealing with these thoroughly and completely.

If we choose not to do so, this aspect remains relatively benign.

Quincunx

Chiron-quincunx-Saturn will confer a nagging sense of responsibility for our Healing and evolution of consciousness. This is often mirrored in our efforts to help others to attend to the same. If we are attending to these things in our own lives, we will feel more or less satisfied. If we are not, however, we will feel constantly irritated, uneasy and incomplete, tending to beat ourselves for not doing enough in the direction of sorting out our lives. By projection, we would then tend to beat others for their perceived laziness, inaction, lack of discipline and lack of organization. We would tend to beat them for failing to attend to their issues and Wounds. Do we see who we are really beating?

The Healing path lies in attending to our issues and Wounds *as they arise.* Otherwise, the cumulative effect becomes overwhelming. Healing also lies in acknowledging where we do in fact make efforts towards sorting out our issues. We can tend to be too hard on ourselves and need to see the other side of the picture.

This aspect can be a welcome addition to the chart of a person 'called' to Heal in some form or other. This is particularly so if it forms part of a yod pattern (two quincunxes and a sextile) or a square/quincunx/trine triangle such as in the chart of Sai Baba.

Noted people that share this aspect include Sai Baba, Billy Graham, Hugh Hefner, Auguste Rodin, Joan Sutherland (soprano), Oscar Wilde and Jack Brabham (Australian motor car racer).

Chiron in aspect to Uranus

Chiron/Uranus aspects have a very long cycle due to the long orbits of each of these planets. During the 20th century, we did not experience a Chiron-conjunct-Uranus at all. Sextiles occurred only during 1939–1940. Trines occurred only during 1945–1946 and 1994–95. Squares occurred only during 1943 and 1997. Quincunxes occurred only during 1948–49 and 1992–93. Oppositions of Chiron and Uranus, on the other hand, were more prolific during the 20th century than for hundreds of years prior to this. The 41 occurrences of this opposition spanned the years 1952–1989, a phenomenon we have already explored in depth in previous chapters.

This means that these aspects will exert a more collective and longer-lasting influence than that of the inner planet aspects. Having said this, though, it is necessary to acknowledge that collective movements of the consciousness of Humanity and Gaia are made up of multiple individual movements of consciousness. In short, the action of these aspects works through individuals, but when they are powerful and long lasting, the number and intensity of individuals affected creates mass movements.

So let's look at the way Chiron/Uranus aspects are reflected in our lives personally, against the background of the collective movement of consciousness of the planet Earth.

From the point of view of consciousness, Uranus's theme is *awakening*, i.e. moving to a higher level of consciousness about any given issue. It seeks to bring paradox into metadox (the union of opposites), seeming opposites into synthesis, conflict into harmony, disagreement into agreement and discord into concord. It does this by revealing the larger Plan at work behind the seemingly-disparate fragments that we see before us in our lives. For this reason, Uranus is associated with genius.

Uranus shines a light on those issues related to the planets to which it makes aspects. In Chiron's case, Uranus shines a light upon our Wounds, blockages and unresolved issues, impelling us to come to a higher understanding of these things. It brings that which lies within our Darkness into the Light, so that we may then have an opportunity to Heal and reconcile these issues. It seeks to show us the lessons, blessings, benefits and Gifts that lie behind our misperceptions and lopsided judgments. It seeks to show us the perfection of the Plan of the Universe and the Plan of our lives.

Chiron in aspect to Uranus represents a revolution in our consciousness and understanding of what we call our Wounds, blockages, issues, etcetera. Uranus represents a *revolution* in consciousness, *per se*. This is particularly what this series of books is all about, i.e. Healing and the evolution of consciousness.

We must also acknowledge the role of Chiron/Uranus aspects in the exploration, discovery and development of radical new ideas and technologies for Healing. Many of these ideas and technologies are energetic in nature, such as radiology, acupuncture, bio-electro-magnetic therapy, spiritual Healing and color therapy, etcetera.

Conjunction, Parallel, Contra-Parallel, Occultation

Chiron-conjunct-Uranus occurred last in 1898. The next time will be in 2042–43 and 2066–67. For those born with this aspect, there is a continual light shone upon their Wounds, blockages and unresolved issues. It takes a highly evolved person to bear this continually. This aspect, if combined with other such aspects of Chiron, would tend to produce a highly sensitive and powerful Healer, capable of delving into the very nature of Wounding and Healing and the human psyche. Psychic and mystical experiences are possible here. This would be particularly so if the pair of planets are in an occultation.

Collectively speaking, this aspect heralds new and revolutionary consciousness around our now favorite themes of Wounding and Healing, taken in their broadest sense, as connected to every aspect of our journey of life.

This aspect can be a tacit indication of considerable work already done on Healing and the evolution of consciousness in past lives.

Declination enhancements will have a similar effect to the conjunction with the occultation being the most powerful.

Noted people with this aspect, most born in 1898, include Emanuel Swedenborg (17th century mystic), Queen Anne, Ernest Hemmingway, Fred Astaire, George Gershwin, Rene Magritte (Belgian painter), Francois Polenc (French composer), William Sheldon (American psychologist), Simon Vestdijk (Dutch writer), Antonio Vivaldi (Italian baroque composer born 1678) and Karl Waldemar Ziegler (German Nobel prize winning chemist who discovered polyethylene plastics).

Opposition

We have dealt with Chiron-opposition-Uranus in detail already, but we will again outline its influence and themes. In opposition, Uranus shines a light – a challenge, in a sense – upon our Wounds, blockages and unresolved issues. By illuminating these, we are given the ultimate opportunity to deal with the Wounds and issues as they come to the fore.

This aspect is perhaps the most *active* of the Chiron/Uranus aspects barring the conjunction. The opposition causes us to run in the opposite direction to our Woundedness. In doing so, we run into Uranus, who then proceeds to show us the higher view of that from which we were running. When Uranus's Truth and its bigger Picture become too difficult to handle, challenging us beyond our current capacity, we run again, back into our Woundedness, back to Chiron. Here, due to Uranus's light shining on the Wounds, we find new material to work with, adding to our overall understanding. When what we find there again becomes too Painful, again we run, again bumping into Uranus. So it goes on, in a tic-tocking journey of Healing and evolution of consciousness. The Universe had to have had a sense of humor when it invented this aspect! I can't help thinking of mice in a cage!

If we are not able to deal with the Wounds and Pain that come up and we are not able to deal with the greater Truth that Uranus offers, then we are stuck in a kind of nightmare of constant running. In this case we tend to try to do anything to 'blank out'. We attempt this by using alcohol, drugs, sleep, work, music and all other types of 'escapism' to avoid the Wounds, blockages and unresolved issues. If we try this for too long, however, it will inevitably be reflected in our bodies through illness, disease and general unwellness.

This all-or-nothing kind of psychology is the very reason why Chiron-opposition-Uranus (and Chiron-opposition-Pluto, as we shall see later) is an aspect that confers Healing ability and/or focus in our lives. We cannot avoid it; we cannot run away from it; it follows us wherever we try to go. This is why the generations of people born between 1952 and 1989 have altered the consciousness of the planet via the Healing modalities (taken in their broadest sense). The mid-1960s represented the fulcrum point. The late 1970s represented the culmination. The 1990s represented the peak, particularly as this time encompasses not only Chiron's perihelion and perigee, but also Chiron's own half-Return. This psychology, combined with the sheer number of oppositions Chiron and Uranus made during this time, is one of the major contributors to the discovery of Chiron, as we have already seen.

Due to the vast number of people with this aspect, we will offer only a few examples. It is important to point out that there are not so many famous people with this aspect, a point that fails to support our assertion that the aspect is associated with the Healing and new-age movements. However, if we consider that 1) the aspect itself does not confer fame or notoriety, 2) the Healing and new-age movements were not about fame and notoriety – they were about inner Healing – and 3) the bulk of Healers and new-age facilitators were part of a grass-roots phenomenon, then we can understand the deficit of noted persons that follows. I can show hundreds of charts supporting the connection, but most are for people of whom no one has heard.

Noted people with this aspect include Ji Maharaj (Indian guru who made the 'big time' in the US from 1972 onwards), Nick Campion (British astrologer), Annie Lennox, Bill Gates, Carrie Fisher, Denzel Washington, James Ingram, Shannen Doherty, David the Bubble-Boy (rare disorder of immune deficiency) and Bo Derek.

It is interesting that an unusual number of athletes possess this aspect. Perhaps they are literally trying to run away from their Wounds, blockages and unresolved issues. This may sound implausible. However, consider that 1) our outer activities mirror our inner state and that 2) one of the means we use to avoid having to sit down and think deeply about our issues is to stay busy and physically active all the time. I know many people like this and can see this tendency in myself.

These sportspeople include Martina Navratilova, Chris Evert Lloyd, Frederi Deburghgraeve (Belgian athlete named Sportsman of the Year and given an Award of Merit, 1995), Eddie Edwards (British athlete called "The Eagle;" participated in the winter Olympics 1988), Jim Harbaugh, (American quarterback and athlete), Kathy McMillan (American track and field champion), Ed Moses (American athlete, a hurdler who won Olympic gold at Montreal in 1976 and in Los Angeles August 1984), Gianni Poli (Italian field and track star, winner of the marathon in New York 11/02/1986) and Paolo Rossi (Italian soccer player; helped Italy win the World Cup 1982).

Trine

It is interesting that Chiron's last 2 trines to Uranus (1945–1946 and 1994–95) both occurred very close to when Chiron was at its perigee and perihelion (closest to the Earth and the Sun, respectively) and in the sign of Libra in 1945 and 1996. This fact makes it a little difficult to separate the influence of the trine from the perigee/perihelion in Libra. Uranus was in Gemini during the 1945–46 trine and in Capricorn and Aquarius during the 1994–95 trine.

In general, though, Chiron-trine-Uranus brings our Wounds, blockages and unresolved issues into sharp focus, much in the same way as the Chiron/Uranus opposition. However, it does so in a more harmonious way inasmuch as the higher internal logic and underlying Plan behind our Wounds and issues is more easily accessed. Having said this, though, when we combine this trine with the perigee/perihelion of Chiron, the extreme visibility – nakedness, in a sense – of our Wounds, blockages and unresolved issues makes it all the more difficult for us to bear. In this case, we would tend to run away from the Wounds and towards Uranus's other themes, i.e. technology, global networking and communications, and humanitarian themes. If we cannot 'fix' ourselves, we try to 'fix' the world and make it a 'better' place to live. This (combined with the Saturn-square-Chiron aspect aforementioned) accounts, in part, for the post-WWII era of material and economic stability. This was further combined with technological advances that were built upon the discoveries of the first half of the 20th century. As we have said previously, this era of materiality had its peak in 1970–71 with Chiron's apogee/aphelion.

This trine, personally speaking, gives us an enormous opportunity to delve into our Wounds, blockages and unresolved issues. Whether we do or not will depend on the other Chiron aspects in our charts and upon our general willingness to pursue them or, alternately, to run from them.

Those born during the 1945–46 trine represent the advance scouts, so to speak, of the coming shift of consciousness of the 1960s. Many were actively involved in this shift, being, as they were, in college at the time during the mid-1960s.

In a sense, those born during this trine (1945–46) would fall dramatically into two camps. The first camp consisted of the advance scouts of the coming 'new age' (Libran Chiron), the second of those that became materially oriented, scientifically-minded and technologically-inclined (Gemini Uranus).

Those born during the 1994–95 trine have yet to blossom into measurable trends and patterns. We can predict, however, that these children will contribute, in their later years, to two vastly polarized trends as we approach the next Chiron apogee/aphelion of 2020–21. Some will turn towards a new 'new-age' movement. They will tend back towards spirituality and a more global consciousness. This time, however, it will have a more practical basis than the previous 'new age' (Chiron in Libra again and, to a lesser degree, Uranus in Capricorn/Aquarius). Others will turn to the more practical and economic path (Uranus in Capricorn/Aquarius) and seek to solidify the material, economic, social and political state of the world as it becomes increasingly global in outlook.

Lastly, this aspect can be a tacit indication of considerable work already done on Healing and the evolution of consciousness in past lives.

Noted people with this trine aspect of Chiron and Uranus include James Joyce, Barry Gibb, Bill Clinton, Donald Trump, Franklin D. Roosevelt (1882 trine), Goldie Hawn, Oscar Wilde, Stuart Wilde (new age teacher and speaker), Lorne Johndro (Canadian astrologer interested in the research of electromagnetic fields and their astrological correspondence), Antoine Becquerel (French physicist, whose early studies were concerned with the magnetic and polarization properties of light. He shared the Nobel Prize in physics with Pierre and Marie Curie in 1903 for the discovery of radioactivity), Jules Massenet (French composer) and William Blake (poet and visionary, 1757 trine).

Square

Chiron-square-Uranus (1943 and 1997) indicates that we are initially blocked from gaining a higher understanding of our Wounds, blockages and unresolved issues. This, in itself, creates a feeling of even deeper Pain and separation from a sense of connectedness. In other words, it *increases* our drive to grow, Heal and evolve.

If, by virtue of the other aspects or lack thereof to Chiron in our charts, we are unable or unwilling to deal with these things as they arise, then we are *still* driven towards our Divine Design. In this case, however, the Wounds act as a powerful, but *unHealed,* motive force. Our Divine Design will reflect this. We have discussed this scenario in relation to Chiron-square-Saturn. In the case of Chiron-square-Uranus possible avenues of expression include delving into technology, the information age, space, invention and innovation as a defence against our issues and Woundedness (in particular, those born in 1943).

If, on the other hand, we are able and/or willing to try to deal with these things, we are driven on a Healing path, one that *also* takes us to our Divine Design. The Healing aspect will be naturally reflected in the 'flavor' of that Divine Design. The depth of the Wounds and the level of the challenge in approaching these Wounds are balanced in the level of Healing and evolution of consciousness possible with this difficult aspect.

If this square forms part of a T-square or other angular pattern then its resolution can be thus facilitated; it can also be an addition to the chart of a person 'called' to Heal as a specific life's path.

Noted people who share this aspect include Percy Bysshe Shelley (poet), Janis Joplin, John Newcombe (tennis star), Julio Iglesias, Hans Christian Andersen, Charles Baudelaire (French poet tormented by religion and the struggle between good and evil in man), Louis Braille (inventor of Braille script for the blind), Antoine Becquerel (French physicist – see Chiron trine Uranus), Emily Dickinson (poetess), Martin Heidegger (German existentialist philosopher), Walther Model (German General Field Marshall to Hitler) and Lech Walesa (Polish union leader who led the Polish Solidarity Movement).

Interestingly, Chiron squared Uranus in 1997 during Chiron's own half-Return (opposition to its own natal position of 1977).

Sextile

Chiron-sextile-Uranus (1939–40) indicates an open channel to discover the higher meaning, logic and Plan behind our Wounds, blockages and unresolved issues. Like all sextiles, however, it must be activated consciously and intentionally by our Wish for Healing and evolution of consciousness. Otherwise, this aspect remains relatively benign.

It is, in any case, a welcome addition to the chart of a person wishing to pursue a specific life's path of Healing, whatever the specific modality.

Quincunx

Chiron-quincunx-Uranus (1948–49 and 1992–93) acts almost in the same way as the Chiron/Uranus opposition (see Chiron opposition Uranus). However, there are two differences. The first is that the influence of the quincunx is not as acute a challenge or confrontation as the opposition. The second is that there is a constant nagging feeling, an uneasiness, irritation, restlessness, etcetera, in the background of our consciousness. These feelings arise from a belief that we are never doing enough towards our Healing and evolution of consciousness.

This aspect impels us to attain a higher understanding, a new level of consciousness, with respect to our Wounds, blockages and unresolved issues.

Noted persons that share this aspect include Bernadette Peters (Broadway performer), Bruce Springsteen, Cheryl Kernot (long-time leader of the Australian Democrat Party), John Carpenter (film director of "Dark Star", "Halloween" and "Star Man"), Rick Springfield (singer) and Jean-Baptiste Troppman (French homicidal homosexual sociopath).

Chiron in aspect to Neptune

Again, due to the slow-moving nature of Neptune, aspects of Neptune and Chiron are rare, having global significance as well as personal impact in our natal charts.

Generally, Neptune relates to our potential for a Return to Spirit, a merging with Oneness, a Return Home from whence we came and the actual experience of Unconditional Love. It intimates, wordlessly, of a supra-consciousness, of a divine order that goes beyond ideas, images, concepts and logic, even beyond *meaning*, as such. It is *felt* in the Heart and *known* in the Soul. It intimates the Suchness of Love.

Manifested in our lives, Neptune's influences can seem strange, mysterious, confusing, illusive and ethereal. Its influences, meeting our fragmented consciousness, can create confusion, delusions, fantasies, irrationalities and disassociative states of consciousness. Nonetheless, it constantly challenges us to acknowledge Spirit, to acknowledge the Divine within us and around us and to wake up to the Love that is the essence of existence in all its manifest forms.

When aspecting Chiron, Neptune's influence seeks to bypass our intellect, our rationalizations, our justifications and our protective mind-games in order to allow us to access, recognize, acknowledge, embrace and finally Love our Wounds, blockages and unresolved issues a little more. It is, in essence, the call of Spirit, encouraging us to move through our Wounds, blockages and unresolved issues by seeing all sides of otherwise negatively-judged happenings and circumstances, thus emerging into a more unified state and experiencing Unconditional Love. The steps are: recognition, acknowledgment, forgiveness, acceptance, inclusion and finally, beyond forgiveness, Oneness and Unconditional Love.

The ultimate message of Chiron aspecting Neptune is that Love is the greatest Healer.

Conjunction, Parallel, Contra-Parallel, Occultation

Chiron-conjunct-Neptune (1879–80, 1945 and 2010) indicates that there is a clear and resonant channel between our Soul and its experience of Unconditional Love on the one hand and the Wounds, blockages and unresolved issues of our lower nature on the other.

Depending on our level of Healing and evolution of consciousness, this can affect us in one of two ways (or a proportional balance of both ways). Firstly, it can entirely disassociate us from reality and make it virtually impossible for us to touch the ground, so to speak. In this case, we would expect to see all manner of escapist behavior, from drugs to organized religion. (We will explore the many ways we attempt to escape from our Wounds and issues in Book Two.) Alternately, it can create an extraordinary channel for the Healing and resolution of our Wounds, blockages and unresolved issues. The former case is more likely the less evolved we are, the latter case more likely the more evolved we are. In Truth, each of us is a combination of both and, with this aspect, we would have aspects of each polarity with respect to different areas of our lives.

Ultimately, this aspect confers the need to connect with Spirit as an answer to our inner Woundedness. Neptune encourages us to Love our Wounds Unconditionally, bringing them Lovingly back into the Light. This aspect can be the mark of a true mystic inasmuch as we are driven to the mystic and ethereal realms by our need for Healing.

This aspect can be a tacit indication of considerable work already done on Healing and the evolution of consciousness in past lives.

Declination enhancements will, as always, have a similar influence to the conjunction with the occultation being the most powerful.

Noted persons with this aspect include Edgar Cayce (the "Sleeping Prophet"), Alan Page (American footballer), Albert Einstein, Marie Stopes (birth control crusader), Michelangelo, Steve Martin, Upton Sinclair (socialist writer), Luigi Boccherini (Italian baroque musician and composer), John Dee (astrologer and British double-agent to Queen Elizabeth I), Guy Ballard (American co-founder of "The Mighty I Am" religion, who claimed to hear spirit messages, see 70,000 years of reincarnations and heal 5,000 people a year), Joseph Stalin, Bela Bartok (Hungarian composer) and Arturo Bocchini (occultation, head of the Fascist police).

Opposition

Chiron-opposition-Neptune (1900–01, 1990 and 2048–55) indicates the initial tendency to try to escape our Wounds, blockages and unresolved issues, going into places of escapism, fantasy, illusion, delusion, self-deceit and imagination. Psychologically speaking, this would tend to have us creating an alternate or virtual reality within the spaces of our mind, distanced from reality and from the parts of ourselves that we feel are too Painful to approach.

If, however, we are able and willing to deal with our Wounds, blockages and unresolved issues (this may be supported by other aspects of Chiron in the chart), then the effect of the Neptune opposition would be to constantly encourage us to look into our Darkness and Love what we see there. By doing this, we are allowing the fragments of ourselves to rejoin with the whole of ourselves. For this to be effective, though, we must have a framework in which to put our feelings that arise from Neptune's influence. This means a certain level of conscious evolution and a certain amount of work on ourselves towards the goal of Healing and the evolution of consciousness. Neptune, like Chiron, can only be reliably accessed via Saturn. As we support ourselves in this effort, so we are supported by the Love of the Universe.

Noted people that share this aspect include Barbara Cartland (novelist), Karl Ernst Krafft (Astrologer and advisor to Hess, Krafft fell from grace when his predictions did not match Hitler's ambitions for himself), Louis Armstrong, Erich Fromm (psychologist), James Kirsch (Jungian analyst and author) and Spencer A. Paterson (Scottish physician and psychiatrist, the author of "Electrical and Drug Treatments in Psychiatry," 1963).

Trine

Chiron-trine-Neptune (1895, 1920–26, 1963–68 and 1994–95) indicates that there is a high degree of resonance between our spiritual nature or Soul and our Wounds, blockages and unresolved issues. Even if we do not consciously and intentionally deal with these things, they will tend to find expression through our creative, artistic and spiritual pursuits. In addition, they may find expression through our exploration and experimentation with altered states of consciousness. These themes were the hallmark of the explosion of creativity and experimentation in the trines of the 1960s.

With this aspect, if we choose to deal with our issues, we may tend more towards spiritual, Healing and creative pursuits whereas, if we choose not to, then we may tend more towards escapist and consciousness-altering or consciousness-dulling pursuits and devices. *Either way, as always, our Divine Design is expedited, consciously or unconsciously.*

There can be the tacit indication of considerable work already done on Healing and the evolution of consciousness in past lives.

Essentially, this aspect is speaking the Truth that Love is the greatest Healer. This aspect is a welcome addition to other Chiron aspects in the chart of people wishing to pursue Healing as a specific life's path.

Noted people that share this aspect include Gene Roddenberry (Star Trek), Pope John Paul II, Kurt Cobain (Nirvana), Lee Iaccoca (Chrysler CEO), Lyle Menendez (homicide with brother), Matt Biondi (Olympic swimmer), Robert Kennedy, Whitney Houston and Marcel Marceau.

Square

Chiron-square-Neptune (1849–50, 1893, 1935–37, 1954–55, 1996–97 and 2042) indicates an initial sense of being cut off from our Soul/Spirit/divinity/Home/Source. This aspect would tend to accentuate the feeling of being abandoned by Spirit, left in a world without meaning or connection. This feeling will tend to impel us to seek Spirit even more or, conversely, to entirely deny Spirit and live an existentialist and/or atheistic life. In actuality, we live between these two extremes, particularly with this aspect.

This aspect bears a lot in common with Chiron in the sign of Pisces (see Chiron in Pisces) inasmuch as it makes us feel as though the Universe has betrayed or abandoned us. In response, we tend to shut the door to our Soul. This, in itself, will take us on a journey whereby the compassion, mercy and Love of the Universe/Spirit will be gradually revealed to us if we are willing to listen with open ears and look with open eyes.

If this square forms part of a T-square or other such angular pattern, it can offer a more obvious Healing path. As such, it would be a useful addition to the chart of a person wishing to pursue Healing as a specific life's path, whatever the modality.

Noted people who share this aspect include Annie Lennox, Chris Evert Lloyd, John Travolta, Luciano Pavarotti, Patty Hearst, Ron Howard, Tony Blair, Charles Baudelaire (French poet tormented by religion and the struggle between good and evil in man), John Milton (poet), Cardinal Richelieu (French ecclesiastic and politician) and Barbara Stabiner (American psychic).

Sextile

Chiron-sextile-Neptune (1891, 1940–41, 1950, 1999 and 2038–39) indicates an open channel between our Wounds, blockages and unresolved issues and our Soul-guided higher self, i.e. Spirit. As with all sextiles, however, we must be the ones to activate and use this channel. Otherwise, this aspect remains relatively benign.

Quincunx

Chiron-quincunx-Neptune (1897–98, 1905–07, 1981–84, 1992–93 and 2046–47) indicates that a new level of consciousness is sought regarding our Wounds, blockages and unresolved issues. Neptune seeks to help us to Love all our Dark, repressed, unacknowledged, denied, disowned, ignored, unseen, negatively-judged and otherwise unLoved parts, reminding us that all things are a Service of Love.

There will be a nagging feeling in the background of our consciousness that there is an unseen meaning and providence behind those things that we judge, blame and/or condemn. This feeling will ever impel us to seek out the deeper meaning for the happenings in our lives.

If we do not heed this call consciously, as a substitute, we will unconsciously tend to seek to 'fix' others, 'saving' them from their Wounds, blockages and unresolved issues. This often involves the creation or imagining of some evil force, against which we are fighting. This can lead us to promoting extreme religious beliefs and practices. Alternately, our own denial of a Healing path, whilst still being impelled by this aspect, can lead us to seek to vehemently 'disprove' Spirit or react violently against Spirit in some way.

This aspect is a welcome addition to the charts of those of us wishing to pursue our Healing and evolution of consciousness in a more conscious way. It is also a welcome addition in the chart of a person wishing to pursue Healing as a more specific life's path and purpose.

Noted persons with this aspect include Jean Paul Sartre, Johannes Keplar, Joseph McCarthy (ignited Communist paranoia – McCarthyism – in the 1950s), Auguste Renoir (painter), Albert Speer (German Nazi architect, author and Hitler's Minister for Armaments and War Production), Hermann Bauer (German astrologer and esoteric publisher) and Lucky Luciano (Sicilian-American gangster).

Interestingly, Chiron and Neptune were quincunx at the release of the film "ET".

Chiron in aspect to Pluto

Pluto represents death and rebirth, ends of old cycles and beginnings of new cycles, transformation, transmutation, nuclear energy, quantum physics, etcetera. In terms of consciousness, Pluto represents the potential for moving into new octaves of understanding. In this way, Pluto stands as a guardian, turning back those who have not yet transformed themselves sufficiently to merit entry into this new octave. Sometimes it is even necessary to 'plough' in old forms that have become 'stuck' in their evolution, preparing the soil for the growth of new forms that will better Serve our aim of Healing and evolution of consciousness.

When Pluto aspects Chiron, our Wounds, blockages and unresolved issues are maximally challenged, confronted and stirred up, particularly those that are the most long-standing and deeply-ingrained. Pluto is seemingly without mercy or respite in this task. To make sense of it, we must remember that Spirit will do everything it can to ensure our ultimate Healing and evolution of consciousness. We are not allowed by the nature of the laws of the Universe to remain static for too long. We must be moving either toward or away from the Light. Ultimately, it is our choice. Pluto, when aspecting Chiron, forces our hand, so to speak, impelling us to choose our direction.

Conjunction, Parallel, Contra-Parallel, Occultation

Chiron-conjunct-Pluto (1883–84, 1941 and 1999) confers the maximum pressure upon our Wounds, blockages and unresolved issues. It challenges us to move through these things and into a new level of consciousness. Alternately, if we are not yet ready for this quantum leap, Pluto wipes away the old forms of the preceding cycle and initiates a fresh tack, still dealing with the same Wounds and issues.

This aspect represents a major turning point. In the natal chart, it represents a person who is constantly challenged to make every moment a turning point. This can be either an untenable aspect or an extraordinary Gift, depending on the evolution, preparedness and willingness of the native.

If we are unprepared or unwilling, we may take our Wounds, blockages and unresolved issues out of the world in violent ways. Alternatively, we may seek to change the world to such a degree that, if we could, it might make recompense for the Woundedness that we feel inside. Still further, we may make all attempts to self-destruct ourselves in order to escape our Wounds, blockages and unresolved issues.

If, however, we are to some degree prepared and willing, we will be able to make major leaps of Healing and evolution of consciousness.

As part of the aspect set of a person wishing to pursue Healing as a specific life's path, this aspect is extremely powerful. It may even need to be tempered with caution, reserve and wisdom.

This aspect can be a tacit indication of considerable work already done on Healing and the evolution of consciousness in past lives.

Declination enhancements confer similar features with occultations being the most powerful. I have yet to discover a person who has Pluto and Chiron in occultation.

Noted people who share this aspect include Bruce Lee, Coco Chanel (perfume mogul), Karl Marx, Benito Mussolini, Armand Hippoly Fizeau (physicist who first successfully measured the speed of light – see Chiron conjunct Saturn, too. This person's chart is certainly worth studying. Born 23 September 1819, 4am LMT, Paris.), John Maynard Keynes (British economist and financial expert, he published "Economic Consequences of Peace" in 1919), Edgar Varese (French-American 20th century avant-garde composer), Pierre Laval (French lawyer and socialist politician. The Minister of France in October 1945, he was called "the Evil Genius of France."), Riccardo Muti (Italian orchestral conductor), Peter Joseph William Debye (Nobel Prize winning Dutch-American physiochemist) and Walt Whitman.

Opposition

Chiron-opposition-Pluto (1899, 1961–1965 and 2043–45) is one of the major aspects involved in the lead-up to Chiron's discovery in 1977. We have already discussed this aspect in some detail, but let's review and expand upon our previous work, putting it into the context of our lives personally.

With the opposition aspect, we tic-tock between the two planetary poles, in this case between Chiron and Pluto. If our Wounds, blockages and unresolved issues become too Painful or difficult to deal with, we run towards Pluto. This can mean towards change, violence, conflict, war, challenge, confrontation and death, within us or outside us. Again, finding this new pole too Painful and/or difficult to deal with, we retreat once more into our Woundedness. Finding no relief here, we bounce back towards Pluto, and so on and so forth. We are caught in a game that *demands* that we evolve by attending to our Wounds, blockages and unresolved issues. If we cannot, we lash out, self-destruct or retreat within. In all cases, we tend to be decidedly self-destructive.

This is certainly the case with so many people that I have worked with who have this aspect. It acts in a similar way to the Chiron/Uranus opposition, but much more acutely and intensely. For this reason, with this aspect, we tend to take much longer coming to a point of acknowledging, embracing and actively pursuing our journey of Healing and evolution of consciousness.

When we eventually come to this point, however, the power of transformation at our fingertips is unparalleled. This aspect has the potential to create extremely Gifted Healers, providing the other aspects in the chart support this and providing this is our wish and active intention.

Noted people who share this aspect include Annie Besant (British-Indian social reformer and feminist and former head of the Theosophical Society in India), Matt Dillon, Chris Farley (American comedian who died bingeing on booze, cocaine and heroin in 1997), Elias Hutter

(16th century German writer and Orientalist, also a renowned editor of Bibles of the time), Princess Stephanie of Monaco and Fritz Werle (German psychologist, astrologer and author).

Interestingly, during the opposition in the 1960s we saw the release of the Beatles 1st album, the USSR pulling out of Cuba, the Aberfan slag heap disaster, the Apollo disaster, Martin Luther King Jnr's famous "I have a dream . . ." speech and his winning a Nobel Peace Prize, the Sharpeville massacre, Indira Gandhi becoming Prime Minister of India, anti-Vietnam riots, Berlin Wall riots, the 1st man in space, the release of the original Star Trek series and the 1st heart transplant. Coincidence?

Trine

Chiron-trine-Pluto (1895, 1909–10, 1950, 1989–90 and 2037–38) represents a high degree of resonance between our Wounds, blockages and unresolved issues and our powers of transformation and conscious evolution. Like the conjunct and the opposition aspects of Chiron and Pluto, this aspect manifests in several possible directions. In the first case, it can cause us to actively lash out or seek to change the outside world as an answer to our Woundedness. In the second case, we lash out against ourselves, attempting to self-annihilate or 'blank out'. In the third case, it can give us the Gift of personal Healing and evolution of consciousness to a degree paralleled only by the conjunction and opposition. Overall, this aspect is more harmonious than the other two.

There can be the tacit indication of considerable work already done on Healing and the evolution of consciousness in past lives.

This aspect is a welcome addition to those of us who wish to pursue a path of Healing and evolution of consciousness, for ourselves alone or as a specific life's path and purpose.

Noted persons who share this aspect include Barbara Castle (tough, uncompromising British politician), Johannes Keplar, J. Edgar Hoover, Richard Branson (Virgin Records), Brenda Crenshaw (British-American psychic and medium to the Hollywood stars), Bette Davis, Herbert von Karajan (conductor), Gurudev Muktananda Baba (Indian mystic and guru), Emperor Mutsohito of Japan, Eva Peron of Argentina and Josephine Stevens (American mystic, astrologer, clairvoyant, co-author of the book, "The Rainbow Bridge" and student Alice A. Bailey).

Square

Chiron-square-Pluto (1893, 1919–21, 1947, 1992–93 and 2028–30) indicates an initial inability to transform our Wounds, blockages and unresolved issues. The evolutionary path seems blocked. However, Pluto, being what it is, will constantly try to break through to us with a new understanding. In a square aspect (Saturnian influence), it does this by bringing crises that cause us to have to sit down and reassess our lives. It will keep tripping us up until it births a new consciousness.

In this aspect, Pluto will continue to trip us up, stopping the smooth and comfortable flow of our otherwise uneventful and stagnant lives, until we see our Wounds, blockages and unresolved issues in a new light. After all, it is our Wounds, blockages and unresolved issues that are stopping us from moving forward, at the same time as impelling us towards a new understanding and, ultimately, towards our Divine Design. Pluto is merely pointing this out to us.

If we refuse to expand our consciousness, Pluto will continue to mirror our Wounds, blockages and unresolved issues via the external calamities of our lives. Our reactions will be similar to the negative reactions to the other Chiron/Pluto aspects, aforementioned (See Chiron conjunct Pluto, Chiron opposition Pluto and Chiron trine Pluto).

If, on the other hand, we choose to work in a positive way with Pluto's calamitous demonstrations, we will reap the fruits of accelerated Healing and evolution of consciousness. The Healing path consists of transforming our perceptions and illusions, i.e. of seeing our Wounds and issues and their associated events and circumstances in a new light, of seeing a larger picture, of seeing the balance, harmony, perfection and Love behind every aspect.

Noted people who share this aspect include Eleanor Bach (American astrologer, publisher/editor of "Planet Watch", author of "Asteroid Ephemeras", she was called "the mother of asteroids"), Howard Cosell (controversial American broadcaster), Dino De Laurentiis (Italian-American major film producer), Betty Friedan (American feminist pioneer and organizer, lecturer and writer, the author of "The Feminine Mystique" in 1963), Mario Lanza, Liberace, George Bernard Shaw, Spike Milligan and writer, Ray Bradbury.

Sextile

Chiron-sextile-Pluto (1891, 1931–32, 1945, 1995 and 2012–14) indicates that there is an open channel that we can use for the conscious and intentional transformation and Healing of our Wounds, blockages and unresolved issues. We must, however, as with all sextiles, consciously activate this aspect with our conscious intention and Wish for Healing. Otherwise, this aspect remains relatively benign.

Quincunx

Chiron-quincunx-Pluto (1897, 1903, 1953–54, 1981–85 and 2041–42) indicates an incessant, nagging, irritating and frustrating feeling in the background of our consciousness, impelling us to transform and Heal our Wounds, blockages and unresolved issues. It impels us to achieve new perspectives on those Wounds and issues, seeing their hidden blessings, benefits, lessons and Gifts, seeing the flip-sides to issues and happenings that we otherwise see only negatively or positively.

If we fail to attend to the call of this aspect, we will tend to take out our frustration and irritation upon others. We will either seek to 'fix', change or destroy them and their lives or we will unconsciously 'stir the pot', so to speak, for no other reason than to discharge our negative feelings.

If, on the other hand, we turn the power of this aspect inwards and attend to our issues, this aspect can be a constant blessing, never failing to provide new material for our spiritual growth. The Healing path consists of attending to each Wound and/or issue *as it arises.* Otherwise, the cumulative effect gradually becomes unbearable. A new perspective, a new level of consciousness pertaining to our Wounds and issues is sought.

Noted persons that share this aspect include Dr. John Demartini, teacher and Healer of whom we have previously spoken, Oprah Winfrey, Paul Joseph Goebbels (Hitler's head of the Ministry of Public Enlightenment and Propaganda), Whoopi Goldberg, Bill Gates, Chaka Khan, Tony Blair and David Berkowitz (American homicide, "Son of Sam")

A surprising number of noted athletes have the aspect. The nervous energy of this aspect is obviously discharged physically through their sport. They include Chris Evert Lloyd, Archie M. Griffin (footballer),

Venus Williams, Susan Butcher (American sled racer), Patti Catalano (American field and track champion), Janet Lynn (Olympic skater) and Sara Simeoni (Olympic high jumper).

Chiron in aspect to MC

Chiron aspects to the MC (Midheaven) indicate that, in some way, we are destined to express our journey of Healing and evolution of consciousness in a public way and/or through our career path. This can be for us alone, for our own Healing path, not necessarily indicating a career in the specific field of Healing. Alternatively, it can also be that our journey of Healing and evolution of consciousness directs us to a career/vocation with a specific Healing emphasis and Service to others.

In any case, when our Chiron aspects the MC, we will tend to be seen by others to be involved in a Healing journey of some kind in our lives. (Bear in mind that Healing can take many forms, some quite removed from what we might generally associate with the Healing professions).

Conjunction

(Conjunction simultaneously opposing IC)

Chiron-conjunct-MC indicates that our journey of Healing and evolution of consciousness is potentially in perfect alignment with our chosen vocation. In fact, our career path will tend to be fraught with difficulties, false starts and disappointment until we align it with this Healing path.

The career path/public image is ultimately the exterior visage of who we are, why we are here, where we come from and where we are going. As such, it will ultimately reflect our life's path and purpose, seen through the Moon's Nodes. It will reflect our way of expressing this path, seen through the Sun. It will reflect our exterior masks, seen through the Ascendant. It will reflect our lower emotional nature, seen through the Moon. Lastly, particularly in this case, it will reflect our Wounds, blockages and unresolved issues, seen through Chiron.

As we evolve, our personal/inner path becomes increasingly an outward path of Service to others and, as it does, it is reflected through our vocation and through our public persona.

In Truth, the distinctions we make between our life's path and purpose, its expression, its arena of execution, our Healing journey and our career *are illusory distinctions. All are part of our total Divine Design.* Chiron-conjunct-MC merely illuminates this Truth by bringing our journey of Healing and evolution of consciousness into greater alignment with our career path/public persona.

This aspect can be a welcome addition to the chart of persons wishing to pursue a specific life's path and purpose of Healing. It can also be the indication of substantial work done in the past and/or in past lives on Healing and the evolution of consciousness.

Noted persons who share this aspect include Dane Rudhyar (Sabian Symbols), George Michael, Peter Sculthorpe (Australian 20th century composer), Don Drysdale (baseball player), Frantz Fanon (French-American psychiatrist and revolutionary writer), Joan Grant (American metaphysical novelist), Edmond Halley (astronomer), Harpo Marx, Josephine Stevens (American mystic, co-author of "The Rainbow Bridge") and Alfred Lord Tennyson (poet).

Opposition

(Same as conjunction with IC)

Chiron-opposition-MC initially indicates Wounds, blockages and unresolved issues relating to the past, parents, grandparents, heredity, genetics, etcetera. These Wounds, blockages and unresolved issues tend to cause us to try to escape by burying ourselves in our careers or seeking a public life. Inevitably, our Wounds, blockages and unresolved issues (and hence the Healing journey thereof) will become a part of the career or public persona we strive for, even if our career is not strictly speaking a career in Healing.

This opposition can also mean tension, conflict or a dilemma between our vocation and our Wounds, blockages and unresolved issues. One will necessarily aggravate the other. This, however, will impel us to resolve the Wounds, blockages and unresolved issues. If we try to escape and put all our energy and focus into our career, the same Wounds, blockages and unresolved issues we tried to escape from will emerge in our vocation path, still demanding attention.

Of course, we can make the choice consciously to attend to our Wounds, blockages and unresolved issues within the context of the career path. If we do attend in this way, our career will have a Healing element, even if this is not the primary element.

Alternately, if we do not attend to our Wounds, blockages and unresolved issues, we may play out their drama in dramatic, sometimes violent and often public ways.

Noted persons who share this aspect include Angus Young (AC/DC), Katharine Hepburn, Phil Donahue, Sean Connery, Ralph Abernathy (American Civil Rights Activist and founder of the Southern Christian Leadership Conference with Dr. Martin Luther King, Jnr in 1957), Jomanda (renowned Dutch psychic and Healer), Salvatore Luria (Nobel prize winning Italian biologist, virologist) and Emil Edmund Kemper (American serial killer and necrophiliac).

Trine

(Simultaneously sextiling IC)

Chiron-trine-MC indicates a high degree of resonance between our Wounds, blockages and unresolved issues and our vocation and/or public profile. In a sense, our Wounds, blockages and unresolved issues are put out front in a way that attracts others to our cause through empathy, sympathy, vulnerability and a feeling of a common bond and/or cause.

This can manifest as a *reaction* to the Wounds, blockages and unresolved issues, in which case we may find ourselves championing a cause or trying to 'fix' or change people or situations. Conversely, it can manifest as an *action* along Healing lines, in which case we may end up expressing our journey of Healing and evolution of consciousness through our career and/or publicly.

In this case, this aspect can indicate a career in a Healing (taken in the broadest sense) field. It can also indicate substantial work done towards our Healing and evolution of consciousness in the past and/or in past lives.

Noted persons who share this aspect include Germaine Greer, Woody

Pittman (American comedy-magician who took his pathological shyness and has made from it a successful stage act), Eleanor Roosevelt, Tipper Gore (political wife of Al Gore), Eva Braun, Spike Milligan, George Adamski (Polish-American alleged UFO contactee and author), Brother Charles (former chela of Muktananda Paramhansa, now a new-age high-tech meditation teacher), Joe Cocker, Che Guevarra, Ruth Rendell and Sulamith Wulfing (German mystical painter).

A surprising number of politicians and leaders and their partners have this aspect, too, aside from the ones mentioned above.

Interestingly, Chiron trined the MC during Hitler's very first political speech in 1927.

Square

(Simultaneously squaring IC)

Chiron-square-MC indicates that our Wounds, blockages and unresolved issues will initially block our career path and thwart our efforts to step out into the public eye. Alternately, our Wounds, blockages and unresolved issues may become a public affair and/or may create the circumstances for a career to be born, although, for all visible purposes, Healing and resolution may not ever take place.

In the first case, we will not understand why our career and/or public life seem to be blocked or thwarted. Consequently, we may simply not develop this area of our lives. It may be that the focus of our life's path and purpose and its expression is in another area and our Wounds, blockages and unresolved issues drive us there as a kind of seeming default. In Truth, it is all part of a larger Plan.

In the second case, our Wounds, blockages and unresolved issues become public property and may even give us a career. These areas of our lives will then become the arenas upon which the drama of our Wounds, blockages and unresolved issues will be played out. Our Wounds, blockages and unresolved issues will reflect those of the greater populace, the Healing journey played out upon a public stage.

A final case, a further step from the first case, is where, impelled by our frustrations about a blocked or thwarted career path or public life, we delve deeply into our Wounds, blockages and unresolved issues in an effort to unlock this area of our lives. The result will be the expression, to a greater or lesser degree, of our Healing path through our career and/or public life, either just for our own Healing or also for the Healing of others in a professional capacity.

Noted persons who share this aspect include Albert Schweitzer, Jimmy Hoffa, Johannes Keplar, Karen Silkwood (plutonium fuel plant scandal), Liza Minnelli, Muhammad Ali, Sir Joh Bjelke-Peterson (Australia, Queensland state premier), Ludwig Beck (Chief of Staff of the Armed Forces to Hitler, 1935–1938, later opposed the Nazi regime and Hitler's invasion plans, becoming the leader of the German Resistance Movement. Taken into custody, he was ordered to shoot himself on 20 July 1944 in Berlin), Donovan (Scottish musician), Princess Grace, Ronald Kray (British homicide along with his twin brother), Shaquille O'Neal and Gearge Washington.

Sextile

(Simultaneously trining IC)

Chiron-sextile-MC indicates an open channel for the expression of our Wounds, blockages and unresolved issues through our career and/or public life. It can also indicate the expression of our Healing journey through these same areas. However, this aspect must be consciously activated by our intention and wish for Healing and evolution of consciousness. Otherwise, this aspect remains relatively benign.

Quincunx

Chiron-quincunx-MC indicates that our Wounds, blockages and unresolved issues continually nag us, irritate and frustrate us, constantly poking their heads into our career and/or public lives. The impulse for career and/or public life may stem from a deep need for the Healing and resolution of these things. In this way, we may seem driven, because the uneasiness and unrest within us is never completely allayed, even if we consciously attend to our Wounds, blockages and unresolved issues.

The expression of our innermost Wounds, blockages and unresolved issues may take a publicly creative and artistic form, performance being the natural Healing ground for us. Without such expression, we may end up in despair. Persons with this aspect are encouraged to find outward expression of their innermost feelings.

One way that we may unconsciously find expression for our Wounds, blockages and unresolved issues with this aspect is by seeking to 'fix' and/or change others and the world around us in publicly demonstrative ways.

However, if we *attend* to our Wounds, blockages and unresolved issues, it is likely that we will express the *Healing journey* through our career and/or public life, whatever form that may take.

Noted people who share this aspect include Burt Bacharach, Carl G. Jung, Joan Baez (folk singer), Jodie Foster, Jason Donovan, Tom Wolfe (American writer), Charles Aznavour, Clifford Brown (jazz trumpeter), Nicholas Cage and Getulio Vargas (Brazilian President, dictator and suicide).

Chiron in aspect to IC

Quincunx

Chiron-quincunx-IC indicates that we will see our Wounds, blockages and unresolved issues reflected in our past, our parents, grandparents, genetics and general heredity. We may hearken back to bygone eras and/or expound the virtues of the past compared to the present as an unconscious way of trying to allay the Pain of our Woundedness. We may feel incomplete without a fuller resolution and knowledge of the past and its connection to our present feelings and our Woundedness.

In some ways, this aspect can make us feel as though the past often comes back to haunt us.

Inasmuch as our Wounds, blockages and unresolved issues have their ultimate origins in the past, this makes this aspect highly useful in terms of inspiring and impelling a path of Healing and evolution of consciousness. In this way, this aspect may be a welcome addition to the chart of a person wishing to pursue Healing as a life's path and purpose.

Noted persons that share this aspect include Christopher Isherwood (novelist of pre-Hitler Berlin, one novel inspiring the musical "Cabaret"), Errol Flynn, F. Scott Fitzgerald, Fred Schepisi, Martina Navratilova and Michelangelo.

(For all other aspects of Chiron to the IC, see Chiron in aspect to the MC)

Chiron in aspect to Ascendant

The Ascendant is our window to the world. Initially, it represents the exterior mask(s) we wear, for the most part unconscious. In this way, it represents the way we see ourselves and the way the world sees us, particularly at first meeting. This image may be partly or entirely illusory, depending on our degree of awakening to our true Selves. However, it Serves 1) to protect us from greater Truth until we are ready and 2) to mirror our illusions back to us so that we might transcend them and see the greater Truth of our higher Self and Soul.

As we work through our unresolved issues and Heal our Wounds, evolving and awakening, this mask becomes increasingly transparent. As this happens, we are then able to invoke our different masks consciously and use these masks when and where they are appropriate to the fulfillment of our Divine Design. The Ascendant is our interface with the outside world, the material world, the world of forms and the world of other people in earthly incarnation. It acts as a kind of 'stepping-down station' for the Soul that resides in higher realms to become manifest in the lower earth realms.

When Chiron aspects the Ascendant it indicates that we act as a kind of *persona* for Chiron, i.e. an interface for Chiron to interact with the lower realms. In a sense, Chiron is 'seen' in our countenance. When we are relatively unawakened, in this lifetime or in our overall evolution, Chiron's manifestation through the Ascendant primarily expresses the Wounding. Conversely, when we are relatively awakened, in this lifetime or in our overall evolution, Chiron's manifestation through the Ascendant primarily expresses the Healing.

Conjunction

(Conjunction simultaneously opposing Descendant)

Chiron-conjunct-Ascendant indicates that we are destined to personify Chiron in some way in our lives. In a sense, we unconsciously and continuously channel Chiron and its issues and messages.

Initially, our Wounds, blockages and unresolved issues are worn upon our outer countenance, for all to see and feel, whether we are aware of it or not and whether others can consciously identify it or not. We may find that others want to rescue us, wrap us up in cotton wool, nurture us and soothe our Woundedness.

Our own reaction may be the antithesis of this, i.e. a total denial of our sensitive inner nature, a stoic posture and/or a cynical, suspicious and/or even atheistic attitude towards spiritual matters. Conversely, we may play out the drama of our Woundedness to the maximum, taking out our Wounds, blockages and unresolved issues upon others. It will all depend on the other aspects involved with Chiron in the chart and Chiron's sign placement.

With this aspect, our Woundedness tends to become our first mask; i.e. we unconsciously hide behind our Wounds, blockages and unresolved issues. We may even believe that our Wounds, blockages and unresolved issues *are* us until we attend to the journey of Healing and evolution of consciousness.

When we consciously acknowledge and embrace this journey, we then *live* the Healing journey in the first person, an example for all to see and aspire to. In this case, this aspect becomes a boon to those wishing to pursue Healing as a specific life's path and purpose, conferring empathy, deep understanding and an Unconditionally Loving manner.

Noted persons who share this aspect include Belinda Carlisle, Bjorn Borg, Dennis Nilsen (serial killer), Karen Silkwood (nuclear fuel plant scandal), John Bradshaw (American psychologist, therapist, philosopher and author on methods of Healing the Inner Child and dealing with additions), Reinhold Ebertin (German astrologer and developer of Cosmo biology), Rollo May (American psychoanalyst and lecturer, pioneer of existential psychology) and Joan Pio Prado (Brazilian psychic channeling composer).

Opposition

(Same as conjunction with Descendant)

Chiron-opposition-Ascendant indicates that we stand at the threshold of awakening to a larger picture of ourselves and our lives. This aspect tends to illuminate our Wounds, blockages and unresolved issues around relationship with others, the way others see us and the way we see ourselves in relation to others.

Ultimately, Chiron teaches us that the world is a mirror. Others are a reflection of ourselves. We are all connected and we are all essentially the same, despite the differences in the nature of our individual Divine Designs.

Chiron sitting on the Descendant, as it does in opposition to the Ascendant, indicates a potential awakening to the Other, i.e. the world outside us. This awakening has within it the seeds of the ultimate Truth that we are all One. We go through the stage of separating Self and Other in order to become awakened to the ultimate Truth of Oneness and Love. This is the purpose of the Wounding. This is the purpose of the reflection we call the outside world.

In practical terms, this aspect will constantly throw our Wounds, blockages and unresolved issues around our relationship with ourselves and with others back in our faces. This Serves to impel us to attend to these Wounds, blockages and unresolved issues, to see ourselves as we truly are and to see ourselves in others whom we might otherwise be judging negatively or perhaps infatuating.

Noted people who share this aspect include Albert Schweitzer, Janis Joplin, Michael Gudinski (controversial CEO of Mushroom Records, Australia), Ted Kennedy Jnr, John J. McLeod (Nobel prize winning Scottish physiologist, jointly discovered insulin) and Douglas Block (American astrologer, metaphysician, psychologist and writer of books of affirmations, etcetera).

Trine

(Simultaneously sextiling Descendant)

Chiron-trine-Ascendant indicates a high degree of affinity and resonance between issues of Wounding and Healing in our lives on the one hand and our self-image on the other. For this reason, this aspect can confer a certain charisma, empathy and sensitivity that others may find attractive.

Like the conjunction of Chiron and the Ascendant, this trine indicates that Chiron lives through us, is 'channeled' through us, is present upon our countenance. In this way, we will tend to play out the Wounding and Healing journey through all our interactions with the outside world, as well in the private spaces of our self-image and personal fantasies about ourselves.

Noted persons who share this aspect include Joan Baez, Ringo Starr, Barbara Streisand, Charlie Chaplin, Meryl Streep, Shirley MacLaine, Bonnie Prince Charlie, Rene Crevel (French Dadaist playwright, openly gay, poet obsessed with death, suicide), Arthur Conan Doyle (creator of Sherlock Holmes), Joseph F. Goodavage (American journalist and writer on numerous 'new-age' subjects) and Wassily Kandinsky (Russian artist).

Square

(Simultaneously squaring Descendant)

Chiron-square-Ascendant indicates that, initially, our Wounds, blockages and unresolved issues block, inhibit or limit the free expression of our inner nature. This will be so until we attend to our journey of Healing and evolution of consciousness to some degree.

Conversely, our image of ourselves and the way others see us can tend to stand in the way of us accessing our Wounds, blockages and unresolved issues. In this case, we tend to mistake our masks for our true nature, believing our own publicity, so to speak. This can drive us to try to create masks and personas that protect us from having to deal with our Wounds, blockages and unresolved issues and that hide our true nature from others. This could be a blessing for those wishing to go into show business or be in the public eye.

Alternately, this aspect may tend to make us overly shy and fearful of contact with others due to us trying to hide and/or avoid triggering our sensitive and Wounded inner nature.

With this aspect, we may also tend to see the world in terms of Woundedness, Pain and despair, with little possibility of Healing or reconciliation, i.e. in a fatalistic and/or existentialist way.

This aspect can bring us to the point of asking the question, 'who I am *really*?' The ultimately dissatisfying nature of our masks brings us to this question, engendering a wish to touch something within us that is more true, more permanent and closer to Spirit.

Noted persons who share this aspect include Ernest Hemingway, Barry Humphries (Dame Edna Everage), Liberace, Ron Howard, Rona Barrett (controversial American gossip columnist), J. G. Bennett (British occultist and proponent of the work of Gurdjieff and Ouspensky), John Dryden (17th century poet, dramatist, critic and astrologer), Huey Newton (American political activist, co-founder of the Black Panthers black militant group in the 1960s) and Prince Philip (consort to Queen Elizabeth II).

Sextile

(Simultaneously trining Descendant)

Chiron-sextile-Ascendant indicates that there is a potential pathway for the expression of journey of Wounding and Healing through the vehicles of our masks, our self-image and our public persona.

If we consciously and intentionally activate this aspect by our wish for Healing, our Wounds can be seen upon our countenance as can our efforts and results from attending to these Wounds, i.e. the Healing Journey. Otherwise, this aspect remains relatively benign.

Due to the simultaneous trine with the Descendant, this aspect can confer a good deal of empathy, rapport and sensitivity with others. This is particularly so in terms of being able to feel others' Wounds, blockages and unresolved issues and being able to offer them support, nurturing and/or Healing.

This sextile can be a welcome addition to the charts of those wishing to pursue Healing as a specific life's path and purpose.

Quincunx

Chiron-quincunx-Ascendant indicates a nagging, frustrating, irritating and incessant surfacing of our Wounds, blockages and unresolved issues into our relations with others, into our feelings about ourselves and into the way others perceive us. This can manifest simply as an underlying self-doubt and low self-esteem. This, combined with the fear that others, too, may see us as incomplete or see something 'wrong' with us, will tend to drive us to perfectionism.

A new level of consciousness is sought here concerning who we truly are inside, as opposed to who we think we are in our masks and personas. Until such time, we will tend to attract happenings and situations into our lives that will stir up our Wounds, blockages and unresolved issues. This will impel us to attend to these things and thus to 'clear' the glass of our Ascendant window to the world, allowing our true nature to Shine through.

This can be a welcome aspect in the chart of a potential Healer.

Noted persons who share this aspect include Anita Cobby (murder victim), Arnold Palmer, Claudia Schiffer, Jane Fonda, Shirley Temple Black, Karl Bohm (Austrian musician and conductor), Leonardo Conti (Swiss-German Third Reich Health Leader, responsible for the Nazi euthanasia programs), A. J. Foyt (racing driver), Howard Hughes and Sai Baba.

Chiron in aspect to Descendant

Quincunx

Chiron-quincunx-Descendant indicates that we may have the nagging, frustrating, irritating and incessant feeling that we cannot have a totally fulfilling and/or 'normal' relationship with others. We tend to beat ourselves for our failings and/or judge others for theirs. Our Wounds, blockages and unresolved issues will tend to emerge in our relationships, seeking Healing and resolution through this vehicle. Although this can be very difficult, it can also be very rewarding with the right partner.

We innately seek to bond with others, but in order to do so we must Heal the Wounds, blockages and unresolved issues that isolate and disconnect us from others. Until we do so, we will tend to feel incomplete. This is because relationship mirrors our own inner fragmentedness. The journey of Healing and the evolution of consciousness is the journey of 'wholing' ourselves once more. The vehicle of relationship provides the mirror of this fragmentedness, allowing us to see, acknowledge, embrace and finally Love each of our fragments, bonding them into Oneness and Love.

This aspect illuminates the aforementioned points, providing an opportunity and impetus for Healing through relationships.

This can be a welcome aspect in the chart of a potential Healer.

Noted persons who share this aspect include Agatha Christie, Karl Marx, Roseanne, Heather Locklear and Michael Caine.

(For all other aspects of Chiron to the Descendant, see Chiron in aspect to the Ascendant)

Chiron in a T-square

In a T-square (an opposition connected by two squares), the planet at the junction of the two squares Serves as the vehicle for the reconciliation of the issues of the opposing planets. Simultaneously, the two opposing planets Serve as the catalysts for raising our consciousness around the issues associated with the squaring planet. In this way, where Chiron is situated in a T-square will determine its role in the pattern.

If Chiron is one of the opposing planets, then the squaring planet will offer aid and assistance in Healing and resolving our Wounds, blockages and unresolved issues as indicated by Chiron and as illuminated and challenged by the opposing planet. At the same time, Chiron and the opposing planet will act as catalysts in the raising of our consciousness around the issues of the squaring planet. Let's take an example, ignoring house placements for the sake of simplicity:

Let's suppose we have Chiron in Pisces opposition Uranus in Virgo, both squaring Venus in Gemini.

Firstly, Chiron in Pisces, as we now know, indicates a Wound of feeling as though the Universe/God has betrayed or forsaken us, indicating possible early childhood happenings or circumstances that seem unforgivable. Uranus in Virgo, in this opposition, acts as a light shining upon our Wounds, blockages and unresolved issues, encouraging us to see them in the greatest possible detail and to attend to them in a Healing way. Venus in Gemini, in this T-square, might assist the Healing and resolution of these Wounds, blockages and unresolved issues by giving some intellectual objectivity to our emotional nature. Furthermore, it may influence us towards having multiple relationships instead of getting stuck in the potential stagnation of a single relationship. In this way, we will reap the benefit of a variety of perspectives that will tend to help us see a bigger picture of our lives. This, in turn will ultimately help us to gain a greater consciousness around those things that we previously judged in solely negative ways, i.e. those things that constitute the reasons why we feel the Universe/God betrayed or forsook us. In short, Venus will give us perspective and objectivity.

Secondly, Chiron in Pisces and Uranus in Virgo will act as catalysts to bring our Venus issues to a higher level of consciousness. The lower octave of Venus in Gemini can be fickleness in relationships, shallowness of the Heart and a lack of perseverance and loyalty when thing get difficult in relationship. In this T-square, Venus squaring Chiron indicates that we may be like this as a defence against people getting too close to us and thus having our Woundedness exposed. It can also be that we are unwittingly betraying and forsaking others (another interpretation of the fickleness of Venus in Gemini) as an unconscious revenge against the Universe/God for doing this to us. *We must become what we condemn in order to learn to Love it.* Uranus, squaring Venus and illuminating our Wounds, blockages and unresolved issues through Chiron, seeks to show us a different picture. What we call being betrayed and forsaken has hidden blessings, benefits, lessons and Gifts. With this T-square, we will unconsciously play out our Wounds, blockages and unresolved issues through relationship, repeatedly and in many different circumstances (Venus in Gemini), until the penny begins to drop. As it does and we gradually resolve our issues and Heal our Wounds, our sensitive inner nature will be revealed, our Heart opened and our true Self allowed to Shine through.

Next, if Chiron in a T-square pattern is at the junction of the two squares, then, on the one hand, Chiron will help us to resolve the issues around the opposing planets. At the same time, the opposing planets will act as catalysts for the Healing and resolution of our Wounds and issues indicated by Chiron. That is, the opposing planets will help to bring our Wounds, blockages and unresolved issues into a higher state of consciousness.

Again, let's take an example:

Let's say we have Sun in Cancer opposition Mercury in Capricorn, both squaring Chiron in Libra.

Firstly, the issues of Sun in Cancer opposing Mercury in Capricorn may be that we wish to be caring, nurturing, loving and kind to others (Sun in Cancer). However, our head tells us that this is being too soft, too wishy-washy, too sentimental and too easily swayed by others' emotional problems (Mercury in Capricorn). Furthermore, we may be extremely practical, pragmatic, responsible and unemotional in our way of thinking (Mercury in Capricorn), but we tend to sabotage this by following random emotional impulses (Sun in Cancer). Chiron in Libra will help us to overcome this dilemma by showing us the hidden blessings, benefits, lessons and Gifts that each way of being affords us. It will help us to connect head and Heart, realizing that each represents but a part of the greater whole of ourselves.

Secondly, Chiron in Libra may represent a Wound of feeling alone and/or incomplete without another with whom to share our life. Mercury in Capricorn, squaring Chiron, initially represents an intellectual fortress of protection against our Woundedness. However, it will seek to give us a more down-to-earth understanding of our predicament, also inspiring us to get practical, organized and serious about dealing with our Wounds, blockages and unresolved issues. Sun in Cancer, squaring Chiron, will initially cause us to pine away, feeling as though the Wound of aloneness can never be filled. However, it will also seek to show us that, ultimately, the love, nurturing and care that we may seek from companionship are already within us. In short, it will try to teach us to Love ourselves. It will try to awaken us to the Truth that there is nothing missing within us. Head (Mercury) and Heart (Sun) will join in this T-square to teach us that balance and wholeness already exist in the world and in our lives and that, most importantly, we are never truly alone.

It is important to point out that, as with any specific pattern or aspect, having this pattern does not guarantee that we will attend to our journey of Wounding and Healing. This is a choice that we ourselves make or not make.

Obviously, there are innumerable possible T-square arrangements, more than we can deal with here. However, if we remember and apply the principles we have just laid out, we can discover the essence of each possible T-square arrangement of planets.

It is impossible to give more than a few examples of noted people with T-squares involving Chiron due to the innumerable possible combinations of planets and due to limitations of space. However, here are a few: Charles Samuel Addams (American cartoonist, creator of "The Addams Family"), Muhammad Ali, Louis Braille (inventor of Braille script for the blind), Nat "King" Cole, Jeffrey Dahmer (American serial killer, necrophiliac cannibal), Michael Jordan, Douglas Adams (sci-fi writer, author of "Hitchhikers Guide to the Galaxy"), Chris Evert Lloyd, Bill Gates, Whoopi Goldberg and George Bernard Shaw.

Chiron in a Grand Trine

In a Grand Trine, three planets make mutual trines, generally within one element, i.e. earth, water, air or fire. They mutually enhance each other, resonating at a higher vibration than any of the three planets in isolation. A Grand Trine represents some Gift or other in our lives, the nature of which is determined by the element, sign and house placements of each planet and by the other aspects made to these three planets.

When Chiron is involved in a Grand Trine, the specific themes of Wounding and Healing become emphasized in the areas of life indicated by 1) the other two planets and 2) by the element, sign and house positions of all three planets. A Grand Trine involving Chiron would generally tend to indicate specific Healing themes in our lives. It may also indicate substantial work done on our Healing and evolution of consciousness in the past and/or in past lives.

Let's give an example of a Grand Trine involving Chiron:

Let's say we have Chiron in Aquarius trine Moon in Gemini trine Jupiter in Libra. In isolation, Chiron in Aquarius may indicate a Wound of feeling isolated, cut-off, disconnected and/or alienated from society. Moon in Gemini may indicate talkativeness and a chameleonesque emotional nature. Jupiter in Libra may indicate an obsessive need for balance and companionship arising from Inner Child issues around feeling alone.

Chiron in Aquarius trining Moon in Gemini may indicate a talent for being able to see our Woundedness from others' perspective, to put ourselves in their shoes and to share our understandings with them.

Chiron in Aquarius trining Jupiter in Libra may indicate the potential for a Healing return to the childlike wisdom of the Inner Child that knows that we are never truly alone.

Jupiter in Libra trining Moon in Gemini may indicate a capacity for networking on a large scale.

Taken together, these three planets in the Grand Trine might indicate a potential Gift for large-scale sharing with others the journey of the Inner Child, from aloneness and isolation back to a feeling of togetherness and connectedness. How this might manifest in practical terms would be seen in the house placements of the three planets involved, particularly Chiron's house placement.

It is important to point out that, as with any specific pattern or aspect, having this pattern does not guarantee that we will attend to our journey of Wounding and Healing. This is a choice that we ourselves make or not make.

Again, it is not possible to give numerous examples of noted people who share Grand Trine aspects due to innumerable possible arrangements of planets and due to limitations of space. However, here are a few: Benjamin Creme (Scottish metaphysician, student of Alice Bailey), Andre Gide (French writer, novelist, essayist, critic, playwright, Nobel Prize winner), Richard Speck (American mass murderer), Hank Williams, Troy Aikman (American footballer, Dallas Cowboys), Jean Eugene Atget (French photographer of Paris in the 1890s and early 20th century), and Sylvia Kars (American Sensuality Therapist).

Chiron in a triangle of Trine and two Sextiles

This planetary pattern represents a kind of miniature Grand Trine. Refer to the notes on Grand Trines, above. Further to this, the planet at the junction of the two sextiles is doubly enhanced by the two trining planets and forms the focal point of the pattern. In addition, the trining planets will be further enhanced by the focal planet.

If Chiron is the focal planet, then our journey of Healing and evolution of consciousness will be enhanced by the trining planets. For example, if Chiron, as the focal planet, sextiles Saturn and the Moon, our Healing journey will be enhanced by a sense of seriousness and responsibility (Saturn). It will also be enhanced by a direct connection between our deepest hidden Wounds and our visible lower emotional nature (Moon). Conversely, enhanced control (Saturn) of our lower emotional nature (Moon) will aid our journey of Healing and evolution of consciousness (Chiron).

If Chiron is one of the trining planets, then, in combination with the other trining planet, it will help us to see the benefits, blessings, lessons and Gifts that are hidden within the issues of the focal planet. For example, if Chiron were trining Venus and both were sextiling the Sun, Chiron and Venus would enhance the Sun. In practical terms, this might mean that Chiron would help us to reveal, acknowledge, embrace and finally Love our sense of self, our creativity, our will power and our willingness to let ourselves Shine. Venus would help us to express beauty, balance, warmth and harmony. Chiron-trine-Venus indicates a close connection between our journey of Wounding and Healing and our emotional nature, i.e. our capacity to love and be loved. This can tend to enhance the openness of our self-expression and our potential for the free expression of our Inner Light and Love.

It is important to point out that, as with any specific pattern or aspect, having this pattern does not guarantee that we will attend to our journey of Wounding and Healing. This is a choice that we ourselves make or not make.

A few examples of noted persons who share this planetary pattern include Lena Horne (singer and actress), Auguste Rodin, Richard Branson (Virgin Group), Jean Piccard (Swiss scientist, chemist and aeronautical engineer) and Phoebe Snow (American singer/songwriter).

Chiron in a Grand Cross

A Grand Cross consists of two planets in opposition to each other squaring two other planets also in opposition to each other. Each pair of planets in each opposition represents a catalyst for the raising of consciousness around the issues of the planets in the other opposition.

In general, the Grand Cross initially represents an *impasse* of consciousness. For a transcendence of this planetary pattern, the issues of all four planets involved must be attended to relatively simultaneously. If this is done, the potential for Healing and the evolution of consciousness is unparalleled.

This being so, when Chiron is involved in a Grand Cross, it is almost an irrevocable requirement that we attend to our Woundedness in order to free up our lives and in order to fulfill our life's path and purpose. Of course, this can be difficult. We must attend not only to our Woundedness, represented by Chiron in this pattern, but also simultaneously attend to the issues raised by the other three planets. An understanding of the mechanics of this planetary pattern can assist greatly. Even without such understanding, these mechanics will tend to impel us in a certain direction, unconsciously driving the journey of Healing and the evolution of consciousness. Let's take an example, ignoring house and sign positions for the sake of simplicity:

Let's say we have Chiron-opposition-Uranus both squaring Mercury-opposition-Jupiter. Firstly, the Chiron/Uranus opposition indicates that our Wounds, blockages and unresolved issues are constantly being illuminated, encouraging us to attain a new level of consciousness about them. The Mercury/Jupiter opposition will act as a catalyst for the attainment of this aim. In this case, Mercury-opposition-Jupiter indicates a dilemma between the childlike and seemingly-naïve, but ultimately-wise knowings of the Inner Child and our adult mental attitudes and thinking. This opposition will give two opposing but complementary perspectives to the issues brought up by the Chiron/Uranus opposition. The Jupiter side will encourage us to delve into our childhood issues and see a greater wisdom thereof. The Mercury side will help us to develop objectivity and to see all sides of the issues that we previously judged primarily negatively. In this way, the Jupiter/Mercury opposition will help us to attend to the Wounds, blockages and unresolved issues illuminated by Uranus.

Now let's look at our example pattern from the other angle. The Jupiter/Mercury opposition, as we have said, indicates a dilemma between the childlike and seemingly-naïve, but ultimately-wise knowings of the Inner Child and our adult mental attitudes and thinking. The Chiron/Uranus opposition might assist the resolution of this dilemma by showing us ways in which these seemingly-opposing views are actually connected. It might show us how they both Serve us in different ways to come to a more complete picture of reality, closer to Truth and Actuality. In other words, Chiron and Uranus will show us that these two ways of viewing the world are *complementary*, much the same as the fact that we require both thought and emotion to have a complete picture of anything.

It is important to point out that, as with any specific pattern or aspect, having this pattern does not guarantee that we will attend to our journey of Wounding and Healing. This is a choice that we ourselves make or not make.

•

A few examples of noted persons who share the Grand Cross pattern include Diane C. Chechik (American writer, bestseller book on breast cancer), Kathy McMillan (American Olympic track and field athlete), Jack Riley (American actor, writer, voice-man, mostly comedy), Billy Connolly (Scottish comedian), Riccardo Patrese (Italian Grand Prix winning Formula 1 driver) and Charlene McCarthy (American newswoman and anchorwoman).

Chiron in a Star of David

The Star of David planetary pattern consists of six planets in a necklace of six sextiles. It is a highly balanced pattern allowing open correspondence between the issues of our lives in six different areas. Whether we make use of this psychological gridwork of interconnections is up to us. A Star of David pattern would tend to indicate that we have done substantial work of our Healing and evolution of consciousness in the past and/or in past lives.

Chiron's presence in a Star of David pattern would indicate that conscious access to our journey of Wounding and Healing would be increased six-fold, with five extra planets offering assistance. The journey of Healing and the evolution of consciousness would be an integral part of our lives and one which we would tend to be more conscious of than not. After all, in Actuality, in Truth, *all* things are leading us, guiding us, helping us and impelling us to grow, Heal and evolve. It is just that, in lower levels of consciousness and awakening, we are not so aware of this and tend to see things in our lives as being separate and disconnected.

It is important to point out that, as with any specific pattern or aspect, having this pattern does not guarantee that we will attend to our journey of Wounding and Healing. This is a choice that we ourselves make or not make.

Chiron in a Yod

The yod planetary pattern (also referred to as "the finger of God") consists of a triangle formed from two quincunxes and a sextile. The focal point of the yod is the planet at the junction of the two quincunxes. The two sextiling planets assist in bringing our consciousness around the issues of the focal planet into a higher state.

When Chiron is involved in a yod pattern, the elements of Healing and the evolution of consciousness are emphasized. Chiron role in the pattern will change according to its placement.

If Chiron is the focal point, the two sextiling planets will impel us to attain a higher state of consciousness around our specific Wounds, blockages and unresolved issues as indicated by Chiron. For example, if Jupiter sextiles Mars and they both quincunx Chiron, then Jupiter and Mars will impel us to attend to our Wounds, blockages and unresolved issues. Jupiter will tend to impel us to see the hidden 'rightness' and wisdom that lay behind those things that we call our Wounds, i.e. to see the benefits, blessings, lessons and Gifts. Mars will give us an extra kick, an extra impulse, to get on with the journey of Healing and evolution of consciousness.

If Chiron is one of the sextiling planets, then, in combination with the other sextiling planet, it will impel us to attain Healing and evolution of consciousness concerning the issues of the focal planet. For example, if Chiron sextiles Saturn and they both quincunx Venus, Chiron and Saturn will impel us to raise our consciousness around the issues of earthly love, relationships, beauty, balance, harmony, etcetera. (These issues will be modified by any other aspect that Venus might make in the chart as a whole.) In this example, Chiron will impel us to Heal Wounds of relationship, the feelings of being loved or not and the feelings of being able to love or not. Saturn will encourage us to get serious about these same issues and the take responsibility for their Healing and resolution.

It is important to point out that, as with any specific pattern or aspect, having this pattern does not guarantee that we will attend to our journey of Wounding and Healing. This is a choice that we ourselves make or not make.

A few examples of noted people who share the yod planetary pattern include Richard Schultz (American astrologer, author of "Cosmic Connection"), Florence Baggett (British test tube baby), Paul Martin Simon (American liberal Democrat politician, ex-counterintelligence agent) and James Alexander Lamond (Scottish M.P.).

Chiron in a triangle of Trine, Square, Quincunx

This triangular mixture of aspects has the best of all possible worlds. It contains a blockage or limitation to overcome (square), an enhancement to aid us on our journey (trine) and an impelling force to drive us to attend to that journey (quincunx). When Chiron is involved in this pattern, then the themes of Healing and the evolution of consciousness will be apparent in the pattern's issues.

The first step in interpreting this pattern is to interpret each individual aspect separately, i.e. the trining planets, the squaring planets and the quincunxing planets. Then we can look at the pattern as a whole. The focal planet is the planet at the quincunx/trine junction. This planet will assist the breaking down of the *impasse* of consciousness reflected in the issues of the squaring planets. This focal planet will assist in bringing about a new level of understanding and awareness.

If Chiron is the focal planet, it will help us to see the all sides of the issues of the squaring planets, revealing the hidden benefits, blessings, lessons and Gifts of each. In this way, it will help us to Heal the issues that otherwise maintain the *impasse* of consciousness indicated by the square.

If Chiron is one of the squaring planets, the focal planet will assist us in Healing and resolving our Wounds, blockages and unresolved issues, enabling us to unlock the higher potential of the other squaring planet.

It is important to point out that, as with any specific pattern or aspect, having this pattern does not guarantee that we will attend to our journey of Wounding and Healing. This is a choice that we ourselves make or not make.

Chiron in a triangle of Opposition, Trine, Sextile

The opposition in this planetary pattern is already resolved to a degree by the trining/sextiling planet. The trining/sextiling planet – the focal planet – will assist in further integrating the issues of the opposing planets and bringing about a higher, more unified, understanding and awareness.

If Chiron is the focal planet, then the integration and resolution of the opposition issues are dependent on our journey of Healing and evolution of consciousness. The opposition issues will impel us to attend to this journey.

If Chiron is one of the opposing planets, then the focal planet will offer assistance on the journey of Healing and the evolution of consciousness, called to action by the planet opposing Chiron.

A few examples of noted persons who share this planetary pattern include Tracy Austin, Annie Besant (British-Indian social reformer and feminist and former head of the Theosophical Society in India), Nicholas Cage, Boris Becker, Leonardo Conti (Swiss-German Third Reich Health Leader, responsible for the Nazi euthanasia programs) and Whitney Houston.

Chiron in a Kite formation

The kite formation is one of the most advanced of planetary patterns, rarely seen. It consists of a Grand Trine where one of the trines is also part of a trine-and-two-sextiles pattern. It can also be viewed as two opposition-trine-sextile patterns placed back to back, their respective focal points also trining.

The focal point of the kite pattern is the tip of the kite, i.e. the planet at the junction of the two sextiles, simultaneously opposing the junction of two of the three trines. The planet that opposes the focal planet will be the major catalyst in this pattern, challenging and confronting us to attain a new level of consciousness at the focal point planet. The three trining planets will represent an inherent Gift we bring into this lifetime. The two trining planets sextiling the focal planet will focus this Gift into the focal planet.

If Chiron is the focal planet, then the journey of Healing and the evolution of consciousness will be one of the major focuses of our life, whatever external form that may take. This would the mark of a person 'called' to Heal in some way.

If Chiron is the planet opposing the focal point, it will act as the catalyst to inspire new levels of consciousness expressed through the focal planet. Said another way, our Wounds, blockages and unresolved issues will drive us along the Healing path which, in turn, will help us open up the expression of the focal planet.

If Chiron is one of the two trining planets that sextile the focal point, then it will Serve to bring Healing and resolution to the issues of the focal planet, thus allowing the focal planet's fullest expression.

In all cases, Chiron's presence in this pattern indicates that the themes of Healing and the evolution of consciousness will be strong in our lives, whether consciously acknowledged or not. It is important to point out that, as with any specific pattern or aspect, having this pattern does not guarantee that we will attend to our journey of Wounding and Healing. This is a choice that we ourselves make or not make.

A few examples of noted persons who share this planetary pattern include Kurt Cobain (Nirvana), Howie Long (American football defensive lineman, actor and TV sports commentator), Harry Curtis (American costume and stage designer), Billy Mitchell (French military man who became the youngest officer ever appointed to the General Staff in 1912 and, by 1920, was a Brigadier General, a pilot and a lifelong advocate of air power) and Wilfried Peeters (Belgian Olympic cyclist).

Interestingly, the chart of the recording of the Beatles' first single – the one that first brought them fame – contains a kite formation. *(See Chart 20 – BEATLES 1ST SINGLE, p. 556.)*

8 ~ CHIRON IN TRANSIT

Having previously suggested specific orbs for transits, it is important to make a distinction here between the applying and separating periods of any given transit.

For practical purposes, it has been common to consider the total period of transit and its influence to be the combined time of applying and separating periods. In this case, the intensity of the transit is determined by the proximity to an exact angle. However, I have found that the transit's influence is actually confined to the applying period up until an exact angle is made. The separating period is, strictly speaking, no longer a period of influence, but rather is a period of aftermath of the effects of the applying period.

This may seem like nit-picking, but when we are exploring actual happenings in relation to the transits, it becomes an important distinction and increases the accuracy and scientific veracity of the process.

It is also important to remind ourselves that the intensity and specific effect of any given transit will be determined by the natal angular aspects made to the planet being transited. The transit of a natal singleton will be less significant than the transit of well-aspected planet in the natal chart.

However, having said this, it is important to note that transits offer natal singletons their only opportunity to become significantly active in a person's life. This makes these specific transits worthy of special attention when reading the chart.

Lastly, we must remember that the house and sign placements of the planets involved in any given transit will give the general influences and themes of the transit a practical context in day-to-day life. Due to limitations of space, however, we will restrict our definitions to the general influences and themes, leaving the context of house and sign placements to you, the reader, to work out and integrate. (For a brief overview of the themes and issues of each of the signs and houses, refer to Appendix C, "Affairs of the Signs" and Appendix D, "Affairs of the Houses".)

Transits to and by Planets, MC & Ascendant, etc.

Conjunct, Parallel, Contra-Parallel, Occultation Transits

In general, these transits are the most powerful and have the most obvious effects in our lives. There is a direct activation of the transited planet and the natal planets in aspect to it. When Chiron is the transiting planet, then it will act as a catalyst for the Healing and evolution of consciousness of the issues around the transited planet and its aspecting companions, as played out through their respective signs and houses. When Chiron is the planet transited, the transiting planet will aid the Healing and evolution of consciousness of our specific Wounds, blockages and unresolved issues as indicated by natal Chiron and its aspecting companions, as played out through their respective signs and houses.

As always, occulting transits will be the most powerful and focused.

Chiron conjuncting, paralleling, contra-paralleling natal North Node

Wounds, regrets, failings, unresolved issues around our life's path and purpose are brought to the surface, impelling us to clear the way for a more conscious pursuit of that path and purpose.

North Node conjuncting, paralleling, contra-paralleling natal Chiron

A call from our destiny, so to speak, to attend to our Wounds, blockages and unresolved issues so that we might more faithfully honor our life's path and purpose.

Chiron conjuncting, paralleling, contra-paralleling natal South Node

Wounds, blockages and unresolved issues from the past and/or past lives surface during this transit, encouraging us to finally Heal and resolve them, moving forward on our life's path and purpose.

South Node conjuncting, paralleling, contra-paralleling natal Chiron

The past comes back to haunt us, triggering our Wounds, blockages and unresolved issues, as indicated by natal Chiron, impelling us to finally Heal and resolve them.

Chiron conjuncting, paralleling, contra-paralleling natal Sun

Residual feelings of shyness, fear of self-expressing, ego-Wounds, loss or lack of will power, thwarted or repressed creativity, etcetera, surface, encouraging Healing and resolution of same.

Sun conjuncting, paralleling, contra-paralleling natal Chiron

Activation and illumination of our Wounds, blockages and unresolved issues, encouraging us to attend to them.

Chiron conjuncting, paralleling, contra-paralleling natal Moon

Old Wounds, regrets, self-depreciation and negative feelings about our emotional protective patterns and the reactions and emotional habits of our lower nature. Chiron's light encourages us to bring our emotional nature into a higher octave, closer to Love.

Moon conjuncting, paralleling, contra-paralleling natal Chiron

Transient (monthly) lower-natured expression and exacerbation of our inner Wounds, blockages and unresolved issues. Brought to conscious light, we are encouraged to attend to our Wounds, blockages and unresolved issues.

Chiron conjuncting, paralleling, contra-paralleling natal Mercury

Residual Wounds, regrets, negative feelings around our ability to communicate, interact with others, express ourselves and/or think clearly and/or being unintelligent are brought to the surface, impelling us to attend to these issues.

Mercury conjuncting, paralleling, contra-paralleling natal Chiron

A time of greater potential to be able to express, communicate and mentally understand our Wounds, blockages and unresolved issues as indicated by natal Chiron.

Chiron conjuncting, paralleling, contra-paralleling natal Venus

Residual Wounds, regrets, self-depreciation and negative feelings around being loved or not, being able to love or not, around relationships and issues of companionship are brought to the surface. This will occur most often within our current relationships, encouraging us to attend to these issues in this area of our lives.

Venus conjuncting, paralleling, contra-paralleling natal Chiron

Venus encourages us to express our feelings arising from our Wounds, blockages and unresolved issues, to share them with others in close personal relationship, trusting the resultant Healing process. We may meet someone special during this transit.

Chiron conjuncting, paralleling, contra-paralleling natal Mars

Residual Wounds, regrets, self-depreciation and negative feelings around action, decisions, intentions we have had in the past and/or that we have failed to act upon, surface during this transit. We are encouraged us to see the reasons behind our past manifestations and to take appropriate action now. What stops us from activating our lives?

Mars conjuncting, paralleling, contra-paralleling natal Chiron

A call to action, concerning our journey of Wounding and Healing.

Chiron conjuncting, paralleling, contra-paralleling natal Jupiter

Residual Wounds, regrets, self-depreciation and negative feelings around 1) issues of freedom or lack thereof, 2) around childhood and Inner Child issues, 3) around excessive behavior and/or 4) around failure to attend to the details of our issues surface during this transit, encouraging our attention to these matters.

Jupiter conjuncting, paralleling, contra-paralleling natal Chiron

Jupiter encourages us to see a bigger picture with respect to our Wounds, blockages and unresolved issues, to see the hidden benefits, blessings, lessons and Gifts within those issues that we previously judged solely negatively. Jupiter coaxes us to return the childlike but wise view of the world as being the best of all possible worlds, everything in its right place and Serving a larger Plan. This is a medium-strength Healing transit.

Chiron conjuncting, paralleling, contra-paralleling natal Saturn

Residual Wounds, regrets, self-depreciation and negative feelings around 'father issues', authority, restriction, limitation, repression, blame, responsibility and discipline surface during this time. We are encouraged us to get serious about our lives and about our higher mission and purpose. We are chided to become more responsible and disciplined on our journey of Healing and the evolution of consciousness.

Saturn conjuncting, paralleling, contra-paralleling natal Chiron

Saturn, via the circumstances of our life, causes us to have to sit down and stay seated in some way until we begin to take stock, becoming serious and responsible about our journey of Wounding and Healing. A call to get serious and face our inner nature. This is a major Healing transit.

Chiron conjuncting, paralleling, contra-paralleling natal Chiron

(This is the Chiron Return – *see **Part Three, Chapter 3, "Life Cycles"**, p. 308.*)

Chiron conjuncting, paralleling, contra-paralleling natal Uranus

Residual Wounds, regrets, self-depreciation and negative feelings surface 1) around our failure to expand our minds, 2) around our network of friends and contacts, 3) around our view of the world and our lives, 4) around our inability to choose a direction in life and stick to it and 5) around past major changes in our lives that we judge primarily negatively. Chiron encourages us to see the perfection and Plan in all these issues and to embrace the changes as a vehicle for our Healing and evolution of consciousness.

Uranus conjuncting, paralleling, contra-paralleling natal Chiron

Uranus shines a direct light upon our Woundedness, as indicated by natal Chiron, encouraging us to attend to what we see. Uranus encourages us to bring our consciousness around our Wounds and issues into a higher state, seeing the perfection and Plan behind it all. This is a major Healing transit.

Chiron conjuncting, paralleling, contra-paralleling natal Neptune

Residual Wounds, regrets, self-depreciation and negative feelings surface 1) around our spiritual life or lack thereof, 2) around our sense of aloneness and/or 3) around feeling abandoned by the Universe/God, etcetera. We are encouraged us to reach out to Spirit, to reach inwards to our Heart and Soul and to see the Divine in all things in our lives, past, present and future.

Neptune conjuncting, paralleling, contra-paralleling natal Chiron

A time when Neptune encourages us to Love ourselves just as we are, to Love those parts of us that have been Wounded, fragmented, separated, judged negatively, condemned, etcetera. Neptune also encourages us to Love our Woundedness and the people involved for the Service they have afforded us and others in the larger Loving Plan of life. This is a major Healing transit.

Chiron conjuncting, paralleling, contra-paralleling natal Pluto

Residual Wounds, regrets, self-depreciation and negative feelings surface around losses, endings, major upheavals, major crises, major changes and deaths we may have had in our lives, metaphoric and actual. We are encouraged to move beyond these illusions and see the new forms that these things now take in our lives. A call to emerge into a new cycle of our lives, activating our innate powers of transformation of consciousness.

Pluto conjuncting, paralleling, contra-paralleling natal Chiron

Pluto most violently and forcefully shakes our Wounds, blockages and unresolved issues, bringing them to the surface in ways we cannot ignore, impelling us to attend to these things immediately or suffer major upheavals in our lives, internally or externally. Pluto encourages us to alter our pre-conceptions, illusions, misperceptions, biases and lopsided attitudes towards those things that we feel created our Wounds, blockages and unresolved issues. It encourages us to see the other side of the picture and to acknowledge the Loving Service behind all things, people, events and places in our lives. This is a major Healing transit.

Chiron conjuncting natal Ascendant

Residual Wounds, regrets, self-depreciation and negative feelings surface around our self-image, our self-confidence, our self-appreciation, our view of ourselves and around the way others see us. We are encouraged to see and Love ourselves just as we are, *masks and all,* for it all Serves us and others in ways that we don't initially see.

Chiron conjuncting natal Descendant

Residual Wounds, regrets, self-depreciation and negative feelings surface 1) around our relationship with others, 2) around our separation from others, 3) around our seemingly-scattered psyches, 4) around our state of health (physical, emotional, mental and/or spiritual) and/or 5) around our deep wish and need for companionship. We are encouraged to attend to these issues in a Healing way.

Chiron conjuncting natal MC

Residual Wounds, regrets, self-depreciation and negative feelings around career and public image issues arise during this transit. We are encouraged us to link our life's path and purpose – our inner passion – with our chosen vocation. We are also encouraged to Heal our Wounds, blockages and unresolved issues around what others think of us, around being seen by others and/or around being on show, so to speak.

Chiron conjuncting natal IC

Residual Wounds, regrets, self-depreciation and negative feelings surface around past Wounds, blockages and unresolved issues of family – parents, grandparents, great-grandparents and other older relatives in particular. We are encouraged to Heal the past so that we can move forward into the future more freely and openly.

Opposing Transits

In general, opposition transits shine a light on the natal planet they oppose, challenging and confronting us to achieve new consciousness around the issues of the natal planet. When Chiron is involved in opposition transits, the themes of Healing and the evolution of consciousness become part and parcel of the issues raised.

Chiron, as the transiting planet, brings up residual Wounds, regrets, self-depreciation and negative feelings around the issues of the transited natal planet. This is similar to a conjuncting transit, but is more challenging and confronting, because it illuminates the flip-sides of issues that we may be reluctant to see and acknowledge.

Chiron, as the natal planet, is challenged and confronted by the opposing transiting planet. The transiting planet, in this case, illuminates particular aspects of our specific Wounds, blockages and unresolved issues as indicated by natal Chiron, challenging us to see the Dark and hidden parts of ourselves more clearly.

Chiron opposing natal North Node

(See Chiron conjuncting natal South Node.)

North Node opposing natal Chiron

(See South Node conjuncting natal Chiron.)

Chiron opposing natal South Node

(See Chiron conjuncting natal North Node.)

South Node opposing natal Chiron

(See North Node conjuncting natal Chiron.)

Chiron opposing natal Sun

Residual Wounds, regrets, self-depreciation and negative feelings surface around failure to express ourselves, to honor our creativity, to exercise our will power and/or to allow ourselves to Shine. They are illuminated and thrown back in our faces, challenging us to deal with them.

Sun opposing natal Chiron

The Sun illuminates and activates our Wounds, blockages and unresolved issues as indicated by natal Chiron, challenging us to see, acknowledge and attend to them.

Chiron opposing natal Moon

Residual Wounds, regrets, self-depreciation and negative feelings surface around our lower-natured emotional reactions and protective devices. They are thrown back at us, challenging us to learn to Love these aspects of ourselves for the Service they have afforded us, keeping us safe until we are ready for greater Truth.

Moon opposing natal Chiron

Our Wounds, blockages and unresolved issues are brought to the fore through our lower-natured emotional reactions, protective patterns, habits and impulses. Illuminated in this way, we are challenged to attend to these Wounds, blockages and unresolved issues.

Chiron opposing natal Mercury

Residual Wounds, regrets, self-depreciation and negative feelings surface around failure to express ourselves clearly, around communication difficulties, around difficulty in making friends, around feeling unintelligent and/or around feeling out of touch. These are brought to the fore and thrown back at us, challenging us to attend to these feelings.

Mercury opposing natal Chiron

Mercury challenges us to gain a greater understanding of our Woundedness, as indicated by natal Chiron. It challenges us to make connections between the seemingly-confusing aspects of these Wounds, blockages and unresolved issues and to communicate our understandings to others around us.

Chiron opposing natal Venus

Residual Wounds, regrets, self-depreciation and negative feelings around perceived failure(s) in relationships, around feeling not loved, around feeling unable to love and around our emotional nature in general are thrown back in our faces. Chiron challenges us to attain a new consciousness about these issues and our feelings around them.

Venus opposing natal Chiron

Venus challenges us to Love our Wounds, blockages and unresolved issues. It challenges us to Love those around us, past and present, who have had anything to do with those Wounds, blockages and unresolved issues. It challenges us to see ourselves, the positive and the negative, in the mirror of others close to us. Someone may come into our lives during this time and challenge our Wounds, blockages and unresolved issues.

Chiron opposing natal Mars

Residual Wounds, regrets, self-depreciation and negative feelings surface around things we have done or not done in the past and around perceived failure(s) to take action, make an intention, carry out a resolve, etcetera. These are thrown back in our faces, challenging us to come to a new level of consciousness around these issues, ultimately seeing how inaction is a form of action, appropriate to certain circumstances and situations.

Mars opposing natal Chiron

Mars calls us to action in the tasks of Healing and the evolution of consciousness, bringing up the most acute aspects of our Wounds, blockages and unresolved issues, challenging us to make a decision to deal with them.

Chiron opposing natal Jupiter

Residual Wounds, regrets, self-depreciation and negative feelings surface 1) around perceived failure to acknowledge and listen to the wisdom of our Inner Child/Heart/Soul, 2) around our excessive negativity, 3) around our excessive nature that swings from one extreme to another and/or 4) around our perceived failure(s) to attend to the details of things we turn our attention. These are thrown back in our faces, challenging us to attend to these issues and our feelings about them.

Jupiter opposing natal Chiron

Jupiter challenges us to see a bigger picture with respect to our Wounds, blockages and unresolved issues. It challenges us to see a larger Plan, to see the inherent 'rightness' of all that befalls us and to see the Service that even our Woundedness affords us and others on the journey of Healing. Jupiter says that, despite our judgments of the past, all's right with the world and there is a Guiding Hand at work behind the scenes.

Chiron opposing natal Saturn

Residual Wounds, regrets, self-depreciation and negative feelings surface 1) around feeling restricted, limited, repressed, oppressed, 2) around authority, discipline, seriousness and responsibility in our lives and/or 3) around the issue of blame. These are thrown back in our faces, challenging us to take responsibility for our lives and to get serious about our journey of Healing and evolution of consciousness.

Saturn opposing natal Chiron

Saturn challenges us to get serious, disciplined and responsible for our Wounds, blockages and unresolved issues by throwing these back in our faces, forcing us to sit down and take stock. This is a major Healing transit.

Chiron opposing natal Chiron

(This is the Chiron *opposition* or *half-Return.* *See Part Three, Chapter 3, p. 303.)*

Chiron opposing natal Uranus

Residual Wounds, regrets, self-depreciation and negative feelings surface 1) around major changes in our lives, 2) around our inability to set a direction and stick to it, 3) around feeling unable to fit in with others or be a part of groups and/or 4) around feeling different from others. These are thrown back at us during this transit, challenging us to find new perspectives on these issues. We are challenged to see the hidden benefits, blessing, lessons and Gifts in these issues in terms of our potential Healing and evolution of consciousness.

Uranus opposing natal Chiron

Uranus shines a challenging light upon our Wounds, blockages and unresolved issues as indicated by natal Chiron. It impels us to attend to these things, encouraging us to see them in a different light, from different angles and from a more inclusive vantage point. This is a major Healing transit.

Chiron opposing natal Neptune

Residual Wounds, regrets, self-depreciation and negative feelings surface 1) around neglect of our spiritual life, 2) around feelings of betrayal by the Universe/God, 3) around feeling abandoned by those who 'should' have loved us more, 4) around our own rejection of spiritual matters and/or 5) around our seemingly-irrational and incommunicable feelings. These are thrown back in our faces, challenging us to see things differently, challenging us to acknowledge the presence of Love, Oneness and Spirit around us and within us.

Neptune opposing natal Chiron

Neptune challenges us to Love ourselves Unconditionally, i.e. all of ourselves including the light and the dark, the 'good' and the 'bad', the hidden and the visible. It challenges us to see the Divine Plan that lies behind those things that we have been judging primarily negatively in our lives, past and present. It challenges us to open our Hearts and allow ourselves to be Healed by the Love that is always around us, hidden from our unseeing eyes. This is a major Healing transit.

Chiron opposing natal Pluto

Residual Wounds, regrets, self-depreciation and negative feelings surface around loss, endings, radical changes, major crises, major upheavals and death in our lives. These are thrown back in our faces violently and forcefully. We are challenged us to transcend our old perspectives and biases around these issues. We are challenged us to see the new forms taken by those things in our lives that we felt we lost. Chiron challenges us to see the benefits, blessings, lessons and Gifts in crises and calamities. This is a major Healing transit.

Pluto opposing natal Chiron

Pluto violently and forcefully shakes up our Wounds, blockages and unresolved issues, challenging us to attend to them immediately or suffer further feelings of loss, endings, crises, death and change. In opposition, Pluto shines a light on the flip-sides of our Wounds, blockages and unresolved issues in an effort to wipe away our lopsided illusions, misperceptions and lies that merely perpetuate our Woundedness. Pluto seeks to evolve our consciousness in dramatic ways. This is a major Healing transit.

Chiron opposing natal Ascendant

(See Chiron conjuncting natal Descendant.)

Chiron opposing natal Descendant

(See Chiron conjuncting natal Ascendant.)

Chiron opposing natal MC

(See Chiron conjuncting natal IC.)

Chiron opposing natal IC

(See Chiron conjuncting natal MC.)

Squaring Transits

In general, squaring transits will bring issues of the transited planet to a head. They do this by somehow stopping us in our tracks, by causing us to have to take stock, think deeply and try to understand the nature of the issues at hand. In this way, square aspects and squaring transits are related to Saturn.

When Chiron makes a transiting square to a natal planet, the Wounds, blockages and unresolved issues around the natal planet are triggered. They are brought to the fore, in some ways suspending the free flowing of the affairs of that planet until we sit down and reassess, take stock and think deeply about the issues at hand.

When another planet makes a transiting square to natal Chiron, the transiting planet will assist in the Healing and resolution of our Wounds, blockages and unresolved issues, according to its specific influences and affairs.

Chiron squaring natal North Node

(Simultaneously squaring natal South Node.)

Our life's path and purpose are seemingly thwarted and brought into question by residual Wounds, regrets, self-depreciation and negative feelings around our path and purpose.

North Node squaring natal Chiron

(Simultaneously squared by transiting South Node.)

Our specific Wounds, blockages and unresolved issues, as indicated by natal Chiron, are brought into question. We are encouraged by the North (and South) Node to examine the ways in which these Wounds, blockages and unresolved issues have thwarted the discovery and fulfillment of our life's path and purpose.

Chiron squaring natal South Node

(See also Chiron squaring natal North Node.)

The transiting square of Chiron to the South Node brings our past Wounds, blockages and unresolved issues into view, encouraging us to take stock, reassess and examine the ways in which these have thwarted our life's path and purpose.

South Node squaring natal Chiron

(See also North Node squaring natal Chiron.)

Old Wounds, blockages and unresolved issues are brought into focus. We are encouraged us to take stock, reassess and examine the ways in which our specific Woundedness, as indicated by natal Chiron, has thwarted our life's path and purpose.

Chiron squaring natal Sun

Our free expression, creativity, will power and ability to Shine are seemingly thwarted or limited by the surfacing of Woundedness around these Sun themes. We are encouraged us to take stock, reassess and think deeply about these Wounds, blockages and unresolved issues.

Sun squaring natal Chiron

A short-term transit (yearly for a few days). The Sun encourages us to express our Wounds, blockages and unresolved issues, as indicated by natal Chiron. Our ego, self-will and pride may get in the way, however, causing us to question these aspects of ourselves and their role in keeping our Wounds, blockages and unresolved issues unHealed and unresolved.

Chiron squaring natal Moon

Chiron questions our lower-natured emotional reactions, patterns and habits and their role in keeping us from Healing and resolving our Wounds, blockages and unresolved issues. We may find our emotional reactions during this transit keep us from functioning normally in our lives, impelling us to question, take stock, reassess and examine our emotional life.

Moon squaring natal Chiron

A short transit (monthly, for less than a day). The Moon will trigger our Wounds, blockages and unresolved issues, as indicated by natal Chiron. It will stop us for a short time from functioning normally, encouraging us to question, take stock, reassess and examine our emotional life.

Chiron squaring natal Mercury

Chiron questions the Wounds, blockages and unresolved issues around our mental life, around our ability to communicate with others, around feeling out of touch and around our feelings of being unintelligent, encouraging us to delve into these issues. We may find ourselves seeking solitude and silence during this time.

Mercury squaring natal Chiron

Mercury will tend to hijack our mental processes for the purpose of causing us to think more deeply about our Wounds, blockages and unresolved issues, as indicated by natal Chiron. We may seem preoccupied during this time, seeking solitude and silence.

Chiron squaring natal Venus

Chiron brings our Wounds, blockages and unresolved issues around relationships, being loved or not, being able to love or not and around our need for companionship into focus. This can take the form of *impasses* in dealings with others close to us. It can also indicate the surfacing of long-past issues – i.e. resentments, regrets, blame, hurt, etcetera – particularly in long-term relationships.

Venus squaring natal Chiron

Venus, more often than not through relationship, will tend to trigger our Woundedness, as indicated by natal Chiron. This will force us to pause for a moment. It will force us to take stock, to reassess and examine the role of our Woundedness in our relationships. It will cause us to question our ability to give and receive love or not.

Chiron squaring natal Mars

Chiron will tend to bring us to a halt in our lives. It will do this in order to impel us to delve into the reasons why we might thwart, sabotage, limit, interfere and repress our life's activity, our drive, momentum, intentions and actions in general.

Mars squaring natal Chiron

Mars calls us to action by triggering our Wounds, blockages and unresolved issues, as indicated by natal Chiron. We may find ourselves expressing anger at ourselves and others for thwarting our attempts to get on in life, to get certain things done and to make certain decisions. We will be impelled to understand the ways in which our Wounds, blockages and unresolved issues hold us back and why.

Chiron squaring natal Jupiter

Chiron will bring to the fore Wounds, blockages and unresolved issues 1) around our Inner Child, 2) around our sense of injustice in the world, 3) around our doubts about there being a larger Plan and/or 4) around our failure to attend to the details of things to which we turn our attention. We may find that we lose a sense of meaning and *joie de vivre* during this time, inspiring us to search for meaning and to discover a larger picture of life.

Jupiter squaring natal Chiron

Jupiter will inspire us during this time to see a larger picture and Plan to our Wounds, blockages and unresolved issues, as indicated by natal Chiron. It will seek to expand our consciousness, to awaken us to the Guiding Hand in our lives and to the 'rightness' of all that transpires in our lives. We may not be able to concentrate on the details of these things during this time, as Jupiter seeks to help us see the whole picture at a glance.

Chiron squaring natal Saturn

Chiron will bring our Wounds, blockages and unresolved issues around restrictions, limitations, repressions, oppressions, authority, responsibility and discipline to the fore. This will put the brakes on our lives in some way, impelling us to take stock, reassess, and re-examine our lives, past, present and future. It encourages us to ask the questions, "Who am I? Where do I come from? Where am I going? Why am I here?" It encourages us to see the ways in which Saturn's issues have Served us, despite their frustrating nature and sometimes-Painful processes.

Saturn squaring natal Chiron

Saturn impels us, during this transit, to take stock, accept responsibility, cease blaming, start attending to and working seriously with our Wounds, blockages and unresolved issues, as indicated by natal Chiron. It will tend to create conditions in our lives that will force us to stop and do this. It represents a time to think, reflect, ponder, plan and make resolutions. This is a relatively major transit.

Chiron squaring natal Chiron

(See Part Three, Chapter 3, p. 301 (1st square) and p. 307 (2nd square)).

Chiron squaring natal Uranus

Chiron will tend to thwart higher understanding during this time, impelling us to search for deeper meaning and connections in our Wounds, blockages and unresolved issues. It will encourage us to attend to our Woundedness 1) around radical change in our lives, past and present, 2) around being a part of society and community, 3) around our place within groups, 4) around feeling different from others, 5) around fitting in or not fitting in and/or 6) around not feeling like we can get a grasp of a higher meaning in the seeming chaos of our lives.

Uranus squaring natal Chiron

Uranus impels us to seek a higher consciousness around our specific Wounds, blockages and unresolved issues, as indicated by natal Chiron. It will tend to create unexpected blockages, restrictions, limitations and closed doors in an effort to get us to go within and ponder our Wounds, blockages and unresolved issues. It will encourage us to see larger connections, see the flip-sides and see the overall Plan behind these things. This offers us a way of moving beyond the apparent blockages of this square. This is a relatively major transit.

Chiron squaring natal Neptune

Chiron will tend to bring our Woundedness to the surface 1) around spirituality or lack thereof, 2) around the nature and existence of Love, 3) around our misperceptions and illusions of our lives, inner and outer, 4) around the fantasies and escapisms of our inner life and/or 5) around any feeling of betrayal or abandonment in our lives to the fore. It will tend to give us pause and reason to ponder these important issues.

Neptune squaring natal Chiron

Neptune will act in a mysterious and unpredictable way upon our Wounds, blockages and unresolved issues, as indicated by natal Chiron. We are being called to stop and go within, to hear the small voice within our Hearts, to hear our Soul/Spirit and to acknowledge the Guiding Hand of Love in our lives. We are being impelled to see the Love that lies hidden within our Wounds, blockages and unresolved issues. This Love drives us constantly towards our ultimate Healing and evolution of consciousness and towards a Return to Oneness and Love. Ultimately, the Wound is a Gift of Love. This is a relatively major transit.

Chiron squaring natal Pluto

Chiron will bring the Wounds, blockages and unresolved issues to the surface around loss, endings, death, major crises, major upheavals and radical change in our lives. This will tend to stop us in our tracks via some outer or inner circumstances. This, in turn, will tend to impel us to break through our judgments, blockages and Wounds around these issues. Chiron and Pluto will work together to birth a new level of consciousness within us, one that sees the new forms that are birthed from what we initially perceived as loss, endings, death, major crises, major upheavals and radical change.

Pluto squaring natal Chiron

Pluto will forcefully bring our Wounds, blockages and unresolved issues, as indicated by natal Chiron, to our immediate attention. This will tend to stop us in our tracks by sometimes-radical external circumstances. This, in turn, will tend to force us to delve into our Woundedness and find new answers to old *impasses* of consciousness. This is a major transit.

Chiron squaring natal Ascendant

(See also Chiron squaring natal Descendant. See also Chiron conjunct MC or IC, accordingly, if in orb.)

Chiron will bring our Wounds, blockages and unresolved issues to the surface around self-image, sense of self, how we see ourselves and/or how we think others see us. This will tend to cause us to question these issues by placing doubt into our mind and into our feeling concerning the truth of our previous notions thereof. Who are we, as opposed to our masks? Where is the real "me"? We may experience shyness, reticence, fear of what other's think of us and/or low self-confidence during this transit. It may also bring up past and forgotten Wounds around these same issues.

If Chiron is in the lower hemisphere, internal issues will be emphasized. If Chiron is in the upper hemisphere, external issues will be emphasized.

Chiron squaring natal Descendant

(Simultaneously squaring natal Ascendant. See also Chiron conjunct MC or IC, accordingly, if in orb.)

Chiron will bring to the fore our Wounds, blockages and unresolved issues 1) around relating to others, 2) around being in relationships, 3) around being alone and/or 4) around health and disease (physical, emotional, mental and/or spiritual). We will tend to be impelled to attend to these things during this transit.

If Chiron is in the lower hemisphere, internal issues will be emphasized. If Chiron is in the upper hemisphere, external issues will be emphasized.

Chiron squaring natal MC

(See also Chiron squaring natal IC. See also Chiron conjunct Ascendant or Descendant, accordingly, if in orb.)

Chiron will bring up our Wounds, blockages and unresolved issues around vocation and/or our public persona. It will tend to put the brakes on these areas of our lives. It will impel us to think more deeply about the things in our lives that have been holding us back from fully activating and expressing these areas.

Chiron squaring natal IC

(Simultaneously squaring natal MC. See also Chiron conjunct Ascendant or Descendant, accordingly, if in orb.)

Chiron will tend to bring up issues to do with the past, family, parents, grandparent and other older relatives. These things may slow us down during this transit, impelling us to delve into these Wounds, blockages and unresolved issues more deeply than we might otherwise be inclined.

Trining Transits

In general, trining transits represent a time of increased opportunities, possibilities, meetings, connections and affinities. Things will just seem to fall into place during this time in the areas indicated by the transiting and natal planets.

When Chiron is the transiting planet, it will bring about increased opportunities, possibilities, meetings, connections and affinities in relation to the Healing and evolution of consciousness of the issues pertaining to the natal planet.

When Chiron is the natal planet, the transiting planet will help open up increased opportunities, possibilities, meetings, connections and affinities in relation to the Healing and resolution of our specific Wounds, blockages and unresolved issues, as indicated by natal Chiron. The way in which the transiting planet does this is dependent upon the planets specific characteristics.

Chiron trining natal North Node

Chiron will inspire increased opportunities, possibilities, meetings, connections and affinities in relation to our journey of Healing and the evolution of consciousness and in relation to our specific life's path and purpose.

North Node trining natal Chiron

The North Node will bring increased opportunities, possibilities, meetings, connections and affinities for the Healing and resolution of our specific Wounds, blockages and unresolved issues, as indicated by natal Chiron. It will help us to Heal and resolve those particular Wounds, blockages and unresolved issues that have been holding us back in our life's path and purpose.

Chiron trining natal South Node

Chiron will assist us in the Healing and resolution of Woundedness 1) around the past, 2) around past lives and/or 3) around our unfulfilled life's path and purpose. It will assist us by bringing increased opportunities, possibilities, meetings, connections and affinities to illuminate past issues that may have become hidden or forgotten.

South Node trining natal Chiron

The South Node awakens old Wounds, blockages and unresolved issues around the past, past lives and unfulfilled life's path and purpose, bringing increased opportunities, possibilities, meetings, connections and affinities for their Healing and resolution.

Chiron trining natal Sun

Chiron presents us with increased opportunities, possibilities, meetings, connections and affinities for the Healing and resolution of Wounds, blockages and unresolved issues around self-expression, creativity, will power and allowing ourselves to Shine.

Sun trining natal Chiron

The Sun helps us to Heal and resolve our Wounds, blockages and unresolved issues by bringing increased opportunities, possibilities, meetings, connections and affinities to illuminate our Darknesses. By Darknesses, we mean our repressions, Wounds, blockages, judgments, biases, blame, etcetera. The Sun inspires us to exercise our will and self-determination towards the goal of Healing and the evolution of consciousness.

Chiron trining natal Moon

Chiron illuminates our lower emotional nature – i.e. our lopsided perceptions, misperceptions, judgments, biases, illusions and lies. It does this via increased opportunities, possibilities, meetings, connections and affinities that bring our emotional patterns, habits and reactions into view, giving us the opportunity to Heal and resolve these issues.

Moon trining natal Chiron

The Moon, in this short transit, awakens our Wounds, blockages and unresolved issues, as indicated by natal Chiron. It does this via increased opportunities, possibilities, meetings, connections and affinities that illuminate these Wounds, blockages and unresolved issues through the vehicle of our Moon nature.

Chiron trining natal Mercury

Chiron assists us in the Healing and resolution of our Woundedness around communication, networking, thinking processes and feeling unintelligent. It does so by offering us increased opportunities, possibilities, meetings, connections and affinities for exchange, interaction, communication and mental stimulation, etcetera.

Mercury trining natal Chiron

Mercury gives us increased opportunities, possibilities, meetings, connections and affinities for the Healing and resolution of our Wounds, blockages and unresolved issues, as indicated by natal Chiron, creating an enhanced environment for exchange, interaction, communication and mental stimulus.

Chiron trining natal Venus

Chiron offers us increased opportunities, possibilities, meetings, connections and affinities for the Healing and resolution of our Wounds, blockages and unresolved issues around loving, being loved, relationship, companionship, aloneness, harmony, peace, etcetera.

Venus trining natal Chiron

Venus gives us increased opportunities, possibilities, meetings, connections and affinities for the Healing and resolution of our specific Wounds, blockages and unresolved issues, as indicated by natal Chiron. It shows us how to Love ourselves a little more and how to accept the Love of others, most often through the vehicle of relationship.

Chiron trining natal Mars

Chiron provides increased opportunities, possibilities, meetings, connections and affinities for the Healing and resolution of our Woundedness 1) around what we have done or not done in our lives, 2) around our past and present actions and reactions and/or 3) around our past and present decisions and intentions.

Mars trining natal Chiron

Mars opens up increased opportunities, possibilities, meetings, connections and affinities for the Healing and resolution our specific Woundedness, as indicated by natal Chiron. It inspires us to make resolutions and take action towards our journey of Healing and the evolution of consciousness.

Chiron trining natal Jupiter

Chiron creates increased opportunities, possibilities, meetings, connections and affinities for the Healing and resolution of our Woundedness

1) around childhood, 2) around our Inner Child, 3) around our feelings of meaninglessness, 4) around our loss of faith in a Divine Plan and/or 5) around our lack of close attention to our life's meaning and purpose.

Jupiter trining natal Chiron

Jupiter creates increased opportunities, possibilities, meetings, connections and affinities for the Healing and resolution of our specific Woundedness, as indicated by natal Chiron. It draws our attention to a larger picture of our lives. It seeks to reveal the meaning and purpose behind those things in which we previously saw no meaning and purpose. It seeks to awaken the knowing and wisdom of the Inner Child that knows all is 'right' with the world.

Chiron trining natal Saturn

Chiron assists in offering increased opportunities, possibilities, meetings, connections and affinities for the Healing and resolution of our Wounds, blockages and unresolved issues around 'father' issues, around authority, responsibility, repressions, limitations, restrictions, seriousness and discipline.

Saturn trining natal Chiron

Saturn brings about increased opportunities, possibilities, meetings, connections and affinities for the Healing and resolution of our specific Woundedness, as indicated by natal Chiron. It does so by inspiring seriousness and a sense of responsibility towards our journey of Healing and the evolution of consciousness.

Chiron trining natal Chiron

(See Part Three, Chapter 3, p. 302 (1st trine) and p. 306 (2nd trine).)

Chiron trining natal Uranus

Chiron opens up increased opportunities, possibilities, meetings, connections and affinities for the Healing and resolution of our Woundedness 1) around radical change in our lives, past and present, 2) around fitting in, 3) around feeling different and/or 4) around seeking a higher understanding of our lives. It inspires us to make new connections, make new efforts to understand a bigger picture and make contact with other sources of knowledge.

Uranus trining natal Chiron

Uranus brings about abrupt and increased opportunities, possibilities, meetings, connections and affinities for the Healing and resolution of our specific Woundedness, as indicated by natal Chiron. It inspires us to delve deeper into the higher meanings behind those things in our lives that we have been judging primarily negatively and blaming for our life's predicaments. It inspires us to see a larger Plan behind the seeming chaos of our lives. This is a major Healing transit.

Chiron trining natal Neptune

Chiron awakens increased opportunities, possibilities, meetings, connections and affinities for the Healing and resolution of our Woundedness 1) around our spirituality, 2) around loss or absence of faith in divinity, 3) around the seeming absence of Love in our lives and/or 4) around our emotional nature that longs for a Return to Oneness and Love. It inspires us to pursue spiritual matters, higher understanding and/or solace for the Heart and Soul.

Neptune trining natal Chiron

Neptune opens increased opportunities, possibilities, meetings, connections and affinities for the Healing and resolution of our specific Woundedness, as indicated by natal Chiron. It inspires deep thought, pondering, meditation, the seeking of spiritual and/or psychological advice and, ultimately, the Loving of the whole of ourselves. This is a major Healing transit.

Chiron trining natal Pluto

Chiron creates increased opportunities, possibilities, meetings, connections and affinities for the Healing and resolution of our Woundedness around radical change, loss, endings and death in our lives. It inspires a deep and intense search for higher meaning and understanding around these issues. Ultimately, it seeks to show us the births and new forms that arose from the perceived losses, deaths, endings, major crises, major upheavals and radical changes.

Pluto trining natal Chiron

Pluto brings swift and sometimes drastic occasions of increased opportunities, possibilities, meetings, connections and affinities for the Healing and resolution of our specific Woundedness, as indicated by natal Chiron. It inspires us to shift our consciousness around these issues. It inspires us to leave behind old illusions, allow judgmental attitudes to die, see the flip-sides of these issues and end old cycles in our lives. In this way, we are making room for new birth of higher consciousness. This is a major Healing transit.

Chiron trining natal Ascendant

Chiron brings increased opportunities, possibilities, meetings, connections and affinities for the Healing and resolution of our Woundedness around self-image, sense of self, the way we see ourselves and how we think others see us. It inspires a new appreciation for who we are, as we are, beyond the illusions of our masks, beyond illusions about ourselves.

Chiron trining natal Descendant

Chiron opens up increased opportunities, possibilities, meetings, connections and affinities for the Healing and resolution of our Woundedness 1) around relating to others, 2) around relationships in general, 3) around our feeling of aloneness and/or 4) around the issues of health and disease. It inspires us to make our peace with others, resolve our differences, make new contacts and connections and attend to our general health and disease (physical, mental, emotional and/or spiritual).

Chiron trining natal MC

Chiron creates increased opportunities, possibilities, meetings, connections and affinities for the Healing and resolution of Woundedness around our vocation and around our public persona. It inspires us to make connections between our specific life's path and purpose and our career. It encourages us to see the way in which our specific Woundedness in these areas have Served us on our Healing journey.

Chiron trining natal IC

Chiron opens up increased opportunities, possibilities, meetings, connections and affinities for the Healing and resolution of Woundedness around the past, past lives, genetic history, family, parents, grandparents and other older relatives. It inspires us to delve into this past, make our peace with our relatives and Heal past issues. It encourages us to identify issues that have been holding us back from pursuing our life's path and purpose, in particular, ones related to vocation and our public persona.

Sextiling Transits

In general, sextiling transits open possibilities in our lives, like windows of opportunity. Whether we take these opportunities or not is up to us. Otherwise, sextiling transits are relatively benign. For this reason, they can come and go with or without our noticing it.

Chiron making sextiling transits to our natal planets will open possible avenues of Healing and evolution of consciousness for the affairs pertaining to the natal planet being transited.

When other planets make sextiling transits to Chiron, these other planets will open possible avenues of Healing and evolution of consciousness for our specific Wounds, blockages and unresolved issues, as indicated by natal Chiron (in its natal sign, house and aspects). Each planet, according to its specific affairs, will offer different possibilities and opportunities, illuminating different aspects of our specific Woundedness.

Chiron sextiling natal Chiron

(See Part Three, Chapter Three, "Life Cycles", p. 300 (1st Chiron-sextile-natal Chiron transit) and p. 308 (2nd Chiron-sextile-natal Chiron transit)).

Quincunxing Transits

In general, quincunxing transits tend to impel us to raise our consciousness of the affairs of the natal planet to new levels. They impel us to leave behind our old ways of seeing things, much in the same way as an opposition transit. However, quincunxing transits are not so challenging and confronting. They are more nagging, irritating, frustrating and insistent. In this way, the quincunxing transit, particularly when made by Chiron or the outer planets, is akin to a kind of miniature Pluto transit. It is also akin to the zodiac sign of Virgo.

When Chiron makes a quincunxing transit to a natal planet, it impels us in the aforementioned way to raise our consciousness to new levels around the Wounds, blockages and unresolved issues pertaining to the affairs of the natal planet (in its natal sign, house and aspects).

When another planet makes a quincunxing transit to natal Chiron, it impels us in the aforementioned way to raise our consciousness to new levels around our specific Wounds, blockages and unresolved issues, as indicated by natal Chiron.

Chiron quincunxing natal Chiron

(See Part Three, Chapter 3, "Life Cycles", p. 303 (1st Chiron-quincunx-natal Chiron transit) and p. 305 (2nd Chiron-quincunx-natal Chiron transit)).

Transits of Houses

In general, Chiron transiting a house will tend to bring up our Wounds, blockages and unresolved issues around the affairs of that house during the transit. We are encouraged to attend to these things and to bring our consciousness in this area of our lives into a higher state.

1st House

(See also Chiron transiting natal Ascendant, particularly conjuncting.)

Chiron transiting the 1st house will tend to bring to the surface our Woundedness 1) around self-image, our sense of self, how we see ourselves and how we feel others see us, 2) around issues of physical health and disease and/or 3) around issues of past and/or present physical abuse. This gives us the opportunity to deal with these things and to attain a higher state of consciousness in this area of our lives.

2nd House

Chiron transiting the 2nd house will tend to bring to the surface our Woundedness 1) around our material affairs (and our psychological transference and projection of material affairs to our emotional life), 2) around material and/or emotional security, safety, comfort, values, and/or 3) around being loved, cared for and looked after. This gives us the opportunity to deal with them and attain a higher state of consciousness in this area of our lives.

3rd House

Chiron transiting the 3rd house will tend to bring to the surface our Woundedness 1) around issues around our mental affairs, 2) around our ability to communicate, network and interact with others, 3) around feeling smart or stupid and/or 4) around our capacity or inability to remain focused on one thing at a time. It can also bring up issues around siblings, early learning, gossip and publicity. This gives us the opportunity to deal with them and attain a higher state of consciousness in this area of our lives.

4th House

(See also, Chiron in transit to the IC, particularly conjuncting.)

Chiron transiting the 4th house will tend to bring to the surface our Woundedness around our family life. This can mean Woundedness around immediate family, extended family, community, Humanity, Earth (Gaia), Nature, heritage, roots, our children, our parents, our spouses, etcetera. This gives us the opportunity to deal with them and attain a higher state of consciousness in this area of our lives.

5th House

Chiron transiting the 5th house will tend to bring to the surface our Woundedness around our expression of self. By this, we mean around self-expression, ego, child within, love, romance, sexuality, creativity (including children as the product of our creation), will power, self-determination and around allowing or not allowing ourselves to Shine. This gives us the opportunity to deal with them and attain a higher state of consciousness in this area of our lives.

6th House

Chiron transiting the 6th house will tend to bring to the surface our Woundedness around work, service to others, methods of doing things, ingrained habits and around health and disease (physical, mental, emotional and/or spiritual). This gives us the opportunity to deal with them and attain a higher state of consciousness in this area of our lives.

7th House

(See also, Chiron in transit to the Descendant, particularly conjuncting.)

Chiron transiting the 7th house will tend to bring to the surface our

Woundedness around relationship. By this, we mean around being alone, around companionship, marriage, social life, social justice, our place in society and around our psychology in general. This gives us the opportunity to deal with them and attain a higher state of consciousness in this area of our lives.

8th House

Chiron transiting the 8th house will tend to bring to the surface our Woundedness around loss, death, endings, major crises, major upheavals, major changes in our lives, joint finances, sexuality, taxation and some spiritual matters (metaphysics, life-after-death, esotericism, the occult). This gives us the opportunity to deal with them and attain a higher state of consciousness in this area of our lives.

9th House

Chiron transiting the 9th house will tend to bring to the surface our Woundedness around education, philosophy, religion, spirituality in general, morals, ethics, racism, travel, adventure and sources of wisdom in general. This gives us the opportunity to deal with them and attain a higher state of consciousness in this area of our lives.

10th House

(See also Chiron transiting the MC, particularly conjuncting.)

Chiron transiting the 10th house will tend to bring to the surface our Woundedness around vocation, career, work, status, station, being seen in public, public persona and public image, being recognized, appreciated, respected and acknowledged for our achievements. This gives us the opportunity to deal with them and attain a higher state of consciousness in this area of our lives.

11th House

Chiron transiting the 11th house will tend to bring to the surface our Woundedness around fitting into society or not, collective expression, humanitarian ideals, networking, extended family, hopes and dreams, feeling different from others, feeling like a stranger or an alien, around technology and progress and around feeling lost in the crowd.

This gives us the opportunity to deal with them and attain a higher state of consciousness in this area of our lives.

12th House

Chiron transiting the 12th house will tend to bring to the surface our Woundedness 1) around feeling abandoned by the Universe/God, 2) around feeling victimized and/or covertly manipulated (secret enemies), 3) around our inner life, dreams, fantasies and dark secrets, 4) around past lives and sub-conscious impulses (karma) and/or 5) around our feelings of being exiled, separate, closed-in, locked-up and/or incarcerated. This gives us the opportunity to deal with them and attain a higher state of consciousness in this area of our lives.

Transits Setting off Natal Aspects & Patterns

Not only do transits trigger the planets they are transiting, but also the planets that are natally aspecting the transited planet. This is another way of describing the effect of multiple angles made by a single transit. For example, if we have Chiron-opposition-Uranus in our natal chart and Jupiter makes a conjuncting transit to Chiron, it simultaneously makes an opposing transit to Uranus.

Transits that makes multiple angles such as this are much more powerful than transits of singletons, because they set of our natal planetary aspects and patterns. In these cases, we need to look, not only at the transits and their multiple angles, taking into consideration the affairs of each planet involved, but we also need to then look at the way the transiting planet affects the whole natal pattern.

In these cases, where a natal pattern is triggered by a transit, the *conjuncting* transit will be the focal point of the pattern for the purposes of the transit, *even if the focal point of the natal pattern is elsewhere.* If no *conjuncting* transit by the planet in question is in evidence, then we must consider the *house* transited and the possible natal *midpoints* conjuncted by the transiting planet, etcetera. In any case, when a natal pattern is activated by a transit, the lesser angles of transit – opposition, trine, square, sextile and quincunx – will become more powerful than they would otherwise be if they were on their own.

If we remember the rule of *synergy* – that the total effect is always greater than just the sum of the parts – we will have a good rule of thumb for judging the power and importance of particular transits involving natal patterns, their aspects and the planets involved.

Lastly, if the transiting planet is making aspects and patterns to other transiting planets, then the combined influence of the current aspects and current patterns upon our natal planets and their aspects and patterns must be considered, too. Furthermore, we must consider the dynamic picture, taken over the period of the transits, i.e. which transit and/or follows which and how this contributes to the unfoldment of a psychological drama.

The Psychology of Retrograde & Multiple-Pass Transits

Often, particularly with the outer planets, a transit will occur more than once, due to the retrograde motion – i.e. the apparent backwards motion – of the transiting planet. The transiting planet will make the first pass in direct (forward) motion, the second pass in retrograde motion and the third and final pass in direct motion once more.

Multiple-pass transits, such as these, are much more powerful in their final effect due to the increased length of the overall transit.

The first pass tends to introduce the issues and initially trigger the affairs of the natal planet and its attendant aspects and patterns. With sufficient readiness, preparation and willingness, we may be able to deal fully with the issues that come up during this first pass. The second pass will tend to deepen the influence, probing deeper into our psyches and bringing up deeper and more detailed aspects of the issues at hand. The second pass tends to be more difficult to deal with and more difficult to resolve at the time. Often, we must be content (if that is at all possible!) to sit and wait this out until direct motion is reestablished. In this way, the second pass is akin to a Saturnian influence. The third and final pass gives us the opportunity to finally deal with and resolve the issues at hand, to a much deeper level than we might have been able with just a single-pass transit.

All this does *not* ensure that we will be able or willing to deal with the issues brought up by the transit at all. This always depends upon our degree of readiness, preparation and willingness, which, in turn, is heavily dependent upon our current stage of Healing and evolution of consciousness.

When Chiron is involved in a multiple-pass transit as the transiting planet, the first pass will bring our Wounds, blockages and unresolved issues *pertaining to the natal planet transited* to the surface. The second pass will go even deeper. It may exacerbate the Wounds, blockages and unresolved issues brought up in the first pass. Even then, it may give us no obvious path of Healing and resolution. Instead, it may simply leave us to ponder, reflect and try to understand these Wounds and issues. The third pass will open the door for deeper Healing and for resolution of these deeper Wounds, blockages and unresolved issues.

When Chiron is the natal planet transited, the first pass will bring up our Wounds, blockages and unresolved issues, *as indicated by natal Chiron,* giving our first opportunity to deal with them. The second pass will go deeper and may exacerbate these core Wounds, blockages and unresolved issues, giving us no obvious path of Healing and resolution, instead leaving us to ponder, reflect and try to understand them. The third pass will open the door for deeper Healing and resolution of these core Wounds, blockages and unresolved issues.

9 ~ RETROGRADES, INTERCEPTS & PAST LIVES

Retrogrades

Some astrologers, Martin Schulman being perhaps the most well known, hold that retrogrades in the natal chart are an indication of past-life influences coming through in this lifetime. They hold that retrogrades represent areas of our life, which we have neglected in past lives. Alternatively, they represent areas where we have commenced work in previous lives, but have not yet finished and where we have brought the related issues into this lifetime.

Other astrologers hold that retrogrades in the natal chart simply represent a repression of the given issues in this lifetime, not requiring the idea of past lives to explain it.

Still others, such as the Magi Society of astrologers, hold that retrogrades mean nothing unless the given retrograde planet is making an applying aspect, progression or transit to other planets. In this case, it is treated essentially the same as a direct motion applying aspect, progression or transit.

I suggest that it is a combination of all these ideas. If we take our previous discussions regarding multiple-pass transits, we can get an idea of what a retrograde might mean in the natal chart. We said that the first direct motion contact, in this case to a natal aspect, represents the initial broaching of the themes and issues around the two planets and their aspecting companions. The second pass, now in retrograde motion, represents a deepening of the same issues. It represents a time where we may feel unable to resolve these issues, leaving us to think, reflect, ponder and/or meditate upon them. The third pass, again in direct motion, gives us the opportunity to resolve the issues at hand to a greater depth than the first direct motion pass.

We must also consider that a retrograde increases the total length of a given planetary encounter.

Having said all this, when we are born, the only thing that matters from a natal perspective is whether the given planet is applying or separating from given aspects. Natally speaking, it makes no difference whether a planet was in retrograde or direct motion, as we were not present, i.e. incarnate, before this happened. However, what does make a difference is the fact that we are born into an environment *where the planetary encounter has already been going on,* i.e. it has a history and has created earthly conditions into which we are born. Bearing in mind the psychology of multiple-pass transits, discussed previously, the people, circumstances, situations and happenings around us when we are born will definitely affect us, albeit indirectly.

In the final analysis, retrograde planets in our charts *do* affect us. However, they only affect us by virtue of applying aspects they might make in the natal chart and/or by virtue of the indirect influences of the people and conditions around us at the time of birth.

As far as retrogrades indicating real past-life influences, I have found no logic or evidence that supports this assertion. What I have found, however, is that retrogrades can bring up symbolism within us that we can *ascribe* to past lives. This is due primarily to the indirect influences of the people and conditions around us at the time of birth. These influences are more unconscious, more reflective, deeper and generally more hidden. What we thought were past-life influences are actually the symbolism of our issues in this lifetime in disguise. One possibility is that they can be the issues of the people around us just before our birth. Please refer to the later section, "Past-life Symbolism". This explains what we are hinting at more fully.

So what does Chiron retrograde in the natal chart indicate? Again, if Chiron retrograde is making applying aspects to other planets in the chart, it is read the same as a direct motion applying aspect. With respect to the indirect influences of those people and things around us at the time of birth during a retrograde Chiron, we can say that this definitely must be taken into consideration. People around us at our birth, who are experiencing the second pass of Chiron in transit to their natal planets, will be in the throes of the deepening effect of the transit. They will be unable to do anything except ponder and wait. With Chiron, this means that their deepest Wounds, blockages and unresolved issues will be in full view, but with little possibility of dealing with them at the time. This 'atmosphere' will definitely make its stamp upon us and our own Chiron issues, by transference[69], encouraging us to be more pensive, thoughtful, philosophical, inwardly-focused and possibly fatalistic and negative about our Wounds, blockages and unresolved issues. This can seem, from an outside perspective, to be like a repression or denial of expression of the issues indicated by natal Chiron. In actual fact, we are being given the Gift of introspection, packaged with our Wounds, blockages and unresolved issues.

Intercepted Houses

Again, different astrologers have different views on the interpretation of intercepted houses and the planets within them. Intercepted houses occur when a zodiac sign and its polar opposite fall completely *within* a house and its opposing house. The general view is that this means the zodiac signs in question are not given full expression through the specific affairs of our lives. Some astrologers feel that this, like retrogrades, indicate a repression of the issues of these zodiac signs and the issues of the planets within these signs. Others believe that intercepts are an indication of past-life failings and neglects coming through in this lifetime.

The *raison d'être* behind this attitude is the fact that the zodiac signs in question do not sit on the first degree of any given house. Most astrologers feel, for some reason, that the first degree of any given house is the most important degree and colors the affairs of the whole house. Given this, they then feel that the zodiac sign on the first degree of a house *rules* this house.

I tend to disagree with this formulation for various reasons. Firstly,

---

[69] That is, by the fact that consciousness consists of overlapping fields of electromagnetic (Light) energy, as we shall explore in depth in Books Two and Three.

house cusps are, for the most part, arbitrarily calculated and are subject to the personal views of the astrologer. This can be seen in the vast number of different house systems of all colors, shapes and sizes that fill the shelves of the modern astrology supermarket, so to speak. Secondly, the definitions of houses and their attendant affairs are culturally determined. They change over time as the collective consciousness of Humanity (Gaia) changes over time, despite what some modern astrologers may think. Thirdly, why should any one degree of a house be more important than another except when it makes true angular aspects to real planets in the sky? I know that the 1st degree of a given house is the first to be touched by transiting planets. This gives an argument in favor of the 1st degree's important in transits to houses, but does not make its zodiac sign automatically the ruler of the house. Lastly, if a zodiac sign lies wholly within a house, rather than being shared between two houses, surely this would indicate a *strengthening* influence rather than a diluting or repressing influence on the given house. As far as past-life indications, I can find little logic in supposing that intercepted houses relate to this. If there seem to be past-life indications in intercepted houses and the planets within them, I would have to say that we should treat these indications as *symbolism* of the issues of this current lifetime. This leads us to our next topic of discussion . . .

Past-life Symbolism

How do we determine if Chiron in the natal chart indicates past-life Wounds, blockages and unresolved issues? The answer, when considered from a certain perspective, is simple: it always does. In order to understand why this is so, we need to understand what Wounds are, even beyond what we have already asserted. From Chiron's perspective, *Wounds mirror areas of our life that we have not yet learned to Love Unconditionally.* We will explore the psychology behind this in Book Two and the metaphysics behind it in Book Three.

We suggest that the only things we take from lifetime to lifetime are those things we have learned to Love Unconditionally. We will explore why we say this in detail in Book Three. The rest represents a kind of unawakened void, i.e. our Wounds in an unconscious embryonic state.

Having said this, though, if we have not worked through a particular issue in a given lifetime, learning how to Love it Unconditionally, *it is bound to show up in our next lives as a Wound until we learn to Love it.* However, unlike the things we *have* learned to Love Unconditionally, it will not necessary show up in the same *form* as in previous lives and certainly not in the same circumstances.

In Books Two and Three, we will explore the fact that we are a collection of frequencies of Light/energy. Bearing this in mind, each time we incarnate, we are attracted to a time and a place that corresponds to the overall net sum of those frequencies. That is, we are attracted to a time and place with specific energies corresponding to our psychic signature and to specific planetary patterns. The areas of our life we have not yet learned to Love will show up in the planetary patterns of our natal horoscope until we have transcended them. Chiron is one of the primary places where our Wounds show up, the house and sign placement giving context to the general themes.

Having said all this, it is important to dispel a certain illusion that has been perpetuated by the new-age community in particular. This illusion is based, in part, on an incorrect interpretation of the Eastern concept of *karma.* It is said that if we do something 'wrong' or 'bad' in a particular lifetime, we will be subject to the same treatment ourselves in our next lives. In addition, it is said that if we have a particular character trait in a given lifetime, we will have that character trait in our next lifetime. Still further, it is said that the specific circumstances of one lifetime are transferred into the next, in a continuous drama. It is also said that we repeat exact circumstances, situations and happenings from lifetime to lifetime until we 'get it right'. Still further, it is said that we will journey from lifetime to lifetime with the same people. *Much of this constitutes a misinterpretation . . .*

To repeat, *all we take from one lifetime into the next is the things that we have learned to Love Unconditionally.* We will not have to deal with these issues again, even if we are predisposed to them by virtue of the planetary features of our charts. This is because we are already awakened to the issues' true and full nature, as aspects of ourselves, Healed, rejoined, 'wholed' and integrated with our Higher selves. These things are already a more or less permanent part of our Higher selves.

What we have not yet learned to Love in a given lifetime will show up in our next life, yes, but, in all likelihood, in different circumstances, different guises, different character aspects and with different people. In short, the themes will be the same, but the specific manifestation in our lives (the *forms)*, in all likelihood, will be entirely different.

Why? Firstly, because *the themes,* as general energetic patterns, are seen in the planets' own energies and their angular aspects to each other. These patterns are more universal, *without specific material manifestation until we incarnate,* and relate to cosmic time frames that cover many lifetimes. Secondly, *the specific manifestation* of these themes in a given lifetime are seen in the house and sign positions of the planets at the time of birth, *which change from lifetime to lifetime.* The specific manifestation of these themes is the earthly context into which the themes are put.

Put another way, the longer the planetary time frame, the more permanent the corresponding aspects of our psyches and the closer to Unconditional Love we are in these aspects of ourselves. Recall that we said that, as we approach the solar system's magnetopause, we approach timelessness, spacelessness, Oneness and Love? *These aspects are our Soul, mirrored in our higher Self.* Conversely, the shorter the planetary time frame, the more impermanent and transient the corresponding aspects of our psyches and the more emotionally fragmented and Wounded we are in these aspects of ourselves. *These aspects are mirrored in our lower nature, i.e. in our personality.*

For these reasons, we suggest that the planetary energies themselves, particularly of the outer planets, and their angular aspects relate more to our higher Self that incarnates from lifetime to lifetime. The signs and houses (combined with the Moon, the inner planets, the Ascendant and the MC) relate more to the lower-natured personality, which *dies at the death of the body after each incarnation.*

Nothing of the *personality* remains after physical death. It breaks down and disperses in the same way as the physical body. What remains is our essence, enlightened to a greater or lesser degree by the things we have learned to Love.

This is why we do not remember our past lives, for the most part. What we *can* remember, as we become more evolved, is memories of what we have learned to Love Unconditionally. *We do not remember traumas, crises, calamities, pain, suffering, abuse, etcetera, because these things are judgments made by our lower nature – our personalities – that do not survive from lifetime to lifetime.* If we do remember these things, it is only because we have Loved them and no longer see them as negatives, but as Loving aspects of a greater Plan of perfection.

I can hear the cries of objection! What about past-life regression? Doesn't this prove that we remember past lives? Yes and no, I say. I have personally experienced and studied past-life regression therapy. Again, I say that the only things we take from lifetime to lifetime – *the only things we remember from lifetime to lifetime* – are the things that we have learned to Love Unconditionally.

Therefore, memories of past lives that come up in a past-life regression therapy session that invoke the deep and uncommon experience of Unconditional Love are likely to be *real* past-life memories. Furthermore, such real memories may be our own memories *or they can be the memories of others' that we are tuning in to, because we are resonating at a similar frequency.*

All other so-called past-life memories that engender any other emotions apart from Unconditional Love are not real past-life memories.

So, if these other so-called past-life memories are not real, what are they? I suggest that they constitute the symbolism of our minds, giving form to those things that we have not yet learned to Love Unconditionally, *i.e. our Wounds, blockages and unresolved issues.* They are the mind's way of communicating these issues in a form to which we can relate. In this way, past-life regression therapy – let's now simply call it "regression therapy" – represents a perfect Chiron-based therapy. We will explore this subject in greater detail in Book Two.

The other possibility is that we are connecting, psychically, to the Wounds and issues of other people resonating at a similar frequency to us.

The 'memories' that arise from regression therapy are mostly the *symbols* of our Wounds, blockages and unresolved issues, mirroring the things we have yet to Love Unconditionally. In the same way, *our life's circumstances, situations and happenings are also the symbols of what we have not yet learned to Love Unconditionally.* From this perspective, *sym-*

bolic 'memories' arising from regression therapy mirror the same Wounds, blockages and unresolved issues as the real circumstances of our present lifetimes.

Leading on from the preceding statement, why would we need regression therapy if the symbols that arise mirror the same issues that are already mirrored in our present life circumstances, situations and happenings? There can be several answers to this. Firstly, regression therapy gives us a different perspective on the Wounds, blockages and unresolved issues that we may have become stuck on in our present life. Secondly, regression therapy puts *distance* between us and our Wounds, blockages and unresolved issues, allowing us, perhaps, to approach them a little better and begin the journey of their Healing and resolution. Lastly, in cases where we are in extreme denial about our responsibility and participation in our own Woundedness, i.e. we are in blame, *regression therapy gives us the chance to place blame outside our present lives.* Although this may seem like a negative step in the Healing process, it positively represents a step forward. It does so inasmuch as it *still* gives us a new perspective on Wounds, blockages and unresolved issues that we may have lost the ability to process in this lifetime.

Lastly, it is important to mention that there is a deep connection between so-called past-life memories and dreams. Dreams, too, offer us a symbolic window into the depths of our psyche. The symbolism brought to light in regression therapy and the symbolism of dreams is often very similar and can both be used as tools in the Healing process. We will discuss all these topics at length in Book Two. For now, we must move on.

However, below, I have offered some symbolic past-life/dream scenarios that are designed to connect with our specific Woundedness, thus giving us new perspectives on our Wounds, blockages and unresolved issues and triggering the Healing process. They are a compilation of the many symbols, dreams and 'past-life memories' of those with whom I have worked over the years, including my own. They can be used in a similar way to the Sabian Symbols.

Note that some of the symbols may be seen in more than one sign or house, as the symbolisms are often complex and cross the established boundaries of definition. In addition, as we have mentioned before, each one of us has within us, holographically, every aspect of every planet, every sign, every house in every possible pattern. In this way, we each have all possible Wounds and are connected to all possible past lives, our own and others'.

Chiron, in the chart, is the primary place of our Woundedness and, hence, of our potential Healing. This is because it stands between the inner and outer planets, between the lower-natured personality and the higher Self and Soul. It stands between illusion and Truth, between fragmentedness and Oneness and between lower-natured emotions and Unconditional Love. Seen through the prism of the zodiac signs and houses, it offers us unparalleled insight into the deepest recesses of the psyche.

Here are the symbolisms . . .

Chiron in Aries or in the 1st House

- *A person is beaten, robbed, raped and/or left for dead.*
- *A person is kidnapped, sold as a slave and worked to the point of death.*
- *A child is constantly told that they are useless, worthless and no good.*
- *A person is sacrificed by the tribe, for the tribe, to appease the gods.*
- *A person, having committed a 'crime', lives their life trying to make up for it.*
- *A person is unintentionally responsible for others' death and/or loss.*
- *A child is abandoned by their parents and lives in the streets.*
- *A person is born into the lowest untouchable caste of society.*
- *A person is exiled and left for dead, due to leprosy or the plague.*

Chiron in Taurus or in the 2nd House

- *A natural disaster destroys a person's home, village, city or nation.*
- *A family cannot afford their child and adopts it out.*
- *A person loses everything they own through litigation.*
- *A child feels like a burden to their struggling parents and family.*
- *A person's closest love is killed. Or a person loses their parents.*
- *A person experiences a revolution where all accepted values are wiped away.*
- *Famine creates starvation in a person's village.*
- *An aristocrat loses everything in a revolution.*
- *A rich person dies rich, unhappy and unloved.*
- *A person is left out of an inheritance.*

Chiron in Gemini or in the 3rd House

- *A person with a speech impediment is deemed a moron by society.*
- *A person is wrongly accused in a foreign country and cannot explain his innocence due to a language barrier.*
- *A person's public statement is misinterpreted and they become a laughing stock.*
- *A breakdown in communications leads to loss of lives.*
- *A war refugee loses touch with their friends and family.*
- *A gossip's machinations backfire, causing disgrace and dishonor.*
- *A war captain, under sudden attack, cannot think fast enough to save his men.*

- *A person, misunderstood and different from others, becomes the village idiot.*
- *Twins or siblings are separated at birth or in early childhood.*
- *A politician is destroyed by a slanderous media campaign.*

Chiron in Cancer or in the 4th House

- *A person's parent's die and they are raised under duress by close relatives.*
- *A shy person keeps to themselves, feeling as though love will never come.*
- *A person's children are slaughtered in full view.*
- *A person's mother emotionally tortures them throughout childhood.*
- *A native witnesses the felling and burning of their forest homeland.*
- *A conservationist, trying to save a species is defeated by poachers.*
- *A person's baby dies in their arms of an unknown disease.*
- *A child wishing for love is raised in a cold, disciplinary, cruel environment.*
- *A person is forcibly exiled from their homeland.*
- *A person's spouse dies. They remarry and the second spouse dies, too.*
- *A person falls in love with another who is unattainable by marriage, station, class, age, race or* distance.

Chiron in Leo or in the 5th House

- *A child is prevented by draconian parents from pursuing their creativity through art and/or music.*
- *An orphaned child loses its sense of individuality in an orphanage.*

- *Heavy expectations from parents and teachers cause a person's breakdown and/or abandonment of their creative expression.*
- *A person is required to subjugate themselves to the needs of family and/or community in times of hardship, sickness and/or crisis.*
- *A person is passed over in the selection process for awards or a position of accolade, public recognition, special privileges and/or leadership.*
- *A person sees others of lesser talent and worthiness gain exponentially more fame, fortune and success.*
- *A person lives in the shadow of their siblings' success and accolades.*
- *An artist's creations are condemned and/or misunderstood by society.*
- *A gambler is unable to curb his addiction and dies in abject poverty.*

Chiron in Virgo or in the 6th House

- *A person leaves their life's work unfinished due to terminal illness.*
- *A child is broken in spirit by parents' incessant criticism and unattainable expectations.*
- *A person's spouse leaves them, despite love, unable to live up to their unreasonable standards.*
- *A doctor is unable to save his patients from an unknown disease.*
- *A social/political/green activist is condemned, imprisoned and/or exiled for trying to change the status quo.*
- *An underling is beheaded for criticizing or questioning the king/queen.*
- *A person admits themselves into a psychiatric institution for depression and for feeling scattered and they are drugged, given electroshock therapy, becoming a virtual vegetable.*

- *A person's sense of completeness and stability is shattered by war, their family scattered as refugees.*
- *A person wastes their life living hedonistically and like a bohemian.*
- *Venereal disease or Alzheimer's leaves a person confused and unable to function in their lives.*

Chiron in Libra or in the 7th House

- *Family, partner and friends die in a plague or war, leaving a person utterly alone.*
- *A person is ostracized and/or exiled by a society with rigid social expectations for not fitting in.*
- *A person is imprisoned and/or condemned to die for taking a stand.*
- *Physical deformity prevents a person ever having a partner.*
- *A person's spouse dies slowly of a terminal illness and then they themselves die of heartbreak.*
- *Soul-mates recognize each other, but one is very young and another is very old, consummation impossible.*
- *The entire Romeo and Juliette story.*
- *A person following their inner calling is hated by all, condemned by society and ostracized by those close to them, leaving them feeling alone.*
- *Conflict between a person and their spouse or family creates unrest, disharmony and* cancer.

Chiron in Scorpio or in the 8th House

- *A person loses their family and friends in the plague or in war.*
- *A person witnesses the massacre of their village.*
- *Drought and famine forces a person out of work.*

- *A person's wealth is confiscated by the monarchy, church or state.*
- *Twins are separated and lost from each other.*
- *A person's mentor/teacher/guardian/parent passes away, leaving them empty and forlorn.*
- *A mother loses her young baby.*
- *A person suffers sexual mutilation at the hands of a ritualistic cult.*
- *A 'happy' period of life is abruptly ended.*
- *A long marriage ends abruptly in divorce.*
- *A person realizes that they have been secretly used and manipulated for years.*

Chiron in Sagittarius or in the 9th House

- *Bombarded by a lifetime of calamities, a person gives up trying to understand why.*
- *Living in the wake of heavy religious dogma and ritual, a person's Heart languishes, starved for personal Contact with the Divine.*
- *A person feels unenlightened, living in the shadow of the great wisdom and divine inspiration of a society governed by a religious order, e.g. ancient Tibet.*
- *A person who, as a child, wished to adventure far and wide over the globe, lives and dies in a small and remote village.*
- *A person feels thwarted by people and/or circumstances from expanding their life.*
- *A person has a vision or dream that others cannot see and discard peremptorily.*
- *A person's adventure/exploration to new lands ends in failure, death, loss and/or disgrace.*
- *A person feels their life is meaningless and withers away, physically, mentally, emotionally* and/or spiritually.

Chiron in Capricorn or in the 10th House

- *A person's achievements are not respected, recognized or valued in their own lifetime.*
- *A person is silenced for sociopolitical reasons.*
- *A person's need for power and recognition leads them to sacrifice their own morals, ethics and values, leading ultimately to disgrace and disrespect.*
- *Economic recession puts a person's life into chaos and disorder.*
- *A person raised in a religious/spiritual order feels disconnected from the real material world, longing to be 'normal'.*
- *A person seeking to help others is thwarted from gaining the power and authority to do so.*
- *A child is ignored, just one of dozens of others vying for attention in an orphanage.*
- *A person watches helplessly as events beyond his/her control dissects their life and the lives of those close to them, one piece at a time.*
- *A person freed from prison after countless years, cannot cope on their own, their life a sha*mbles.

Chiron in Aquarius or in the 11th House

- *A person is locked up and left to die for speaking their inner Truth.*
- *A person is left alone after their family and/or tribe has been destroyed.*
- *A person is ostracized from society for being different.*
- *A person is burned at the stake for their blasphemous viewpoints and occult practices.*
- *A person's new invention is boycotted, condemned and ridiculed.*
- *A person is born in unpopulated wastelands, having to eke out a meager existence.*

- *A person is born of two conflicting cultures and is ostracized by both.*
- *A long voyage takes a person to a strange new land, cut off from all they have known.*
- *A strange person lives in a dark overgrown house, feared and teased by children, ignored by adults, forgotten by the world.*

Chiron in Pisces or in the 12th House

- *After their village/nunnery/monastery is ransacked by invaders, a person relinquishes their faith in God.*
- *A person is institutionalized, unable to get a grasp of reality, unable to function in the normal world.*
- *A person, having committed a 'crime', is left in the remote wilderness to die.*
- *A person is taken advantage of by unscrupulous confidence tricksters, losing everything.*
- *A person, Wounded in love, vows to never open their heart again.*
- *A person of high psychic ability loses touch with normal living.*
- *A person maimed/raped/mugged sees their aggressor get off 'scot-free' in legal proceedings.*
- *A person's secret enemies bring about their demise.*
- *A person opens their whole inner life to another, only to be used, abused and discarded.*
- *The story of Jesus Christ: accusation, trial and crucifixion. "Eli, Eli, lama sabachthani?", i.e. "My God, My God, why hast thou forsaken me?"*[70]

[70] Matthew 27:46.

10 ~ MISCELLANY

Chiron and Relationship

This book would not be complete without a short exploration of Chiron and its place in relationships. Relationship is generally associated with Libra and the 7th house. Although it seems somewhat removed from our discussions so far, there is sound logic for presuming that Chiron plays not a small part in determining our relationships and in the psychology of their goings-on. Zane B. Stein suggested the linkage in his earliest work on Chiron.[71] The Magi Society, aforementioned, has also done extensive study in this area and affirms that Chiron in aspect, progression and transit to other planets in our charts, particularly Venus, is a major player in this area. Although we will not explore the finer details of their study, we will set out a *raison d'être* for their assertions. In my own studies, I have found their assertions to be accurate and in line with Chiron's musings in relation to Healing and the evolution of consciousness.

To begin with, we have asserted that Chiron represents our deepest and most primal Wounds, blockages and unresolved issues. Further, we have suggested that our Wounds – i.e. our Voids – determine our Values, i.e. what we seek and what we try to run from in life. We have also suggested in our discussions on past-life symbolism that our Wounds, blockages and unresolved issues can resonate to those of others. We tend to be attracted to others for a number of different reasons. Some of these reasons may be empathy, sympathy, a common ideal or a common way of looking at the world. On an unconscious and emotional level, we may be attracted to someone particular because we wish to rescue them,

---

[71] Stein, *op cit.*

wrap them up in cotton wool, soothe their Wounds and protect them from harm. Conversely, we may be attracted to someone particular who can offer us these same things. Lastly, we may be attracted to someone with whom we feel a kinship due to similar Wounds, blockages and unresolved issues.

Another consideration is that, as we have said, our Woundedness takes us to exactly the circumstances, situations and environments we need in order to facilitate our Healing journey. This includes attracting us to or repelling us from specific people. It is through the mirror of relationship with others that we gradually see what we need to see about ourselves. We learn to Love ourselves. We begin to see the hidden, repressed and denied aspects of ourselves, which constitute our Wounds, blockages and unresolved issues.

Furthermore, taking our discussions on the rulership of Chiron into account, the seeking of Libran balance and harmony and its attendant longing for union with our Soul-mate is expressed primarily through relationship. The Libran ideal of completeness through the merging of two people is actually the first step in the Piscean ideal of merging with the All. This is the essence of our journey of Healing and the evolution of consciousness, i.e. the Return to Oneness, the Return to Love. Our Woundedness drives us towards these ideals, hence Chiron's role in relationship.

In terms of seeing Chiron's relationship role in our lives through the natal chart, progressions and transits, the most telling feature would be Chiron's relationship to Venus. In fact, a study of long-lasting relationships will reveal a higher-than-average statistical predominance of Chiron/Venus aspects. These aspects show up in their synastry, in their composite charts (mid-point) and in the transits at the time of meeting. Particular aspects include trine and conjunction aspects and enhancements of declination, i.e. parallels, contra-parallels and occultations.

From this perspective, we can suggest that, in the same way the Moon represents the outer face of Chiron in the area of our lower emotional nature, Venus represents the outer face of Chiron in the area of relationship, attraction, romance and earthly love (as distinct from Unconditional Love). Taken together, Venus and Chiron in our natal charts, in composite charts (mid-point) and in transit will reflect 1) who we will be naturally attracted to, 2) who will be a long-lasting partner for us, 3) when, where and how we will meet, react, get along with and interact with potential or current partners and 4) what the respective benefits, blessings, lessons and Gifts in the relationship are likely to be.

The further exploration of Chiron in relation to Venus and to relationship is the subject of a future study, beyond the scope of this present work.

Chiron/North Node Conjunctions

I feel a special mention of Chiron-conjunct-North Node of the Moon is appropriate. If Chiron represents our Woundedness and its potential path of Healing and the North Node represents our life's path, purpose, destiny, etcetera, then the conjunction of the two represent the potential and destiny for Healing as a life's path and purpose. We have defined this already in terms of the natal chart. What does this mean from a larger perspective, though?

To put it simply, every time this conjunction occurs, a new batch of Healers is 'let loose' on the world. A new batch of Healers pass their final exams, so to speak, 'graduate' and are ready to go out into the world to begin their mission, to start practicing what they came here to do, to honor their higher purpose. This does not mean to say that new Healers are not constantly becoming active. It is simply that, around these conjunctions, there are graduations *en masse.*

The specific nature and exact blend of Healing and life's path and purpose of the Healers activated around each of these conjunctions can be seen in the zodiac sign placement of the conjunction.

For example, the conjunction of February 1969 was in Aries. The 1960s, as we have explored, occurred as Chiron approached aphelion – its most distant point occurring in the sign of Aries, representing the most acute inner expression of our Woundedness. The 1960s was the beginning of a revolution of consciousness. It was the beginning of new cycle of emphasis on spiritual and Healing matters. The conjunction of Chiron and the North Node in 1969 in Aries was the birth of Healers who marked the beginning of this new paradigm. This was the beginning of the so-called new-age, the beginning of the prelude to the Age of Aquarius. These people were the advance party, so to speak, whose task it was to take new and bold steps into uncharted territory. The territory was *personal Healing.*

In the process of evolution, we all reach a point where we are stopped until we look back and look within, doing so with the intention of clearing away the residue and backlog of Wounds, blockages and unresolved issues. The Healers who were activated in 1969 began this process, further setting the scene for the birth of Chiron into our consciousness in 1977. Once Chiron was discovered, our Healing could become more conscious and intentional. The key had been given. All we had to do was use it.

The next conjunction of the North Node and Chiron occurred in July 1984 in Gemini. This was the graduation, so to speak, and activation of Healers whose task it was to be *messengers* of Healing. Their messages came not only from their own personal journeys of Healing and the evolution of consciousness, but also from channeled sources. This was the fulcrum point for the connection of the Earth to channeled sources from around and beyond the world as we know it. These Healers were the messengers for the higher consciousness of spirit guides and discarnate entities. The overall message was simple: "You have the power and capacity to become citizens of the galaxy, as you were meant to be. You can Heal yourselves. You can clear away the debris of your Wounds, blockages and unresolved issues and become Whole again. You are Divine and limitless. All you have to do is choose."

The next Chiron/Node conjunction occurred in Libra in 1996, in the year of Chiron's perihelion and perigee – its closest point to the Sun and Earth, respectively, and its point of greatest expression of Healing. The Healers who graduated, so to speak, during this time, who were activated and empowered by this conjunction, were people who had lived through co-dependency, abandonment, deprivation, relationship failure, aloneness, alienation and separation. Having Healed and resolved these Wounds and issues in their own lives, these Healers began sharing what they had gained with others in similar need. Their ultimate message was that *separation is a lie.* In Truth, we are all connected to one another, whether we see it or not. Healing is seeing it, embracing it and living it.

Their mission was to help us re-establish a balance between Self and Other. Towards this end, they recognized that we must attend to our own Wounds, blockages and unresolved issues before the Healing of others becomes possible. Our own Healing is a pre-requisite to a healthy and harmonious relationship with others. When we establish a balanced and harmonious relationship with ourselves, we can then establish the same with the world at large and with others in a personal way. The mirror of relationship is the perfect vehicle for seeing what we need to see about ourselves in order to establish balance and harmony. The end result is the capacity to recognize the benefits, blessings, lessons and Gifts inherent in all relationships, and to experience Unconditional Love and Gratitude within these relationships.

The next Chiron/North Node conjunction takes place in 2008 in Aquarius. We can speculate that this will represent the graduation and activation of Healers whose calling will be to Heal the Wounds of separation, alienation, distance, isolation, etcetera, all brought about by the Age of Technology. Although we have made the world far smaller and far more connected by technology and communications, it has also produced the paradoxical effect of making us feel more alone, cut-off and removed from each other. During the present stage of the Chiron Cycle, the world appears to be becoming more impersonal . This is evident in the age of the Internet, email, on-line shopping, chat-rooms, cable TV, satellite TV, etcetera. We may feel more connected, technologically, but we also feel more disconnected physically and emotionally from others. Healers of the year 2008 will most certainly be called to deal with these issues.

To sum up, each time Chiron conjuncts the North Node, it represents a fulcrum point – a cycle within larger cycles such as the Chiron Cycle. It represents a fulcrum point for the outward expression of Healing, particularly through individuals with an inner calling to Heal as an expression of their life's path and purpose.

Chiron's Own Natal Chiron Cycle

If we trace Chiron's own natal Chiron Cycle (taking its discovery event as its natal chart), we will begin to see the pattern of its expression in the world and the evolution of its musings and messages in relation to Healing and the evolution of consciousness.

Chiron's first square to its natal position occurred on August 17, 1991. This represented perhaps the first conscious recognition of Chiron's own Wounds. What are Chiron's own Wounds? Its natal chart tells us that Chiron was in Taurus at the time, indicating a Wound of feeling insecure, unloved, lacking in Trust and incognizant of the form of Love being given it. Its natal 4th house placement tells us that this Wound is played out in the area of family. For Chiron, we might imagine that its family consists of the other planets and astrology and astronomy in general. We might speculate that Chiron's Wound means it feels insecure around, unloved by and does not Trust the other planets, astrologers and astronomers. Chiron is incognizant of the form of Love that the Universe is giving it. These Wounds would become consciously apparent for the first time during this first transiting square.

Translated into worldly terms, astrologers and astronomers, after their initial elation and interest in the newly discovered planet, became less and less interested in Chiron in the wake of further discoveries of other planetesimals and withdrew their attention from it. Chiron's Wound, however, will constantly drive it to become tangibly recognized, to be accepted as equal, to be loved as a part of the family, so to speak. Its Wound will drive it to bring its musings and messages into a tangible form, readily acceptable and digestible by Humanity at large.

Interestingly, the beginning of the end of the Soviet Union was with the attempted, but failed coup in Russia in August 1991, a day after the Chiron/natal Chiron square was exact. The former stability and security of the USSR dissolved into separate states only months after this with the resignation of Soviet leader, Mikhail Gorbachev. That was in December of the same year. The world was simultaneously upset and hopeful for the future of international relations with Russia.

Chiron's first trine to its natal position occurred on September 9, 1993. This represented a time of increased possibility of Healing on a global scale, Chiron's work becoming more apparent upon the global stage.

Interestingly, on September 13, 1993, Yitzhak Rabin, the Prime Minister of Israel, and Yasir Arafat, the chairman of the PLO, sealed the first agreement between the Jews and the Palestinians to end their conflict. They agreed to share the holy land along the river Jordan, sealing the accord in the presence of US President, Clinton. The world rejoiced at the prospect of greater peace in the Middle East. Some factions, including many Palestinians, were, nonetheless, incensed by Arafat's conciliation. Now, into the new millennium, we see an escalation of conflict and tensions.

Other events of 1993 included: Presidents Bush and Yeltsin signed the START II Treaty, Bill Clinton was sworn in as US President, Russian government conservative lawmakers attempted a coup, Yeltsin dissolved the Russian parliament, the Mississippi River broke its banks in the USA, creating some of the worst floods in US history, the Waco siege, Spielberg's film, "Schindler's List" was released, the Hubble Space Telescope was repaired, the Dalai Lama visited the USA and Nelson Mandela and F. W de Klerk won the Nobel Peace Prize.

Chiron's half-Return (opposition to its natal position) occurred on September 28, 1997. This was shortly after Chiron's perigee and perihelion (1996). This represented a time of exacerbation of long-standing Wounds, blockages and unresolved issues of Chiron, reflected in the events, circumstances and situations upon the global stage. From these conflicts and poignant re-surfacing of old Wounds, blockages and unresolved issues, came the possibility for deeper Healing. This was a time when many Wounds, blockages and unresolved issues were identified, becoming more consciously recognized. It was a time for looking back and finding Gratitude and Love for those things and people that were previously taken for granted or that were previously judged negatively. It was a time for recognizing the form that Love took, beyond our narrow expectations and blinkered judgments. It was a time for rekindling our inner vision for the future and our faith in the possibility of Healing.

Interestingly, on the August 31, 1997, only a month before this transit, Diana, Princess of Wales was killed in an automobile accident, the world mourning her death. In July 1997, NASA's Sojourner beamed back pictures from the surface of Mars. Also in July, Great Britain ceded control of Hong Kong back to China. In October, the Dow Jones Industrial Average crashed on Wall Street, losing 554.26 points. Deaths during 1997 included Jacques-Yves Cousteau, Robert Mitchum, Jimmy Stewart, Gianni Versace and John Denver. Also in 1997, George Lucas's trilogy, Star Wars, was updated and re-released. It was also the year infant Matthew Eappen died in the charge of British nanny, Louise Woodward, sparking a highly-publicized murder trial in the USA. 1997 also saw chess grandmaster, Gary Kasparov, defeated by IBM supercomputer Deep Blue. In addition, the world watched the comet, Hale-Bopp, discovered in 1995, make its closest pass to Earth. Lastly, 1997 was the year geneticists first cloned a living animal, resulting in Dolly, the cloned sheep.

Chiron's second trine to its natal position will occur in January 2002. This will be a time of increased opportunity and manifestation for the Healing of Chiron's own Wounds, blockages and unresolved issues. Chiron's place in the consciousness of Humanity will almost certainly grow, most probably through astrology rather than through astronomy. This will be mirrored in Healing events, situations and circumstances on the global stage.

Chiron's second square to its natal position will occur in April 2005. This will be a time of resurfacing of the Wounds, blockages and unresolved issues of Chiron. It is likely that there will be events, circumstances and situations on the global stage that will create doubt in the consciousness of Humanity concerning the possibility of complete and lasting Healing. This will reflect Chiron's own doubt concerning the on-going success of its mission on Earth.

Chiron's Return to its natal position will occur in June 2027. This is likely be a time when much of Chiron's work with Humanity will bear fruit or not. It could be a time of great Healing, reflected in the events, situations and circumstances on the global stage. Alternatively, it could be a time a deep regrets and a re-grouping of intentions and sentiments for the Healing of the planet and the consciousness of Humanity. In any case, by this time, Chiron's place in the astrological palette will be more in accordance with the importance of its mission.

Group Wounds

Let's now consider groups of people – families, circles of friends, companies, clubs, communities, churches, other organizations, etcetera – as collective consciousnesses. There is every reason to suggest that these groups have collective Wounds, blockages and unresolved issues in the same way that they have collective goals, aims, desires and directions. The only complicating factor, as far as astrology goes, is determining the date of 'birth' of the group in question. Given this, the group is driven by the same forces as an individual, i.e. by its Wounds (Voids) as indicated by Chiron and its chief 'spokes-planet', the Moon. In addition, its Values arise from its collective Wounds. This is reflected in a group's beliefs, political preferences, religious attitudes, morals, laws and ethics.

As an example, let's look at the incorporation chart of Australia's biggest airline, Qantas (November 16, 1920, 9am, Brisbane, Australia). Here, we see a life's path and purpose (North Node in Scorpio) of overcoming material preoccupation and moving into higher realms of consciousness. Preempting our explorations in Book Three, we can say that this corresponds to moving into higher levels of the Earth's atmosphere, i.e. flying and space travel. This life's path and its outward expression (Sun and Mercury, also in Scorpio) all lie in the 10th house of companies, business, the public eye, etcetera. The Moon and Mars conjunct in Capricorn (physical and emotional resources applied to the material question, i.e. business). They both sit on the Ascendant (seeing themselves as a stable, responsible and well-managed business). They both trine Saturn in Virgo (disciplined and responsible attention to detail) in the 9th house (holding a vision for the future). All these planets sextile the Sun and Mercury (focusing the elemental earth energy into tangible creation and expression). This is an extraordinary chart in anybody's terms. What drives it, though?

Chiron sits in Aries (Wound of self-worth), retrograde in the 3rd house (feeling unable to communicate or share its deep Wound of self-worth). It squares Pluto in Cancer (the Wound seemingly blocked, but simultaneously stirred up, nurturing and Healing seemingly absent), retrograde in the 6th house (the house of work and service). In addition, Chiron quincunxes the North Node in Scorpio in the 10th house (a new level of consciousness around their life's path and purpose (Node) and around their deep self-doubt (Chiron) is sought).

The face of the Moon in Capricorn on the Ascendant attempts to hide this deep Woundedness by seeking respect, recognition, accolade and achievements. Its fear of letting others see its Woundedness (Chiron in the 3rd house) drives it to create massive structures that disguise itself and, at the same time, prove its worthiness, in this case, a large corporation.

What will these Wounds and protective patterns drive it to do? To seek to justify its own self-worth. To discover, recognize, acknowledge, embrace and finally Love itself for its special and unique Gifts. It does this through achievement in the public eye in the area of business in the sky. *This is its Divine Design.* Its Wounds (Voids) and their outer expression determine its Values and their tangible manifestation. As we have said all along, the Gift is in the Wound.

On a larger scale, we have the Wounds of entire nations and races. The natal charts of nations are not so hard to establish, the data being available through various astrological books and astrologers' research. The origin of races is, by contrast, almost impossible to trace to a date. The Wounds of nations and races will determine what will drive them to fulfill their Divine Design.

As an example, let's look briefly at the birth of the USA (taking the birth time to be July 4, 1776, 2:14am, LMT, Philadelphia, Pennsylvania). Here Chiron sits in Aries in the 11th house. The Aries Wound is the ultimate Wound of self-worth and identity. It drives the USA to seek self-worth and identity at all costs. Initially, this expresses as belligerent and puffed-chest band-standing about its virtues, gifts and talents. The outward show seeks to diguise the fact that, inside, the USA doubts its own self-worth. It battles with fear of being seen, fear of being worthless, fear of being upstaged, fear of losing the competition, fear of not appearing worthy and fear of not being recognized for its unique identity. In short, it drives the USA to try to excel in the eyes of others, to be seen as a unique, special and valuable identity. It plays out this Wound in the 11th house, i.e. through its posturing on an international stage. It also plays it out by espousing the Aquarian ideals of freedom, liberty and justice for all, one for all and all for one.

The Moon in Aquarius, trining Chiron, combined with the Gemini Ascendant, reflects the USA's tendency towards outward insincerity, plasticity and chameleonesque personality. It seeks to disguise its Wounds and unresolved issues by dressing up its appearances. The USA's success in the entertainment business is one of the Gifts arising from this. However, there is an inner distance kept between its people and others, protecting its vulnerability at all costs. Its low self-worth, which sees others as potential enemies or rivals, causes it to build up its defenses, metaphorically and actually.

The triangle of Chiron sextiling the trine of Mars and Moon indicates that Mars and Moon will assist in the Healing of the USA's Wounds and unresolved issues. The Moon in Aquarius will ever seek to give the USA emotional objectivity. Mars in Gemini will cause it to diversify its activities and always to see new ways in which the USA is unique, special, worthy of Loving itself and worthy of being Loved by others.

There is a very loose kite formation arising out of this aforementioned triangle. Chiron forms the focal point with Mars and Moon at the sides and Saturn at its base. Saturn drives the pattern in Libra by impelling the USA to seek balance through hard work, seriousness and responsibility. In this way, it will ultimately Serve to give the USA something to be proud of and something that will soothe its Wounds of low self-worth.

Interestingly, the 11th house where Chiron sits and the 5th house where Saturn sits are intercepted houses. This, in my opinion, *accentuates* the virtual rulership of those houses by Aries and Libra, respectively. (We explored intercepted houses earlier on and suggested that the usual way of looking at them was illogical.) This intercept brings the issues of Self and the Other into acute focus, particularly with Chiron and Saturn loosely opposing within it. The USA is actually extremely conservative *inside* (Saturn at the base of the kite in the 5th house of personal self-expression) but *expresses* radical, innovative, liberal and unusual policies and ideals *outwardly* (Gemini Mars, Aquarius Moon, Gemini Ascendant). An appearance of concern for the welfare of others is what is *expressed* (through the 11th house of collective expression). However, the true focal point is *Self* (Chiron in Aries in the 11th house) and the way the USA looks to others (Gemini Ascendant).

With its North in Leo, the USA's prime purpose in life is to learn how to let its true Inner Light Shine out, beyond its need for others' approval. Rising out of the undifferentiated sea of the collective, the USA's task is to find and express its unique and individual Gifts, thereby becoming a beacon for others to allow their own Inner Light to Shine forth. The Wound of low self-worth, indicated by Chiron in Aries, buried in the collective of the 11th house, ever drives the USA towards fulfilling this Divine Design.

Although the Wounds of races are virtually impossible to trace, we can make educated guesses as to the Wounds that drive them, seeing the outer manifestation of their Wounds, blockages and unresolved issues. Perhaps the most striking example over the last many thousands of years is that of the Jewish people. They wear their Woundedness upon their sleeves. One might speculate that they have Chiron in Pisces (Wound of betrayal by the Universe/God, expressed in being subject to seemingly-unforgivable abuse and betrayal by others). They may also have Chiron the 12th house (secret enemies, victimization, driving them inwards to find their divinity). Lastly, Chiron may make major aspects to Pluto (major calamities, death, transformation, manipulation and betrayal by others).

Whatever the case may be, it is again apparent that the Divine Design of races as a whole and the fulfillment of that Design are driven by the races' innate Wounds (Voids).

And what of the Woundedness of the planet as a whole, i.e. the collective consciousness of Gaia? For this, we need a larger astrology. We need an astrology that encompasses the entire solar system and that can be read in stellar patterns and galactic indicators. Until this kind of astrology is discovered, we can have a general certainty that Gaia, too, as a whole, is driven by collective Wounds, blockages and unresolved issues. This Woundedness drives the planet's collective consciousness towards its ultimate destiny, towards its Divine Design, towards Healing and the evolution of consciousness.

The Ultimate Wound

We have spoken at length about Wounds, blockages and unresolved issues in relation to ourselves and in relation to collective consciousnesses of different magnitudes. What constitutes the ultimate Wound, however, the Wound that underlies all other Wounds, which predates and drives all other Wounds?

Let's reaffirm our definition of "Wound" as a sense of inner hurt, missingness, fragmentedness, injustice, unfairness, incompleteness, etcetera. By "Woundedness" we mean the unresolved, undissolved, unreconciled, unHealed issues that lie buried within our psyches, awaiting the Healing process. In a sense, the Wounding is the dualistic material condition into which we are born. In another sense, our Wounds are the dualistic misperceptions we have had of objectively neutral events, circumstances, situations and people. Further, we have asserted that these misperceptions – our Wounds – drive us, run us and point us in particular directions in our lives.

By this same definition, Healing is the opposite process, the process of integration, 'wholing', synthesis, merging and unifying of our consciousness, mirrored in our physical, emotional, mental and spiritual vehicles. It is a Return to Oneness. It is a Return to our divine origins. It is a Return to Spirit, a Return to the Soul. It is a Return to Love.

Chiron says there is a Gift in the Wound. The Gift is our awakening . . . our awakening to the ultimate perfection of our lives, of the lives of others and of the world around us. This is the purpose of the Wound, i.e. to help us awaken to ourselves, to our true nature and to the perfection of our lives. The Wounding, i.e. the dualistic material condition in which we are born, offers us the mirror in which we can gradually see ourselves and awaken to our true nature. Our true nature is Love and Light.

The ultimate Wound is our initial separation from the All, from God, from Divinity, from pure Light, from Unconditional Love, from Oneness. We will explore this in detail in the next two books.

The further back we trace our Wounds, Healing as we go, approaching the original Wound – what we call the root cause – the closer we come to the ultimate source of our Wounds. If the ultimate goal of Wounds is to awaken us to our true nature as Love and Light, *then the ultimate Wound has its source in the Love that pervades the All.*

Love is the Beginning and the End of our journey of Wounding and Healing.

The Evolution of Consciousness

Our Wounds, i.e. Voids, determine our Values. Our Values point us in a particular direction, the Voids galvanizing us into action. Without such an impetus, would we be inclined to move at all? The promise of a 'better' future, driven by the perceived 'imperfections' of the past, drives us ever onward. Similarly, our rosy view of certain aspects of the past compared to the Wounds of the present drives us to attempt to recreate or return to the past in the future. Either way, our Wounds constitute the motor that drives the evolution of consciousness.

Perceiving imbalance, we seek balance. Perceiving disharmony, we seek harmony. Perceiving imperfection, we seek perfection. Perceiving fragmentation, we seek wholeness. Perceiving separation, we seek connection. Perceiving lack of love, we seek Love. Perceiving Matter, we seek Spirit.

The awakening journey of Healing is realizing that balance, harmony, perfection, wholeness, connection, Love and Spirit already exist and have always existed. We were simply not able to see it. Such is the essence of our Woundedness, i.e. the inability to see. Our blindness in this respect is juxtaposed with the hidden part of us that knows otherwise. *The Void between the part of us that does not see and the part that knows is the Wound.* This is the Wound that drives us, that seeks Healing, that seeks awakening to the Truth and that drives the evolution of consciousness.

Wounding and Healing are the dual aspects of the journey of the evolution of consciousness.

Chiron/Pluto Conjunction and the New Millennium

In December 1999, as Chiron and Pluto approached a conjunction, a number of world events were in evidence. Amongst these were the following:

- *Russia escalated their military efforts against rebels in Chechnya.*
- *Former Russian President, Boris Yeltsin, threatened the USA on their stance on the Chechnya issue, i.e. reminding the USA that Russia was still a nuclear power; rubbing salt into old Wounds from the Cold War era.*
- *Boris Yeltsin resigned as Russian President on the eve of the new millennium.*
- *Meanwhile, a biochemist, having entirely decoded the genetic structure of a simple one-celled organism, announced that we could now create life from scratch.*
- *The so-called "Y2K bug" posed the threat of accidental missile launches due to antiquated software.*
- *Skirmishes between Israel and Hezbollah factions erupted. Elsewhere Tamils clashed with Sri Lankan forces.*
- *Ex-Beatle, George Harrison, was stabbed (not fatally, fortunately).*
- *An Indian airline plane was hijacked New Year's Eve (ending peacefully after New Year).*
- *The Panama Canal was handed over by the USA to Panama.*

Days into the year 2000:

- *Coptic Christians and Muslims clashed in Egypt leaving 20 dead.*
- *Religious violence erupted on the Indonesian island of Lombok.*

- *Sunni Muslim extremists clashed with Lebanese security forces in Beirut, leaving 23 dead.*
- *Chechen rebels in Grozny won various counter-attacks, regaining control of four villages.*
- *Israel and Syria began peace talks, mediated by US President Clinton.*
- *Israel and Palestine reached an accord on the transfer of five percent of the West Bank.*
- *Acting Russian President Putin began rearranging the government of Russia.*
- *The US stock market experienced its greatest consecutive daily falls in history, particularly in technology stocks, only to recover sharply and set new record highs a week later. In May 2000, the markets began a decline that would not bottom out until mid-2001.*
- *The so-called Y2K bug failed to be the devastating crisis that so many had predicted.*

Apart from these issues and events, the Chiron/Pluto conjunction represents a time of revolutionary change in the area of Healing, from medical science to alternative therapies. The completion of the Humane Genome Project, the research and financing of genetic engineering, cloning, stem-cell research, bionic organs, etcetera, all represent a part of the revolution augured by the conjunction.

We stand at the beginning of the end of the accepted paradigm that diseases – physical, mental, emotional and/or spiritual – are somehow outside of us. We stand at the beginning of the end of the paradigm that diseases are caused by outside intruders in the form of viruses and germs or as a result of outside events and circumstances. We stand at the beginning of the end of the myth that genetic defects or so-called hereditary diseases are entirely inherited or entirely environmentally created. We stand at the beginning of a new paradigm that asserts that consciousness and health and disease are inseparable. This new paradigm recognizes that health and disease – physical, mental, emotional and/or spiritual – *are the body exactly mirroring our changing states of consciousness.* The new paradigm will see health and disease for what they truly are . . . as Gifts given to us to help us awaken to our true nature on our journey of Healing and the evolution of consciousness.

I predict that we will eventual discover that *health and disease are created by the electromagnetic fields of our consciousness.* Fields of consciousness turn genes on and off.[72] They excite and/or depress the sympathetic and parasympathetic nervous systems, building up or breaking down our physiology, accordingly. More amazing than this, we will discover that the body itself is 'held together' by electromagnetic and morphogenetic fields that are constantly seeking to reestablish and maintain equilibrium in the organism, attempting to counter-balancing the effects of our consciousness, at the same mirroring that consciousness. Such truths are already being explored until the banner of *complexity theory* and *self-organizing systems.* The electromagnetic and morphogenetic organizing fields required for the creation and maintenance of biological life are also consciousness, *but not ours* . . . We will explore these questions at length in Books Two and Three.

What else lies in store for us in the new millennium? We have already touched on some of the expectations. We have explored the Chiron Cycle and its trough in 2021–22 and its next peak in 2047. We have indicated that we are moving into a material phase of the cycle until 2021–22, during which spirituality will become increasingly material and increasingly integrated with practical matters. As we approach 2021–22, our Wounds becoming increasingly exacerbated, we can expect an internal crisis in the consciousness of Gaia/Humanity, similar to the nineteen-1960s, but far less in magnitude and certainly not expressed outwardly in the same way. From there, the cycle takes us back toward an emphasis on spiritual matters once more, peaking in 2047.

As far as Chiron aspects to the outer planets in the next 50 years, here are a few of the highlights:

---

[72] The elation around the completion of the Human Genome Project as being the ultimate key to the creation of life from scratch will eventually be shown to be misplaced. The missing factor will eventually be found: electromagnetic fields of consciousness manifesting as the consciousness of life-forms themselves and as the environmental womb in which life arises. The Human Genome is but the *dictionary* of building blocks – the *moderating* factors – involved in the creation of life.

- *Saturn-opposition-Chiron 7 times between September 2003 and June 2006.*
- *Neptune-conjunct-Chiron, February 2010.*
- *Saturn-trine-Chiron 4 times between November 2012 and August 2014.*
- *Saturn-square-Chiron 3 times between December 2016 and November 2017.*
- *Saturn-conjunct-Chiron, June 2028.*
- *Pluto-square-Chiron 5 times between July 2028 and April 2031.*
- *Pluto-trine-Chiron 3 times between July 2037 and May 2038.*
- *Saturn-square-Chiron 8 times between December 2040 and May 2044.*
- *Neptune-square-Chiron, August 2042.*
- *Uranus-conjunct-Chiron 3 times between November 2042 and June 2043.*
- *Pluto-opposition-Chiron 3 times between October 2043 and July 2044.*
- *Neptune-trine-Chiron 3 times between October 2044 and July 2045.*
- *Pluto-trine-Chiron 3 times between November 2047 and August 2048.*
- *Neptune-opposition-Chiron 3 times between December 2048 and October 2049.*

What is immediately interesting from this list is the deficit of major aspects around the time of the next trough in the Chiron Cycle (2021–22). Conversely, there is an abundance of major aspect as we approach the next peak of the Chiron Cycle in 2047. This is quite the opposite of the lead-up to the last trough in 1970–71 and to the peak in 1996. This will have the effect of deepening our feeling of Woundedness, isolation, separation and disconnection from Spirit and spiritual matters around 2021–22. This will be unable to be fully expressed at the time, due to the deficit of major aspects to the other outer planets. It will, however, add momentum to the escalating outward expression as we approach the peak of 2047. We could hazard a guess that the 2040s will be a time of extraordinary outpouring from the collective consciousness of Gaia/Humanity. It will be time akin to the 1960s . . . tumultuous, devastating, inspired, creative, revolutionary and extraordinary. The major fulcrum point of this decade will be when Chiron and Uranus conjunct between November 2042 and June 2043.

11 ~ EXAMPLE CHART DELINEATION

In order to give guidance on the interpretation of Chiron in the natal chart, we offer an example natal chart delineation, read from a Healing and spiritual perspective. The chart we have chosen is rich in Chiron aspects, as this gives us the greatest possibility of seeing how Chiron works in a 'focused' chart.

The chart we have chosen is that of a real person, although we have changed their name at their request. We have included their own feelings and thoughts, related to the various aspects of their chart and we have offered some important real-life events and their correlations with Chiron transits in their life.

Milly

(See Chart 29 – MILLY, p. 565.)

Milly is a Healer, singer, midwife and mother.

Her expressed purpose in life is to bring personal Healing/Change to a large number of people. She has worked on personal and planetary Healing since the age of 14.

Her passions include Healing, music, writing, art, nature and learning.

The first thing to look at is the life's path and purpose, i.e. the Nodes of the Moon. All other features of the chart revolve around this.

North Node in Aries indicates a life's path of finding, acknowledging and affirming a sense of Self. The South Node indicates that Milly comes from a background (past-life or otherwise) of denying Self and *giving away her power to others.* Initially, she unconsciously places more importance and value in others than in herself. She tends to have an underlying low self-esteem and can spend much time deprecating and depreciating herself. There is also a tendency to try to please others. In addition, there is a tendency to take the line of least resistance and opt for greatest safety, particularly when in social settings. Furthermore, there is the tendency to avoid conflict, to keep the peace and to strive for harmony and smooth waters. This makes her dependent on the whims and tastes of others. When she does this for too long, she ends up becoming resentful and beating herself up for it.

Milly's journey is a journey back to an acknowledgement of Self. It is a journey back towards true self-worth. Her task in this lifetime is to create solidity, stability, presence . . . a tangible core of self-awareness. It is about focusing her attention and concentration inwards, ultimately realizing that everything that she does for herself benefits those around her. To be spiritually selfish is the highest altruism. Committees and general consensus can only go so far towards co-Creating the world. Individual effort and inspiration are also necessary. As time goes by, she will find that the Universe will increasingly give her conditions where she will be challenged to 'go it alone'.

Furthermore, Milly will find herself increasingly *wishing* to 'go it alone'. There is a place in the world for positive ego. The expression of positive ego is a sacred act of acknowledging the Light within, i.e. of allowing ourselves to Shine in the world without guilt, fear or self-depreciation.

The North Node life's path point in the 3rd house indicates a lifetime aimed towards communicating and sharing the innate wisdom, knowledge and experience that Milly brings with her from other lives. Initially, she will find it difficult to relate to society and difficult to find a way of communicating her inner knowings. In some ways, she will feel like an outsider at first. Her inner knowings will not always be in line with what are accepted paradigms of truth and living. For these reasons, Milly's task is to find a way of sharing what is inside of her in ways that others can relate to, i.e. to learn the language of social and ideological interaction, so to speak.

In a sense, Milly is the adventurer who has traveled the world and experienced life in the raw. Now, in this lifetime, she returns to the 'normal' world to share her tales of adventure, to share the jewels of wisdom that she has picked up along the way.

To find a language with which to communicate this tale, it will be necessary for Milly to gather much information and data across a wide field of knowledge. We all have the answers already; we just need to discover the context in which to put those answers and the language with which to express them. As we gather information, we will gradually recognize the place of each part in the jigsaw puzzle of the universal Plan. When sufficient information is synthesized into this picture, we will gradually know how to communicate it, enabling us to share our inner knowings. This is Milly's path.

When taken together, Milly's North Node life's path point in Aries and in the 3rd house gives her a life's path of striving to acknowledge and validate her true Self. In addition, to share that Self with others, and to communicate her inner knowings and understandings. Her sense of self-worth is intimately connected with the acknowledgement of what she already knows and understands within herself. Her sense of self-worth is also tied to whether or not she is 'out there' doing what her calling dictates, i.e. sharing and communicating her wisdom.

When we are not acknowledging and honoring our true Selves and inner knowings, giving in to others' wishes, ideas and opinions, we beat ourselves up. When we are in situations where we have wisdom, understanding and knowing, but fail to share it due to lack of self-worth, we deprecate ourselves more.

For Milly, learning – gathering knowledge and data – is more accurately called 'remembering'. This is due to the fact that learning is a reflection, from the outside world, of what she already knows inside, but for which she has not previously had words. Milly's true learning in this lifetime is in learning to acknowledge herself and in learning how to communicate with others in a way to which they can relate, according to their current paradigms and belief systems.

The highest expression of Milly's life's path will come when she acknowledges and honors that which comes through her as a messenger. It will come when she acknowledges and honors herself as a messenger. It will come when she consciously participates in the receiving and broadcasting of the divine knowledge and wisdom that comes through the waystation of her Heart.

Note that the Nodes of the Moon in Milly's chart aspect Chiron, Jupiter, Uranus, Neptune and Mars. We will deal with these aspects momentarily.

The next thing we will look at is how Milly's life's path and purpose, as indicated by the Nodes of the Moon, *expresses* in this lifetime. That is, we will look at her Sun sign, house and aspects.

With Sun in Pisces, Milly expresses her life's path primarily through the emotions. The initial tendency to feel like the victim of her life and to be prone to every shift of the wind will gradually give way to the understanding that her life is guided from Above. On one hand, she is ruled by the slightest change of emotion around her. She is extremely sensitive to the energy environment. On the other hand, this gives her enormous powers of perception. She is able to feel what others are feeling, without words. This ability can be a burden at times when she cannot seem to shut out the outside world. This can lead to a retreat into the inner safety of a virtual world. This is the dreamer within her. This can also be a hard shell, masking her inner sensitivity.

Milly has a tendency to take on the Wounds and causes of others, to support and champion the underdog. Her deepest wish, whether acknowledged or not, is to reconnect with the Love and Oneness of her divine origins. In this way, she can sometimes lose herself, allowing others to encroach and to take advantage of her. Milly's lesson is to try to retain her sense of self while listening to the inner voice that speaks to her from her Heart. Individuality and a sense of belonging to the greater whole are both equally necessary. Even the tendencies to feel like a victim and to succumb to self-pity are necessary processes in her, giving her time and space until she is ready for greater Truth.

The 3rd house placement of Milly's Sun indicates that she will express her life, as indicated by the aforementioned Pisces placement, in the area of communication, media, writing, intellectual pursuit, etcetera. She has a message to share. The way she will share it will depend on the other astrological considerations of her chart.

Note that Milly's Sun opposes her Moon. We will look at this aspect in a moment.

Now we will look at Milly's Chiron – the force that drives her along her life's path and purpose (Nodes) and its outer expression (Sun).

Milly's Chiron in Aries indicates that her deepest void or Wound, around which all her other Wounds and Voids revolve, is a profound loss of self-worth. Some event, circumstance or issue, very early in her life, convinced her that she was entirely worthless and unworthy of love, perhaps even that she was undeserving of life itself. The Healing journey involves a Return to self-worth. It involves an affirmation of her worthiness, an affirmation of her right to live, Love and be Loved. The Gift of this journey is that it gives her the opportunity to consciously seek and search for Love for herself.

Milly's original perceptions of worthlessness were misperceptions, but the Gift of those misperceptions has been in the journey on which they have taken her. This journey has brought her to where she is today. It has brought her towards becoming what she has been Divinely Designed to become.

In seeking self-worth, Milly is being given the opportunity to find the core essence of herself – her Spirit – and to affirm and express that essence. Her Gift to others will be the message that the imponderable Spirit within can never be lost, harmed or damaged. Only the outer layers – personality, masks – undergo these processes. Milly's journey will take her beyond the illusions of the personality and into the immortal Truth of her essence, i.e. her true identity. From here, she will express, Shine and communicate this eternal Truth to others so that they, too, can awaken to the Truth of their Spirit.

Without such a Wound/Void – i.e. her lack of self-worth – would she have been impelled in her life to seek to awaken consciousness of her true immortal Being? That is the Gift in this Wound.

Milly's Chiron in the 3rd house indicates that her deepest Wounds, aforementioned, are played out in the area of knowledge and understanding. A deep feeling of not knowing or not being worthy to know afflicts her. The feeling of being stupid, slow, ignorant or uneducated can be evident here as can the feeling of being unable to communicate what is inside of her. The latter feeling arises from her feeling that nothing inside her is worth communicating.

This placement of Chiron drives her towards the pursuit of knowledge, understanding and wisdom. It drives her to find out all she can about all subjects to which she feels connected. In this process, she will gradually realize, by the reflection of that knowledge, that, somewhere deep inside her, she knew it all already. This placement is about seeing, acknowledging and embracing her own inner knowing and wisdom.

Milly's 3rd-house Chiron also drives her to try to find ways of feeling worthy of sharing what is inside of her and ways of communicating this with others, despite her fear and low self-esteem.

The ultimate Gift of Chiron in the 3rd house is the finding, acknowledging, expressing and communicating of our deepest inner wisdom through the interface of language and the associated social paradigms of Humanity today. It is becoming conscious to and awakening to the deep wisdom that lies wordless in our Hearts – the wisdom of Love – and giving it form in the world.

When considered together, Milly's Chiron in Aries and in the 3rd house gives a Wound that equates knowledge, understanding and wisdom with self-worth. Her feeling of lack of knowledge, understanding and wisdom – her feeling of being stupid, slow, ignorant or uneducated – causes her to feel that she is entirely worthless, useless to the world. This drives her to seek knowledge, understanding and wisdom in order to feel worthy to exist, in order to feel worthy to have something to say, in order to feel worthy to participate in life. This drives her to seek all knowledge and wisdom with a fervor and intensity that seems as though her life depends on it.

The net result, apart from the gaining of knowledge and wisdom for its own sake, is for Milly to realize that the knowledge and wisdom gained from the outside world is pale in comparison to the knowledge and wisdom of the Heart. It is to realize that the Heart knew it all along, despite the denials and lack of acknowledgment. The realization of her own inner wisdom – her inner knowing – is, in Milly's case, synonymous with the affirmation of true self-worth. This is the acknowledgement of the inner essence of Self, which is connected to the all-knowing, all-pervading and all-loving Spirit.

When this is sufficiently realized and embraced, Milly will realize that her efforts to try to communicate what was inside of her were not in vain. She will acknowledge what is inside of her and be inspired to communicate it to others, i.e. to share her inner wisdom. Part of Milly's message to others will originate from the very journey that she has undergone. The message will be that we all have 'the knowing' inside of us already. It is simply a matter of acknowledgment. The attainment of this universal Truth is the Gift of this Chiron placement.

Let's now consider the Moon in Milly's chart and its place as the outer lower-natured/emotional face of Chiron.

Milly's Chiron in Aries expresses, as we have said, her Wound of deep loss or lack of self-worth. The external face of Virgo Moon is the perfectionist. It represents the person for whom nothing is ever good enough, who can never be happy or satisfied with the performance of others, who can never be happy or satisfied with the *status quo.* Virgo Moon takes solace and refuge in criticism of self and others. All this derives, in Milly's case, from never being happy or satisfied with herself, her performance or with who she is at any given time. Can we see how Chiron and the Moon are psychologically connected here? This psychology, of course, will ever impel her to try to improve herself. Ultimately, it will ever drive her to learn to Love herself for who she is, exactly as she is.

Now let's widen our perspective of Milly's chart by considering some of the important aspects in her chart, beginning with the North Node/Chiron conjunction.

Any planet that conjuncts the North Node is a special guide in one's life. Chiron is Milly's special planetary guide in this lifetime, one of the reasons that we have chosen her chart to work with in this chapter. Her life is not only guided by Chiron, but her *purpose* is to do Chiron's work, i.e. Healing in some form or other. With Chiron being in the 3rd house, conjunct the North Node and sharing the house with the Sun and Mercury, Milly's primary task is to communicate and express the messages of Chiron. Further, it is to communicate and express these messages in a highly personal way. Milly's journey of acknowledgement of Self and of the Gifts that she brings from Above is the same journey as the sharing. The more she acknowledges this, the more she will Shine and the more others will wish to hear her story, learning from her wisdom and sharing in her Gifts.

Milly's Chiron opposes the South Node conjunct Uranus and Jupiter. Apart from the Chiron/North Node conjunction, this one of the more important features of her chart. The opposition of Chiron and Uranus, as we have said, is a feature of the period between 1952 and 1989. It occurred 41 times during this time at discrete intervals. Those born with this aspect fall somewhere between two extremes:

On the one hand, there is the chance that the degree of difficulty in dealing with their deep Woundedness can create a tendency towards extreme escapism, avoidance and self-destructive behavior. On the other hand, if the challenge of the Wounds is met, it can manifest in amplified Healing gifts and skills.

The nature of this aspect is such that Uranus, the planet concerned with the divine blueprint and with seeing the bigger picture, shines a light directly into the Darkness where the Wounds lie. We cannot escape the Wounds. If we try to avoid or escape from them, they show up again in a different form. Confronted with no place to run, we are given no option but to try to deal with the Wounds or to go off the rails trying to avoid feeling them.

The highest potential of this aspect is to produce the finest Healer, a Healer who transcends the established boundaries of current thinking about Healing. The journey of Healing and the journey of spiritual evolution are the same. Personal Healing takes a quantum leap when we realize, acknowledge and have Gratitude for the perfection of our own lives. Our lives *are* the Healing journey in every aspect. This journey gives us the opportunity to evolve and to become the Divinely-Designed person we are today.

Chiron-opposition-Uranus is the mark of the Healer. Unable to escape or hide from her Woundedness, like Chiron in the myth, Milly will ever seek to learn all about Healing, Healing others as she goes.

For Milly, Jupiter is involved in the equation, too, conjunct the South Node and Uranus and opposing Chiron. Jupiter represents the Inner Child that knows in its Heart that all is 'right' with the world. Milly's Inner Child lies hidden behind the Wounds, calling out to be heard, driving her even more upon the Healing path. Ultimately, Jupiter in opposition to Chiron will seek to give Milly a new view – a larger view – of her Wounds and unresolved issues, showing her the larger Plan of which they are a part. Jupiter promises her the freedom of awakened consciousness if she can transcend the illusions of her judgments, charges and misperceptions that constitute her Wounds and Voids.

Milly's Chiron and North Node opposing her Uranus, South Node and Jupiter all form a trine/sextile aspect to Neptune-conjunct-Mars in Sagittarius in the 12th house.

Mars, from a spiritual perspective, represents action, reaction, intention and motivation. Neptune represents the striving for Oneness, Spirit and Love. Taken together, in conjunction, they represent the potential for active, conscious and intentional pursuit and expression of Spirit. Initially, however, when we are primarily *reactive,* this can cause us to act in mysterious and irrational ways. In the 12th house, this is even truer. Milly is being given the opportunity to delve actively, consciously and intentionally into her psyche, seeking the Spirit within her Heart.

When Milly's Mars and Neptune are considered in relation to their aspects with the Nodes, Chiron, Uranus and Jupiter, this gives her journey *supra-conscious* motivation, power and drive. When transits set off any of the planets involved in this arrangement, all the other associated planets resonant, too. This triangle of planets is a powerful indicator of Milly's Healing ability and focus.

Milly's Pluto in Virgo represents a generation of people destined to revolutionize Healing and Healing methods. Being in a wide-orbed conjunction with the South Node and its attendant aspects, this indicates that Milly brings revolutionary Healing ideas and abilities into this lifetime. It also indicates that she understands, intuitively, the metaphysics of Healing and of the evolution of consciousness.

All the planets in Milly's 9th house reflect the wisdom that she brings through the South Node past-life point, channeled through the 3rd house planets, activated and motivated by the 12th house planets.

Let's now come back to the Sun/Moon opposition we mentioned previously.

The Sun/Moon opposition keeps Milly balanced. It keeps her feet on the ground and head in the heavens. Bless this aspect! It is her God-send. Apart from driving her towards self-improvement and towards learning to Love herself, as we mentioned before, Moon in Virgo is very pragmatic, positively skeptical, discerning, rigorously attending to detail and a positive 'doubting Thomas' if there ever was one! Milly's innate emotional need for order, for knowing all the details and for putting them in their proper place not only keeps her honest, but it gives her credibility. The Pisces Sun can then soar on the firm foundations that the Moon provides, without getting lost in the clouds.

This opposition of Sun and Moon, as with all oppositions, provides an innate balance check. Both sides of the equation demand to be considered. This is what makes oppositions so difficult: they demand that we synthesis what initially seems to be opposite, irresolvable and irreconcilable. Truth lies beyond the paradox that oppositions present. As a general rule and when seen from this perspective, oppositions are the greatest and most obvious Gifts in the chart.

Let's now turn to Milly's Saturn, Venus and their quincunx aspect to Pluto, with Pluto conjuncting the South Node. Normally, I wouldn't allow such a wide orb for a quincunx as we potentially see between Venus/Saturn and the South Node. However, as the South Node conjuncts Pluto, within about 6 degrees orb, we will consider that it also quincunxes Venus/Saturn.

Milly's Venus and Saturn in Aries and in the 4th house, quincunxing the South Node and Pluto, means that she was destined to have her father, symbolically or actually, create dramatic and revolutionary change in her life. (This was enacted most obviously in the real-life circumstance of her father 'stealing' her away from her mother when she was 5 years old.)

For Milly, the 'father' will inevitable show up in her every relationship until she learns to Love every aspect of her father and of her 'father' issues. Every partner will mirror those aspects of her father that she does not yet Love Unconditionally.

There appears to be, by the nature of the quincunx to the South Node, a past-life connection between Milly and her father, i.e. she has past-life issues to resolve. I suggest that she is on a path to resolving things and events concerning her father in a past life. (Remembering what we have said before concerning past-life symbolism, we should take this formulation as symbolic and not actual.)

Milly's journey goes a little like this . . . first, there was negative judgment as a result of deeds 'done to her' by the 'father' person in a past life. Next, there was the failure to resolve these issues in past lives. Next, there was attraction and resonance, bringing Milly and this other person (or someone of very similar resonance) together in this life. Next, there is the lesson of 'accepting' what they 'did to her'. Then, the lesson of learning to 'forgive' them. Finally, there will be the lesson of learning to Love them Unconditionally, knowing that no forgiveness was ever necessary and that everything that transpired between the two of them was part of a larger Plan, Divine and magnificent.

In short, the quincunx aspect demands that Milly attain a new perspective and understanding of unresolved past-life/symbolic issues through the vehicle of present-life interaction with her natural father and/or 'father'-type people in this lifetime. Note that Milly's 'father' in this context may be someone other than her natural father. Indications from Milly herself suggest that her *mother* played part of the role we are suggesting here.

When viewed in the context of her life's path and purpose, as indicated by the Nodes and expressed through the Sun, the role of 'father' in Milly's life takes on a higher meaning. The 'father' in our lives is the one who challenges us (even if 'father' is expressed through the physical mother or even someone else outside the immediate family). The 'father' is the one who questions our self-worth, our right to exist, our beliefs and actions. The 'father' is the mirror of the Universe/God/Creator/All/Spirit, whereas the 'mother' is the mirror of the Creation /Goddess /Mother /Maintainer /World /Matter.

The Wounds Milly bears in the area of self-worth are exacerbated by the 'father' and her 'father' issues in this lifetime. However, the paradox is that her 'father' and 'father' issues will simultaneously act to impel her to ultimately assert, affirm and empower her self-worth. This is doubly emphasized by the fact that Venus and Saturn in her chart are, like Chiron, in Aries. Restrictions, repressions, limitations, cruelty, harshness, coldness, abuse, etcetera, toward us ultimately inspires us to stand up and say "enough is enough!" Furthermore, in the process, we collect some valuable Gifts along the way, i.e. discipline, seriousness, perseverance, fortitude, determination, etcetera. The Love of the Father comes in mysterious ways. The Return to the Love of the Father is the ultimate end of all Healing.

Finally, we come to the singleton in the chart, i.e. Mercury. Normally, we would have dealt with Mercury earlier in the reading, after coming to its aspects to other planets, but when it is unaspected it tends to get left until later.

Milly's Mercury in Aquarius and in the 3rd house, *unaspected to any other planets,* paradoxically adds weight to her purpose of communication. Initially, it remains isolated and Milly will tend to find it hard to give voice to her wisdom and understanding. This is further accentuated by Chiron, also in the 3rd house. The Gift of Mercury's isolation and its Aquarian stance is objectivity, distance, space and perspective. It is the voice of reason, helping her to sense a higher order in what her earth-bound understanding initially perceives as chaos.

Milly's Libran Midheaven indicates that any career or public path she may take will need to offer her a sense of balance and be in line with her chosen life's higher purpose. This is particularly so as it lies so close to the conjunction of Jupiter, Uranus and the South Node.

Her Sagittarian Ascendant initially indicates that Milly sees herself as an adventurer on the journey of life. She sees herself as a free spirit and wishes to embrace life with both hands, so to speak. Whether she can or not will depend on her own degree of serious work on her Wounds and unresolved issues. It will rely on the effort of conscious Healing. We might notice that, although it is not marked in the chart, there is a wide-orbed square of Milly's Sagittarian Ascendant and her Pisces Sun. This indicates that her sensitive nature may initially be at odds with the adventurer spirit in her.

Ultimately, Milly's inner journey of Healing will be embraced with the same sense of adventure as a rock-climber embracing their physical sport.

Now let's deal briefly with the subject of relationship, as this was one of Milly's specific questions in the reading. It will also Serve to illustrate assertions we have made previously with respect to Chiron and its place in relationship.

Firstly, we should take into account the aforementioned comments regarding Milly's Venus/Saturn conjunction quincunxing Pluto and the South Node. That is, the 'father' will 'show up' in her every relationship until she learns to Love him. Paradoxically, by virtue of her Wounds, as indicated by Chiron, Milly will attract people who will beat her up, metaphorically or actually, until she stands up for herself. These people may have similar Wounds and therefore an immediate empathy with Milly. However, as time goes by in the relationship, they will tend to take out their own frustrations and Wounded self-worth upon her (and vice versa). Relationships are a mirror.

Further, we have indicated that our Wounds take us to exactly the places we need to be in order to learn what we need to learn and in order to Heal our Wounds and resolve our issues. This is why Milly would be attracted to people who would eventually challenge her self-worth by them playing out their issues upon her. The lesson of Chiron in Aries is learning to Love Self. Milly's actual relationship experiences affirm the previous indications.

Now let's look at some of the facts, as related by Milly herself in the reading and see how they fit in with the delineation as set out above. We will concentrate on Chiron placements, aspects and transits, as this is our theme in this book. Words in quotations are Milly's exact words.

Natal Placements:

Chiron in Aries: Physical abuse in earliest years (1–5), carrying on throughout childhood and into some adult relationships. Sexual abuse periodically. Prone to "energy crashing and over-giving". Experiences Healing crises very physically. A need to share her 'extraordinary' experiences with others, to feel important and validated by virtue of having experiences that transcend and surpass (even if negatively) the normal experiences of others.

Chiron in 3rd house: Expressed wish to Heal. "A gifted child from a dysfunctional family who didn't achieve worldly academic potential". Concerning her stepmother, Milly relates, "The main way she Wounded me was to make me feel unacceptable for being 'gifted'. The word 'brain' was a put-down in the family." Milly also experienced Wounds in relation to her siblings. Milly expresses a Wish to write globally, inspired by her adversity. She also expresses a Wish to work with schizophrenics and other mentally 'ill' people. She is a self-taught 'psychologist' with a great interest in weighing up and exploring the depths of others. All this has lead to a deep understanding of Healing and an extended ability to communicate Healing ideas.

Natal Aspects:

Chiron conjunct Node: A expressed deep Wish to bring Healing/ Change to as many others as possible. A feeling of destiny, having "worked on personal and planetary Healing since awakening at age 14."

Chiron/North Node opposition Uranus/Jupiter/South Node: Path of the Healer. Inner Child discovery. "Very deep thinker and lover of life's mysteries . . ." Finds herself "unintentionally" working with abused children. Also learning "to Love even the 'Wounder', not just the Wounded". (In addition, see expressed purpose, aforementioned.)

Chiron/Node trine Mars/Neptune in Sag in the 12th: Highly motivated individual in the area of personal and planetary Healing. Expressed purpose: "to receive humility and initiation as a Healer with Unconditional Love for All-that-is".

Chiron Transits:

Early life abuse (age 1–4): It is interesting that Chiron went retrograde four months after Milly's birth and conjuncted natal Chiron in the 10th month *at the same time as the North Node conjuncted natal Sun.* Furthermore, Chiron and Uranus danced around Milly's natal IC and MC for the first few years of life. Her Healing destiny and its imprint as a vocation are set here, her Wounds in place, the Wounds that will drive her Healing journey back to Love.

Pluto-conjunct-Uranus opposed natal Chiron while transiting the 9th house: Moved to Australia.

Chiron conjunct natal Venus/Saturn in 4th house: Father "stole" her away from her mother. In addition, Pluto was conjunct natal Jupiter/ Uranus. This indicates revolutionary change (Pluto) to Inner Child (Jupiter) and overall view of the world (Uranus).

North Node square natal Chiron/North Node & Uranus/Jupiter/

South Node: Milly relates that this was the time she started her personal and planetary Healing journey.

Chiron opposition natal Mars/Neptune: Personal and planetary Healing journey given extra impetus. (This was the year and a half following the previous mentioned transit).

Milly's Children:

1st child: Jupiter-conjunct-natal Sun, shortly after rejoining with her mother. Of this child, Milly says, "I needed to be Loved Unconditionally and she came to give me this".

2nd child: 1st Chiron-square-natal Chiron. Child born to different father than first child, the father being "some sort of dark one, energy vortex, inward collapse, wolf in sheep's clothing." The child's relationship with Milly is, in her own words, "to reflect my own Wounds and search for Truth".

3rd child: Chiron-square-natal Venus/Saturn in the second half of the pregnancy. Same father as 2nd child. This child, as Milly puts it, "knows that persistence pays." "His polarities aren't fully heterosexual . . . also, I remembered my sexual abuse during this pregnancy."

4th child: Saturn conjunct natal Chiron & Chiron opposition natal Venus/Saturn. Different father from the other three children. Milly recalls that when the child was born, the father's "'mental illness' manifest. His extremely traumatic childhood blew up in his face. He became 'paranoid schizophrenic'. He has continued to attack and attempt to Wound me despite every loving effort." During the child's birth, Milly relates that "I made the noise I had always been afraid to make, the noise of my Wound. I could never reproduce that sound and I feel the sadness even now as I recall it." Milly feels that she accessed tools during this birth and from this child subsequently that she could use in the future to defend herself.

1st Chiron square natal Chiron/North Node: Only months after this transit Milly met spiritual teachers, Ma Shivam Rachana and Daricha. Her Healing journey began to gain momentum.

Uranus square natal Chiron/North Node: This was the period of time spent with the aforementioned spiritual teachers.

Chiron opposition natal Mercury (singleton): A guide came to Milly in the form of her English teacher. Recall what we have said about the importance of transits to natal singletons.

Jupiter opposition natal Chiron/North Node: A guide came to Milly. Of this encounter, she relates that it came "just in the nick of time, before I inwardly collapsed. This was my first quantum leap."

Nervous breakdown/transformation: This was a time of monumental spiritual emergency/emergence in Milly's life, between 1992 and 1993. In early 1992, the North Node squared natal Chiron/North Node and Uranus/Jupiter/South Node. Chiron opposed Mercury in late 1992 into early 1993. (Recall again what we have said about the importance of transits to activate natal singletons.) The fulcrum point was in April 1993 when Uranus squared natal Venus/Saturn, while Chiron opposed natal Mercury, while the North Node squared natal Sun and Moon and while Saturn squared natal Neptune/Mars!

As we have said, Healing crises are accentuated in people whose natal Chiron is involved in multiple planetary aspects. During this time, Milly "spent 9 months under a doona for 90% of my waking hours, not sleeping, not awake . . ." She emerged afterwards feeling reborn "like a butterfly".

Chiron conjunct natal Pluto: In late 1994 into 1995 Milly started writing "due to adversity", inspired to share it globally. Saturn conjuncted natal Sun in February 1995. Later in 1995, Chiron opposed natal Chiron/North Node while Pluto conjuncted natal Mars/Neptune.

Chiron conjunct natal Neptune: Experienced "increased spiritual awareness" in late 1998 and into September 1999. In August 1999, Milly experienced an enormous cathartic Healing crisis and cleansing, including past-life recall. During this time, Barbara Hand Clow's book on Chiron came to her.

Chiron conjunct natal Mars: In October 1999, Milly experienced a period of activation and increased motivation for her Healing efforts, personal and planetary. Although she acknowledges that she still has a long way to go, she has a conscious and powerful vision for the future.

It is important to mention once more, at the conclusion of this natal chart delineation, that the degree of correlation between the planets and a person's actual life, inner and outer, depends on the degree of focus of the chart, i.e. on how well-aspected it is with planetary angles. Milly's chart is highly focused and thus presents the perfect vehicle for the exploration of planetary correspondences. Perhaps we would find the chart of someone not so focused a little disappointing if we were expecting a similar result to the above. Nonetheless, the influences of the planets are still there, whether manifest in obvious events in a person's life or not. In cases where the chart is less focused, the delineation must necessarily be more psychological and less concerned with relating actual events to planetary placements, aspects and transits.

APPENDIX A ~ CHARTS

(All charts were calculated and drawn using Solar Fire Astrology software.)

Chart 1 – BIRTH OF CHIRON

Chiron was discovered on November 1st, 1977.

Birth of Chiron—Natal Chart
Nov 1 1977, 9:56 am, PST +8:00
Pasadena CA USA, 34°N05', 118°W09'
Geocentric Tropical Zodiac
Koch Houses, True Node

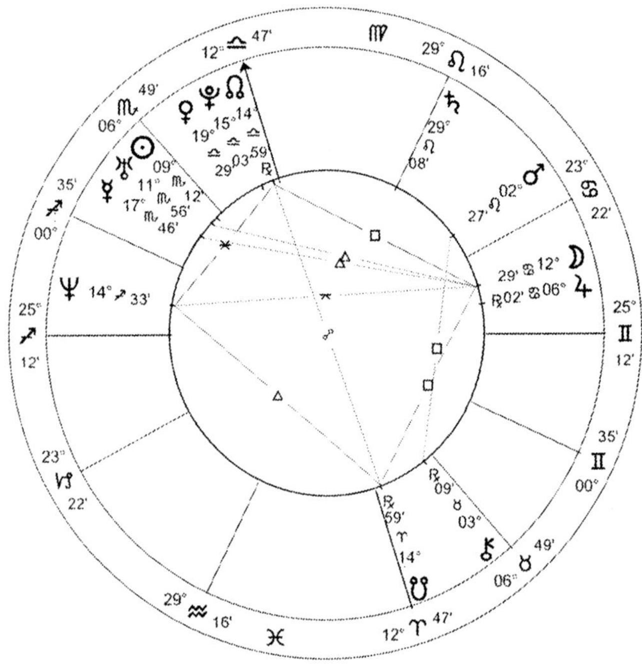

Chart 2 – 1st CHIRON/URANUS OPPOSITION

Chiron and Uranus opposed each other some 41 times between 1952 and 1989, a feature of these times and one that played a large part in the discovery of Chiron in 1977.

1st Chiron/Uranus opposition—Natal Chart
Feb 22 1952, 4:31 am, BST-1:00
London, 51°N00', 000°W12'
Geocentric Tropical Zodiac
Koch Houses, True Node

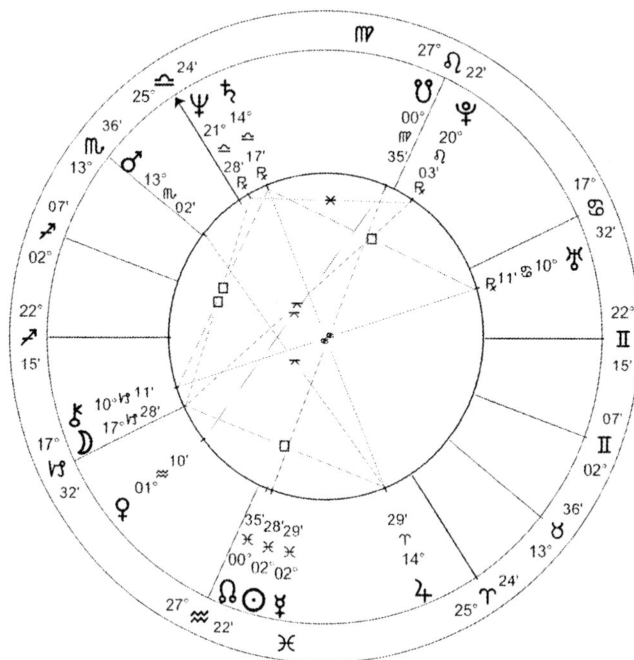

Chart 3 – STAR TREK APPROVED

The approval to go ahead and produce the series, "Star Trek", was, on the surface, not seemingly significant. However, history tells a different story. Behind this series and the later spin-offs and movies lies the eternal quest of Humanity/Gaia to expand its consciousness beyond its present boundaries, to ultimately become a galactic citizen and rejoin with the greater Universe from which all of us were born.

Star Trek—Natal Chart
Feb 15 1966, 10:00 am, PST +8:00
Los Angeles CA USA, 34°N00', 118°W10'
Geocentric Tropical Zodiac
Koch Houses, True Node

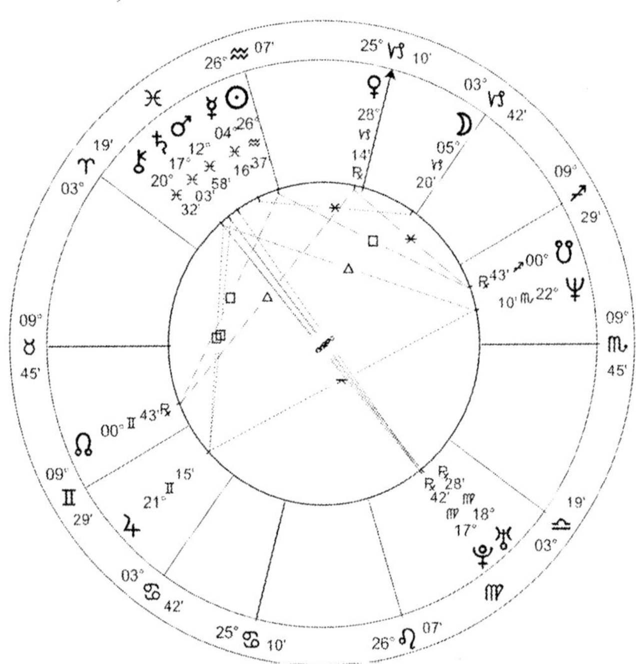

Chart 4 – LAST CHIRON/URANUS OPPOSITION

By the time this last opposition of Chiron and Uranus occurred in the 20th century, Chiron was well and truly established and ready to 'go it alone'. Its themes and messages had been defined to an acceptable degree and its place in the pantheon of planets assured.

Last Chiron/Uranus opposition—Natal Chart
May 18 1989, 6:15 am, PST +8:00
Los Angeles CA USA, 34°N00', 118°W10'
Geocentric Tropical Zodiac
Koch Houses, True Node

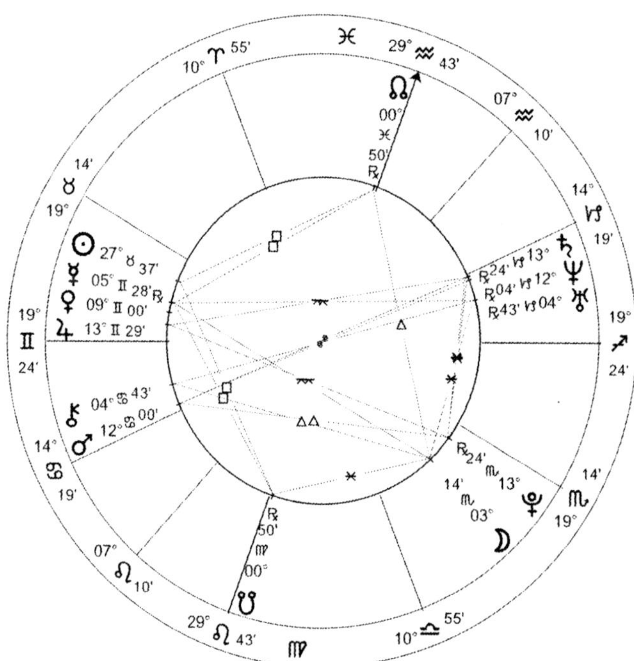

Chart 5 – CHIRON/SATURN OPPOSITION 1989

This opposition represents a parting salute between Chiron and Saturn, Chiron now fully activated as a multi-dimensional bridge between the inner and outer planets.

Chiron opp Saturn 1989—Natal Chart
Jul 12 1989, 2:58 am, BST-1:00
London England, 51°N30', 000°W10'
Geocentric Tropical Zodiac
Koch Houses, True Node

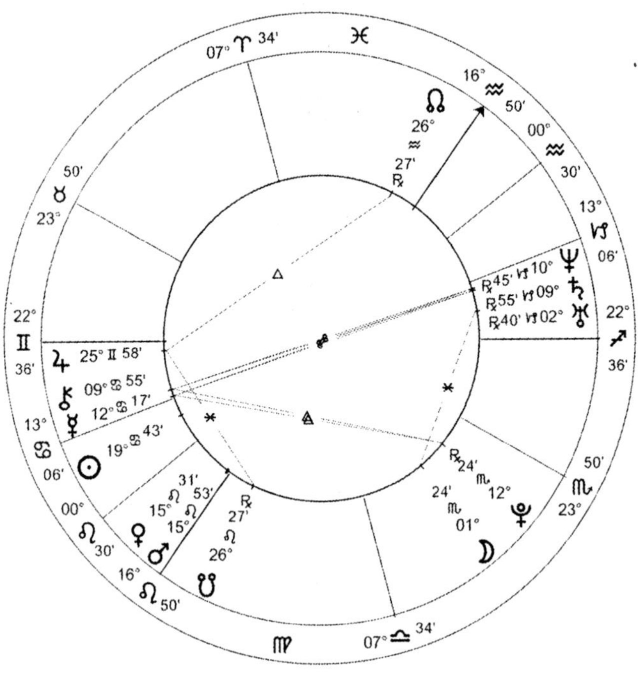

Chart 6 – CHIRON/NEPTUNE OPPOSITION 1989

Chiron and Neptune shake hands, so to speak, Chiron's initiation into the mysteries of conscious planethood complete.

Chiron opp Neptune 1989—Natal Chart
Jul 18 1989, 7:36 pm, BST-1:00
London England, 51°N30', 000°W10'
Geocentric Tropical Zodiac
Koch Houses, True Node

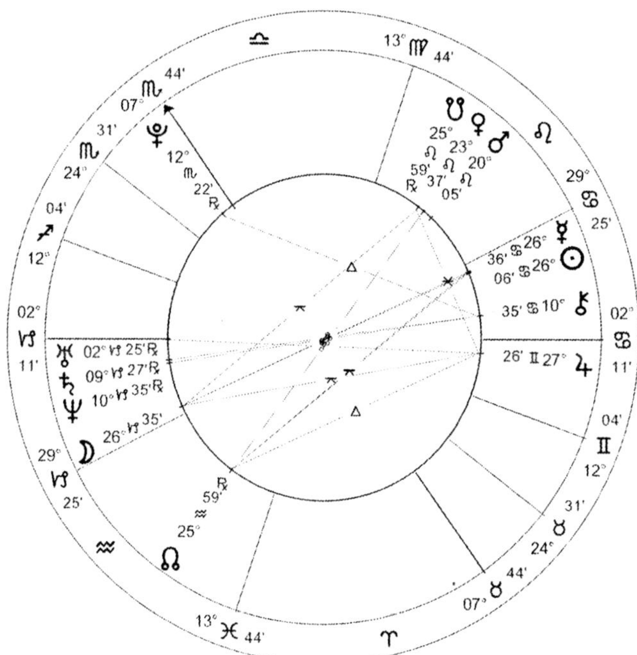

Chart 7 – NOVEMBER 1989

Chiron trines Pluto and Mars. This represents Chiron's final initiation and activation before being left to its own devices, so to speak. Its mission was laid out, its themes and messages defined and its role as a bridge between the inner and outer planets fully in place.

November 1989—Natal Chart
Nov 27 1989, 10:16 am, PST +8:00
Los Angeles CA USA, 34°N00', 118°W10'
Geocentric Tropical Zodiac
Koch Houses, True Node

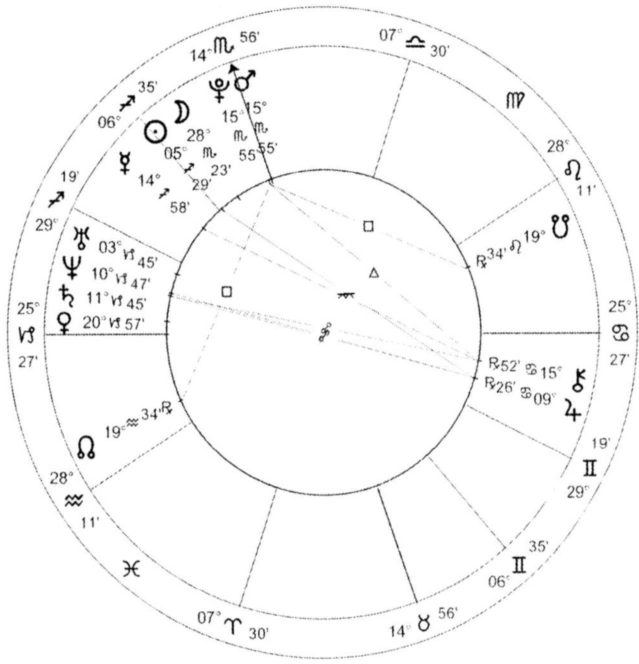

Chart 8 – FIRST MAN IN SPACE

N.B. Exact time of achieving orbit is unknown. The ship landed at 10:55am BAT, an orbit of the Earth took 89.1 minutes, so one may presume that orbit was achieved around 9:26am BAT. Referenced from The New York Times, April 12, 1961.

First man in space—Natal Chart
Apr 12 1961, 9:26 am, BAT-3:00
Moscow > Moskva Russia, 55°N45', 037°E35'
Geocentric Tropical Zodiac
Koch Houses, True Node

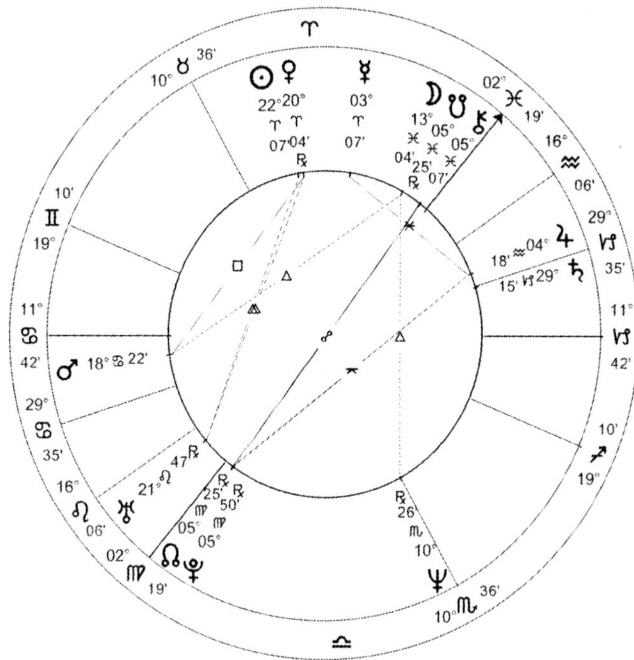

Chart 9 – MAN LANDS ON THE MOON

Referenced from The New York Times, July 21, 1969. Although reported from Houston, the time given is EDT. Man's first step on the Moon occurred at 10:56:20pm on the same day.

For truly accurate charts of these two events, one would have to calculate these charts from a lunar-centric perspective.

Man lands on the Moon—Natal Chart
Jul 21 1969, 4:17:40 pm, CDT +5:00
Houston Texas, 29°N45'47", 095°W21'47"
Geocentric Tropical Zodiac
Koch Houses, True Node

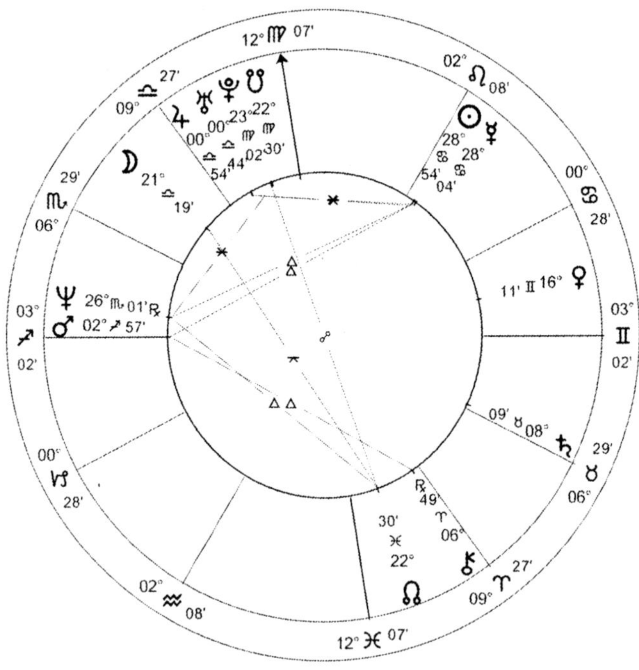

Chart 10 – CHIRON/PLUTO CONJUNCTION 1999

A dramatic start to the new millennium. This augurs revolutionary changes in health, medicine and Healing in general. Some of these ramifications are explored in the chapter, "Miscellany".

Chiron Pluto conjunct 1999—Natal Chart
Dec 30 1999, 10:02 pm, AEDT-11:00
Sydney NSW Australia, 33°S52', 151°E13'
Geocentric Tropical Zodiac
Koch Houses, True Node

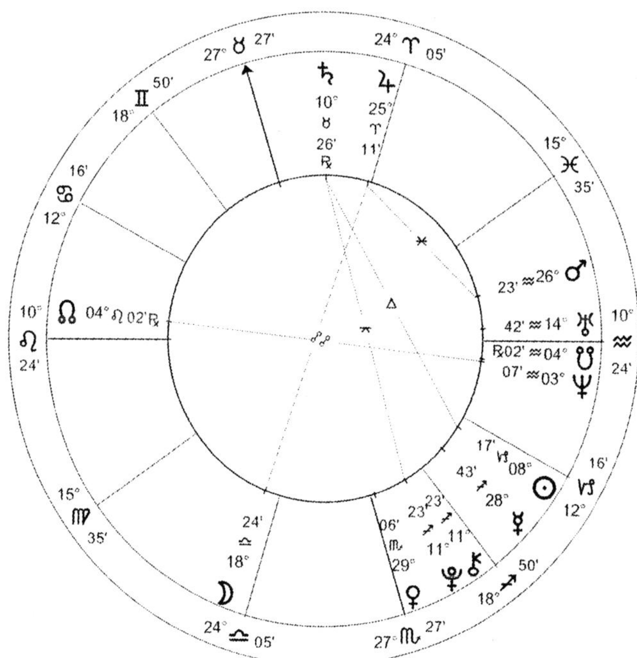

Chart 11 – STAR TREK 1ST EPISODE

The first episode of the original series of Star Trek goes to air.

Star Trek 1st episode airs—Natal Chart
Sep 8 1966, 8:30 pm, PDT +7:00
Los Angeles California, 34°N03'08", 118°W14'34"
Geocentric Tropical Zodiac
Koch Houses, True Node

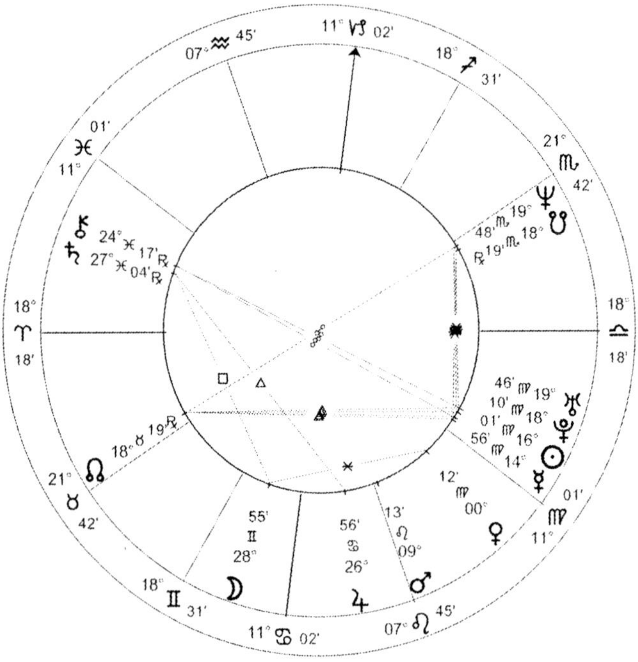

Chart 12 – GENE RODDENBERRY

The creator of Star Trek . . .

Life's path (North Node in Libra) was about finding the balance between self and others in the arena of personal family, community and global family (4th house). Interestingly, his Star Trek character, Spock's, famous saying, "the needs of the many outweigh the needs of the few or the one"[73] was much later contrasted with Captain Kirk's words, "the needs of the one outweighed the needs of the many"[74].

Expressed his life's path through media (TV) and entertainment (3rd house Sun and Mercury in Leo). Wound of low self-worth (Chiron in Aries) and feeling of lack of recognition (in the 10th house) further exacerbated by deep feelings of physical inadequacy and feelings of lack of love (Chiron squaring Pluto and Venus in Cancer in the 1st). His inner self finds expression through fantasizing and creating stories (Leo planets) about the physical meeting (Mars) with higher realms (Neptune), i.e. space travel (Chiron in Aries trine Neptune and Mars).

---

[73] Sherwin, *op cit.*, p.307.

[74] Ibid., p. 133.

Gene Roddenberry—Natal Chart
Aug 19 1921, 1:35 am, MST +7:00
El Paso Texas, 31°N45’31”, 106°W29’11”
Geocentric Tropical Zodiac
Koch Houses, True Node

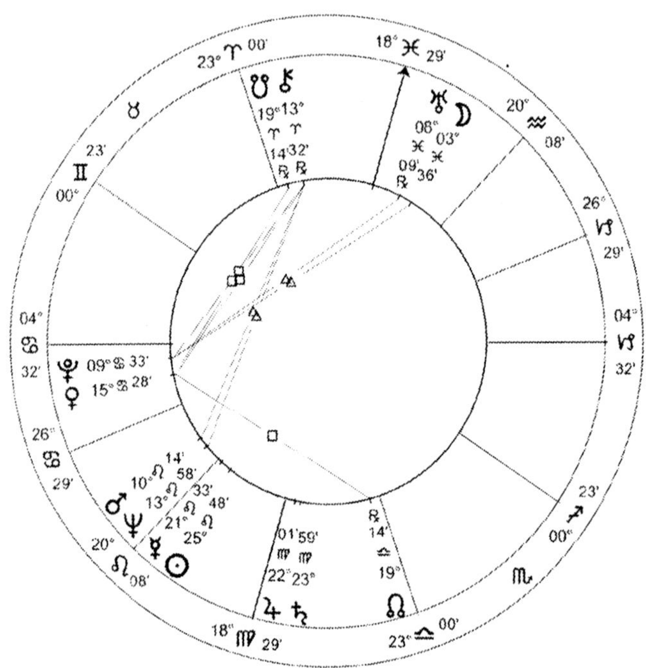

Chart 13 – CLOSE ENCOUNTERS

Classic science-fiction film.

Close Encounters—Natal Chart
Nov 16 1977, 8:00 pm, EDT +4:00
New York New York, 40°N42'51", 074°W00'23"
Geocentric Tropical Zodiac
Koch Houses, True Node

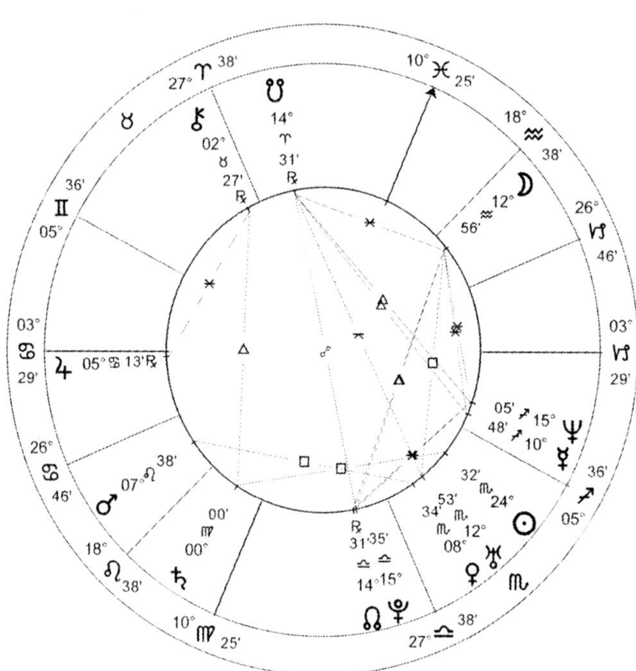

Chart 14 – ET

Another classic science-fiction film. Note the *yod* planetary pattern of Chiron in Taurus with Jupiter and Neptune.

ET—Natal Chart
Jun 13 1982, 8:00 pm, EDT +4:00
New York New York, 40°N42'51", 074°W00'23"
Geocentric Tropical Zodiac
Koch Houses, True Node

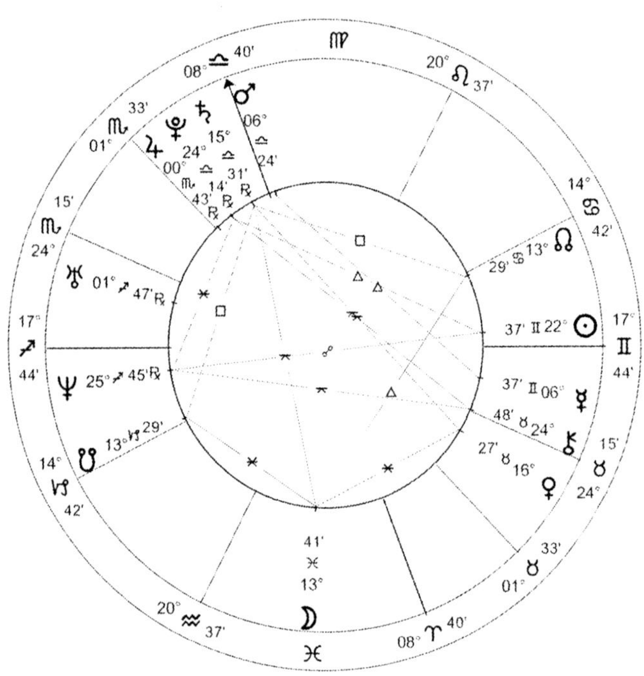

Chart 15 – GHOSTBUSTERS

A seemingly-innocuous and flippant film with deeper ramifications and underlying themes.

Ghostbusters—Natal Chart
Jun 8 1984, 8:00 pm, EDT +4:00
New York New York, 40°N42'51", 074°W00'23"
Geocentric Tropical Zodiac
Koch Houses, True Node

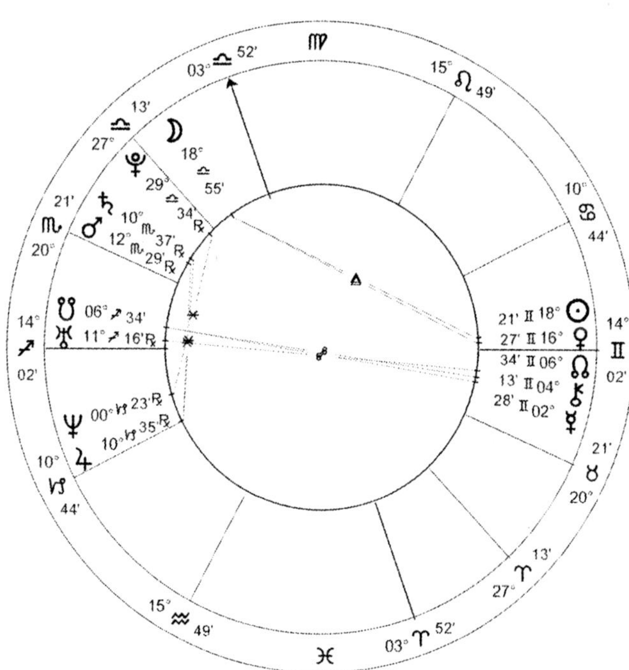

Chart 16 – DEAD POETS SOCIETY

A classic film with obvious Chironic themes.
Dead Poets Society—Natal Chart
Jun 2 1989, 8:00 pm, EDT +4:00
New York New York, 40°N42'51", 074°W00'23"
Geocentric Tropical Zodiac
Koch Houses, True Node

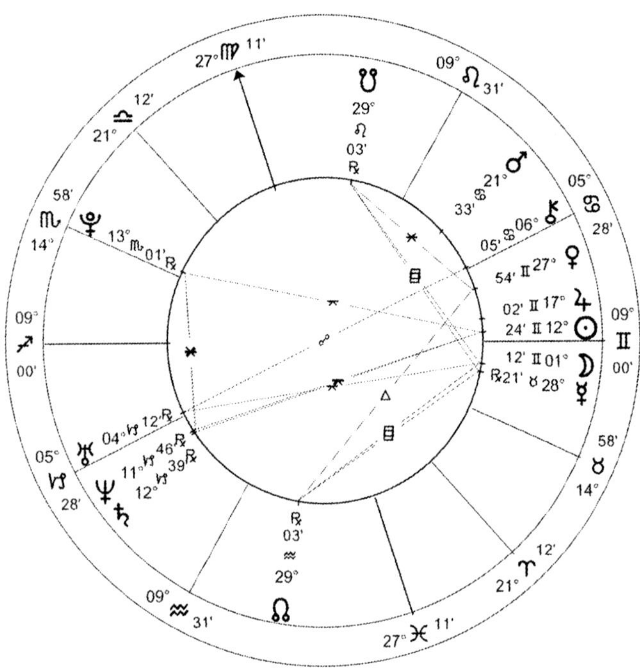

Chart 17 – THE BERLIN WALL

Early manifestation of the Chiron/Pluto oppositions of the 1960s.

Berlin wall—Natal Chart
Aug 13 1961, 2:30 am, EET-2:00
Berlin, 52°N30', 013°E30'
Geocentric Tropical Zodiac
Koch Houses, True Node

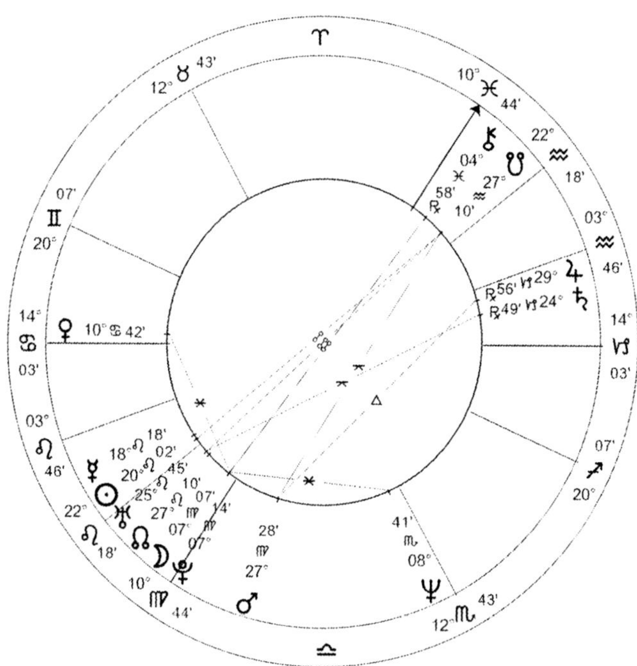

Chart 18 – BERLIN RIOTS

Chiron-opposition-Pluto in full swing in the 1960s.

Berlin riots re: wall—Natal Chart
Aug 15 1962, 11:00 am, GMT +0:00
Sydney, 33°S52', 151°E13'
Geocentric Tropical Zodiac
Solar Sign Houses, True Node

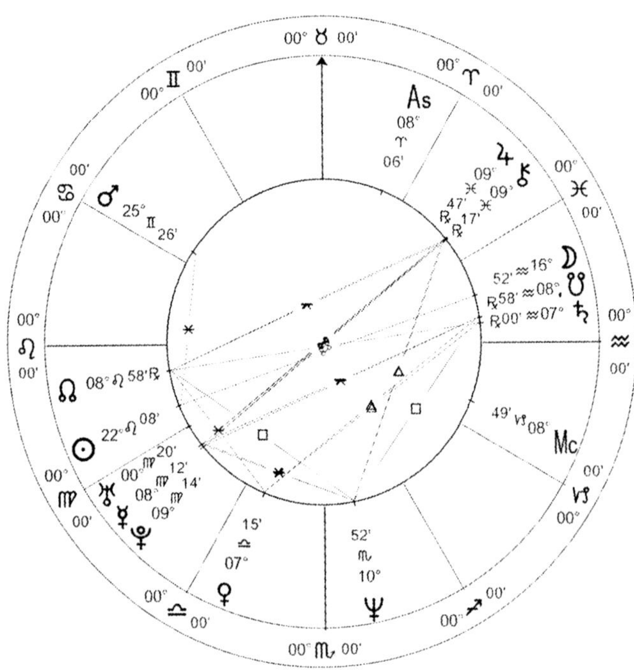

Chart 19 – CUBAN MISSILE CRISIS

More turmoil from the 1960s.

Cuban missile crises—Natal Chart
Oct 22 1962, 11:00 am, EST +5:00
Washington, 38°N53', 077°W37'
Geocentric Tropical Zodiac
Solar Sign Houses, True Node

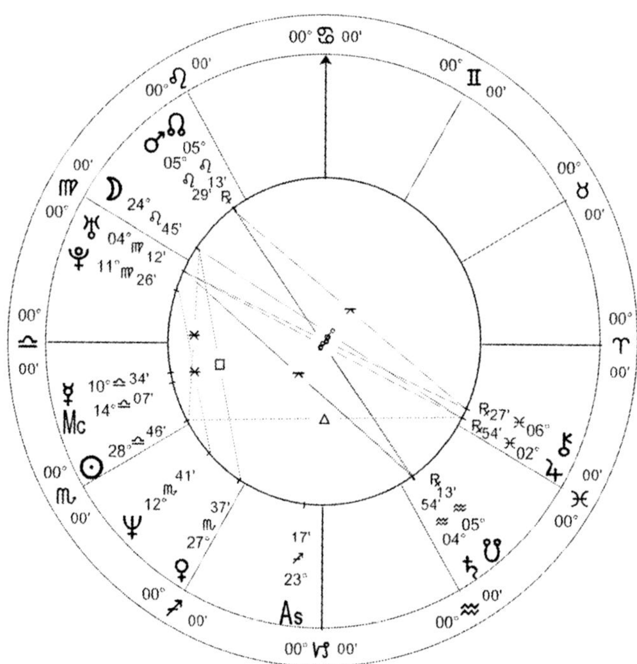

Chart 20 – BEATLES 1ST SINGLE

Here is the extraordinary planetary pattern that started and defined the cultural revolution of the 1960s. Notice Chiron's placement with Jupiter at the root of the kite planetary pattern.

Beatles record 1st single—Natal Chart
Sep 4 1962, 12:00 pm, BST-1:00
Liverpool England, 53°N25', 002°W55'
Geocentric Tropical Zodiac
Koch Houses, True Node

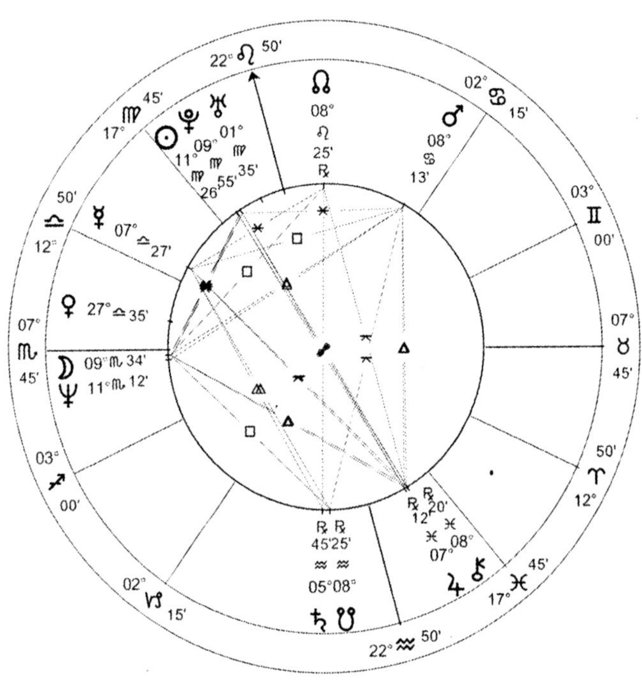

Chart 21 – WOODSTOCK

A cultural baring of Wounds (and other things!). The Wounds of Humanity were expressed through music, art and the hippie culture during the 1960s.

Woodstock opening—Natal Chart
Aug 15 1969, 5:07 pm, EDT +4:00
Bethel New York, 41°N41', 074°W52'18"
Geocentric Tropical Zodiac
Koch Houses, True Node

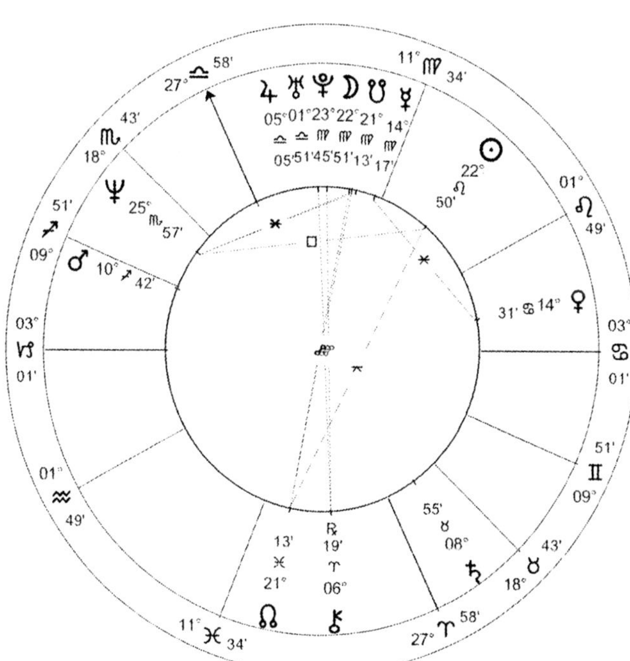

CHART 22 – EICHMANN SENTENCED

Wounds of WWII illuminated.

Adolf Eichmann sentenced—Natal Chart
Dec 12 1961, 11:00 am, GMT +0:00
London, 51°N00', 000°W12'
Geocentric Tropical Zodiac
Solar Sign Houses, True Node

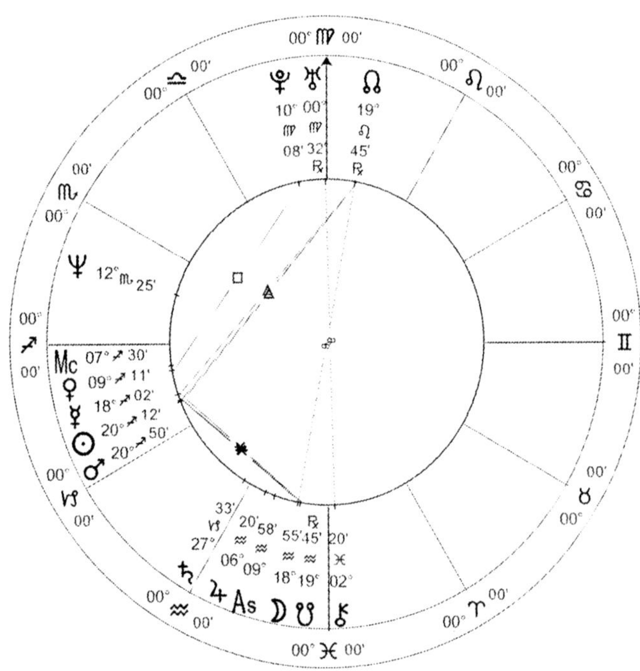

CHART 23 – EICHMANN HANGED

Wounds of WWII further illuminated.

Eichmann hanged—Natal Chart
May 31 1962, 11:00 am, CET-1:00
Israel, 32°N06', 034°E46'
Geocentric Tropical Zodiac
Solar Sign Houses, True Node

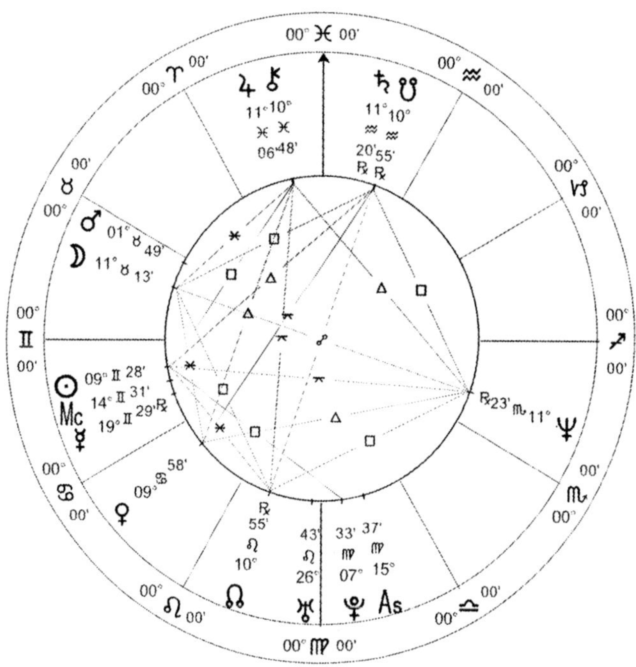

CHART 24 – JOHN F KENNEDY

Kennedy was an icon of the 1960s and a hero of the USA as a nation. Notice Chiron's placement and its indication of charisma and empathy. Kennedy represented and championed the Woundedness of the collective consciousness.

John Fitzgerald Kennedy—Natal Chart
May 29 1917, 3:00 pm, +5:00
Brookline Massachusetts, 42°N19'54", 071°W07'18"
Geocentric Tropical Zodiac
Koch Houses, True Node

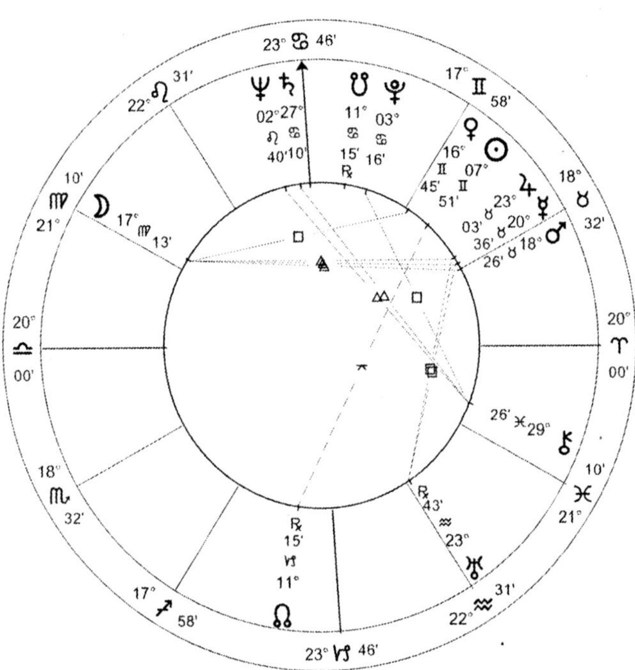

CHART 25 – JFK ELECTED

Destiny at work.

Kennedy elected—Natal Chart
Nov 9 1960, 6:00 pm, EST +5:00
Washington, 38°N51', 077°W02'
Geocentric Tropical Zodiac
Koch Houses, True Node

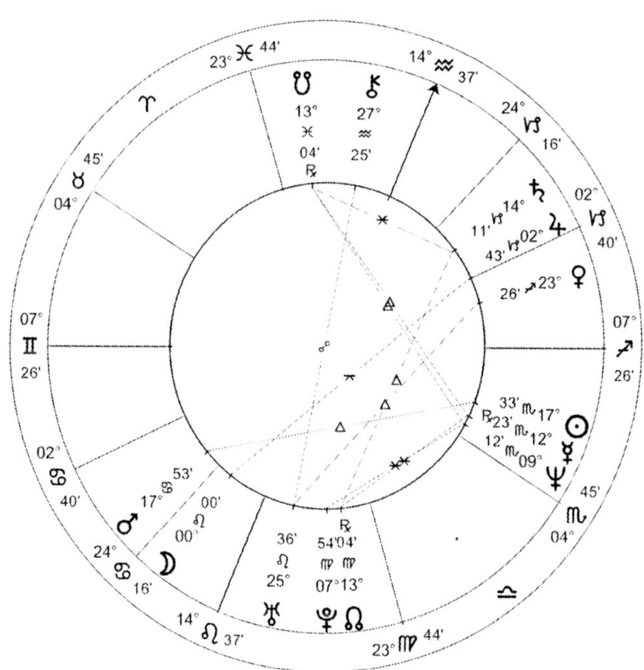

CHART 26 – JFK ASSASSINATED

N.B. Time of assassination is quoted in The New York Times as 12:30pm Central Standard Time. The time of death is disputed. However, the bullet went right through the skull, so it is presumed that death was instantaneous.

Kennedy assassination—Natal Chart
Nov 22 1963, 12:30 pm, CST +6:00
Dallas, 32°N58', 096°W50'
Geocentric Tropical Zodiac
Koch Houses, True Node

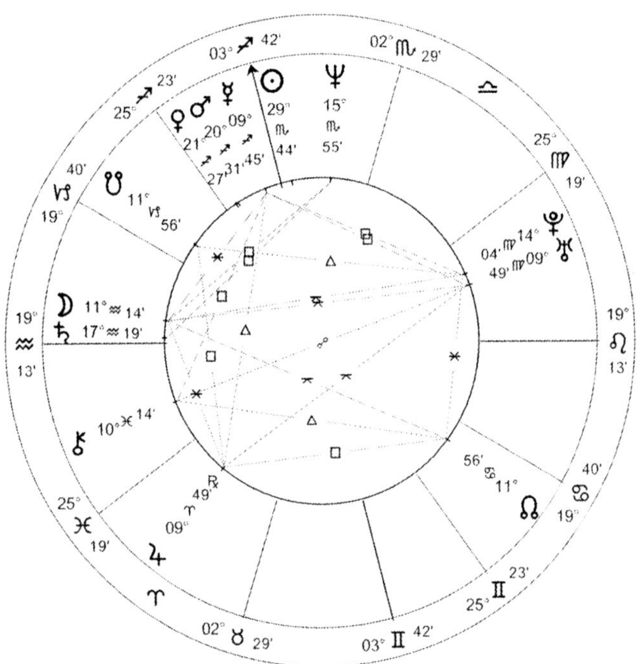

CHART 27 – MARTIN LUTHER KING JNR.

Another champion of the Woundedness of the collective consciousness, this time expressed through the theme of black civil rights.

Martin Luther King—Natal Chart
Jan 15 1929, 0:00 am, CST +6:00
Atlanta Ga, 33°N45', 084°W23'
Geocentric Tropical Zodiac
Koch Houses, True Node

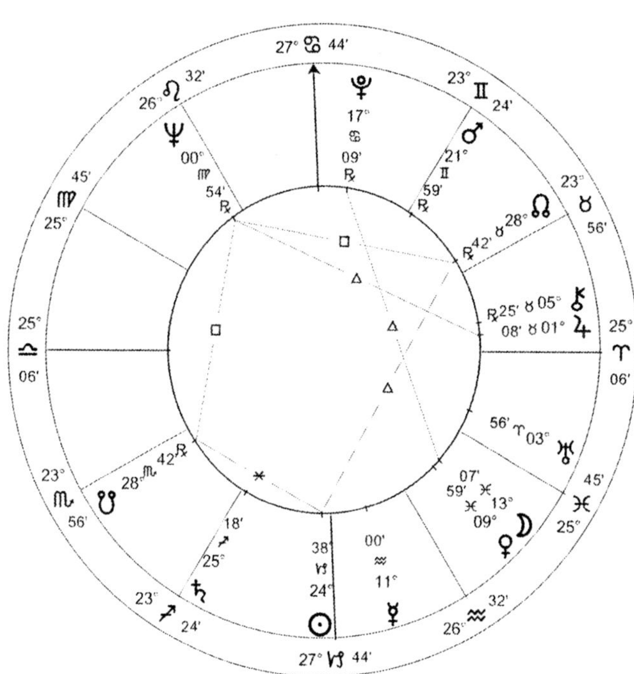

CHART 28 – MARTIN LUTHER KING JNR. KILLED

N.B. Chart drawn based on time of shooting. Time of death was officially quoted as 7:05pm CST.

Again, the Wounds of the collective consciousness are brought into question.

Martin Luther King killed—Natal Chart
Apr 4 1968, 6:00 pm, CST +6:00
Memphis TN USA, 35°N08', 090°W03'
Geocentric Tropical Zodiac
Koch Houses, True Node

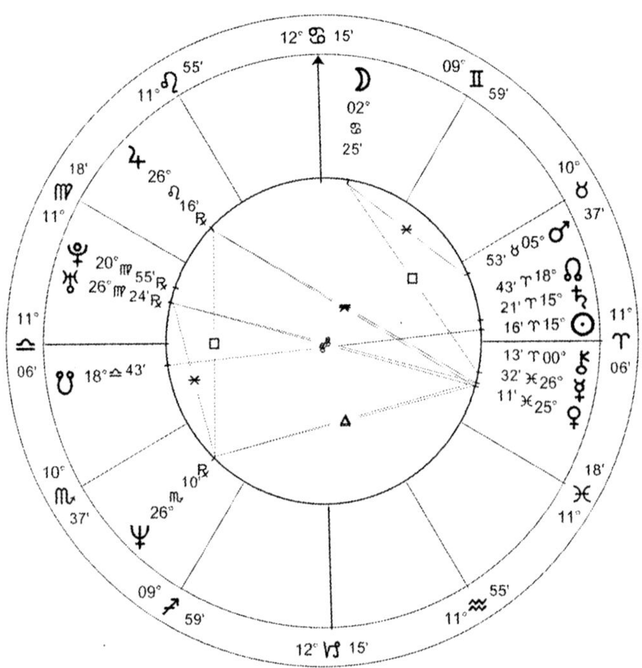

Chart 29 – MILLY

Milly is a pseudonym for the natal chart we have chosen to delineate in Chapter 11. *(See page 518.)*

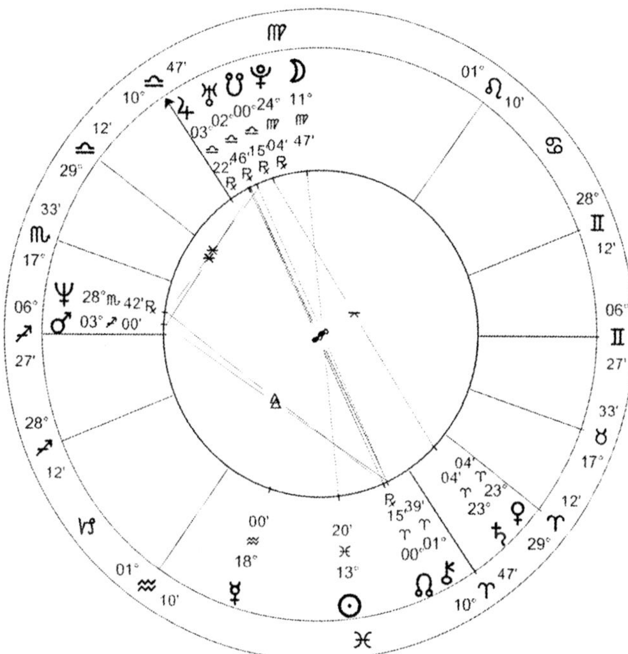

Chart 30 – RICKIE HILDER

Australian Aura-Soma Color Therapy practitioner, Healer, singer/entertainer, writer, numerologist and conscious (not trance) channeler.

She has worked consciously with Chiron energy for many years. Her work is concerned with 'connecting' people, places and things and facilitating peoples' next steps in their growth, evolution and Healing. Also works with children.

Note that she not only has Chiron-conjunct-Sun sextiling both outer planets Uranus and Neptune, but she has Chiron-parallel-Mercury. She is certainly a messenger of Chiron.

A channeling of Chiron by Rickie can be found on p. 177.

Rickie Hilder—Natal Chart
Jul 13 1940, 8:00 am, AEST-10:00
Sydney, 33°S52', 151°E13'
Geocentric Tropical Zodiac
Koch Houses, True Node

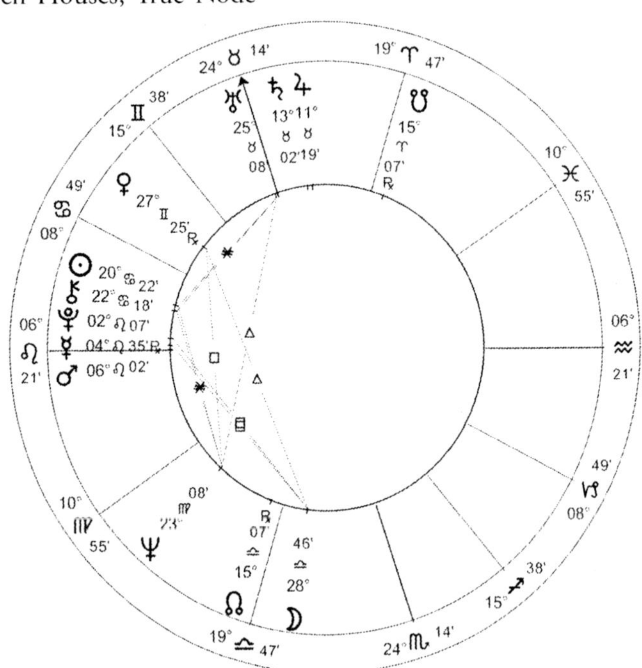

Chart 31 – CHIRONIC DREAM

Sun's daylight consciousness in Cancer in 2nd house is challenged by 8th house Uranian and Neptunian consciousness. Chiron sends messages through conjunct Mercury in the 3rd house (conjuncting native's natal Uranus – see Chart 31a). Pluto trining Venus in Cancer (native's Venus Return – Chart 31a) inspires a new paradigm concerning the juxtaposition of earthly love and Divine Love. The native's rebirth of the feminine side, experienced in the dream state, certainly reflects this.

Chironic Dream—Natal Chart
Jul 8 1992, 4:00 am, AEST-10:00
Sydney Australia, 33°S52', 151°E13'
Geocentric Tropical Zodiac
Koch Houses, True Node

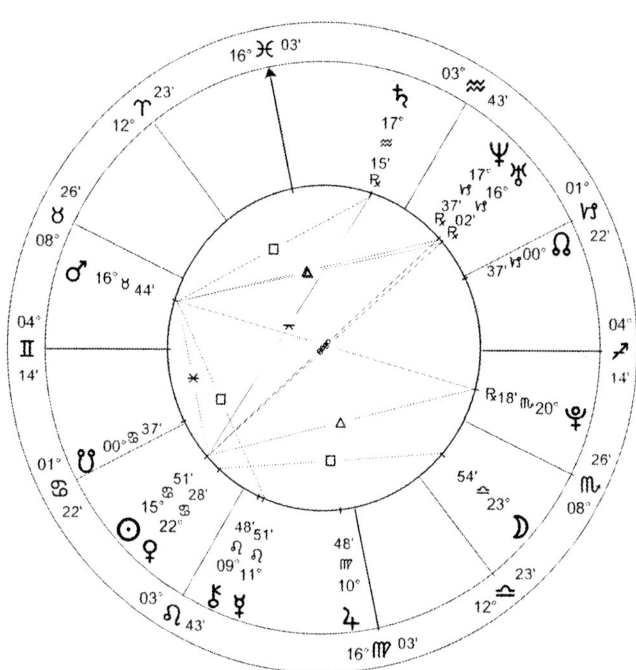

Chart 31a – CHIRONIC DREAM (cont.)

Chiron-conjunct-Mercury transiting natal Uranus awakens native to Chiron's messages. Moon-square-Venus blocks outward expression, but Moon transiting natal North Node-conjunct-Jupiter indicates destiny at work. (The Moon is Chiron's exterior face and relates to the lower emotional nature and dream states.)

INNER WHEEL	OUTER WHEEL
Martin Lass - Natal Chart	Chironic Dream - Natal Chart
Aug 6 1958, 8:33 pm, CST +6:00	Jul 8 1992, 4:00 am, AEST -10:00
Chicago USA, 42°N06', 087°W44'	Sydney Australia, 33°S52', 151°E13'
Geocentric Tropical Zodiac	Geocentric Tropical Zodiac
Koch Houses, True Node	Koch Houses, True Node

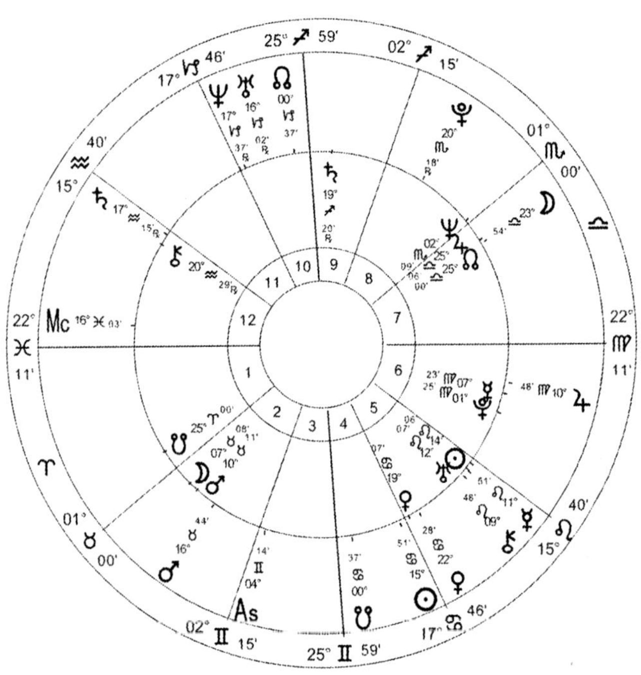

Chart 32 – PAST LIVES REVEALED

A cathartic experience involving the recall of past lives . . .

Note Chiron's exact conjunction of natal Uranus: the Wounds of past lives come through the higher gateway of Uranian understanding. Also note Venus's exact conjunction of natal Sun: the 'remembered' past lives related to the loss of a loved one.

Chiron's message, as always, is to bring the Wound into the Light, thereby giving the opportunity for Healing through higher understanding of the initial event or circumstance.

Neptune, Uranus and Node transiting 10th house indicate the destiny of this experience as a catalyst for bringing Chiron's messages to the world.

INNER WHEEL
Martin Lass - Natal Chart
Aug 6 1958, 8:33 pm, CST +6:00
Chicago USA, 42°N06', 087°W44'
Geocentric Tropical Zodiac
Koch Houses, True Node

OUTER WHEEL
26 July 1992 - Natal Chart
Jul 26 1992, 11:00 am, AEST -10:00
Townsville Australia, 19°S16', 146°E48'
Geocentric Tropical Zodiac
Koch Houses, True Node

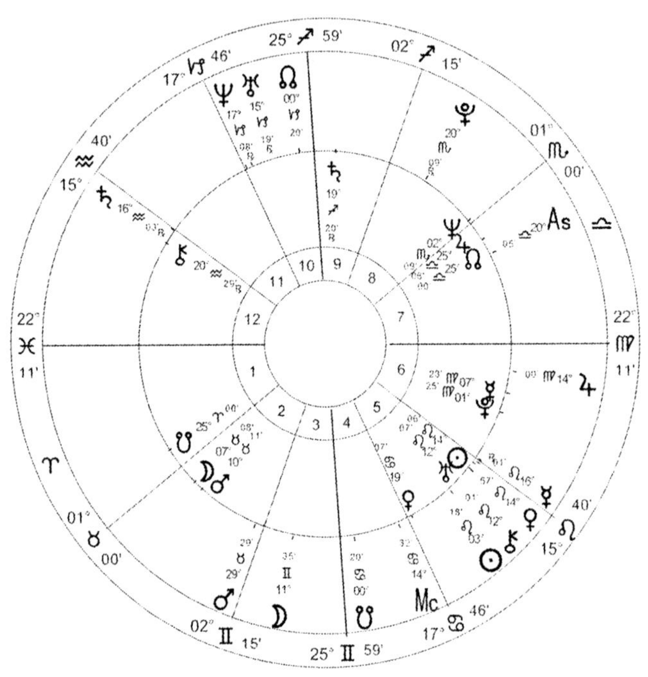

Chart 33 – MARTIN LASS

The author's natal chart. Chiron in Aquarius feels entirely distant from Contact. Chiron in the 12th house requires non-rational leap of consciousness in order to access and Heal Wounds. Mystical bent. Chiron's loose opposition to Sun in the 5th house in Leo gives the challenge of expressing the messages of Chiron. The *yod* between Chiron, Saturn and Venus impels a new perspective on love, being loved and giving love. Saturn says take responsibility for loving self, Chiron says love is all around you. Note parallel of Venus and Pluto and contra-parallel of Venus and Saturn, further amplifying the lessons of Love, via Venus. Note Libran Node-conjunct-Jupiter in the 7th house . . . life of seeking balance, revealing harmony and returning to child-like Trust in the Universe, ultimately Returning to the soul-mate through the Inner Child. Note Jupiter parallel with Chiron, further emphasizing the Healing journey of the Inner Child. Sun-conjunct-Uranus in Leo in the 5th house: unconventional self-expression and creativity, technological bent. Sun-conjunct-Uranus square Moon-conjunct-Mars in Taurus: Braking factor, ensuring that feet remain on the ground while Wounds are Healed and balance sought.

Martin Lass—Natal Chart
Aug 6 1958, 8:33 pm, CST +6:00
Chicago USA, 42°N06', 087°W44'
Geocentric Tropical Zodiac
Koch Houses, True Node

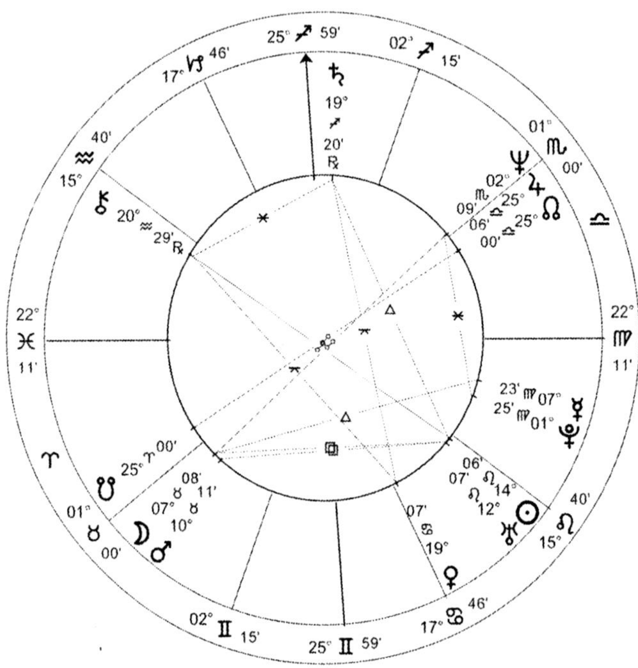

Chart 34 – ZANE STEIN

One of the first and most renowned of the Chiron astrologers. He has an extensive website dedicated to Chiron and the other Centaur planetesimals.

The website URL is *http://www.geocities.com/SoHo/7969/chiron.htm*.

Zane Stein—Natal Chart
Jun 18 1951, 0:43:17 am, EDT +4:00
Germantown Pennsylvania, 40°N02'36", 075°W10'50"
Geocentric Tropical Zodiac
Koch Houses, True Node

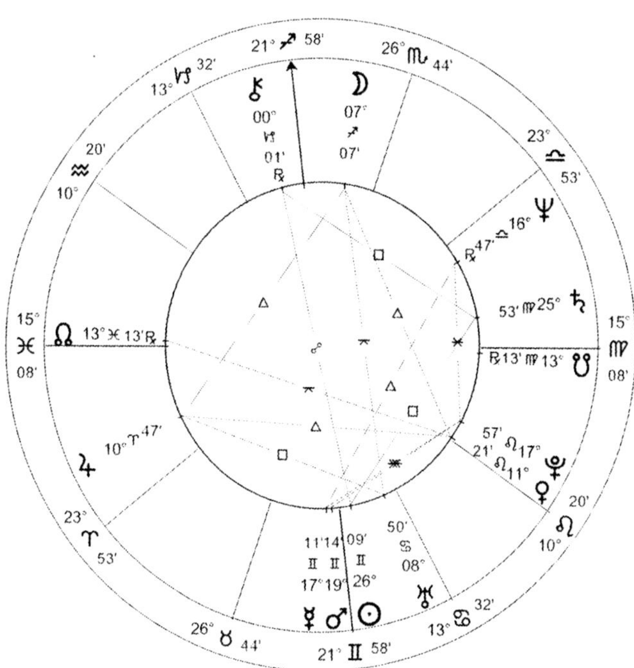

APPENDIX B ~ MISCELLANEOUS GRAPHS

GRAPH 1—CHIRON CYCLE

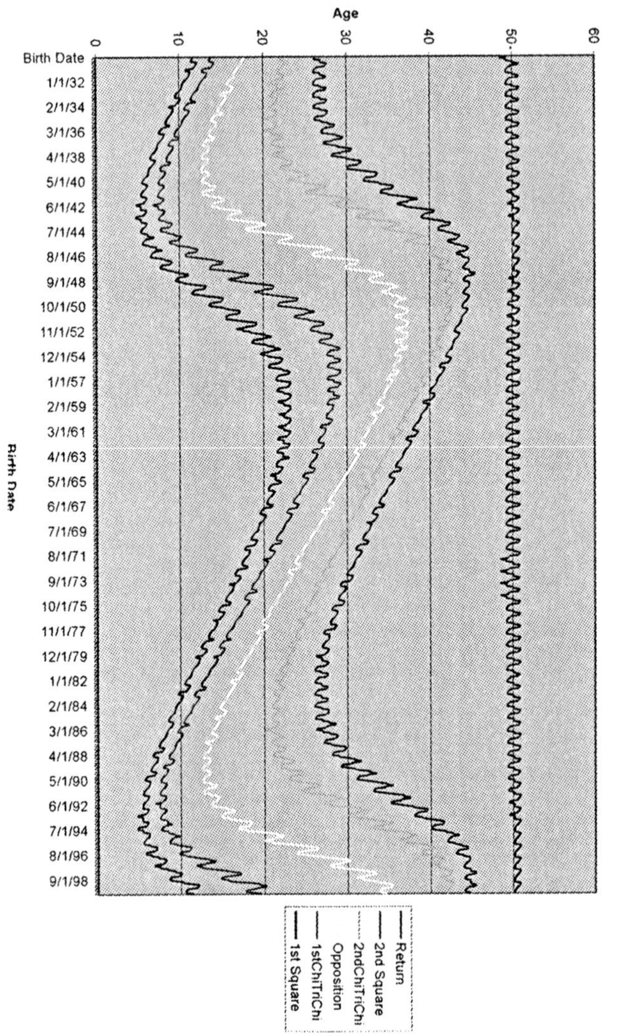

GRAPH 2 – CHIRON CYCLE MAJOR ASPECTS (HISTORICAL)

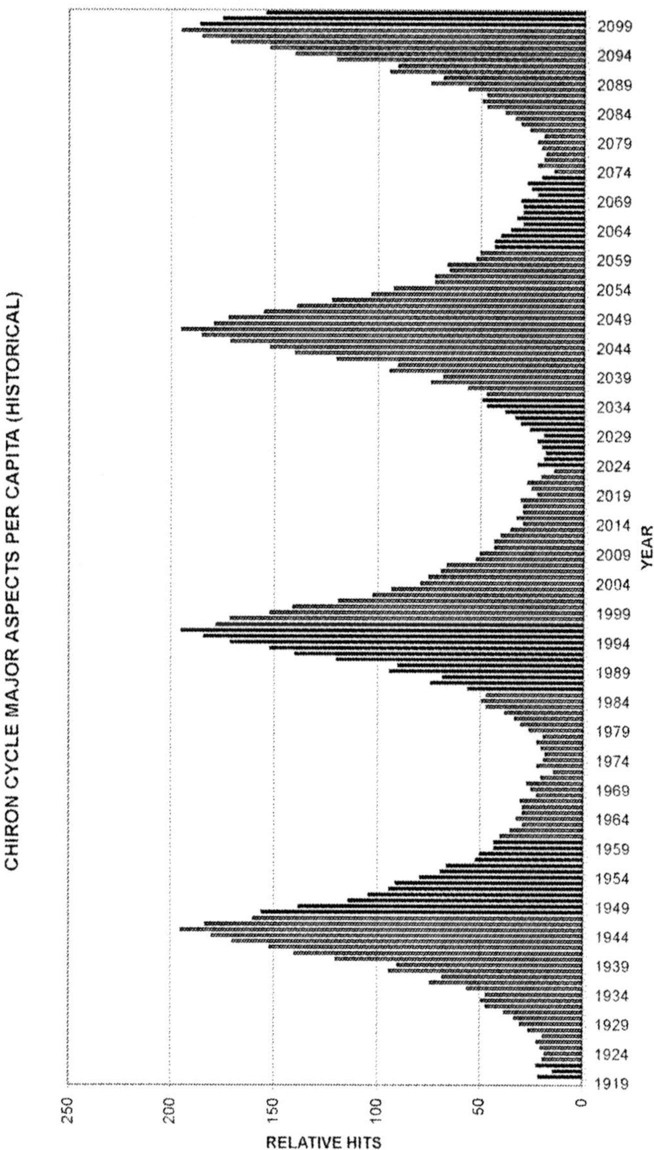

GRAPH 3 – NEPTUNE CONJUNCT NATAL CHIRON (1947–48)

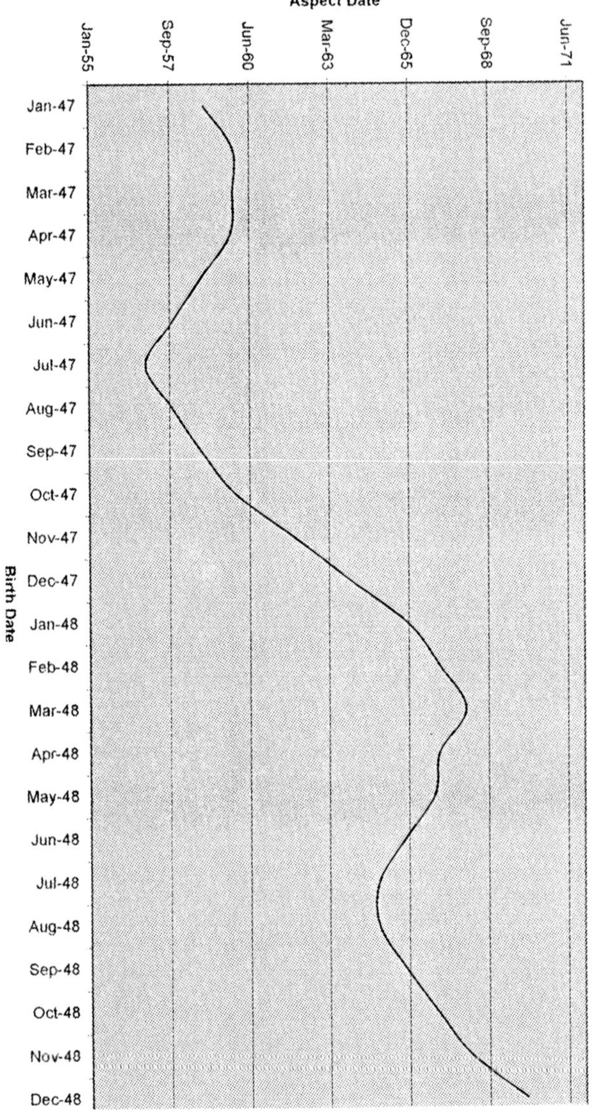

APPENDIX C ~ AFFAIRS OF THE SIGNS

Aries

"I am." Sense of self, individuality, initiative, energy. Affairs of self, physical body, movement, beginnings. Assertive, bold, courageous, decisive, direct, fiery, independent, individual, initiating, pioneering, self-oriented, energetic, self-reliant, single-minded. Can be aggressive, egotistical, failing to complete tasks, impulsive, insensitive, impatient, lacking in persistence, lacking in subtlety, needing to be liked, selfish, volatile.

Higher octave expression: Presence.

Taurus

"I have." Sense of security, abundance, stability, solidity, warmth. Material affairs, affairs of personal finance, long-term planning, the physical arts, comforts, emotional attachments. Stable, acquisitive, determined, earthy, enduring, gentle giant, reliable, steadfast, strong desires, strong values, unyielding. Can be boring, overly possessive, self-indulgent, slow to anger but devastating when pushed to the point, stick-in-the-mud, stubborn, stuck.

Higher octave expression: Unconditional Love.

Gemini

"I know". Sense of knowledge, communication, play, lightness. Affairs of the mind, communication, knowledge, humor, siblings. Agile, airy, communicative, creative, flowing, light-hearted, inquisitive, interested, mentally fertile, versatile, multi-tasking, talkative. Can be changeable, chameleonesque, fickle, flighty, inconsistent, restless, inattentive, scattered, superficial, volatile.

Higher octave expression: Knowledge.

Cancer

"I care." Sense of being looked after and of looking after. Affairs of mothering, nurturing, caring, family, earthly love, ecology. Emotional, nurturing, protective, steadfast, strong roots, sweet, tenacious, watery. Can be clinging, co-dependent, emotionally draining, depressive, lunatic, overly protective, reclusive, timid, uncommunicative.

Higher octave expression: Mothering, the Goddess.

Leo

"I express." Sense of singing, shining, celebration, being seen, being the center. Affairs of creativity, ego, self-expression, children, leadership. Creative, dramatic, generous, magnanimous, powerful leader, self-confident, warm-hearted. Can be arrogant, cruel, extravagant, insensitive, overbearing, selfish, self-centered, self-obsessed, overly proud, vain.

Higher octave expression: Light, Shining.

Virgo

"I work." Sense of progress, Healing, discernment, exactitude, purity. Affairs of work, methodology, Healing, service, details, purity, synthesis. Contained, cautious, discriminating, hard working, health conscious, meticulous, methodical, organized, practical, pragmatic, pure, understated. Can be anal, compulsive, critical, cynical, nagging, obsessive, perfectionistic, petty, sarcastic. Alternately, can be hedonistic, bohemian, lazy, messy, scattered, disorganized, excessive.

Higher octave expression: Healing.

Libra

"We are." "I long." Sense of companionship, partnership, relationship, balance, grace, equity. Affairs of the heart, companionship, relationship, society, social justice, balance, arts, beauty, grace. Altruistic, artistic, balancing, diplomatic, friendly, graceful, even-handed, harmonious, strong sense of fairness. Can be appeasing, give away own power, over-compromising, incapable of working or being alone, indecisive, judgmental, prone to breakdown and inner turmoil, self-sacrificing.

Higher octave expression: Soul-mates.

Scorpio

"I transform." Sense of inner knowing, mystery, sexuality, secretness, intensity, focus. Affairs of spirit, sexuality, birth and death, rebirth, creation and destruction, transformation, secret knowledge, joint material affairs, taxes. Confronting, focused, intense, magnetic, persistent, penetrating, perceptive, single-minded, wishing to get to the essence of a given matter, zealous. Can be back-stabbing, controlling, destructive, dishonest, gossiping, jealous, manipulative, overly dramatic, secretive, vengeful.

Higher octave expression: Creation/Maintenance/Destruction, i.e. the *cosmogonic cycle.*

Sagittarius

"I understand." Sense of knowing, joy, celebration, expansion, optimism, philosophy, adventure. Affairs of knowledge, wisdom, education, travel, the outdoors, morality, ethics, religion, philosophy. Adventurous, confident, encouraging, enthusiastic, goal-seeking, inspiring, motivational, optimistic, truthful, visionary. Can be fanatical, judgmental, naïvely optimistic, obsessive, reckless, proselytizing, tactless, unrestrained.

Higher octave expression: Wisdom, Truth.

Capricorn

"I control." "I build." Sense of structure, organization, solidity, tangibility, seriousness, discipline, control. Affairs of vocation, public image, status, accolade, business, government, responsibility, planning, organization. Achieving, ambitious, conscientious, disciplined, industrious, organized, responsible, reliable, practical, serious. Can be callous, controlling, dull, heartless, lacking in vision, materialistic, overly conventional, pessimistic, rigid, seeking status and station at all costs, uninspired.

Higher octave expression: Fathering.

Aquarius

"We express." "I transcend." Sense of community, culture, society, belonging, togetherness, the bigger picture. Affairs of community, culture, society, Humanity, collectives, group expression, radicals, revolution, revelation, ecology, invention, innovation, technology, genius, seeing the big picture, the new age. Affable, egalitarian, environmentally aware, friendly, group conscious, humanitarian, idealistic, innovative, progressive, serving others. Can be aloof, contrary, eccentric, emotionally superficial, overly extroverted, perverse, rebellious, stubborn.

Higher octave expression: Belonging, seeing the Big Picture.

Pisces

"We merge." "I feel." Sense of empathy, connectedness, Oneness, emotion, sensitivity, the psyche. Affairs of the psyche, the unconscious, the intuitive, the psychic, mysticism, religion, institutions, victims. Compassionate, empathic, gentle, intuitive, sensitive, self-sacrificing, supportive, sweet, sympathetic, understanding, watery. Can be blaming, gullible, escapist, hyper-sensitive, impractical, indecisive, rough diamond, play the victim, poor me, sour, sleazy, vague.

Higher octave expression: Oneness.

APPENDIX D ~ AFFAIRS OF THE HOUSES

1st House

Identity, personality, how we see ourselves, how others see us, the physical (body), new beginnings, early life.

2nd House

Resources, possessions, money, self-esteem, self-worth, values, safety, security, emotional attachments.

3rd House

Communication, the mind, early learning, siblings, knowledge (not necessarily with understanding), short journeys, immediate environment, the media.

4th House

Home, family (particularly the mother), family of community, nature, the Earth, roots, private life, heritage, emotional patterns.

5th House

Creativity, arts, recreation, entertainment, fertility, children, self-expression, lovers, romance, self-fulfillment.

6th House

Work, day-to-day life, Healing, service, habits, small animals, skills, pets and animals.

7th House

Partnerships, relationship, social justice and equality, marriage, the arts (to a small degree).

8th House

Regeneration, birth and death, sex, legal matters, taxes, personal transformation, metaphysics, the esoteric, life after death, support from others, joint resources.

9th House

Higher learning, philosophy, ethics, morals, religion, travel, law, sport, other cultures, publishing, the Way (spiritual).

10th House

Public life, career/profession, business, government, status and standing (in community), parenting, the father, authority, the military, achievement, outward expression of inner calling.

11th House

Groups, group friendships, extended family, acquaintances, networking, hopes and dreams, organizations, welfare, collective expression (culture).

12th house

The psyche, collective unconscious, spirituality, mysticism, cults, past lives, service to Humanity, endings, institutions (psychiatric, hospitals, jails, libraries, military, etcetera), hidden strengths and weakness, secret enemies, self-undoing, karma.

GLOSSARY

Divine Design. The divine blueprint of our lives. Our special calling or mission. Our unique Service to the Creation. The thing we would most Love to do with our lives when we have Loved ourselves and our lives exactly as they are.

Gift in the Wound, The. The miraculous and perfect journey of our lives, leading to our Divine Design and expressing the Suchness of Omnipresent Love.

Grand Unified Theory (GUT) or Theory of Everything. A theory sought by modern science that would bring together all the observable laws of the cosmos into a unified picture, mathematically and scientifically coherent and explaining everything in its most simplified form.

Healing, The. Our journey of consciousness towards Truth, Oneness and Love. Our journey Home to Spirit.

Healing. Physical, emotional, mental and spiritual healing, taken in its broadest sense, beyond mere medical boundaries. The process of integration, unification, merging, individuation, 'wholing', balancing, synthesis, awakening, revealing Truth, raising consciousness, evolving, growing, coming closer to Love and Oneness.

Hermetic. Referring to Hermes and the sacred teachings passed down through the Egyptian Mystery traditions, whether Greek, Latin, Coptic, Gnostic or Renaissance in manifestation. However, the origin of the teachings pre-dates Egypt by thousands of years, ostensibly all the way back to the mythical Atlantis, the time of the Avatars. Pertaining to the Mysteries.

Higher Mind. See Higher Self.

Higher Self. Also known as the Higher Mind. Our consciousness, lying between the Soul and the lower nature (also known as the lower mind), partially awakened to Truth, Oneness and Love. The part of us we call "me" in enlightened moments, that is *relatively* wise and knowing. The part of us that cycles through incarnations, seeking to grow, Heal and evolve. The vehicle of its physical expression is the voluntary nervous system. Its home is in the Heart.

Holographic. The smallest part reflects and contains the whole.

Issues. Our perceptions of events, circumstances and situations, often involving other people, that have thrown us off-center from a place of inner (and hence, outer) balance.

Koan. A paradoxical question that seeks to bring our consciousness into a higher quantum state, resolving all seeming opposites and contradictions into a higher understanding (metadox), closer to Truth and Love.

Lower mind. See Lower nature.

Lower nature. Also known as the lower mind. Lower self. Our animal nature that seeks pleasure and runs from pain, that protects our physical body. Summated in the autonomic nervous system. Its heart is in the solar plexus. Also, our manifested dualistic nature, personality, emotions, masks, personas, charges, judgments, lies, illusions, half-truths. Charged, ionic, fermionic, polarized, kinetic, reactive, semi-conscious in nature. The part of us that we call "me" in unenlightened moments of charge, bias, judgment and blame.

Mysteries, The. Sacred and esoteric Teachings passed down from the Avatars of the Mother Culture that is known today as Atlantis. The Mysteries were passed down through the Egyptian Mystery schools and through the Hermetic teachings of the early centuries AD.

Non-local. Connected beyond normal time and space as we know it. Action at a distance.

Rainbow Bridge. A metaphoric and metaphysical device for bringing our fragmented and Wounded consciousness (the many colors of the material Creation) back into unity, balance, Light and Love (the white Light of Spirit).

Soul. The keeper of our Divine Design represented simultaneously by the most expanded consciousness of the solar system and by the most focused consciousness of the Sun. Our true nature, unmanifest, pure, spaceless, timeless, omnipresent, being Love.

Wound. A sense of inner hurt, missingness, fragmentedness, injustice, unfairness, incompleteness, etcetera. The unresolved, undissolved, unreconciled, unHealed issues that lie buried within our psyches, awaiting the Healing process, arising from our early misperceptions of our lives and the world around us.

Wounding, The. Our journey into duality, the material condition, illusion, Darkness, fragmentation, separation, isolation, disconnectedness.

BIBLIOGRAPHY

There were innumerable references and texts drawn upon in the writing of this series of books. In this first book, for the sake of simplicity, I have only included a limited number of bibliographic entries that have direct and obvious bearing on this first book. Books Two and Three of this series contain more comprehensive bibliographies in keeping with the widened scope of these subsequent works.

Bailey, Alice. *Esoteric Astrology.* Lucis Publishing Company, 1989.

Bellamy, H. S. & Allan, P. *The Calendar of Tiahuanaco.* Faber & Faber Ltd, 1956.

Brennan, Barbara Ann. *Light Emerging—The Journey of Personal Healing.* New York: Bantam, 1993.

Bunyan, John. *"The Pilgrim's Progress"* London, 1678, html version courtesy of Judith Bronte, http://acacia.pair.com/Acacia.John.Bunyan/.

Calaprice, Alice ed. *The Expanded Quotable Einstein.* Princeton University Press, Princeton, 2000.

Campbell, Joseph. Edited by Diane K. Osbon. *A Joseph Campbell Companion.* HarperPerennial, 1998.

Campbell, Joseph. *The Hero with a Thousand Faces.* Fontana Press, 1993.

Demartini, John F. *The Book of Quotations by John.* © John F. Demartini, 1996.

Demartini, John F. *Count Your Blessings – The Healing Power of Gratitude and Love.* Element Books, Inc. 1997.

Eliot, T. S. *Four Quartets.* Faber and Faber, London, 1944, 1959, 1979.

Emerson, Ralph Waldo. *Nature* (1836), edition: *Selected Essays*, ed. Larzer Ziff. Penguin Classics, New York, 1985.

Erdman, David V. ed. *The Complete Poetry and Prose of William Blake.* Anchor Books (Doubleday), New York 1988.

Freke, Timothy & Gandy, Peter. *The Hermetica – The Lost Wisdom of the Pharaohs.* Judy Piatkus Publishers, London, 1997.

Goodwin, Brian. *How the Leopard Changed its Spots – the Evolution of Complexity.* Charles Scribner's Sons, New York, 1994.

Hand Clow, Barbara. *Chiron—Rainbow Bridge Between the Inner and Outer Planets.* USA: Llewellyn, 1987, 1993.

Hermetica, The. The Lost Wisdom of the Pharaohs. Translations by Timothy Freke & Peter Gandy, Judy Piatkus Publishers Ltd, 1997.

Jantsch, Erich. *The Self-organizing Universe.* Pergamon Press, Oxford, 1980.

Jung, Carl G. *Archetypes of the Collective Unconscious.* Orig. 1934; Collected Works, vol. 9, part i; New York and London, 1959.

The Kybalion – Hermetic Philosophy. By Three Initiates. Yogi Publication Society.

Lantero, Erminie. *The Continuing Discovery of Chiron.* Weiser, Maine, 1983.

Leunig, Michael. *Common Prayer Collection.* Harper Collins (Collins Dove), North Blackburn, Victoria, Australia, 1993.

Moore, Thomas. *The Re-Enchantment of Everyday Life.* Hodde & Stoughton, 1996.

New Scientist (magazine). (various issues) Reed Business Information, London.

Nolle, Richard. *Chiron, The New Planet in Your Horoscope: The Key to Your Quest.* American Federation of Astrologers, Arizona, 1983.

Ouspensky, P. D. *In Search of the Miraculous.* USA: Harcourt Brace Jovanovich, 1949, 1977.

Ouspensky, P. D. *The Psychology of Man's Possible Evolution.* Vintage Books, 1974.

Parkhill, Stephen C. *Answer Cancer – Miraculous Healings Explained.* Health Communications Inc., Florida, 1995.

Raine, Kathleen. *William Blake.* Thames and Hudson Ltd., London, 1970, 1988.

Raleigh, A. S. *Occult Geometry and Hermetic Science of Motion & Number.* DeVorss Publications, 1991.

Reinhart, Melanie. *Chiron and the Healing Journey.* UK: Arkana, 1989.

Roob, Alexander. *The Hermetic Museum: Alchemy and Mysticism.* Taschen, 1997.

Rudhyar, Dane. *An Astrological Mandala.* Vintage Books, New York, 1974.

Schulman, Martin. *Karmic Astrology, Vols. 1–4.* Samuel Weiser, Inc., 1984.

Sherwin, Jill ed. *Quotable Star Trek.* Pocket Books, New York, 1999.

Stein, Zane. *Essence and Application—A View from Chiron.* Copyright 1995 Zane B. Stein.

The Hamlyn Pictorial History of the 20th Century. Hamlyn, 1995.

The Mountain Astrologer Magazine. Various issues, 1995–1998.

Three Initiates. *The Kybalion—Hermetic Philosophy.* Yogi Publication Society.

Toms, Michael & Toms, Justine Willis. "*True Work*". Bell Tower, New York, 1998.

Wasson, Gordon & Hoffman, Albert & Ruck, Carl A. P. *The Road to Eleusis.* Hermes Press (William Dailey Rare Books Ltd.), Los Angeles, 1998.

Watson, Lyall. *Supernature.* Coronet Books, 1974.

WellBeing Magazine Astrology Guide 2000. Wellspring Publishers, North Sydney, Australia, 2000.

Whitfield, Stephen E. & Roddenberry, Gene. *The Making of Star Trek.* Ballantine Books, 1968.

CONTACTS

Martin Lass
Astrology, Music & Healing
Email: MartinLass7@aol.com
Website: *www.martinlass.com*

Concourse of Wisdom School of Philosophy and Healing
Dr John F. Demartini
Website: *http://www.drdemartini.com*
TOLL FREE 1–888–336–2784

ss

BOOK ONE

Musings of a Rogue Comet

Chiron, Planet of Healing

A native American prophecy states that when the planet of Healing is discovered in the sky, the ancient sacred warrior teachings will return to the Earth.

Enter planet, Chiron . . .

In a series of four books, Chiron's musings explore health, disease, dysfunction and disorder – our *Wounds* – and their relationship to our spiritual journey through life. Chiron says our Wounds are our *teachers.* They are the *homing beacons* of Spirit, pointing us toward greater wholeness, consciousness, Truth and Love.

Orthodox medicine and psychology approach *dysfunction* from the point of view of symptoms and their root causes. Chiron calls the root cause, the *Wound.* Orthodoxy seeks to fix, correct, cure or get rid of our Wounds. Chiron says there is *nothing* to fix, correct, cure or get rid of . . . further, that every Wound contains a Gift. Discovering the Gift is the Healing journey . . .

As Chiron's message unfolds, we begin to see that Healing is not just about health and disease, but encompasses every area of human endeavor and human expression, from astrology to medicine to mythology to quantum physics.

Chiron takes us on a journey through our Darkness, personally and collectively, seeking the Light, in search of the *Gift in the Wound.*

Musings of a Rogue Comet – Chiron, Planet of Healing

BOOK TWO

Mirror, Mirror, Body and Mind

If you have ever wondered what the origin is of all health, disease, dysfunction and disorder . . . if you have ever been sick of being sick, not knowing why you are sick . . . if you have ever wanted to know what it means to Heal and how to Heal – physically, emotionally, mentally and/or spiritually – then this book is for you.

What if all health, disease, dysfunction and disorder – our *Wounds* – were all a matter of *consciousness?* What if the Body and Mind constituted a perfect mirror of that consciousness? What if our Body/Mind mirror were a Gift given to us specifically for awakening to our True nature? What if health and disease were actually *homing beacons,* pointing us towards Truth, Love, Light and Oneness? Such are the musings of rogue comet, Chiron . . .

Of disease, dysfunction and disorder, Chiron says there is *nothing to fix, nothing to change, nothing to correct or get rid of* . . . they are simply the Body/Mind doing its job, pointing us in the direction of those things that we have yet to learn to Love.

In this book, guided by Chiron, we explore the Body/Mind mirror. Once we understand its nature, we can begin to deal with our issues, attend to our Wounds, bring back balance and harmony into our lives and approach the real experience of Unconditional Love. Chiron says that as we learn to Love, so we Heal. As we Heal, so the *Gift in the Wound* is gradually revealed.

BOOK THREE

The Story of Life

The Journey of Wounding & Healing

Four questions summarize our quest for the meaning of existence:

Who are we?

Where do we come from?

Why are we here?

Where are we going?

The answers to these questions are encapsulated in the Story of Life. The Story of Life tells of our journey of Wounding and Healing, our spiritual journey into Darkness and our Return to Light.

With origins before time began, the Story of Life is written everywhere we look . . . it is written into the fabric of the cosmos, from microcosm to macrocosm. We can see it in psychology, physiology, astronomy, quantum physics, in the nature of Light, in cosmology, in the nature of time, in music, astrology, mythology, religion, philosophy and metaphysics. It is written into our daily lives. It is all around us. It is within us. It *is* us. Everything is a *hologram* of the Story of Life.

As the Truth of the Story of Life begins to dawn upon us, we begin to realize that nothing in our lives is accidental, that there are no mistakes, no wrong paths, and that all things, without exception, Serve our Healing and evolution of consciousness. We begin to become aware of the magnitude of Love that lies at the core of all life.

The awakening to the Story of Life *is* the Healing journey.

Musings of a Rogue Comet – Chiron, Planet of Healing

BOOK FOUR

Practical Healing

A Chiron Workbook

In Book One of this series, we were introduced to Chiron in a highly personal way, we explored the myths and themes of Chiron and we elaborated Chiron's astrology.

In Book Two, we explored the relationship between *consciousness* and our states of health and disease, dysfunction and disorder, seeing how Healing is possible.

In Book Three, we stood witness to the Great Story of Life – the Journey of Wounding and Healing – that lies within every aspect of life from the microcosm to the macrocosm, from before time to the present-day realities of our own lives.

Now, in Book Four, Chiron's musings in relation to Healing and the evolution of consciousness are brought together into a workbook of practical Healing methods. Laid out before us is a step-by-step guide to working through our issues, Healing our Wounds and attaining the real experience of Unconditional Love. With this one book, we are given the rare opportunity of Healing our lives in a lasting and meaningful way.

INDEX

D

E

F

G

Printed in the United States
6526

9 781401 032036